# CATHOLIC
# WOMEN
# WRITERS

# CATHOLIC WOMEN WRITERS

## A Bio-Bibliographical Sourcebook

Edited by Mary R. Reichardt

GREENWOOD PRESS
Westport, Connecticut • London

**Library of Congress Cataloging-in-Publication Data**

Catholic women writers : a bio-bibliographical sourcebook / edited by Mary R. Reichardt.
    p.  cm.
    Includes bibliographical references (p.  ) and index.
    ISBN 0-313-31147-1 (alk. paper)
    1. Women authors—Biography—Dictionaries.  2. Catholic
authors—Biography—Dictionaries.  3. Literature—Women
authors—Bio-bibliography—Dictionaries.  I. Reichardt, Mary R.
PN471.C38  2001
809′.89287′03—dc21
[B]      00-049506

British Library Cataloguing in Publication Data is available.

Library of Congress Catalog Card Number: 00-049506
ISBN: 0-313-31147-1

First published in 2001

Greenwood Press, 88 Post Road West, Westport, CT 06881
An imprint of Greenwood Publishing Group, Inc.
www.greenwood.com

Printed in the United States of America

The paper used in this book complies with the
Permanent Paper Standard issued by the National
Information Standards Organization (Z39.48-1984).

10 9 8 7 6 5 4 3 2 1

# CONTENTS

# PREFACE

This volume examines the extraordinary richness and diversity of over one thousand years of women's writing in the Catholic tradition. A reference guide, it consists of alphabetically arranged entries on sixty-four authors, each written by a scholar in the area. Each entry is divided into five parts: a brief biography of the author; a critical examination of her major themes, particularly as they relate to Catholicism and women's issues; a summary of the critical reception of her works; and a selected primary and secondary bibliography. The volume's introduction places the authors in an historical and literary context, noting how their writings respond to or reflect significant events or movements within the Catholic Church. To direct further study, the book closes with a selected general bibliography.

Like most worthwhile projects, this book arose out of a felt need. After years of teaching and publishing on early American women writers, the area of my graduate training, I found myself gravitating by personal and professional inclination toward my university's interdisciplinary Catholic Studies program, where I now teach a variety of Catholic literature courses on both the undergraduate and graduate levels. Although a long-time reader of a handful of Catholic women writers such as Sigrid Undset and Muriel Spark, I needed rather hastily to expand my repertoire to include more women's texts in my courses. However, I soon discovered that few general resources on the subject exist. Although women have been writing in the Catholic tradition since early medieval times, no source prior to this book has brought together biographical, critical, and bibliographical information on a wide cross section of Catholic women authors. While individual sources on more popular writers such as Katherine Anne Porter abound, no single guide offered me the overview of the field or the sense of the sweep and diversity of writings from across centuries and countries that I was looking for as I began my study.

This gap in scholarship seems at first surprising given the prominence over the last few decades of feminist and revisionist criticism that has succeeded in recovering heretofore forgotten women's literature. As was typical of most pre-1970s literary criticism, scholarship on Catholic writing produced earlier in the century tended to focus primarily, even exclusively, on male authors. During the aftermath of the Second Vatican Council, the turbulence of which has only recently subsided, it was evident that a new type of Catholic writing was emerging, written by artists—many of them women—who were responding to the changes ushered in by Vatican II. As if waiting for a clearer sense of this growing body of post-conciliar fiction, critics produced very little scholarship on Catholic literature throughout the 1970s–1980s. But over the last decade, a new and substantial wave of criticism has emerged. And because the changes wrought by Vatican II coincided with the women's movement and the subsequent broadening of the canon, this recent body of research is far more willing to assess the works of women side-by-side with those of men. We are, it seems, currently in the midst of renewed interest in Catholic literature and Catholic culture, exceedingly ripe areas for further scholarly attention. This volume contributes to this growing body of contemporary scholarship by providing just the kind of reference guide I was searching for as I began my investigation into the expansive and intriguing world of women writing in the Catholic tradition. My hope is that it will serve to introduce scholars, students, and general readers of Catholic literature and of women authors to this world; direct further reading in specific areas; and encourage new avenues for research and writing. For much critical inquiry still lies before us.

This book does not claim to be complete, nor does it attempt to define a specific canon of Catholic women authors. Rather, its much more modest goal is to assemble in one place a generous and representative sampling of such writers. In fact, as I began to research authors for possible inclusion, I quickly discovered that there were many more candidates than space limitations would allow for. My initial list of approximately twenty authors doubled and then tripled several times over as I circulated it among the many scholars who answered my call for contributors and generously proffered their suggestions. To narrow the list to a manageable number, I relied on several selection criteria. The first necessitated evolving a working definition of a "Catholic writer." From the outset, it was clear to me that such extraneous qualifications as the author having been baptized in the Catholic Church or having exhibited an adherence to Catholic doctrine in her lifetime was both unhelpful and unworkable. Wishing to focus on the nature of the literature itself and not on the author's biography, I deemed an author suitable for inclusion if one or more of her important works was informed in a substantial and meaningful way by the structures, traditions, history, spirituality, and/or culture of Catholicism. Perhaps controversially, such a definition allows for the inclusion of authors such as Willa Cather, Christina Rossetti, Dorothy L. Sayers, and Kathleen Norris who were (or are) not members of the Catholic Church but whose major writings participate thematically in a Catholic view of the world. It is, therefore, more accurate to speak of "women writing in the Catholic tradition" than "Catholic women writers," although I use both phrases interchangeably here.

Several other selection criteria were also used to arrive at the final tally of sixty-four entries. Authors were chosen with an eye toward representing most centuries from early medieval to contemporary times; as wide a scope as possible of countries and ethnicities; and a broad spectrum of literary genres, including fiction, poetry, spiritual narrative, drama, essays, children's works, and even performance art. Moreover, authors included here also represent a diverse range of attitudes toward Catholicism and the Catholic Church. Thus, this book includes authors whom the Church has designated saints and even "Doctors of the Church" for the orthodoxy of their writings (e.g., Catherine of Siena, Thérèse of Lisieux). It also includes mystics and spiritual writers who express highly individualistic and sometimes unorthodox responses to Catholic teachings (Margery Kempe, Simone Weil); and it includes authors whose works are critical of the institutional Church or view it primarily as an historical or cultural artifact (Mary Gordon, Rosario Ferré). Readers will discover here writers who are both "major" and "minor," those whose works are well known and those whose writings deserve to be rediscovered. Finally, from a practical standpoint, the list was also pared down to those authors for whom I had contributors. To some extent, therefore, the content of this book reflects the current interests of scholarship in the academy.

A final note is needed on how authors' names are alphabetized. I chose to list writers by their most commonly recognized names or titles, leaving the biographical portion of the entry to provide complete given and family names. Teresa Sánchez de Cepeda y Ahumada is alphabetized, therefore, under the "t's" as Teresa of Avila, and Jeanne-Marie Bouvier de la Motte Guyon is listed under the "g's" as Madame Guyon. A Hispanic writer whose full family name is composed of her maiden and married surnames is also alphabetized accordingly: Emilia Pardo Bazán, for example, is listed under the "p's." In all cases, I have tried to make it as simple as possible for readers to locate authors under their most familiar descriptors.

# ACKNOWLEDGMENTS

A reference volume of this magnitude is the collaborative effort of many people. My thanks go first to the forty-six scholars who have contributed entries to this text and whose enthusiasm for the project has been most gratifying. More than half of the entries here were recommended by contributors, and I am especially grateful for the advice I received as I created the final list of inclusions. Moreover, a delightful benefit of such collaborative scholarship is the number of personal relationships formed as a result of it; I have had the privilege of connecting with many others who, like myself, are fond readers, teachers, and scholars of Catholic women writers. I also thank Greenwood editor George Butler who encouraged the project from the beginning and expedited its production. The Aquinas Foundation of the University of St. Thomas provided me with a generous grant during the 1998–1999 academic year that was used to free up time for research. And last, I am grateful to my students in my interdisciplinary Catholic Literary Tradition class. Their refreshingly open responses to the women writers we studied have helped me grow as a teacher, scholar, and person of faith, and led me initially to conceive of this book.

# INTRODUCTION

To a greater or lesser degree, a Catholic view of the world inspires the work of each writer in this text. It is well, therefore, to begin by considering some of the more distinctive elements of that view that have bearing on Catholic literature. Catholicism traces its roots in an unbroken line to the transforming moment in history, the salvation offered humankind by the death and resurrection of Jesus Christ. Because God chose to redeem us by becoming human and experiencing all aspects of human life, Catholic thought is highly incarnational. It emphasizes the dignity of all people made in the image of God and regards the physical world, the ordinary "stuff" of life, as essentially good and worthy of respect because Christ has sanctified it by going through it. Catholic thought is also highly sacramental. Unlike the dominant direction of Protestant thinking, Catholics stress God's immanence in, not absence from, the world. Rightly regarded and used, all aspects of life that are not explicitly sinful become proofs of God's presence and conduits of his grace. Art and literature, too, reveal the "real presence" of God.[1] In the sacrament of the Eucharist, Catholics even enjoy the ultimate physical contact with God as they consume the bread and wine transformed into the body and blood of Jesus.

Due to its incarnational and sacramental emphases, Catholicism is thus a strongly sensate faith that finds joy in all creation. However, Catholics also remember that the world is passing away, and that the use and enjoyment of the things of earth must be ordered to the greater good, the soul's attainment of heaven. One must, therefore, constantly train the eye to look through created things to discover the divine. In such vision, the spiritual and material are not separate aspects of reality, but rather the "sacred [i]s continuous with the secular."[2] This Catholic sense of continuity also extends to the living and the dead with the doctrine of efficacious intercessory prayers directed to the saints in heaven and for the souls in purgatory. An integrative, analogical habit of mind—the "both/and" rather than the "either/or"—thus characterizes Catholic thought and tends to be reflected in literature as a decided penchant for image, metaphor, symbol, and paradox. The Christian faith is, after all, replete with astonishing paradoxes: Jesus is both divine and human, one finds one's life by losing it, in great weakness is great strength, and so on. Things are, usually, much more than what they seem.

For all Christians, the single most important narrative is the great drama of sin and redemption. As opposed to much Protestant thought, however, Catholicism asserts the need for ongoing conversion and spiritual progress. Conversion is, in fact, a lifelong process in which God rewards good will over results and derives blessings even out of apparent evil for the right-minded person. Because God's loving providence is working secretly in the midst of human limitations, suffering, and sin, nothing, therefore, is to be despaired of except the only true horror, the soul that dies unrepentant. With its communal rather than individualistic emphasis, Catholicism insists on the necessary role of both faith and good works in spiritual progress: love of God is best demonstrated by love of neighbor. While inevitable in this life, such evils as poverty and injustice are to be combated actively by the Catholic, a belief to which the Church's long and well-developed tradition of social justice testifies.

A Catholic view of the world, then, is a richly imaginative and metaphoric one, steeped in both a deep sense of mystery and an intense delight in creation. At once lofty and sensual, heaven directed and earth bound, the Catholic faith has provided countless visual and literary artists throughout the centuries with ready material to engage their imaginations, hearts, and intellects. Because of its sense of sacramentality, Catholicism has always honored artistic endeavor. Human creativity mirrors God's creativity, and Christ himself, the Word of God, taught by story. Both reason and imagination, head and heart, can lead humans closer to God. In fact, these distinct yet compatible paths to truth are witnessed in the two great Catholic writing and teaching traditions of the scholastic rationalists and the mystics. But whether arrived at by reason or imagination, writing that professes to teach Church doctrine has traditionally been subjected to the Church hierarchy to verify its orthodoxy, the *nihil obstat* coveted by numerous theologians and teachers over the centuries including some represented here. Whether viewed as a strong repository of the truth or as a reactionary force against change, in all ages the Church hierarchy has been a formidable factor in the lives of Catholics.

Interestingly, although it upholds the value of literature and several popes, including John Paul II, have themselves engaged in composing imaginative works, the Catholic Church has never promulgated an official theory about the role of literature. Even the long-standing *Index* of prohibited books initiated during the Inquisition was never considered a suppression of literary art but rather a means of protecting the simple faithful from doctrinal error. Modern authors in the Catholic tradition who have reflected on the topic concur to an overwhelming degree that literature must be free of institutional and societal constraint if it is to reach artistic excellence. Fiction written with the overt didactic intent of converting others or proving certain aspects of the faith is, after all, generally tedious stuff. For a like reason, contemporary authors often shrink from being labeled a "Catholic writer" because it implies a certain dogmatism or, even worse, the sentimental "Instant Uplift" that Flannery O'Connor, one of our most astute critics, rightly scorned.[3] Because the expansive and integrative Catholic perspective embraces all reality and is concerned with telling the truth about that reality, Catholic literature is, in O'Connor's words, constantly "pushing its own limits outward toward the limits of mystery." "The more we learn about ourselves," she adds, "the deeper into the unknown we push the frontiers of fiction."[4] In a recent article, Albert Gelpi comments perceptively on this phenomenon:

Faith not only allows but generates the freedom to test and realize the consequences of belief in the crucible of the individual's actual living and thinking and feeling. It is, then, the Catholic artist's particular charism and responsibility within the community to exercise that freedom, even at times to extend the Catholic vision into uncharted areas and contested dimensions of experience. Artists and prophets have a different role in the community than theologians and priests. It should not be surprising, therefore, if the imaginative impulse of Catholic artists . . . gravitates from the center to the more ambiguous peripheries and boundaries of orthodoxy, driven at times to explore volatile and shadowy areas that orthodoxy has shied away from.[5]

Historically, the role of women in the Church has participated to a marked degree in the manifold paradoxes of the faith. Throughout Christian cultures, women have often been viewed in irreconcilable dualities. On the one hand, Christianity's Judeo heritage singles out for exuberant praise such faithful and intrepid women as Esther and Judith. Women were certainly central to Christ's ministry, forming an integral part of his circle of followers. Yet sin entered the world through the temptress, Eve, and, by way of popular interpretation, Mary Magdalene's greatest sin was her dangerous female passion and sexuality. Elevated above all the saints, Mary the Mother of God reigns in Catholic tradition as Queen of Heaven, yet she is, paradoxically, both virgin and mother; both submissive and the preeminent *mulier fortis*. Throughout the centuries, women in the Church have struggled and—as the contemporary Latin American writers presented here demonstrate—continue to struggle with the image of womanhood as at once exalted and debased. Long advised by some clerics to keep silent in imitation of the Virgin and in compliance with such biblical passages as 1 Timothy 2:11–15, women have wrestled with defining themselves and their rightful place in the Church and in society. From Hrotsvit of Gandersheim to Edith Stein, from Julian of Norwich to Julia Alvarez, the majority of the authors presented here have attempted in their writings to envision new images and expanded roles for women. With Vatican II's stress on the importance of the individual conscience coupled with the women's movement of the mid–twentieth century, this discussion is perhaps more intense today than at any other time in history.

Throughout the long tradition of Catholic literature, women have consistently contributed influential and innovative voices. What follows is a brief survey, in more-or-less chronological order, of the authors and major genres and themes that the reader will encounter here. It is fitting that, in terms of chronology, the first writer presented in this volume possessed a name that heralded the arrival of a distinct—and powerful—woman's voice. The Saxon canoness Hrotsvit of Gandersheim (c.935–c.975) delighted in calling herself the "*clamor validus Gandeshemensis*," or the "strong voice of Gandersheim." Poet, historian, and playwright, Hrotsvit also has the distinction of being among the first women writers to challenge contemporary depictions of women. Her sacred dramas featuring fearless and faithful Christian women were designed to counter the negative portraits of womanhood popularized by the Roman poet Terence. Even more remarkable for breaking barriers for women was the astonishingly talented Benedictine abbess Hildegard of Bingen (1098–1179). Theologian, dramatist, poet, natural historian, composer, and prophet, Hildegard received extraordinary spiritual visions from childhood on. Commanded by Christ at the age of forty-two, she recorded her experiences in a trilogy of mystical works that portray salvation history and envision the harmonious interconnection of all elements of the cosmos with *Ecclesia,* or Mother Church, as the fecund feminine principle at its center.

The careers of these early writers, Hrotsvit and Hildegard, focus attention on two principal themes of early Catholic women's works: a defense of women's dignity and capabilities, and the value of the mystical path to God. Because Christianity emphasizes the equal worth of all souls before God, women used their pens insistently and often to counter misogynist suppositions. Christine de Pizan (1365–c.1430), for example, spent much of her literary career defending her sex, especially against Jean de Meun's anti-feminine continuation of the *Roman de la Rose.* De Pizan's utopian city in her *Book of the City of Ladies* is inhabited by heroic women from history and religion with Mary as its Queen. The dramas of the Renaissance playwright Antonia Pulci (1452–1501) also depict Christian women as valiant even when facing persecution. In her plays, Pulci extols the benefits of convent life over marriage, a choice confronting nearly all young women of her day. The first play by a woman composed in English, Elizabeth Cary's (1585–1639) *The Tragedy of Mariam, the Fair Queen of Jewry,* underscores the need for women to fulfill their God-given intellectual capabilities and follow their own consciences, even in marriage. And the Mexican author, Sor Juana Inés de la Cruz (1648?–1695), also celebrates courageous women of faith, especially the Virgin Mary, in her poetry and plays. Written in response to criticism she received that a nun should not pursue intellectual activities, her famous *Reply to Sor Filotea* sharply defends a woman's right to education and to the study and writing of theology.

Following Hildegard of Bingen, a second important strain in early Catholic women's writing is that of the mystical and spiritual narrative. Medieval Europe witnessed a remarkable proliferation of women mystics and spiritual teachers, a phenomenon that reinvigorated Catholic thought and praxis. Although not only women claimed supernatural experiences, in unprecedented numbers both religious and laywomen reported receiving visions of God the Father, Christ, Mary, and the saints and angels. Most often, they recorded their visions at the behest of their superiors or confessors, and they likewise obeyed in composing their spiritual autobiographies, a genre that has its origins in Augustine's fourth century *Confessions,* so that their piety and orthodoxy could be scrutinized. By narrating their revelations for the spiritual benefit of others, women found a voice in teaching in the Church that was otherwise largely unavailable to them. By claiming that their writing was divinely inspired, women gained authority for their instruction whether they possessed any theological training or not. Hildegard's *Scivias,* for example, was submitted to Pope Eugenius III and declared both orthodox and divinely inspired; four centuries later, Teresa of Avila was informally questioned by the Inquisition for the content of her writings. In the typical modesty *topos* that prefaces their works, women took care to deflect accusations that they were teaching from their own knowledge or on their own volition. With its mixed tone of humility and self-respect, Julian of Norwich's statement serves as a classic example:

But God forbid that you should say or assume that I am a teacher, for that is not and never was my intention; for I am a woman, ignorant, weak, and frail. But I know very well that what I am saying I have received at the revelation of him who is the sovereign teacher. . . . But because I am a woman, ought I therefore to believe that I should not tell you of the Goodness of God, when I saw at the same time that it is his will that it be known?[6]

This mysticism involved a direct and emotional approach to the divine that ran parallel to the abstract intellectual scholasticism of such theologians as Thomas Aquinas (d.1274). Far from denying the human aspect of the Incarnation, visionaries often expressed their revelations in strongly physical, even erotic, images. Many such works present variations on the classic tripartite stages of spiritual growth: the purgative (in which the soul through grace realizes her sins and performs penance); the illuminative (in which God leads the soul to higher contemplation through sufferings); and the unitive (in which intimacy with the Godhead is achieved through the soul's perfect conformity to God's will). The latter stage is often marked by intense supernatural occurrences such as ecstasies, the spiritual marriage, and the receiving of spiritual wounds. Many mystics reported participating bodily in aspects of Christ's passion and some, such as Catherine of Siena and Teresa of Avila, bore the stigmata. For all these women, the experience of divine love changed their lives profoundly and gave singular energy and immediacy to their writings.

The mystics and spiritual writers presented in this volume are the following. In her commitment to radical poverty, Clare of Assisi (1194–1253) evolved a

*Rule* for cloistered life that created a new and influential type of women's community. Angela of Foligno (c.1248–1309) underwent a dramatic conversion at age thirty-seven, and her work detailing the path to the heavenly embrace of God, *The Book of the Blessed Angela of Foligno*, influenced theologians, writers, and saints throughout the centuries. The eventful life of Catherine of Siena (1347–1380) involved an extraordinary degree of spiritual phenomena, including ecstasies, the spiritual betrothal, and repeated endurances of the agonies of the crucifixion. Commanded by God, she entered public life, where she played an important role in both Church reform and restoring peace to a divided Italy. Her *Dialogue* is structured as a colloquy between God and the human soul. Unhappy in marriage, Catherine of Genoa's (1447–1510) experience of God's love changed her tepid life into one of active prayer and care for others during the time of the Black Plague in Italy. Like Catherine of Siena's *Dialogue*, her *Spiritual Dialogue* presents its teachings in the form of a conversation, in this case between the Soul, the Body, Self-Love, and other speakers. Teresa of Avila (1515–1582), along with Catherine of Siena the first women to be designated "Doctors of the Church," reformed the Carmelite order to a more austere rule and established numerous convents throughout Spain. She too underwent exceptional mystical experiences, and her *Way of Perfection* and *Interior Castle* are among the Church's most outstanding spiritual documents.

During the fourteenth century, a strong mystical tradition also arose in England. While near death, the anchoress Julian of Norwich (c.1342–c.1413) experienced sixteen visions of Christ's crucifixion. At once a powerfully emotional narrative and a work of carefully reasoned theology, her *Revelations of Divine Love* emphasizes God's delight in dying for a humanity he cherishes and depicts Jesus as representing the maternal face of the Trinity. Marked by startling visions and outbursts of uncontrollable wailing, Margery Kempe's (c.1373–c.1440) unusual life was recorded by an amanuensis in *The Book of Margery Kempe*, considered the first autobiography in English. Kempe was compelled by her visions to undertake a life of penance and pilgrimage to such far off locations as Rome, Danzig, and Jerusalem. Her narrative records her meeting with Julian of Norwich, whom she had sought out for spiritual counsel.

With surprising speed, the Protestant Reformation swept through sixteenth-century Europe, claiming nearly half its inhabitants. By 1561, when the Catholic poet Mary Stuart (1542–1587) ascended the Scottish throne, Calvinism was already fully established in that country. But the Catholic Counter Reformation helped restore a sense of unity to the splintered faith with the Council of Trent (1545–1563), the formation of new religious orders, and the promotion of missionary activities throughout the world. A number of influential women mystics, teachers, and devotional writers arose in seventeenth-century Counter Reformation France. Prompted by her visions, the Ursuline nun Marie de l'Incarnation (1599–1672) undertook missionary work among the Indians in New France, where she produced dictionaries in the Algonquin and Iroquois languages and penned autobiographies that form important historical documents of early European settlement in Quebec. Margaret Mary Alacoque (1647–1690) records in her autobiography how she was ordered by Christ to promote the cult of the Sacred Heart of Jesus, which evolved into one of the most influential devotional practices in the Church. The mother of five children, Madame Guyon (1648–1717) experienced a powerful conversion that led to her teachings about the mystical way in *Spiritual Torrents*. Accused of heresy, she endured eight years in the Bastille, although formal charges were never brought against her. And in the New World, the Columbian "Mystic of Tunja," Madre Castillo (1671–1742), drew upon the works of Catherine of Siena, Teresa of Avila, St. John of the Cross, and Sor Juana Inés de la Cruz in her *Spiritual Feelings* and other writings, evincing her keen awareness of her connection to the mystical tradition of her time.

Finally, one can append to this discussion of mystics and spiritual teachers several writers who carry the tradition into modern times. Thérèse of Lisieux's (1873–1897) autobiography, *Story of a Soul*, is one of the most widely read spiritual works ever, revealing the French saint's "little way" to God amid the ambiguities and tensions of ordinary daily life. At once simple and profound, its teaching, like that of all the mystics, of the primacy of love has exerted a major influence on contemporary Catholic spirituality. The brilliant philosopher, theologian, mystic, and social activist Simone Weil (1909–1943) was preoccupied all her life with such matters as the person of Christ, the mystery of the Incarnation, and the nature of the sacraments. Her collection of essays *Waiting for God* explains her theory of the need for "attentiveness," a contemplative state in the midst of daily affairs that opens a person to the spirit of truth residing in all things.

In the wake of Protestant reform and the foment of Enlightenment rationalistic and deistic thought, Catholic culture reached perhaps its lowest point during the eighteenth century. Religious life was paralyzed in France during the Revolution, and in England years of persecution had reduced Catholics to a tiny fraction of the population. But a strong revival of interest in Catholicism and numerous conversions to the faith took place during the nineteenth century. The Catholic Emancipation Act of 1829 allowed English Catholics to practice their faith openly for the first time in centuries. As a result, thousands of Catholic Irish immigrants resettled in England. But the single most important factor that galvanized Catholic culture was the Oxford Movement of 1833. The movement's original impetus had been to restore elements of Catholicism to the Anglican faith, returning it, among other things, to a belief in apostolic succession. In 1845, however, the movement's most prominent leader, John Henry Newman, converted to Roman Catholicism, prompting a wave of conversions over the next several decades even though turning to Rome remained an act of bravery in the face of continued anti-Catholic sentiment in England.

Products of the rise of secular, pluralistic culture, the new genres of the novel and the short story also developed throughout the nineteenth century. As middle-class women began to have increased opportunities for education and for the option of pursuing a literary career, Catholic literature in a wide variety of modes flourished, much of it written by converts. Some of this literature naturally assumed a didactic or polemic edge, a result of the author's experience of being marginalized as a Catholic in Protestant Europe or in the United States.

Although she never converted to Roman Catholicism, Christina Rossetti (1830–1894), one of the great Victorian poets, was strongly persuaded by the teachings of the Tractarians, adherents to the principles of the Oxford Movement. Her poetry conveys a deep sense of sacramentality as well as themes of the interplay between desire and renunciation and the power of intercessory prayer. After her conversion, Adelaide Anne Procter's (1825–1864) poetry reflected her strong Catholic beliefs coupled with such political issues as a plea to England to spare the persecuted Irish their Catholic faith. Also influenced by the Oxford Movement, Alice Meynell (1847–1922) entered the Church in 1867. Married with eight children, she was an admired and influential poet, essayist, and critic; a partner with her husband in a journalism career; and a crusader for women's rights. The aristocrat Lady Georgiana Fullerton (1812–1885) began to publish novels after her conversion as a way to support her extensive charitable works. Her hugely successful early books such as *Ellen Middleton* and *Grantley Manor* combine Victorian interests with Catholic themes and were read by both Catholics and Protestants alike. And Irish poet and essayist Emily Henrietta Hickey (1845–1924), who lived most of her life in London, also converted to Catholicism through the inspiration of Newman. Unlike Fullerton's writings, however, her work suffered the typical fate of losing a sizable portion of its secular audience once its themes became too ardently "Romish."

Continental authors during this time include the Russian aristocrat and Catholic convert Sophie Rostopchine, Countess de Ségur (1799–1874), who, while living in France, became an author at age fifty-five when she turned her lifelong passion for children's education into a series of children's stories. Influenced by nineteenth-century hagiography, her popular tales combined realism, humor, and catechism, and helped reinvigorate the faith after the French Revolution. Spanish novelist and intellectual Emilia Pardo Bazán (1851–1921) introduced elements of Naturalism into her controversial early works while avoiding the strict determinism that is at odds with Catholic belief. Later, she also penned studies of Catholic saints and Christian epic poets, and her novels reveal her intimate knowledge of the Catholic mystical tradition.

Although present from early on, Catholics in the United States remained a nonthreatening minority until the nineteenth century's huge influx of immigrants, most of whom were Irish. By 1850, Catholics had suddenly become the largest religious denomination in the country. Always latent, anti-Catholic feeling flared from the 1830s through the 1850s with the rise of the Nativists and Know-Nothings; in 1834 following a sermon by Presbyterian minister Lyman Beecher, an angry mob burned the Ursuline convent at Charlestown, Massachusetts. A rash of anti-Catholic literature made its appearance during these decades followed by the earliest Catholic novels, nearly each of which, as David Reynolds puts it, "contains a priest who defends such doctrines as transubstantiation, the Virgin Birth, and apostolic succession with cool wisdom . . . [and who] stresses that Protestantism is hopelessly fragmented and that the final destination for the Protestant is either bewilderment or atheism."[7] Just as English Catholics found a champion in John Henry Newman, so did United States Catholic authors find inspiration in the mid-1840s conversion of former Transcendentalist and Unitarian Orestes Brownson. Like Newman also a novelist, Brownson devoted much of his post-conversion career to formulating standards for and promoting American Catholic literature.

Three nineteenth-century United States writers appear here: Irish immigrant Mary Anne Sadlier (1820–1903), and American-born New Englanders Louise Imogen Guiney (1861–1920) and Rose Hawthorne Lathrop (1851–1926). By 1860 when she moved with her family to New York City from Canada, Sadlier was already the best-selling Irish Catholic writer in America. Her numerous didactic and historical romances such as *New Lights; or, Life in Galway* and *The Blakes and the Flanagans* defended Irish Catholics in North America and addressed such Irish immigrant concerns as the danger of losing the faith in a secular society and the need for a separate Catholic school system. Poet, essayist, and biographer, Louise Imogen Guiney composed lyrics that show her deep sacramental sensibility expressed in reverence for nature. After moving to Oxford, Guiney dedicated her later scholarship to reviving the works of forgotten Catholic literary figures and producing biographies of lesser known Catholic martyrs and reformers. Daughter of Nathaniel Hawthorne, Rose Hawthorne Lathrop scandalized New England society by converting to the faith with her husband in 1891. After the breakup of her marriage, she opened a hospice for indigent cancer patients and became a nun in the Dominican order she founded. Throughout her life, she published stories, poems, and histories, most notably *Memories of Hawthorne* and *A Story of Courage*, a chronicle of the Visitation Convent at Georgetown University.

The first half of the twentieth century witnessed a remarkable Catholic literary renaissance. Leaving behind the naive didacticism that characterized the first stage of fiction, Catholic authors achieved maturity as artists and succeeded in attracting an audience far broader than that confined to the Catholic faithful. Throughout the nineteenth and into the twentieth centuries, conversion to Catholicism was frequently motivated at least in part by dissatisfaction with the rise of industrial, secular society. By contrast to the vulgarity and greed of rampant materialism, the Catholic Church offered a sense of the eternal and the sacred. With Pius IX's 1864 encyclical *Syllabus of Errors*, the Church appeared to adopt a policy of intransigence against the direction of modernity, and Vatican I (1869–1870) affirmed the ultramontane position by strengthening the authority of the papacy as a bulwark against progressivism. What resulted was a Church with a clear sense of identity, coherent and unchanging in its doctrines and devotional practices. Catholics considered themselves countercultural even as they began to permeate all occupations and levels of society. Gene Kellogg has referred to this sense as one of "abrasiveness, an overlapping with the secular world in which the Catholic community was always so conscious of its difference from the outer environment that friction never ceased."[8] It was precisely the dual quality of belonging to and remaining distinct from mainstream society that afforded authors an optimal position from which to observe the human situation. Moreover, Catholics' newfound confidence in themselves resulted in many writers turning a sharp eye on their own community, criticizing the shortcomings of individual Catholics and Catholic practices while affirming the overarching truth of the faith. In a passage that aptly captures this affirmation yet critical self-analysis, Muriel Spark's protagonist Caroline Rose in *The Comforters* opines of another character, "He was her sort of Catholic, critical but conforming. [He] always agreed with Caroline that the True Church was awful, though unfortunately, one couldn't deny, true."[9]

While both fiction and nonfiction of this period evince increasing experimentation, many authors chose to explore their themes through historical works, a genre that emphasizes the timeless values and continuity of Catholicism, or through social satire, a detached stance that highlights the emptiness and futility of a world without faith. Others composed realistic works that examined the various ways in which Catholicism could be lived in modern times. While these themes and techniques were shared by important female and male writers of the era, the latter group including such figures as Graham Greene, Evelyn Waugh, François Mauriac, Georges Bernanos, and G. K. Chesterton, women frequently concentrated on Catholic issues in light of rapidly changing roles for women in society.

One of the most popular and controversial European authors in the early part of the century was the Austrian Enrica von Handel-Mazzetti (1871–1955). Her historical novels of Counter Reformation Austria such as *Jesse and Maria* implicated both Catholics and Protestants in the cruelties of the time and pleaded for a tolerance that transcended Germany's confessional divide and forged the path for modern ecumenical dialogue. Also known for her meticulously crafted historical novels, Scandinavian writer Sigrid Undset's (1882–1949) epic studies of medieval Catholic Norway, *Kristin Lavransdatter* and *The Master of Hestviken*, earned her the Nobel Prize for literature in 1928 and led to her own conversion. Other continental writers presented here include Spanish playwright Pilar Millán Astray (1879–1949), who became well known in the 1920s–1930s for her variations on *sainetes*, comic plays with moralizing endings. In a time of anti-Catholic sentiment in Spain,

Millán Astray's voice dared to champion Catholic and feminist causes. Born to a Jewish family in Germany (now Poland), the brilliant philosopher and saint Edith Stein (1891–1942) converted to Catholicism during her studies under the phenomenologist Edmund Husserl. Stein's philosophical writings worked to synthesize the thought of Aquinas and the phenomenologists, and her essays on women's roles distinguished her as a leader in the progressive feminist movement of her time.

In Britain, the versatile novelist Sheila Kaye-Smith (1887–1956) often focused her plots on courageous women who break class, gender, and religious barriers to follow their consciences. She chronicled both her own conversion process and the return of Catholicism to England in such works as *The End of the House of Alard* and *Superstition Corner.* Although she never converted, Dorothy L. Sayers (1893–1957) demonstrated her interest in Catholic dogma by penning a number of popular sacred dramas such as *The Man Born to Be King* and *The Zeal of Thy House* as well as essays on Christian aesthetics collected in *The Mind of the Maker.* The prolific Rumer Godden (1907–1998) wrote two successful novels with Catholic themes as she herself was taking instruction in the faith. Both *In This House of Brede* and *Five for Sorrow; Ten for Joy* portray convent life as a viable and fulfilling alternative lifestyle for modern women. After her conversion in the early 1950s, Scottish-born satirist Muriel Spark (1918– ) produced a number of novels, such as *The Comforters* and *Robinson,* that explore the travails of converts adjusting to the faith in secular society. Irish writer Mary Lavin (1912–1996) concentrates on the hardship and paradoxes of Irish Catholic women's lives in such works as *Tales from Bective Bridge* and *The House in Clewe Street.* And Modernist writer Antonia White (1899–1980) explores the role of the Church in a young girl's life and the conflict between the artist's vocation and the faith in four related novels beginning with *Frost in May.*

Catholic literature also came of age in the United States at this time. Although not a Catholic, Willa Cather (1873–1947) wrote sympathetically about Catholicism in her historical novels *Death Comes for the Archbishop,* which portrays the missionary Church in New Mexico Territory, and *Shadows on the Rock,* which studies the influence of Catholicism on seventeenth-century French settlers in Quebec. Southern convert Caroline Gordon (1895–1981) addressed the modern existential struggles of humans in the changing South and the transforming possibilities of faith in such works as *Aleck Maury, Sportsman* and *The Malefactors.* Gordon helped nurture a generation of American Catholic writers. Among her protégés was fellow southerner Flannery O'Connor (1925–1964), whose darkly comic depictions of the conflicts of race, religion, and class in southern society coupled with a profound Catholic sense of sacramentality and grace single her out as one of the most intriguing Catholic writers of all time. Texas Modernist and convert Katherine Anne Porter (1890–1980) displays a Catholic sensibility in such works as *Old Mortality, Ship of Fools,* and *Pale Horse, Pale Rider,* where her protagonists betray themselves morally and spiritually by ignoring faith and attempting to rely on themselves alone.

One of the most significant figures in the history of American Catholicism, the journalist and social activist Dorothy Day (1897–1980) had a major impact on the development of contemporary Catholic social thought. Cofounder of the Catholic Worker Movement, Day's autobiographies *From Union Square to Rome* and *The Long Loneliness* are modern spiritual classics. Journalist Katherine Burton (c.1884–1969) was a prolific Catholic apologist who penned nearly forty lightly fictionalized biographies of notable Catholics and Catholic institutions. And Clare Boothe Luce (1903–1987) enjoyed a varied career as a playwright, journalist, editor, politician, and diplomat. Her early Broadway plays satirized modern elite society, and she later shifted her emphasis to public expression of the faith in such works as *Come to the Stable,* turned into a popular 1940s film, and *Saints for Now,* a collection of saints' biographies. Like many writers in this volume, Day, Burton, and Luce were each converts to Catholicism.

While Vatican II (1960–1965) did not alter Church doctrine to any significant degree, its effect on the life of the average Catholic was considerable. On the one hand, the Church's *aggiornamento* inaugurated a welcome dialogue with the modern world, embrace of ecumenism and social justice initiatives, and greater emphasis on conscience and responsibility on the part of the laity. On the other hand, reforms in the liturgy and long-established pious practices proved disruptive and alienating to many. Over night, it seemed, the authority of the Church had eroded and all was in flux. As Catholics began to become indistinguishable from their secular neighbors, an identity crisis of sorts ensued. Moreover, in the United States, the anti-authoritarianism and radical individualism of the 1960s–1970s coincided with the Second Vatican Council and produced a generation of Catholics who relied increasingly on the dictates of their consciences to adjudicate moral matters rather than on the teaching authority of the Church. The concurrent feminist movement also contributed strongly to Catholic women's sense of dislocation. Unable to accept without question older values and roles, women yet lacked clear direction in the present. In *Final Payments,* Mary Gordon (1949– ) reveals this uncomfortable disorientation when her protagonists Isabel and Eleanor discuss their future goals: "What do you want, then, from your life? [asks Isabel.]" "I don't know. I'd like to do something I was entirely sure of." "Like we used to be about the Church. It's so unfair. There's nothing like it, nothing takes its place."[10]

Authors writing during the tumult of the period often recorded an atmosphere of loss, ambiguity, and insecurity. However, the seeds of discontent were already sown in some of the literature that appeared just prior to Vatican II that depicted a stifling and repressive preconciliar Catholicism. Expatriate writer Edna O'Brien (1932– ), for instance, portrays Church injustices and clerical hypocrisies in the lives of restricted rural Irish women struggling to define themselves against religious and cultural forces. Mary McCarthy

(1912–1989) described her rigid Catholic upbringing with bitterness in *Memories of a Catholic Girlhood* and chronicled women's attempts to reconcile contemporary and traditional values in *The Company She Keeps* and *The Group*. Mary Gordon (1949– ) similarly registered an ambiguous reaction to Vatican II's changes in *Final Payments* and *The Company of Women*, where her protagonists strive in vain to adapt older notions of women's goodness and virtue to their liberated modern lives. Finally, in *House of Gold*, Elizabeth Cullinan (1933– ) artfully employs the metaphor of a dying matriarch of a large Catholic family to signify the demise of ritualistic and authoritarian Catholicism. Although now free from their mother's overbearing personality, the six grown children of the novel feel keenly the loss of her sustaining and unifying presence. To varying degrees, all four of these writers—O'Brien, McCarthy, Gordon, and Cullinan—show the pernicious, lingering effect of Jansenist Irish Catholicism in their characters' guilt, self-criticism, fear of punishment, and unhealthy attitude toward sexuality.[11]

While some predicted the end of Catholic literature due to Catholics' loss of a distinct identity in society after Vatican II, this in fact did not occur. Literature infused with a Catholic sensibility appears alive and well today, and women writers have especially dominated the field. As the furor over the Second Vatican Council subsided and the Church gained equilibrium under John Paul II, whose long pontificate was intent on mediating between the old and new, Catholic literature has grown increasingly diverse in theme and genre. Unlike that produced in the first half of the twentieth century, however, this new body of work, especially that coming from the United States, tends to reflect personal experience rather than looking outward to the authority of the Church. "If authoritarianism was the preconciliar model of American Catholicism," Anita Gandolfo has noted, "individualism is rapidly becoming its postconciliar counterpart."[12] In both United States' literature and the emerging literature of the Americas, two clear trends in this individual expression of Catholicism can be detected: a growing sensitivity to how certain cultures have translated Catholicism in ways that contribute to oppression, especially for women; and a quest for renewed spirituality and a sense of the sacred in a society characterized by materialism, moral relativity, pluralism, and rapid change.

In the postmodern world where a monolithic conception of historical truth is shattered, criticism of the missionary Church appears in the fiction of Louise Erdrich (1954– ), whose multilayered sagas of Native American communities examine the injustices perpetrated by imposed white culture and the almost surreal mixture of Catholic and Indian spirituality that has resulted. The notable body of literature arising by women of the Americas frequently scrutinizes the ingrained *machismo* of Latin culture and views the Church as complicit in that culture in reinforcing stereotypes of women. Nevertheless, Catholicism's spirituality, symbols, and rituals usually remain vital supports in the protagonists' lives. These works often contrast traditional Latino Catholic culture with

United States secular culture as they highlight the manifold difficulties of biculturalism and assimilation. Julia Alvarez (1950– ), for example, examines these issues for Dominican American women in such works as *How the García Girls Lost Their Accents*. Sandra Cisneros (1954– ) also discusses cultural assimilation in *The House on Mango Street*, where she merges traditional Catholic and Mexican imagery to create new symbols for contemporary womanhood. Puerto Rican writers Rosario Ferré (1938– ) and Judith Ortiz Cofer (1952– ) likewise revise traditional iconography from Latino Catholic culture to evolve new patterns of relating to the modern world. And the autobiographies of the human rights activist Rigoberta Menchú (1959– ) consider the plight of indigenous peoples, the position of women, and the role of the Catholic Church in war-torn Guatemala.

In a society oblivious, if not hostile, to such basic Christian beliefs as the need for redemption and the possibility of communion with the divine, several recent authors have used their writings to interpret these beliefs anew and evoke the deeper spirituality and contemplative habit of mind that are at Catholicism's core. Southerner Valerie Sayers's (1952– ) characters in such novels as *Who Do You Love* move through the suffering of modern alienation and confusion from exile to salvation; like Flannery O'Connor before her, Sayers is convinced of the vital importance of faith, grace, and redemption in today's world. Sister Carol Anne O'Marie's (1933– ) mystery stories featuring an elderly Catholic nun turned sleuth can be read as modern morality plays that address matters of the destructive nature of sin, the important of social justice, and God's unfailing mercy on fallen human nature. Informed by a Catholic aesthetic, Theresa Hak Kyung Cha's (1951–1982) *Dictee* mingles traditional Korean images with classical and religious motifs, including excerpts from Thérèse of Lisieux's autobiography, to express the Asian American immigrant experience of physical and spiritual exile from the homeland. Costa Rican poet Eunice Odio (1919–1974) infused her lyrics with Christian mysticism and her intense devotion to St. Michael the Archangel. One of the twentieth century's finest poets, Denise Levertov (1923–1997) created a multidimensional body of work, which, in such collections as *The Stream and the Sapphire* and *A Door in the Hive,* explored her own faith journey to Catholicism. Also a convert to the faith, Annie Dillard (1945– ) seeks God through the study of nature and contemplates the pervasive mystery of violence and suffering in creation— "the thorny beauty of the real"—in such books as *Pilgrim at Tinker Creek* and *Holy the Firm*. And last, one of the most intriguing contemporary writers on spirituality, Kathleen Norris (1947– ), who is not Catholic, promotes a spirit of ecumenism and introduces a generation of Americans to the value of Catholic monastic life—to silence, contemplation, prayer, chastity, poverty—in *The Cloister Walk*. If indeed in every age the Church is renewed not primarily by institutional decrees but by reinvigorated and re-imagined spirituality, women writers from the time of the great mystics to today have contributed powerfully to such renewal by giving voice to the Spirit's promptings.

## NOTES

1. Used by Catholics to describe the Eucharist, this phrase is also the title of George Steiner's book (*Real Presences,* Chicago: University of Chicago Press, 1989).

2. Ross Labrie, *The Catholic Imagination in American Literature* (Columbia: University of Missouri Press, 1997): 4.

3. Flannery O'Connor, *Mystery and Manners,* ed. Sally and Robert Fitzgerald (New York: Farrar, Straus & Giroux, 1969): 165.

4. O'Connor, 41, 165.

5. Albert Gelpi, "The Catholic Presence in American Culture," *American Literary History* 11.1 (Spring 1999): 202–03.

6. *Julian of Norwich Showings,* trans. Edmund Colledge and James Walsh (New York: Paulist Press, 1978): 134–35, short text.

7. David S. Reynolds, *Faith in Fiction: The Emergence of Religious Literature in America* (Cambridge, Massachusetts: Harvard University Press, 1981): 154.

8. Gene Kellogg, *The Vital Tradition: The Catholic Novel in a Period of Convergence* (Chicago: Loyola University Press, 1970): 225–26.

9. Muriel Spark, *The Comforters,* in *A Muriel Spark Trio* (New York: J. B. Lippincott, 1962): 93–94.

10. Mary Gordon, *Final Payments* (New York: Random House, 1978): 57.

11. Although the Catholic Church officially condemned the heresy of Jansenism in 1653, its legacy throughout French and Irish Catholicism in particular has been persistent. Jansenist influence on American Catholicism has been strong due to the fact that its negative view of human nature resonated with the Puritan/Calvinist view of natural depravity.

12. Anita Gandolfo, *Testing the Faith: The New Catholic Fiction in America* (Westport, Connecticut: Greenwood Press, 1992): 142.

# CATHOLIC
# WOMEN
# WRITERS

# MARGARET MARY ALACOQUE
# (1647–1690)

## BIOGRAPHY

The Catholic Counter Reformation was in full flower in France when, on July 22, 1647, Margaret Mary was born into the Alacoque family in the provincial town of Lauthecourt. Her childhood was marked by difficulties. The death of her father left her mother with five small children and few means. Thus Margaret Mary received little education until she was placed in a convent of Poor Clares at the age of eight. Continual illnesses cut short her convent stay. Subsequently, she and her mother were reduced to a state of virtual domestic captivity by relatives who assumed charge of their affairs. Being shy and of an imaginative nature, the young girl began to seek out solitude and the consolation of prayer with her beloved Jesus. This prayer, which took various forms, including conversations, visual imagery, and divine appearances, would continue to be the focal attraction of her entire life.

Despite her mother's entreaties, Margaret Mary avoided an adolescent proposal of marriage and clung to her growing desire to enter religious life. This she did in June of 1671 when she entered the Visitation Monastery in Paray-le-Monial, a community founded as part of loyalist Catholic efforts to counteract the powerful Protestant presence in the region. Her early years in the monastery were trying ones, as her superiors were wary of her singular inner life. They sought to teach her more normative methods of mental prayer, which she seemed incapable of learning, and stressed exact obedience to the monastic rule, which seemed to elude her. Gradually, through interior instruction from Jesus, Margaret Mary Alacoque was able to submit to the discipline of the monastery. She came to understand her sufferings as part of the plan that he had for her.

Taking final vows in 1672, the rest of Margaret Mary's life was spent, to all outward appearances, in the daily routine of prayer and work that characterizes the monastic life. However, her inner life was far from routine. Gradually, the inner drama that was her chief preoccupation became public. The narrative that gave shape to Margaret Mary Alacoque's self understanding was one whose elements had long been articulated in Christian hagiography but which voiced the singular spiritual perspective of the late seventeenth century. She saw herself as a chosen spouse who shared Christ's bed of sufferings, as well as a beloved disciple commissioned to spread the burning flames of his charity. Her inner experiences came often in the form of imaginative visions. In this she was encouraged by Jesuit Claude de la Colombière, the monastery's confessor from 1675–1676 and her spiritual advisor via letter until his death in 1682. It was through the posthumous dissemination of his retreat notes, which made anonymous but recognizable reference to the Visitandine's visions, that Alacoque's story became known.

Under obedience to her superiors, including one of the monastery's later Jesuit confessors, Father Rolin, Alacoque began to record the drama of her inner life. This resulted in a manuscript that has become known variantly as *Vie par elle-même*, or in English, the *Life* or *Autobiography*. Central to this narrative were the accounts of a series of "great revelations" in which Christ revealed to her the secrets of his Sacred Heart and requested that devotional practices—a Thursday holy hour of adoration, communion on the first Friday of each month, and a feast on the Friday following the feast of Corpus Christi (Christ's body and blood)—be instituted to honor that Heart and make reparation for the indifference and disdain it was shown.

Sister Alacoque held several offices within her community before her death in October 1690 at the age of forty-three: novice mistress (1685–1686) and assistant to the superior (1690). During her term as novice mistress, she introduced the Sacred Heart devotion that had been the focus of her visions. Soon the devotion spread throughout the Visitation order. When in the eighteenth century the papacy promoted the Sacred Heart as a devotion to be embraced by the universal Church, Margaret Mary Alacoque's particular formulation of the devotion served as its basis. Sacred Heart piety spread rapidly in the nineteenth century, that era in which devotionalism virtually defined Roman Catholicism. Margaret Mary Alacoque was seen as the font of the diffusion of the graces of the Sacred Heart into the global community. It was in this climate that the Paray nun was canonized in 1920 by Pope Benedict XV.


## MAJOR THEMES

Margaret Mary Alacoque did not think of herself as a writer nor did she aspire to the renown to which circulation of her words might lead. Writing an account of the intimate events that transpired within her was, to use her own words, a "repugnant" activity to which she submitted only under order from her superiors (*Autobiography*, TAN 1986, p. 19). In fact, she ceased writing her *Autobiography* once the confessor who had ordered it ceased his ministry in her community. Nevertheless her words, especially the *Autobiography*, have been widely circulated, both in the original French and in numerous translations, in the three centuries since they were authored.

As literature, the *Autobiography* belongs to the genre of what might now be termed spiritual autobiography. On a first reading, the descriptive term "autobiography" might strike the modern reader as ill suited. Alacoque does include some information about her family and her life in religion. But the trajectory of the narrative is guided not by the outward events of her life but by the spiritual drama going on within. The story chronicles her growing intimacy with Christ and describes the remarkable visitations, insights, visions, and exterior and interior trials that accompanied that intimacy. At the heart of the narrative are her descriptions of the "great revelations."

A central theme that permeates the *Autobiography* is that of loss of self or *anéantisement* (annihilation). This theme threads through the Christian spiritual tradition from its inception but finds its most emphatic articulation in seventeenth-century France. Thus Alacoque was not alone among her contemporaries in seeing herself as achieving intimacy with and conformity to Christ by recognizing herself as an "abyss of unworthiness" who could "thank my Sovereign Lord for making me appear such as I really was in order to annihilate me in the esteem of creatures" (*Autobiography*, p. 104). This language of loss of self was ubiquitous in spiritual literature at the end of the century, and was found in both male and female writers as well as in different streams of spiritual thought. It was grounded in a wider cultural discourse of absolutism, strengthened during the reign of Louis XIV and under the impetus of the French Counter Reformation, which stressed hierarchical order and obedience in things civil and religious.

Such radical identification with the crucified Christ achieved through one's own suffering had, however, a redemptive end. Alacoque perceived her pain to be united to Christ's: a pain engendered by an immeasurable love, which ached to redeem the world. Thus she could write,

A large cross was shown me, the extremity of which I could not see, but it was all covered with flowers. [Jesus said] "Behold the bed of My chaste spouses on which I shall make thee taste all the delights of My pure Love. Little by little these flowers will drop off, and nothing will remain but the thorns, which are hidden because of thy weaknesses. Nevertheless, thou shalt feel the pricks of these thorns so keenly that thou wilt need all the strength of my love to bear the pain." These words delighted me, as I thought I should never find enough suffering . . . for my love for Him gave me no respite day or night. (*Autobiography*, pp. 62–63)

Margaret Mary Alacoque claimed, in union with Christ, to be the chosen disciple of the Sacred Heart who decried a world that rejected and neglected the God of Love made manifest on the cross, prodigally available in the Eucharist, and symbolized in the Sacred Heart.

Spiritual autobiography was a familiar literary genre in Alacoque's day, especially within devout circles. It can be included in the larger genre of inspirational writing, including hagiography, that has enjoyed lively circulation from Christianity's beginnings. Her account has much in common with medieval writing about and by saintly women, especially visionaries. Several motifs central to her narrative—the mystical exchange of hearts between herself and Christ, the engraving of the divine name on her breast, visions of Jesus requesting the institution of a liturgical feast—are found in earlier lives of saintly women. Similarly, the language of spiritual espousal that frames her self-identity is ubiquitous among medieval and early modern writers, a self-identity that is not exclusively female but which is almost always claimed by women.

Margaret Mary Alacoque's narrative is unique in that it became the foundation for the public devotion to the Sacred Heart. Although devotion to the Heart was an ancient private Christian practice, one with which both the founders of the Visitation as well as later Visitandines were familiar, the specific liturgical and visual forms of the devotion advanced by the saint were singular. News of her visions and the later circulation of her narrative and its promotion by well-placed Jesuit ecclesiastics gave encouragement to the devotion. During the eighteenth and nineteenth centuries, the annual feast and liturgical practices urged by Margaret Mary Alacoque were promoted by the papacy and became one of the defining devotions of the pre-Vatican II Church.

## SURVEY OF CRITICISM

As literary efforts, Margaret Mary Alacoque's writings are unremarkable. Her translators have complained that her words are difficult to render into another language, that her grammar and syntax are faulty, that she strings together disparate thoughts in a single sentence, and that her style is rustic. Their author had only two years of formal schooling, wrote only under obedience, and was forbidden to reread or correct what she had written for fear she might destroy it. Her importance as a Catholic woman writer, therefore, lies less in the artfulness of her words than in the experience they express, the spiritual authority they imply, and the influence they have had on the Church since she committed them to paper.

The *Autobiography*, along with her collected letters and fragmentary words of advice and instruction, composes the full corpus of Alacoque's work, none of which was published before her death. The content of her "great revelations" was known during her lifetime, as was her love for the Sacred Heart and her desire that it be adored in her community and beyond. A report of her revelations was included in a treatise written by Jesuit Father Croiset under the title *La devotion de Sacré-Coeur de Jesus* in 1694, as well as in the posthumous notice in the annual Circular sent to all the Visitation monasteries. However, the existence of an autobiographical manuscript only came to light some time after the author's last illness during which she had asked her superior to write to the confessor who had ordered its writing and forbidden its destruction and ask for permission to burn the sixty-four page copybook stored in her cup-board. The superior denied the request and the manuscript was saved.

The *Autobiography,* under the title *Life of the Servant of God,* was first pub-lished in 1726 (in Latin), then again in 1733 (in French), with some changes in style and diction, by Jesuit Father Gallifet in a treatise on the Sacred Heart. Several editions followed. The original text was mostly restored in 1867 when the sisters of the Visitation of Paray-le-Monial published their first edition of Alacoque's works, *Oeuvres de la Bienheureuse* [Collected Works of the Blessed]. However, for "fluency's" sake, some words and passages were omit-ted and others added in this and an 1876 edition.

It was not until the nineteenth century that a critical edition of Sr. Alacoque's work was undertaken. In part, interest in this new edition was sparked by the popularity of numerous pious biographies that were circulat-ing. The scholarly sensitivities of François-Leon Gauthey, a cleric and later archbishop of Besançon, were aroused. He, in collaboration with archivists from the Paray monastery, began collecting documents in 1890 for a first scholarly edition of her works. Despite the fact that great archival losses had been incurred during the French Revolution when monastic communities were disbanded, the original *Vie par elle-même* had survived, as had memoirs of many of Margaret Mary Alacoque's contemporaries. Father Gauthey's 1915 edition remained the standard until the 1990 Saint-Paul edition was published in Paris under the supervision of Professeur Darricau. The latter was occa-sioned by the tercentenary of Margaret Mary Alacoque's death.

The Gauthey edition served as the basis of the innumerable translations of the *Autobiography* that were circulated in the nineteenth and early twentieth centuries. Virtually every language in which Catholic devotional literature has been published has enjoyed an edition of the Paray nun's narrative. Multiple European language editions were produced. Always, Alacoque's popularity as a writer has been linked to her reputation as a saint and visionary, a "chosen disciple" who received revelations destined to change the face of Catholic de-votion by securing a place in the public liturgy, in theological speculation, and in sacred art for the Sacred Heart of Jesus.

## BIBLIOGRAPHY

### Works by Margaret Mary Alacoque

*Vie et oeuvres de Sainte Marguerite-Marie Alacoque* [Life and Works of Saint Margaret Mary Alacoque]. 1915. Presentation du Professeur Darricau. 2 vols. Paris-Fribourg: Éditions Saint-Paul, 1990.

*The Autobiography of Saint Margaret Mary.* Trans. by the Sisters of the Visitation. Partridge Green, Horsham, West Sussex, England: Sisters of the Visitation, 1930. Rockford, Illinois: TAN Books and Publishers, 1986.

*The Letters of Saint Margaret Mary Alacoque.* Trans. Father Clarence A. Herbst, S.J. Chicago: Henry Regnery Company, 1954. Rockford, Illinois: TAN Books and Publishers, 1997.

### Works about Margaret Mary Alacoque

Bougaud, Rt. Rev. Émile. *The Life of Saint Margaret Mary Alacoque.* Trans. by a Visitandine of Baltimore. New York: Benzinger Brothers, 1890. Rockford, Illinois: TAN Books and Publishers, 1990.

Callahan, Annice. "The Visions of Margaret Mary Alacoque from a Rahnerian Perspective." *Modern Christian Spirituality: Methodological and Historical Essays.* Ed. Bradley C. Hanson. Atlanta, Georgia: Scholars Press, 1990. 183–200.

Darricau, R., and B. Peyrous, eds. *Sainte Marguerite-Marie Alacoque et le message de Paray-le-Monial* [Saint Margaret Mary Alacoque and the Message of Paray-le-Monial]. Paris: Éditions Desclée, 1993.

WENDY M. WRIGHT

# JULIA ALVAREZ
## (1950– )

## BIOGRAPHY

Dominican American writer Julia Alvarez was born in New York City in 1950. Although tied to the United States by birth, Alvarez spent the length of her childhood with her parents and three sisters in the family's native home of the Dominican Republic. Island life for the young Alvarez was full of privileges and comforts. Not only was her family financially well off, but she was also surrounded by a host of nearby aunts, uncles, cousins, and grandparents—family whose adjacent properties combined to form an extended compound in which Alvarez and her sisters were lavishly indulged.

Life changed drastically for Alvarez when she was just ten years old. Her father's activities as a political insurgent working to oust then-dictator Rafael Trujillo were suddenly discovered, and the family was forced to flee the country. Their new home in Queens, New York, was a particularly hostile place of exile. Gone was the affluent lifestyle of the Dominican Republic as well as any semblance of Latin culture. In an attempt to cope with this new environment, Alvarez threw herself into her schoolbooks and set about mastering the English language. By the time she entered Connecticut College in 1967, she was already a fledgling writer, capturing the school's Benjamin T. Marshall Prize in poetry shortly after her arrival, an award she would win two years in a row. Alvarez continued writing even after transferring to Middlebury College in 1969. She won Middlebury's Creative Writing Prize during her final year of school and went on to earn her M.F.A. at Syracuse University, graduating in 1975.

For the next several years, Alvarez crisscrossed the country, hopping from one temporary appointment to another—conducting poetry workshops, attending writing seminars, teaching college courses, and tirelessly honing her craft. Finally, in 1984, Grove Press published Alvarez's first book of poetry, a slim volume of works entitled *Homecoming*. After its release, Alvarez began to dedicate more time to fiction instead of verse. By the late 1980s, she had also exchanged her life of frequent upheaval for one of professional and personal stability, accepting a tenure-track teaching position with the Department of English at Middlebury College and marrying her third and current husband, a doctor from Nebraska. Perhaps the most defining moment in her writing career occurred two years later, in 1991, when she succeeded in publishing her first "novel," a series of interconnected short stories entitled *How the García Girls Lost Their Accents*. The work was immediately praised for its insider's account of the tensions and anxieties associated with Latino biculturalism, and it all but established Alvarez as a prominent figure among contemporary Latina women writers.

Today, Alvarez continues to live and work in Vermont. Although raised a strict Catholic and even educated in Catholic institutions, she has long distanced herself from the Church, explaining in her autobiographical compilation of essays *Something to Declare* (1998) that Catholicism's "ban against the ordination of women, its stance on birth control, [and] its system of indulgences and penances" (p. 254) have all caused her to renounce Church doctrine and redefine her religious status as that of a "lapsed and divorced Catholic" (p. 231).

## MAJOR THEMES

Much of Julia Alvarez's work is semi-autobiographical, and therefore it foregrounds the same themes that figure prominently in the author's own life: the importance of family and the complexities of biculturalism. For most of Alvarez's texts, these two themes are interconnected; that is to say, family becomes the space in which the trials and anxieties of cultural assimilation are played out, tested, and negotiated. The mediating function of the family as such appears most visibly in *How the García Girls Lost Their Accents*, a text that centers on each of the four García sisters as they make the difficult transition between island life in the Dominican Republic and American life in New York City. The focused vignettes of the novel reflect a family unit that weakens and rallies in close sync with each daughter's attempt to find her own compromise between the old way of life and the new. Papi's outrage at Yolanda's proposed Teacher's Day speech—a speech in which Yolanda borrows from Whitman, writing, "The best student learns to destroy the teacher" (1992, p. 145)—offers a telling example of this dynamic, for Yolanda's thrill over having written something in which "[s]he finally sounded like herself in English" (1992, p. 143) prompts outrage in her father, a man whose old-world paranoia over acts of institutional rebellion prevents him from allowing Yolanda to speak the American voice she has so lately discovered.

While Alvarez treats family and biculturalism in ways that emphasize the interplay between these two categories of experience, both themes also highlight other issues the author routinely deals with in her works. Specifically, the theme of cultural assimilation allows Alvarez to critique the social construction of women in the male dominant societies of both the Dominican Republic and the United States. In *Something to Declare*, for example, Alvarez's experience watching the annual Miss America pageant forces her to consider the restrictions placed on the women of her native culture ("We were being groomed to go from being dutiful daughters to being dutiful wives with hymens intact" [p. 42]) and, surprisingly, those placed on American women as well. She learns that, despite the array of career opportunities available to them, American women are regularly judged by standards of beauty that enact the same methods of exclusion and oppression imposed by institutionalized gender roles.

Alvarez's second novel speaks even more forcefully as a feminist text. The only one of her works set exclusively in the Dominican Republic, *In the Time of the Butterflies* (1994) relates the tragic true story of the four Mirabal sisters, three of whom were murdered on November 25, 1960, in retaliation for their organized resistance against the leadership of Dominican Dictator Trujillo. The sisters of this particular novel are insurrectionists of a political and cultural kind, for they openly challenge both the patriarchal rule that governs their country and that which governs their churches, their families, and their entire life prospects. The third eldest, Minerva, embodies the sisters' subversive spirit the best, appearing before the reader as a woman who not only demands for herself a university education but has the courage to critique the behavior of her philandering father, to reject the sexual advances of the dictator, and to privilege the activist impulse inside her over a forced sense of maternal obligation.

Rooted in Alvarez's critique of the phallocentric rule that controls women in Dominican society is a critique of the dominant Catholic religion that also participates in such an oppressive order. Minerva, in *In the Time of the Butterflies*, by far the most involved of the sisters in the plot to precipitate a national revolution, rejects the Catholic Church, having observed in the case of her school friend, Lina, the manner in which organized religion functions as a tool of the dictatorship. Alvarez's treatment of Catholicism in this text, however, is notably complex. At the same time that she implicates the institution as a proponent of a repressive status quo, she also shows the incalculable power that underwrites a strong Catholic faith. The spirituality shared by the sisters in this text, for example, poses no obstacle to female self-empowerment; it functions on the contrary as a force that renders these women practically omnipotent—a force that allows them to endure intimidation, separation, imprisonment, and loss. Dedé understands this fact implicitly, using prayer during one incident to help Patria cope with the capture of her son and husband: "In a soothing voice, [Dedé] reminded her sister of the faith that had always sustained her. 'You believe in God, the Father Almighty, Maker of heaven and earth . . .' Sobbing, Patria fell in, reciting the Credo" (1995, p. 192).

Catholicism as a theme undergirds this novel as it does all of Alvarez's works. Unlike in *In the Time of the Butterflies*, however, where the Catholic religion figures as a concrete political issue, Catholicism enters Alvarez's other texts in much more subtle ways, generally surfacing, once again, as a distinctly cultural concern. In *How the García Girls Lost Their Accents*, for example, Catholicism is a piece of "old world" ideology that must be stretched and reconfigured by the author's characters as they construct themselves anew in their foreign American setting. Yolanda's rejection of the persistent sexual advances of an American boyfriend finds her reflecting on just such a process of renegotiation: "I saw what a cold, lonely life awaited me in this country. I would never find someone who would understand my peculiar mix of Catholicism and agnosticism, Hispanic and American styles" (1992, p. 99).

As this passage demonstrates, Alvarez often uses religion to accentuate the social, political, and cultural differences between the United States and the Dominican Republic. Notably, Catholicism and Catholic iconography are employed almost exclusively as symbols of the Dominican Republic, symbols that are meant to contrast with the relative secularism of America and thus render explicit the gaping discrepancies between the two countries. The use of religion as such is aptly illustrated in Alvarez's poem "Proof," a text in which a young Dominican speaker mistakes New York City's Statue of Liberty for "a giant Virgin" (*The Other Side* 1996, p. 19). The speaker's error in this instance is somewhat amusing, and yet it also succeeds in making a graphic statement about the discrete and conflicting nature of the two cultures symbolized by the famous female patrons associated with each.

Just as in *In the Time of the Butterflies*, however, implicit in Alvarez's use of Catholicism as a cultural marker is also a veiled critique of the Catholic Church in general. Many of Alvarez's references to her own religious upbringing suggest a dissatisfaction with the way the Church thwarts opportunities for self-actualization and restricts the freedoms of women. This critique is readily apparent in the following observation of Sandi in *García Girls*: "The Catholic sisters at Our Lady of Perpetual Sorrows Convent School were teaching me to sort the world like laundry into what was wrong and right. . . . Before I could ever get to my life, conscience was arranging it all like a still life or tableau" (1992, p. 248). Sandi's complaint in this passage about losing control of her own powers of self-determination echoes the sentiments of the protagonist of *Yo!* (1997), a thinly disguised Alvarez who listens in horror as a dutifully Catholic mother draws on Church teachings to persuade her daughter to bear the beatings of an abusive husband (pp. 106–107).

As heavy-handed as this latter indictment of Catholicism may be, Alvarez is not entirely negative in her treatment of the Church. Her poem "Anatomy Lesson," for example, may be read as a partial protest against Catholicism's stance on premarital sex, but it openly validates other precepts of the Church by using aspects of Catholic doctrine to communicate the sacred nature of the love the speaker feels for her future husband (*The Other Side* 1996, pp. 74–78). In other instances, Catholicism takes on an equally positive function, supplying emotional if not spiritual comfort to the various characters in Alvarez's fiction. The fact that Jesus encountered trials in life at age thirty-three, for example, is recalled by the speaker of Alvarez's poem "33" to help her feel more at ease with her own despondency at the same age (*Homecoming* 1996, p. 70). Similarly, Yolanda of *García Girls* clings to her crucifix in times of despair, despite having "laps[ed] from [her] heavy-duty Catholic background" (1992, p. 102). Neither Yolanda nor the speaker of "33" displays a serious commitment to Catholicism, and yet in a final assessment of Alvarez's works, such a point becomes entirely irrelevant. What is important in her texts is not the extent to which a person subscribes to and embraces the Catholic faith, but the extent to which her identity is implicitly informed and shaped by it. Catholicism, for better of worse, figures prominently in this regard, imprinting itself on Alvarez's characters as a persistent reminder of the roots from which they come and of the tangled and complex nature of that grounding.

## SURVEY OF CRITICISM

Unfortunately, no scholarship to date has centered on Alvarez's treatment of Catholicism per se. Of the few essays published on her works, Ilan Stavans and Gus Puleo offer two of the most compelling (if somewhat partial) feminist readings of *In the Time of the Butterflies*, both essays making visible the "gender battlefield" that underwrites Alvarez's fictional retelling of Dominican history. Not of a feminist bent but equally insightful is Joan Hoffman's analysis of language in *How the García Girls Lost Their Accents*. Hoffman's argument that Yolanda's obsession with words is bound up in her "cross-cultural search for identity" (p. 22) is very similar to Julie Barak's analysis of the same book, in which Barak argues that the non-linear narrative structure of the novel effectively dramatizes the task of realizing a non-fractured self in a distinctly fractured cultural setting.

In addition to textual criticism, Jonathan Bing's "Julia Alvarez: Books that Cross Borders" offers one of the most delightful peeks at the personal life of Alvarez. Bing's essay is nicely complemented by Heather Rosario-Sievert's interview transcript "Conversation with Julia Alvarez," a simple but substantive summary of Alvarez's thoughts on her craft and her role as a Dominican American writer.

## BIBLIOGRAPHY

### Works by Julia Alvarez

*Homecoming*. New York: Grove Press, 1984. Reissued as *Homecoming: New and Collected Poems*. New York: Plume, 1996.

*How the García Girls Lost Their Accents*. Chapel Hill, North Carolina: Algonquin Books, 1991; New York: Plume, 1992.

*In the Time of the Butterflies*. Chapel Hill, North Carolina: Algonquin Books, 1994; New York: Plume, 1995.

*The Other Side: El Otro Lado*. New York: Dutton, 1995; New York: Plume, 1996.

*Yo!* Chapel Hill, North Carolina: Algonquin Books, 1997.
*Something to Declare.* Chapel Hill, North Carolina: Algonquin Books, 1998.

### Works about Julia Alvarez

Barak, Julie. "'Turning and Turning in the Widening Gyre': A Second Coming into
    Language in Julia Alvarez's *How the García Girls Lost Their Accents.*"
    *MELUS* 23.1 (1998): 159–76.
Bing, Jonathan. "Julia Alvarez: Books that Cross Borders." *Publishers Weekly* 16 De-
    cember 1996: 38–39.
Hoffman, Joan M. "'She Wants to Be Called Yolanda Now': Identity, Language, and
    the Third Sister in *How the García Girls Lost Their Accents.*" *Bilingual Re-
    view/La Revista Bilingue* 23 (1998): 21–27.
Puleo, Gus. "Remembering and Reconstructing the Mirabal Sisters in Julia Alvarez's
    *In the Time of the Butterflies.*" *Bilingual Review/La Revista Bilingue* 23
    (1998): 11–20.
Rosario-Sievert, Heather. "Conversation with Julia Alvarez." *Review: Latin Ameri-
    can Literature and Arts* 54 (1997): 31–37.
Stavans, Ilan. "Las Mariposas." Rev. of *In the Time of the Butterflies,* by Julia Alvarez.
    *Nation* 7 November 1994: 552–55.

TERESA DERRICKSON

# ANGELA OF FOLIGNO
## (c.1248–1309)

### BIOGRAPHY

Angela, a mystic of the Franciscan tradition, was born in Foligno, a central Italian town not far from Assisi in the region of Umbria. Almost everything we know about Angela is narrated in *The Book of the Blessed Angela of Foligno.*

In 1285, the thirty-seven-year-old Angela underwent a dramatic conversion, the first of many steps in her spiritual journey. Details regarding her life previous to 1285 are virtually unknown. Local tradition has it that she was probably born in 1248 into a wealthy and noble family, and that her father died while she was still very young. When she was probably around twenty years old, Angela married a man who remains anonymous. Although we know no details, we do know that she had several sons and that shortly after her conversion they, along with her husband and mother, all died. According to her own account, she had prayed for their deaths. Although this seems extraordinary, we can surmise from her writings that her family had seemed an obstacle to her, preventing further progress along her spiritual journey.

Passages in Angela's *Book* indicate that previous to her conversion, she seems to have enjoyed the extravagant social life of the wealthy—fancy food, beautiful and expensive clothing, and fine perfumes. They also indicate that she may have had a tendency toward anger, pride, gossiping, and illicit seductive behavior. A local tradition indicates that she was unfaithful to her husband, but no document exists to confirm this claim. However, upon close study of her writings, it does appear that the sin she felt obligated to confess at the onset of her conversion may have been of a sexual nature.

The only explicit motives for her conversion, mentioned in her *Book*, simply indicate that in 1285, she wept sorrowfully, greatly fearing damnation. She was then inspired to go to confession, but in her shame, was unable to confess all of her sins. In her despair, she prayed to St. Francis to help her find a confessor. The next morning she encountered a Franciscan friar, a man who happened to be a relative of hers and who was also chaplain to the local bishop. Angela then decided this was the man for whom she had prayed and made a full confession to him. Biographical tradition refers to this Franciscan simply as "Brother Arnaldo."

Most likely Angela received no formal education, but we can gather from her *Book* that she was an exceptionally cultivated woman. Not unlike other women of her time, she was probably able to read but not write. She dictated the first part of her *Book*, the *Memorial*, to Brother Arnaldo. From probably 1292–1296, Arnaldo, as her confessor, met regularly with Angela in a local church in Foligno, writing down what she told him of her spiritual journey.

Although it was a slow and difficult process, after her conversion Angela began a new life, embarking on the way of penance. From 1285 until 1291, she struggled to liberate herself from her sinful past. Although counseled against it by her religious advisors, Angela desired to follow the example of St. Francis in his poverty. She gave up her extravagant way of life, and distributed most of her belongings to the poor. She made a pilgrimage to Rome in 1291 in order to ask the apostle Peter to help her become truly poor. Upon her return to Foligno, she gave up almost all of her remaining possessions and sold her home to give to the destitute. Sometime in 1291 Angela also became a Franciscan Tertiary. She made another pilgrimage, traveling to Assisi to pray to St. Francis that he might help her remain poor to the end.

Despite the fact that she appears quite frequently in Angela's *Book*, very little is known concerning Angela's companion Masazuola. Initially, Masazuola may have been Angela's servant, but she eventually became her constant companion and spiritual confidante. There are numerous references to the purity and piety of Masazuola in the *Memorial*. We know that she was in direct rapport with Arnaldo and also related to him some of the mystical phenomena she had observed in Angela. Both Angela and her companion cared for the sick and poor.

Angela's life was marked by intense, startling visions and mystical experiences that she related to Brother Arnaldo. She also experienced intermittent periods of agony and joy. From 1296 to her death in 1309, very little is known of her life. In 1300, she made another pilgrimage to Assisi and in 1301 she traveled to Spello, a small town near Foligno, to visit the Poor Clares. We know that a group of disciples and devotees had begun to gather around her to listen to her teachings, and it is to them that the second part of her *Book*, the *Instructions,* are addressed. The last of the *Instructions* narrates what she told her disciples during her final illness and records her death in 1309. Angela was never canonized by the Church, but she was given the title of "Blessed" in 1701.

## MAJOR THEMES

The *Memorial*, which Angela dictated to Brother Arnaldo, narrates the steps or transformations the soul makes as it advances along its spiritual journey. Arnaldo wrote down as best he could what she dictated to him in her

Umbrian dialect and then later translated her words into Latin. Arnaldo asserts on more than one occasion that he was very conscientious while copying Angela's *Memorial*, often times rereading to her what she had dictated to him to be sure he had transcribed it correctly. Angela acknowledged that, while what he wrote was somehow "weakened," it was basically faithful to what she had told him.

Drawing from her own experience, Angela originally designated thirty steps. Arnaldo transcribed nineteen steps and part of the twentieth. Unsure how to describe and enumerate the remaining material, he assembled the rest of her revelations into seven "supplementary" steps. The first twenty steps describe Angela's purification through suffering and her subsequent intimacy with God. She experiences increasingly intense visions of Christ's passion and crucifixion, and becomes acutely conscious of her sins. She emphasizes an awareness of divine mercy, self-knowledge, and an understanding of the meaning of the cross. Determined to align her life with Christ's and follow the example of St. Francis, she pledges perpetual chastity and ardently desires to become poor. Feeling such intense delight in prayer and in love of God, she experiences physical illness, mystical consolations, and loss of her power of speech.

In the first five supplementary steps, Angela's ascension is characterized by increasingly intense visions and experiences of Christ crucified, the Eucharist, the universe filled with the presence of God, and various other formless visions of the Godhead. Through these powerful and even shocking divine revelations, Angela grows even more intimate with Christ, whom she calls the suffering "God-Man." Despite the nature of her intense visions, she endures periods of emptiness, doubts, uncertainties, and temptations from the devil. These periods are interspersed with feelings of immense joy and certitude of God's love.

The sixth supplementary step describes various torments upon her body and soul inflicted upon her by demons, as well as the deep abyss into which she was plunged. The seventh supplementary step, however, relates lofty visions of God in and beyond the divine darkness. This marks the highest point of her mystical ascent and recalls the negative theology of the Pseudo-Dionysius, which defines God in terms of what he "is not" rather than what he "is."

The thirty-six *Instructions* contain Angela's teachings and admonitions, offered to her devotees to whom she had become a spiritual mother. They also contain other mystical experiences that presumably occurred after the first part of her *Book* was written. The *Instructions* were addressed to and transcribed by anonymous disciples. Most of them are undated, and some may be additions and glosses composed by various disciple scribes. The teachings that appear in the *Instructions* are grounded in the *Memorial*, although they are frequently amplified. The various themes of the *Instructions* include but are not limited to these: the following of Christ, the suffering God-Man and his cross, Christ's poverty, prayer, the Eucharist, and knowledge of God and self.

## SURVEY OF CRITICISM

Paul Lachance's critical edition of Angela's *Book* in *Angela of Foligno: Complete Works* contains an excellent and thorough introduction that gives a complete panorama of Angela's life and times as well as the historical, cultural, and spiritual currents surrounding them. Lachance discusses Angela's direct influence on her contemporary disciples, and also points out that her *Book* was perhaps used for polemical purposes in the struggle between various factions of the Franciscan movement in the early fourteenth century. He mentions the early manuscripts of her works and the influence of her teachings through the centuries. Angela's influence extended to many philosophers, saints, and theologians, including Teresa of Avila, Ignatius of Loyola, Francis de Sales, Alphonsus Liguori, and the French philosopher Ernest Hello. Lachance also considers various critical editions and translations of her works.

Angela's writings have lately enjoyed a good deal of scholarly interest. I limit discussion to only those most noteworthy. Bynum examines Angela in the framework of other medieval holy women, emphasizing the role of food, the Eucharist, female imagery, and the body in their writings and religious devotional practices. Petroff also discusses Angela alongside other medieval female religious. Sagnella investigates Angela's writings in light of the negative medieval perception of the female body as vile, while Archangeli attempts to disentangle Angela's voice from that of Arnaldo in the *Memorial*. Archangeli argues that Angela's voice is filtered; thus we as readers remain somewhat removed from it. Mooney also examines the role of Arnaldo in the transcribing of the *Memorial*. And finally, Lavalva considers the role of language in Angela's attempt to narrate her mystical visions to Arnaldo.

## BIBLIOGRAPHY

### Work by Angela of Foligno

*Angela of Foligno: Complete Works.* Ed. and trans. Paul Lachance. New York: Paulist Press, 1993.

### Works about Angela of Foligno

Arcangeli, Tiziana. "Re-reading a Mis-known and Mis-read Mystic: Angela da Foligno." *Annali d'Italianistica* 13 (1995): 41–78.

Bynum, Caroline Walker. *Fragmentation and Redemption: Essays on Gender and the Human Body in Medieval Religion.* New York: Zone, 1991.

Lavalva, Rosamaria. "The Language of Vision in Angela da Foligno's *Liber de vera fidelium experientia.*" *Stanford Italian Review* 11.1–2 (1992): 103–22.

Mooney, Catherine M. "The Authorial Role of Brother A. in the Composition of Angela of Foligno's Revelations." *Creative Women in Medieval and Early Modern Italy.* Ed. Ann E. Matter and John Coakley. Philadelphia: University of Pennsylvania Press, 1994. 34–63.

Petroff, Elizabeth Alvilda. *Body and Soul: Essays on Medieval Women and Mysticism.* New York: Oxford University Press, 1994. 204–23.

———, ed. *Medieval Women's Visionary Literature.* New York: Oxford University Press, 1986. 231–41.

Sagnella, Mary Ann. "Carnal Metaphors and Mystical Discourse in Angela da Foligno's *Liber.*" *Annali d'Italianistica* 13 (1995): 79–90.

MOLLY MORRISON

# KATHERINE BURTON
# (1884?–1969)

## BIOGRAPHY

Katherine Burton (née Kurz), one of the twentieth century's most prolific Catholic biographers, was born near Cleveland around 1884.[1] After graduating from (Case) Western Reserve University, Burton briefly taught private school. In 1910, she married Harry Payne Burton, a newspaper reporter who later became a magazine editor. Early in her marriage, Burton also worked as a newspaper reporter. Once she had three children, she became a stay-at-home, suburban mother. Burton's comfortable life was upended in the late 1920s when her husband had a nervous breakdown and left his family. To support herself and her children, she began working as an associate magazine editor, for *McCall's* from 1928 to 1930 and for *Redbook* from 1930 to 1933.

Burton was raised as a nominal Lutheran. When she married, she began attending Episcopal services with her husband. Burton first took an interest in Catholicism after her husband's breakdown. Drawn several times to the local Catholic parish, Burton experienced great peace inside the sanctuary. On one occasion, she stated that she felt inexplicably sustained by a presence outside of herself, presumably the Real Presence (*Next Thing*, p. 98). She slowly approached Catholicism, heading first for the Anglo-Catholic wing of the Episcopal Church and then entering the Catholic Church in 1930, moved by the witness of Catholic friends and awed by "the beauty of the Catholic faith" (*Next Thing*, p. 118).

In 1933, Burton resigned from *Redbook* and began pursuing a freelance career in earnest. Before her conversion, she had published some poetry and written occasionally for an Episcopal periodical. After her conversion, she published poems, a short story, and monthly columns in the Catholic magazine *Sign*, essays in *Catholic World* and *Commonweal*, forty biographies of notable Catholics and Catholic institutions, a cookbook for feast days, and her own autobiography. In the words of her colleagues at *Catholic World*, her pen was "indefatigable" ("Our Contributors," p. 209).

Burton was a tertiary in the Dominican order, received therein by the same priest who had received Rose Hawthorne Lathrop, the subject of the first book Burton wrote after her conversion. Burton published her last book in 1965 and died on September 22, 1969.[2]

## MAJOR THEMES

All of the poems Burton wrote, even those published before her conversion, explicitly convey her religious convictions. Her two pre-conversion poems, published in 1927, convey the Catholic nature of Burton's Anglicanism: "'So Died a True Christian'" refers to a crucifix and "A Prayer for Ronald" refers to the intercession of the saints. Two of Burton's post-conversion poems convey her beliefs while commenting on current events: "To the Soviet Rulers," published in 1933, predicts the triumph of the cross over the hammer and sickle, and "November Eleventh," published in 1938, pleads for the intercession of "Mary, Queen of Peace" on Veterans Day.

Burton's short story "The Leper Who Sought His Lord" features a leper healed by Christ who pursues him to express his gratitude. This story, published in 1935, exhibits two traits that would be prominent in Burton's columns, biographies, and histories. The story takes fictional liberties with a factual story (e.g., the leper encounters one of the shepherds who was present at Christ's birth), and it emphasizes Christian humanitarianism (Christ heals the sick, and in turn, the sick strengthen Christ).

Burton's most engaging writings are her columns in Catholic periodicals, especially those in *Sign*. In her monthly "Woman to Woman" columns for that magazine, Burton ventured opinions on matters ranging from war to women in politics, from birth control to the education of children. The keynote of all her columns is moderation. Consistently avoiding extremes, she rendered opinions in keeping with Church teaching. For instance, on the issue of birth control, Burton denounced Planned Parenthood and stated her conviction that the Pill had sown a "crop of disaster" (*Woman*, p. 100). But she also decried Catholics who were oblivious to the challenges couples face in remaining open to God's will regarding the size of their families, and she promoted the rhythm method soon after it was developed. Similarly, on the issue of war and peace, Burton was an ardent pacifist until World War II but she believed that war was necessary (pp. 142–43). She did, however, oppose the atomic bombings of Hiroshima and Nagasaki (p. 158).

Burton's moderation is also evident in her many columns about women and their possible vocations. When her husband left his young family, she quickly learned to balance the vocations of motherhood and authorship in her own life. Thus, while she believed that being a stay-at-home mother is "the greatest job in the world" (*Woman*, p. 64), she commended women who work outside the home to support themselves or their husbandless families (*Woman*, p. 85; *Next Thing*, p. 112). Likewise, Burton defended St. Paul against charges of sexism but also advocated greater responsibility for women in the world and in the Church. Burton believed that "equality of sexes does not mean identity"; that is, that God gave men and women different but equally important roles to play in the world (*Woman*, p. 85). In Burton's opinion, women's role was to be humble, yet assertive. Her personal role models were the Blessed Virgin Mary, St. Catherine of Siena, and St. Bernadette, all of whom submitted to God but courageously adhered to their convictions before men. Burton herself did not hesitate to reveal strong opinions on topics heated in her day and ours: school violence, economic exploitation, American materialism, and racial integration.

Burton's columns do not simply express the Catholic faith; they show that faith alive in love. Fond of Martin Luther King's command to "Walk—but walk with God" (quoted in *Woman*, p. 33), Burton advocated good works grounded in deep faith. She championed ordinary people "living quiet lives full of affectionate care for others" (p. 20). And she sought to be such a person, using her columns to solicit Christmas gifts for the elderly and relief packages for victims of World War II.

Katherine Burton is most remembered for her prodigious output of Catholic biographies and histories, which will be discussed interchangeably here. According to her autobiography, Burton believed most Catholic biographies were irrelevant and colorless (*Next Thing*, pp. 192–93), and she thought most Catholic women writers were "too moralistic and preachy" and thus off-putting to readers (p. 228). Setting herself against these tendencies, Burton attempted to write subtle biographies that would read like fiction and relate to contemporary life.

Fictionality is the hallmark of Burton's biographies. For the most part, her books have their facts straight and are, as she intended, "fictional in style only" (*Next Thing*, p. 200). Her books read like novels insofar as they contain a great deal of dialogue, feature numerous anecdotes, and revel in quirky details. In writing dialogue, Burton envisioned herself as re-creating "what might well have been said" between the subjects of her books (p. 201). For instance, she imagined what Rose Hawthorne Lathrop and her estranged husband might have said to each other as he was dying (*Sorrow*, pp. 179–81).[3] Dialogue fills Burton's earliest biographies to the point of distraction, but it was used more sparingly in her later works.

At times, Burton's anecdotes seem unnecessary, but some do lead readers to a better comprehension of an important aspect of the subject's life. For example, Burton begins *Witness of the Light* (1958), her biography of Pope Pius XII, by depicting a little boy listening to his grandfather read a newspaper. The boy is the future pope, the grandfather is the founder of the newspaper, and the newspaper is the Vatican's *L'Osservatore Romano*. This anecdote establishes Pius XII's papal destiny. Likewise, Burton's fondness for novelesque detail can irk as well as engage. Some of her books, such as *Sorrow Built a Bridge* (1937), become so bogged down in detail that readers may lose sight of the narrative

Burton purports to tell. Yet other books bring characters to life by revealing their quirks. For instance, *Witness of the Light* endears readers to Pope Pius XII by reporting that he treasured his electric shaver. *The Next Thing* (1949), Burton's autobiography, profiles the spiritually restless aunt who took Burton only to sermons proffered by "youthful and romantic deliverers" (p. 25).

Burton sought to engage readers not only by fictionalizing her biographies but also by relating them to her readers' lives. Nearly half of her biographies center on American Catholics, and even those that center on non-Americans gravitate towards Americans. In *Witness of the Light*, for example, Burton minutely records the visit of future Pope Pius XII to the United States and reports that he was ecstatic "to learn the progress of the Faith" in this country (p. 101). One of Burton's most nationalistic books is *The Dream Lives Forever* (1960), a history of St. Patrick's Cathedral. Therein, she emphasizes how "American" the Cathedral was designed to be, speaks of the affection of popes for the United States, and mentions many American clerics who were made cardinals. Evidently, Burton was determined to prove, along with Isaac Hecker, the founder of the Passionist order, that "a Catholic can be a good American, just as an American can be a good Catholic" (paraphrased in *Woman*, p. 129).

Determined as Burton was to defend American Catholics, she promoted Catholicism quite subtly. On only rare occasions, she referred to the Catholic Church as "the true fold" (*Make the Way Known*, p. 21) and spoke of Catholicism's "true value" (*Sorrow*, p. 50). More commonly, Burton let facts speak for themselves. For instance, she recorded what the subjects of her biographies did and let readers infer why they did so. In *Make the Way Known* (1959), for example, she profiles a nun who risks her own safety to save her convent, and in *Sorrow Built a Bridge* she depicts Rose Hawthorne Lathrop as caring for a man who vomited blood on her. While Burton does not directly attribute such heroic acts to Catholic convictions, the Catholic emphasis on self-abnegation comes across clearly in her description of the acts. Burton further exemplifies subtlety by a conciliatory approach to non-Catholics. Her books highlight ecumenical endeavors, and assume interest in but not knowledge of Catholicism on the part of readers. Burton patiently explains the Stations of the Cross, the process of papal elections, and other "long and lovely rituals of the Church" (*The Dream*, p. 219).

In sum, Katherine Burton aspired to weave facts into stories, relate these stories to her readers' lives, and evangelize with mitigated fervor.

## SURVEY OF CRITICISM

Intent as Burton was on steering clear of irrelevance, tedium, and didacticism, many early critics of her biographies believed she did not entirely avoid these pitfalls. Critics generally agreed that her books would serve ordinary readers well but would be irrelevant to scholars. Her books were considered unscholarly because they contained some inaccuracies and were fictionalized. In fact, fictionality was the most disputed aspect of Burton's works. Some critics found it dull or confusing; others considered it amusing and enlightening. Partiality was another debated feature of Burton's writings. Several reviewers said only Catholics would appreciate her works, and even a presumably Catholic critic, writing for *Commonweal,* found one of Burton's biographies cloying, naive, and clichéd (Moody, p. 284). Yet both religious and secular reviewers admired the author's enthusiasm for her subject material. A critic for the *Saturday Review* offered a typical response to Burton's writing when he said one of her books had "flat pages" but nonetheless provided "pleasant reading" (Jones, p. 26).

Although Burton evoked more interest in her time than in ours, she has not been forgotten. She was included in both the 1989 and 1998 editions of the highly selective *Catholic Lifetime Reading Plan.* Here, author Father John Hardon praises her "intensely personal biographies" for their "painstaking research" (1998, pp. 205, 206).

## NOTES

1. Reference sources widely disagree on the year of Burton's birth. Several sources indicate 1884, but others list 1887 and 1890. Burton's *New York Times* obituary states that she died at the age of 82 in 1969, suggesting she was born in 1886 or 1887. Burton did not give her year of birth in her autobiography.

2. Some publications have erroneously reported that Katherine (Kurz) Burton taught at Wheaton College in Massachusetts. On July 16, 1999, Wheaton's archivist, Zeph Stickney, confirmed that a different Katherine Burton—a Katherine Alice Burton who died in 1994—taught at Wheaton.

3. Unfortunately, Burton did not have her facts straight when she re-created this deathbed conversation of the Lathrops. Such a conversation never occurred; Rose Hawthorne Lathrop herself said that her husband died "'about half an hour before I reached him'" (quoted in Patricia Dunlavy Valenti, *To Myself a Stranger: A Biography of Rose Hawthorne Lathrop.* Baton Rouge: Louisiana State University Press, 1991, p. 146).

## BIBLIOGRAPHY

### Works by Katherine Burton

"A Prayer for Ronald." *Bookman* 65 (July 1927): 518.
" 'So Died a True Christian.'" *Literary Digest* 9 July 1927: 31.
"To the Soviet Rulers." *Commonweal* 15 March 1933: 547.
"The Leper Who Sought His Lord." *Catholic World* 141 (April 1935): 61–69.
*Sorrow Built a Bridge: A Daughter of Hawthorne.* London: Longmans, Green and
        Co., 1937.
"November Eleventh." *Catholic World* 148 (November 1938): 147.

*The Next Thing: Autobiography and Reminiscences.* New York: Longmans, Green and Co., 1949.

*Witness of the Light: The Life of Pope Pius XII.* New York: Longmans, Green and Co., 1958.

*Make the Way Known: The History of the Dominican Congregation of St. Mary of the Springs, 1822 to 1957.* New York: Farrar, Straus, and Cudahy, 1959.

*The Dream Lives Forever: The Story of St. Patrick's Cathedral.* New York: Longmans, Green and Co., 1960.

*Woman to Woman.* Ed. Julie Kernan. New York: P. J. Kennedy & Sons, 1961.

### Works about Katherine Burton

Hardon, John A., S.J. *The Catholic Lifetime Reading Plan.* Royal Oaks, Michigan: Grotto Press, 1998.

Jones, Howard Mumford. Rev. of *Celestial Homespun*, by Katherine Burton. *Saturday Review* 29 May 1943: 26.

Moody, Joseph N. Rev. of *Mother Butler of Marymount*, by Katherine Burton. *Commonweal* 7 July 1944: 284.

"Our Contributors." *Catholic World* 157 (May 1943): 209.

Schlesinger, Arthur M., Jr. Rev. of *Celestial Homespun*, by Katherine Burton. *New England Quarterly* 16 (September 1943): 534–35.

REBECCA L. KROEGER

# ELIZABETH CARY
## (1585–1639)

---

## BIOGRAPHY

Born Elizabeth Tanfield in Oxfordshire to the lawyer Laurence Tanfield, Elizabeth Cary was by all accounts remarkably precocious. She mastered French, Spanish, Italian, Latin, and Hebrew independently, and reportedly read and disputed Calvin's *Institutes* at the age of twelve. Her first surviving work is a manuscript translation of Abraham Oretelius's *Le Miroir du Monde* (1598). At the age of seventeen, Elizabeth was married in an arranged match to Sir Henry Cary, Viscount of Falkland. Soon after her marriage, Elizabeth read Hooker's *Ecclesiastical Policy* but, instead of finding it an exemplary defense of the Anglican Church, found herself unconvinced of its persuasiveness and turned instead to the writings of the early Church fathers and the counsel of Richard Neale, Dean of Westminster. Her play *The Tragedy of Mariam, the Fair Queen of Jewry*, acknowledged as the first play written in English by a woman, was written at some point between 1603 and 1612.

Cary's sympathy with the Catholic Church was a source of much contention between herself and her husband, who, in aspiring toward the role of courtier, recognized the political danger of having a wife who often refused to attend Anglican services and who spoke publicly of the superiority of the Catholic Church. Falkland's appointment as Viceregent of Ireland in 1622 was a cause of further contention, as his duties entailed the enforcement of Anglican authority over the Catholic Irish. Unable to reconcile her community projects in Ireland (including training children in trades) with her husband's political oppressiveness, Elizabeth returned to England in 1625 without her husband. In 1626, after a year's separation, Cary converted publicly to Catholicism, and Falkland wrote letters to the king and members of the Privy Council claiming his disillusionment with and separation from his wife. At the time, Elizabeth Cary managed to secure the favor of several prominent women at court, including the Duchess of Buckingham and Queen Henrietta Maria, to whom she dedicated her translation of the French Catholic Jacques Davy du Perron's response to James I's attack on his work, *The Reply of the Most Illustrious Cardinall of Perron* (1630).

Despite Henry's death in 1633, Elizabeth Cary's Catholicism continued to be a political concern at court. Archbishop Laud wrote to Charles I, requesting him to have Cary's children tended by the second Viscount Falkland, so as to prevent their being unduly influenced by their mother's religious tendencies. Despite Laud's attempts, Cary saw her daughters become nuns at the Benedictine Convent of Cambrai between 1638 and 1639, and her sons take holy orders in France. Her son Lucius entertained open intellectual and liberal religious discussion in his houses. Despite her son's efforts to offer her financial aid, Cary died in poverty and illness, largely (according to the seventeenth-century biography *The Lady Falkland: Her Life*) as a result of her own charitable contributions.

Aside from writing *The Tragedy of Mariam* and being the presumed author of the play *Edward II*, Cary also translated work by Flemish mystic Louis de Blois, the text of which remains in manuscript. *The Lady Falkland: Her Life* also mentions Cary's numerous verse biographies of female saints and hymns to the Virgin. These works are now considered lost. Cary is also presumed to have been the author of a funeral elegy on the Duke of Buckingham.

## MAJOR THEMES

Cary's most famous work, *The Tragedy of Mariam*, dramatizes the difficulties of a wife in asserting her intelligence and ability within domestic confines. These conflicts not only are indicative of Cary's feminist concerns, but can also be seen as figurative representations of her awareness of the religious and political difficulties of a Catholic in conflict between a desire to serve and a moral need to challenge authority based on an inherent understanding of what is morally, politically, and spiritually "right."

Set during the biblical reign of King Herod, *The Tragedy of Mariam* explores and implicitly condemns the politics of a society that allows a married man to be lord and master over his wife. Cary delineates the freedom and intellectual joy that everyone (particularly the women) experience when Herod leaves the court and is presumed dead. While Cary does not go so far as to have her intelligent female characters take over, she condemns any overly authoritative political structure that inhibits freedom of self-expression and the desire to marry for love. In her play, this political structure is implied to be that of a monarchy. When Herod returns, violence and death ensue, and Mariam, the only character of integrity, dies in her inability to live under oppressive patriarchal rule. In this single work, therefore, Cary condemns the categorization of females as "unruly" in their desire for freedom from societal (and necessarily patriarchal) restraints; implicitly questions the spiritual validity of a monarchical system that causes death and intellectual confinement to those most expressive of virtue; and, in limiting the action of the text to a decidedly domestic sphere, emphasizes the similarities between the injustice of Herod and that imposed on women by men in marriage.

Always concerned with linking what would now be perceived as feminist concerns with her political and religious convictions, Cary's work consistently enacts this connection between the position of women, the role of the monarchy, and the importance of Catholicism. By dedicating her translation of du Perron to the Queen, Cary to a certain extent recognizes the importance of the Queen over her husband. Similarly, by singling out a Queen considered at the time as "troublesome" for her Catholic sympathies witnessed by her translation of a defense of Catholicism, Cary implicitly encourages not only Catholicism but also the self-expression of married women despite the political and social authority of their husbands.

In her work, therefore, Cary consistently validates the importance of women and exemplifies their scholarly and intellectual potential. She does this while questioning a political structure that encourages the suppression not only of women but of what her writing consistently attests to be the true and virtuous religion, that is, Catholicism. Cary's reasons for conversion are not known, nor are her opinions regarding political enactments of religious toleration. Instead, her work stresses the importance of virtue, integrity, and expression of conscience and belief, a belief that her conversion and her raising of her children indicate to have been strongly Catholic. Known for her charity work and advocation of tolerance, Cary exemplified in her life the concerns that she delineated in her writing. Cary's work comes dangerously close to questioning the validity of monarchical government and, more explicitly, condemns the imposition of social, political, and intellectual restraints on women, restraints with which she was herself very familiar in interactions with her husband, the clergy, and the court.

## SURVEY OF CRITICISM

The facts of Cary's life are known primarily through her biography, *The Lady Falkland: Her Life* (c.1645–1650), written by one of her daughters, a nun in the Benedictine Convent at Cambrai (and published in a modern edition, along with *The Tragedy of Mariam*, by Weller and Ferguson). Interesting more as a historical example of an implied saint's life than as a meticulous account, the biography is primarily concerned with Cary's exemplary Catholic faith, and does little to emphasize her importance as a political or literary figure. The work remained a historical curiosity into the nineteenth century, and it has not been until the past two decades that Cary has been seriously considered for her literary output. Despite early twentieth-century discussion of the authorship of *Edward II*, little had been produced on the known writings of Cary until feminist critics approached her as the first English woman writer of a play, thus leading to such studies as those by Lewalski in *Writing Women in Jacobean England*. Many critics have taken a primarily historical approach to

Cary's work, deducing from her writings the social state of women at the time, and the implications of marriage in Jacobean England. Others, such as Gutierrez and Krontiris, have more firmly explored the effects of gender in the historical reception and contemporary analysis of Cary's works. Still others, such as Brashear, are more concerned with placing her work in a literary context.

To date, there is remarkably little that directly addresses the religious elements of Cary's work apart from her social and political concerns; Fischer's paper, "Elizabeth Cary and Tyranny, Domestic and Religious," is a rare example. In fact, the most satisfying treatments remain those provided in such general studies as John Bossy's *The English Catholic Community, 1570–1850* (1975), and Diane Willen's "Women and Religion in Early Modern England." The most satisfying general accounts of Cary's life, work, and thematic emphases are provided by the Wright and Weller-Ferguson editions of *The Tragedy of Mariam*, both of which (particularly the latter) include extensive bibliographies and discuss various critical approaches.

## BIBLIOGRAPHY

### Works by Elizabeth Cary

*The Tragedy of Mariam, the Fair Queen of Jewry with The Lady Falkland: Her Life.* Ed. Barry Weller and Margaret W. Ferguson. Berkeley: University of California Press, 1994.

*The Reply of the Most Illustrious Cardinall of Perron, to the Answeare of the Most Excellent King of Great Britaine.* Trans. by Elizabeth Cary. Douay: Martin Bogard, 1630.

*Edward II.* In *Renaissance Women: The Plays of Elizabeth Cary and the Poems of Emilia Lanyer.* Ed. Diane Purkiss. London: W. Pickering, 1994.

### Works about Elizabeth Cary

Brashear, Lucy. "A Case for the Influence of Lady Cary's *Tragedy of Mariam* on Shakespeare's *Othello*." *Shakespeare Newsletter* 26 (1976): 31.

Fischer, Sandra K. "Elizabeth Cary and Tyranny, Domestic and Religious." *Silent But for the Word: Tudor Women as Patrons, Translators, and Writers of Religious Works.* Ed. Margaret P. Hannay. Kent, Ohio: Kent State University Press, 1985. 225–37.

Fullerton, Lady Georgiana. *The Life of Elisabeth, Lady Falkland.* London: Burns and Oates, 1883.

Gutierrez, Nancy. "Valuing Mariam: Genre Study and Feminist Analysis." *Tulsa Studies in Women's Literature* 10 (Fall 1991): 233–51.

Krontiris, Tina. *Oppositional Voices: Women as Writers and Translators of Literature in the English Renaissance.* New York: Routledge, 1992.

Lewalski, Barbara Kiefer. *Writing Women in Jacobean England.* Cambridge: Harvard University Press, 1993.

Willen, Diane. "Women and Religion in Early Modern England." *Women in Reformation and Counter-Reformation Europe*. Ed. Sherrin Marshall. Bloomington: Indiana University Press, 1989. 140–65.

Wright, Stephanie J., ed. Introduction. *The Tragedy of Mariam, The Fair Queen of Jewry*. Staffordshire: Keele University Press, 1996.

IRENE MORRA

# MADRE CASTILLO
# (1671–1742)

## BIOGRAPHY

Colombia's "Mystic of Tunja" was born Francisca Josefa on October 6, 1671. Her family were members of the local ruling elite in Tunja, magistrates and assistants to the Spanish *corregidores*, or district governors. Her father, Francisco Ventura de Castillo y Toledo, a jurist, had been raised in Spain. Her mother, Doña María, a *criolla* (creole), was the daughter of a city councilman. Francisca was one of the couple's three daughters.

In addition to being a powerful family in New Granada (the colonial name for Colombia), the Castillos were devoutly religious. Several of Francisca's female cousins and nieces professed vows in the community of Poor Clares in Tunja. The presence of several family members in the same religious community was not unusual in colonial Spanish America, and it ensured that the Castillos exercised influence in the affairs of both the state and Church. This proved advantageous for Francisca when she herself entered the convent of Santa Clara in 1689 and began her rise towards the position of abbess.

Other than a certificate of baptism and a few details in her autobiography, no documentation on Francisca's life prior to entering the convent exists. We have no clear picture of her childhood, or the influences on her vocation. As a socially prominent woman, she may have been attracted to the religious community's promise of autonomy and artistic development. We do know that when she joined the Poor Clares at age eighteen she had received a high degree of education and was soon entrusted with many of the managerial responsibilities of the convent, including bookkeeping. Francisca took the habit of novice in 1692. In 1694, she made her profession as a black veiled nun, the highest rank in her community. She was entrusted with more and more leadership, including positions as secretary, nurse, mistress of novices, parlor chaperone, director of music, and convent organist. In 1718, she was elected abbess, the first of three such elections (the others being in 1729 and 1738).

Early in her monastic career, Madre Castillo began to experience mystical visions. At the urging of her confessors, she wrote them down through at least 1728. These writings formed the basis for her most famous work, *Sentimientos espirituales* [Spiritual Feelings], also known as *Afectos*. Her *Vida*, or *Life*, was probably written at the command of her confessor around 1715; in order to check the orthodoxy of the mystic, such a command was standard practice in the Counter Reformation Church. The date of composition of a later work, the *Cuaderno de enciso* [Guidebook], is uncertain, but in it Madre Castillo copied several of her *Afectos*, poetry by John of the Cross and the Mexican nun Sor Juana Inés de la Cruz, passages from the *Spiritual Exercises* of Ignatius of Loyola (a favorite author of hers), and the writings of Saint Teresa of Avila. It's possible that she used this manuscript as a spiritual guide in her instruction of the novices.

As abbess, Madre Castillo had to deal with the convent's severe debts (a sign of economic trouble throughout New Granada) and accusations by various sisters of her unorthodox behavior, including alleged manifestations of demonic possession. As a result, Madre Castillo was constantly under the supervision of confessors and investigators from the archbishop's office. Despite her spiritual and interpersonal struggles, she managed to improve the convent's financial status, oversee the renovations of the chapel, and arrange for the donation of an expensive gold monstrance in 1737 for use by the Poor Clares in their meditations before the Eucharist. Although her early terms as abbess were marked by painful power struggles and questions about her mystical ecstasies, her last term and final years at Santa Clara, by contrast, showed that she had consolidated her authority in her community. After fifty-three years as a nun, Madre Castillo died in 1742 at the age of seventy.

Strangely, there was no fanfare in Tunja over her passing. No further inquiry into her mysticism was conducted. The manuscripts of her three works remained in the possession of the Convento Real de Santa Clara until 1813 when they were given to one of her nephews. He arranged for the publication of the *Life* in Philadelphia in 1817. The first edition of her *Spiritual Feelings* was published in 1843 and was heralded as a classic of mystical literature. An imprint of her complete works was finally published in 1968.

## MAJOR THEMES

The major themes of Madre Castillo as a Catholic woman writer are contained in her three texts: *Spiritual Feelings*, *Life*, and *Guidebook*. These works reflect the nature of her mystical visions and teachings. They manifest an intimate knowledge of the Scriptures and the writings of Teresa of Avila, Catherine of Siena, John of the Cross, Ignatius of Loyola, and other Spanish theologians and spiritual writers. They also demonstrate a familiarity with the Divine Office and various liturgical prayers. Madre Castillo expertly weaves these sources into a conflicted dialogue between her soul and Christ, and she fashions a voice that is uniquely her own while articulating the feminine mystic's desire for submersion in and sensual union with God, her divine husband-lover.

In the *Spiritual Feelings*, Madre Castillo speaks of herself as God's amanuensis. Her mystical knowledge is a record of the relationship of God, Christ, and Mary to mortal creatures. As secretary to the Divine, she notes how Christ seeks to be the lover-husband of the mystic's soul. This is the most prominent theme in the work. Through a recollection of her visions (with glosses to liturgical prayers), she instructs her soul to renounce the world, be ever more humble, and to decry the corruption of humanity in order to be worthy of the promised union with Christ. Each meditation, or *affect* (the Spanish noun *afecto* refers to a "lovable" truth that is encountered and not just "known" in the sense of "understood"), is a soliloquy that expresses her pain at separation from God, pleads for his mercy and care, and thanks him for his occasional consolations. Madre Castillo also uses her role as a conduit of divine knowledge to scold her sister Poor Clares for their spiritual laxity.

Madre Castillo's *Life* reads as a journal of spiritual exile in the midst of *murmuración* (slanderous gossip) in the convent, and describes her inner conflict as she tries to defend herself and yet reject the sin of boastful pride. The speaking voice is at times a bitter one, placing its pain on the written page and encouraging itself to be outwardly calm and humble. The author refers to the gossipers in her community as pawns of the devil who seek to disturb her communications with God and call into doubt the sincerity of her Catholic faith. Moreover, she laments her status as a "public woman" and finds consolation in the memory of Mary Magdalene, the prostitute who, despite her reputation, received Christ's welcome into his company and became his "lover." The trials she endures as an object of malicious rumors within the walls of the convent and on the streets of Tunja make her long for death, the overcoming of the painful exile in this world, and final union with her "celestial spouse." The psychological and physical torments she experiences are ever present reminders of death's promised release, and her lover's future total embrace—her soul's chief longing.

The *Guidebook* is an overtly orthodox work, a patchwork of Catholic dogma and copied poetry, liturgical prayers and commentary, and biblical exegesis. The text uses an unidentified female "I" as narrator to instruct her soul, and to teach an unnamed "you" on the proper way to reach God. The work seems to be partially modeled on Saint Teresa's classic instruction to her Carmelite sisters, the *Camino de perfección*, or *Way of Perfection*. It has a more public dimension than Madre Castillo's other writings, for in it she acts as teacher and preacher, exhorting her student-congregation to follow her steps toward perfect unity with God. With a confident and authoritative voice, she uses profoundly sensual metaphors to express her teachings. The world is depicted as a landscape of both dangers and benefits; the soul needs to humble itself in order to climb the mountain of suffering and reach the divine landscape of eternal joy. The soul's final destination is to seek its comfort in the tomb of Christ and its home in his wounded side. In this journey, God assists us with the Lord's Prayer, the Eucharist, and confessors or earthly guides so that we can achieve the soul's consummation with the Crucified Lover.

## SURVEY OF CRITICISM

To date, no definitive English translation of Madre Castillo's complete works has been published. As a result, she remains mostly unfamiliar to English-speaking readers. The majority of criticism is in Spanish, but even this is minimal.

With the publication in 1997 of Kathryn Joy McKnight's *The Mystic of Tunja*, a wider readership has been introduced to Madre Castillo. McKnight's book is a combination of biography, an insightful analysis of the nun's major texts, and a feminist primer on how to read Spanish colonial women's writing. It has served to spur interest in Madre Castillo among Latin American colonial and feminist scholars, and it promises to have the same intellectual (and promotional) impact as did Octavio Paz's 1980s quasi-biography of the seventeenth-century Mexican nun Sor Juana Inés de la Cruz. McKnight includes generous samplings of the author's writings in English translation.

Other English-language studies that readers may find of interest include the works by Flores and Antoni listed in the bibliography. Flores's piece is a short introduction to a selection of poems by Madre Castillo, including her *villancico* (song of praise) on the Redeemer's birth. Antoni's article is actually a prologue to his translations of chapters from the *Life* and the *Spiritual Feelings*. However, some caution should be exercised in reading the biographical interpretations of both Flores and Antoni. In fact, one of McKnight's valuable contributions is to correct and revise the many false facts and misleading information about the life of Madre Castillo. Still, in the case of Antoni, it is helpful to have any translations of Madre Castillo's work.

For Spanish readers, the bibliography also lists key studies that discuss the religious influences on Madre Castillo. The lengthy introduction by Dario Achury Valenzuela to Madre Castillo's *Obras completas* goes into depth on such topics as the impact of Ignatius of Loyola, Teresa of Avila, and Sor Juana Inés de la Cruz on the nun's thought. Valenzuela also investigates Madre Castillo's relations with the Inquisition in New Granada and the political turmoil within the Santa Clara community. He includes copious notes and indexes concerning the locations within her works of Madre Castillo's numerous scripture citations.

In other studies, Gimbernat de González provides an excellent analysis of Madre Castillo's conflicted voice in her confessional writings, a theme further developed by McKnight. Morales Borrero downplays any spiritual conflict in Madre Castillo's life and subjects her work to prescribed theological and scriptural categories: Madre Castillo on God, salvation through Christ, and so on.

The overall effect is a catechism based on the writings of the mystic. Written by a Colombian, the book is nationalistic in tone and hagiographic, taking pride in Madre Castillo as a Spanish American mystic in the tradition of European mystics of the Middle Ages and the Renaissance. Perricone, too, is somewhat uncritical of Madre Castillo and accepts her writing at face value. However, she provides a valuable listing of key themes in the author's work, including her mastery of the Divine Office. Finally, Robledo comments on the impact of Madre Castillo's confessors' demands on her writing, noting how the author manipulated the male clerics' expectations to generate drama in her life narrative and show her special status as one of the elect in God's divine order.

## BIBLIOGRAPHY

### Work by Madre Castillo

*Obras completas.* 2 vols. Ed. Dario Achury Valenzuela. Bogotá: Talleres Gráficos del Banco de la República, 1968.

### Works about Madre Castillo

Antoni, Claudio G. "Women of the Early Modern Period: A Late Baroque Devotional Writer: Madre Castillo." *Vox Benedictina* 4.2 (April 1987): 155–68.

Flores, Ángel, ed. *The Literature of Spanish America.* Vol. 1. New York: Las Américas Publishing Co., 1966.

Gimbernat de González, Ester. "El discurso sonámbulo de la Madre Castillo." *Letras Femeninas* 13.1–2 (1987): 43–52.

McKnight, Kathryn Joy. *The Mystic of Tunja: The Writings of Madre Castillo, 1671–1742.* Amherst: University of Massachusetts Press, 1997.

Morales Borrero, María Teresa. *La Madre Castillo: Su espiritualidad y su estilo.* Bogotá: Instituto Caro y Cuervo, 1968.

Perricone, Catherine R. "La Madre Castillo: Mística para América." *Santa Teresa y la literatura mística hispánica.* Ed. Manuel Criado de Val. Madrid: Edi-6, 1984.

Robledo, Ángela I. "La Madre Castillo: autobiografía mística y discurso marginal." *Letras Femeninas* 18.1–2 (1992): 55–63.

JOHN F. CROSSEN

# WILLA CATHER
## (1873–1947)

## BIOGRAPHY

Willa Cather was not a Catholic, but she wrote so seriously and sensitively about the Catholic Church—particularly in her historical novels *Death Comes for the Archbishop* and *Shadows on the Rock*—that many readers assume she was.

Cather was born December 6, 1873, the first of Charles and Virginia Boak Cather's seven children, in Back Creek, Virginia, a scruffy backcountry hamlet west of Winchester and the Blue Ridge Mountains. It was one of the most bitterly torn regions of the Civil War, and the conflict had divided Cather's family as it did most others. Although very few people there owned slaves, Cather's maternal great-grandmother was one of those few; Cather remembered and memorialized her, together with her own ambivalent feelings about the Southern part of her past, in her last novel, *Sapphira and the Slave Girl* (1940). By Willa's tenth year, after tuberculosis had claimed several members of the family, most of two generations of Cathers had moved west to the dryer air of the newly opened Nebraska Territory. Willa's great childhood trauma was this dislocation—being uprooted from an established community in the flowering and forested Appalachian foothills to a bumptious new settlement in the endless sameness of a vista she described as being as "bare as a piece of sheet iron" (*Willa Cather in Person*, p. 10). But, as she later told an interviewer, she and the prairie "had it out together" that first year; she developed an unshakable passion for the shaggy grass country (p. 32).

After a year on a prairie farm, the Cathers moved into the booming railroad town of Red Cloud. Willa was precocious, outgoing, theatrical, and unintimidated by convention. She easily made friends with adults, and in adolescence apprenticed herself to the local physician. For this male-dominated profession she dressed the part: cropped her hair, wore trousers and suspenders, and signed her name "William Cather, M.D." Not until 1892, when at the University of Nebraska she decided to become a writer and not a doctor, did she abandon cross-dressing.

The neighboring prairie immigrants from Scandinavia and Bohemia gave the adolescent Cather her first exposure to other tongues and customs, and their foreign ways interested her far more than those of her bland American neighbors. She became passionately interested in European culture, and majored in classics at the university. There she was also active in theater, editor of the campus literary magazine in which she published her first stories, and a prolific arts reviewer, not just for the campus paper but also for the *Nebraska State Journal*, whose editor took her on as a protégé.

Cather's craving for the refinements of Old World culture—learning, music, art, and theater—later drove her to the eastern cities to live, first in Pittsburgh, where she worked for ten years as a journalist and teacher, then in New York, where in 1906 she became managing editor of the prominent muckraking magazine *McClure's*. Only in 1912, when she was thirty-eight, did Cather follow the advice of Sarah Orne Jewett (who just before her death had befriended the younger writer) and give up her job to write full time. The following year Cather published her breakthrough novel, *O Pioneers!*, and dedicated it to Jewett's memory.

Willa Cather was very close to her family, especially her father and brothers, but she did not marry. The great romance of her life was Isabelle McClung, with whom she lived for six years in Pittsburgh. When Isabelle married in 1916, the unsuspecting Cather went into deep depression. They re-established their friendship, but heartbreak and disillusionment darkened all her later writing about romantic love. For her last forty years, Cather lived with Edith Lewis, a fellow Nebraskan.

In 1922, at the age of forty-nine, Cather left the Baptist congregation of her childhood and was confirmed in the Episcopal Church in Red Cloud. As all of her novels from the 1920s show, she was also exploring Roman Catholicism at this time. By the 1930s, however, she became increasingly irritated by presumptuous mail from Catholic readers, and sometimes responded sharply to it. After that the Catholic Church all but disappeared from her fiction, though religious questions did not.

During the 1930s Cather financially assisted a number of her Nebraska farm friends who were badly hit by the Depression. She also began to suffer from health problems, and carpal tunnel syndrome kept her from writing for months at a time. In this decade too she grieved the loss of her parents, a favorite brother, and in 1938 Isabelle, whom Cather had nursed through her final illness. As the decade closed and the rumblings of war made her fearful for her beloved Europe, she wrote *Sapphira and the Slave Girl*, about the Old South and the evil of subjecting one race of human beings to another.

In the 1940s losses and health afflictions only accelerated, and to them were added the real destructions and privations of war. The few stories she wrote in this decade were published posthumously, and at her death on April 23, 1947, she left unfinished another historical novel, set in fourteenth-century Avignon during the "Babylonian Captivity" of the popes of Rome.

## MAJOR THEMES

Five overlapping themes dominate Cather's fiction: childhood (especially in her most autobiographical works); art and the artist's life; landscape (especially that of the American West); love and romantic friendship; and history and religion, including serious explorations of Catholicism.

Childhood experience is particularly important in *The Song of the Lark* (1915), *My Ántonia* (1918), and the novella "Old Mrs. Harris" in *Obscure Destinies* (1932), all of which have strong autobiographical elements. Characters in Cather's other prairie novels and stories—including *O Pioneers!* (1913), *A Lost Lady* (1923), *Obscure Destinies,* and *Lucy Gayheart* (1935)—are based on people she knew in her Nebraska childhood, and all have either a child narrator or an important child character. *Shadows on the Rock* (1931), written during the years Cather lost both of her parents, also has a child heroine, and Cather includes herself as an undisguised five-year-old witness to events in the last chapter of her Virginia novel, *Sapphira and the Slave Girl.*

Art and the artist's life was already a central concern in Cather's first published piece, a romantic essay on Thomas Carlyle written at age sixteen, where she first proclaimed her credo of art as a religion, and acknowledged the conflict between personal relationships and the demands of an artist's craft (*Kingdom of Art,* p. 423). She knew that this conflict was particularly acute for female artists, and in *The Song of the Lark* she explores both the costs and rewards of an operatic soprano's training and triumphant career. *Lucy Gayheart,* however, portrays another, less driven musician for whom the conflict of personal and professional needs is never happily resolved.

To most people Cather is best known as the first writer to give serious artistic attention to the landscape of the Western prairie; in *My Ántonia* and *O Pioneers!* her characters—like the young Cather herself—learn to love the subtleties of the wild grassland that at first seems so monotonous and forbidding. Cather's imagination was also fired by the deserts and canyons of the Southwest, where material culture and spiritual imagination merged in the cliff-dweller ruins of civilizations as old as those in medieval Europe. In *The Song of the Lark, The Professor's House* (1925), and *Death Comes for the Archbishop* (1927), she portrays the desert and its native cultures with a religious reverence.

From the beginning of her writing career, Cather was determined to break out of the sentimental romance formula of the "lady scribblers" of her time. She did not avoid writing about love, but she wrote most often about kinds of love then unconventional in women's fiction: love for art and for creative work, love between friends and family members, love for God, and *caritas,* or human compassion. When she did write courtship tales, she broke with expectation by exposing the illusions and dangers at the heart of romantic love (e.g., in *A Lost Lady* and *My Mortal Enemy* [1926]). The soundest relationships in her fiction are not erotic infatuations but friendships, some of which accommodate marriage (Fathers Latour and Vaillant in *Death Comes for the Arch-*

*bishop*; Alexandra Bergson and Carl Linstrum in *O Pioneers!*). Cather's hesitance to celebrate erotic passion is most often interpreted as a sign of confused or repressed sexuality, though other factors, such as her deep disappointment in Isabelle McClung, and her close intellectual affinity with ancient Rome and the European Middle Ages (when celibacy was regarded as a noble choice), were also important.

Willa Cather had already given serious attention to tensions between science, art, and religion in her early journalism, and she continued to scrutinize different Christian denominations in her fiction. She had little use for stern Protestant sects that disapproved of physical and aesthetic pleasure. To her, art was not a sign of frivolity and moral degeneration, but one of the highest spiritual achievements, whether expressed in a cathedral facade or a salad dressing. She often wrote admiringly about Catholic faith and rituals—the beauty of the funeral Mass in *O Pioneers!*, Papa Shimerda's spontaneous genuflection to the crèche figures in *My Ántonia*, Godfrey St. Peter's unanticipated comfort from the family seamstress's piety in *The Professor's House*, and Myra Henshawe's deathbed efforts to return to the Catholic ceremonies of her youth in *My Mortal Enemy*.

In her historical novels Cather delved more deeply into Catholic culture. *Death Comes for the Archbishop* portrays the Church as a timeless repository of European culture, adapting endlessly to challenging political and spiritual circumstances in new settings. In this unconventional narrative about two nineteenth-century missionaries in New Mexico Territory, Cather makes clear the interrelation of material and spiritual realms through her use of relics, visions, legends, and the celebration of Mass as vehicles of divine love: "where there is great love there are always miracles," explains Bishop Latour (p. 50). She also conveys a mutual respect between her idealistic Latour (based on the historical Archbishop Jean Lamy) and his Pecos and Navajo friends, from whom he absorbs both human wisdom and reverence for nature.

In the seventeenth-century Quebec of *Shadows on the Rock*, Cather illustrates ways that familiar images (e.g., the Holy Family), artifacts, and rituals of the Church helped structure the lives of French settlers in the American wilderness. This is a world seen through ten-year-old Cécile Auclair's eyes, and as Terence Martin observes, Cather deftly weaves the child's understanding of the safety and security of her own family with that of the Holy Family, as well as with experiences of martyrs and mystics, whose "radical spiritual ventures [were] clearly outside the range of [Cécile's] domain, and then convert[s] these singular odysseys to communal stories, to the stuff of legend, for Cécile's edification" (p. 32). Historical characters in this novel include Bishop Laval, the Montreal anchorite Jeanne Le Ber, and Mère Juschereau, mother superior at the Hôtel Dieu; Cécile also hears many tales about the founders of Quebec's Ursuline convent and Fathers Brébeuf, Jogues, and Lalemant, North America's own Jesuit martyrs.

## SURVEY OF CRITICISM

There are several biographies and memoirs of Cather, and much criticism of her work is biographically inflected. Important memoirs are Elizabeth Shepley Sergeant's *Willa Cather, A Memoir*; Edith Lewis's *Willa Cather Living*; and Mildred Bennett's *The World of Willa Cather*. E. K. Brown's *Willa Cather, A Critical Biography* had the cooperation of Edith Lewis, who was Cather's literary executor. Sharon O'Brien explores gender and sexuality issues as factors in the development of Cather's literary voice in *Willa Cather: The Emerging Voice*. Hermione Lee's *Willa Cather, Double Lives* focuses on tensions and contradictions in Cather's work and personality, and Merrill Maguire Skaggs's *After the World Broke in Two: The Later Novels of Willa Cather* is a psychological/biographical study of Cather's mature work. The most recent fully documented biography is James Woodress's *Willa Cather: A Literary Life*.

Critical literature treating gender issues in Cather's writing is vast, as the question of Cather's sexual identity generated heated debate for over two decades. Blanche Gelfant's 1971 article "The Forgotten Reaping Hook: Sex in *My Ántonia*" established the ground, and by the mid-1970s several critics had proposed that Cather was lesbian, a claim endorsed in Sharon O'Brien's detailed psychological study. In the abundant feminist criticism of Cather's fiction, Susan J. Rosowski's readings set a consistently high standard. Deborah Carlin's *Cather, Canon, and the Politics of Reading* and Marilee Lindemann's *Willa Cather: Queering America* both focus on the deliberately unsolved tensions and resistances in Cather's characters and narrative design that invite queer readings.

John J. Murphy has done the most work on Cather's relation to Catholicism, most frequently by identifying biblical references, Christian symbolism, and Catholic teachings in her work. In "The Faith Community in *Death Comes for the Archbishop*," for example, he explores the Holy Family as the model for both her biological and communal families, and in "Gilt Diana and Ivory Christ," he argues Christian charity as the central theme of *My Mortal Enemy*. He is author of the historical essay and textual notes to the Scholarly Edition of *Death Comes for the Archbishop*, and is editor of the 1988 Willa Cather issue of *Literature and Belief* (which includes significant essays by Mildred R. Bennett on Cather and religion, Susan J. Rosowski on Cather's matriarchal Christianity, and Marilyn Arnold on Bishop Latour, among others).

Other important discussions of Cather and religion appear in the Spring 1975 issue of *Renascence*, which is devoted to Cather; in Judith Fryer's *Felicitous Space*, which examines female spirituality and orientations to physical place; in Terence Martin's "'Grande Communications avec Dieu': The Surrounding Power of *Shadows on the Rock*"; and in Guy Reynolds's "The Ideology of Cather's Catholic Progressivism."

# BIBLIOGRAPHY

## Works by Willa Cather

*O Pioneers!* Boston: Houghton Mifflin, 1913.
*The Song of the Lark.* Boston: Houghton Mifflin, 1915.
*My Ántonia.* Boston: Houghton Mifflin, 1918.
*A Lost Lady.* New York: Knopf, 1923.
*The Professor's House.* New York: Knopf, 1925.
*My Mortal Enemy.* New York: Knopf, 1926.
*Death Comes for the Archbishop.* New York: Knopf, 1927. Scholarly Edition: historical essay and textual notes by John J. Murphy; text edited by Charles Mignon, with Frederick M. Link and Kari A. Ronning. Lincoln: University of Nebraska Press, 1999.
*Shadows on the Rock.* New York: Knopf, 1931.
*Obscure Destinies.* New York: Knopf, 1932.
*Lucy Gayheart.* New York: Knopf, 1935.
*Sapphira and the Slave Girl.* New York: Knopf, 1940.
*The Kingdom of Art: Willa Cather's First Principles and Critical Statements, 1893–96.* Ed. Bernice Slote. Lincoln: University of Nebraska Press, 1966.
*The World and the Parish: Willa Cather's Articles and Reviews, 1893–1902.* Ed. William M. Curtin. Lincoln: University of Nebraska Press, 1970.
*Willa Cather in Person: Interviews, Speeches, Letters.* Ed. L. Brent Bohlke. Lincoln: University of Nebraska Press, 1986.


## Works about Willa Cather

Bennett, Mildred. *The World of Willa Cather.* 1951. Lincoln: Bison-University of Nebraska Press, 1961.
Brown, E. K., and Leon Edel. *Willa Cather, a Critical Biography.* New York: Knopf, 1953.
Carlin, Deborah. *Cather, Canon, and the Politics of Reading.* Amherst: University of Massachusetts Press, 1992.
Fryer, Judith. *Felicitous Space: The Imaginative Structures of Edith Wharton and Willa Cather.* Chapel Hill: University of North Carolina Press, 1986.
Gelfant, Blanche H. "The Forgotten Reaping Hook: Sex in *My Ántonia.*" 1971. *Critical Essays on Willa Cather.* Ed. John J. Murphy. Boston: G. K. Hall, 1984. 147–64.
Lee, Hermione. *Willa Cather: Double Lives.* New York: Vintage, 1989.
Lewis, Edith. *Willa Cather Living.* 1953. Foreword by Marilyn Arnold. Athens: Ohio University Press, 1989.
Lindemann, Marilee. *Willa Cather: Queering America.* New York: Columbia University Press, 1999.
*Literature and Belief.* Willa Cather Issue. Ed. John J. Murphy. 8 (1988).
Martin, Terence. "'Grande Communications avec Dieu': The Surrounding Power of *Shadows on the Rock.*" *Cather Studies* 3. Ed. Susan J. Rosowski. Lincoln: University of Nebraska Press, 1996. 31–50.
Murphy, John J. "The Faith Community in *Death Comes for the Archbishop.*" *Willa Cather: Family, Community, and History.* Ed. John J. Murphy, with Linda

Hunter Adams and Paul Rawlins. BYU Symposium, Provo, Utah: Brigham Young University Humanities Publications Center, 1990. 311–19.

———. "Gilt Diana and Ivory Christ: Love and Christian Charity in *My Mortal Enemy.*" *Cather Studies* 3. Ed. Susan J. Rosowski. Lincoln: University of Nebraska Press, 1996. 67–99.

———. "Willa Cather and the Literature of Christian Mystery." *Religion and Literature* 24.3 (Autumn 1992): 39–56.

———. "Willa Cather's City of God: *Shadows on the Rock.*" *Literature and Belief* 15 (1995): 119–35.

O'Brien, Sharon. *Willa Cather, The Emerging Voice.* New York: Oxford University Press, 1987.

*Renascence.* Willa Cather Issue. 27.3 (Spring 1975).

Reynolds, Guy. "The Ideology of Cather's Catholic Progressivism." *Cather Studies* 3. Ed. Susan J. Rosowski. Lincoln: University of Nebraska Press, 1996. 1–30.

Rosowski, Susan J. "Willa Cather's Subverted Endings and Gendered Time." *Cather Studies* 1. Ed. Susan J. Rosowski. Lincoln: University of Nebraska Press, 1990. 68–88.

———. "Willa Cather's Women." *Studies in American Fiction* 9.2 (Autumn 1981): 261–75.

Sergeant, Elizabeth Shepley. *Willa Cather: A Memoir.* 1953. Lincoln: Bison-University of Nebraska Press, 1963.

Skaggs, Merrill. *After the World Broke in Two: The Later Novels of Willa Cather.* Charlottesville: University Press of Virginia, 1990.

Woodress, James. *Willa Cather: A Literary Life.* Lincoln: University of Nebraska Press, 1987.

*Women's Studies.* Willa Cather Issue. Intro. Margaret Anne O'Connor. 11 (December 1984): 219–372.

SHERRILL HARBISON

# CATHERINE OF GENOA
# (1447–1510)

## BIOGRAPHY

Catherine of Genoa was both a mystic and a heroic woman who spent a good deal of her life caring for the poor and sick. She established a tradition that was embraced by members of lay movements of the time, including the Oratories of Divine Love and the Theatines. Catherine was the youngest of five children born into the powerful and aristocratic Fieschi family in the northern Italian city of Genoa in the region of Liguria. Her father, Jacopo Fieschi, was Viceroy of Naples and his family was the most powerful of the Guelph families of Genoa. He was a descendant of Roberto Fieschi, the brother of Pope Innocent IV. Her mother, Francesca di Negro, also belonged to an ancient, aristocratic family of Genoa.

As a pious young girl of thirteen, Catherine desired to enter an Augustinian convent, but was denied entrance because of her age. In 1463, two years after the death of her father, her brother Giacomo married her off to the aristocrat Giuliano Adorno for political and financial motives. Catherine was only sixteen years of age. Since Giuliano's family was Ghibelline, the marriage was an attempt to reconcile the two families divided by politics. Giuliano proved to be unfaithful, frequently absent from home, and a spendthrift. He gambled and squandered not only his own finances but Catherine's as well, and fathered an illegitimate child with his mistress. Catherine was extremely miserable, spending the first five years of her marriage in isolation and loneliness. During the next five years, she made an attempt to return to the social life of Genoa, spending her time in various amusements. But she again plunged into a depression and in 1473 sought help from a priest-confessor at the convent where her sister, Limbania, was a nun. While about to make her confession, Catherine experienced a sudden and overwhelming love of God that subsequently caused her radical conversion and determination to live a life of devotion.

Although a married laywoman, Catherine's life underwent profound changes as she entered into a period of intense personal penance and prayer.

She did not remain in isolation, however, but rather led a life of outward piety, caring for the poor and sick of the slums of Genoa. Her husband, meanwhile, went bankrupt and shortly thereafter followed her footsteps in humble conversion. He became a Franciscan Tertiary, and the two agreed to live in continence while spending their lives caring for the poor and sick. Initially, they moved into a small house near the Pammatone hospital, but from 1479 on, they lived within the hospital itself, serving without pay and at their own expense. Catherine became director of the hospital and held that post for six years, between 1490 and 1496. In 1493, the plague struck Genoa, and Catherine turned the open space behind the Pammatone into a huge outdoor hospital for the sick and dying.

During the plague, Catherine began an extraordinary friendship with Ettore Vernazza, a wealthy notary and businessman. He dedicated himself to the care of the sick and dying, becoming the spiritual disciple of Catherine as well as the source of much of what is known about her. He became the founder of the Oratory of Divine Love, as well as various institutions in Italy dedicated to the care of the destitute.

In 1497, Giuliano died and shortly thereafter, in 1499, Catherine accepted Don Cattaneo Marabotto as her spiritual director and confessor. She refused, however, to join a Third Order and remained independent. Frequent ecstatic absorptions, penance, mortification, and in particular long, mysterious fasts in which she was unable to take any food had characterized Catherine's life since her conversion. But shortly before she accepted Marabotto as her director, her great fasts had come to an end and along with them her spiritual isolation. During this period Catherine shared the experiences of her inner life with Vernazza, Marabotto, and other disciples.

After a period of poor health and physical suffering, Catherine died in 1510 surrounded by her disciples and friends. She was not canonized until 1733. Catherine herself never wrote any books, and the writings attributed to her are really the work of her disciples who wrote down what they knew of or had heard from Catherine. These works include her *Life, Purgation and Purgatory* (or *Treatise on Purgatory*), and the *Spiritual Dialogue*. Thus these works must be referred to as containing her "teachings" rather than having been actually written by her. They were completed by 1522, about twelve years after her death. It is virtually impossible to decipher where Catherine's actual words lie, and which are the additions and glosses of the authors. However, her principle thoughts and teachings come through and do manage to convey Catherine's spirit.

## MAJOR THEMES

Catherine's *Life*, probably written by Marabotto and Vernazza, contains her legend as well as many of her sayings, experiences, and teachings. The notable teachings in the *Life*, however, are also contained in *Purgation and Purgatory* and the *Spiritual Dialogue*.

*Purgation and Purgatory*, whose first redactor was probably Vernazza, is a collection of Catherine's teachings on the theme of spiritual purgation, both in this life and in the next. The historical context surrounding *Purgation and Purgatory* arose from the Lutheran controversy regarding the doctrine of purgatory that intensified shortly after the saint's death; her teaching was used for polemical purposes and was widely read and studied. Early redactors may have tampered with some of her phrases, rendering them more conventional.

In *Purgation and Purgatory*, Catherine sees the life of the deceased individual as a continuation of this life except for certain differences resulting from passing through death itself. In essence, the purgation of the dead soul has the same primary goal as that of the devout striver in this life; namely, attaining the purity necessary for union with God. Therefore, the victory of pure Love over the false self is a struggle that continues beyond the death of the body. Purgatory is seen as a "loving" place that reflects God's justice. The book is filled with many such interesting paradoxes. In fact, the soul itself, at the moment of death, flings itself into purgatory, and if it were to do otherwise it would suffer even further. In purgatory, the soul has no sin in it, but is cleansed of any remaining "rust" of sin. The soul feels joy and pain simultaneously and does not consider punishment as suffering but rather is content in God's will. The soul gradually draws upwards, casting off any imperfection so that it can be united with God.

Catherine also contrasts the souls in purgatory with those in hell. In purgatory, a soul suffers and feels fire, but no guilt. On the other hand, the soul in hell, remaining in a state of evil will, feels guilt, and infinite blame and suffering. While the soul in purgatory knows it will one day see God, the damned soul knows it has no hope of ever doing so. Nevertheless, God's mercy shines on even those in hell, since he could have imposed even more suffering than he has.

Marabotto, Vernazza, and Vernazza's daughter Battista have all been proposed as possible authors for either all or part of the *Spiritual Dialogue*, but no authorship can be established with certainty. It was most likely composed by more than one of her disciples. At any rate, it contains the inner history and development of Catherine, and represents various stages of her spiritual life. Various characters represent different aspects of the same person. It takes the form of dialogues spoken by the Soul, the Body, Self-Love, the Spirit, Human Frailty (Humanity), and the Lord God. These characters converse about the needs each one of them has, and how they will survive with one another along the journey of life.

In part one of the *Spiritual Dialogue*, the Soul, the Body, and Self-Love struggle to have their needs met, which involves the participation of all three of them. Following the wishes of the Body and Self-Love, the Soul becomes increasingly unhappy as it moves further and further away from God. The Soul realizes, through the help of God, that only God can save and rescue the Soul, and that had it listened to the Body and Self-Love, it would have been led to its death. In part two, the Soul, as well as Human Frailty and the Spirit, converse. The Soul knows it has sinned and feels great distress, but after visions of Christ and God's love, it turns away from all other imperfect love. The Spirit eventually wins over Human Frailty. Part three narrates the end of Catherine's life and her death, describing her various strange illnesses that baffle doctors and lead them to believe that her sickness is of a supernatural nature.

Catherine's many teachings are found throughout the *opus catharinianum* and include but are not limited to the following: (1) God is pure love and he perceives this same love in the rational soul; (2) humans must accept the divine will and trust totally in God; (3) the conflict between self-love and pure love is lifelong; and (4) purgatory occurs both in this life and in the next.

## SURVEY OF CRITICISM

The volume *Catherine of Genoa*, edited by Serge Hughes, contains a good introduction by Father Benedict Groeschel C.F.R., which summarizes Catherine's life and various teachings, as well as the influence of those teachings throughout history. Groeschel discusses the various Catholic reformers, mystics, and theologians who were inspired by Catherine, as well as those Protestant leaders of nineteenth-century America who considered her an example of the perfect Christian. To those in the Protestant Perfectionist Movement, also of the nineteenth-century, Catherine was an example of a woman who filled a position of leadership in the Church and did so with charity. In the same volume, Hughes, in his "Notes on the Translation," discusses the various manuscripts of Catherine's works and the question of their authorship. This volume also contains translations of *Purgation and Purgatory* and the *Spiritual Dialogue* because these two works contain all the salient points of her teachings.

In 1908 Friedrich von Hügel published an exhaustive and lengthy study on Catherine's life, experiences, teachings, and relationships with her disciples. Umile Bonzi's comprehensive and thorough study followed in 1961–1962. Hughes, as well as Kenneth Jorgensen, discusses the merits and contributions of each of these scholars, and the various corrections and redactions of Catherine's works. Jorgensen's article also discusses events surrounding Catherine's life and experiences, framing them in an approach that addresses Catherine's experiences in relation to those of other mystics. Donald Christopher Nugent has suggested that Catherine's "doctrine" of annihilation of the self has analogies with the Buddhist doctrine of *annatta*, or "no-self" (p. 67). More generally, Amy Oden's and Bridget Mary Meehan's anthologies contain short reflections on Catherine's life and brief excerpts of her works.

# BIBLIOGRAPHY

## Works by Catherine of Genoa

*Life and Doctrine of Saint Catherine of Genoa*. Trans. Mrs. G. Ripley. Preface by Isaac Hecker. New York: The Catholic Publication Society, 1874. Rpt. as *The Spiritual Doctrine of St. Catherine of Genoa*. Rockford, Illinois: Tan Books and Publishers, 1989.

*Catherine of Genoa*. (Contains *Purgation and Purgatory* and the *Spiritual Dialogue*.) Ed. and trans. Serge Hughes. New York: Paulist Press, 1979.

## Works about Catherine of Genoa

Bonzi da Genova, P. Umile. *S. Caterina Fieschi Adorno*. 2 vols. Torino: Marietti, 1961–62.

Hug, P. L. "Catherine of Genoa, St." *New Catholic Encyclopedia*. Prepared by an editorial staff at the Catholic University of America. New York: McGraw-Hill, 1967. 254–56.

Jorgensen, Kenneth. "'Love Conquers All': The Conversion, Asceticism and Altruism of St. Caterina of Genoa." *Renaissance Society and Culture*. Ed. John Monfasani and Ronald G. Musto. New York: Italica, 1991. 87–106.

Meehan, Bridget Mary. *Praying with Passionate Women: Mystics, Martyrs, and Mentors*. New York: Crossroad Press, 1995. 87–90.

Nugent, Donald Christopher. "Mystic of Pure Love: Saint Catherine of Genoa." *Women Writers of the Renaissance and Reformation*. Ed. Katharina M. Wilson. Athens: University of Georgia Press, 1987. 67–80.

Oden, Amy, ed. *In Her Words: Women's Writings in the History of Christian Thought*. Nashville: Abingdon, 1994. 204–15.

von Hügel, Friedrich. *The Mystical Element of Religion as Studied in Saint Catherine of Genoa and Her Friends*. London: J. M. Dent and Sons, 1908.

MOLLY MORRISON

# Catherine of Siena
## (1347–1380)

## BIOGRAPHY

Catherine of Siena was a remarkable woman who was not only a mystic and a theologian, but a spiritual counselor, a caretaker to the sick and poor, and an energetic advocate for peace, justice, and Church unity. She was born in 1347 in Siena, an Italian town not far from Florence in the region of Tuscany. She was the twenty-fourth of twenty-five children born to Giacomo Benincasa and Lapa Piagenti. Her twin sister died in infancy. Even from an early age, Catherine was attracted to a life of devotion and piety. When she was around seven years of age, she experienced a vision of Christ and subsequently vowed her chastity to him. At the age of fifteen, as the result of her parents' insistence that she marry, she cut off her hair in protest. She endured persecution from her family until her father, eventually convinced of her genuine piety, ordered that a small room on top of the house be given to her for her own prayerful meditation.

In 1365, at the age of eighteen, she joined the Mantellate, a group of Third Order Dominican women, most of them elderly widows dedicated to prayer, penitential acts, and service to the sick and poor. After joining the Mantellate, Catherine remained in her father's house in solitude, devoting herself to prayer and the practice of strict austerities. Although she never received a formal education, it was perhaps during this period that, by engaging a friend to teach her, she learned to read, at least enough to understand liturgical texts. Whether or not she ever learned to write many years later is conjectural. In 1368, at the age of twenty-one, she experienced a "mystical marriage" to Christ and consequently left her solitude to serve others through offering both physical care of the sick and poor and spiritual assistance. Catherine soon acquired a growing group of devotees and disciples whom she called her *famiglia*. This group, who referred to her as "mamma," was made up of men and women, both priests (Dominicans naturally predominated) and laypeople, many of them more advanced in age than Catherine but all in some way her spiritual pupils.

The formation of Catherine's group led to the beginning of the great number of letters which she dictated to her various disciple-scribes. Her letters, initially written to instruct and encourage, eventually began to touch on political and ecclesiastical matters. In 1370, she underwent a "mystical death," a period of four hours of ecstasy during which she outwardly appeared dead. Her extraordinary penances included rigorous fasting to the point of near starvation. She became increasingly in demand as a spiritual counselor, and soon her personality and influence gave rise to opposition and slander. Accused of hypocrisy and presumption, in 1374 she was called to Florence to give an account of herself to the general chapter of the Dominican Order. Satisfied with their investigation of her, the chapter appointed Raymond of Capua as her spiritual director. From then on, Raymond was closely associated with her activities, becoming both spiritual son and father to Catherine. That same year witnessed another outbreak of the plague, the "Black Death," and she and her followers tended to the sick and dying.

From 1374–1378, Catherine's influence on political and ecclesiastical affairs was at its greatest, and her activity began to reach out beyond Siena to various cities in Italy. These years witnessed her involvement in various matters of Church and state: the conflict between the city-states and the papacy, Church reform, the return of the Pope to Rome, and the crusades. In 1375, she was instrumental in persuading Pisa and Lucca not to join the anti-papal league. She was also active in preaching the crusade to the Holy Land. During this same year, in Pisa, she received the stigmata, although the wounds were not visible to anyone but herself. In 1376, at the request of the Florentine government, she went to Avignon, France, where Pope Gregory XI was then residing in exile. She had gone there attempting to make peace between Florence and the Pope, and while this attempt failed, she did manage to influence Gregory's decision to return to Rome that same year. Back in Siena in 1377, Catherine founded a convent of strict observance, and spent time in the nearby areas preaching reform. She also began her principal work, the *Dialogue*.

The so-called Great Schism, which occurred in 1378 after the death of Gregory XI that same year, brought about the election of Urban VI as Pope in Rome and a rival set up in Avignon. Urban VI called Catherine to Rome to work for his cause. Along with some members of her *famiglia*, she set up her household there, living on alms. She occupied herself with pleading on behalf of Urban VI and arguing for Church unity. It is during this period that most of Catherine's *Prayers* were composed. Throughout her life Catherine had imposed austere penances on herself, frequently practicing severe fasting, but by the beginning of 1380 she was unable to eat anything at all. She died in April of that year. Catherine was canonized in 1461, and in 1970, along with Teresa of Avila, she was declared a Doctor of the Church.

## MAJOR THEMES

Catherine's 382 surviving *Letters*, dictated to various disciple-scribes between about 1370 until shortly before her death in 1380, reflect her involvement in ecclesiastical and political matters, as well as her concern for others.
Dictating her letters rapidly, and often several at once to different scribes, she
never proofread or checked transcriptions of her correspondence. Her *Letters*
give us insight into Catherine's personality and illustrate her personal growth.
Through their demonstration of the more practical side of Catherine, they remind us that she was not just enraptured in celestial visions and experiences.
Written with a personal touch to each person to whom they are addressed, they
provide interesting autobiographical and historical facts as well as immense
spiritual value. They are written to anyone on whom she felt she could have a
positive influence, and illustrate her convictions and opinions. The letters are
addressed to people as diverse as popes, cardinals, prisoners, queens, kings, intimate friends and relatives, prioresses, prostitutes, public figures, poets, and
artists. Often lengthy and forceful, they demonstrate Catherine's unique type
of preaching and instruction, and they reveal her as one of the great letter writers of the fourteenth century. Catherine's letter writing is considered one of
her most important forms of apostolic activity. Unlike her *Dialogue*, they possess a familiar tone and frequently deal with just one or two topics.

Catherine's *Dialogue* was composed a few years before her death, between
1377 and 1378. Through the *Dialogue*, Catherine intended to share with her
disciples all that she had learned about life with God in Christ; it contains all of
her theological teaching. Contrary to pious legend, it was not written during
the space of a single five-day ecstasy. The book did, however, involve a great
deal of dictation on her part during those times she was in ecstasy. Additionally,
Catherine herself may have edited it, although it was her disciples who later divided the book into chapters.

The inspiration for the composition of Catherine's *Dialogue* lay in an intense mystical experience she described in a letter to her spiritual director, Raymond of Capua. This experience provided the framework and content for her
book: a dialogue between herself and God. In her book, Catherine (referring
to herself in the third person) speaks with God. God is most often addressed as
"father," while she, in turn, is addressed as "daughter." Catherine begins the
work by making four petitions to God: for herself, for the reform of the
Church, for the whole world, and for assurance of God's providence in all
things, and in particular with regard to a certain person whose needs Catherine
is aware of. The rest of the book is composed of God's responses to these petitions, with an occasional interjection by Catherine. The conclusion brings together the principal themes addressed throughout the book. The *Dialogue* can
be difficult in parts, as its style involves frequent repetition of previously stated
arguments, although there is almost always an addition of new elements. It
deals with such themes as the centrality of truth and love, the human being as

an image of the triune God, Christ as redeemer, love for God and neighbor, and knowledge of God and self.

Catherine's twenty-six *Prayers*, composed during the last four years of her life, were copied down by disciple-scribes as she prayed aloud in ecstasy. She was probably not aware that these prayers were being recorded. Various themes found in the *Dialogue* and *Letters* reappear in her *Prayers*. Her *Prayers* demonstrate Catherine's most mature thought. They are characterized by their simplicity and their concentration on God who is continually praised and thanked. They also demonstrate Catherine's desire for the salvation of others, as she earnestly pleads for God's mercy on the world, the Church, the Pope, and her friends and followers.

Strictly theologically speaking, there is nothing new or original in Catherine's teaching. Her teachings stem from traditional Christianity, and her religious views were shaped by her belief in and devotion to the Church, headed by the Pope. However, it is the noteworthy way in which she expressed herself that is truly unique and inspiring. While most of Europe's scholars wrote and taught in Latin, Catherine dictated and taught in her own Sienese dialect, and she had a wonderful capacity for vivid, fresh, and illuminating expression. Catherine is the first woman to have produced extensive writings in that vernacular.

At the center of all of Catherine's teaching is her conception of God as truth and love. She often uses everyday images, weaving them together. Her favorite themes are expressed in fascinating imagery such as drowning in the sea of God's Being, cutting out the root of self-love with the knife of self-hatred, the well of the soul, the cell of self-knowledge, and Christ the Bridge.

## SURVEY OF CRITICISM

There is a large body of secondary work on Catherine's writings, including critical editions, translations, and scholarly articles. Of late, the foremost scholarship is represented by Suzanne Noffke and Giuliana Cavallini, who have produced translations, book-length studies, and critical editions of Catherine's works. Noffke's translations of the *Dialogue* and *Prayers* contain good introductory essays on Catherine's life, mysticism, and sources. Her book *Catherine of Siena: Vision Through a Distant Eye* provides an extensive discussion on Catherine, and an inclusive bibliography. Noffke has begun a translation project of all of Catherine's *Letters*. To date, she has published the first of four volumes that will eventually make up the only complete English translation of the *Letters*. Cavallini established the original structure of Catherine's *Dialogue*, which she follows in her critical edition. Cavallini conclusively shows that there is a recurring pattern of petition-response-thanksgiving that characterizes Catherine's *Dialogue*.

Rudolf Bell and Caroline Walker Bynum have discussed Catherine in light of other medieval holy women, emphasizing some of her more ascetic practices regarding fasting and food. Karen Scott has examined how Catherine's career exemplified both the mystical and apostolic opportunities available to women in fourteenth-century Italy and the limitations they experienced.

Shorter essays and summaries on Catherine and her works abound. Those that give a historical framework with regard to the piety and religious practices of the Middle Ages are most noteworthy. Also not to be ignored are those that provide explanations of Catherine's teachings, style, and language, as well as those that discuss her theology in relation to other spiritual writers of the age. Such essays include, but are not limited to, those published by Madigan, Woods, O'Driscoll, and Wolfskeel.

## BIBLIOGRAPHY

### Works by Catherine of Siena

*Catherine of Siena: The Dialogue.* Trans. Suzanne Noffke. New York: Paulist Press, 1980.
*The Prayers of Catherine of Siena.* Trans. Suzanne Noffke. New York: Paulist Press, 1983.
*The Letters of Catherine of Siena.* Trans. Suzanne Noffke. Binghamton, New York: Center for Medieval and Early Renaissance Studies, State University of New York at Binghamton, 1988.

### Works about Catherine of Siena

Bell, Rudolph M. *Holy Anorexia.* Chicago: University of Chicago Press, 1985.
Bynum, Caroline Walker. *Holy Feast and Holy Fast.* Berkeley: University of California Press, 1987.
Cavallini, Giuliana. *Catherine of Siena.* London: Geoffrey Chapman, 1998.
Foster, K. "Catherine of Siena, St." *New Catholic Encyclopedia.* Prepared by an editorial staff at the Catholic University of America. New York: McGraw-Hill, 1967. 258–60.
Madigan, Shawn, ed. *Mystics, Visionaries, and Prophets.* Minneapolis: Fortress, 1988. 209–26.
Noffke, Suzanne. "Caterina da Siena (Catherine of Siena) (1347–1380)." *Italian Women Writers: A Bio-Bibliographical Sourcebook.* Ed. Rinaldina Russell. Westport, Connecticut: Greenwood Press, 1994. 58–66.
——. *Catherine of Siena: Vision Through a Distant Eye.* Collegeville: Liturgical Press, 1996.
O'Driscoll, Mary, ed. *Catherine of Siena: Passion for the Truth, Compassion for Humanity.* New Rochelle, New York: New City Press, 1993.
Raymond of Capua. *The Life of Catherine of Siena.* c.1395. Trans. Conleth Kearns. Wilmington, Delaware: Michael Glazier, 1980.
Scott, Karen. "'Io Catarina': Ecclesiastical Politics and Oral Culture in the Letters of Catherine of Siena." *Dear Sister: Medieval Women and the Epistolary Genre.* Ed. Karen Cherewatuk and Ulrike Wiethaus. Philadelphia: University of Pennsylvania Press, 1993. 87–121.

——. "Urban Spaces, Women's Networks, and the Lay Apostolate in the Siena of Catherine Benincasa." *Creative Women in Medieval and Early Modern Italy.* Ed. E. Ann Matter and John Coakley. Philadelphia: University of Pennsylvania Press, 1994. 105–19.

Wolfskeel, Cornelia. "Catherine of Siena." *A History of Women Philosphers.* Vol. 2. Ed. Mary Ellen Waithe. Boston: Kluwer Academic Publishers, 1989. 223–58.

Woods, Richard. *Mysticism and Prophecy: The Dominican Tradition.* Maryknoll: Orbis, 1998.

MOLLY MORRISON

# THERESA HAK KYUNG CHA
# (1951–1982)

————•◦•◦•————

## BIOGRAPHY

Performance artist, filmmaker, and poet, Theresa Hak Kyung Cha was born in Pusan, Korea, on March 4, 1951. Her parents and their five children (Cha was the third child) immigrated to Hawaii in 1962 and then to San Francisco in 1968, where she attended high school at the Convent of the Sacred Heart. After a year at the University of San Francisco, Cha transferred to the University of California at Berkeley from which she received a B.A. in comparative literature in 1973, a B.A. in art in 1975, an M.A. in art in 1977, and an M.F.A. in 1978. During this time, she created a number of performance pieces drawing on Korean dance and themes of language, silence, and memory with such titles as "Barren Cave Mute" (1974), "A Ble Wall" (1975), "Aveugle Voix" (1975), "Vampyr" (1976), "Reveille Dans la Brûme" (1977), "Other Things Seen, Other Things Heard" (1978), and "Recalling Telling Re Calling" (1978); she also published a mail art piece, "Audience Distant Relatives" (1978). In 1976, Cha studied in France at the Centre d'Études Américaine du Cinéma à Paris. Her first video, *Passages Paysages*, was shown at the University Art Museum in Berkeley in 1976. From this point, Cha began to concentrate on making videos and films and on writing.

Cha was naturalized as a United States citizen in 1977 and moved to New York in August of 1980. She edited an anthology of structuralist film theory, *Apparatus/Cinematographic Apparatus: Selected Writings*, that was published by Tanam Press in 1980. Two texts, "Exilées" and "Temps Morts," were also published in that year in an anthology, *Hotel*. Cha's films, whose themes of loss and displacement are apparent in their titles (*Re Dis Appearing*, 1980; *Exilée*, 1980; *Permutations*, 1982) were shown at museums in San Francisco, New York, and Europe. In 1981 Cha went to Korea (she had previously traveled there and also to Japan in 1978) to begin work on a film project, *White Dust from Mongolia*; this project was later abandoned. In May 1982, she married the photographer Richard Barnes. Cha's book *Dictee*—the work through which most readers first encounter her—was published in October 1982 by Tanam Press. A piece entitled "Pravda/Istina" was also published in that year in *Heresies: A Feminist Publication on Art and Literature.*

Tragically, Cha was raped and murdered on November 5, 1982, in New York by Joey Sanza, a security guard suspected in a number of Florida assault attacks. She was thirty-one years old. At the time of her death, she was working on a film, a book, a critical study of advertising, and a study of hands as represented in Western painting.

## MAJOR THEMES

A Catholic aesthetic informs many of Cha's works, which focus on the fragmentation of experience, silence, and the redemption that comes through speech, through the word. The word "redemption" is central to the performance piece "Other Things Seen, Other Things Heard." The title of this piece also points to the theme of displacement, the sense that one is in exile from one's true home—as an immigrant in a foreign country, as a woman in a society historically dominated by men, and as a soul on this earth yearning to return to heaven.

Performance art, the first genre Cha worked in, relies directly on the physical presence of the artist, of her body. Except for some notes and materials (slides, texts), Cha's work as a performance artist is lost to us. Yet, this loss can be read as part of the message of her performance pieces, in which the artist uses her body as a medium in a literal reenactment of the "word being made flesh," of the Incarnation.

The reader of Cha's book, *Dictee*, is made to feel that something is missing, that the text is looking outward for its performance by its lost author. In *Dictee*, Cha intermixes motifs and images from classical mythology, Korean history, and Roman Catholicism to depict the immigrant's journey from silence back to a sense of self in a new, foreign land. "Mother," "motherland," and "mother tongue" or language are all confused in Cha's work. *Dictee* is structured around the nine Muses of Greek mythology; a list of each Muse's name across from whatever genre of Greek literature she presides over appears at the beginning of *Dictee* (e.g., Clio for history, Melpomene for tragedy, Polymnia for sacred poetry). Cha evokes the Greek poet Sappho at the beginning of *Dictee* as a comment on the untold lost voices and persons of women in the course of history. She makes up a "quote" by Sappho ("May I write words more naked than flesh, / stronger than bone, more resilient than / sinew, sensitive than nerve"), as if to underline the loss not only of so much of the Greek poet's work, but of the details of her life that are lost to history. Sections of liturgy and quotes from *Story of a Soul (Histoire de'une âme)*, the autobiography of St. Thérèse of Lisieux, are used to portray the psychological and spiritual dimensions of the Asian American experience.

Throughout *Dictee*, Christ's resurrection comes to represent the immigrant's "death" in leaving her native land for America and "rebirth" as she reclaims her identity and self through language. Cha learned the French language in Catholic high school. In an early section of *Dictee*, she implicitly compares instruction in this foreign language to her indoctrination in the catechism: "First Friday. One hour before mass. Mass every First Friday. Dictée first. Every Friday. Before mass. Dictée before. Back in the study hall. It is time" (p. 18). In the section "CALLIOPE EPIC HISTORY," the "epic" journey narrated is that of a young Korean woman sent to be a teacher in Manchuria. She falls ill and dreams of being tempted by three women bearing plates of food in a scene recalling Christ's temptation in the desert by Satan (Cha includes the passage from Luke 4); she awakens holding her parents' hands. In the final section of *Dictee* (entitled "POLYMNIA SACRED POETRY"), a little girl is on a journey to obtain medicine for her sick mother; a mysterious woman at a well provides her with it. The last page of *Dictee* is a child's request to her mother to be carried, so she can see out the window: "Lift me to the window to the picture image unleash the ropes tied to weights of stones . . . to break stillness bells fall a peal to sky" (p. 179).

Cha's evaluation of history leads to the inclusion of documents and photographs of historical realia (letters, maps, petitions, the author's own handwritten rough drafts for *Dictee*), set alongside a theoretical discussion of historiography ("CLIO HISTORY") and the lessons that can be drawn from the study of history ("TRAGEDY MELPOMENE"). *Dictee* thus fuses abstract concepts through analogy to the concrete and material. But Cha takes *Dictee* to more than a philosophical, theoretical level, as she addresses suffering and pain, and their reality. While *Dictee* at first seems to be about literature and film, these are ultimately seen of use only inasmuch as they train the speaker and the reader in the ways of the sacred, of the spirit. Like St. Thérèse of Lisieux's autobiography, *Dictee* is itself "the story of a soul," the spiritual autobiography of its author. The text presents a highly personal and personalized spirituality in the moments of the inner life of one writer's psyche as she grapples with the world's unexplainable chaos of pain and suffering and death. The section containing the quotes from St. Thérèse, "ERATO LOVE POETRY," is headed by a photograph of the saint playing the role of St. Joan of Arc while in the convent; in "CLIO HISTORY," Cha identifies the martyred saint with Yu Guan Soon, a Korean girl who was executed by the Japanese for her patriotism. Writes St. Thérèse as quoted in *Dictee*: "Martyrdom was the dream of my youth and this dream has grown with me within Carmel's cloisters. But here again, I feel that my dream is a folly, for I cannot confine myself to desiring one kind of martyrdom. To satisfy me I need all" (p. 117). This emphasis on suffering and self-sacrifice is also apparent in a quote from Cha's high school yearbook: "There is but one thing I dread, not to be worth my sufferings" (quoted in Young-Nan Kim, p. 76).

Self-identification of the author with the mystic St. Thérèse is also readily suggested in Cha's English name, Theresa. And the identification goes beyond the name: with its traits of silence, quietude, and a sternly regulated self-discipline, a certain religiosity tinged with mysticism imbues Cha's works, her writing and films, and the remembrance of her performance pieces. Art in *Dictee* becomes a vessel pointing toward an answer beyond literature, beyond language, text, and the written word; an answer that perhaps resides in Cha's never again to be re-created performance pieces.

## SURVEY OF CRITICISM

Throughout the 1990s, interest in Cha's work has increased with the development of Asian American studies. Retrospective exhibitions of her films and other artwork occurred in 1989 at Mills College in Oakland, California; in July–September 1990, at the University Art Museum/Pacific Film Archive at the University of California at Berkeley; and in December–January 1993, at the Whitney Museum of Modern Art in New York (along with a panel discussion of Cha's life and work on January 19, 1993). *Dictee* went out of print in the mid-1980s; Third Woman Press of Berkeley published a second edition in 1995 that was preceded by a collection of essays by four Asian American women, *Writing Self Writing Nation*, edited in 1994 by Kim and Alarcón. The earliest discussions of *Dictee* focused principally on its postmodern techniques of assemblage and fragmentation and its adherence to *l'écriture féminine*; that is, on its literary aspects (Stephens, Wolf, Martin). More recently, Cha's work has been the subject of an increasing number of scholarly papers and dissertations that highlight its representation of the Asian American woman's experience, displacement, and silence (Minh-ha, Rinder, Wong, Chew, Lowe). Any history of Asian American writing has become incomplete without reference to Cha's enigmatic films and to *Dictee*, with their aesthetic of silence and fragments as central themes of what it means to be an Asian American woman.

## BIBLIOGRAPHY

### Works by Theresa Hak Kyung Cha

"Composition." *Apparatus/Cinematographic Apparatus: Selected Writings.* Ed. Theresa Hak Kyung Cha. New York: Tanam Press, 1980.
"Exilées," "Temps Morts." *Hotel.* New York: Tanam Press, 1980.
*Dictee.* New York: Tanam Press, 1982. Berkeley: Third Woman Press, 1994.

### Works about Theresa Hak Kyung Cha

Chew, Kristina. "Pears Bearing Apples: Vergil's *Georgics—Plato's Phaedrus—*Theresa Hak Kyung Cha's *Dictee*." Diss. Yale University, 1995.
Kim, Elaine H. and Norma Alarcón. *Writing Self Writing Nation.* Berkeley: Third Woman Press, 1994.
Kim, Young-Nan Nancy. "Memorable Losses: Writing in exile and the lessons of writing in *Dictee*." B.A. Thesis. Princeton University, 1991.

Lew, Walter K. *Excerpts from Δικτη/Dikte for "Dicte."* Seoul: Yeul Eum Publishing Company, 1992.

Lowe, Lisa. *Immigrant Acts: On Asian American Cultural Politics.* Durham: Duke University Press, 1996.

Martin, Stephen Paul. *Open Form and the Feminine Imagination (The Politics of Reading in Twentieth-Century Innovative Writing).* Washington, D.C.: Maisonneuve Press, 1988.

Minh-ha, Trinh T. *Woman, Native, Other: Writing Postcoloniality and Feminism.* Bloomington: Indiana University Press, 1989.

Rinder, Lawrence. "The Theme of Displacement in the Art of Theresa Hak Kyung Cha and a Catalogue of the Artist's Oeuvre." M.A. Thesis. Hunter College, 1990.

Stephens, Michael. *The Dramaturgy of Form: Voices in Short Fiction.* Carbondale: Southern Illinois University Press, 1986.

Wolf, Susan. "Recalling Telling Retelling." *Fire Over Water.* Ed. Reese Williams. New York: Tanam Press, 1986.

Wong, Shelley Sunn. "Unnaming the Same: Theresa Hak Kyung Cha's *Dictée.*" *Writing Self Writing Nation.* Ed. Elaine H. Kim and Norma Alarcón. Berkeley: Third Woman Press, 1994. 103–40.

KRISTINA CHEW

# SANDRA CISNEROS
# (1954– )

## BIOGRAPHY

As the daughter of Mexican American parents with close family ties to Mexico, Sandra Cisneros is at home on both sides of the national and cultural borders. As the only daughter among six brothers, Cisneros is well aware of the patriarchal culture of Chicano society. Her life and writings illustrate the tensions of a woman's life on the cultural and social borders between exclusion and inclusion, restriction and success.

Born in Chicago in 1954, Cisneros attended Catholic elementary and high schools, and graduated from Loyola University of Chicago in 1976. During her childhood, the family moved frequently from one rented apartment to another, and often visited family in Mexico. While studying at the University of Iowa Writers' Workshop, Cisneros discovered the uniqueness of her urban, Hispanic, female experience and voice. After completing her M.F.A. at Iowa, she worked with Latino youth in academic settings in Chicago until she moved to San Antonio, Texas, where she still makes her home. In the note on the author that appears in her two novels, a note that she herself almost certainly wrote, Cisneros is described as "nobody's mother and nobody's wife," emphasizing her commitment to women's asserting individual identities rather than defining themselves in relation to men. She has earned fellowships from the National Endowment for the Arts, one each in fiction and poetry, and she received a MacArthur Foundation "genius grant" in 1995. She occasionally works as a guest professor or writer-in-residence at universities throughout the country. In addition to writing poetry, fiction, and essays, Cisneros is committed to supporting local arts efforts and Hispanic cultural projects, particularly in the San Antonio area.

## MAJOR THEMES

The life and work of Sandra Cisneros illustrate the borderland metaphor that Gloria Anzaldúa uses to characterize the experience of Hispanic women in the Americas. In *Borderlands/La Frontera* (1987), Anzaldúa describes the shifting territory between two established cultures as a forbidden zone occupied by outcasts; specifically, where Anglo and Mexican cultures overlap, the mixed-blood occupants enacting the struggles of the conflicted cultures belong in neither culture. Anzaldúa argues that women especially bear the burden of this cultural ambivalence (pp. 12, 31, 48–49). A native of both Anglo and Chicana worlds who is completely at home in neither, Sandra Cisneros voices the experience of women seeking their place in culture, in relationships, and in artistic production so that, free of patriarchal oppression, they can achieve identity, relational independence, and professional success on their own merits, rather than under the constraints of the traditional expectations and limitations of culture, family, and church.

In an essay entitled "Only Daughter," Cisneros describes herself as "the only daughter and *only* a daughter," revealing her understanding of the culture which values sons and expects a daughter to become, first and foremost, a wife and mother (p. 119). In the male dominated household of her childhood, she felt she had seven fathers protecting her; however, that protection confined her within the patriarchal assumptions of Mexican American Catholic culture. Cisneros's poetry and fiction demonstrate a fierce commitment to feminism, but it is a feminism inseparable from issues of race and class. Her working class immigrant background compels Cisneros to write in gratitude to those whose manual labor made it possible for her to enjoy the privilege of education, and to challenge the cultural assumptions that perpetuate injustice based on ethnicity, gender, and economic class. A poem entitled "I Awake in the Middle of the Night and Wonder If You're Still There" expresses the speaker's solidarity with the women of war-torn Sarajevo: half a world away, those women are intimately connected to the speaker because, a woman like them, "I don't count either" (*Loose Woman,* p. 64).

A key theme in Cisneros's fiction and poetry is feminist resistance to patriarchal oppression. The central characters in her stories, and the speakers in her poems, are Hispanic girls and young women who struggle with the restrictions placed on their lives and ambitions by the men they love. In the poem which prefaces the collection *My Wicked Wicked Ways* (1987), the speaker identifies herself as a woman who chose poetry instead of the conventional options of "rolling pin or factory" (p. x). The preteen narrator of *The House on Mango Street* (1984) understands that, in her urban barrio, a woman's place is in the home, but Esperanza Cordero is already looking for more opportunity than her culture allows. Her mother tells her to study hard in school so that she will not be trapped in domestic drudgery; the girl's grandmother, also named Esperanza, "looked out the window her whole life, the way so many women set their sadness on an elbow" (p. 11). Like Cisneros herself, the narrator and her family move often from one rented flat to another, leading Esperanza to realize how much she longs to live in a real house: "Not a man's house. Not a daddy's. A house all my own" (p. 108). Commenting on the significance of the house as a symbol of the psychic development of the self, a number of critics have linked this longing with Virginia Woolf's image of a woman writer's room of her own.

Cisneros also writes of the tenderness of family life, the close connections of loving family members. Esperanza's Papa is clearly modeled on Cisneros's own father, who instilled in his children ambition to succeed academically, to work with their heads rather than as manual laborers like himself. Many of the mother figures in Cisneros's stories are loving, self-sacrificing women who raise their daughters to aspire to a greater degree of freedom than they themselves have had. Cisneros treasures her Mexican American heritage, and celebrates family life, love, and devotion as a precious legacy, without denying the limitations of romantic ideals. In a poem entitled "Old Maids,"while admitting the attractiveness of married life, the thirty-something speaker gives more credence to the cautionary tales of entrapped married women, including the Greek Penelope, the Hindu Vashti, even the wife of Peter Pumpkin Eater.

This fusion of cultural references illustrates Cisneros's practice of adapting and reconfiguring images and literary genres, a practice characteristic of the borderland aesthetic. A number of critics have argued that in *The House on Mango Street* Cisneros consciously reshapes the male centered *bildungsroman*, following Esperanza as she comes of age, discovers her artistic vocation, and eventually leaves the neighborhood to seek her fortune in the wider world. In *Mango Street* and in *Woman Hollering Creek* (1991), the female characters break out of the molds assigned to them by the culture in search of new roles and new kinds of relationships. Cisneros portrays women who challenge stereotypes and break taboos, sometimes simply for the sake of shocking the establishment, but most often because the confining stereotypes prevent them from achieving their own identity.

Among Cisneros's cultural refigurations are her adaptations of traditional Catholic symbols of faith and worship. In a poem dedicated to her nephew on his baptismal day, "Arturito the Amazing Baby Olmec Who Is Mine by Way of Water," the aunt-godmother-speaker makes three wishes for the boy, whom she compares to a tiny prince of ancient Mexico: that he have the nobility of the Mexican freedom-fighter Zapata, the wisdom of Gandhi, and the generosity of Mother Teresa (*Loose Woman*, pp. 98–99). The borderland aesthetic here not only intertwines cross-cultural images but also shows how "the aunt who dislikes kids and Catholics" nevertheless recognizes the value of a religious tradition despite her rejection of its misogynistic theology and moral regulations. Similarly, in the story "Little Miracles, Kept Promises" (*Woman Hollering Creek*), Cisneros pays tribute to the faith of simple people who express their petitions and gratitude in *ex voto* offerings at a shrine to the Virgin Mary. The final voice in the story belongs to Rosario, a young woman who disappoints her mother and grandmothers by cutting off her braids as she creates an identity of her own. Changing her name to Chayo and pursuing an art career, the speaker discovers the links between the image of the Virgin of Guadalupe and those of the ancient Aztec fertility goddess Coatlaxopeuh and the good mother goddess Tonantzín. In this cultural fusion, Cisneros illustrates her hope that women will come to wholeness in their self-understanding, transcending the images of meekness and purity demanded by a male-dominated religious tradition.

Cisneros often plays with the three-fold Mexican images of woman as La Malinche (the Aztec who betrayed her people to Cortés, initiating their submission to the conquering European influences), La Llorona (the raped and victimized woman whose children have been taken from her or killed), and La Virgen de Guadalupe (the saintly mother, always self-sacrificing, obedient, demure). In the story "Woman Hollering Creek," Cisneros exposes the emptiness of the images of romantic love promoted by soap opera culture, and gives new meaning to the traditional myth of La Llorona. Cleofilas, a young Mexican mother abused by her philandering, drinking husband, is unable to find support from her neighbors Dolores and Soledad who believe that physical abuse is an unfortunate but normal part of husband-wife relationships. Finally, afraid for her children's lives, Cleofilas flees to a woman's center where staff members Felice and Graciela agree to help her return to her father's home. En route to the bus station, as they drive over La Gritona creek, Felice explains that it is not "Woman Weeping" but "Woman Hollering," and gives a Tarzan-like, liberated cry of power that convinces the humble Cleofilas that women can not only drive their own trucks but also take charge of their own lives. Cisneros transforms the traditional Christian and Indian myths of submissive, suffering womanhood into images of healing and liberation, giving new meaning to ancient symbols as women cope with new cultural and social situations.

While Cisneros readily admits that her devotion to the Virgin of Guadalupe is not exactly the same as traditional Catholic devotion, it is clear that she values this image of Mary, and many other traditional symbols of Catholicism, for their spiritual content. She told an interviewer that "the work of women and minorities and working class people has spiritual content and political content, and that's their strength," a strength which gives such writing a substantial and enduring quality (Jussawalla and Dasenbrock, p. 306). For Cisneros, Catholic images transcend denominational borders, carrying symbolic—even political—weight, which gives them power to transform society.

## SURVEY OF CRITICISM

At this writing, while no full-length study of Sandra Cisneros has been published, a significant number of journal articles and book chapters are devoted to her work, particularly her feminist themes, her challenges to established literary genres, and her place in Chicano literary studies. While it is claimed that her poetry collection *My Wicked Wicked Ways* is her most widely read book, it is Cisneros's fiction that has earned the most critical attention.

Cisneros is among the most prominent figures in the burgeoning field of Chicano/a literary studies, a significant expansion of American literary history. In *Chicano Narrative: The Dialectics of Difference*, Ramón Saldívar shows how Cisneros, Cherríe Morága, and Isabella Rios challenge the exclusion of Chicana voices from "the racist, classist, patriarchal bourgeois world that founds itself on the notion of a fixed and positive identity and on specified gender roles based on this positive fixation" (p. 175). However, with the chapter on Chicana writers appearing last in his book, almost as an addendum, it might be argued that Saldívar seems to perpetuate the very exclusions he critiques.

Recent studies in women's fiction emphasize feminist and Latina themes in Cisneros's work. In *Women Singing in the Snow* (1995), for example, Tey Diana Rebolledo discusses the wicked woman motif in Cisneros's poetry and fiction, arguing that rebellion against the constraints of Mexican cultural *machismo* and Catholic sexual morality allows the Chicana to "seize both the public space and public language" en route to freedom (p. 203). Similarly, in *Home Girls* (1996), Alvina Quintana argues that Cisneros and other authors challenge literary constraints on genre and topic in order to expose women's isolation and oppression, revise women's history, and contribute to a Chicana aesthetic. And Ellen McCracken, in *New Latina Narrative* (1999), claims that Cisneros reconfigures the traditional iconography of Mexican American Catholicism by applying it to the contemporary social issues of *Woman Hollering Creek*.

## BIBLIOGRAPHY

### Works by Sandra Cisneros

*Bad Boys*. San Jose: Mango Press, 1980.
*The House on Mango Street*. New York: Vintage-Random, 1984.
*My Wicked Wicked Ways*. Berkeley: Third Woman Press, 1987.
*Woman Hollering Creek and Other Stories*. New York: Vintage-Random, 1991.
*Loose Woman*. New York: Knopf, 1994.
"Only Daughter." *Máscaras*. Ed. Lucha Corpi. Chicana/Latina Studies Series. Berkeley: Third Woman Press, 1997. 119–23.

### Works about Sandra Cisneros

Gonzales, Maria. *Contemporary Mexican-American Women Novelists: Toward a Feminist Identity*. Frankfurt: Peter Lang, 1997.
Gutiérrez-Jones, Leslie S. "Different Voices: The Re-*Bildung* of the Barrio in Sandra Cisneros' *The House on Mango Street*." *Anxious Power: Reading, Writing, and Ambivalence in Narrative by Women*. Ed. Carol J. Singley and Susan Elizabeth Sweeney. Albany: State University of New York Press, 1993. 295–312.
Herrera, Andrea O'Reilly. "'Chambers of Consciousness': Sandra Cisneros and the Development of the Self in the BIG House on Mango Street." *Bucknell Review* 39.1 (1995): 191–204.

Jussawalla, Feroza, and Reed Way Dasenbrock, eds. "Sandra Cisneros." *Interviews with Writers of the Post-Colonial World*. Jackson: University Press of Mississippi, 1992. 286–306.

McCracken, Ellen. *New Latina Narrative: The Feminine Space of Postmodern Ethnicity*. Tucson: University of Arizona Press, 1999.

Mullen, Harryette. "'A Silence Between Us Like a Language': The Untranslatability of Experience in Sandra Cisneros's *Woman Hollering Creek*." *MELUS* 21.2 (Summer 1996): 3–20.

Olivares, Julián. "Entering *The House on Mango Street* (Sandra Cisneros)." *Teaching American Ethnic Literatures: Nineteen Essays*. Ed. John R. Maitino and David R. Peck. Albuquerque: University of New Mexico Press, 1996. 209–35.

Quintana, Alvina E. *Home Girls: Chicana Literary Voices*. Philadelphia: Temple University Press, 1996.

Rebolledo, Tey Diana. *Women Singing in the Snow: A Cultural Analysis of Chicana Literature*. Tucson: University of Arizona Press, 1995.

Saldívar, Ramón. *Chicano Narrative: The Dialectics of Difference*. Madison: University of Wisconsin Press, 1990.

Wyatt, Jean. "On Not Being La Malinche: Border Negotiations of Gender in Sandra Cisneros's 'Never Marry a Mexican' and 'Woman Hollering Creek.'" *Tulsa Studies* 14.2 (Fall 1995): 243–71.

EILEEN QUINLAN, S.N.D.

# CLARE OF ASSISI
# (1194–1253)

## BIOGRAPHY

Clare of Assisi is one of the greatest women of the Franciscan tradition and the foundress of the Order of the Poor Ladies, or Clares. She was the third of five children born to a relatively noble and wealthy family in the Italian town of Assisi in the region of Umbria. Even before her "conversion," she appears to have been a pious young woman. She was probably around seventeen years old when she first heard St. Francis preaching in the town square of Assisi, but it is unknown when she first actually met him. When her uncle made arrangements for her to marry, she refused and was able to arrange a secret meeting with St. Francis and consult with him for advice. She followed his admonitions to live a life of virginal purity, and in March 1212 she went to join him at the chapel of the Portiuncula (Santa Maria degli Angeli), where she committed herself to follow him in his pursuit of Gospel perfection. Initially, he escorted her to a Benedictine monastery not far from the Portiuncula. Despite the anger of her father, Clare remained firm in her resolve to live a life of piety. St. Francis later moved Clare to San Damiano, the first of the little run-down churches he had restored. Clare would remain at San Damiano for the rest of her life.

At San Damiano, others— including Clare's mother, Ortolana, and her two sisters, Agnes and Beatrice—joined her. She became abbess in 1215 of this community of women who wished to follow her in her desire to live according to the spirit and ideals set forth by St. Francis. Their way of life was one of extreme poverty, and they lived entirely by alms. The development of Clare's community is quite remarkable in light of the fact that by 1215, the Church forbade the establishment of any new religious orders. Clare and her sisters gained recognition as a religious community, and in 1217 the Cardinal Deacon Ugolino provided them with a Rule based on that of the Benedictines. This Rule, however, lacked an aspect that Clare considered extremely important: austere poverty. From this point onward, Clare's life was characterized by an ongoing effort to follow a way of life that was based on the principles that

St. Francis had given her. With a papal document in 1228, Cardinal Ugolino (now Pope Gregory IX) decided to give Clare the *privilegium paupertatis*, the privilege to practice complete poverty and to live without any possessions and without any sure means of income. This is especially noteworthy considering that previous to this, Rules for women had been based on the principle that religious communities would have to support themselves from income from their corporate possessions. This unique "privilege" was the first one of its kind ever issued by the papacy. Eventually, however, in 1247, Pope Innocent IV bound Clare and her sisters to a new Rule that allowed property and income, regardless of any previous regulations. Clare then began to write her own Rule that was based on the premise of poverty and the ideals espoused by St. Francis.

Clare bravely continued to seek the approval of her Rule from Pope Innocent IV. Two days before her death, she won her struggle to create a new kind of community for women. She received a papal bull approving her Rule which included the "privilege of poverty," reaffirming the right of her convent to live in strict and absolute poverty. Clare died at San Damiano in 1253. She was canonized just two years after her death, in 1255.

Throughout her life at San Damiano, Clare courageously maintained a determined effort to retain the ideal of radical poverty, despite the fact that Franciscan friars had begun to relax somewhat their practice of it. Clare remained steadfast in her convictions and challenged the Pope when he attempted to oblige her to adopt a Rule that contrasted with her firm beliefs. In essence, Clare created a new type of convent community—one that was supported entirely by alms and manual labor just like the original followers of St. Francis. Clare lived long enough to witness the foundation of convents of Poor Clares throughout Europe. Her followers continue today as a contemplative Order living in poor, enclosed communities throughout the world.

This remarkable woman left us only five known writings: her *Rule* and four *Letters to the Blessed Agnes of Prague*. The authenticity of other writings, the *Testament*, *Blessing*, and the *Letter to Ermentrude of Bruges*, has been disputed.

## MAJOR THEMES

Clare's *Rule*, the first in the history of the Church written by a woman for a female religious community, expresses her strong dedication to the vision of St. Francis, and is clearly based on his teachings. It should be emphasized, however, that Clare was not simply a female version of St. Francis. She had her own ideas about how women should live together, and her theology tends to focus more on Christ (the poor and suffering Christ, or the beloved bridegroom) while St. Francis emphasized the Trinity.

While its foundations lie in the Rule of St. Francis, Clare's *Rule* differs from it in that it describes the cloistered life. Her *Rule* outlines a life completely tied to a monastery, the practice of separation from the world in the enclosure. Clare sets out a way of life for the sisters based on the observance of the Gospel of Christ, the absence of possessions, and chastity. She outlines how women may join the order, maintaining that they must be accepted by the majority of the sisters, unmarried (or sworn to a mutual vow of chastity and living separately), and free to pursue an observance of the religious life. Furthermore, they should sell all their goods and distribute them to the poor. Clare gives specific requirements and describes the various conditions of the penitential life in the community, including the daily life of the sisters. She also outlines the duties of the abbess and the responsibilities of other officers of the convent.

Clare describes a daily life in the convent that is completely influenced by the sisters' pursuit of radical poverty. Throughout her *Rule*, Clare underscores the poverty of Christ. She envisions the spiritual life as conforming oneself to the poor Christ, thus enabling one to enter upon the way that leads toward the kingdom of heaven. Her *Rule* is also characterized by efforts to preserve the unity of the mutual love of the sisters. Clare was concerned with the spiritual, interior life of each sister and its demonstration in the community of the sisters as a whole. Mutual love is also seen as the way to solve problems. Sisters who sin are to be humbly admonished by the abbess, and punished only if absolutely necessary.

The four *Letters to the Blessed Agnes of Prague*, written to a woman of royal descent over the span of nineteen years, demonstrate the development of Clare's teaching on religious life. Agnes had come to know the Friars Minor, and had become attracted to the spiritual life they advocated. Desiring to imitate the life and ideals of Clare, she entered a monastery and began to correspond with her. Clare's letters highlight her understanding of the spiritual life in the Franciscan tradition, as well as her desire to guide another in a life of piety and poverty. She contrasts secular and spiritual lives and discusses poverty and contemplation. Moreover, she identifies prayer and evangelical poverty with economic poverty—to be receptive to God's love, one must let go of material possessions. She attempts to strengthen Agnes in her determination to endure the hardships of the Franciscan way of life, encouraging her to remain steadfast in her love for the suffering Christ.

The other writings attributed to Clare reflect her vision and spirit despite the fact that their authenticity has been questioned. The *Letter to Ermentrude of Bruges*, addressed to a woman in Flanders who had founded several monasteries and who wished to pattern her life after Clare and her sisters, is written in a more simple and impersonal style than Clare's other writings. In it, she emphasizes the deceptiveness of the world. Doubts concerning Clare's *Testament* have arisen because of the weakness of the manuscript tradition. Nevertheless, this work exemplifies Clare's spirituality and contains expressions of gratitude and thanksgiving as well as encouragements directed toward her sisters. Just like a mother to her daughters, Clare wishes to admonish and encourage both present and future sisters, advising them to continue their life of simplicity, humility, and poverty, with St. Francis as their spiritual model. The Poor Clares, as a remembrance of their Foundress, have always cherished Clare's *Blessing*, allegedly addressed to her sisters at San Damiano as well as those in other monasteries and those who would come in the future.

## SURVEY OF CRITICISM

Regis Armstrong and Ignatius Brady's critical edition, entitled *Francis and Clare: The Complete Works*, contains a good introduction to Clare and her writings. They discuss her life and works as well as her spirituality. Their annotated translations of her works also include those whose authenticity has been called into question. However, their introduction lacks any information regarding some important innovations in Clare's *Rule*.

Elizabeth Petroff's article highlights how Clare's *Rule* established a new kind of community for women, arguing that it represents a utopian narrative of a unique kind. Petroff shows how Clare's community differed from those that were more traditional. She points out that, while the Rule of the Benedictines provided an abbess with complete authority, Clare's *Rule* adopts a nonhierarchical structure; in Clare's community, an abbess has a number of experienced sisters ("discreets") to advise and help her. Clare's vision of community life thus included sharing and cooperation among all the sisters. Moreover, the punishments Clare prescribes for disobedient sisters are mild compared to those prescribed by other medieval convent communities, where imprisonment and beatings were common. Petroff argues that Clare's emphasis on poverty illustrates that women do not need protection from men and can provide for themselves, a break from traditional medieval ideas regarding women.

Rosalind and Christopher Brooke discuss the relation of Clare's movement to the wider issues of female involvement in contemporary medieval religious movements. Bridget Mary Meehan, Elizabeth Petroff, Amy Oden, and Monica Furlong all include short discussions and reflections on Clare and her works, as well as excerpts from her writings.

## BIBLIOGRAPHY

### Work by Clare of Assisi

*Francis and Clare: The Complete Works*. Ed. and trans. Regis J. Armstrong and Ignatius C. Brady. New York: Paulist Press, 1982.

### Works about Clare of Assisi

Brooke, Rosalind B. and Christopher N. L. "St. Clare." *Medieval Women*. Ed. Derek Baker. Oxford: Basil Blackwell, 1978. 275–87.
Furlong, Monica, ed. *Visions and Longings: Medieval Women Mystics*. Boston: Shambhala, 1996. 117–35.

Meehan, Bridget Mary. *Praying with Passionate Women: Mystics, Martyrs and Mentors*. New York: Crossroad, 1995. 75–77.

Oden, Amy, ed. *In Her Words: Women's Writings in the History of Christian Thought*. Nashville: Abingdon, 1994. 127–39.

Petroff, Elizabeth. "A Medieval Woman's Utopian Vision: The Rule of Saint Clare of Assisi." *Feminism, Utopia and Narrative*. Ed. Libby Falk Jones and Sarah Webster Goodwin. Knoxville: University of Tennessee Press, 1990. 174–90.

——, ed. *Medieval Women's Visionary Literature*. New York: Oxford University Press, 1986. 231–41.

Robinson, Paschal. "Clare of Assisi, Saint." *The Catholic Encyclopedia*. Vol. 4. Ed. Charles G. Herbermann, et al. New York: Robert Appleton, 1908. 4–6.

Thomas of Celano. *The Life of Saint Clare*. In *The Legend and Writings of Saint Clare of Assisi*. n.d. Trans. Ignatius Brady. St. Bonaventure, New York: Franciscan Institute, 1953.

MOLLY MORRISON

# JUDITH ORTIZ COFER
# (1952– )

## BIOGRAPHY

Judith Ortiz Cofer's bicultural background and American assimilation experience are the most prominent themes in her writing. Because she dealt with adjusting to a new culture early, the process of adapting to new surroundings became a dominant characteristic of her childhood. Judith was born on February 24, 1952, to J. M. and Fanny Ortiz, in Hormigueros, Puerto Rico. Judith's family was devoutly Catholic with deep roots in the religious community. She was immediately baptized into the same church her mother and grandmother had been baptized in and then placed in Catholic school early on.

Judith's father joined the U.S. Navy while she was young and was subsequently posted to the Brooklyn Naval Yard. Taking his family with him, J. M. moved to New York, settling the family into a Puerto Rican community in Paterson, New Jersey. His career with the Navy meant that J. M. often went to sea for extended periods of time, and whenever he left, Judith's mother would pack up Judith and her brother and return to Puerto Rico to their grandmother's house. Through frequent trips between Puerto Rico and the United States, Cofer quickly adapted to her constantly changing surroundings. She learned to speak English and, together with her brother and father, actively took the role of facilitating American life and culture for her mother. Very early on, Cofer's sense of heightened cultural awareness meant that she noticed cultural differences and problems that even now continue to influence her writing.

After graduating from Florida Atlantic University with an M.A. in English, Cofer began teaching, writing poetry in her spare time. She showed her first creative efforts to a colleague who urged her to send her work out, resulting in the publication of her first poem. Encouraged by her success, she continued to write and send out her work. Cofer's first collection of poetry, the chapbook *Peregrina*, won the first place award in the Riverstone International Chapbook Competition in 1985. Its subsequent publication by Riverstone Press in 1986 launched her career as a poet. *Peregrina* was followed by *Terms of Survival* and *Reaching for the Mainland*, poetry collections published in 1987. In 1989, Cofer published her first novel, *The Line of the Sun*, to critical acclaim, and it was subsequently nominated for the Pulitzer Prize. A PEN/Martha Albrand Special Citation in Non-Fiction followed the publication of her autobiographical memoir *Silent Dancing: A Partial Remembrance of a Puerto Rican Childhood* in 1990. *The Latin Deli* (prose and poetry collection, 1993), *An Island Like You: Stories of the Barrio* (children's stories, 1998), and *The Year of Our Revolution: Selected and New Prose and Poetry* (1998) followed, bringing her more awards and recognition for her writing.

Cofer currently lives in Georgia, where she is the Franklin Professor of English and Creative Writing at the University of Georgia in Athens. When not teaching at the university, Cofer and her husband Charles live on a farm in rural Louisville, Georgia, where she raised her daughter, Tanya, and continues to write about Puerto Rico, *"la isla de mis sueños"* (the island of my dreams).[1]

## MAJOR THEMES

It is impossible to read almost any full-length work by Judith Ortiz Cofer and not notice Catholic images, rituals, and symbols that enrich her prose and anchor her writing. The presence of Catholicism as a dominant theme initially suggests that Cofer is primarily engaged with exploring her relationship to the religious elements of her upbringing and identity. However, the same Catholic images and themes that give her work purpose and balance also become problematic in trying to determine how Cofer's religion has influenced her writing. Namely, what do we as readers make of the extensive Catholic presence in her work? Why is Cofer's Catholicism important in understanding the dominant themes in her writing? By examining the Catholic images and themes in her work, a clearer understanding of the relationship between Cofer's Catholicism and writing can be gained. In the process, we may also move closer to understanding what role religion plays in determining identity on levels more immediate to ourselves.

The chronological progression of Cofer's writing reveals a complex but evolving relationship with Catholicism. Although her early poetry registers her discontent with Catholicism and its rituals, as her writing career progresses her view becomes generally more accepting of and circumspect about the religious circumstances that shaped her life. For example, several poems in her early collection *Terms of Survival* exhibit her recognition that the Catholic codes of religious conduct often contradict human urges and tendencies. In the poem "La Fe" [Faith], Cofer invokes with an almost reverential tone images of the saints, church bells, and the proper attitude and demeanor required while attending Mass. But instead of using this setting to affirm her faith, her prayer becomes a petition of release from Catholicism's strict rules. She prays "to be released from rituals," an image and request that indicates her feeling of captivity (p. 12). Furthermore, the women characters in Cofer's early writing often have a disconnection between their faith and behavior. For example, the woman who engages in an adulterous affair in "Las Malas Lenguas" [Bad Tongues] does so after "being caught on her knees" making a deal with the devil for her body and soul, and her mistakes become legendary in her hometown (p. 15). Through these types of characters, Cofer explores the contradictions and outcomes of being raised a Catholic and willfully not behaving as one should.

The theme of discontent with Catholicism that marks Cofer's early work generally evolves into more complex considerations of Catholic issues in her later writing. For example, Cofer also experiments with and explores the ever-present theme of the Madonna-whore dichotomy that has its roots in Catholicism and is reinforced by her Puerto Rican culture. While in *Terms* that dichotomy is revealed as an often unquestioned reality in Catholic women's lives, Cofer's poetry in *The Latin Deli* begins to examine more fully this contradiction by exposing the faulty reasoning behind blind acceptance of the stereotype. In particular, the poem "Las Magdalenas" clearly problematizes the stereotype by considering a real-life example of apparent contradiction. The prostitutes in this poem attend morning Mass before going home to sleep after a night of work. In doing so, these women represent the dichotomy most clearly—Madonna-like by day and whores by night—and the cleansing ritual of the Mass they engage in marks a stark contrast with their chosen lifestyle. The suggestion that their confessions have become ritualized to the point of becoming meaningless lies just slightly below the surface of the poem. Although the poem initially appears to be a meditation on the contrast between prostitution and religion, what becomes most apparent is Cofer's suggestion that blindly engaging in religious rituals does not guarantee a change in wayward behavior, a complex comment on the relationship of Catholicism to everyday life.

Cofer's relationship with Catholicism again plays a dominant role in *The Line of the Sun*, but her concerns in this novel are more of a presence rather than a central theme. Here Catholicism functions as a touchstone for Cofer's version of reality in the novel. She makes comparisons to Catholic images and art works and also uses saints and religious images to anchor her descriptions. For example, Mama Cielo's problem with her son Guzmán hinges on her rigid adherence to Catholic principles and his unwillingness to be bound by those rules. She consistently makes the sign of the cross after discussing her son's waywardness and consults the aid of a spiritualist and healer to help rid him of the "malicious spirit" that she is sure is causing his misbehavior (p. 23). But this conflict is only a sidelight to the central narrative of Guzmán finding his way in the world. Cofer also explores the relationship of Catholicism and spiritualism in this novel, since Mama Cielo's husband works as a spiritual healer in their town, as well as being a devout Catholic himself. The intersection of the

Catholic faith with the other systems of belief that these Puerto Rican characters develop to describe the inexplicable remains a constant theme.

In a recent interview with me, Cofer indicated that her evolving identity as a Catholic woman has led her to make religious comparisons and invoke images that exclusively rely on her experience as a Catholic. She stated, "If I want to describe Ramona as particularly calm and beautiful, I call her a Madonna. If I want to say that somebody looks beautiful in a particular way I'll say that they remind me of the portraits or the paintings of the Virgin. These are not conscious choices, I don't say 'now I am going to make a parallel,' these images are just there" (see Note 1). For Cofer, Catholicism is inextricably tied to gender issues and what it means to be a woman, but she is quick to point out that she does not consider herself just a "Catholic writer." "I consider myself a Catholic writer in a similar way if not in an exact way that I consider myself a woman writer," she stated in the same interview. "I don't sit down when I'm starting a poem or an article and say to myself—you are a woman writer. Every time I put down a word it's imbued with my being and certainly not with my *machismo*. Being Catholic was a condition of my life, more of a condition than a situation. I can't help my connection to it." Aside from the noticeable patterns of images and Catholic reference points in her work, what remains constant is how Cofer's religious heritage continues to enrich and enlarge her writing.

## SURVEY OF CRITICISM

Cofer's writing has generated much critical acclaim, although her work did not attract much attention until her first novel, *The Line of the Sun*, was published. In his review of the book for the *New York Times Book Review*, Roberto Marquez noted that Cofer's writing "confirms the continuing efflorescence and enlarges the resonance and reach of [Hispanic] literature." She is "a prose writer of evocatively lyrical authority," he continued, "a novelist of historical compass and sensitivity" (p. 46). Sonja Bolle's review for the *Los Angeles Times Book Review* echoed Marquez's praise and also pointed out how Cofer's eye for detail "brings alive the stifling and magical world of village life" (p. 6).

*The Latin Deli* was also followed by warm and vigorous praise. Writing for *Studies in Short Fiction*, Michael O'Shea enthuses, "Buy this book for the profound, poignant, funny, universal and moving epiphanies between its covers" (p. 502). O'Shea also notes that Cofer's "essays and poems are highly personal and as powerful as her stories," and he is the only critic and reviewer to mention the presence of strong Catholic imagery structures and themes throughout her work (p. 503). "Several poems evoke the power of Catholic symbol and mysticism recalled through some secular distance, yet retaining not only the power of vivid recollection but also that conferred by artistic transformation," he adds (p. 503).

One general theme of most reviews of Cofer's work is her tremendous sense of accessibility to a wide reading audience—her stories seem to speak to all levels of readers. This type of praise and admiration continues through reviews even in cyberspace. For example, one Internet reviewer of *Silent Dancing* on the Amazon.com web site notes "Cofer's conversational tone is engaging and unintimidating despite the deep issues she raises and the hard questions she subtly asks. Throughout *Silent Dancing*, Cofer takes the reader along for a very enlightening journey through self-exploration and self-definition. She discusses the ways that race, class, gender, and culture interact to shape her life experiences without sounding dogmatic or naïve" ("Silent Dancing," Amazon.com, p. 1).

Academic critics have also focused on Cofer's writing, especially the bicultural themes in her works. Juan Bruce-Novoa, for example, examines the roots of Cofer's identity in his article "Judith Ortiz Cofer's Rituals of Movement." Specifically, Bruce-Novoa considers how the "habit of movement" Cofer describes between two cultures ultimately places the identity development process into the act of movement itself. Laurie Grobman expands on this line of inquiry by examining the role of memory in the creative process, and concludes that the act of remembering returns Cofer to her cultural past in order to create the present. While these two critics focus primarily on the process of developing identity, there has also been new interest in Cofer's role in the debate regarding border literature. In a forthcoming article for *MELUS*, Teresa Derrickson examines the problems of applying Gloria Anzaldúa's perceptions of border identity to Cofer's writing, since the Puerto Rican experience differs on fundamental levels from the Chicano existence that primarily concerns Anzaldúa.

In addition to these critical considerations, Cofer has granted a number of interviews that shed light on her image of herself as an author. She has answered questions about her responsibilities as an "ethnic" woman and writer, her creative process, and the role of teaching in her work, among other issues. Perhaps more than most authors, her continued accessibility as an author is a tribute to her commitment to her writing and readers.

## NOTE

1. I am indebted to Judith Ortiz Cofer for these comments during my personal interview with her for this article on August 12, 1999.

## BIBLIOGRAPHY

### Works by Judith Ortiz Cofer

*Peregrina*. Golden, Colorado: Riverstone Press, 1986.
*Reaching for the Mainland*. Tempe, Arizona: Bilingual Review Press, 1987.
*Terms of Survival*. Houston: Arte Publico Press, 1987.
*The Line of the Sun*. Athens: University of Georgia Press, 1989.

*Silent Dancing: A Partial Remembrance of a Puerto Rican Childhood*. Houston: University of Houston Arte Publico Press, 1990.
*The Latin Deli*. Athens: University of Georgia Press, 1993.
*The Year of Our Revolution: Selected and New Prose and Poetry*. Houston: University of Houston Arte Publico Press, 1998.
*An Island Like You: Stories of the Barrio*. New York: Troll Books School Book Club Publications/Penguin, 1998.

## Works about Judith Ortiz Cofer

Bolle, Sonja. "Fiction: *The Line of the Sun* by Judith Ortiz Cofer." *Los Angeles Times Book Review* 6 August 1989: home ed. 6.
Bruce-Novoa, Juan. "Judith Ortiz Cofer's Rituals of Movement." *The Americas Review* 19.3–4 (1991): 88–99.
——. "Ritual in Judith Ortiz Cofer's *The Line of the Sun*." *Confluencia: Revista Hispanica de Cultura y Literatura* 8.1 (1992): 61–69.
Derrickson, Teresa. "'Cold/Hot, English/Spanish': The Puerto Rican-American Divide in Judith Ortiz Cofer's *Silent Dancing*." Forthcoming in *MELUS*, 2001.
Grobman, Laurie. "The Cultural Past and Artistic Creation in Sandra Cisneros' *The House on Mango Street* and Judith Ortiz Cofer's *Silent Dancing*." *Confluencia: Revista Hispanica de Cultura y Literatura* 11.1 (1995): 42–49.
Marquez, Robert. "University Presses; Island Heritage, *The Line of the Sun*." *New York Times Book Review* 24 September 1989: late ed., sec. 7: 46.
Ocasio, Rafael. "The Infinite Variety of the Puerto Rican Reality: An Interview with Judith Ortiz Cofer." *Callaloo: A Journal of African American Arts and Letters* 17.3 (1994): 730–42.
——. "Puerto Rican Literature in Georgia? An Interview with Judith Ortiz Cofer." *The Kenyon Review* 14.4 (1992): 43–50.
O'Shea, Michael. "*The Latin Deli*: Prose and Poetry by Judith Ortiz Cofer." *Studies in Short Fiction* 31 (1994): 502–3.
Piedra, Jose. "His and Her Panics." *Disposito: Revista Americana de Estudios Comparados y Culturales/American Journal of Comparative and Cultural Studies* 16.41 (1991): 71–93.
"Silent Dancing." Online posting 4 August 1999. Amazon.com book reviews. 27 December 1999. http://www.amazon.com/exec/obidos/ASIN/1558850155/.

LISA TREVIÑO ROY-DAVIS

# ELIZABETH CULLINAN
# (1933– )

## BIOGRAPHY

Elizabeth Cullinan joins company with other important Irish American writers such as F. Scott Fitzgerald, Brendan Gill, and James T. Farrell. She was born in 1933 to Irish parents and raised in New York City where she attended Catholic schools and, later, Marymount College in Manhattan. Many of her early experiences as an Irish American Catholic inform her writing. In 1955, Cullinan began working for *New Yorker* magazine as a secretary while at the same time launching her literary career. Her early stories were published in the *New Yorker*; these were later collected in *The Time of Adam* (1971). During the 1960s, Cullinan lived for several years in Ireland. Throughout the 1960s–1970s, she continued to publish stories in the *New Yorker* as well as in other magazines. In 1970, her first novel, *House of Gold*, appeared; it was the Houghton Mifflin Literary Fellowship Novel for that year. In 1977, Cullinan became a faculty member at the Writers' Workshop at the University of Iowa, where she taught for one year. A second collection of short stories, *Yellow Roses*, was published that year. Cullinan's second novel, *A Change of Season*, a story of an Irish American woman's sojourn in Dublin, appeared in 1982.

## MAJOR THEMES

Elizabeth Cullinan's most important work, *House of Gold*, develops the themes that are found throughout the author's canon. These include the domineering Irish American matriarch, the dutiful daughter, and the strong influence of ritual Catholicism on the Irish American family. Catholic themes and symbols abound in Cullinan's works and are interconnected, lending her writings a sense of continuity.

The basic premise of *House of Gold* revolves around the death of the elderly matriarch of a large Irish American family, Mrs. Julia Devlin. Although the events of the novel occur at an unspecified time, the atmosphere evoked is clearly pre–Vatican II, probably the mid-1960s. The action takes place over two days. As Mrs. Devlin lays dying, her six surviving adult children (three others have died earlier), their spouses, and her four grandchildren gather together in the Devlin family home to prepare for the end. *House of Gold* provides an intimate view of individuals in a close-knit family facing the reality of death. By deftly shifting her point of view and exploring the interior thought processes of several characters, Cullinan succeeds in presenting both a philosophical and moral novel, one underpinned by issues of life, death, and religion. Each family member must deal with his or her feelings for the dying woman, for each other, and for his or her status as insiders or outsiders to the complex Devlin clan.

The novel's title is significant, functioning as a metaphor for the work's major themes. On a literal level, the phrase "house of gold" refers to the golden-hued decorations that draped the home's interior for Mr. and Mrs. Devlin's fiftieth wedding anniversary that took place several years prior to the novel's action. Symbolically, however, the title points to Julia Devlin's fiercely held Catholic beliefs and the strict manner in which she has raised her children to conform to these beliefs. As the novel makes explicit, "house of gold" is one of the titles applied to the Virgin Mary in the "Litany of the Virgin Mary." Although their relationship with her has been complicated, Mrs. Devlin's children and extended family regard her as a saintly Madonna-like figure and her house an almost holy place. Daughter-in-law Claire Devlin provides perhaps the clearest view of the family we receive. Discovering Julia Devlin's gold and rose trimmed china service in a cabinet, she meditates on its significance:

There were things like this on [God's] table, the sacred vessels on the altar: ciborium, chalice, patten, monstrance—the sacraments given artful shapes, intricate designs. Here it was the other way around. Simple domestic objects, a cup, a saucer, a teapot, became vaguely sacramental, symbolic. Of what? No, not of what. Of whom? Of her, Mrs. Devlin. There was a line in the Litany of the Blessed Virgin—Claire smiled to herself at the thought of it. Literally, figuratively, ironically, every way and any way that one phrase fit. . . . Mystical Rose. Tower of David. Tower of Ivory. House of Gold. (p. 213)

But as critic Anita Gandolfo rightly notes, "house of gold" can likewise denote the so-called "Golden Age" of Catholicism that Julia Devlin represents, a veneer-covered, repressively pious attitude that has exacted an "enormous physical and psychological cost" from her offspring (p. 120). A stereotypical Irish matriarch, Mrs. Devlin wields authority in her household, and her children, even as adults, obey her without question. Although her husband has been dead for a number of years when the novel opens, there is evidence that he, too, submitted to her command. A self-sacrificing mother who raised nine children in relatively straitened circumstances, Mrs. Devlin's unquestioned piety has made her totally unable to see herself, her children, and the world in anything but the most conventional, sugar-coated terms. Perhaps no incident brings this fact to the forefront better that Claire's surreptitious perusal of

Mrs. Devlin's "autobiography," a notebook manuscript entitled "The Story of a Mother" that Claire discovers as she helps set the house in order. Reading through Mrs. Devlin's descriptions of her "saintly" children (especially the five who have become priests or nuns), Claire comments to herself,

"More like a Fairy Tale than True Life," the author had written, but it was the other part of the story, the family part, that read like the fairy tale—the clear lines and brilliant colors of the surfaces; tragedy and triumph and nothing in between . . . past boredom, irritation, triviality . . . What unshakeable belief you'd need if you were to eliminate all that, belief in yourself and in True Life. (p. 169)

Unable to live up to their mother's expectations—to the saintly Mrs. Devlin—each of the Devlin children gathered in anticipation of her death reveals the fears, loneliness, and insecurities that have resulted from growing up in the household. Justin, the middle son, unmarried, middle-aged, and moorless, is an alcoholic. The youngest son Tom, Claire's husband, is hot-tempered and spoiled. Sister Mary James, a nun, finds her only comfort in her collection of pills, Librium and Butasol, to keep her calm. Mrs. Devlin's guilt-inducing presence extends to her children's spouses and her grandchildren. While they regard her authority with respect and a certain awe, they have always been made to feel of little or no account, as perpetual outsiders to the Devlin family. Upon seeing Mrs. Devlin in a coma, Elizabeth's husband Edwin is stunned that the woman who had always dominated others is now so helpless. And as Claire observes, "[H]ere in the house you always felt the weight of [Mrs. Devlin's] presence, her overbearing possessiveness. You couldn't stay here for long without beginning to feel physically oppressed" (p. 138).

The Devlin child who has experienced her mother's oppression most forcefully is Elizabeth. Although a married woman with two adult children, she was "more a daughter than she was anything else" (p. 14). She has obeyed her mother in everything throughout her life, with only one exception. For the first several years of their married life, she and Edwin lived with their children on the upper floor of Mrs. Devlin's house, but then, against the older woman's wishes, they moved to a nearby apartment. Although quarrels and tension between mother and daughter were constant when the two lived together, and her family was never allowed to feel welcome in the house, Elizabeth remains guilt-ridden at her "abandonment" of her mother. As the only daughter who has not entered religious life, she has been the perpetual caretaker, the child who has dutifully born the family burdens. But her mother has never allowed Elizabeth to feel she was good enough, and has never expressed her appreciation for all Elizabeth has done.

To the end, Elizabeth is unable to express her frustration to her mother. Right before she dies, Mrs. Devlin holds a conversation with Elizabeth that leaves Elizabeth distraught: her mother asks her if she ever "held her back" in life. Elizabeth vehemently denies it (p. 81). In reality, however, Julia Devlin has repressed Elizabeth in many ways. Elizabeth remains unable to break the strong hold her mother exerts over her and in fact replicates Julia Devlin's controlling behavior with her own daughters: "She had to be firm. . . . To her [being a daughter] meant obedience" (p. 87). Nevertheless, the end of the novel presents some hope that the younger generation of women may yet break free of such oppression and act more truthfully and spontaneously when Elizabeth's daughter Winnie confronts the wife of the doctor who (the novel implies) has misdiagnosed Mrs. Devlin's illness. In breaking through the woman's "fairy-tale" hypocrisy and standing up fearlessly for the truth, Winnie demonstrates symbolically that the older generation is passing; the dominant matriarch is dying. While the older women in the text are submissive and docile, the younger generation of women represented by Winnie, Cullinan implies, has the potential to break free of stereotyped Irish American behavior patterns for women. Cullinan's is, therefore, a tempered feminist statement.

The letter if not the spirit of Catholicism dominates the Devlin household. Mrs. Devlin considers herself to be a specially blessed woman: "Surely there was something marvelous in store for a mother who had sacrificed so much" (p. 3). She surrounds herself with statues and pictures of Jesus, Mary, and the saints, with crucifixes and rosaries. Even the house itself is situated directly across the street from a Catholic church. The Devlin children accept this ritualistic Catholic atmosphere with little question: it is natural to their upbringing. Cullinan's tone regarding Catholicism is superbly complex. On the one hand, inseparable from the figure of Mrs. Devlin, Catholicism's demand for unquestioning loyalty and obedience has produced the anxious, guilt-ridden Devlin children. On the other hand, especially in the scenes of Mrs. Devlin's annointing and the aftermath of her death, Catholic beliefs and rituals lend comfort, stability, and support to the grieving family members. Although hungover from a fling, the alcoholic son Justin cannot stop sobbing when his mother dies. As the family gathers to pray the rosary at the wake, he badly wants to sneak away but is, rather, inescapably drawn toward it: "Kneeling was better than standing. Saying the Hail Marys was better than talking. It would make the time pass. It would help fill up the hours" (p. 328). Ultimately, Cullinan's tone, while critical, upholds Catholicism as a stabilizing and unifying force in times of crisis, perhaps the only factor that allows the Devlin children to truly come together in spirit.

One of the great appeals of *House of Gold* is in its minute delineation of domestic details. A fair share of the action during the two days Mrs. Devlin lays dying revolves around cleaning and food preparation. As is natural to such a setting, these activities are dominated by the women; the men, sent outside the house for groceries or for other duties, become—and feel—superfluous. In the level of detail she provides, Cullinan succeeds in making readers one with the family, understanding how family rank is quietly determined by who undertakes which chores. Mostly, these domestic duties are repetitive and boring, and readers see more fully the endless routine the female characters like Elizabeth have been forced to carry out. But, similar to Catholicism's rituals—Mass, rosary, novenas—such routine domestic work becomes an outlet for grief.

Most of Cullinan's short stories deal with similar themes of Catholicism's influence and the domestic details of family life. "The Power of Prayer" concerns a daughter who prays that her father might come home early to celebrate her mother's birthday. "The Old Priest" discusses Vatican II changes in the Mass. "The Ablutions" concerns a wealthy family's embrace of the social and cultural aspects of Catholicism, but they prove indifferent to its spirituality even when a family friend, Father Fox, tries to bring them to a deeper faith. None of these stories, however, adequately portrays as does *House of Gold* what is perhaps the most noteworthy characteristic of Cullinan's writings, namely, her remarkable skill in capturing the intricacies of human relationships, especially when those relationships involve a family's complex mixture of love, hate, desire, and repression.

## SURVEY OF CRITICISM

The critical response to Cullinan's works, though sparse, has been mainly favorable. In "Elizabeth Cullinan: Yellow and Gold," Maureen Murphy discusses the Joycean influences on Cullinan's short stories, and the themes of domesticity and religion in *House of Gold*. She analyzes the parallels drawn between the Holy Family and the Devlin family, and she concludes that the comparison is valid given the typical Irish American devotion to the Virgin Mary. Murphy also discusses the various ways the color gold is used in the novel, and the satiric value of Mrs. Devlin's autobiography, which she calls "a comic masterpiece—sentimental, pretentious, lugubrious" (p. 145). In addition, Murphy presents a helpful analysis of the image of the train in the novel. Set near train tracks, the Devlin household is interrupted several times every day by the noise of the passing train. Murphy notes, for example, that the disruptive passing of the train does not bother Julia Devlin's hired nurse, a nun, because she has had the courage to leave her disapproving family behind—or, metaphorically, "jump on the train"—when deciding to enter the convent. The Devlin children, on the other hand, afraid to defy their mother by exerting their independence, are continually annoyed by the trains. Finally, Murphy accurately sums up the overall theme of *House of Gold* in pointing out that Elizabeth's daughter Winnie holds the key to the novel's tension between individual expression and family loyalty: "It is Winnie Carroll's understanding that people have the right to be themselves, to their own identity, that is at the heart of *House of Gold*, for it urges the claims of the individual over the twin bonds of faith and family in Irish-American life" (pp. 147–48).

In "Historical and Fictional Stereotypes of the Irish," Margaret Conners concludes that Cullinan's *House of Gold* provides a narrow and stereotyped view of the contemporary Irish American lifestyle. Connors first traces the history of the various stereotypical views of Irish Americans from the nineteenth through the twentieth centuries. "Mothers dominate and daughters obey; or if they rebel, they are forever guilt-ridden," Connors writes; "Cullinan's young women, despite liberated lifestyles, are unable to escape Elizabeth Devlin's plight" (p. 8). According to Conners, Irish American authors like Cullinan "have propped up tired stereotypes for too long and they have steadfastly refused to confront the cultural issues that have shaped their fiction" (p. 9).

In his important study, *The Irish Voice in America*, Charles Fanning also discusses the matriarchal theme in and the Irish American influence on Cullinan's writings, but his view of the author's work is much more positive. Fanning calls Cullinan's work "remarkable for its combination of precise craftsmanship and authenticity to felt experience" (p. 334), and he praises her ability to capture in fiction the intricate nature of close relationships. Fanning finds that while *House of Gold* may employ a stereotyped version of the Irish American family, it is accurate in demonstrating how such a typical household both suffocates and supports its family members. While Mrs. Devlin "imposes a rule of duty, controls her family by withholding love, and dominates her children into sharing her distorted vision of the world . . . she is not a caricature, but a fully realized human being whose plausible neuroses evoke sympathy and understanding, not ridicule and bitterness" (p. 335). Fanning uses Mrs. Devlin's autobiography as well as the thoughts and conversations of her children as springboards for his keen insights into her character. Moreover, Fanning explains the novel's theme in its ironic juxtaposition of the images of gold and trains: "Against the power of Mrs. Devlin's self-sustaining gold-leaf dream of herself as a kind of Virgin Queen, Cullinan has placed in realistic counterpoint one recurrent brute fact of life in this house, a fact so insistent that even the Devlins cannot ignore it: the trains. . . . In a brutal irony, Mrs. Devlin dies as a freight train is passing, and . . . the noise undercuts the conventional deathbed tableau of the family gathered for the last farewell" (p. 339). Fanning concludes, rightly, that *House of Gold* "exemplifies contemporary Irish-American domestic fiction at its best" (p. 335).

## BIBLIOGRAPHY

### Works by Elizabeth Cullinan

*House of Gold.* Boston: Houghton Mifflin, 1970.
*The Time of Adam.* Boston: Houghton Mifflin, 1971.
*Yellow Roses.* New York: Viking, 1977.
*A Change of Scene.* New York: W. W. Norton, 1982.

### Works about Elizabeth Cullinan

Conners, Margaret E. "Historical and Fictional Stereotypes of the Irish." *Irish-American Fiction: Essays in Criticism.* Ed. Daniel J. Casey and Robert E. Rhodes. New York: AMS, 1979. 1–12.

Fanning Charles. *The Irish Voice in America: Irish-American Fiction from the 1760s to 1980s.* Lexington: University Press of Kentucky, 1990.

Gandolfo, Anita. *Testing the Faith: The New Catholic Fiction in America.* Westport, Connecticut: Greenwood Press, 1992.

Murphy, Maureen. "Elizabeth Cullinan: Yellow and Gold." *Irish-American Fiction: Essays in Criticism.* Ed. Daniel J. Casey and Robert E. Rhodes. New York: AMS, 1979. 139–51.

ELLEN C. FRYE

# DOROTHY DAY
# (1897–1980)

## BIOGRAPHY

When Dorothy Day died in 1980 at the age of eighty-three, the historian David J. O'Brien called her "the most significant, interesting, and influential person in the history of American Catholicism" (p. 711). For many years the daily routine of the writer and activist had consisted of "daily Mass, the rosary, and at least two hours a day of meditation on Scripture" (Ellsberg, p. xviii). A deep Catholic spirituality infused all Day's writing after she became a Catholic in 1927. In *From Union Square to Rome* (1938), her early account of her conversion, she wrote: " 'All my life I have been [haunted] by God,' a character in one of Dostoevsky's books says. And that is the way it was with me" (pp. 11, 18).

Dorothy Day was born in Brooklyn, on November 8, 1897, the third of five children born to Grace Satterlee and John I. Day, an itinerant sportswriter and cofounder of the Hialeah racetrack in Florida. John Day worked as the sports editor of Chicago's *Inter Ocean* and also as racing editor of New York's *Morning Telegraph*. At age six, Dorothy moved with her family to California, first to Berkeley and then to Oakland. Her leanings toward spirituality and social activism were apparent from a young age; in her autobiography *The Long Loneliness* she recalled that her child's "heart leaped when I heard the name of God" (p. 12). The family was marginally Episcopalian, and once when young Dorothy attended a church service by herself, she found the Psalms and the formal prayers deeply moving. At eight, she experienced the 1906 San Francisco earthquake and was struck by the "warmth" and "kindliness" the cataclysm elicited as it broke down the usual barriers between people (*On Pilgrimage*, p. 47; *From Union Square*, pp. 23, 32).

Two years later, the family moved to Chicago, where Dorothy attended public high school and was deeply influenced by reading the social novels of Jack London and Upton Sinclair. She later wrote, "the very fact that *The Jungle* was about Chicago where I lived, whose streets I walked, made me feel from then on that my life was to be linked to theirs [the poor's], their interests to be mine; I had received a call, a vocation, a direction to my life" (*Long Loneliness*, p. 38). Indeed she had: her feeling for the poor led to her passionate involvement in the Old Left and ultimately, at least in part, to her conversion to Roman Catholicism in 1927.

After a year at the University of Illinois, where she wrote for both the campus and the town newspapers, Day moved with her family to New York City. There she joined Greenwich Village's literary and social avant-garde. She became a card-carrying Wobbly (International Workers of the World) and socialist, and she attended Communist meetings while serving her journalistic apprenticeship at the socialist *Call*. She had approached the editor of the *Call* for a job because her father had told all his journalism cronies not to hire her, as he vehemently opposed career women, let alone women in journalism (*Long Loneliness*, p. 52). Living cheaply in a Cherry Street tenement on the Lower East Side, Day earned five dollars a week covering strikes, pickets, and community demands for better housing, school, and health care. She interviewed Leon Trotsky while he was in the United States, and heard thrilling speeches by the likes of Emma Goldman, Alexander Berkman, and the famous anarchist Bill Haywood. She also wrote for the *Masses*, the brilliant radical literary magazine edited by Max Eastman, and later for its successor, the *Liberator*.

In the evenings, Day sat in Greenwich Village restaurants and bars with the other young intellectuals, activists, and artists of the day, including Claude McKay, Mike Gold, and Maurice Becker. Often Eugene O'Neill sat with her all night in the Hell Hole, a Village saloon located at Sixth Avenue and West Fourth Street, where, in his cups, he would sometimes recite the Francis Thompson poem "The Hound of Heaven." "Gene would recite all of it," Day later recalled, "and he used to sit there, looking dour and black, his head sunk on his chest. . . . The idea of this pursuit by the Hound of Heaven fascinated me. The recurrence of it, the inevitableness of the outcome made me feel that sooner or later I would have to pause in the mad rush of living and remember my first beginning and my last end" (*From Union Square*, p. 88; *Long Loneliness*, p. 84). Frequently, after spending such a night, she would stop at St. Joseph's Church on Sixth Avenue for the early morning Mass.

Day was not yet a Catholic, but her reading of the New Testament, Thomas à Kempis's *The Imitation of Christ*, and Dostoevsky's novels, particularly *The Brothers Karamazov*, were all leading her to ponder the deeper meaning of her secular social activism. In 1927, following the birth of her only child, a daughter, Day underwent a profound conversion experience and was baptized a Roman Catholic. To the bafflement of her radical friends, Day chose a church characterized by a bourgeois, hierarchical organization, holding vast amounts of property. But as she explained many times, including in her autobiography, she chose the Catholic Church because it was the church of the masses, the church of the poor.

Thereafter Day sought to combine the secular social activism of her youth with a profound spirituality. A major expression was her cofounding, with Peter Maurin, of the Catholic Worker Movement in 1933 in New York City; it advocated principles of social justice, peace, and personal responsibility. Catholic Workers opened a soup kitchen and a homeless shelter near the Bowery, endeavors soon emulated in cities around the country. Another expression was the *Catholic Worker*, the movement's monthly newspaper that Day edited from her room at the New York Catholic Worker from 1933 until her death in November 1980. She wrote a column that became the heart of the paper; it was also the basis for several book-length collections, among them *On Pilgrimage* (1948) and *On Pilgrimage: The Sixties* (1972). She also wrote considerable reportage for the *Catholic Worker*, especially during the 1930s. *From Union Square to Rome* recounts her conversion, which is treated again, with other themes, in her autobiography, *The Long Loneliness* (1952). *House of Hospitality* (1939) deals with the Catholic Worker's first years, while *Loaves and Fishes* (1963) is a more extensive account. *Thérèse* (1960) is a biography of St. Thérèse of Lisieux, "The Little Flower," one of Day's favorite saints; other contemplative writing includes *Meditations*, edited by longtime Catholic Worker Stanley Vishnewski (1960). *By Little and By Little: The Selected Writings of Dorothy Day* (1983), edited by former *Catholic Worker* managing editor Robert Ellsberg, presents an extensive sampling of her work culled from the *Catholic Worker* and most of her books, as well as her articles in such magazines as *Commonweal* and *Liberation*.

## MAJOR THEMES

After a pre-conversion, immature novel (*The Eleventh Virgin*, 1924), Day concentrated on nonfiction that would advance Catholic Worker principles of social justice, peace, personal activism, and communitarian Christianity. But this was hardly utilitarian advocacy prose. Day had a well-developed literary sensibility and took pride in producing writing of high quality. Unlike some advocacy writers, Day instinctively recognized the importance of style in enhancing the impact of substance. It was a lesson she had certainly learned at the *Masses*, the first radical publication to pay serious attention to literary style in communicating its strong viewpoints (Roberts, p. 69). Thomas Cornell, a *Catholic Worker* editor in the early 1960s, observed of Day that "[w]riting was her craft and she took it very seriously" (Interview, 1981). Father John J. Hugo, Day's close friend and confessor, similarly disclosed that "[s]he considered herself a writer; she always mentioned that. She considered writing not an avocation but a vocation" (Interview, 1981).

Because Day lived at the Catholic Worker house in New York in voluntary poverty for nearly fifty years, eating the soup kitchen's meals and taking her dresses from the common clothing bin, her prose has an uncommon authenticity. Because she spent every day among the poor, the homeless, and the terminally ill, "[t]here was," as Robert Ellsberg has written, "absolutely no distinction between what she believed, what she wrote and the manner in which she lived" (p. xv). Such daily, direct experiences were the catalyst for both her social activism (including civil disobedience activities for which she was jailed several times) and her nonfiction writing.

Day's writing often addresses the Catholic Worker tenets of social justice, peace, and personal activism, especially their spiritual roots in such sources as Christ's Sermon on the Mount. Typical of Day's *Catholic Worker* pieces are her many detailed portraits of the poor. In Day's prose, they emerge as fully real-ized individuals with innate, God-given dignity. Often she wrote eloquent obituaries for the forgotten poor who died in the care of the Catholic Worker, such as an alcoholic farm worker named John Ryder:

John, like the prodigal son, came home to us after feeding off the husks of the swine. And he could not be feasted because he was dying. Instead, he had that real feast, the bread of the strong [the Eucharist], and he died and was laid out in the chapel at Maryfarm [the Catholic Worker farming commune/retreat center in Newburgh, New York], and each night before his burial we said the office of the dead as though he were one of the mightiest of the sons of God. ("For These Dear Dead," *Catholic Worker*, No-vember 1946, p. 6)

Day's compassion for the poor and especially for workers can be seen in much of her *Catholic Worker* reportage in the 1930s. A classic piece is her 1936 account of a speech by the Reverend Stephen Kazincy, the so-called "labor priest," in Braddock, Pennsylvania. With a matter-of-fact tone, Day empha-sized the gravity of the steel workers' plight:

The steel workers spoke first and the sun broiled down and the men and their wives stood there motionless, grave, unsmiling, used to hardship, and thinking of the hard-ships to come if the steel masters locked them out.

And then Father Kazincy was announced. He got up before the microphone, a broad, straight man of about sixty. His hair was snow white, his head held high . . . his words came abrupt, forceful, and unhesitating. . . .

"Remember that you have an immortal soul," he told them. "Remember your dig-nity as men."

"Do not let the Carnegie Steel Company crush you." ("Father Kazincy, Workers' Friend, Speaks for Labor," *Catholic Worker*, August 1936, p. 4)

Another important theme in Day's writing is the spiritual basis of peacemak-ing. She worked out her theology of nonresistant pacifism especially during World War II, when the Catholic Worker Movement came under considerable attack from the general public as well as the Catholic hierarchy for its pacifist stance. Day writes about the atomic bombing of Japan in 1945 by beginning in the immediate aftermath with an image of President Harry Truman: "Mr. Tru-man was jubilant. He went from table to table on the cruiser which was bring-ing him home from the Big Three conference, telling the great news, 'jubilant,' the newspaper said. *Jubilate Deo.* We have killed 318,000 Japanese." Day continues,

That is, we hope we have killed them, the Associated Press, page one, column one, of the Herald Tribune says. The effect is hoped for, not known. It is hoped they are vaporized, our Japanese brothers, scattered, men, women and babies, to the four winds, over the seven seas. Perhaps we will breathe their dust into our nostrils, feel them in the fog of New York on our faces, feel rain on the hills of Eason [a Catholic Worker farm in Pennsylvania]. ("We Go On Record," *Catholic Worker*, September 1945, p. 1)

A passionate concern with peace and nonviolence, thoughtful analysis, and a warm, at times homespun, narrative that draws on her personal experiences as a mother and grandmother to create an intimate connection with her readers is typical of Day's writing. Part of her genius was to remain what Robert Ellsberg calls "a most personal writer, even when dealing with large and sometimes abstract issues" (p. xvi).

Finally, another frequent theme in Day's writing is contemplation of God's presence in the beauty of the natural world. After all, it was in the midst of the Staten Island beaches' pristine serenity in the mid-1920s that Day felt a profound spiritual call. Years later she recalled that "[t]he beauty of nature which includes the sound of waves, the sound of insects, the cicadas in the trees—all were part of my joy in nature that brought me to the Church" ("On Pilgrimage" *Catholic Worker*, October–November 1976, p. 4). Her writing has a rich sensory quality that stems from an acute awareness of nature's divine revelations. One of innumerable examples is her November 1936 *Catholic Worker* column "Thanksgiving," which begins: "The trees are getting bare, but still it stays warm. Coming down at night from the city, the warm, sweet smell of the good earth enwraps one like a garment. There is the smell of rotting apples; or alfalfa in the barn; burning leaves; of wood fires in the house; of pickled green tomatoes and baked beans."

## SURVEY OF CRITICISM

Since Dorothy Day's death in 1980, several Church leaders, including the late Cardinal John O'Connor of New York, have urged that she be considered for canonization as a saint in the Catholic Church. Much was written about her life and work during her centenary year, 1997; in fact, in October the United States' Catholic bishops issued a statement praising Day as "a woman whose life was rooted in her commitment to her Catholic faith, to prayer and sacraments." Also that month, Marquette University sponsored a symposium to celebrate and reflect on her legacy. Over the years, many have offered commentary on her contributions as a writer. For instance, in 1939 the *Dublin Review* said of Day's *From Union Square to Rome*, "It would be difficult to exaggerate the interest of this book, or the capability with which it is written" (vol. 204, p. 410). Of *The Long Loneliness*, a *New Yorker* reviewer in 1952 wrote, "The book is emotionally written, but it has wit, humility, and humanity, and is a good cut above the run of inspirational literature" (vol. 28, March 8, 1952, p. 108). In evaluating the same work, *Kirkus Reviews* described Day as "a writer of experience and competence . . . [whose] story of her life is interestingly told" (January 15, 1952, p. 36); while the *New Republic* asserted that Day's "clear and simple style enhances the value of her book" (August 4, 1952, p. 21). And reviewers of Day's selected writings, *By Little and By Little*, used language such as this: "penetrating author" (*Library Journal*, vol. 108, May 1, 1983, p. 912); "direct and vivid prose style . . . a fine eye for the aphorism and maxim" (*Commonweal*, vol. 120, February 12, 1993, p. 26).

To date, one of the more thoughtful analyses of Day's writing is given by Sally Cunneen, who focuses on Day as a storyteller. Also insightful is Robert Ellsberg's work. He notes her natural tendency toward "digression and repetition," especially in the day-to-day writing that she did, sometimes in great quantity, to fill the pages of the *Catholic Worker.* "Such criticism," Ellsberg observes, "was not as likely to be made of that work which represented her most careful and deliberate efforts" (p. xii). Similarly, writing in *Commonweal*, Patrick Jordan (former managing editor of the *Catholic Worker*) comments that "in all the recent studies that deal with Day (and the same will hold true here), the passages that invariably stand out for their notable insight, clarity, and grace are those from her hand" (p. 665).

Significantly, a sample of Day's *New Masses* writing is presented in *Writing Red: An Anthology of American Women Writers, 1930–1940*, edited by Charlotte Nekola and Paula Rabinowitz (with a foreword by Toni Morrison). Day is included in the section entitled "Reportage, Theory, and Analysis" along with writers such as Josephine Herbst, Agnes Smedley, Meridel LeSueur, Mary Heaton Vorse, and Anna Louise Strong. Like many of these women, Day hit her journalistic stride in the 1930s, writing about social reform, and labor and peace issues. In advocacy journalism, women found one of their few opportunities to contribute in a meaningful public way to revolutionary movements such as communism, socialism, and the International Workers of the World, as these movements usually channeled women into traditional, behind-the-scenes support activities such as housekeeping and child care.

Since 1984, Day has been included (in both text and photograph) in the definitive text of U.S. journalism, *The Press and America*. In the most recent edition of that volume, she is likened to the advocacy journalist I. F. Stone in demonstrating "a compelling, tenacious, and consistent journalistic purpose." She is also said to enjoy an "influence [that] reached far beyond the circulation of her *Catholic Worker*" (p. 419). In Thomas B. Connery's *A Sourcebook of American Literary Journalism: Representative Writers in an Emerging Genre*, Day takes her place among such literary journalists as Mark Twain, John Hersey, Ernest Hemingway, Gay Talese, and Joan Didion. As I state in my chapter on Day in this text, while she is "Usually thought of as an apostle of the homeless,"

she should also be remembered as a gifted storyteller who communicated the realities of poor people's lives in a thoughtful and compelling way. The result is a large body of writing that transcends conventional journalism in both the gravity of its themes, which more commonly are literature's province, and in its degree of insight into human beings, who are vividly and compassionately evoked. (p. 184)

## BIBLIOGRAPHY

### Works by Dorothy Day

*The Eleventh Virgin.* New York: A. and C. Boni, 1924.
*From Union Square to Rome.* Silver Spring, Maryland: Preservation of the Faith Press, 1938.
*House of Hospitality.* New York: Sheed and Ward, 1939.
*On Pilgrimage.* New York: Catholic Worker Books, 1948.
*The Long Loneliness: The Autobiography of Dorothy Day.* New York: Harper and Brothers, 1952.
*Thérèse.* Notre Dame, Indiana: Fides, 1960.
*Loaves and Fishes.* New York: Harper and Row, 1963.
*Meditations.* Ed. Stanley Vishnewski. New York: Newman Press, 1970.
*On Pilgrimage: The Sixties.* New York: Curtis Books, 1972.
*By Little and By Little: The Selected Writings of Dorothy Day.* Ed. and intro. by Robert Ellsberg. New York: Alfred A. Knopf, 1983.

### Works about Dorothy Day

Coles, Robert. *Dorothy Day: A Radical Devotion.* Reading, Massachusetts: Addison-Wesley, 1987.
Cornell, Thomas. Personal interview with Nancy L. Roberts. Milwaukee, Wisconsin, 6 November 1981. Tape recording available at Dorothy Day–Catholic Worker Collection, Memorial Library Archives, Marquette University, Milwaukee, Wisconsin.
Coy, Patrick, ed. *"A Revolution of the Heart": Essays on the Catholic Worker Movement.* Philadelphia: Temple University Press, 1988.
Cunneen, Sally. "Dorothy Day: The Storyteller as Human Model." *Cross Currents* 34 (Fall 1984): 283–93.
Emery, Edwin, Michael Emery, and Nancy L. Roberts. *The Press and America: An Interpretive History of the Mass Media.* 9th edition. Boston: Allyn and Bacon, 2000.
Forest, Jim. *Love Is the Measure: A Biography of Dorothy Day.* New York: Orbis, 1994.
Hugo, Father John J. Personal interview with Nancy L. Roberts. Milwaukee, Wisconsin, 5 November 1981. Tape recording available at Dorothy Day–Catholic Worker Collection, Memorial Library Archives, Marquette University, Milwaukee, Wisconsin.
Jordan, Patrick. "Dorothy Day: Still a Radical." *Commonweal* 29 November 1985: 665.
Klejment, Anne, and Alice Klejment. *Dorothy Day and "The Catholic Worker": A Bibliography and Index.* New York: Garland, 1986.
———, and Nancy L. Roberts, eds. *American Catholic Pacifism: The Influence of Dorothy Day and the Catholic Worker Movement.* Westport, Connecticut: Praeger, 1996.

Miller, William L. *Dorothy Day: A Biography*. San Francisco: Harper and Row, 1982.

———. *A Harsh and Dreadful Love: Dorothy Day and the Catholic Worker Movement.* New York: Liveright, 1973.

Nekola, Charlotte, and Paula Rabinowitz. *Writing Red: An Anthology of American Women Writers, 1930–1940*. New York: Feminist Press, 1987. 279–81.

O'Brien, David. J. "The Pilgrimage of Dorothy Day." *Commonweal* 19 December 1980: 711.

Piehl, Mel. *Breaking Bread: The Catholic Worker and the Origin of Catholic Radicalism in America*. Philadelphia: Temple University Press, 1982.

Roberts, Nancy L. "Dorothy Day." *A Sourcebook of American Literary Journalism: Representative Writers in an Emerging Genre*. Ed. Thomas B. Connery. Westport, Connecticut: Greenwood Press, 1992. 179–85.

———. *Dorothy Day and the "Catholic Worker."* Albany: State University of New York Press, 1984.

NANCY L. ROBERTS

# ANNIE DILLARD
# (1945- )

## BIOGRAPHY

Annie Dillard was born Meta Ann Doak on April 30, 1945, the eldest of the three daughters of Frank and Pam Lambert Doak. Affluent and well connected in Pittsburgh society, the Doaks were energetic, free-spirited people who raised their daughters to be independent and adventurous. Not churchgoers themselves, they still made sure their daughters went to the Presbyterian Church, Sunday school, and church camp in the summers. The girls attended Pittsburgh's prestigious Ellis School and were involved in their country club's social activities.

As a child, Annie explored the natural world in the neighborhood and through the public library. Discovering *The Field Book of Ponds and Streams*, Annie began her methodical studies of insects, plants, and rocks, using her microscope and making drawings of what she observed. She briefly rebelled against her Presbyterian upbringing and the hypocrisy of churchgoers, and was suspended from high school for smoking. In her autobiographical *An American Childhood* (1987), Dillard recalls being encouraged by the Ellis headmistress to apply to Hollins College in Roanoke, Virginia, where "her rough edges" would be smoothed off; Annie herself hoped that those rough edges would be "a can opener, to cut . . . a hole in the world's surface" through which she could escape (p. 243).

In the fall of 1963, Annie entered Hollins where she studied literature, writing, Christian theology and philosophy, and the natural sciences. The idealism and liberal social consciousness absorbed from her parents prompted Annie to work in antipoverty programs, read for the blind, and challenge paternalistic restrictions in the women's college. In 1965, at the end of her sophomore year, she married R. H. W. Dillard, one of her writing professors. She earned a bachelor's degree at Hollins in 1967, and a master's degree in 1968, writing her thesis on Thoreau's *Walden*. In 1974, her first books were published: *Tickets for a Prayer Wheel*, a collection of poems, and *Pilgrim at Tinker Creek*, which became a Book-of-the-Month Club selection and won the 1974 Pulitzer Prize in general nonfiction. Shortly thereafter, when her marriage to Dillard ended in divorce, she moved to Western Washington University in Bellingham as scholar-in-residence (1975–1979, 1981–1982). She was married to Gary Clevidence, a novelist and anthropologist, from 1980 to 1988; their daughter Cody Rose was born in 1984.

After two years as a visiting scholar at Wesleyan University in Middletown, Connecticut (1979–1981), Dillard has taught nonfiction prose writing there since 1983. She married Robert D. Richardson, Jr., a Thoreau scholar, in 1988, and joined the Roman Catholic Church. In 1999 Dillard was inducted into the American Academy of Arts and Letters, and the Modern Library included *Pilgrim at Tinker Creek* among the 100 Best Nonfiction books in English. Her writing is widely anthologized in collections of nature writing and in readers for college composition classes.

## MAJOR THEMES

The Jesuit weekly *America* awarded Dillard its 1994 Campion Award "for her craft but also for her religious commitment" (Torrens, p. 2). Throughout her life, Dillard has sought God through close study of the natural world; through wide reading in science, literature, and theology; and through writing. Her books are laced with quotations from Scripture, philosophy, poetry, and mystical texts of Christian, Jewish, and Hindu traditions. Although pervasive, inexplicable violence and suffering challenge human belief in a loving God, Dillard finds her faith sustained by the evident order and beauty of the natural world. Her conversion to Catholicism continues her journey through the ritual, belief, and spirituality of the Church.

Dillard's essays, rather than her fiction or poetry, offer the most insight into her faith and spirituality. In *Pilgrim at Tinker Creek*, tracing the progress of the seasons in a valley of Virginia's Blue Ridge, Dillard interweaves close observations of sky and water, plants and animals, with quotations and reflections on the significance of the beauty and violence which she witnesses. Critics consistently compare the book to Thoreau's *Walden*, as both texts look beyond observable phenomena to the mystery of human existence; Dillard, however, maintains that *Pilgrim* is primarily a book of theological reflections. Indeed, many recent studies focus on Dillard's Christian mysticism and her use of images that represent the soul's approach to God in contemplative prayer.

The search for God in creation and the probing of the mysteries of human suffering are themes continued in her later essays. She wrote *Holy the Firm* (1977) about three days of observing and reflecting on nature and events in a solitary seaside cabin. The book's three sections have been compared to the three days of Christ's suffering, death, and resurrection, and to the purgative, illuminative, and unitive stages of mystical prayer. In a misty, wooded setting, Dillard introduces images of flame that destroy and transform: the moth dying in the candle flame, the girl burned in a plane crash, and the soul seeking peace in God. In *Teaching a Stone to Talk* (1982), Dillard ranges further afield, exploring far-flung locales such as the Galapagos Islands and a polar ice floe, and reflecting on human insignificance in relation to the power behind solar eclipses, and on the paradox of human love's challenge to mortality. She also reflects on the Church, the vehicle through which humanity shares the common search for God and the flawed but genuine worship of the divine.

In *For the Time Being* (1999), Dillard presents her most complex weaving of observations and data in an effort to probe the apparent "mistakes" in God's creation. Observations of natural phenomena—clouds, sand, birth defects—lead into reflections on the mystery of evil in a world created by a benevolent God. Dillard parallels her reflections with the faith struggles of priest-anthropologist Teilhard de Chardin and the eighteenth-century Hasidic Rabbi Baal Shem Tov, who both sought God in the clay of the earth and struggled with the apparent futility of their efforts to do good. With its beauty and deformity, creation is for Dillard a sacrament revealing the presence of God. Her poetic prose becomes the prayer of contemplation, praise, and reparation for the imperfections of human striving.

Similar themes mark Dillard's *Tickets for a Prayer Wheel* (1974), a collection of twenty-four poems arranged as a cohesive meditation on prayer, grace, and suffering, and illustrating the attention to natural detail and the finely crafted language that mark all her texts. Dillard has also written two books about writing, *Living by Fiction* (1982) and *The Writing Life* (1989). In the former, she explores the purpose and methods of literary criticism in search of something that will "interpret for us the world at large" (p. 143) and in order to explain, as science alone cannot, the significance of the observable phenomena of human experience. *The Writing Life* is a reflection on the risks, pain, and elation of the creative process.

While Dillard's all-women educational background has not made her a women's rights activist, her style and themes reflect the "different voice" described by Carol Gilligan, a voice sensitive to particularity, concreteness, relatedness, and ambiguity, in contrast to the abstraction associated with the dominant masculinist approach. Sandra Humble Johnson argues that the core of Dillard's work is to transcend created limits, showing the human person "in touch with the merging of time and eternity, unpolitical, leaping beyond the idea of gender into the idea of the artist in touch with the infinite" (p. 61).

Not explicitly feminist, Dillard shows respect for assertive, self-possessed womanhood in the portraits of her mother, Pam Lambert Doak, in *An American Childhood*, and of the pioneer women in her novel *The Living* (1992). Dillard's mother was a housewife whose job was raising the children, but her energy, verbal power, practical jokes, social conscience, and independent spirit had an undeniable formative influence on Annie. While the central characters of *The Living* are men, Dillard also presents a significant number of courageous female characters who brave the harshness of frontier life, endure the illnesses and accidental deaths of children and husbands, and battle through astonishing adversity to maintain their families, homesteads, and businesses. In *Encounters with Chinese Writers* (1984), a collection of her experiences and impressions as a member of the U.S. State Department's 1982 cultural exchange program with China, Dillard also makes telling observations on the status of female writers, both Chinese and American, in the company of their male peers.

Linda Smith identifies three central concerns in Dillard's work: the nature of human awareness; the nature of suffering and death, particularly in light of her belief in a loving God; and the pattern of life one ought to follow, given the certainty of suffering and death (pp. 125–27). Dillard recalls writing a high school essay on the Book of Job in which she began to probe these issues: "If the all-powerful creator directs the world, then why all this suffering?" (*American Childhood,* p. 228). In her essays, fiction, and poetry, Dillard presents her struggles to come to some resolution of that dilemma.

## SURVEY OF CRITICISM

Two book-length studies approach Dillard's work from different angles. In a 1991 Twayne study, Linda Smith offers a comprehensive review of Dillard's life and career, with chapters devoted to each of her major texts through 1988. In *The Space Between: Literary Epiphany in the Work of Annie Dillard* (1992), Sandra Humble Johnson presents a thematic study of Dillard's pursuit of the nature of human insight into the mysteries hidden in the visible creation. Johnson places Dillard in the Romantic tradition of Wordsworth, Keats, Gerard Manley Hopkins, and Modernists such as James Joyce and Virginia Woolf.

Suzanne Clark claims in *Sentimental Modernism: Women Writers and the Revolution of the Word* that contemporary female writers are restoring sensibilities sacrificed in the spare Modernist world of ideas. Clark devotes a chapter to Dillard's essays, arguing that the speaker's invisibility and anonymity is a subversive tactic that challenges the masculine voice characteristic of essay and memoir. Clark links Dillard with Emerson's Transcendentalism, Rimbaud's symbolism, and Eliot's Modernism, and associates Dillard's punning, parodic wordplay with the *jouissance* of *l'écriture féminine*. Margaret Loewen Reimer also analyzes qualities of the feminine in the particularity of Dillard's reflections on creation and redemption.

Nancy Parrish locates Dillard and her peers at Hollins College in the worlds of women's higher education and the New Critical publishing industry in the mid-1960s. In the community at Hollins, Parrish argues, young female writers—including Dillard—had a unique opportunity to clarify their vision and to find their voice as they responded to contemporary changes in literary studies and social systems.

While some critical attention is paid to feminist issues in Dillard's work, most of the scholarship deals with Dillard's place in the tradition of

Emersonian Transcendental nature writing, or her connection to the environmental movement. Of these, James I. McClintock's study associates Dillard with Aldo Leopold, Joseph Wood Krutch, and Edward Abbey, noting her distinctive Christian hope and ritual engagement with nature. Dillard's synthesis of faith and science has also drawn the attention of journals of religion and philosophy such as *America* and *Journal of Feminist Studies in Religion*. Articles published in such journals describe Dillard's theological reflections as mystical theology or ecotheology and link her to the Judeo-Christian concept of contemplative prayer.

Whether they analyze her science or her spirituality, her environmentalism or her feminism, critics agree on the excellence of Dillard's prose style, and her use of Modernist and Imagist techniques to illuminate the paradox of human hope in the midst of suffering. Critics observe that her prose incorporates the essentials of poetry: carefully crafted language, powerful metaphors, compression, and emotion. Trained as a poet, Dillard has written memoir and fiction, but has found her niche as one of the nation's premier essayists and as a woman of faith who continues to ask the difficult questions.

## BIBLIOGRAPHY

### Works by Annie Dillard

*Pilgrim at Tinker Creek*. New York: Harper, 1974.
*Tickets for a Prayer Wheel*. Columbia: University of Missouri Press, 1974.
*Holy the Firm*. New York: Harper, 1977.
*Living by Fiction*. New York: Harper, 1982.
*Teaching a Stone to Talk: Expeditions and Encounters*. New York: Harper, 1982.
*Encounters with Chinese Writers*. Middletown, Connecticut: Wesleyan University Press, 1984.
*An American Childhood*. New York: Harper, 1987.
*The Writing Life*. New York: Harper, 1989.
*The Living*. New York: HarperCollins, 1992.
*Mornings Like This: Found Poems*. New York: HarperCollins, 1995.
*For the Time Being*. New York: Knopf, 1999.

### Works about Annie Dillard

Breslin, John B. "The World According to Annie." Rev. of *For the Time Being*, by Annie Dillard. *America* 14 August 1999: 25–26.
Cheney, Jim. "'The Waters of Separation': Myth and Ritual in Annie Dillard's *Pilgrim at Tinker Creek*." *Journal of Feminist Studies in Religion* 6.1 (Spring 1990): 41–63.
Clark, Suzanne. *Sentimental Modernism: Women Writers and the Revolution of the Word*. Bloomington: Indiana University Press, 1991.
Johnson, Sandra Humble. *The Space Between: Literary Epiphany in the Work of Annie Dillard*. Kent, Ohio: Kent State University Press, 1992.

Major, Mike. "Annie Dillard, Pilgrim of the Absolute." *America* 6 May 1978: 363–64.

McClintock, James I. *Nature's Kindred Spirits: Aldo Leopold, Joseph Wood Krutch, Edward Abbey, Annie Dillard, and Gary Snyder.* Madison: University of Wisconsin Press, 1994.

———. "'Pray Without Ceasing': Annie Dillard Among the Nature Writers." *Earthly Words: Essays on Contemporary American Nature and Environmental Writers.* Ed. John Cooley. Ann Arbor: University of Michigan Press, 1994. 69–86.

Parrish, Nancy C. *Lee Smith, Annie Dillard, and the Hollins Group: A Genesis of Writers.* Baton Rouge: Louisiana State University Press, 1998.

Peterson, Eugene H. "Annie Dillard: With Her Eyes Wide Open." *Theology Today* 43 (July 1986): 178–91.

Reimer, Margaret Loewen. "The Dialectical Vision of Annie Dillard's *Pilgrim at Tinker Creek.*" *Critique* 24 (Spring 1983): 182–92.

Ross-Bryant, Lynn. "The Silence of Nature." *Religion and Literature* 22.1 (1990): 79–94.

Scheick, William J. "Annie Dillard: Narrative Fringe." *Contemporary American Women Writers: Narrative Strategies.* Ed. Catherine Rainwater and William J. Scheick. Lexington: University Press of Kentucky, 1985. 50–67.

Smith, Linda L. *Annie Dillard.* New York: Twayne, 1991.

Smith, Pamela A. "The Ecotheology of Annie Dillard: A Study in Ambivalence." *Cross Currents* 45 (Fall 1995): 341–58.

Torrens, James S. "Of Many Things." *America* 19 November 1994: 2.

Yancey, Philip. "Annie Dillard: Pointing to the Vision." *Catholic Digest* 60 (April 1996): 82–88.

EILEEN QUINLAN, S.N.D.

# LOUISE ERDRICH
## (1954– )

---

## BIOGRAPHY

The eldest of seven children of an Ojibwe mother and a German American father, Louise Erdrich explores Native American themes in her works, with major characters representing both sides of her heritage. Raised in North Dakota, Erdrich is a member of the Turtle Mountain Band of the Anishinabe (Ojibwe, or Chippewa) people, of which her grandfather was once tribal chairman. In four of her novels, Erdrich explores both Native American and white families losing faith in Christian and Native American religious traditions. And because Christianity was imposed on Native Americans, they suffer doubly, estranged from traditional shamanism and warped by an often distorted Catholicism.

In 1972, Erdrich began attending Dartmouth College, a member of the first class of women admitted to the previously all-male institution. On the same day, Michael Dorris, who was partly of Modoc descent, arrived to teach in the anthropology department. Although they knew each other, their romantic relationship did not begin until several years after Erdrich graduated. In 1981, after conducting poetry workshops in North Dakota and winning awards for her poetry, Erdrich was named writer-in-residence at Dartmouth and became involved with Dorris, who was then director of the Native American Studies Program. When they married in October 1981, Erdrich became the mother of three Native American children Dorris had adopted earlier as a single parent; together, they had three more children.

Both writers claimed in many interviews that their writing was collaborative, although they would publish a work under the name of the one who wrote the first draft. The single exception is *The Crown of Columbus* (1991), a book they published under both names and one that allowed both writers to retire from teaching.

In 1992, the couple quietly split up temporarily, and in 1995 Erdrich left the marriage for good, again quietly, sharing custody of their three daughters.

In 1997, Dorris committed suicide in a motel room. Today, Erdrich lives in Minneapolis with her children.

## MAJOR THEMES

Erdrich's first novel, *Love Medicine* (1984) won the 1984 National Book Critics Circle Award for Best Work of Fiction. The novel is composed of inter-related short stories about the lives of the Kashpaws, Lazarres, Lamartines, Nanapushes, and Morrisseys, the Chippewa and part–Native American families living on the Chippewa reservation in North Dakota. Many of the characters were raised Catholic and sent to Catholic schools, but most are only superficially Christian, influenced more by ancient tribal traditions and superstitions. All of the characters, however, struggle with the imposition of a culture and spirituality that are not native. A pivotal chapter in the novel is the dramatic relationship between the teenaged Marie and the bedeviled nun Leopolda. Marie's ambition is to escape the reservation by joining the Church. She tells us, "I had the mail-order Catholic soul you get in a girl raised out in the bush, whose only thought is getting into town" (1993, p. 44). The sadistic Sister Leopolda abuses Marie at the convent, where she is scalded and stabbed in an attempt to rid her of the devil. In order to avoid scandal, Leopolda explains Marie's stab wound as the holy stigmata, and Marie has her revenge when Leopolda is forced to kneel to her along with the other nuns. Sister Leopolda represents what can happen when Catholic beliefs meet Chippewa beliefs. As Lydia Schultz puts it, "Through Sister Leopolda, Erdrich satirically demonstrates how the white folks' religion fails to make sense of the world for Ojibwes (Chippewas); it appeals primarily to American Indians who are already distancing themselves from their own community" (p. 87). However, some characters, like the adult Marie, are able to choose only those aspects of Catholicism that peacefully coexist with their traditional values, and thus they are not destroyed by it.

Yet, on the post-Vietnam reservation, even the traditional gods are losing their effectiveness to alcohol, poverty, and despair. The only direct reference to Chippewa gods in *Love Medicine* is when Lipsha muses,

Now there's your God in the Old Testament and there is Chippewa Gods as well. Indian Gods, good and bad, like tricky Nanabozho or the water monster, Missepeshu, who lives over in Lake Turcot. That water monster was the last God I ever heard to appear. It had a weakness for young girls and grabbed one of the Blues off her rowboat. She got to shore all right, but only after this monster had its way with her. She's an old lady now. Old Lady Blue. She still won't let her family fish that lake.

Our Gods aren't perfect, is what I'm saying, but at least they come around. (pp. 194–95)

Lipsha fears the results of having two gods, the Christian and the Chippewa, neither of whom seems to be listening very carefully to his people's prayers.

*Love Medicine*'s chapter titles, such as "The World's Greatest Fisherman," "Saint Marie," "Flesh and Blood," "Crown of Thorns," and "Crossing the Water," illustrate the power of Catholic imagery in the Chippewa world. Each chapter sets up a conflicting relationship between Christian values and traditions and their Native American shamanic counterparts. For example, June Kashpaw is depicted, in part, by Christian images such as her Easter weekend rebirth and death. And she is also seen as a presence on the reservation, "where her spirit, according to Native American beliefs, mingles with the living and carries out unfinished business" (Rainwater, p. 412). She is a Christ-like figure caught between two worlds. When young June is adopted by the Kashpaws as a child, her only possession is a string of Cree prayer beads. When June leaves home, she leaves the beads with Marie, the same Marie who once wished to be a nun and who calls the beads a "rosary" in the Catholic tradition. The beads are thus both shamanic and Catholic, like Marie herself, who is a healer. As Marie tells us,

I don't pray, but sometimes I do touch the beads. . . . I never look at them, just let my fingers roam to them when no one is in the house. It's a rare time when I do this. I touch them, and every time I do I think of small stones. At the bottom of the lake, rolled aimless by the waves. I think of them polished. To many people it would be a kindness. But I see no kindness in how the waves are grinding them smaller and smaller until they finally disappear. (p. 73)

By comparing the beads to humans and to stones, Erdrich is de-sanctifying the "rosary" beads and, at the same time, connecting them to despair and destruction (Rainwater, p. 415). Also, by juxtaposing religious symbols, Erdrich seems to suggest that neither is exclusive and that all religious myths and symbols are equal.

But Catholicism's presence in Erdrich's fictional world is not always negative—institutionalized Catholicism is, but not Catholicism as represented by specific individuals. Reflecting the Church's commitment to justice, "young Fr. Damien, in Erdrich's *Tracks*, does his best to help the Ojibwe families with food, fuel, rent and legal advice as well as with sacramental ministry" (Quinlan, p. 31). And in *Love Medicine*, Sister Mary Martin attempts to come to Gordie's aid when he begs for forgiveness after accidentally killing a deer, an animal that, in his inebriated state, he thinks is his late wife June. Sister Mary Martin fails to recognize the deer's transubstantiation for Gordie, thus does not succeed in relieving his misery and guilt, yet she does try. For Erdrich, then, Catholicism as practiced by individuals—even if they don't succeed—is often more humane than institutionalized Catholicism.

*Tracks* (1988) is more political than *Love Medicine* and its main events precede those in the earlier novel. Sister Leopolda is seen as the young Pauline, and we discover how she became the near-mad nun. In this novel, Erdrich depicts the original success of Catholicism with the Chippewa: the Chippewa reluctantly embrace the new religion in return for help in recovering their lost land from the fur traders. The novel illustrates the tension between Catholic and Chippewa beliefs. Pauline, of course, is an extreme example: hers is the story of a mixed-blood girl who wants to be white, and finds Catholicism as a way out of the reservation and away from the Indians she despises. But the sadder effect depicted is that the Chippewa people themselves are fragmented by the events of the novel.

*The Bingo Palace* (1994) continues where *Love Medicine* leaves off: Lipsha Morrissey returns home to the reservation where he accepts a job in his uncle Lyman's bingo parlor. The two are romantic rivals for the love of Shawnee Ray, who has Lyman's child, but who is smitten by the charming Lipsha. As in Erdrich's first novel, Lipsha again searches for love medicine, but this time for himself. He first looks within his tradition by searching for Fleur, the mysterious woman of *Tracks* and *The Beet Queen* (1986). She can't be found. He next tries a traditional sweat lodge that also does not succeed. Finally, he steals a Gideon Bible in a desperate attempt to find answers through Christianity. But as in *Love Medicine*, neither god is listening. The loss of traditional religion is more intense here than in *Love Medicine*: in *The Bingo Palace*, traditional spirituality must fight the fatalism of the bingo game. Through numerous trials, Lipsha discovers the spiritual emptiness of his dreams for material success. He realizes that luck fades, so tradition and spirituality must stay alive, and he discovers—as he did in the earlier novel—that having "heart" and "staying power" allow him to retain connections with those he loves. He is able to help his father escape imprisonment, and he is able to continue to love Shawnee Ray after she leaves to continue her education and become more independent from the fated Chippewa reservation. Lipsha is the sole narrator of this novel and, fittingly, Erdrich's theme is the individual's struggle with his or her fate; the bingo game is a game of fate, yet life, unlike bingo, allows for free will. The central metaphor of bingo thus brings together both Catholic and Native American ideas of fortune.

*Tales of Burning Love* (1996) tells the story of five women united by their love for one weak man, Jack Mauser. Jack is the same man who the Christ-like June meets at a bar at the start of *Love Medicine*. June, as we now find out, was Jack's first wife, and he still suffers from her death as she wandered off drunkenly in a blizzard just hours after the wedding. *Tales* charts Jack's subsequent life and marriages. His four surviving wives wind up together in another blizzard, the night before Epiphany, trapped in Mauser's truck only hours after what they thought was his funeral. They survive by talking about Mauser, presenting him as a fully human, multifaceted man who seemed to change, trickster-like, with each wife, and through their talk they learn to forgive him, the enclosure of the truck acting as a confessional. As Michael Lee has noted, "the tales call into question courtly and romantic ideals of altruistic love, suggesting that to some extent human love is an exercise in reciprocal narcissism" (p. 30). As several critics have also pointed out, the novel reminds us that, like Mauser, we are able to redeem ourselves and resurrect our lives, a theme that resonates with Erdrich's Catholic heritage. After the tales have been told, one of the ex-wives, Eleanor, has a vision of Sister Leopolda who mocks the tales of love and whose image warns Eleanor that she will freeze to death unless she follows the image back to life. At the same time, Jack has visions of his first wife, June, who also brings him home. The novel ends with Jack and Eleanor, the wife with whom he shared the deepest relationship, returning to their love and their home.

## SURVEY OF CRITICISM

Reviewers have generally responded positively to all of Erdrich's work, but her first published novel, *Love Medicine*, is by far the most critically acclaimed. The novel has been compared favorably with William Faulkner's *As I Lay Dying* for its multivoiced structure and its poetic style: as Dan Cryer notes, "If Faulkner's Snopeses and Compsons are burned into our collective memory, so too . . . are Erdrich's Kashpaws, Morrisseys and Lamartines" (p. 32). Like Toni Morrison, Erdrich is able to write lyrically about her people without sentimentalizing them. However, some critics are uncomfortable with the multiperspective format that leaves the reader to piece together the "true" story. When Erdrich came out with the expanded edition of the novel in 1993, containing chapters that had previously been cut, the readers and critics who had complained of the puzzling connection between the chapters—and of the book's forty-year time frame—were less confused.

*Tracks* is considered quite different in that the time frame is shorter (a few years) and the plot more focused on the effects of the contact of Catholic and Chippewa values, and the struggle over American fur traders' and Chippewa lands. Although it shares many of the themes in *Love Medicine*, some critics found this novel to be too didactic and melodramatic, less poetic and multifaceted than the earlier work. Other reviewers, however, found the work more grounded, perhaps because of its more limited focus.

With *The Bingo Palace*, Erdrich returns to contemporary North Dakota, and reviewers have often placed this novel within the context of the Chippewa series composed of *Love Medicine*, *Tracks*, and *The Beet Queen*. Almost all the reviewers love the character of Lipsha, whose voice, and sometimes surrealistic ideas, are very appealing. Many find the single narrator approach to be much more focused than Erdrich's usual style.

Erdrich's most recent novels have received less positive criticism. *Tales of Burning Love* is more accessible than many of her novels: like a romance, it has been described as "a bright, loud book. . . . *One Hundred Years of Solitude* rewritten by Terry McMillan" (Max, p. 117). Although they praise the work's depiction of male and female relationships, some critics miss the literary richness of Erdrich's earlier novels, seeing *Tales* as merely a book about women sitting around talking about sex. *The Antelope Wife* (1998) returns more explicitly to Erdrich's theme of the alienation of Native Americans in the modern world, a theme that reviewers clearly expect from the author. However, some critics have found the magical realism disturbing (e.g., a dog who thinks like Socrates), while others are pleased at Erdrich's return to the question of fate. Toward the end of *The Antelope Wife*, the narrator speculates, using the beadwork imagery seen in several earlier novels, "Are we working out the minor details of a strictly random pattern? Who is beading us? . . . Who are you and who am I, the beader or the bit of colored glass sewn into the fabric of this earth?" (p. 240).

Several critics, such as Eileen Quinlan, Michelle Hessler, John Desmond, and Michael Lee, have explicitly placed Erdrich among the new Catholic writers. Quinlan and Hessler focus on the Catholic Church's role in *Tracks*; Desmond emphasizes the erosion of both Catholic and Native American values in *Love Medicine* and *Bingo Palace*; and Lee briefly examines the themes of redemption and resurrection in *Tales of Burning Love*. All the critics conclude that Erdrich's portrayal of the Church as an institution is a negative one, although certain individual representatives of the Church (such as young Father Damien in *Tracks*) are quite sympathetic and helpful to those victims of the institutional Church. Yet the kindness of some Catholic priests and nuns is overshadowed by the distorted Catholicism of Pauline/Sister Leopolda in Erdrich's early novels. Ultimately, for Erdrich, holding on to orthodox Catholicism is not in the best interests of the Ojibwe community.

## BIBLIOGRAPHY

### Works by Louise Erdrich

*Love Medicine*. New York: Holt, Rinehart & Winston, 1984. Rev. ed. New York: Holt, 1993.
*The Beet Queen*. New York: Holt, 1986.
*Tracks*. New York: Henry Holt, 1988.
*The Crown of Columbus* (with Michael Dorris). New York: HarperCollins, 1991.
*The Bingo Palace*. New York: HarperCollins, 1994.
*Tales of Burning Love*. New York: HarperCollins, 1996.
*The Antelope Wife*. New York: Harper Perennial, 1998.

### Works about Louise Erdrich

Barak, Julie. "Blurs, Blends, Berdaches: Gender Mixing in the Novels of Louise Erdrich." *Studies in American Indian Literatures* 8 (Fall 1996): 49–62.
Barry, Nora, and Mary Prescott. "The Triumph of the Brave: *Love Medicine*'s Holistic Vision." *Critique: Studies in Contemporary Fiction* 30 (Winter 1989): 123–38.
Cryer, Dan. "Chippewas' Struggle with Fate and a Harsh World." *Newsday* 27 December 1993: 32.
Desmond, John F. "Catholicism in Contemporary American Fiction." *America* 170 (14 May 1994): 7–11.

Ferguson, Suzanne. "The Short Stories of Louise Erdrich's Novels." *Studies in Short Fiction* (Fall 1996): 541.

Hessler, Michelle R. "Catholic Nuns and Ojibwa Shamans: Pauline and Fleur in Louise Erdrich's *Tracks.*" *Wicazo Sa Review* 11 (Spring 1995): 40–45.

Larson, Sidner. "The Fragmentation of a Tribal People in Louise Erdrich's *Tracks.*" *American Indian Culture and Research Journal* 17.2 (1993): 1–13.

Lee, Michael. "Erdrich's Dakota as Metaphor for American Culture." *National Catholic Reporter* 24 May 1996: 21, 30.

Max, D. T. Rev. of *Tales of Burning Love*, by Louise Erdrich. *Harper's Bazaar* 1 April 1996: 116–17.

Quinlan, Eileen. "New Catholic Literature Sails in Open Sea." *National Catholic Reporter* 24 May 1996: 31–32.

Rainwater, Catherine. "Reading Between Worlds: Narrativity in the Fiction of Louise Erdrich." *American Literature* 62 (September 1990): 405–22.

Schultz, Lydia A. "Fragments and Ojibwe Stories: Narrative Strategies in Louise Erdrich's *Love Medicine.*" *College Literature* 18 (October 1991): 80–95.

Silberman, Robert. "Opening the Text: *Love Medicine* and the Return of the Native American Women." *Narrative Chance: Postmodern Discourse on Native American Indian Literatures.* Ed. Gerald Vizenor. Norman: University of Oklahoma Press, 1989. 101–20.

Wong, Hertha. "Adoptive Mothers and Thrown-Away Children in the Novels of Louise Erdrich." *Narrating Mothers: Theorizing Maternal Subjectivities.* Ed. Brenda O. Daly. Knoxville: University of Tennessee Press, 1991. 174–92.

STACEY DONOHUE

# ROSARIO FERRÉ
## (1938– )

## BIOGRAPHY

Although recordings of the year of Rosario Ferré's birth vary between 1938 and 1942, the best evidence lists the date as September 28, 1938, in Ponce, Puerto Rico. Her mother, Lorenza Ramirez, was born to the landowning elite, and her father, Luis A. Ferré, was a businessman and engineer who served as governor of Puerto Rico from 1968 to 1972. Rosario Ferré was raised and educated as a Catholic: she first attended a Jesuit boys' school, during which time she started to write. She later transferred to the School of the Sacred Heart, a Catholic girls' school, and continued her writing, inspired by the fairy tales and stories taught to her by her black nanny, Gilda Ventura.

Throughout most of her young adulthood, Ferré led the privileged yet limited life of an upper-class woman, the contradictions of which she addresses in much of her writing. After high school, she studied English and American literature in the United States at Wellesley and Manhattanville Colleges. After completing her studies in the States, Ferré married Benigno Trigo, a merchant, and had three children, Rosario, Benigno, and Luis. Several years later, she divorced her husband and resumed her education at the University of Puerto Rico, where she received her M.A. in Spanish. While there, Ferré met Uruguayan critic Angel Rama and Peruvian novelist Mario Vargas Llosa, both of whom encouraged her in her writing. Also during this time, her mother died; subsequently, Ferré moved in with her father and served as hostess of the governor's residence. Although her father remained politically invested in seeking statehood for Puerto Rico, Ferré began to explore her own politics and openly embraced Puerto Rican independence.

In the early 1970s, Ferré founded and directed *Zona de carga y descarga* [Loading and Unloading Zones], a literary magazine dedicated to new Puerto Rican literature. She then moved to Mexico, where her first work, *Papeles de Pandora*, was published in Spanish in 1976. Translated into English as *The Youngest Doll* in 1991, this collection of short stories offers a transgressive, explicit exploration of female sexuality and social positions. Ferré's first work translated into English was *Sweet Diamond Dust* in 1989; in 1993, *The Battle of the Virgins* was also translated from Spanish. *The House on the Lagoon* (1995), a 1996 National Book Award Finalist, was Ferré's first novel written in English.

Ferré earned a Ph.D. from the University of Maryland in 1986, having written a dissertation on the short stories of Julio Cortázar. After teaching at Georgetown University for five years and lecturing throughout the United States, Ferré moved back to Puerto Rico permanently. She has since been married twice more, to Mexican novelist Jorge Augilar Mora, and more recently to Augustin Costa. In 1998 Ferré published another novel, *Eccentric Neighborhoods*, she continues to be a prolific writer.

Considered Puerto Rico's leading woman of letters, Ferré has written several novels as well as books of poetry, short fiction, children's stories, biography, and feminist criticism, and in doing so has broken the stereotype of the Puerto Rican woman writing only love poems. Inspired by such writers as Simone de Beauvoir and Virginia Woolf, Ferré is credited with having brought feminism to Puerto Rico, as well as with serving as the most significant spokesperson of the women's movement emerging on that island since the 1970s. Known for her use of magical realism to reread traditional mythology and folktales, Ferré offers a new vision of Puerto Rican—as well as international—womanhood.

## MAJOR THEMES

Ferré's work has been anthologized in texts addressing fields as varied as women's literature, Caribbean literature, Latin American literature, Spanish American literature, Puerto Rican literature, women's incest literature, and international feminist fiction. With its recurrent use of magical realism and surrealism, Ferré's writing confronts issues of selfhood and identity, of feminism and nationhood, of sexuality and race. She revises sexist, colonialist folklore and fairy tales, compelling both her characters and her readers to work their way through these forces in her fiction. Ferré deals with such issues more directly in her nonfictional articles and theoretical writings, including *El coloquio de las perras* (1990) [The Colloquy of the (Female) Dogs (in reference to Cervantes' "El coloquio de los perros")], a collection of eight essays of feminist literary criticism, selections of which are translated and reprinted in *The Youngest Doll*. In such essays, she discusses the differing themes between male-authored and female-authored literature, and criticizes the different treatment of male and female authors, particularly within a Latin American context.

The main focus of Ferré's thinking concerns gender roles. One image that emerges throughout much of her work is that of the doll, the ultimate representation of woman as decoration, of female objectification and fragmentation, and of loss of self and identity. In *The Youngest Doll*, stories such as

"Amalia," "Marina and the Lion," and "The Youngest Doll" explore the often fatal effects of such trivialization of women's lives, as well as examine the potential for revolt and ensuing unity among women as they subvert their traditional roles within patriarchy. In her book of poetry, *Fábulas de la garza desangrada* (1982) [Fables of a Bleeding Crane], Ferré draws on female mythical figures of Western civilization, such as Ariadne, Antigone, Daphne, Mary Magdalene, Desdemona, Medusa, and Helen of Troy, rewriting their victim status and remaking them into rebels against the misogynistic forces intent upon mistreating and misreading them. *Sitio a Eros* (1980) [Eros Besieged], a collection of biographical and critical essays stressing the importance of women in literature and culture that includes her famous piece "The Writer's Kitchen," unites with the poetry in *Fábulas de la garza desangrada* and the short stories of *The Youngest Doll* to create what has been called Ferré's trilogy of feminist manifestos.

Another significant tradition that Ferré relies on and plays with in her writing is Catholicism. Her story "The Gift" in *Sweet Diamond Dust* offers a satire upon the alliance between the wealthy elite and the Catholic Church; her novella, *The Battle of the Virgins*, addresses religious fanaticism and class difference. Ferré problematizes religious female figures in her work as well, such as Eve, both first mother and first sinner; the Blessed Virgin Mary, redeemed mother and asexual—therefore sinless—woman; and Mary Magdalene, sexualized woman and redeemed whore. *The Youngest Doll* is largely informed by these images. Stories such as "When Women Love Men" explore the doubling of femalehood into the image of the Madonna/whore that the Catholic Church seems to perpetuate: Isabel Luberza and Isabel la Negra represent each side of this dichotomy, yet this story joins these two alleged aspects of womanhood in ways that question sexual, racial, and class differences. Both critical of the upper classes and sympathetic toward the restricted lives of wealthy women—whom she envisions as equally marginalized as poor, working-class women—Ferré interrogates our notions of womanhood and of how women function within both the agrarian and industrial classes in Puerto Rico.

"Sleeping Beauty," another short story from *The Youngest Doll*, provides a prime example of how Ferré employs Catholic traditions to rethink the stereotypes placed on women today and to reconsider the role of Catholicism in current understandings of race, class, gender, nationality, and politics. This story invokes and reworks such myths and fairy tales as Sleeping Beauty, Coppélia, Giselle, and The Red Shoes. Ferré's "Sleeping Beauty," however, relies equally on stories, tales, and traditions from Catholicism. Here Ferré rewrites fairy tales as revisions of Judeo-Christian stories, revising them to reveal a new story about female sexuality. The protagonist, María de los Angeles, awakens to her sexuality through dance, only to find both her dancing and her sexuality suppressed by her worldly father Don Fabiano and her mother in religion, the Reverend Mother Martínez. Both Don Fabiano and Mother Martínez are intent on preserving the virginity of their young charge until it can be offered to the appropriate buyer: either a husband who can assume responsibility for the family business, or the convent. But while María's desire to dance is considered insanity, it remains her only hope for mental and emotional soundness. Attempting to balance these opposing images of Catholic womanhood—virgin, mother, whore—María is quite literally left walking a tightrope without a net.

Religion is central to Ferré's writing because it remains central to her homeland of Puerto Rico. In "On Language, Destiny, and Translation; or, Ophelia Adrift in the C. & O. Canal," she argues that "Latin American society is still rooted in Thomistic, Aristotelian beliefs, which attempt to reconcile Christian thought with the truths of the natural universe and of faith" (*The Youngest Doll*, p. 157). She contends that, unlike North America, "Spain (and Latin America) have never really undergone a scientific or an industrial revolution, and they have never produced the equivalent of a Hobbes or a Locke, so that theories such as that of pragmatism, individual liberty, and the social contract have been very difficult to implement" (p. 157). Ferré's writing demonstrates how Puerto Rico, with its continuing Catholic influence, must confront the connections and contradictions between religion and sexual, social, racial, and class liberation.

Sweeping family sagas in such texts as *The House on the Lagoon* and *Eccentric Neighborhoods* tend to address the complex relationship between personal identity and family history, as well as the question of who is finally allowed to write that history. The problematic relationship between Puerto Rico and the United States is also central to Ferré's writing, particularly within her discussions of the American presence in her native country's developing culture. These issues are especially emphasized in *Eccentric Neighborhoods*, which explores the complicated social, political, and economic intersections within contemporary Puerto Rico. Ferré's literary bilingualism, her recognition of audiences in both the United States and Puerto Rico, places her in the difficult position of confronting issues that remain keenly debated at the beginning of the twenty-first century, particularly Puerto Rico's continuing commonwealth status. Janice Jaffe argues that Ferré alters the negative portrayal of the United States when she translates her work from Spanish to English, painting the country in a more positive light for her American audience. She contends that Ferré "'prostitutes' herself as a Puerto Rican writer," although Jaffe draws on Ferré's own non-pejorative use of the term as an "emblem . . . of linguistic and sexual marginalization and mutability" (p. 66). Yet readers and critics alike often find that Ferré deftly addresses both audiences, offering a vision of Puerto Rico that rings true for its residents and captures its sense of place for foreign readers.

## SURVEY OF CRITICISM

Critics generally regard Ferré's fiction with high esteem; her novels and short stories are internationally acclaimed, including in her home country.

Ferré's work is considered original and often daring, invoking language that challenges our perceptions of women's literature and exploring social taboos that directly inform women's lives. Patricia Hart terms Ferré's fiction "magic feminism," finding in it a contemporary magical realism that blends with feminism to attend to women's experiences. Ferré's poetry, like her fiction, has also been well received. However, responses to her literary criticism and theory vary from favorable to disparaging; for example, her biographies of women artists in *Sitio a Eros* have been called imprecise and subjective. Her children's literature has also been debated, not on the basis of its value, but rather in terms of its audience. Some critics argue that her children's fairy tales are intended for adult audiences, and that the social and political critiques would be inaccessible to young readers. But Margarite Fernández Olmos asserts that children's literature has long been a venue for such commentary, and that many writers consider children the appropriate starting point for such socialization.

Suzanne Hintz's *Rosario Ferré: A Search for Identity* contains the most detailed and lengthy discussion to date of Rosario Ferré's life and work. Hintz's biography of Ferré is authoritative, with an extensive bibliography of Ferré's *oeuvre*. Her discussion of Ferré's works largely examines the author's theoretical and literary growth, foregrounding her politics, her feminism, and the autobiographical aspects of her writing.

The critical attention given to Rosario Ferré's literature, beginning immediately after her first publications and continually increasing, suggests that her works will progressively become even more widely read. Ferré has already come a long way toward achieving her goal of moving women's stories and writings from the margin to the center.

## BIBLIOGRAPHY

### Works by Rosario Ferré

*Sitio a Eros: Trece ensayos literarios.* Mexico City: Joaquín Mortiz, 1980.
*Fábulas de la garza desangrada.* Mexico City: Joaquín Mortiz, 1982.
*Sweet Diamond Dust.* [*Maldito amor*]. New York: Ballantine Press, 1988.
*El coloquio de las perras.* Rio Piedras, Puerto Rico: Cultural, 1990.
*The Youngest Doll.* [*Papeles de Pandora*]. Lincoln: University of Nebraska Press, 1991.
*Las batalla de las virgenes.* San Juan, Puerto Rico: Editorial de la Universidad de Puerto Rico, 1993.
*The House on the Lagoon.* New York: Plume, 1995.
*Eccentric Neighborhoods.* New York: Farrar, Straus & Giroux, 1998.

### Works about Rosario Ferré

Acevedo, Ramón Luis. "Rosario Ferré." *Spanish American Authors: The Twentieth Century.* Ed. Angel Flores. New York: H. W. Wilson Co., 1992. 313–17.

Chapman, Jeff, and John D. Jorgenson, eds. *Contemporary Authors: New Revision Series*. Detroit: Gale Research Corporation. Vol. 55. 167–69.

DelRosso, Jeana. "Veiled Threats: Contemporary International Catholic Girlhood Narratives." Diss. University of Maryland, 2000.

Hart, Patricia. "Magic Feminism and Inverted Masculine Myths in Rosario Ferré's *The Youngest Doll.*" *Studies in Honor of Maria A. Salgado.* Ed. Millicent A. Bolden and Luis A. Jimenez. Delaware: Juan de la Cuesta, 1995. 97–108.

Hintz, Suzanne S. *Rosario Ferré: A Search for Identity.* New York: Peter Lang, 1995.

Jaffe, Janice A. "Translation and Prostitution: Rosario Ferré's *Maldito amor* and *Sweet Diamond Dust.*" *Latin American Literary Review* 23.46 (1995): 66–82.

Olmos, Margarite Fernández. "Rosario Ferré." *Spanish American Women Writers: A Bio-Bibliographical Sourcebook.* Ed. Diane E. Marting. Westport, Connecticut: Greenwood Press, 1990. 165–75.

Rivera, Carmen S. "Rosario Ferré." *Dictionary of Literary Biography: Modern Latin-American Fiction Writers.* Vol. 145. A Bruccoli Clark Layman Book. Ed. William Luis and Ann Gonzalez. Detroit: Gale Research, 1994. 130–37.

*World Authors 1985–1990.* Ed. Vincenta Colby. Wilson Author Series. New York: H. W. Wilson Co., 1995. 262–64.

JEANA DELROSSO

# LADY GEORGIANA FULLERTON
# (1812–1885)

## BIOGRAPHY

Born an aristocrat and surprised by literary celebrity, Lady Georgiana Fullerton led a charmed early life, suggesting the plot of a fashionable romance novel. Fullerton's continual struggles to reconcile secular realities with her other-worldly religious devotion, however, endows her life story with a complexity and hybridity that—much like Fullerton's fiction—belies easy categorization. Fullerton, a Catholic convert and a lay member of the Third Order of Saint Francis, would have preferred being remembered for her extensive works of charity rather than for her novels. Accordingly, Fullerton's early biographers, hoping to bring about her official canonization within the Catholic Church, constructed hagiographies which emphasized Fullerton's piety and altruism over her considerable literary accomplishments. These biographies have set the tone for subsequent critical appraisal of Fullerton; she has been remembered (or more often, forgotten) as a pious woman who also happened to be a "minor religious novelist." Yet just as Fullerton's austere black dress and ungloved hands (the half-crown for gloves was better spent on the poor, she claimed) belied in later years her true social standing, so also have literary historians overlooked the extent of her reputation and influence in mid-Victorian Britain. For not only were Fullerton's first three novels reviewed prominently, and favorably, alongside those of Dickens, Thackeray, and Charlotte Brontë, but they also illustrate in vivid relief many of the same religious, spiritual, and moral concerns that preoccupied other female writers, both canonical and noncanonical, of her generation.

Born Georgiana Charlotte Leveson-Gower at Tixhall Hall in Staffordshire in 1812, Fullerton was the daughter of Lord Granville Leveson-Gower and his wife, Lady Harriet Cavendish. Georgiana was named after her maternal grandmother, the fifth Duchess of Devonshire, who was immortalized on canvas by Sir Joshua Reynolds. Although young Georgiana's upbringing was, by her own recollection, rather austere and regimented by an overzealous governess, she and her siblings enjoyed all the privileges of wealth and social standing, on both sides of the English Channel (Lord Leveson-Gower was appointed the British ambassador to France in 1824). George IV bounced four-year-old Georgiana on his knee at a children's party ("I told him I should not stay any longer with him," she recalled, "or I should lose a dance" [quoted in Taylor, p. 4]); King Louis-Philippe helped the child to *pommes de terre* at the Palais Royal; and she also took piano lessons from Franz Liszt (during which, she later stated, "he sometimes started up and ran about the room, stopping his ears!" [quoted in Coleridge, p. 32]).

In 1833, Georgiana married Alexander George Fullerton (1808–1907), a Guards' officer and heir to large estates in Ireland and Gloucestershire. The marriage took place in Paris, and the Fullertons lived for a time with Lord and Lady Leveson-Gower at the British embassy. They also traveled extensively, alternating rambles on the Continent with periods of fixed residence in both Paris and England. An only child, William Granville, was born in 1834.

The 1840s were important formative years for Fullerton, whose writing career seemed to evolve alongside her search for a viable religious and spiritual identity. Fullerton and her husband both converted to Roman Catholicism (Alexander in 1843, Georgiana in 1846), and she began writing in order to support her extensive charitable activities. Fullerton's first three novels (*Ellen Middleton*, 1844; *Grantley Manor*, 1847; *Lady-Bird*, 1852) were phenomenally successful. Although all three works addressed contemporary religious issues, their engaging plots and complex characters captivated readers and critics. William Gladstone wrote a twenty-five page review essay of *Ellen Middleton* for the *English Quarterly*, in which he claimed that the novel exhibited "the mastery of all human gifts of authorship" (p. 356). This work also received enthusiastic praise from Queen Victoria, Harriet Martineau, and, across the Atlantic, from Emily Dickinson and Edgar Allan Poe. Actress Fanny Kemble reported being so enthralled with Fullerton's second novel, *Grantley Manor*, that while reading the book at dinner, she reached for her wine and accidentally brought the mustard-pot to her lips.

Fullerton's complete body of work includes eight novels, four biographies, and an assortment of novellas, plays, poems, and short stories. Her literary prominence seems to have diminished considerably after midcentury, although she retained a great popularity in France and among Catholic circles in England. This abrupt change in Fullerton's literary reception roughly coincided with a new trajectory in her personal and spiritual life. In 1855, Fullerton's son William died suddenly of a brain tumor, a devastating loss from which she would never recover. Always pious, Fullerton now devoted herself to the poor more than ever; upon joining the Third Order of St. Francis, she took a vow of poverty and even, according to biographer Frances Taylor, a vow of chastity within marriage. Although Fullerton continued to write and publish books until 1883, she found it increasingly difficult to reconcile her identity as an author with her religious and spiritual ideals. The achievements for which she was most celebrated, upon her death in 1885, were her efforts in bringing the Sisters of Charity of St. Vincent de Paul into England in 1859, and her establishment of a religious order for women without dowries, the Poor Servants of the Mother of God Incarnate.

## MAJOR THEMES

Fullerton's three most popular novels all demonstrate an engagement with religious issues from a Roman Catholic (or, before her conversion, an Anglo-Catholic) standpoint. However, they appealed to Protestants as well as Catholics, partly because the themes central to Fullerton's fiction touched on religious and spiritual concerns shared by Victorian women of faith across denominations. In particular, Fullerton's work foregrounds an anxiety voiced by a number of her female contemporaries: that the domestic ideals of a culture that encouraged women to obey their husbands in matters religious and spiritual, as well as temporal, might compromise women's spiritual integrity and, at worst, lead to the ruin of their souls.

Accordingly, each of the heroines in *Ellen Middleton, Grantley Manor,* and *Lady-Bird* evolves through seeking an autonomous moral and spiritual authority, one freed from the supervision and control of husbands and lovers. *Ellen Middleton,* implicitly suggesting a Tractarian argument in support of auricular confession in the Anglican church, features a young woman who comes to ruin because she is unable to confess that she has accidentally killed her cousin. Ellen considers confessing to her husband, but Edward's moral rigidity—combined with his idolatrous conviction of Ellen's perfection—ultimately drives Ellen and her dark secret from home, a flight leading Edward to wrongly suspect his wife of adultery. Ellen finally receives solace through her confession to an Anglican clergyman, "one who neither loved nor hated me" (p. 106), who brings about the dying Ellen's reconciliation with her husband and family.

The suggestion of marriage and domesticity as a potential obstacle to women's spiritual integrity is reiterated in *Grantley Manor,* Fullerton's first novel following her conversion to Roman Catholicism. The novel's plot hinges on a secret marriage between Edmund Neville, a Protestant, and Ginevra Leslie, a Catholic. Edmund insists on secrecy because his father has forbidden him, on the pain of disinheritance, to marry a Catholic. Throughout the course of the narrative, Edmund prevails upon his wife to renounce her faith, so that his family might recognize and accept their marriage. Ginevra steadfastly clings to her Catholic faith, but not without an enormous sacrifice. The novel's conclusion, although allowing for a felicitous resolution of the secrecy plot, suggests that Ginevra—now debilitated by severe psychological and spiritual turmoil—will not live much longer.

Marital strife again appears in *Lady-Bird,* a novel in which the heroine, Gertrude Lifford, rashly enters into marriage with a man she despises. Although

Gertrude passionately loves another, her spiritual maturation requires that she learn, through prayer and noble self-sacrifice, to love her husband and to renounce the object of her unlawful passion. So successful is Gertrude in her efforts, that when her husband dies—leaving her free to marry her first love—she nonetheless remains single and devotes her life to serving the poor.

In *Ellen Middleton, Grantley Manor,* and *Lady-Bird,* women's religious and spiritual needs continually clash with secular cultural ideals of romantic love, marriage, and domesticity. All these conflicts are, in Fullerton's fiction, always resolvable, but only through the means of prayer and self-sacrifice on the part of the heroine. The modern day secular reader might not understand or relate to the religious imperatives in Fullerton's works. These novels are, however, nonetheless remarkable in their consistent challenge to societal ideals; their strikingly complex, multifaceted female characters; and their resistance to the dominance of the marriage plot in midcentury Victorian fiction.

## SURVEY OF CRITICISM

In the 1840s and 1850s, Fullerton's novels received a great deal of attention from critics, and reviews of her work appeared in such publications as the *London Times,* the *North British Review, Tait's Edinburgh Magazine, Fraser's,* and the *Atheneum.* Reviewers expressed admiration for the interest and complexity of Fullerton's characters as well as her talent for constructing gripping and sensational plots. Interestingly, most reviews, while often noting the religious dimensions of Fullerton's novels, do not characterize them as works of religious controversy. Rather, in an era when Victorian readers demanded just the right balance of entertainment and moral edification, Fullerton was lauded for her ability to present religious opinions without compromising the literary quality of her work.

Critics less appreciative of Fullerton's novels complained of their excessive melodrama, their religious and doctrinal errors (a review in a Catholic periodical, for example, complained that *Grantley Manor's* Ginevra Leslie embraced a heretical doctrine of salvation for Catholics and Protestants alike), and, perhaps most frequently, their "excessively painful" characters. Although the extraordinary self-renunciation practiced by such characters as Ginevra Leslie and Gertrude Lifford seems to have been consistent with Fullerton's religious views, this otherworldly ethos unsettled at least a few readers and critics. Emily Dickinson's brother Austen, for example, despite having enjoyed *Grantley Manor,* could not help but regard *Lady-Bird* as "a story full of only wretchedness & misery. . . . [A] story of deeper suffering than . . . any should know till they are obliged to" (quoted in Jaeger, p. 302). A reviewer for the *Atheneum,* similarly affected by *Lady-Bird,* condemned it as "thoroughly morbid" (quoted in Jaeger, p. 302).

Lady Georgiana Fullerton's literary reputation did not long survive her death. In 1895, Charlotte Yonge wrote an essay on Fullerton's life and work for a collection entitled *Women Novelists of Queen Victoria's Reign*, which, despite its praise for Fullerton and her work, characterized her rather dismissively as "having written one first-rate book [*Ellen Middleton*] and a number fairly above average" (p. 203). Twentieth-century literary criticism has taken virtually no notice of Fullerton, other than as a minor novelist associated with the Oxford Movement. Margaret Maison devotes just one paragraph to Fullerton in her book *The Victorian Vision: Studies in the Religious Novel*; Joseph Baker, in *The Novel and the Oxford Movement*, characterizes *Ellen Middleton* as "contemptible" (p. 19); and Robert Lee Wolfe, although expressing admiration for *Ellen Middleton* as "a textbook Freudian case-history" (p. 80), considers Fullerton's fiction only in regard to the role it played in Victorian religious controversy. These cursory treatments of Fullerton acknowledge neither the extent of her literary reputation at mid–nineteenth century, nor the fact that her early novels, despite their Anglo- and Roman Catholic sympathies, appealed to a wide spectrum of contemporary readers, who clearly regarded them as much more than religious arguments cloaked in melodrama.

Presently, the best source of information on Fullerton and her works can be found in early biographies (Craven, Coleridge, Taylor), and in a handful of doctoral dissertations. Of the dissertations focusing exclusively on Fullerton, few attempt to place the author and her works in a broad literary, religious, and social context. Raymond Leonard has argued that Fullerton's work laid an important foundation for the Catholic novel in England; other studies, however, have focused more specifically on Fullerton's life (Kathleen Jaeger's study being the most useful in this regard) and on the plots of her novels.

## BIBLIOGRAPHY

### Works by Lady Georgiana Fullerton

*Ellen Middleton.* London: Edward Moton, 1844.
*Grantley Manor.* London: Edward Moton, 1847.
*Lady-Bird.* London: Edward Moton, 1852.
*The Life of St. Frances of Rome.* London: Burns & Lambert, 1855.
*Laurentia: A Tale of Japan.* London, 1861.
*Too Strange Not to Be True.* London: Richard Bentley, 1864.
*Constance Sherwood.* London: Richard Bentley, 1865.
*A Stormy Life.* London: Richard Bentley, 1867.
*Mrs. Gerald's Niece.* London: Richard Bentley, 1869.
*The Gold-Digger's Story and Other Poems.* London: Burns & Oates, 1872.
*Seven Stories.* London, 1873.
*A Will and a Way.* London: Richard Bentley & Son, 1881.
*The Fire of London; or Which Is Which. A Play.* London, 1882.
*The Life of Elisabeth Lady Falkland, 1585–1639.* London: Burns & Oates, 1883.

## Works about Lady Georgiana Fullerton

Baker, Joseph. *The Novel and the Oxford Movement*. 1932. New York: Russell and Russell, 1965.

Barker, John. *Lady Georgiana Fullerton: A Bournemouth Benefactor*. Bournemouth: Bournemouth Local Studies Publications, 1991.

Belloc, Bessie Rayner. "Lady Georgiana Fullerton." *In a Walled Garden*, by Bessie Rayner Belloc. London: Ward and Downey, 1895. 100–11.

Coleridge, Henry James. *Life of Lady Georgiana Fullerton*. Rev. trans. of Craven's biography, listed below. London: Richard Bentley & Son, 1888.

Craven, Augustus, Mme. *Lady Georgiana Fullerton. Sa Vie et ses Oeuvres*. Paris, 1888.

Dornseifer, Elizabeth. "Lady Georgiana Fullerton (1812–1885): A Critical Approach." Diss. Freiburg University, 1967.

Driscoll, Annette Sophia Hoogs. *Tertiaries of Our Day: Lady Georgiana Fullerton and Lady Herbert of Lea*. Chicago: Franciscan Herald Press, 1926.

Gladstone, William. Rev. of *Ellen Middleton*, by Lady Georgiana Fullerton. *English Review* 1 (1844): 336–61.

Jaeger, Kathleen. "Lady Georgiana Fullerton (1812–1885): A Reassessment." Diss. Dalhousie University, 1985.

LaMonaca, Maria. "Paradise Deferred: Religion, Domesticity, and Realism in the Victorian Novel." Diss. Indiana University, 1999.

Leonard, Raymond S. "Lady Georgiana Fullerton." Diss. St. John's University (New York), 1955.

Maison, Margaret. *The Victorian Vision: Studies in the Religious Novel*. New York: Sheed & Ward, 1961.

Taylor, F. M. *The Inner Life of Lady Georgiana Fullerton*. London: Burns & Oates, 1899.

Yonge, Charlotte. "Lady Georgiana Fullerton, Mrs. Stretton, Anne Manning." *Women Novelists of Queen Victoria's Reign: A Book of Appreciations*. Ed. Margaret Oliphant. London: Hurst and Blackett, 1897. 195–203. Rpt. Norwood, Pennsylvania: Norwood Editions, 1977.

Wolfe, Robert Lee. *Gains and Losses: Novels of Faith and Doubt in Victorian England*. New York: John Murray, 1977.

MARIA LAMONACA

# RUMER GODDEN
# (1907–1998)

## BIOGRAPHY

Rumer Godden's life was marked by the peripatetic activity and search for a stable home that figures thematically in much of her fiction. Born Margaret Rumer Godden in Sussex on December 10, 1907, she was the second daughter of Arthur Leigh and Katherine Hingley Godden. While she was yet an infant, her parents moved to India where her father worked as a shipping agent. In 1913, the five-year-old Godden and her older sister Jon were briefly returned to England to live with relatives, but the advent of World War I with the threat of air raids over London necessitated their return to India the following year. The next six years of Godden's childhood were, as she later stated, a "halcyon" time. As British colonists in Narayangunj, the Godden family lived a gracious, upper-class "Raj" lifestyle. The Godden children received no formal schooling although they were tutored in a haphazard way by their aunt. Godden looked back on this unrestrained period of childhood as one that liberated her imagination and fostered her literary creativity: "All of us wrote: poems and stories poured out of us," she recalled in her autobiography, *Two Under the Indian Sun* (p. 195).

In 1920, the halcyon days came to an abrupt end as Godden, now aged twelve, and Jon were sent back to England to attend boarding school. By contrast to the freedom of life in India, Godden's next few years proved confining and miserable. She attended five schools in five years, leaving each because of her inability to adjust to the rote drills and strict discipline. By far her worst experience was at an Anglican convent boarding school in London; she detested the rigid and formal High Anglicanism she experienced both there and while summering with relatives. Finally, at a school named Moira House, Godden met an inspirational English teacher who nurtured the teenager's writing abilities. The creative Godden, however, also had a passion for dance. After graduation, she trained herself to become a children's ballet teacher. In her early twenties, she returned to Calcutta to open a ballet school, the first of its kind in India and a pioneer effort for an independent young woman in 1928.

Having become pregnant, Godden married the baby's father, stockbroker Laurence Sinclair Foster, in Calcutta in 1934. From the outset, as she later remarked, Godden knew the marriage was a sham. Nevertheless, the couple remained together until separating in 1942 and divorcing four years later. During this time, Godden gave birth to two daughters and began to indulge in her early passion for writing. *Black Narcissus* (1939) was her first best seller and the first of her books to be published in the United States. Although it earned her a great deal of money, Godden was left responsible at the time for paying off Laurence's huge debts. With her two daughters, she returned to India to escape the onset of World War II and to live as simply as possible while continuing her writing career. For several years she rented a farmhouse in the isolated Kashmir region. In 1945, she revisited her childhood home in Narayangunj, a location that would become central to her next best seller, *The River* (1946). Returning to England that year, Godden penned the first of what would become a long succession of highly acclaimed children's books, *The Doll's House* (1947). She also continued to write many novels for adults, and she completed three autobiographies, *Two Under the Indian Sun* (written with Jon Godden, 1966), *A Time to Dance, No Time to Weep* (1987), and *A House with Four Rooms* (1989).

Godden married for a second time in 1949, wedding James Haynes-Dixon. His death in 1973 left her in a severe depression for several years. However, she never ceased writing, her career at her death spanning nearly six decades and her corpus consisting of seventy books. As critic Lynne M. Rosenthal put it in *Rumer Godden Revisited*, "even at seventy [she was] wandering shady Parisian quarters from midnight until 3 a.m. (followed by a friend in a taxi) to research *Five for Sorrow; Ten for Joy*," a novel concerning Paris's prostitutes (p. 16). Godden moved to Scotland to be near her daughters and her grandchildren in 1977. She died there in 1998 at the age of ninety-one.

## MAJOR THEMES

In her autobiography *A House with Four Rooms*, Godden explains that her title refers to the four "rooms" of the self: the physical, mental, emotional, and spiritual. "All of us tend to inhabit one room more than another but I have tried to go most days into them all—each has its riches," she states (p. 314). The primary theme of the majority of Godden's fiction is the scattered self's quest to regain a sense of wholeness in the midst of the chaos of contemporary life or after a tragedy. The search for a stable home, room, or sanctuary where one can find such tranquillity figures prominently in Godden's fiction, reflecting in part the author's own restless life.

Among Godden's best and most representative adult novels are two with overtly Catholic themes. Both *In This House of Brede* (1969) and *Five for Sor-*

*row; Ten for Joy* (1979) concern a woman's search for emotional and spiritual healing after a time of trauma; both protagonists regain a sense of completeness after entering a Catholic convent. *Black Narcissus*, also about convent life, can be viewed as a prelude to Godden's continuing interest in women seeking fulfillment by living a dedicated life in community.

Growing up in India, Godden received no religious training from her free-thinking parents, although being surrounded by a variety of believers, including Hindus, Muslims, Buddhists, and Catholics, fostered in her a lifelong respect for and interest in religion. As noted, however, her childhood years at an Anglican convent school made her despise what she regarded as the repressed and arid life of the nuns who instructed her. Years later, remembering that experience, Godden penned the potboiler *Black Narcissus*. The novel concerns a small group of British Anglican nuns who are sent as missionaries to an isolated area of India. Once there, the sisters' ritualized lifestyle and Western sense of decorum are severely tested by the spontaneity, disorder, and superstitions of the native population; they find themselves utterly unable to adapt to the situation and their mission soon fails. Another major reason for their failure is the personalities of the maladjusted nuns themselves. As their circumstances worsen, the women become self-absorbed, petty, and angry; one even attempts to murder another. Though the plot of *Black Narcissus* is too melodramatic for today's tastes, it was a popular best seller both in Britain and in the United States, and in 1947 was turned into a successful film starring Deborah Kerr.

Although Godden participated in the production of the movie, she was ultimately displeased by it. For one thing, she was dismayed to find it completely false, "counterfeit," in its depiction of India (*House,* p. 52). Moreover, by the time the film was released she had already taken steps toward her own conversion first to Christianity and then to Catholicism, and she regretted her novel's bleak portrayal of convent life. Her conversion came about gradually, fostered by the increasing need for a secure anchor in the world. At first she turned to the Anglican Church. But, as she recounts in *House with Four Rooms,* a meeting with the Jesuit Archbishop of Bombay, himself a convert, proved an influential step in her eventual decision to enter the Catholic Church (pp. 240–43). She began taking instruction in the faith in the late 1950s although, since both she and her husband were divorced, it was only later that she could be fully received into the Church.

While contemplating her own conversion, Godden explored the traditions and spirituality of the Catholic faith in two major novels written in the 1960s–1970s. The genesis for both came when she befriended a Benedictine nun, of whom she had requested prayers, at Stanbrook Abbey in Worcestershire. At one point, the sister remarked to her, "I wish . . . that someone would write a book about nuns as they really are, not as the author wants them to be." "I thought of *Black Narcissus*," Godden later related, "and blushed" (*House,* p. 239). This chance remark proved to be the germ of her subsequent novels about convent life. Both *In This House of Brede* and *Five for Sorrow; Ten for Joy* portray nuns realistically, as women no better or worse than others but set apart merely because of their determination to respond to the call to a particular lifestyle. Because of Godden's refusal to stereotype convent life either sentimentally or negatively, these novels remain highly readable today. Moreover, each is a fine example of Godden's use of multiple points of view in revealing character, interwoven dialogue, and flashbacks in developing a suspenseful plot.

In order to research *In This House of Brede* (which was turned into a successful television film starring Diana Rigg), Godden spent many weeks at the English Benedictine Abbey of Stanbrook where she was permitted to interview individual nuns at length. The book took five years to complete and is rightly considered Godden's most mature novel stylistically. Though the nuns at the fictional Brede Abbey are an enclosed order who gather six times daily to pray, each struggles at times with doubts about her vocation, with envy of others, and with other human faults. The novel succeeds in illustrating the difficulties and satisfactions of religious life as lived by women who do not abandon their individuality at the monastery door as they enter. Remarkably, through employing multiple voices, Godden manages to individualize the lives of at least thirty of the ninety-nine nuns at Brede Abbey.

The main plot of the novel is slender. In the preface, we learn that Philippa Talbot, an educated, widowed, forty-two-year-old woman in a promising career, has converted to Catholicism and then has found herself answering a call to a religious vocation. The novel proper begins four years after she has entered the convent; by now, she is thoroughly acclimated to its rhythm of daily life. Although her story is now intimately interwoven with that of the other nuns, we are gradually made aware of a mystery connected with Sister Philippa. Haunted by some element from her past, she is disturbed by nightmares and bouts of depression. These related occurrences essentially tie the novel's several strands of plot together as readers anticipate what the secret sorrow could be. Finally, it is revealed that, years earlier, Philippa's five-year-old son died in a horrific accident caused by the negligence of his nursemaid. When the daughter of that nursemaid seeks entrance to Brede Abbey, Philippa must deal with the tensions of her unresolved memories.

*Five for Sorrow; Ten for Joy* is similar in theme and technique to *In This House of Brede*. An older, worldly-wise woman named Lise enters a French convent and gradually, through multiple points of view and flashbacks, her mysterious past comes to light. What makes this work different than the former novel, however, is the nature of the order of nuns Lise joins. The Dominican Sisters of Bethany is an order half composed of women who are paroled ex-criminals: murderers, drug addicts, prostitutes, and the like. The other half consists of ordinary women who have entered religious life in the normal manner. Like many of the sisters in the first category, Lise's past is complex. Seduced by the pimp Patrice when she was a naive teenager, she becomes ensconced in his Parisian brothel as his special mistress. When she is displaced from her position by Patrice's new favorite, the young Vivi whom Lise has found starving on the streets, Lise kills Patrice in a fit of both jealousy and sincere concern over the fate of Vivi. Immediately arrested, she pleads guilty at her trial and serves fifteen years in the penitentiary.

All this history we learn by flashback. When the novel opens, Lise has just been released from prison and, similar to *In This House of Brede*, is on her way to enter the convent. In jail, she has been converted to Catholicism through the influence of the Sisters of Bethany. We follow Lise, therefore, from the moment she enters the monastery through approximately twenty years of her religious life. Once again, the story presents a kind of tapestry in relating the interwoven lives of the nuns. This time, however, the events are even more dramatic because of the extremes of highs and lows that naturally occur among such an odd mixture of women. The climax of the book occurs when Vivi, who has also served time in prison, stalks Lise and attempts to kill her. She is unsuccessful, but the novel ends on a note at once hopeful and ominous as it is anticipated that she will return one day to try again.

A thread that winds its way throughout *Five for Sorrow; Ten for Joy* is that of the symbolism of the rosary. Godden explains the significance of her title in the book's preface: five decades of sorrowful mysteries in the rosary, and ten for joy and glory. When Lise first finds the young Vivi on the street, Vivi is clutching a cheap rosary. That rosary haunts Lise; somehow it foreshadows, perhaps even influences, her conversion to Catholicism and entrance into religious life. Only after Vivi attempts to murder her and leaves as her calling card the same cheap rosary does Lise achieve through a special grace, it is implied, the rosary's benefit of peace of mind and soul.

Herself an independent career woman and a single mother at a time when such roles were frowned upon, Godden focuses these novels on strong-willed, complex, and intelligent women who search for and discover a level of fulfillment beyond that of marriage and motherhood. Both Philippa and Lise find in communal life a home in which all aspects of the self—the physical, mental, emotional, and spiritual—can achieve a sense of wholeness.

## SURVEY OF CRITICISM

Considered more popular stories than major works of literary art, Godden's novels have not attracted a substantial body of critical scholarship. Although most of her books have remained continuously in print, she is perhaps still best known for *Black Narcissus*, *The River*, and *In This House of Brede*, the three mid-career best sellers turned into popular films. The fullest discussion of Godden's adult works to date can be found in Hassell A. Simpson's *Rumer Godden*. Simpson includes chapters on *Black Narcissus* and *In This House of Brede*; his chronological approach to Godden's large and uneven canon is useful in highlighting the author's experimentation and development in between these two novels. Simpson praises Godden for the range and diversity of her subject matter, the intricacies of her "symphony-like" plot structures, her well-developed dramatic sense, and "the subtlety and power of her sensitive analysis of character under stress" (p. 131). He also notes correctly that in less successful works Godden tends toward contrived plot solutions and stereotyped characters and situations. However, because it was published in the early 1970s, Simpson's book does not consider the more than two dozen works Godden produced after that date.

Among other early criticism, Orville Prescott's *In My Opinion: An Inquiry Into the Contemporary Novel* contains a laudatory chapter on Godden. Prescott concludes that the author is a perceptive writer of universal truths, a refreshing voice in an era of degenerating values. William York Tindall's "Rumer Godden, Public Symbolist" places Godden in the context of the "great symbolist movement of our time" for her repeated use of images of the house, river, and the immenseness and complexity of India itself. Although in his opinion Godden falls short of true artistic excellence, her best work contains "a surface so pleasing and limpid that it makes the depths immediately apparent" (p. 118).

In more recent critical appraisal, Janette Turner Hospital's *New York Times* review, "Adventure Was What She Got," compares Godden to Isak Dineson in her independence as both a woman and a creative artist. Hospital concludes that despite her sometimes elitist assumptions, Godden is a "first-rate story-teller" and a satisfying popular writer (p. 13). Thomas Dukes's "Evoking the Significance: The Autobiographies of Rumer Godden" takes a welcome look at Godden's three substantial autobiographies and notes how their intertwining of life and art have the effect of creating a complex and intriguing female *bildungsroman*.

Over the last decade, Godden has particularly been commended as a fine children's author. Lynne M. Rosenthal's *Rumer Godden Revisited* revises and updates Simpson's earlier Twayne volume but focuses its attention primarily on Godden's works for children, although brief mention is given to most of the adult novels as well. Rosenthal's use of feminist and revisionist criticism is a necessary balance to Simpson's more formalist approach to Godden's canon. Likewise, Patricia Ward's recent *Dictionary of Literary Biography* entry on Godden discusses the writer mainly as a sensitive teller of children's tales. Whether her books were written for children or adults, however, Ward concludes that Godden's best work succeeds in conveying "the plight and triumph of children separated from their parents, the difficulty of adjusting to new cultures and situations, the need for love and belonging, the importance of place and a stable home life, and the power and responsibility of the individual . . . to solve problems and overcome obstacles" (p. 173).

Finally, Anne Chisholm's biography, *Rumer Godden: A Storyteller's Life*, is a welcome addition to Godden studies. Although it does not, for the most part, deal in depth with Godden's writings, it provides clear insight into an author whose life story was often as dramatic and complex as her plots.

## BIBLIOGRAPHY
### Works by Rumer Godden

*Black Narcissus.* London: Peter Davies, 1939; Boston: Little, Brown, 1939.
*The River.* London: Michael Joseph, 1946; Boston: Little, Brown, 1946.
*Kingfishers Catch Fire.* London: Macmillan, 1953; New York: Viking, 1953.
*An Episode of Sparrows.* New York: Viking, 1955; London: Macmillan, 1956.
*Prayers from the Ark,* by Carmen Bernos de Gasztold. Trans. and preface by Rumer Godden. New York: Viking, 1962; London: Macmillan, 1963.
*Two Under the Indian Sun,* with Jon Godden. London: Macmillan, 1966; New York: Viking, 1966.
*The Kitchen Madonna.* London: Macmillan, 1967; New York: Viking, 1967.
*In This House of Brede.* London: Macmillan, 1969; New York: Viking, 1969.
*Five for Sorrow; Ten for Joy.* London: Macmillan, 1979; New York: Viking, 1979.
*A Time to Dance, No Time to Weep.* London: Macmillan, 1987; New York: William Morrow, 1987.
*A House with Four Rooms.* London: Macmillan, 1989; New York: William Morrow, 1989.

### Works about Rumer Godden

Chisholm, Anne. *Rumer Godden: A Storyteller's Life.* New York: Greenwillow Books, 1998.
Dukes, Thomas. "Evoking the Significance: The Autobiographies of Rumer Godden." *Women's Studies* 20 (1991): 15–35.
Hospital, Janette Turner. "Adventure Was What She Got." *New York Times Book Review* 3 January 1988: 13.
Moss, Elaine. "Rumer Godden: Prince of Storytellers." *Signal Magazine* 17 (May 1975): 55–60.
Prescott, Orville. *In My Opinion: An Inquiry Into the Contemporary Novel.* Indianapolis: Bobbs-Merrill, 1952.
Rosenthal, Lynne M. *Rumer Godden Revisited.* New York: Twayne, 1996.
Simpson, Hassell A. *Rumer Godden.* New York: Twayne, 1973.
Tindall, William York. "Rumer Godden, Public Symbolist." *English Journal* 41 (March 1952): 115–21.
Ward, Patricia H. "Rumer Godden." *Dictionary of Literary Biography.* Vol. 161: British Children's Writers Since 1960. Ed. Caroline C. Hunt. Detroit: Gale Research Inc., 1996. 171–80.

MARY R. REICHARDT

# CAROLINE GORDON
# (1895–1981)

## BIOGRAPHY

Born in Kentucky in 1895, Caroline Gordon developed a passion for storytelling at an early age. From her maternal grandmother and namesake, Gordon
learned to cherish stories about her family "connection"—their experiences
settling Kentucky and the devastation of the Civil War and Reconstruction.
From her parents, James Morris Gordon and Nancy Minor Meriwether,
Gordon developed a love for heroes of Greek and Roman myth. A consummate storyteller, J. M. Gordon ran a boys' classical preparatory school with his
wife in Clarksville, Tennessee, before becoming a Disciples of Christ minister.
He also delighted his middle child and only daughter with vivid tales of his experiences hunting and fishing.

After graduating in 1916 with a degree in classical studies from Bethany
College in West Virginia, Gordon taught high school until 1919. Then, inspired by her great-aunt Elizabeth Meriwether Gilmer (1861–1951), known
as Dorothy Dix, a celebrated advice columnist and crime reporter, Gordon
went to work for newspapers, first in Tennessee and later in West Virginia. She
also began writing fiction during this period. Her numerous book reviews for
*Chattanooga News* and *Wheeling Intelligencer* reveal her interest in contemporary literature. Her February 10, 1923, column in the *News* on the southern
little magazine, the *Fugitive*, was one of the first serious reviews the magazine
received.

In 1924, Gordon met Allen Tate (1899–1979), one of the Fugitive poets,
whom she once described as "the most radical member of the group" (quoted
in Jonza, p. 37). The attraction was mutual. Gordon moved to New York City
that fall, and Tate soon followed, although their affair did not last long. Employed by Johnson Features, Gordon continued writing fiction in her spare
time. Discovering she was pregnant in early 1925, Gordon convinced Tate to
marry her. They intended to separate after their daughter was born, but did
not do so.

By 1926, Gordon completed her novel, *Darkling I Listen*. Dissatisfied, she destroyed it but started another. She also began writing short stories and working periodically as a secretary for British novelist Ford Madox Ford. In 1929, Gordon published her first fiction, "Summer Dust: Four Episodes," in the little magazine *Gyroscope*.

In 1930, Gordon was again living in Clarksville, Tennessee, when Maxwell Perkins of Scribner's agreed to publish her new novel, *Penhally* (1931). In the next decade, she wrote and published four novels—*Aleck Maury, Sportsman* (1934), *None Shall Look Back* (1937), *The Garden of Adonis* (1937), *Green Centuries* (1941)—despite repeated emotional and financial crises. From 1933 on, Tate had numerous affairs, wounding Gordon deeply. Although Tate and Gordon garnered good reviews for their writing, they could not support themselves. Gordon went abroad on a Guggenheim Fellowship in 1932 but returned early when her funds ran out. In 1938, Tate and Gordon took the first of many academic positions, teaching creative writing at the University of North Carolina in Greensboro.

Gordon and Tate moved frequently between 1939 and 1944, living in Princeton, New Jersey; Monteagle, Tennessee; Washington, D.C.; and Sewanee, Tennessee. Their marital problems increased, and when Tate asked for a divorce in 1945, Gordon reluctantly agreed. Four months later, however, they remarried, although by early 1947, their marriage and financial affairs were again in chaos.

In the fall of 1947, Gordon converted to Catholicism. Her decision amazed some, but Gordon believed her conversion was inevitable. "I have lived most of my life on the evidence of things not seen—what else is writing a novel but that?—and my work has progressed slowly and steadily in one direction," she wrote. "At a certain point I found the Church squarely in the path. I couldn't jump over it and wouldn't go around it, so had to go into it" (quoted in Jonza, p. 272). Gordon further explained her conversion by writing "The Presence," the last of a series of short stories about Aleck Maury. In "The Presence," Maury comes to understand the importance of faith after a crisis. As another character in the story points out, "when the hard core of the personality is shattered, . . . the real self has a chance to emerge" (*Collected Stories*, p. 119). Gordon's later fiction—*The Women on the Porch* (1944), *The Strange Children* (1951), and *The Malefactors* (1956)—reflected the turmoil in her life. In the latter two novels, Gordon explores the importance of faith in modern life.

In addition to her novels, Gordon published a significant amount of non-fiction as well as three short-story collections. With Tate, she edited the influential textbook *The House of Fiction*, and she also became well known in Catholic intellectual circles. From the 1950s on, she gave lectures and served as a writer-in-residence at Catholic colleges and universities. Gordon also nurtured Catholic writers informally, especially Flannery O'Connor and Walker Percy, both of whom approached Gordon in the fall of 1951 with manuscripts they wanted her to evaluate. Gordon's relationship with O'Connor developed into a friendship that lasted until O'Connor's death in 1964.

Although Gordon hoped that her prayers and Tate's own conversion to Catholicism in 1950 would save their marriage, the couple separated again in 1956 and were divorced in 1959. Gordon continued writing and teaching although she published only one other novel, *The Glory of Hera* (1972). In the fall of 1973, she joined the faculty at the University of Dallas, remaining there until poor health forced her retirement in 1978. She died in San Cristóbal de las Casas, Mexico, in 1981.

## MAJOR THEMES

Most critics identify the central focus of Gordon's fiction to be the study of "heroic characters struggling to assert order and meaning in an unstable world" (Brinkmeyer, p. 80). While true, there are other aspects of Gordon's writing that bear examination. All of Gordon's work explores some part of her personal or family history. In *Penhally*, Gordon creates a fictional account of her maternal ancestors, the Meriwethers, beginning just before the Civil War and ending in the twentieth century. Later novels recount her father's life (*Aleck Maury, Sportsman*), the Civil War experiences of her grandfather and great uncles (*None Shall Look Back*), and the exploits of her pioneer ancestors (*Green Centuries*). Gordon includes a humorous portrayal of her marriage in *Aleck Maury*, and she examines the impact of infidelity in *Green Centuries* and *The Garden of Adonis*. But in later novels, Gordon becomes overtly autobiographical—Catherine and Jim Chapman in *The Women on the Porch*, Sarah and Stephen Lewis in *The Strange Children*, and Vera and Tom Claiborne in *The Malefactors* are thinly disguised portraits of Gordon and Tate, their difficulties and failures.

Through her family stories, Gordon explores two interrelated themes. The most obvious is the importance of a right relationship to the land. The tragedy of *Penhally* derives from the unnecessary division of one family's land. *The Garden of Adonis* shows the degeneration and death of those who lose touch with the land, while *Green Centuries* demonstrates how people destroy themselves with itinerant, rootless lives. Even *None Shall Look Back*, ostensibly a Civil War novel, develops this theme. As Katherine Anne Porter observes in a letter to Gordon, Gordon's "real hero is the same as it was in *Penhally*—the Land," and those who respect it, who love it, cannot truly be defeated (quoted in Jonza, p. 179).

Gordon's second and equally important theme was first identified by Andrew Lytle in a 1949 article: "what Life, the sly deceiver, does to womankind but particularly to the woman of great passion and sensibility" (p. 578). Gordon disagreed with Lytle, insisting her works demonstrated how women created chaos and disaster whenever they were given or took control of life. Yet Gordon often uses women's stories to judge her heroes.

Sometimes this judgment is gentle, as in *Aleck Maury* where the female characters point out the limitations of Maury's selfish pursuits. But more often, Gordon depicts the pain in women's lives as a harsh indictment of her heroes. *Penhally* begins and ends with women's screams, brought on by the stubbornness and selfishness of men. *None Shall Look Back* measures the devastation of the war by contrasting her accounts of a soldier's life with that of Lucy Allard, the young woman he left behind. In *Green Centuries* and *The Women on the Porch*, Gordon juxtaposes the suffering of women (from men's infidelity, selfishness, and rootlessness) with images of the wisdom women could offer a world in chaos.

Although some see a drastic change in "the shape and texture" of Gordon's art after her conversion to Catholicism (Brinkmeyer, p. 74), what differs is primarily Gordon's attitude toward the role faith could play in the lives of her characters. In her earlier fiction, religious faith is either an oddity, one that can change an individual's habits but not affect the greater community (Ed Mortimer in *The Garden of Adonis*), or a more destructive force, a narrow-minded extremism that isolates and destroys (Reverend Murrow in *Green Centuries*). But beginning with "The Presence," Gordon creates more positive images of the power of religious faith.

These images, however, do not reveal a significant reshaping of Gordon's fictional concerns. In "The Presence," Gordon picks up story lines and characters she had intended to use in *Aleck Maury, Sportsman* more than a decade earlier, specifically the impact that Maury's Aunt Victoria, a devoutly religious woman, had on his character development. In this final story, Maury is still selfish and self-absorbed, yet, as Gordon foreshadowed in her earlier novel, his passion for hunting and fishing cannot sustain him. Too old and infirm to pursue sport, Maury is increasingly dependent on others. Consequently, when his landlady's marriage is shattered by her husband's infidelity, Maury wallows in self-pity, worrying about where he will live if the couple divorces and sells the boardinghouse. And he blames the women involved. "*Women!*" Maury shouts. "They'll rock the world if they don't look out!" (*Collected Stories,* p. 119). Yet just as Gordon once used the women in her novel to correct Maury's perspective, in "The Presence" she undercuts Maury's views with allusions to the Virgin Mary and Juno. Ultimately, the memory of his favorite aunt, her faith, and her death leads Maury to the verge of religious conversion.

Gordon develops the idea that women of faith can lead men to salvation in her subsequent novels, although she does so by the indirection characteristic of her earlier fiction. None of the female characters in *The Strange Children* are cast in sympathetic light: they are helpless, ineffectual, or even insane. Yet the men are no better, relying solely on themselves and their intellects. Through references to Saint Martha and the Virgin Mary, Gordon exposes the limitations of such reliance.

She continues this critique in *The Malefactors,* using a quote from Jacques Maritain's essay "The Frontiers of Poetry"—"It is for Adam to interpret the voices that Eve hears"—as her novel's epigraph. Combining Jungian archetypes with stories of Christian saints and classical heroes, Gordon creates a highly symbolic world underpinning her conversion story. Several new themes develop from Gordon's Catholic faith—including, as Ross Labrie notes, themes of acceptance (p. 46) and the need for "balance between the rational/analytical and the creative/affective sides" of human nature (p. 44) as well as a "belief that the ancient Greeks reached a degree of wisdom just short of the Christian revelation" (p. 45). Yet these ideas can also be seen as extensions of Gordon's earliest fictional concerns. Dream sequences recall her preoccupation with underground streams, literal and metaphorical, present in her fiction from *Penhally* onward. Overt and symbolic references to Greek mythology highlight Gordon's love for the classics. And her focus on the need for balance between the analytical (male) and creative (female) aspects of humanity reiterates Gordon's earlier examinations of the differences in men and women's lives.

Gordon discusses her conversion and her views on the relationship between art and faith in several essays, including "The Art and Mystery of Faith," "Letters to a Monk," and "Some Readings and Misreadings." Drawing on Jacques Maritain's work in *Art and Scholasticism*, Gordon asserts that "the fiction writer's imagination often operates within the pattern of Christian symbolism" although it may do so sometimes "without the artist's conscious knowledge [and] almost against his will" ("Some Readings," pp. 385, 388). According to Gordon," there is only [one] plot (the scheme of Redemption) and . . . any short story, or novel, any fiction . . . is a splinter, so to speak, of that plot—if it's good" ("Letters," p. 10). Yet Gordon disparages writers like Evelyn Waugh who place the demands of religious orthodoxy above the craft of fiction.

## SURVEY OF CRITICISM

Of the early criticism, Andrew Lytle's 1949 article for the *Sewanee Review* stands out, containing a perceptive reading of Gordon's fiction. In 1966, Frederick P. W. McDowell published the first book-length study of Gordon, but this volume suffers from the fact that both Gordon and Tate manipulated public perception of their lives and works. For example, McDowell erroneously describes Gordon's marriage as "a happy and understanding relationship" in which Gordon was "encouraged to devote herself, without dissipation of her energies, to the artist's career" (p. 7). W. J. Stuckey's 1972 book includes similar inaccuracies, due in part to his reliance on McDowell and on Gordon's haphazard memory for dates. More useful is Louise Cowan's 1956 article which offers a perceptive analysis of Gordon's female characters, proposing that Gordon is writing only "one story . . . [of] man's search for grace in a fallen world" (p. 26). Many of the works published after Gordon's death rely on McDowell and Stuckey. Rose Ann C. Fraistat's *Caroline Gordon as Novelist and Woman of Letters* gives a thoughtful account of Gordon's journalistic career. Echoing earlier critics, however, Fraistat overlooks influences other than Tate.

The spring 1990 issue of the *Southern Quarterly* features a collection of essays on Gordon given at a November 1985 symposium at Austin Peavy State University in Clarksville, Tennessee. Most notable is Anne Boyle's essay in which she looks at "the gradual disappearance or devaluation of the female voice" in Gordon's fiction (p. 85).

Three biographies of Gordon exist which attempt to correct earlier misperceptions and misrepresentations of Gordon's life and work. Ann Waldron's 1987 work is a very accessible narrative biography. Although it includes no critical discussion of Gordon's writing, Waldron's book is especially effective in revealing the disparity between Gordon's life and the increasingly conservative maxims she espoused. Veronica Makowsky's 1989 biography of Gordon includes new information on Gordon's first, unpublished novel, gleaned from interviews with Gordon shortly before her death. Suggesting Gordon was important only in her connection to Tate, however, Makowsky virtually ignores the first thirty and last twenty-five years of Gordon's life.

My 1995 biography, *The Underground Stream: The Life and Art of Caroline Gordon*, offers a more complete account of Gordon's life. Through careful analysis of unpublished letters, previously overlooked newspaper columns, and manuscript revisions, *The Underground Stream* provides a study of Gordon's development as a writer as well as her deliberate attempts to fashion and control her personal and professional reputation.

Robert Brinkmeyer is one of only a few critics to focus on Gordon as a Catholic writer. His *Three Catholic Writers of the Modern South* offers some useful comparison between the fictional concerns of Gordon and Flannery O'Connor, yet Brinkmeyer clearly dislikes Gordon's post-conversion writing. He sees her "artistic vision" as "noticeably diminished," suffering from "thinness" and "absence . . . of the many tensions that had earlier fired her imagination and had added depth to her fiction" (p. 100).

More useful is Ross Labrie's study of Gordon in *The Catholic Imagination in American Literature*. Basing his observations on more accurate and comprehensive biographical knowledge, Labrie places Gordon's fictional concerns in historical and theological contexts, differentiating between Gordon's views and those of Tate. His analysis of Gordon's later novels is thorough and thought provoking, highlighting both achievements in and problems with her work.

## BIBLIOGRAPHY

### Works by Caroline Gordon

#### *Novels*

*Penhally.* 1931. New York: Cooper Square, 1971.

*Aleck Maury, Sportsman.* 1934. Carbondale: Southern Illinois University Press, 1980.
*The Garden of Adonis.* 1937. New York: Cooper Square, 1971.
*None Shall Look Back.* New York: Charles Scribner's Sons, 1937.
*Green Centuries.* 1941. New York: Cooper Square, 1971.
*The Women on the Porch.* 1944. New York: Cooper Square, 1971.
*The Strange Children.* 1951. New York: Cooper Square, 1971.
*The Malefactors.* New York: Harcourt, Brace and Company, 1956.
*The Glory of Hera.* Garden City, New York: Doubleday and Company, 1972.

### Short-Story Collections

*The Forest of the South.* New York: Charles Scribner's Sons, 1945.
*Old Red and Other Stories.* New York: Scribner's, 1963.
*The Collected Stories of Caroline Gordon.* New York: Farrar, Straus, and Giroux, 1981.

### Nonfiction

*The House of Fiction,* with Allen Tate. New York: Charles Scribner's Sons, 1950.
"The Art and Mystery of Faith." *Newman Annual* (1953): 55–62.
"Some Readings and Misreadings." *Sewanee Review* 61 (1953): 384–407.
"How I Learned to Write Novels." *Books on Trial* 15.3 (November 1956): 111–12; 160–63.
*How to Read a Novel.* New York: Viking Press, 1957.
"Flannery O'Connor's *Wise Blood*." *Critique* 11.2 (Spring 1958): 3–10.
"Flannery O'Connor—A Tribute." *Esprit* 8 (Winter 1964): 28.
"Katherine Anne Porter and the ICM." *Harper's* 229 (November 1964): 146–48.
"Letters to a Monk." *Ramparts* 3 (December 1964): 4–10.
"Foreword." *Flannery O'Connor: Voice of the Peacock,* by Kathleen Feeley. New Brunswick, New Jersey: Rutgers University Press, 1971. ix-xii.
*The Southern Mandarins: Letters of Caroline Gordon to Sally Wood, 1924–1937.* Ed. Sally Wood. Baton Rouge: Louisiana State University Press, 1984.

### Works about Caroline Gordon

Boyle, Anne M. "The Promise of Polyphony, the Monotony of Monologue: Voice and Silence in Caroline Gordon's Later Novels." *Southern Quarterly* 28.3 (Spring 1990): 71–87.
Brinkmeyer, Robert H. *Three Catholic Writers of the Modern South.* Jackson: University Press of Mississippi, 1985.
Cowan, Louise. "Nature and Grace in Caroline Gordon." *Critique: Studies in Modern Fiction* 1.1 (1956): 11–27.
Fraistat, Rose Ann C. *Caroline Gordon as Novelist and Woman of Letters.* Baton Rouge: Louisiana State University Press, 1984.
Jonza, Nancylee Novell. *The Underground Stream: The Life and Art of Caroline Gordon.* Athens: University of Georgia Press, 1995.
Labrie, Ross. *The Catholic Imagination in American Literature.* Columbia: University of Missouri Press, 1997.
Lytle, Andrew. "Caroline Gordon and the Historic Image." *Sewanee Review* 57 (Autumn 1949): 560–86.

Makowsky, Veronica A. *Caroline Gordon: A Biography.* New York: Oxford University Press, 1989.

McDowell, Frederick P. W. *Caroline Gordon.* Minneapolis: University of Minnesota Press, 1966.

Stuckey, W. J. *Caroline Gordon.* New York: Twayne, 1972.

Waldron, Ann. *Close Connections: Caroline Gordon and the Southern Renaissance.* New York: G. P. Putnam's Sons, 1987.

NANCYLEE NOVELL JONZA

# MARY GORDON
# (1949– )

## BIOGRAPHY

Born in Far Rockaway, Long Island, in 1949, Mary Catherine Gordon, the daughter of a Jewish immigrant, David Gordon, and a woman of Italian Irish descent, Anna Gagliano, grew up in Valley Stream, a working-class, Irish Catholic neighborhood. Her father, who had converted from Judaism to orthodox Catholicism before she was born, raised her to be educated and devout: he taught her to read when she was three, and introduced her to Latin, Greek, and literature. Due to illness, he stayed home with young Mary while her mother, despite the effects of polio, worked full time. He founded a number of unsuccessful right-wing Catholic magazines before he died in 1957, when Mary was eight. After her father's death, Mary and her mother lived with Mary's Irish grandmother and aunt. Gordon describes this time as painful: she was sent to an academically weak Catholic school, and was rarely given the opportunity to discuss the literature, art, and ideas that her father had sparked within her. As Gordon wrote in her memoir about her father, *The Shadow Man* (1996), whenever she did something that the cloistered sisters at the school did not like, they would say to her, "That's the Jew in you" (p. 20).

In the late 1960s, Gordon escaped to Barnard College, where she had won a scholarship, in order to experience the non-Catholic world. She promptly lost her virginity, her political naiveté, and her Catholic faith. Although she has since compromised with Catholicism, she was very disturbed by the sexual puritanism of the Church that she faced during college: "I think that the tragedy of the Catholic Church in the twentieth century is that it has put so much energy into forbidding sexual freedom. It turned itself into a kind of very perverse sexual policeman, and it's eroded its own moral authority for that reason," she has stated (Lee, p. 221).

After Barnard, Gordon attended graduate school and drafted her dissertation on Virginia Woolf while also publishing poems and short stories. While researching her dissertation in London, Gordon wrote her first novel, *Final*

*Payments* (1978). After the novel was published to much acclaim, Gordon was able to leave her $11,000 a year teaching job in Poughkeepsie, New York, and begin work on her second novel, *The Company of Women* (1980).

Today, with six novels, a collection of short stories, and a memoir—in addition to numerous uncollected essays and reviews—Gordon is married to Arthur Cash, and lives with her two teenaged children, Anna and David. She also teaches classes at Barnard where she is Millicent C. McIntosh Professor of English.

## MAJOR THEMES

Gordon was reared in the orthodox Irish Catholic Church that drastically changed with Vatican II. She is an identifiable Catholic writer in both her moral sensibility and her subject matter. In her fiction and essays, Gordon explores the relationship between being a woman, a Catholic, and a writer, and the tensions that result from these very different roles. From a feminist perspective, Gordon portrays a Church whose morality is based not on Jesus' *compassionate* ethic of care, but on an often abstract ethic of judgment; yet, paradoxically, she then reveals the immaturity of an *extreme* ethic of care. Ultimately, it is only by integrating both ethics (transformed into orthodox Catholicism and secular feminism in Gordon's fiction) that her heroines have a chance to take responsibility for their own lives. In *Final Payments*, the heroine is formed by religion and is dominated by the letter rather than the spirit of the Catholic concept of goodness. Catholicism is gendered in *The Company of Women*, where the heroine fights the battle between the spirit, enforced upon her by a well-meaning yet domineering father figure, and the flesh, inherent in human relations. In *Men and Angels* (1985), where the non-Catholic heroine again tries to achieve a balance between the spirit and the flesh, religion becomes a potentially dangerous fanaticism. Gordon's collection of short stories, *Temporary Shelter* (1987), covers similar moral themes of faith and love, and anticipates the author's next novel with several stories on being Irish in America. *The Other Side* (1989) is a portrait of the indelible influences of family, religion, and culture on several generations of the MacNamara family. And in *The Rest of Life* (1993), Catholicism is firmly in the past, a piece of nostalgia more than a powerful force.

One of the most important and controversial results of Gordon's Catholic themes is that they have opened the doors to the uninitiated and allowed them to see Catholicism as both a way of thought and a "discipline of life with rituals and restraints" (Breslin, p. xiv). It is this disclosure of secrets, especially to a perceived secular, and hostile, audience, that most disturbs Gordon's Irish American Church and her own family. As Gordon later related, at a family funeral her uncle expressed to her his opinion of her work: "I just want to tell you that I can't stand your books. None of us can. I tried the first one, I couldn't get past the first chapter. The second one I couldn't even get into; I didn't even want to open it up. I didn't even buy it; I wouldn't waste my money" (*Good Boys*, p. 200). Gordon's latest works, however, cover slightly different ground. *The Shadow Man* is a memoir detailing Gordon's search for the truth about her father, a man who—ambiguously—once told Gordon "I love you more than God" (p. xviii). And *Spending: A Utopian Divertimento* (1998), a fairy tale about a Catholic woman artist who gains the freedom to paint when a wealthy man offers to be her muse, continues Gordon's moral questioning, this time about the effects of money, power, gratitude, and obligation.

Gordon creates heroines who try to redefine the Church's definitions of faith, hope, and love—the three Cardinal Virtues—in the modern world. They are unable to go backwards, yet are not comfortable leaving behind their traditions completely. However, her heroines usually come to terms with these tensions and attempt to integrate the Church's moral standards with their feminist perspectives.

Gordon's sense of morality is strongly influenced by her Catholic upbringing: her fiction often examines the concept of goodness, and her heroines realize that a fallible human being has a difficult path in achieving it. For Gordon, the definition of "good" is not the passive state conditioned in the "good Catholic girl," but a much more active moral stance that requires a decision. In *Final Payments*, for example, Eleanor admits that she hates persuading people to do what she requests, and when Isabel asks, "How do you get what you want?" Eleanor replies, "I suppose I still think that if I'm very good things will come" (p. 53). And Isabel backs out of making a decision when she accepts her lover's wife's definition of herself as a "good person gone wrong," who can get back on track simply by leaving the man alone. In *Men and Angels*, Anne Foster recognizes that people consider her to be a good person, but "She knew, though, that that was wrong; she knew that goodness shouldn't be confused with safety" (p. 10). All three characters are made to suffer because they have adopted a passive state of goodness, just as they have passively accepted others' definitions of themselves.

The concept of goodness as a passive state is not morally valid, according to Gordon's fiction and essays. In an essay on American literature, Gordon distinguishes between the American concept of goodness or innocence and the European sense of the word. In American fiction, Gordon states, innocence is often portrayed as a passive state that a character stoically maintains despite evil circumstances, whereas in European and British fiction, innocence is viewed as an active and conscious choice not to do evil (*Good Boys*, p. 4). Part of the development of Gordon's heroines thus requires a dismantling of the "good girl" image, and a reexamination of the deeper definition of the term. In *Men and Angels*, Anne and Jane have a conversation about goodness that reflects this idea:

"How I hate the word 'goodness.' What an obstacle it is to the moral life," said Jane.
"Do you find goodness and morality incompatible?" Anne asked.

"Of course not. But the term 'goodness' has been so perverted, so corrupted, it now covers only two or three virtues when there are hundreds." (p. 200)

In other words, the Jansenist Irish Catholic dualistic moral code is too simplistic. Terms such as "good" and "evil" need to be more complex, because the world is so complex. The Baltimore Catechism's questions and stock answers do not take into consideration that there is often more than one answer, that there is more to being "good" than self-sacrifice and passivity. Gordon recognizes the need to be morally relative, but without losing the old codes. In her story "Safe," for example, the narrator looks back on her two divorces and wonders, "Broke all sorts of laws: the state's, the church's. Caused a good man pain. And yet it has turned out well. Everyone is happier than ever. I do not understand this. It makes a mockery of the moral life, which I am supposed to believe in" (*Temporary Shelter*, p. 171).

In an essay on abortion (she is pro-choice), Gordon wrote, "The desire for security of imagination, for typological fixity, particularly in the area of 'the good,' is an understandable desire" (*Good Boys*, p. 144), but it is not an acceptable one. In other words, in order to be moral, one must admit a little chaos in life; the answers aren't always clear. But the fear of chaos is quite human. Gordon's characters desperately try to order the naturally chaotic world. In *Men and Angels*, Anne's old, heavy furniture is ruined by the overflowing water and blood from the bathtub where Laura kills herself. Anchoring herself to physical structures does not protect Anne from the chaos of life. In *The Other Side*, Magdalene fears the world outside her room. According to critic Marcia Bundy Seabury, "A physical structure gives her life shape. She is immobilized within it; her relationships with her mother and daughter too have set, have hardened into paralysis" (p. 50).

Many of Gordon's heroines think longingly of a near-death, or passive state, where moral responsibility is irrelevant. Images of drowning, fog, and invisibility are found throughout her fiction. In *Final Payments*, Isabel often feels as if she is drowning in feelings or in the disorder of life she can't control, which is why she cries upon finding some rotten broccoli in her father's refrigerator. In the story "Immaculate Man," where the nameless narrator passively watches herself have an affair with a priest, images of drowning and fog play a significant role. When the narrator drives with Father Clement to the Motherhouse, she foreshadows the sex they will later have while she is laid up at the convent because of the flu: "The fog came around the car like water. It was as though we were drowning in silver air" (*Rest of Life*, p. 15). She will not accept moral responsibility for their affair.

In Gordon's novels, although Catholicism is not completely rejected, neither is a full return to the Catholic life a positive option for the protagonists. In the battle between the sacred and the secular, neither wins; only a combination of the two can offer Gordon's heroines any hope of happiness.

## SURVEY OF CRITICISM

Most literary critics either love or hate Mary Gordon's work. She is regarded as either relentlessly honest in her portrayal of the cold Irish Catholic family or she is superficial and angry in her depiction of anything Catholic. Some critics, surprised by a twentieth-century novel with nineteenth-century themes of morality, goodness, and self-sacrifice, compare Gordon to Jane Austen, Doris Lessing, or Flannery O'Connor. However, not all critics agree. Charles Fanning argues that novels like *The Other Side* and *Final Payments* are filled with hostile generalizations about the working-class Irish and, in the former book, about the Irish people as a whole. For example, religious working-class Irish are portrayed by Gordon as fearful of intellectualism, and as for the Irish people in general, "Unhappiness was bred into the bone" (*Other Side,* p. 160). For Fanning, these stereotypes are not only not true, but also "mean-spirited" (*Irish Voice,* p. 330). On the other hand, John Leonard admits that Mary Gordon's depiction of Irish Catholics made him face the coldness of Irishness that "I ought to know and wish I didn't" (p. 655).

Several critics are otherwise disturbed by Gordon's fiction: Francine DuPlessix Gray complains that Gordon's characters are either "cardboard figures" or "as flimsy as bookmarks" (p. 24); James Wolcott notes that her "Catholic imagery is used decoratively, for ticky-tack symbolism" (p. 21); and Brenda Becker complains of *The Company of Women* that "[h]ere again is a wilted flower of Catholic girlhood just aching for defloration at the hands of modernity" (p. 29). Finally, Carol Iannone is disturbed by Gordon's version of Catholicism, and writes that all Gordon is really doing is replacing Catholic orthodoxy with feminist orthodoxy. But Marcia Bundy Seabury asserts that this is not true: Gordon's fiction always ends on an ambiguous note, feminism is not presented as the new orthodoxy, and there is "no easy, self-centered resolution" in her works (p. 37).

Other critics see Gordon's work as affirming Catholic values. Anita Gandolfo suggests that Gordon's first three novels mirror Teilhard de Chardin's pattern of spiritual development: "*Final Payments* offers a vision of inner unification; the *Company of Women* is about the nature of affiliation and its importance; and *Men and Angels* indicates the need for a relationship with the Absolute to achieve full humanity" (p. 169). Writing for the *Christian Century*, critic Trudy Bush describes *The Rest of Life* as an exploration of the "intelligent, reflective woman at midlife who is trying to make sense of a world that is, for her, bereft of transcendent meaning" (p. 1164). Although most critics admired this collection, Bush confirms one concern that several critics voiced: the over-preoccupation with sex and the desire for it to transform one's life. Religion and women's friendships, even motherhood, are minor issues in these stories, and the overwhelming focus on sexuality seems unrealistic. Other critics, like Kathryn Hughes, gush over the novellas, for the quality of the prose and for Gordon's reliance "on minute observation and a personal, poetic language to create narratives that are as dense, mysterious and compelling as any more extrovert tale" (p. 39).

As with her earlier works, *The Shadow Man* and *Spending: A Utopian Divertimento* have also received mixed critical response. Sara Maitland gives *Shadow Man* an "F" grade: "The book is not simply ill-conceived, it is badly structured, sloppily written, and deplorably self-indulgent" (p. 5). Meanwhile, John Leonard, who has reviewed nearly every Gordon work for the *Nation*, highly praises the memoir: he compares it to Nabokov's acclaimed *Speak, Memory*, and calls it "wounding, refulgent and redemptive" (p. 27). *Spending* has surprised most critics and readers: here, Gordon's moral sensibility is still apparent, but the novel itself is described by critic Mary McNamara as "[a] combination bodice-buster, economic inquiry . . . a hedonistic romp that also carefully considers the nature of money and power, of gratitude and obligation" (p. 2). In fact, McNamara reports that Gordon once defended the book as "a very Catholic novel": "For one thing, [Gordon] argues, Catholicism, with its reliance on mystical ritual, its use of parable and metaphor, its emphasis on the physical manifestations of the spirit, is one of the more sensual religions" (p. 2). Dan Cryer, a long-time Gordon fan, believes that the novel's strength is in its depiction of the moral dilemma of its protagonist, Monica. But he also believes that she is the work's only fully developed character and that reading *Spending* is like reading an essay rather than fiction.

## BIBLIOGRAPHY

### Works by Mary Gordon

*Final Payments*. New York: Random House, 1978.
*The Company of Women*. New York: Random House, 1980.
*Men and Angels*. New York: Random House, 1985.
*Temporary Shelter*. New York: Random House, 1987.
*The Other Side*. New York: Penguin Books, 1989.
*Good Boys and Dead Girls and Other Essays*. New York: Viking, 1991.
*The Rest of Life*. New York: Viking, 1993.
*The Shadow Man: A Daughter's Search for Her Father*. New York: Random House, 1996.
*Spending: A Utopian Divertimento*. New York: Scribner's, 1998.

### Works about Mary Gordon

Becker, Brenda L. "Virgin Martyrs." *American Spectator* 14 (August 1981): 28–32.
Breslin, John B., S.J., ed. *The Substance of Things Hoped For: Short Fiction by Modern Catholic Authors*. New York: Doubleday, 1987.
Bush, Trudy. Rev. of *The Rest of Life*, by Mary Gordon. *Christian Century* 17 November 1993: 1162–64.
Cryer, Dan. "A Feminist Steps Lightly into the Romantic." *Newsday* 5 March 1998: B2.

DuPlessix Gray, Francine. "A Religious Romance." *New York Times Book Review* 15 February 1981: 1.

Fanning, Charles. *The Irish Voice in America: Irish-American Fiction From the 1760s to the 1980s.* Lexington: University Press of Kentucky, 1990.

Gandolfo, Anita. *Testing the Faith: The New Catholic Fiction in America.* Westport, Connecticut: Greenwood Press, 1992.

Hughes, Kathryn. Rev. of *The Rest of Life,* by Mary Gordon. *New Statesman and Society* 28 January 1994: 38–40.

Iannone, Carol. "The Secret of Mary Gordon's Success." *Commentary* 6 June 1985: 62–66.

Labrie, Ross. *The Catholic Imagination in American Literature.* Columbia: University of Missouri Press, 1998.

Lee, Don. "About Mary Gordon." *Ploughshares* 23 (22 September 1997): 218–25.

Leonard, John. "Booknotes." *Nation* 27 November 1989: 655.

——. "Booknotes." *Nation* 6 May 1996: 24–27.

Mahon, John. "Mary Gordon: The Struggle with Love." *American Women Writing Fiction.* Ed. Mickey Pearlman. Lexington: University Press of Kentucky, 1989. 47–68.

Maitland, Sara. Rev. of *The Shadow Man,* by Mary Gordon. *Commonweal* 17 May 1996: 17–19.

McNamara, Mary. "Mary Quite Contrary." *Los Angeles Times* 7 April 1998: E2.

Payant, Katherin B. *Becoming and Bonding: Contemporary Feminism and Popular Fiction by American Women Writers.* Westport, Connecticut: Greenwood Press, 1993.

Seabury, Marcia Bundy. "Of Belief and Unbelief: The Novels of Mary Gordon." *Christianity and Literature* 40.1 (Autumn 1990): 37–55.

Ward, Susan. "In Search of 'Ordinary Human Happiness': Rebellion and Affirmation in Mary Gordon's Novels." *Faith of a (Woman) Writer.* Ed. Alice Kessler-Harris. Westport, Connecticut: Greenwood Press, 1988. 303–8.

Wolcott, James. "More Catholic Than the Pope." *Esquire* 3 March 1981: 21, 23.

## STACEY DONOHUE

# Louise Imogen Guiney
# (1861–1920)

## BIOGRAPHY

As America's Southern states seceded from the Union and the threat of war loomed over the country, Louise Imogen Guiney was born to Julia and Patrick Guiney on January 17, 1861, in Roxbury, Massachusetts. Guiney's earliest memories are of the American Civil War and her family's fierce allegiance to the Union. Encamping with her father's unit in Virginia, the young Louise cultivated a hero worship of her father, who led the Ninth Massachusetts Volunteers and who eventually attained the rank of General, the first Irish Catholic to hold such a position in the Union army. In 1865, however, Patrick Guiney was shot in the head and was rushed back to Massachusetts, where he was to suffer miserably until his death in 1877. Although her father's military career came to an end with his return to the North, Louise Guiney was profoundly affected by General Guiney's wartime experience. Military valor continued to be one of her chief fascinations as a child, and later as a poet and essayist. A good student at the convent schools she attended, Guiney nevertheless displayed a martial spirit, a resistance to conventional "female" activities such as cooking and sewing, and a strong identification with literary and historical warriors.

After her 1879 graduation from Elmhurst, a school owned by the Convent of the Sacred Heart in Providence, Rhode Island, Guiney pursued a career in poetry and essay writing. Her first several books—*Songs at the Start* (poems, 1884), *Goose-Quill Papers* (essays, 1885), and *The White Sail and Other Poems* (1887)—met with critical success among the Boston literati. In 1893, however, Guiney decided to try her hand at more prosaic work and was appointed local postmistress at Auburndale, Massachusetts. Unfortunately, Guiney's post office was boycotted in 1894 by many of Auburndale's Protestant residents who resented having a Roman Catholic in charge of their mail. Because Guiney depended on the proceeds of stamp sales to eke out her meager living, she was obliged to live on the kindness of richer friends, such as

Keats collector Fred Holland Day. Despite her penury and her postal martyr-dom, Guiney was still creatively prolific in this period, publishing both another book of verses and a collection of biographies, *A Little English Gallery* (1894).

In 1895, Guiney was given a six-month leave of absence which she spent in England and Wales, making pilgrimages to literary sites such as the dilapidated grave of poet Henry Vaughan, for which she began a restoration campaign. Also at this time, Guiney began to collaborate with Gwenllian Morgan, of Brecon, Wales, a fellow Vaughanian. The two women planned to publish a de-finitive biography of Vaughan, which was never completed.

After her return to the United States, Guiney continued working in the post office until 1897, when she resigned shortly after recovering from a mental and physical breakdown. She then held a position at the Boston public library until 1900. In February of 1901, Guiney boarded a ship bound for England. She took up residence in Oxford, where she would live for the rest of her life, with the exception of two years, 1908–1910, when she returned to Massachu-setts to care for her dying mother. At Oxford, Guiney dedicated her time to compiling editions of relatively obscure, mostly seventeenth-century poets. Putting her scholarly work above all else, she spent long hours in the Bodleian, taxing her already poor eyesight and forgoing meals and fuel to scrape together enough money to buy books. The relative popularity of her work seems to have declined after 1910 or so, and from this period until her death on Novem-ber 2, 1920, Guiney lived in poverty and poor health.

Although she has never been widely read, Guiney did enjoy a certain popu-larity in her time among the literati of Boston, London, Dublin, and Oxford. She was acquainted with such luminaries as Henry Wadsworth Longfellow, Edmund Gosse, Oliver Wendell Holmes, Lionel Johnson, Katherine Tynan, Dora Sigerson, Clement Shorter, and even William Butler Yeats when he was still a poetic neophyte. Especially in her later years, Guiney was a recluse, choosing to spend her time with her books, but she maintained a lively corre-spondence with many poets, priests, and other intellectuals.

## MAJOR THEMES

Guiney's early poetry, to a large extent, mimics the style of nine-teenth-century male poets, such as Wordsworth and Longfellow, and employs "masculine" themes of adventure and martial valor rather than adopting the more domestic themes typical of Victorian women's poetry. Much of Guiney's fascination with war and military heroism stems from her own identification with her father and his military glory. This identification with the masculine marks much of Guiney's writing throughout her career. She sympathizes with male protagonists as diverse as Charles II, Blessed Edmund Campion, and Wil-liam Hazlitt, among others, but has very few sympathetic women as protago-nists in her work.

Around 1894, Guiney's heroic ideal shifted from the ultra-masculine mili-tary hero to the more contemplative literary and spiritual hero. In this year,

Guiney published *A Little English Gallery*, which contains biographies of Lady Danvers, Henry Vaughan, George Farquhar, Topham Beauclerk, Bennet Langton, and William Hazlitt. These more contemplative heroes, and the sixteenth, seventeenth, and eighteenth centuries in which they lived, became the chief subject of Guiney's later scholarship. Guiney's poetry also becomes more contemplative with *England and Yesterday* (1898), a book of meditations on the history of various sites in England, Wales, and Ireland, and the *Nine Sonnets Written at Oxford* (1895), which was privately published as a Christmas gift for her friends.

When Guiney moved to Oxford in 1901, she turned her attention from her poetry writing to reviving the work of "lost" poets. As early as 1897, she had published an edition of the poems of James Clarence Mangan, the mid–nineteenth century Irish poet and "translator." At Oxford, however, Guiney looked to the more distant past and focused her energies on sixteenth and seventeenth poets including Katherine Philips, Thomas Stanley, and Henry Vaughan. She worked on numerous editions of the works of these poets and of others, but many of her projects—including a life and works of William Alabaster, a biography of John Donne, and what was to be the definitive biography of "Henry Vaughan, Silurist"—were abandoned due to nervous strain and consequently never published.

In her later writing, Guiney turned her attention to more religious, usually Catholic, themes. Her last volume of new poetry, *The Martyr's Idyl*—which included a verse drama of the same name and shorter poems—deals with the themes of martyrdom and the presence of divinity in nature. The verse drama is based on the lives of Saints Theodora and Didymus and explores the tensions between indigenous religion and Christianity in pre-Constantinian Rome through their martyrdom. The shorter poems, such as "Virgo Gloriosa, Mater Amantissima" and "Orisons," demonstrate how Christianity—and in particular Roman Catholicism—can be practiced through observation of and reverence for the natural world. This identification of nature-spirituality with Catholicism is also evident in her editions of the works of other Catholic poets, especially that of Lionel Johnson to whom she ascribes a "Franciscan" spirit.

Guiney was dedicated to establishing the voices of lesser-known Catholic poets, especially of the early modern period. She spent her last days working on *Recusant Poets* (1938), which was only published posthumously. Co-edited by the Jesuit Father Geoffrey Bliss, this volume contains poetry by English Catholic poets of 1535–1735, from Saint Thomas More to Ben Jonson. The poetry Guiney and Bliss chose for this volume varies widely in content and form, the most common themes being laudatory odes for Catholic monarchs and nobles, contemplative poems on biblical themes, and songs and prayers dedicated to saints and the Blessed Virgin Mary.

Guiney also engaged in biographical work concerning less canonical Catholic reformers and martyrs. In 1904, she published *Hurrell Froude*, a biography

of the Oxford Movement reformer who was far less well known than colleagues such as John Henry Newman. Several years later, she also published
*Blessed Edmund Campion* (1908), a biography that explores both the devout
Catholicism and the love of England harbored by the sixteenth-century recusant martyr. Both of these works, along with her selections in *Some Poems of
Lionel Johnson* (1912), explore the connection between Catholicism and England, both of which Guiney loved deeply but sometimes found hard to reconcile in light of the Reformation and subsequent persecution of Catholics in
England. Guiney's biographical and editorial work gave her a way of dealing
with this tension as seen in the lives of exemplary martyrs and in the writings of
poets who were devoted to both country and Church.

In addition to these biographical and editorial works, Guiney also published widely in Catholic periodicals such as *Catholic World, America, Ecclesiastical Review, Ave Maria,* and *American Catholic Quarterly Review.* In these
periodicals, she drew connections between modern and historical Catholic
spirituality, informing lay readers of the practices of Elizabethan Catholics, the
intersections of Church liturgy and English poetry, and the wisdom and works
of forgotten saints and poets. Always the advocate of other writers, Guiney
contributed biographical essays about fellow poets such as Gerard Manley
Hopkins and Paul Claudel. She also penned several biographical articles on
Chaucer, Edmund Campion, General Guiney, and Lionel Johnson for the
1907–1912 *Catholic Encyclopedia.*

## SURVEY OF CRITICISM

Because of Guiney's relative obscurity, most of what has been written
about her and her work has been highly biographical. E. M. Tenison's 1923
*Louise Imogen Guiney: Her Life and Works 1861–1920* is still the most comprehensive examination of Guiney's work itself. Tenison approaches
Guiney's life both as a literary friend and as a critic of her work. Excerpting
extensively from the author's letters and her writings, Tenison reconstructs
Guiney's methodology and philosophy of reading and writing and adds an
annotated bibliography of her major works at the end of the volume. Poet,
essayist, and good friend of Guiney's, Alice Brown also wrote an early biography. Although Brown's biography discusses the thought and diligence that
went into Guiney's work, it is much more a chatty personal recollection than
a scholarly endeavor. Henry G. Fairbanks's 1972 biography of Guiney is the
most thorough historical reconstruction of the writer's personal life and has a
useful bibliography that includes all the essays she published in popular,
scholarly, and religious periodicals, as well as the location of much archival
material. James B. Colvert's "Fred Holland Day, Louise Imogen Guiney, and
the Text of Stephen Crane's *The Black Riders*" discusses the little-known editorial role that Guiney played in the production of Crane's verse, and H.
Pearson Grundy's "Flourishes and Cadences: Letters of Bliss Carman and

Louise Imogen Guiney" considers the relationship, both intellectual and personal, that developed between the two poets in their epistolary correspondence.

Several other pieces of criticism examine Guiney as a product of her literary and historical contexts, especially with respect to gender issues. Sheila A. Tully's "Heroic Failures and the Literary Career of Louise Imogen Guiney" argues that Guiney's work never met with popular success because she attempted to embody a masculine ideal of martial heroism which hampered her career as a female. In her dissertation, "Convention and Counterpoint: Nineteenth-Century Women's Poetic Language," Janna Marie Knittel touches upon the contradictions between modernity (and modernism) and Victorian conventions that made it difficult for poets such as Guiney to achieve popular success. Laura Christine Wendorff's dissertation, "Race, Ethnicity, and the Voice of the 'Poetess,'" also examines Guiney in the context of other nineteenth-century women writers, arguing that Guiney, like Frances E.W. Harper, Emma Lazarus, and Ella Wheeler Wilcox, transformed the mythological construction of the nineteenth-century sentimental "poetess" by drawing on the ethnic and literary traditions of Irish Catholicism.

Guiney has also been examined as a Roman Catholic writer. Some earlier Catholic critics, such as Father Alexander Calvert and Katherine Brégy, contextualize Guiney's work within specific traditions. In *The Catholic Literary Revival*, Calvert categorizes Guiney with other *fin de siècle* American Catholic writers who had no truly appreciative audience, who were forced into exile, and who identified with Catholic traditions of other countries. Brégy, in *Poets and Pilgrims from Chaucer to Paul Claudel*, places Guiney in loose spiritual fellowship with writers as diverse as Chaucer, Katherine Tynan, and Thomas Lodge, in a series of essays more popularly biographical than scholarly. Brégy also sang Guiney's praises to a broader American Catholic audience in "The Catholic Note in Contemporary Poetry. IV. Louise Imogen Guiney," in which she goes so far as to call Guiney a "Christian Valkyrie" (p. 201). The most thorough treatment of Guiney as a contributor to Catholic thought is Pamela Nakis Schaeffer's dissertation, "The Countercultural Theology of Louise Imogen Guiney (1861–1920): American Catholic Poet, Expatriate and Social Critic." This work argues that not only was Guiney a scholar of Catholic poets, martyrs, and theologians, but that, in her resistance to progressivism and nationalism, Guiney herself contributed greatly to the formation of contemporary Catholic theology. Schaeffer argues that Guiney demonstrated this resistance by using individual heroic figures, instead of the monarchies or other establishments for which they fought, as exemplars of active faith.

## BIBLIOGRAPHY

### Works by Louise Imogen Guiney

*Songs at the Start*. Boston: Cupples, Upham & Co., 1884.

*Goose-Quill Papers.* Boston: Roberts Bros., 1885.
*The White Sail and Other Poems.* Boston: Ticknor & Co., 1887.
*A Roadside Harp: A Book of Verses.* Boston: Houghton, Mifflin, & Co., 1893.
*A Little English Gallery.* New York: Harper, 1894.
*Nine Sonnets Written at Oxford.* Cambridge: Cambridge University Press, 1895.
*Patrins.* Boston: Copeland & Day, 1897. Boston: Small, Maynard, & Co., 1901;
    London: David Nutt, 1901.
*England and Yesterday.* London: Grant Richards, 1898.
*The Martyr's Idyl and Shorter Poems.* Boston: Houghton, Mifflin, & Co., 1900; Cambridge: Riverside Press, 1900.
*Hurrell Froude: Memoranda and Contents.* London: Methuen & Co., 1904.
*Katherine Philips, "The Matchless Orinda."* Hull, Yorkshire: J. R. Tutin, 1904.
*Thomas Stanley: His Original Lyrics.* Hull, Yorkshire: J. R. Tutin, 1907.
*Blessed Edmund Campion.* London: Macdonald & Evans, 1908. Second edition, London: Burns, Oates & Washbourne, 1914.
*Happy Ending: The Collected Lyrics of Louise Imogen Guiney.* Ed. Louise Imogen Guiney. Boston: Houghton, Mifflin & Co., 1909.
*Some Poems of Lionel Johnson.* London: Elkin Matthews, 1912.
*Letters of Louise Imogen Guiney.* Ed. Grace Guiney. 2 vols. New York: Harper & Brothers, 1926.
*Recusant Poets, Vol. I.* Ed. Louise Imogen Guiney. London: Sheed & Ward, 1938.


## Works about Louise Imogen Guiney

Brégy, Katherine. "The Catholic Note in Contemporary Poetry. IV. Louise Imogen Guiney." *America* 12.8 (5 December 1914): 200–01.
——. "Louise Imogen Guiney." *Poets and Pilgrims from Chaucer to Paul Claudel.* New York: Benziger Brothers, 1925. 169–90.
Brown, Alice. *Louise Imogen Guiney.* New York: Macmillan Co., 1921.
Calvert, Alexander, S. J. *The Catholic Literary Revival.* Milwaukee: Bruce Publishing Co., 1935. 205–09.
Colvert, James B. "Fred Holland Day, Louise Imogen Guiney, and the Text of Stephen Crane's *The Black Riders.*" *American Literary Realism* 28.2 (Winter 1995–96): 18–24.
Fairbanks, Henry G. *Louise Imogen Guiney: Laureate of the Lost.* Albany, New York: Magi Books, 1972.
Grundy, H. Pearson. "Flourishes and Cadences: Letters of Bliss Carman and Louise Imogen Guiney." *Dalhousie Review* 55 (1975): 205–06.
Knittel, Janna Marie. "Convention and Counterpoint: Nineteenth-Century Women's Poetic Language." Diss. University of Oregon, 1995.
Schaeffer, Pamela Nakis. "The Countercultural Theology of Louise Imogen Guiney (1861–1920): American Catholic Poet, Expatriate and Social Critic." Diss. Saint Louis University, 1991.
Tenison, E. M. *Louise Imogen Guiney: Her Life and Works, 1861–1920.* London: Macmillan & Co., 1923.
Tully, Sheila A. "Heroic Failures and the Literary Career of Louise Imogen Guiney." *American Transcendental Quarterly* 47–48 (Summer–Fall 1980): 171–86.

Wendorff, Laura Christine. "Race, Ethnicity, and the Voice of the 'Poetess' in the Lives and Works of Four Late-Nineteenth-Century American Women Poets: Frances E. W. Harper, Emma Lazarus, Louise Guiney, and Ella Wheeler Wilcox." Diss. University of Michigan, 1992.

ANNE M. ENENBACH

# MADAME GUYON
# (1648–1717)

## BIOGRAPHY

In Catholic circles, Jeanne-Marie Bouvier de la Motte Guyon's name has been chiefly associated with the Quietist controversy that raged in late-seventeenth-century France. In Protestant circles, she has long been esteemed as an inspiring spiritual writer who overcame adversity to live the life of faith. She seems to have seen herself simply as a believer touched by God and impelled to tell of that irresistible touch. She was, to use her own image, a "spiritual torrent": "We who are believers are like rivers. There are rivers that flow very slowly, arriving late to their destination. Others move more rapidly than that. The third type moves so fast that none dare sail upon it. It is a mad, headlong torrent" (*Spiritual Torrents,* p. 2).

Jeanne was born in Montargis, France, in 1648, the daughter of a royal procurator and his second wife. She recalled feeling neglected in childhood. From the age of two, she was a frequent boarder at a series of monasteries, receiving there little intellectual training but rather a fervent, if eclectic, spiritual formation. In these years she was introduced to the life of Jeanne de Chantal, a widow-become-religious, which served as an inspiration and her introduction to interior prayer. Her early desire to enter religious life was thwarted by illness, and just before her sixteenth birthday her family arranged a marriage with Jacques Guyon, a wealthy businessman twenty-eight years her senior.

The marriage was a sad one, plagued by illness, loss, and the domination of a jealous mother-in-law. The union produced five children, two of whom died young, intensifying Jeanne Guyon's sorrows. During these difficult married years, she developed an intense devotional life and, in 1668, experienced an inner transformation which resulted in a form of non-conceptual prayer she termed the "prayer of faith." Guided by a Benedictine abbess and a priest renowned as a spiritual director, Madame Guyon's interior life blossomed.

In 1676 Guyon's husband died, leaving his young widow a considerable fortune. Her intention was never again to lose her liberty, so she pursued an unusual course for women of the time by devoting herself to charitable works and piety outside the confines of cloister and marriage. She began the peripatetic lifestyle that was to be hers for much of the next twenty years. On July 22, 1680, Madame Guyon underwent another seminal inner event, which left her with the assurance of being led by a will greater than her own. This led her to Gex where she was invited to endow a community, the "New Catholics," which ministered to converts from Protestantism. Meanwhile, Madame Guyon became reacquainted with a Barnabite priest, Francis LaCombe, who became her spiritual director. Questionable practices in the "New Catholics" led her to withdraw support, and soon she found herself embroiled in a disagreement with the bishop and her half-brother priest, both of whom had an interest in the disposition of her wealth. This caused her to relinquish legal responsibility for her children and inheritance but left her with a generous lifetime pension.

A 1682 retreat under the direction of LaCombe produced the first of her voluminous writings. *Les Torrents spirituels* [Spiritual Torrents] came from her pen as automatic writing under the compulsion of a spirit she felt was not her own. This early work, considered by some to be her finest, circulated in manuscript form. In the same period, Madame Guyon claimed for herself the gift of spiritual maternity and came to believe that she was destined to an apostolic life dedicated to the spread of concepts of mystical prayer and abandonment of self. She seems to have enjoyed success, for soon she attracted the disapproval of local ecclesiastics sensitive to the anti-mystical sentiment then spreading throughout France.

With LaCombe, Madame Guyon moved to Grenoble where laity and religious alike enthusiastically received her teachings. The opposition of the bishop there curbed neither her apostolic activities nor her creative inspiration. Within six months in 1684, she produced the bulk of her mystical commentary on the Bible that would later be printed (1713–1715) in twenty volumes. And her first published book, *Moyen court et très facile de faire oraison* [A Short Method of Prayer], written previously, appeared. Peregrinations through France and a refusal from the Bishop of Geneva to allow her to settle in his diocese finally found her in 1686 in Paris.

In the capital, Guyon became intimate with the moral elite of the French court, especially the Dukes Beauvillier and Chevreuse and their wives. But their enthusiasm for her teachings did not prevent conflict once again with her half-brother priest who was assisting in a plan to marry Madame Guyon's daughter to the great-nephew of Harlay, Archbishop of Paris. When Madame Guyon refused her consent, the charge of Quietism provided a lever intended to dislodge her. It was a grave charge. In Rome in that year, the Spanish priest Miguel de Molinos was formally condemned for his Quietist teachings.

Both LaCombe and Madame Guyon came under suspicion. He began an imprisonment that was to last until his death. She was confined to a Parisian convent. Her *Short Method of Prayer*, along with her confiscated unedited pa-

pers, came under scrutiny by ecclesiastical officials. Her writing was not formally condemned, but her release did not come until the powerful secret wife
of Louis XIV, Madame de Maintenon, urged by Guyon's friends, interceded
with the king on her behalf. Then began a period during which Madame
Guyon's fortunes seemed to prosper. Under Maintenon's aegis, she was introduced to François Fénelon, future Archbishop of Cambrai. He gradually
formed a great admiration for the widow.

Madame Guyon's writings were circulated in the influential school of St.
Cyr that was Maintenon's pet endeavor. But misuse of her ideas caused the
king's wife to dissociate herself and, for a variety of political reasons, turn on
her former friend. Anti-mystic sentiments were gaining ground in the waning
years of Louis XIV's reign, and Guyon's works were submitted for examination to several ecclesiastics including Benigne Bossuet, Bishop of Meaux. To
him, Guyon entrusted not only her circulating works but also the private
manuscript of her *Vie par elle-même* [Autobiography] with the understanding
that it was of a confessional nature. Bossuet's initial verdict was
non-committal. But the mood of the time would not permit the issue to remain there. Bossuet became more hostile and in 1694 condemned her ideas.

During this period Madame Guyon tended to retire, either to the country
or to her Paris apartments where she received few visitors. New accusations began to circulate, now concerning her moral as well as her doctrinal integrity,
and so she requested of Maintenon and the king an official examination. In
preparation, she prepared her *Justifications*, which attempted to explain the
true meaning of her words. Throughout her life, the widow maintained the
orthodoxy of her teachings and admitted only to the possibility that she may
have poorly expressed concepts already found in the Christian tradition.

At the trial at Issy, the examiners were Bossuet; Fénelon; the superior of
Saint-Sulpice; and Noailles, Bishop of Châlons. The issues generating the
gathering were larger than the writings of one woman. In fact, Madame
Guyon was never indicted as a heretic by the commission, although both
Bossuet and Noailles wrote pastoral letters in their dioceses condemning her
*Short Method of Prayer.* Simultaneously, Harlay, Archbishop of Paris, con-
demned both that work and her *Commentary on the Canticle of Canticles.*

Madame Guyon had trusted Bossuet, yet he broke the confessional seal that
had been set on her *Autobiography* and had her incarcerated in the Visitation
monastery in his diocese. There he attempted to have her sign a declaration admitting heresy. She refused, and he freed her with a letter of approval, which he
immediately sought to retract. Arrested in Paris, she finally ended up in the
Bastille where she remained eight years, undergoing up to eighty grueling examinations of her beliefs and morals. The widow stood firm, never losing her
dignity or coherence despite ill health. She interpreted all as a radical process of
self-annihilation, which had as its end the possession of God alone in "pure
love."

During her imprisonment, Bossuet and Fénelon engaged in a scandalous feud that rocked Christendom—the "Quietist affair"—at the end of which Fénelon's *Maxims of the Saints*, which defended ideas like Guyon's, was condemned. To the end, he never accused or lost his admiration for his former friend. After Bossuet's death, Madame Guyon was released, no formal charges having been brought against her. She retired to Blois, under the supervision of her son, and for the remaining twelve years of her life pursued the mission to which she had always felt called. Her fame spread, especially among Protestants with Pietist sympathies. The celebrated Pastor Poiret was especially influential in having her works circulated, and she gathered about her a mixed (and not always compatible) group of disciples, some Roman Catholic, some Scotch Protestant, some English, and some German, who called her "Our Mother." While she remained convinced that the Roman Catholic Church was the one true Church, she also believed that a Protestant of faith and piety could find salvation. She died in 1717 surrounded by her children and several disciples.

## MAJOR THEMES

Seventeenth-century France has become known as an era in which women writers defined a literary and historical space. Women's memoirs (a literary genre focused on "particular" rather than public history) flourished. In writing her *Vie par elle-même*, Jeanne Guyon participated in this effort. But the work also draws on the older genres of hagiography and spiritual narrative that had long been vehicles for women's stories.

The one theme that runs through all the French spiritual schools of that century is that of the loss of self, referred to variantly as annihilation, abandonment, dispossession, servitude, or victimhood. This is the spiritual theme that runs through Madame Guyon's major works. This emphasis places her firmly within the venerable Christian tradition of "negative mysticism."

Guyon's *Autobiography* recounts her personal trials up until her final years of imprisonment and interprets those events in light of the gradual spiritual dispossession that they afforded her. She rests, in the end, in faith alone and the affirmation: Thy will be done!

The *Short Method of Prayer* teaches that one must search for God present in the depth of the soul, and practice a methodless prayer not of the mind but of the heart, which surrenders utterly to the activity of the Spirit. In this work, Guyon stresses that any intermediary between the soul and God must be relinquished and a "holy indifference" cultivated.

Perhaps Madame Guyon's finest work is *Spiritual Torrents*. It characterizes the progress of the soul deeply touched by God as a transforming cruciform annihilation. Like all of Guyon's work, it was written in part to describe her own spiritual experiences and in part to instruct and encourage others in their search for intimacy with God. In it, she likens the chosen soul to a river that moves with torrential force toward its destination (God). The pattern she describes—a progressive stripping of the self of all attachments, including spiritual consolations—is a classic one in the Christian tradition. Guyon thus stands firmly in the tradition of "negative mysticism." The figures she uses, however, are unique to her. The pattern of crucifying death to self and eventual union with God is imaged as a tumultuously descending river that passes through various stages (cataracts, shallows, caverns, etc.) on its way to its ultimate destination: "As a torrent empties into the sea, its waters can be distinguished from the sea . . . but gradually the waters of this river mix with the sea completely. Likewise . . . little by little . . . you lose your own life" (*Spiritual Torrents,* p. 77). Guyon's passionate, evocative prose in this, as in all her works, gained her a devoted following.

## SURVEY OF CRITICISM

The reception of Madame Guyon's writing among Roman Catholics was so tied to conflicts within the Church that to this day in France her collected works, first posthumously published between 1712 and 1720 (in thirty-nine volumes), then between 1761 and 1790 (in forty), have never been reissued in a critical edition. This is true despite the fact that thinkers of the early-twentieth-century French Catholic revival sought to restore her reputation. Moreover, we know that these editions, the first shepherded by her Protestant admirer Poiret, were not complete. In the 1990s, Marie-Louise Gondal discovered and published the hitherto unknown final chapters of the *Autobiography.* It is only very recently, then, that Madame Guyon has come into the purview of serious Catholic readers, and this primarily in academic circles.

The furor that surrounded Madame Guyon's writing is classically seen from the doctrinal perspective. The controversy centers on the charge of "Quietism" (the prayer of quietude which relinquishes reason, imagination, and will, and rests in faith alone) and the practice of "pure love" (a love of God that is disinterested in seeking reward for the self). These were condemned on the grounds that the former denies human activity and responsibility, and the latter is incompatible with the active practice of virtue.

Contemporary scholars analyze the anti-mystic reaction in Madame Guyon's lifetime differently. Marie-Florine Bruneau especially sees that the new experiential religious spirit of which she was a part, which crossed denominational boundaries, challenged the authority of Church institutions and dogmas. Drawing upon the thinking of Michel de Certeau (*The Mystic Fable,* 1992), who has claimed that the development of a rationalized language of science unanchored in faith created a specialized mystical discourse—the "science of the saints"—which then became culturally marginalized and devoid of authority, Bruneau explores the deconstructive effects of this new mystical discourse and shows how the intense reaction against Guyon was due to these effects. Further, Bruneau explores de Certeau's insight that Madame Guyon's rearticulation of the ancient teaching of "pure love" subverted an emerging economic-ethical worldview characterized by the "law of exchange." These contemporary attempts to analyze Madame Guyon's works focus less on the specifically spiritual and religious contributions she made and not at all on the "Catholicity" of her doctrine. For this analysis, one must look to early-twentieth-century interpreters, especially Henri Bremond.

In Protestant circles, Guyon's fate has been utterly different. Her writings were promoted by her Protestant disciples and circulated widely in the eighteenth and nineteenth centuries among German Pietists, Swiss and Dutch Protestants, Quakers, and Methodists. Multiple editions and translations of her unabridged and extracted writings were produced. Through the 1819–1827 Philadelphia reprinting of John Wesley's *Christian Library*, which contained an excerpt from her life, her story became known in the United States. Since they were first published, her writings have remained in print in Protestant devotional circles worldwide where they are seen as eloquent testimonies to the life of faith.

## BIBLIOGRAPHY

### Works by Madame Guyon

*J. M. Guion: Les Opuscules spirituels* [Spiritual Writings]. 1720. Intro. Jean Orcibal. Hildesheim: Georg Olms Verlag, 1978.
*Spiritual Torrents.* 1704? Sargent, Georgia: Seedsowers, 1990.
*Récits de captivité: inédits* [Notes from Captivity]. Ed. Marie-Louise Gondal. Grénoble: Jérôme Millon, 1992.
*Jeanne Guyon: An Autobiography.* 1720. New Kensington, Pennsylvania: Whitaker House, 1997.

### Works about Madame Guyon

Bremond, Henri. *A Literary History of Religious Thought in France from the Wars of Religion Down to Our Own Times.* New York: Macmillan, 1928.
Bruneau, Marie-Florine. *Women Mystics Confront the Modern World: Marie de l'Incarnation and Madame Guyon.* Albany: State University of New York Press, 1998.
De la Bedoyere, Michel. *The Archbishop and the Lady: the Story of Fénelon and Madame Guyon.* New York: Pantheon Books, 1956.
Gondal, Marie-Louise. *Madame Guyon (1648–1717): Un nouveau visage.* Paris: Beauchesne, 1989.

WENDY M. WRIGHT

# ENRICA VON HANDEL-MAZZETTI
# (1871–1955)

## BIOGRAPHY

Born into an aristocratic Austrian household in 1871, Enrica von Handel-Mazzetti developed a vibrant, if complicated, Catholicism that made her one of the most controversial female authors in Central Europe. Her spiritual perspective developed in the intellectually demanding environment created by her widowed mother, who supervised Handel-Mazzetti's education until the age of fifteen. Highly cultivated and knowledgeable in art and literature, she gave her children strict Catholic principles but also trained them in Goethe and Schiller and introduced them to the classic authors of the Western canon. With lively piety and liberality of temper, Enrica flourished amid the challenges presented at home, and was a student of marked precocity when she matriculated at the Institute of the English Girl in Saint Pölten, Austria, in 1886.

Handel-Mazzetti embraced the serenity of the Institute's cloistered life to refine her talents as a writer, which had already brought forward a number of plays and short stories. She also continued her instruction in foreign languages and literature, music, and art. She took religious instruction under the Jesuits, who emphasized scholastic Thomism, the spirituality of Saint Ignatius, and the ethics of Thomas à Kempis. Her piety and intellectual training reinforced each other, stimulating beliefs in the fundamental dignity of human individuals as children of God and in the eternal nature of their souls. She nurtured feelings of solidarity with her fellow human beings, and understood Christian love as a duty and demand of the soul. This demand trumped any other claims made on the human conscience, including those asserted by religious dogma. "*Magna res est caritas*," Thomas à Kempis wrote, "The greatest law is love." Handel-Mazzetti's deployment of this law in her fiction was the source of her renown and notoriety as a writer.

Handel-Mazzetti never married, preferring uninterrupted domestic quiet for writing. She was not a recluse, however. In 1915 she volunteered as a nurse at the local war hospital, was a frequent participant in pilgrimages and religious folk life, made numerous public appearances to discuss her writing, avidly maintained a vast correspondence, and entertained guests often in her small but elegant home in Linz near the Danube. There she wrote over fifty novels, critical essays, and books of poetry well into the 1930s for a large and faithful audience, who celebrated her as an eminent German Catholic novelist. On her sixtieth birthday, the German government presented the Goethe Medal to her in recognition of her literary abilities and her efforts to promote peace and harmony among her fellow human beings. She died in 1955 after a brief illness.


## MAJOR THEMES

Although known for her poems and ballads, Handel-Mazzetti is recognized above all for her historical novels of Counter Reformation Austria, which provided the setting and afforded the plot for her development of religious character. (Due to the signal role the memory of the Reformation played in German national identity creation, however, her novels enjoyed their widest readership in Wilhelmine and Weimar Germany.) Themes of confessional reconciliation, overarching human love, the inviolability of conscience, and the centrality of suffering for redemption pervade her most important work. With a gift for vivid description and significant powers of characterization, Handel-Mazzetti created rancorous and spiritually taxing situations in which individuals speak with conviction in defense of their arguments, despite the significant psychological burdens they carry. In her inaugural novel, *Meinrad Helmpergers denkwürdiges Jahr* [Meinrad Helmperger's Memorable Year], which first appeared in 1897, an atheist nobleman, under suspicion of heresy, blasphemy, and witchcraft by the Lutheran authorities, is hanged for his beliefs in Berlin. His son, who comes under the influence of a Benedictine monk, then converts to Catholicism after acquiring a personal devotion to the Virgin Mary. Consistent with her Thomist education, Handel-Mazzetti reproves the error inherent in an irreligious spirit and rejects the brutality often involved with violations of rights of conscience. In her 1906 masterpiece *Jesse und Maria*, she presents a disturbing account of seventeenth-century Austria, describing in detail the cruelties Catholics and Protestants suffered at each other's hands. Her starkly negative depiction of the inquisition of the Protestant Jesse under the Catholic "Religious Commission," which places justice over mercy, dogmatic assent over sympathy, and confessional discipline over love and understanding, leaves an excruciating impression of a world without Christian charity and fraternal concord. Her greatly popular 1910 novel *Die arme Margaret* [Poor Margaret], which was adapted for both stage and screen by 1920, sounded these same tones in an unsettling narrative of Counter Reformation Styria. Margaret, a Lutheran, defends her martyred husband before the Catholic governor of Linz, for which she is severely persecuted and harassed. Brutal behavior on both sides follows as the Gospel message is subordinated to vengeance and personal gain. Here Christianity is portrayed with stains and warts in a way that shocked Catholic and Protestant readers, who were not used to seeing fictional representations of their faiths in such frenzied, ugly hues. "It is no disavowal of the truth," the author wrote in defense of her impartiality toward the confessions, to argue that "in a comprehensive view of the world all parties according to even-handed justice must be apportioned an equal share of light and darkness" (quoted in Muth, "Enrica," p. 624).

In each of these novels, as in her 1913 trilogy *Stephana Schwertner*, which tackles the issue of religious liberty, one protagonist, either a Protestant or a Catholic, commits a public crime, faces a court trial, and finally undergoes capital punishment. In his last hours, the despairing culprit is consoled by a mediatrix, usually a woman, who effects his spiritual transformation and renewal. Yet unlike the virtuous, submissive, and delicate women so often portrayed in Catholic literature of the time, Handel-Mazzetti's heroines speak with verve and assurance and remain unconquered even by the strongest men. Maria in *Jesse und Maria*, for example, is the noble wife, the self-sacrificing mother, and the defender of Catholic piety—the very model of Christian womanhood. But she is also the *mulier fortis* who overcomes the crafty and learned Jesse by expressions of spiritual depth and intellectual comprehension. Stephana Schwertner, a charismatic peasant girl who leads her community against a prejudiced state official, confronts the officer in command of the troops sent to halt their pilgrimage and, in a moment of principled rage, breaks his drawn sword with her banner.

Handel-Mazzetti's women exhibit supple judgment of human character in historical epochs known for endemic violence and Manichean assessments of good and bad, faithful and heretic. With subtlety of human understanding and command of historical context, she invites her readers into the narrative and asks them to perceive her characters objectively. Such fair-minded sophistication encouraged some contemporary critics to associate Handel-Mazzetti with Germany's most noted historical novelists, like Heinrich von Kleist and Gustav Freytag. Her deft management of the strong emotions occasioned by criminality, spiritual anxiety, and personal unrest, however, situates her novels more closely in relation to those of Jean-Paul Sartre, or even of the world's master of existential psychology, Feodor Dostoevsky.

## SURVEY OF CRITICISM

To suggest that Handel-Mazzetti's writing encountered a mixed and volatile audience would understate the case. For while personal redemption, forgiveness, charity, and the beauty of self-sacrifice attracted wide approbation, themes of religious conversion and clerical corruption agitated authorities on both sides of Germany's confessional divide. Conservative Protestants, drawing upon a fierce anti-Catholicism that had subsided little since the *Kulturkampf*, vehemently opposed Handel-Mazzetti's novels, especially

*Meinrad Helmpergers denkwürdiges Jahr* and *Stephana Schwertner. Meinrad,* for example, was denounced for trying to "prove" that Protestant inquisitors could be as cruel as Catholics, for being a Catholic apology written to effect Protestant conversions, and for representing a false understanding of confessional tolerance. When many of their co-religionists were reading Handel-Mazzetti with interest, these critics saw only Catholic bigotry, which was even more to be regretted since it highlighted their failure to carry out Catholic cultural integration on their own terms.

To Handel-Mazzetti's lifelong distress, however, the most uncordial and piercing criticism came from fellow Roman Catholics. Already with *Meinrad Helmpergers denkwürdiges Jahr,* some Catholics seized upon her "criminal tolerance" and ridiculed the supra-confessional Christianity she seemed to promote. They rejected the representation of inner religious experience without clear doctrinal referents for its apparent immanentism. And they took exception to a literary style that portrayed historical characters and events objectively, which might lead to the subjection of sacred history to critical evaluation or even to an understanding of the Church as an historical and therefore evolving entity. These criticisms congealed into a unified cry of conservative outrage in 1906 after the publication of *Jesse und Maria,* which was denounced by a Roman "Committee of Vigilance" for its "modern tendencies" and threatened with placement on the Index of Forbidden Books.

For all this elite hand wringing, however, Handel-Mazzetti's novels attracted an enthusiastic popular readership. Most Protestants applauded the work of a Catholic author who wrote without bias, without "*Tendenz.*" And literate Catholics recognized in Handel-Mazzetti the kind of writer whose discernment and balance would improve their cultural standing with the Protestant majority and overthrow the punishing stereotypes associated with their alleged "deficit in cultivation." Indeed, in a society in search of cultural integration after years of religious conflict, Handel-Mazzetti's appeal for dogmatic and social tolerance struck a note that resonated among important factions within both confessional groups, addressing a significant felt desire to put a stop to the "centrifugal tendencies" of a religiously cantankerous Germany.

More recently, scholars have debated Handel-Mazzetti's place in modern German literary history. In 1993 the Bonn Germanist Jutta Osinski argued that Karl Muth, who published *Jesse und Maria* as a serial in his journal *Hochland* in 1903–1904, had essentially deluded himself in regarding Handel-Mazzetti as the consummate modern Catholic author. In fact, Osinski stated, Handel-Mazzetti's novels actually fulfilled the fundamental model of nineteenth-century clerical literature by representing themes of sin, redemption, and conversion to Catholicism, while embodying tender and pious virtues in women of heroic faith, like Maria, Margaret, and Stephana Schwertner. One sees this interpretation in the work of Bernhard Doppler as well, who tends to stress the anti-modern, anti-liberal accents of her literature. In 1994, Susanna

Schmidt recovered the alternative voice of earlier critics like Eduard Korrodi, Johann Ranftl, and Paul Siebertz, who viewed Handel-Mazzetti as an innovator. As Schmidt observes in her excellent study, the Catholic novel of the nineteenth century placed the purity of belief over all, even over human love. The standard Catholic novel of the twentieth century, however, like those written by Handel-Mazzetti, justified violations against Catholic cultural assumptions and teachings with an undivided human, though God-inspired, love of others. Representative nineteenth-century Catholic novels, like Edward Georg Bulwer's 1834 *The Last Days of Pompey*, Lewis Wallace's 1880 *Ben Hur*, or Henryk Sienkiewicz's 1896 *Quo Vadis*, present characters who display the possibility of personal conversion and champion the cause of Catholicism over the secular order. Yet Handel-Mazzetti's novels, especially *Jesse und Maria*, emphasize the challenges of spiritual commitment and the virtues of confessional toleration in the interest of social peace and cultural integration (Schmidt, p. 179). Handel-Mazzetti thus played an important role in triggering the attitudinal shifts related to the process, both conscious and unconscious, of conceptual approximation between Catholics and Protestants in the twentieth century that would bear fruit in such later developments as ecumenical dialogue and, after World War II, a pan-Christian social democracy in the West.

In addition to these literary-critical aspects of her writing, Handel-Mazzetti was a model for other Catholic women authors who increasingly challenged the monopoly religious authorities enjoyed over the power to define cultural goods. In articulating a cultural critique that was not necessarily in solidarity with the Catholic struggle against Modernism, Handel-Mazzetti assumed a bold position in the field of religious commentary. Although never disloyal to her faith, she spoke and wrote without asking permission, departing from the hoary Catholic tradition of finding legitimation and authenticity in authority. Her example helped prepare the way not only for a new autonomy and individualism in Catholic literature asserted, for example, by twentieth-century Catholic Expressionists, but also for the greater participation of women in Catholic cultural production in general. Her books inspired a large number of progressive-minded yet faithful women to examine critically themes such as confessional difference, religion in society, and the possibilities for modern women in church and culture. It came as no surprise to her contemporaries when an admirer called Handel-Mazzetti "the *magistra magna* of modern German literature" (Siebertz, p. 467).

## BIBLIOGRAPHY

### Works by Enrica von Handel-Mazzetti

*Meinrad Helmpergers denkwürdiges Jahr*. 1897. Third edition. Munich: Allgemeine Verlags-gesellschaft, 1904.
*Jesse und Maria. Ein Roman aus dem Donaulande*. 2 vols. Kempten and Munich: Josef Kösel'sche Buchhandlung, 1906.

*Deutsches Recht und andere Gedichte* [German Justice and Other Poems]. Kempten
and Munich: Josef Kösel'sche Buchhandlung, 1908.
*Die arme Margaret. Ein Volksroman aus dem alten Steyr.* Kempten and Munich: Josef
Kösel'sche Buchhandlung, 1910.
*Stephana Schwertner. Ein Steyrer Roman.* 3 vols. Kempten and Munich: Josef
Kösel'sche Buchhandlung, 1912–1914.
*Der Deutsche Held* [The German Hero]. Kempten, Regensburg, Munich: Josef
Kösel'sche Buchhandlung, 1920.

## Works about Enrica von Handel-Mazzetti

Doppler, Bernhard. *Katholische Literatur und Literaturpolitik. Enrica von Handel-
Mazzetti: Eine Fallstudie.* Literatur in der Geschichte, Geschichte in der
Literatur series. Vol. 4. Ed. Friedbert Aspetsberger and Alois Brandstetter.
Königstein/Ts.: Hain, 1980.
Korrodi, Eduard. *Enrica von Handel-Mazzetti: Die Persönlichkeit und ihr
Dichterwerk.* Münster in Westfalen: Alphonsus-Buchhandlung, 1909.
Muth, Karl. "Enrica von Handel-Mazzetti." *Hochland* 7.1 (1909–1910): 624–26.
——. "*Jesse und Maria.* Ein literarischer Rück- und Ausblick." *Hochland* 3.2
(1905–1906): 691–708.
Osinski, Jutta. *Katholizismus und deutsche Literatur im 19. Jahrhundert.* Paderborn:
Ferdinand Schöningh, 1993.
Ranftl, Johann. "Enrica von Handel-Mazzetti." *Heimgarten* 30 (1906): 515–25;
597–608.
Rothenfelder, Franz. "Das religiöse Kunstwerk Enrica von Handel-Mazzettis." *Über
den Wassern* 2 (1908–1909): 397–405; 434–42.
Schmidt, Susanna. *"Handlanger der Vergänglichkeit." Zur Literatur des katholischen
Milieus 1800–1950.* Paderborn: Ferdinand Schöningh, 1994.
Siebertz, Paul, ed. *Enrica von Handel-Mazzettis Persönlichkeit, Werk und Bedeutung.*
Munich: Verlag Josef Kösel & Friedrich Pustet, 1930.

JEFFREY T. ZALAR

# EMILY HENRIETTA HICKEY
## (1845–1924)

## BIOGRAPHY

Emily Henrietta Hickey was born on April 12, 1845, near Enniscorthy, County Wexford, Ireland at Macmine Castle, the ancestral home of her mother, a former Miss Newton-King. Her father, Canon John Hickey, was the Church of Ireland parson in Goresbridge, County Kilkenny, and later in Clonmulsh, County Carlow. Emily gained her first knowledge of Catholicism from the household staff.

Emily was sent to boarding school at thirteen. Here Madame Stuart, her teacher and lifelong friend, opened new literary vistas, introducing her to Sir Walter Scott, Elizabeth Barrett Browning, and Tennyson. Shakespeare was reserved for later study since Canon Hickey considered the Bard of Avon inappropriate for young girls. Hickey showed an early penchant for poetry. Her first poem, "Told in the Firelight," appeared in *Cornhill Magazine* before her twenty-first birthday. An invitation by Alexander MacMillan, publisher of *Macmillan's Magazine*, to come to England brought her into contact with many of the period's literary giants, especially Robert Browning. While honing her artistic skills in London, Hickey found work, ranging from tutoring to companioning. At one point, she was employed by the Charity Organisation Society, composed of women desirous of improving the lot of working women through access to higher education. She also earned a first class honors certificate from Cambridge University. Part-time teaching led to an appointment as lecturer of English language and literature at Frances Mary Buss's North London Collegiate School for Girls, a post she held for eighteen years. During this time, she also published short stories, essays, and several volumes of poetry. In 1881, Hickey and Frederick Furnivall founded the Browning Society and she became its honorary secretary. Her friendship with Browning resulted in several biographical and critical articles as well as an annotated edition of his *Strafford*.

An unspecified breakdown forced Hickey to take a long sabbatical. Biographers have suggested that during this period she underwent some sort of religious experience, perhaps under the guidance of her friend Harriet Hamilton-King, a recent Catholic convert. Previously a nominal member of the official church, Hickey first became an ardent Anglo-Catholic. She was subsequently received into the Roman Catholic Church on July 22, 1901, having decided "[i]t was an untenable position, that of an Anglo-Catholic, so I have gone to the old Mother" (Dinnis, *Emily Hickey: Poet, Essayist—Pilgrim*, p. 42). A comment by Katharine Tynan illustrates how thoroughly Catholic Hickey considered herself: describing Hickey dressed in a lovely green dress at a party in 1889, Tynan stated, "We could not have foreseen the day in the far future when Miss Hickey should become a fervent daughter of the Catholic Church, devoted to its service and dressing as nun-like as might be" (*Twenty-Five Years: Reminiscences*, p. 342). Enid Dinnis revealed that Hickey's spiritual life was guided by the Third Order of St. Dominic. According to Dinnis, she memorized most of the Little Office of Our Lady (*Emily Hickey: Poet, Essayist*, p. 51).

After her conversion, Hickey disavowed two of her earlier volumes of poetry that she now deemed inconsistent with Catholic doctrine. Because of her preference for using religious themes in her texts, her poetry no longer fit the secular requirements of either the public or literary critics, and slowly she faded from view. By the time of her death, few would even remember her name.

Hickey, who never married, devoted most of her later years to writing and editing for the Catholic Truth Society. In 1912, Pope Pius X awarded her the Cross *Pro Ecclesia et Pontifice* [For Church and Pontiff] for her contribution to the Church and to literature (Dinnis, "Emily Hickey—In Memoriam," p. 735). She was also placed on the Civil Pensions List for her literary and educational contributions. Working almost until the end, Hickey was blind for the last two years of her life. She died in London on September 9, 1924.

**MAJOR THEMES**

Religious motifs are located throughout the texts Hickey produced before and after her conversion. The difference between the two periods is that her focus shifts from one that seeks answers within the context of a generalized Christianity to another that has found them in the narrow confines of Catholic dogma. Her novel *Lois*, first serialized in 1906–1907, especially fictionalizes this spiritual journey.

Hickey's search for religious truths can be observed in her pre-conversion poetry. The narrator of "What Have I to Do with Thee?" in *Verse-Tales, Lyrics, and Translations* (1890) initially refuses to be moved by the suffering and death of Christ but ultimately acknowledges a deep desire for forgiveness and salvation (pp. 90–91). In "Per Te Ad Lucem" [Through You to the Light] (*Verse-Tales*, pp. 92–93), the narrator wishes to know the result of following

Christ. Realizing the way may be fraught with pain, suffering, and death, the narrator admits that only by trust will salvation be gained. "Why?" (*A Sculptor and Other Poems*, 1881, pp. 129–30) considers what occurs when youthful self-denial in the service of others fails to satisfy the soul. Having worked diligently for God and humans, the narrator discovers old age approaching. Worn out, she asserts she no longer wishes to serve either God or humankind. As she waits for death, she contemplates what lies beyond the grave, uncertain that her efforts have been worthwhile. Self-sacrifice for the good of others is a repeated theme in Hickey's works. "Father Damien of Molokai" eulogizes the priest who ministered to the lepers in Hawaii and eventually died of the same disease (*Verse-Tales*, pp. 2–6). The heroine of "The Ballad of Lady Ellen" sells her soul to the emissaries of Satan in exchange for food and seed for the starving poor (*Poems*, 1896, pp. 1–11). Roden Noel, the subject of "The Children's Knight," was a dedicated social reformer whose particular concern was for the welfare of children (*Poems*, pp. 29–30).

With Hickey's conversion in 1901 came a new focus in her writings. Her pre-conversion secular love poems, biographical and critical articles, and short stories were replaced by an effort to locate Catholicism in every topic she addressed. Hickey pointed out Catholic influences on English literature in several articles, for example, "Catholic Principles and English Literature," "Catholicity in Spenser," and "Catholicism and Happiness." She theorized that authors known not to be members of the faith, such as Shakespeare and Milton, nevertheless employed ideas and motifs derived from a Catholic heritage.

Hickey also revised her views on women's place in society, as seen by the change in attitude the central figure of *Lois* undergoes. Lois is devoted to her writing career until laid low by an accident. On the brink of suicide, she has an epiphany that transforms her life. At the novel's conclusion, she has become a tertiary in a convent, much as Hickey was reported to have assumed a nun's habit and rule. Hickey had earlier urged women to embrace Christianity, that is, Roman Catholicism, in *Thoughts for Creedless Women* (1905). There, she argued that religion and morality were inseparable, and that religion was the "only perfect safeguard for chastity" (p. 18). *Lois* demonstrates how fully she believed in this idea. When Katey, Lois's free-thinking friend, announces her plan to live with a married man, the women argue. After Katey dies as the result of saving her from a fire, Lois makes a disturbing remark, "But I know it was best that she should die" (p. 643). To Hickey, death is better than living in sin.

Formerly a staunch supporter of women's rights, Hickey now argued that the advances in education which allowed women to support themselves financially had created wrong thinking. Education and the financial independence it offered meant a woman need not marry and fulfill her destiny as a mother. Further, an educated woman who did marry would probably limit the number of children she bore. In Hickey's opinion, this type of woman was blind to the "consequences of the race-suicide" she was committing (*Thoughts for Creedless Women*, p. 17).

Hickey's post-conversion poetry also displays an intense Catholic spirituality. Six volumes published between 1902 and 1924 are primarily or totally devoted to religious motifs, the most frequent of which is the Virgin Mary. Earlier published was *Ancilla Domini: Thoughts in Verse on the Life of the Blessed Virgin Mary* (1898). The portrayal of Mary takes many forms, from her birth in "Our Lady's Birthday" (*Later Poems*, pp. 42–43), to her presentation in the temple in "After Our Lady's Presentation" (pp. 46–49). She is the sinner's intercessor with God in "To the Mother, for Those Who Are in Bonds" (*Devotional Poems*, pp. 18–19). Equally important is Christ who appears in many forms, from babe in the manger in "This Day Is Born to You a Saviour" (p. 25), to the innocent man crucified for sinners in "Behold Your King!" (pp. 31–33), to the savior of the world in "Inveni Quem Diligit Anima Mea" [I Have Found Him Whom My Soul Loves] (pp. 7–8).

## SURVEY OF CRITICISM

Having removed herself after her conversion from the mainstream British literary establishment through a new emphasis on sacred subjects, Hickey found she was increasingly ignored by critics in the major periodicals. Colman, for example, remarks that Hickey sacrificed "craft for content" in her later poems (p. 547).

Reviewers of Hickey's post-conversion period tended to be Catholic friends. Commenting on Hickey's Catholic tendencies even before her formal reception into the Church, Father Matthew Russell wrote about Hickey's volume *Ancilla Domini*, "Almost every line might have been written by a devout Irish maiden who had been saying the Hail Mary all her life" ("Poets," p. 201). Katharine Tynan praised Hickey for being "a feminine personality and a feminine Muse, yet . . . [possessing] something of the best of masculine, its frankness, its courage, its simplicity in her work and herself" (p. 338). Henrietta Knight called Hickey's poetry "[t]ender, full of colour and of music, and of love for all that is good and noble" (p. 42). She urged Catholics to buy *Our Lady of May and Other Poems* (1902), commenting, "It is so real and so simple; the poems are sermons written in poetry and not in stone" (p. 43). Eleanor Hull commented that Hickey's poetry had always been religious, but since the author's conversion it had taken on a "more doctrinal" nature (p. 210). *Later Poems*, she remarked, was filled with "very tender religious poems" (p. 210). Enid Dinnis asserted Hickey was not a propagandist even though she dedicated her talents to the Church. Dinnis said the verse contained in *Later Poems* "no longer won approval by being 'unsectarian'—the muse of the poet who had made a bid for the laurels assigned by the world's judges had been commandeered by Holy Church" (p. 734).

Emily Henrietta Hickey suffered the consequences of her religious convictions. Consciously choosing to abandon a secular career that had rewarded her with fame and financial success could not have been easy. She truly believed she was doing God's work by devoting her skills and talents to the Church. In no way should her decision be minimized. She lived at a time when Catholics still existed on the fringes of "polite society" in England.

Hickey's achievement continues to be noted in major reference works, as Catharine Weaver McCue points out (p. 277), because she dared to examine English literature from a point of view deemed radical by the standards of her time. Today's increased interest in women writers will inevitably lead to a deeper study of her ideas and texts.

## BIBLIOGRAPHY

### Works by Emily Henrietta Hickey

*A Sculptor and Other Poems.* London: Kegan Paul, 1881.
*Verse-Tales, Lyrics and Translations.* London: Arnold, 1889.
*Poems.* London: E. Mathews, 1896.
*Ancilla Domini: Thoughts in Verse on the Life of the Blessed Virgin Mary.* London, privately published, 1898.
*Our Lady of May and Other Poems.* London: Catholic Truth Society, 1902.
*Thoughts for Creedless Women.* London: Catholic Truth Society, 1905. Rpt. in *The Catholic Church and Labour.* London: Catholic Truth Society, 1908. 1–24.
"Lois." Ser. in *The Month* 108–9 (July 1906–June 1907). Rpt. as novel *Lois.* London: Washbourne, 1908.
"Catholicity in Spenser." *American Catholic Quarterly* 32 (July 1907): 490–502.
"Catholicism and Happiness." *Irish Monthly* 38 (September 1910): 525–28.
*Our Catholic Heritage in English Literature.* London: Sands, 1910.
"Catholic Principles and English Literature." *Catholic World* 95 (May 1912): 145–52.
*Later Poems.* London: G. Richards, 1913.
*Devotional Poems.* London: Murray, 1922.

### Works about Emily Henrietta Hickey

Colman, Anne. "Emily Henrietta Hickey." *Dictionary of Irish Literature.* Vol. 1. Rev. ed. Ed. Robert Hogan et al. Westport, Connecticut: Greenwood Press, 1996. 546–47.
Dinnis, Enid. "Emily Hickey—In Memoriam." *Catholic World* 120 (March 1925): 732–36.
———. *Emily Hickey: Poet, Essayist—Pilgrim.* London: Harding and More, 1927.
Furlong, Alice. "Emily Hickey." *Irish Monthly* 55 (January 1925): 16–20.
Hayes, Richard J., ed. *Sources for the History of Irish Civilization.* Vol. 2. Boston: G. K. Hall, 1970.
Hull, Eleanor. "The Poetical Works of Emily Hickey." *Catholic World* 104 (November 1916): 202–13.
Knight, Henrietta. "The Poems of Emily Hickey." *Bookman* 47 (November 1914): 42–44.

McCue, Catharine Weaver. "Emily Hickey." *The 1890s: An Encyclopedia of British Literature, Art, and Culture.* Ed. George A. Cevasco. New York: Garland, 1993. 276–77.

Russell, Matthew. "Poets I Have Known, IV: Emily Hickey." *Irish Monthly* 31 (April 1903): 192–202.

Tynan, Katharine. "Emily Hickey: A Catholic Poet." *Catholic World* 93 (June 1911): 328–40.

——. *Twenty-Five Years: Reminiscences.* New York: Devin-Adair, 1913.

Woodall, Natalie Joy. "Emily Henrietta Hickey." *An Encyclopedia of British Women Writers.* Ed. Paul and June Schlueter. 1988. Rev. ed. New Brunswick, New Jersey: Rutgers University Press, 1998. 318–19.

NATALIE JOY WOODALL

# HILDEGARD OF BINGEN
## (1098–1179)

## BIOGRAPHY

A unique figure in the history of Catholic women writers, the Benedictine abbess Hildegard of Bingen exemplifies the twelfth-century renaissance in secular learning and spiritual living. Visionary, preacher, composer of liturgical music, correspondent of emperors and popes, and foundress of two monastic communities, Hildegard was renowned among contemporary religious sisters, male ecclesiastical superiors, and secular authorities as well as by later generations for her spiritual insights and prophetic gifts.

Hildegard was born in 1098 to a noble German family at Bermersheim, south of Mainz. According to Hildegard's biography, her parents offered her as the youngest of ten children to God as a tithe. Jutta of Sponheim, a recluse who lived in a women's hermitage near the male monastery on the Disibodenberg (Mount Disibod), assumed care of the eight year old and provided her with instruction in Latin. The monk Volmar, who became Hildegard's personal friend and amanuensis, saw to her later education. Between 1112 and 1115, Hildegard professed her vows as a Benedictine nun. As Jutta's spiritual fame grew, a religious community for women led by the recluse was established; upon Jutta's death in 1136, Hildegard was elected head of the community.

In 1141, at the age of forty-two years and seven months, Hildegard heard a voice from heaven that directed her to record the visions she had experienced since early childhood. At first reluctant, Hildegard finally acquiesced to the bidding of the Living Light. As her writings became well known, Hildegard developed a reputation as a prophetess and healer. However, her prophetic ability did not manifest itself in predictions of the future but rather in an understanding and interpretation of contemporary events.

Around 1147 Hildegard had a visionary experience in which she was directed to found an independent convent at the Rupertsberg (Mount St. Rupert) near Bingen. Foreseeing the spiritual and material loss for his community if Hildegard were to depart, Abbot Kuno of Disibodenberg at first blocked the move. However, Hildegard eventually prevailed, and in 1150 she moved with about twenty nuns to the Rupertsberg; the convent was dedicated by the Archbishop of Mainz two years later.

In addition to her spiritual duties, Hildegard was engaged in the secular events of her day. She corresponded with temporal and religious leaders, providing advice and urging reform. Although Frederick I Barbarossa had invited her to his imperial palace at Ingelheim, Hildegard later admonished the emperor because of his support of three anti-popes. Nonetheless, she obtained letters of protection from Frederick that saved the Rupertsberg community when fighting broke out between imperial troops and those loyal to the Pope.

Hildegard undertook three preaching tours between 1158 and 1163 and a final one in 1170–1171; her travels took her to cathedral cities and monastic communities along the Upper and Lower Rhine as well as to more distant venues like Würzburg and Bamberg. The purpose of the tours was to promote monastic and clerical reform and to combat heretical sects, in particular the Cathars. As the Benedictine abbess's reputation grew, the Rupertsberg community flourished. With the increased number of residents, a second community to accommodate young women of a less noble background was established in 1165 across the Rhine River near Eibingen.

Because Hildegard intervened to bury a man who purportedly had died excommunicated, the Eibingen and Rupertsberg communities were placed under interdict in 1178, unable to hear Mass, receive the Eucharist, or sing the Divine Office. The matter was resolved and the interdict lifted just six months before the abbess's death on September 17, 1179. A canonization process was begun in 1233 but never concluded. Nonetheless, Hildegard's name is included in the Roman Martyrology and the Benedictine abbess is venerated locally. Her feast day is September 17.

## MAJOR THEMES

In her letters, Hildegard characterizes her age as an "effeminate" one, an age whose leaders lack the discernment and the vision to advance Church reform and growth. Thus, it becomes the purview of a "poor woman" to proclaim the Word, as revealed to her by God through visions. It is the weakest of God's creatures through whom he reveals his strength. Around 1146 Hildegard wrote to St. Bernard of Clairvaux to seek his support for the recording of her visions, and within a year Pope Eugenius obtained a copy of Hildegard's first, and at the time still incomplete, visionary work. The approval and endorsement of Hildegard's writing by these two ecclesiastical luminaries validated her divine gift and shielded her from criticism for disobeying the vow of silence and disregarding the Church's sanction against teaching by women.

Like other prophets and mystics before and since, Hildegard asserts that it is not her voice but that of God speaking through her. Although the meaning of her visionary experiences is often difficult to grasp, her orthodoxy remains indisputable. Nonetheless, Hildegard introduces original metaphysical ideas and focuses on aspects of theology less commonplace in her day. Of equal importance to the masculine images of God and Christ as father and son or as creator and redeemer are the images of feminine entities who serve to link divinity and humanity. Synagogue, Church, Wisdom, Knowledge of God, and the virtues Charity, Humility, and Peace are among the principal female allegorical figures described by Hildegard in her writings.

God's revelations to the Benedictine nun focus on an understanding of the relationship between the macrocosm and the microcosm, and of the role of humankind in the divine plan. Hildegard's universe is filled with harmonies that manifest themselves among the elements, in music, with connections between the earth and the human body, and even in the relationship between the sexes. At the center of Hildegard's cosmic vision stands humankind, chosen to rule the earth and responsible for its preservation. Individuals of both genders assume these duties because men as well as women are created in the image of God. Earthly discord results from imbalances in the elements that have their genesis in the Fall, but harmony can be achieved again. As humankind seeks to reestablish unity, it discovers *viriditas*, the greening or life-giving principle inherent in the physical universe, which is central to the spiritual realm as well.

These themes play an integral part in the three visionary-theological works, the letters, the nearly eighty vocal pieces, and the liturgical drama Hildegard produced. Her encyclopedic knowledge also manifests itself in her scientific and medical writings. In addition, the Benedictine nun penned two saints' lives and several theological tracts.

Hildegard's trilogy of visionary works contains God's revelations to her that explain the creation of the world, its evolution, and its final days. Most well known and widely disseminated even during Hildegard's lifetime is the *Scivias* (1141–1151) [*Scito vias Domini*, or Know the Ways of the Lord]. Begun when Hildegard was forty-two, the tripartite work begins with a Declaration in which she describes the experience of the Living Light calling her to write what she sees and hears: "Heaven was opened and a fiery light of exceeding brilliance came and permeated my whole brain, and inflamed my whole heart and my whole breast, not like a burning but like a warming flame" (*Scivias*, p. 59). The result is a depiction of the relationship between the macrocosm and the microcosm, the world as created by God and in its postlapsarian form (Book I, six visions); a characterization of Ecclesia (Mother Church) and the sacraments of redemption (Book II, seven visions); and a chronicle of salvation history through the Last Judgment (Book III, thirteen visions). Hildegard first describes each vision, then explicates it in the tradition of the spiritual senses, focusing on the allegorical sense. Incorporated into her interpretations is advice and guidance for religious and secular people seeking to lead holy lives. Her descriptions reflect a variety of sensory experiences and are replete with references to colors and sounds. Although Hildegard's work is part of the tradition of medieval apocalyptic literature, her visionary interpretations are unique in their variety and depth.

The illuminations included in some *Scivias* manuscripts vitalize Hildegard's descriptions. The oldest extant manuscript, the Rupertsberg Codex (Hessische Landesbibliothek, Hs. 1) dating from around 1165, was preserved in the Eibingen convent. Before its disappearance during World War II, the Eibingen nuns copied the text and prepared faithful renderings of its thirty-five illustrations. The miniature accompanying the Declaration portrays Hildegard recording the divine words onto wax tablets as she is inspired by the Living Light. Her secretary, the monk Volmar (and elsewhere Richardis of Stade, a sister at Rupertsberg until 1151), edits the texts and transcribes them onto parchment.

The six visions of the *Liber Vitae Meritorum* (1158–1163) [Book of the Rewards of Life] are informed by Hildegard's own experiences as a spiritual director; her concern with ethics and penitence dominates the explications of the visions. Cast in the mold of the *Psychomachia* of Prudentius, the work depicts the struggle in the soul between the virtues and the vices, the latter of which are described in detail and are represented in the form of animals and human body parts. The broader context is the interaction of the virtues and vices in the universe.

In the final visionary work, the tripartite *Liber Divinorum Operum* (1163–1173/74) [Book of Divine Works], also called *De Operatione Dei* [On the Workings of God], Hildegard offers a somewhat different and more fully developed perspective of her world vision. Written after the composition of her scientific works, the *Book of Divine Works* is less contemplative and allegorical and offers more concrete and detailed descriptions of the cosmos. Whereas in the *Scivias* Hildegard describes the universe as egg-shaped, she revises her characterization in the *Book of Divine Works* in favor of the more prevalent idea of her day, the cosmos as a circle or wheel. At the center of the universe is humankind, God's ultimate creation, arms outstretched in a manner reminiscent of the crucified Christ but also a pose that suggests the power over all elements and nature God has bestowed on humanity. The thirteenth-century Lucca manuscript of the *Book of Divine Works* offers detailed depictions of Hildegard's world vision. Most include Hildegard herself at the foot of the miniature engaged in recording the experience.

Around 1151, having completed the *Scivias*, Hildegard turned her attention to the chronicling of scientific matters. Later editors divided her *Subtilitates diversarum naturarum creaturarum* (c. 1151–1158) [Nine Books on the Subtleties of Different Kinds of Creatures] into two parts, the *Physica* [Natural History or Book of Simple Medicine] and the *Causae et curae* [Causes and Cures or Book of Composite Medicine]. The *Natural History* summarizes ideas of the age concerning natural science; this encyclopedic work includes books on animals, herbs, trees, and precious gems. The *Causes and Cures* offers details on diseases and their treatment; it includes herbal and magical remedies as well as astrological lore and distinctive observations on sexuality. Traces of the same cosmic ideas found in the visionary works are apparent, but Hildegard does not claim any divine inspiration for the scientific writings.

The majority of the more than three hundred extant letters by Hildegard date from her later years (1147–1179), and it is her correspondence with ecclesiastical and secular figures that provides insights into her personal life and her fame. In many cases, a letter is not so much a personal exchange with the correspondent as it is an epistle in the Pauline tradition intended for an entire religious community or group of persons. Although Hildegard characterizes herself as an unlearned "poor little woman," she does not shirk from giving voice to the Living Light bestowed upon her. In several missives to Pope Eugenius, Hildegard intercedes on behalf of Henry, Archbishop of Mainz, an ardent supporter of Hildegard who had been removed from office. The abbess utters sharp words against Pope Anastasius, whom she feels is too easily swayed by his fellow clerics from advocating a more rigorous religious life. Ever vigilant in her struggle against ecclesiastical corruption, Hildegard speaks out against the Cologne clerics, whose laxity is allowing the heretical Cathars to gain a foothold and thrive. The epistolary invective against the clerics is in fact a sermon Hildegard preached during her third homiletic tour. Later reformers exploited the ideas found here to campaign against the mendicant orders as corrupters of the Church, interpreting Hildegard's prophecies against the pseudo-prophets of her age as predictions pertaining to the Dominican and Franciscan orders that flourished in subsequent centuries.

Recent interest in Hildegard is due in part to a rediscovery of her music. Hildegard gathered her liturgical songs and her liturgical drama into a collection called the *Symphonia armoniae celestium revelationum* (1150s, with later additions and revisions) [Symphony of the Harmony of Celestial Revelations]. All of these pieces are part of the Divine Office (the *Opus dei*) or the celebration of the Mass. The liturgical drama, the *Ordo virtutum* (1150s?) [Order of the Virtues] is an expanded version of the final vision included in the *Scivias*. It chronicles the struggles of the Soul to overcome the temptations of the world with the assistance of the Virtues. As the Soul and Virtues are ultimately reunited in celestial harmony, the devil, who is denied a singing voice throughout the drama, is bound and cast out. Hildegard's music reflects practices of contemporaneous Gregorian chant, but she introduces innovative elements such as unusually large leaps in the melodic line and a remarkable thirteen note range that lend a particularly ethereal quality to her works. There is little doubt that the Rupertsberg and Eibingen sisters sang Hildegard's songs, thus according religious women center stage in the performance of the liturgy.

## SURVEY OF CRITICISM

The publication of critical editions and translations of Hildegard's works in recent years makes her writings accessible to a broader and non-German speaking audience. The abbess's community of Eibingen has been at the forefront of scholarly endeavors. Maura Böckeler has provided a modern German translation of the *Scivias*. Marianna Schrader and Adelgundis Führkötter offer careful studies of the manuscript transmission of Hildegard's writings and a detailed investigation of the authenticity of her works.

Sabina Flanagan's monograph on Hildegard provides a general introduction to the accomplishments and ideas of the twelfth-century visionary, balancing the historical, literary, and spiritual aspects of Hildegard's life. Flanagan maintains that Hildegard "sought to understand the divine in its human and natural aspects," and her writings demonstrate that "her interests were intellectual rather than mystical" (p. 200). Barbara Newman champions the original contributions of the Benedictine abbess to twelfth-century intellectual and spiritual life in her examination of Hildegard's theology of the feminine and its relationship to the sapiential, or wisdom, tradition. Much of Newman's study *Sister of Wisdom* focuses on the representations of Eve, Mary, the Church, and Wisdom in Hildegard's writings. In Hildegard's sapiential theology of creation, Newman states, "the feminine is the immanent divine principle that mediates between the transcendent God and his creatures" (p. 250).

Other aspects of Hildegard's work have also been examined by critics. Barbara Thornton provides commentary on Hildegard's musical style and offers performances of the abbess's songs and liturgical drama with the Cologne-based medieval vocal-instrumental ensemble Sequentia, and Barbara Newman's critical edition of the *Symphonia* describes Hildegard's theology of music and examines the poetics of the songs. The abbess's poetic style is a theme in studies by Peter Dronke. With his publication in 1984 of previously unedited Hildegard texts, Dronke draws attention to the still unexamined primary sources of her writings. Christel Meier inquires into allegorical interpretations of the visionary works as well as the relationship between Hildegard's text and the manuscript illuminations. With regard to the scientific works, Heinrich Schipperges examines the Benedictine nun's understanding of the role of humanity in the cosmos and the relationship between healing and salvation in her writings. And finally, theories regarding possible origins of Hildegard's visions are a source of great debate. Charles Singer offers a neurophysiological explanation for Hildegard's visionary experiences, ascribing them to migraine headaches.

Recent English translations of the letters and collections of essays commemorating the anniversary of Hildegard's birth and death such as those edited by Anton Brück and Edeltraud Forster provide insights into various aspects of the theological, scientific, artistic, and social contributions of the twelfth-century "sibyl of the Rhine."

## BIBLIOGRAPHY

### Works by Hildegard of Bingen

*The Ordo Virtutum of Hildegard of Bingen*. Ed. Audrey Ekdahl Davidson. Kalamazoo, Michigan: Medieval Institute Publishers, 1985.

*Symphonia: A Critical Edition of the "Symphonia armonie celestium revelationum."* Ed. and trans. Barbara Newman. Ithaca: Cornell University Press, 1988.

*Scivias.* Trans. Columba Hart and Jane Bishop. New York: Paulist Press, 1990.

*Wisse die Wege. Scivias.* Ed. and trans. Maura Böckeler. 1954. Sixth edition. Salzburg: Otto Müller, 1976.

*The Book of the Rewards of Life [Liber Vitae Meritorum].* Trans. Bruce W. Hozeski. Garland Library of Medieval Literature. Vol. 89. New York: Garland, 1994.

*The Letters of Hildegard of Bingen.* Trans. Joseph L. Baird and Radd K. Ehrman. Vol. 1 and 2. New York: Oxford University Press, 1994, 1998.

*Hildegard of Bingen's Book of Divine Works with Letters and Songs.* Abridged and trans. by Matthew Fox. Santa Fe: Bear, 1987.

*Physica.* In *Sanctae Hildegardis Abbatissae Opera Omnia.* Ed. Charles Daremberg and F. A. de Peuss. Patrologia Latina. Vol. 197. Paris: Migne, 1855.

*Hildegardis Causae et Curae.* Ed. Paul Kaiser. Leipzig: Teubner, 1903.

## Works about Hildegard of Bingen

Brück, Anton, ed. *Hildegard von Bingen, 1179–1979: Festschrift zum 800. Todestag der Heiligen.* Mainz: Selbstverlag der Gesellschaft für mittelrheinische Kirchengeschichte, 1979.

Davidson, Audrey Ekdahl, ed. *The "Ordo Virtutum" of Hildegard of Bingen: Critical Studies.* Kalamazoo, Michigan: Medieval Institute Publishers, 1992.

Dronke, Peter. *Women Writers of the Middle Ages. A Critical Study of Texts from Perpetua (+203) to Marguerite Porete (+1310).* Cambridge: Cambridge University Press, 1984. 144–201.

Flanagan, Sabina. *Hildegard of Bingen: A Visionary Life.* London and New York: Routledge, 1989.

Forster, Edeltraud, and the convent of the Benedictine Abbey St. Hildegard, Eibingen, eds. *Hildegard von Bingen: Prophetin durch die Zeiten: Zum 900. Geburtstag.* 1997. Second edition. Freiburg: Herder, 1998.

Gottfried of Disibodenberg and Theodoric of Echternach. *The Life of the Saintly Hildegard.* ca. 1180s. Trans. Hugh Feiss. Toronto: Peregrina Publishing, 1996.

McInerney, Maud Burnett. *Hildegard of Bingen. A Book of Essays.* New York: Garland, 1998.

Meier, Christel. "Die Bedeutung der Farben im Werk Hildegards von Bingen." *Frühmittelalterliche Studien* 65 (1972): 245–355.

——. "Zwei Modelle von Allegorie im 12. Jahrhundert: Das allegorische Verfahren Hildegards von Bingen und Alans von Lille." *Formen und Funktionen der Allegorie: Symposien Wolfenbüttel 1978.* Ed. Walter Haug. Germanistische Symposien, Berichtsbände. Vol. 3. Stuttgart: Metzler, 1979. 70–89.

Newman, Barbara. *Sister of Wisdom: St. Hildegard's Theology of the Feminine.* Berkeley: University of California Press, 1987.

——, ed. *Voice of the Living Light: Hildegard of Bingen and Her World.* Berkeley: University of California Press, 1998.

Schipperges, Heinrich. *Hildegard of Bingen: Healing and the Nature of the Cosmos.* Princeton: Markus Wiener, 1997.

Schrader, Marianna, and Adelgundis Führkötter. *Die Echtheit des Schrifttums der Heiligen Hildegard von Bingen.* Archiv für Kulturgeschichte. Beiheft 6. Cologne: Böhlau-Verlag, 1956.

Sequentia. *Hildegard von Bingen: 900 Years.* BMG/Deutsche Harmonia Mundi, 1998.

Singer, Charles. "The Scientific Views and Visions of Saint Hildegard." *Studies in the History and Method of Science.* Vol. 1. Oxford: Clarendon, 1917. New York: Arno Press, 1975. 1–55.

DEBRA L. STOUDT

# HROTSVIT OF GANDERSHEIM
## (c. 935–c. 975)

## BIOGRAPHY

Hrotsvit (also Hrotsvitha or Hroswitha or Roswitha) of Gandersheim was one of the most talented writers of the Middle Ages. She lived in tenth-century Saxony during the peak of the Ottonian Renaissance. She wrote eight legends (saints' lives), six plays, and a pair of epics. Hrotsvit has earned the multiple distinctions of being "the first poet of Saxony, the first female German poet, the first dramatist of Germany, the first female German historian, and the first person in Germany to employ the Faust theme" (Wilson, *Plays*, pp. xii-xiii).

Little is known about this amazing woman. Even her name was a subject of dispute until a recent translator pointed out that the medieval writer "records the nominative form of her name as being Hrotsvit and the inflected forms as Hrotsvitham and Hrotsvithae" (Wilson, *Medieval Women Writers*, pp. 30–31). Hrotsvit's birth date is unknown, but since she writes that she was born long after the death of Duke Otto of Saxony (912) and before her abbess, Gerberga II (c. 940), it has been surmised that she was born shortly before the fourth decade of the tenth century. Hrotsvit was a canoness in the Saxon Imperial Abbey of Gandersheim, an abbey established for noblewomen in 850 by the Saxon nobleman Liudolf and his wife Oda. Thus, it is almost certain that Hrotsvit was of noble birth. Abbess Gerberga II, under whose rule Hrotsvit lived, was niece to Emperor Otto the Great (Wemple, p. 44). It seems likely that Hrotsvit received her excellent education at the abbey although she could have received additional instruction at Otto's court (Dronke, p. 56). Since Hrotsvit was a canoness, she probably lived under a Benedictine Rule but also would have enjoyed more liberties, including the right to keep property.

It is unclear whether Hrotsvit's writings had any effect on later medieval authors. Apparently, she had been forgotten by 1493, the year in which poet-humanist Conrad Celtis claimed credit for "discovering" the codex of writings in the Emmeram monastery in Regensburg, Germany. In 1501, Celtis published an edition of Hrotsvit's *Opera* [Works], and it was the only complete edition until the twentieth century (Zeydel, "Reception," p. 239; Wilson, *Plays,* pp. xxix-xxx).


## MAJOR THEMES

Underlying all of Hrotsvit's writings are her fundamental religious beliefs. Her view of the world was essentially Augustinian. Hrotsvit perceived all creation as good and believed *superbia* (pride) the cause of sin and evil in the world. She acknowledged that on earth there was a continuous struggle between good and evil, and, as did St. Augustine, believed that the Christian "bears a divine obligation to combat the work of the Devil . . . and [should] fight against pagans, rebels, and other enemies of the *civitas dei*" (Wilson, *Plays,* pp. xxii-xxiii). Hrotsvit's most dominant theme, introduced in her first legend and repeated in nearly all her subsequent work, is "the exaltation of the virtue of steadfast and pure virginity" (Wilson, *Plays,* p. xiv).

Hrotsvit's earliest works are her legends, and they comprise the first book of the Emmeram codex. Hrotsvit begins the book with a preface followed by a dedication to Abbess Gerberga II. In the preface, she admits that "poetic expression may seem difficult for female frailty," a version of the modesty topos so often found in the writings of medieval women, but in the same preface Hrotsvit also defends her craft, stating that she will not permit her God-given talent to "be destroyed by the rust of neglect" (Wilson, *Medieval Women Writers,* p. 32).

The struggle between good and evil is evident in Hrotsvit's legends along with the theme of virginity. "Mary," the first legend, is an apocryphal tale about the Virgin. The Ascension of Christ is the subject of the second legend, based on a Greek source. The third legend, "Gongolfus," presents the story of a Frankish knight who is murdered by his unfaithful wife and her lover. The fourth legend, "Pelagius," tells the story of a young man living in Christian Galicia; he is murdered because he refuses a caliph's homosexual advances. Here Hrotsvit has varied her predominant theme by depicting a young man rather than a woman dying for the sake of virginity. The legends of "Theophilus" and "Basilius" follow. Both focus on men who made pacts with the devil, the Faust theme. The seventh legend deals with the martyrdom of Dionysius, the first bishop of Paris. The subject of the eighth and final legend, St. Agnes, is martyred for the sake of her virginity.

The second book of the Emmeran codex contains Hrotsvit's six plays. In this book, Hrotsvit reiterates her favorite theme of virginity, and the struggle between good and evil forces is essential to the plots. Here again Hrotsvit includes a preface, and this is followed by a prose letter to her "learned patrons." In the preface, Hrotsvit explains why she wrote the plays, stating that she has noticed many Catholics falling prey to pagan literature and enjoying it more than Sacred Scripture. Even those dedicated to reading Scripture, Hrotsvit maintains, turn aside when given the opportunity to read Terence; attracted by the ancient playwright's "sweetness of style," they are thus inadvertently influenced by the wickedness contained in his writing. Therefore she, "the strong voice of Gandersheim," decided to compose "Christian subject matter in Terentian garb . . . so that in that selfsame form of composition in which the shameless acts of lascivious women were phrased/the laudable chastity of sacred virgins be praised" (Wilson, *Plays,* p. xi). In the letter, Hrotsvit wishes her patrons "everlasting joy" and immediate pleasure; she describes her plays as insubstantial works, intended for friends. But she also notes conflicting emotions of joy and fear when writing because she does not wish "to deny God's gracious gift" to her, nor does she wish to appear to be "more" than she is (Wilson, *Plays,* pp. 4–5).

Each of the six plays, written in rhymed prose, begins with a brief summary. The titles assigned to them by Celtis are still in use. *Gallicanus* is the first of the plays and focuses on the conversion and martyrdom of a Roman general. The second, *Dulcitius,* is a melodramatic "tragicomedy." In it Dulcitius, an evil executioner for the emperor Diocletian, is determined to have his way with three Christian virgins. The girls pray for protection, and Dulcitius is overtaken by confusion. He goes into a pantry and makes love to the cooking vessels, mistaking them for the girls. He emerges covered with soot, external evidence of the darkness of his soul, and the guards that he has placed outside the building mistake him for the devil. Eventually, the three girls are martyred, but each dies in joyful anticipation of union with the heavenly Bridegroom.

The third play, *Calimachus,* focuses on the sin and eventual conversion of a pagan youth who has fallen in love with a married Christian woman, Drusiana, who has taken a vow of chastity. When Drusiana learns of the young man's determination to seduce her, she prays to die. Her prayer is answered, and she is quickly taken up into heaven. In the meantime, Calimachus has bribed the guards at her tomb so that he can have intercourse with her dead body. But he becomes converted and refrains from the unnatural act. In this play, as Elizabeth Petroff observes, "Female characters do not have a monopoly on virginity or celibacy, because for Hrotsvit virginity is not a gender-linked quality" (p. 84).

The "fallen woman" is Hrotsvit's subject in the next two plays, *Abraham* and *Pafnutius.* In both, a harlot is converted largely because of prayers offered up by saintly anchorites. In the final play, *Sapientia,* Hrotsvit deals with the martyrdom of three allegorical sisters—Faith, Hope, and Charity. In all three of the final plays, Hrotsvit adds classroom "lessons" within the dialogue. There is a lesson in "musica" presented in *Pafnutius,* a lesson on arithmetic in *Sapientia,* and a lesson in etymology in *Abraham* (Wilson, "Hrotsvit's Abraham," p. 2).

The last book of the Emmeram codex contains Hrotsvit's two extant epics. The subject matter of each is in some way linked to Hrotsvit's world, and they seem to be connected. *Carmen de Gestis Oddonis Imperatoris,* often referred to as *Gesta Ottonis* [The Song of the Ottonian Emperors], for the most part glorifies the deeds of Otto I, to whom it is dedicated, even though it begins with Henry the Fowler, the first King of Saxony and father of Otto I, and ends with the marriage of Liudolf, Duke of Swabia. It is preceded by an address to Gerberga and letters of dedication to Otto I and Otto II (Haight, pp. 27–28). Earlier critics believed that the letter to the second Otto indicated that an epic based on his life was to follow. However, Katharina Wilson suggests that the letter to Otto II was intended for Hrotsvit's final work, the *Primordia Coenobii Gandeshemensis* [The Origins of the Gandersheim Community], a narrative history of the Gandersheim abbey from its founding in 846 until the death of Abbess Christina in 919 (*Plays,* p. xv).

## SURVEY OF CRITICISM

Criticism of Hrotsvit's writings begins with Celtis's discovery of the Emmeram manuscript. The German humanists were enthusiastic about the discovery, finding in Hrotsvit a reason for national pride. But after the Thirty Years War, Hrotsvit was virtually ignored until the nineteenth century. In 1831, Jakob Grimm explained the etymology of her name, a subject of confusion for the humanists. Grimm noticed that in the preface to her plays, Hrotsvit describes herself as "*clamor validus Gandeshemensis*" [the strong voice of Gandersheim]; he realized that she was making a pun on her name. Her Old Saxon name was derived from two words, "*hruot = clamor* = voice and *suid = validus* = strong" (Wilson, *Medieval Women Writers,* p. 31).

Another nineteenth-century scholar, Joseph von Aschbach, a Viennese, argued that Hrotsvit never existed and that the Emmeram codex was a forgery created by Celtis. As a result of this charge, much Hrotsvit criticism in the early part of the twentieth century was devoted to proving the authenticity of her work. In 1902, a medieval manuscript was discovered that contained the play *Gallicanus,* and subsequently more manuscripts containing works by Hrotsvit were found (Wilson, *Plays,* p. xxx). In addition, critics like Edwin Zeydel turned to internal evidence within the writings themselves to prove their authenticity ("Ego," pp. 281–82).

Discoveries of medieval manuscripts containing works by Hrotsvit presented critics with yet another question: did Hrotsvit have any influence on later medieval literature, especially on the development of medieval drama? This question is still under debate. An early twentieth-century critic, Cornelia Coulter, supports such a probability and cites Coffman, who had suggested that Hrotsvit's plays "may conceivably have furnished a hint for the later miracle plays" (p. 529). More recently, Katharina Wilson has found a "free" translation of *Dulcitius* in Hungarian, in a manuscript tentatively dated 1521, making it the oldest medieval play in the Hungarian language ("Old Hungarian," p. 177). Yet more than a manuscript is needed to prove that Hrotsvit played a direct role in the development of medieval drama.

Another question that has intrigued critics for more than a century is whether Hrotsvit's plays were actually performed. Charles Magnin, a nineteenth-century French critic, suggested that they were staged (Zeydel, "Were," p. 443), but contemporary critics offer more conservative suggestions: the plays "were simply read, or read aloud, or recited with the accompaniment of mimicry" (Wilson, *Plays*, p. xxviii). The extent to which Hrotsvit imitated Terence is another area of critical interest. Hrotsvit wrote six plays, as did Terence. Coulter argues that there is little in Hrotsvit's plays that "can justly be called Terentian" (p. 526), but Wilson has found a number of similarities. Wilson also expands on the idea, introduced by Peter Dronke, that the plays are interconnected. By means of an elaborate numerological study, Wilson argues that a circular structure binds the plays together as a symbol of Christian perfection. She suggests that Hrotsvit intended a kind of "analogical paralleling" inspired by "exegetical as well as iconographic inspiration" (*Plays*, p. xxi). Wilson's recent criticism, more than any other, reveals the sophistication and complexity of Hrotsvit's writing. During the last decades of the twentieth century, Hrotsvit has been given a great deal of attention by critics and translators. It is somewhat ironic that the genius of a tenth-century canoness was never fully realized until the dawning of the second millennium.

## BIBLIOGRAPHY

### Works by Hrotsvit of Gandersheim

Strecker, Karl, ed. *Hrotsvithae Opera*. 1906. Second edition. Leipzig: Teubner, 1930.

Homeyer, Helena, ed. *Hrotsvithae Opera*. Munich: Schöningh, 1970.

Bonfante, L., trans. *The Plays of Hrotsvitha von Gandersheim*. New York: New York University Press, 1979.

Wilson, Katharina, trans. *The Plays of Hrotsvit of Gandersheim*. New York: Garland, 1989.

### Works about Hrotsvit of Gandersheim

Butler, Marguerite. *Hrotsvitha: The Theatricality of Her Plays*. New York: Philosophical Library, 1976.

Chamberlain, David. "Musical Learning and Dramatic Action in Hrotsvit's *Pafnutius*." *Studies in Philology* 77.4 (1980): 319–43.

Coffman, George R. "A New Approach to Medieval Latin Drama." *Modern Philology* 22 (1925): 239–71.

Coulter, Cornelia C. "The 'Terentian' Comedies of a Tenth-Century Nun." *Classical Journal* 24 (1929): 515–29.

Dronke, Peter. *Women Writers of the Middle Ages*. Cambridge: Cambridge University Press, 1984.

Haight, Anne Lyon, ed. *Hroswitha of Gandersheim: Her Life, Times, and Works, and a Comprehensive Bibliography*. New York: The Hroswitha Club, 1965.

Petroff, Elizabeth. *Body and Soul: Essays on Medieval Women and Mystics*. New York: Oxford University Press, 1994.

Pollack, Rhoda-Gale. *A Sampler of Plays by Women*. New York: Peter Lang, 1990.

Thiébaux, Marcelle, ed. *The Writings of Medieval Women: An Anthology.* Second edition. New York: Garland, 1994.

Wemple, Suzanne Fonay. "Monastic Life of Women from the Merovingians to the Ottonians." *Hrotsvit of Gandersheim: Rara Avis in Saxonia?* Ed. Katharina Wilson. Ann Arbor: MARC Publications, 1987.

Wilson, Katharina. "Hrotsvit's *Abraham*: A Lesson in Etymology." *Germanic Notes* 16.1 (1985): 2–4.

——— ed. *Medieval Women Writers.* Athens: University of Georgia Press, 1984.

———. "The Old Hungarian Translation of Hrotsvit's *Dulcitius*: History and Analysis." *Tulsa Studies in Women's Literature* 1.2 (1982): 177–87.

Zeydel, Edwin H. "'*Ego Clamor Validus*'—Hrotsvitha." *Modern Language Notes* 61.4 (1946): 281–83.

———. "The Reception of Hrotsvitha by the German Humanists after 1493." *Journal of English and Germanic Philology* 44 (1945): 443–56.

———. "Were Hrotsvitha's Dramas Performed During Her Lifetime?" *Speculum* 20 (1943): 443–56.

DEANNA DELMAR EVANS

# MARIE DE l'INCARNATION
## (1599–1672)

## BIOGRAPHY

Marie de l'Incarnation was born in Tours on October 28, 1599, the fourth of eight children of Florent Guyart, a master baker, and Jeanne Michelet, whose family had become nobility in the previous century. Even as a child, Marie frequented the Mass and festivals of the Church. Preachers fascinated her, and she often followed them through the streets. At home she would summarize their words for her family, adding her own thoughts as well. This practice "gave me a certain eloquence," she later wrote (Sullivan, p. 8).

At fifteen she sought a religious vocation, but her parents felt her vivacious spirit was not suited to the cloister. Rather, when she was seventeen, they married her to Claude Martin, a silk manufacturer. When he died two years later, he left Marie with their year-old son, Claude, and with a business deeply in debt.

After settling her husband's business affairs, Marie lived in seclusion for a year in her father's house. Later she worked eight years for her brother-in-law, managing his large transport business. The business prospered under her hand, but inwardly during this time she fled in her heart to her first love, "a continual colloquy with our Lord" (Sullivan, p. 24). On January 25, 1631, Marie took the name Marie de l'Incarnation and entered the Ursuline convent in Tours. Her son, but ten years old, went to the care of her sister and later to the Jesuit school at Rennes (Sullivan, p. 76).

In 1639 Marie forsook the comforts of France, in obedience to visions from God, and pioneered an Ursuline mission in New France. Arriving at Quebec, then just a small trading post, she began her mission in a meager, two-room hut by the river, taking in six Indian girls to teach them reading and arithmetic, the domestic arts, and the knowledge of Christ (Sullivan, p. 125). For the next thirty-three years, she worked among the Indian tribes of New France, administering the mission. Marie mastered the Algonquin, Huron, and Iroquois languages, and she wrote both an Iroquois dictionary and a large

French-Algonquin dictionary. She also found time to write two autobiographies, several catechisms in Amerindian languages, an extensive sacred history in Algonquin, and an estimated 20,000 letters, 278 of which are preserved in Oury's 1971 edition. Marie fell ill in January of 1672 and died peacefully on April 30 of the same year in the mission to which she had dedicated the last half of her life.

## MAJOR THEMES

Marie de l'Incarnation's devotional and instructional works in Tours, her two autobiographies (both commonly entitled *La Relation*, 1633 and 1654), and her correspondence—important historical documents—quickly reveal twin themes of passion for God and love for others. From these spring the early histories of the exotic new world, and the images of the *femme forte*.

Marie's passion for God appears immediately in her writings in Tours. These works include her commentary on the *Song of Songs*, an instructional work for Ursuline novices in her convent that uses the figure of the Bride in this biblical book as a model of devotion to Christ through the contemplative life. This divine love also appears in Marie's autobiography in the first of many visions she received. When just seven years old, Marie states, she saw Jesus descending from the heavens. He approached her, kissed her, and asked, "Will you be mine?" She writes, "'Yes,' I replied. When he had heard my consent we saw Him return to heaven" (Sullivan, pp. 3–4). In a later vision dated March 24, 1620, Marie saw herself immersed in the blood of Christ (pp. 14–15). Other visions focused on the Trinity and on spiritual marriage.

Motivated by her visions and scripture, which she cites on nearly every page of her autobiography, Marie describes her life as thirteen stages of prayer through which she passes "from my childhood" to death (Sullivan, p. 3). Her goal is complete unity with Christ, the divine marriage. She describes this union as "a gentle and loving respiration which continues without interruption. It is a communication of spirit to spirit and spirit in spirit . . . Jesus Christ is my life and my life is Jesus Christ. It is not I who live, but Jesus Christ who lives in me" (p. 177). She finds this "ravishing" beyond words: "all I can say is that during it I am in God, possessed by Him, and that He would soon consume me by the intensity and force of His love if I were not sustained by another impression which . . . tempers its splendor, which is too great for one to bear in this present life" (p. 180).

Marie's adoration of "the Divine Spouse" led naturally to her love of others. In Tours it produced her service to the workers she managed, and later to the sisters she lived among. In New France it produced her devotion to the Ursulines, Jesuits, and the Amerindians. She learned native languages in order to speak to tribes in their own tongues, and her letters bear out her affection for the Amerindians. For example, shortly after reaching Quebec, Marie wrote, "What a joy to find oneself with a great troop of native women and girls, whose miserable coverings—a skin or an old rug—do not smell so pleasant as those of the ladies of France but whose candor and simplicity is so unspeakably attractive" (Oury, p. 108). Her love of others also shows in her extensive correspondence with her son, Claude. In 1640 she wrote, "You have gained much in losing me, and my abandonment has been useful to you. And I likewise, having left in you what was most dear and unique to me in the world. . . . I have found myself with you in the bosom of this kind God through the holy calling that you and I have both followed" (Oury, pp. 115–16). When Claude complained in 1649 that he had no idea what she looked like, she raised her veil for the messenger who would bring her letter to him (Oury, p. 384). When Claude confessed to sexual temptation, Marie replied calmly but firmly, requiring him to treat the woman with all chasteness, yet not to withhold any courteous regard. She urged him, "Even if it is difficult all your life you should not stop being kind" (Oury, pp. 533–34, 549–50).

Of the wonders of forested New France, Marie records much. Her accounts of icebergs on her voyage, the life and customs of the Amerindians, native wars, famine, fire, and martyrs stirred all of France. She recounts in fascinating detail a major earthquake in 1663 and the visions that warned both converts and missionaries of the impending disaster (Oury, p. 687ff.). She writes, "We learned from some gentlemen that came from Tadaussac that the earthquake made a strange disorder there. For the space of six hours it rained ashes in such quantity that they lay an inch thick on the ground and in the barks. . . . The ashes were like burned sugar" (Marshall, pp. 291–92). A 1670 letter states, "There was still ice in our garden in the month of June; our trees and our grafts, which bore exquisite fruit, are dead from it. . . . The trees bearing wild fruit are not dead" (Oury, p. 877).

Through all her works, Marie de l'Incarnation's writing reveals a remarkable *femme forte*, as her sisters called her and as she describes the women around her. Marie's autobiography demonstrates her skills as administrator and financial manager in Tours. After her husband's death, she must resolve his troubled business affairs, and she does so by going to the factory every day to oversee production, managing funds from the guild, and facing lawsuits and creditors (Sullivan, p. 14). During the eight years she worked for her brother-in-law's shipping firm, she notes how she honed the skills she would later need when she directed the mission in Quebec. Marie balanced this "confusion of temporal affairs" and her inner life of devotion, she states, through "a new gift of prayer, that of a union with Him" (pp. 17–18). She writes knowledgeably of economics, affairs of state, and religious hierarchy (Oury, pp. 398, 873).

Marie de l'Incarnation's accounts of the vigorous Amerindian women confronted Europe with new social structures more compatible with the tremendous abilities Marie herself demonstrated. During the peace negotiations of 1654–1655 between the French and the Iroquois and other tribes, Marie reports favorably about a chief's wife who influenced decisions at local councils and had authority to name ambassadors (p. 546). She also reports a woman chief at the negotiations (p. 556). When speaking of French girls, she especially praises the often-ignored working classes: "We no longer want to ask for anyone but village girls suitable for work like men. Experience shows that those not raised in this way are not right for here" (p. 832).

## SURVEY OF CRITICISM

Five years after Marie de l'Incarnation's death, her son, Claude Martin, published an extensive biography using material from her letters and her *Relations* of 1633 and 1654. In 1681 he published 221 of her letters, all heavily edited. A number of biographical and hagiographical works followed in French, with little notice in English during the nineteenth century.

This century has seen dramatic new interest in Marie de l'Incarnation and her writings. Henri Bremond published a critical edition of her works in the sixth volume of his history of religious literature (1922). This sparked new studies, including Albert Jamet's two-volume critical edition, *Écrits spirituels et historiques* (1929). This excellent edition includes the letters; meditations, a commentary on the *Song of Songs*, and a catechism written by Marie in Tours; *La Relation* of 1654; Jamet's reconstruction of *La Relation* of 1633 based on Martin's biography; and some brief devotional writings.

In 1964 John J. Sullivan translated the only complete work by Marie available in English, *La Relation* of 1654. Dom Guy Oury published Marie's known correspondence, 278 letters of the thousands she wrote, in a critical edition in 1971.

Readers have noted the logic and clarity of Marie's writings. Anya Mali writes, "Because they were written informally and were not subject to official scrutiny, they present a more candid, personal view of the Indians as well as of the nature, mechanics, and consequences of conversion" (p. 113). In addition, Marie's autobiographies are highly praised, especially *La Relation* of 1654. James Broderick calls the author "one of the most attractive of profound mystics" who "dared to be humorous even when treating of the high things of God" (quoted in Sullivan, p. vii). Bremond praises her style and judgment, and devotes nearly half a volume to her work. Mali says *La Relation* "ranks among the finest in the spiritual literature of the day" (p. xiv).

Until recently most critics placed Marie de l'Incarnation in the mystical tradition, or viewed her mainly as a European woman building a mission in the New World. The last two decades have seen increased interest in her from feminist critics. Three recent books in English consider Marie at length. Natalie Zemon Davis studies Marie as a writer both of history and passionate lyrics, "words of fire" as Marie's son called them (p. 69). She offers an interesting analysis of Claude's response to those words as he edits his mother's works (pp. 128–32). Davis also critiques Marie's attempts to convert the Amerindians, comparing abduction and politeness in France and New France (pp. 132–38).

Mali studies Marie's writing in terms of conversion experiences. While some dismiss supernatural visions, Mali weighs Marie's own analysis of her experience closely: Marie, like us, Mali notes, is a "self-interpreting animal" (pp. 34–36, 172). Mali discusses the new substance that Marie interjects into both mystical literature and contemporary reports of the New World.

Marie-Florine Bruneau, however, takes a more skeptical view of Marie's mystical experience. She posits the Ursulines' religious confinement as a metaphor for their restricted thought and inability to understand the "savages." Where Mali concludes that Marie's experience in Quebec produces her works' originality (as Oury terms her, she is "a spiritual master unbeknownst to herself," pp. 165–66), Bruneau cites Oury to support her assessment that Marie produces "the same discourse, the same representation of the body, the same description of piety as that found in female mysticism from the thirteenth century onward" (p. 39). She understands Marie's writing as primarily "useful" in persuading her superiors that she should undertake the mission to Quebec and later to continue there (p. 42).

But Bruneau also discusses helpful particulars, showing new ground broken by Marie's life and writing. To Bruneau, Marie honored women and their labors, though "circumscribed" by paternal structure (pp. 86–99). Bruneau concludes that Marie's religious mission failed, and finds traces in Marie's texts to prove that "[t]he civilized woman is confined, like the Ursulines who were trying to civilize Indian women; the native woman roams freely in the woods and 'paddles a canoe like a man'" (p. 122).

## BIBLIOGRAPHY

### Works by Marie de l'Incarnation

Sullivan, John J., trans. 1654. *The Autobiography of Venerable Marie of the Incarnation, O.S.U. Mystic and Missionary.* Chicago: Loyola University Press, 1964.

Martin, Claude. *La Vie de la Vénérable Mère Marie de l'Incarnation. Première Supérieure des Ursulines de la Nouvelle-France, tirée de ses lettres et ses écrits.* 1677. Solesmes-Paris: Jouve, 1982.

Jamet, Albert, ed. *Marie de l'Incarnation, Ursuline de Tours: Foundatrice des Ursulines de la Nouvelle-France. Écrits spirituels et historiques.* 2 vols. 1929. Quebec: Les Ursulines de Quebec, 1985.

Marshall, Joyce, trans. and ed. *Word from New France: The Selected Letters of Marie de l'Incarnation.* Toronto: Oxford University Press, 1967.

Oury, Guy-Marie, ed. *Marie de l'Incarnation, Ursuline (1599–1672) Corréspondance.* Solesmes: Abbaye Saint-Pierre, 1971.

——. *Marie Guyart (1599–1672).* Trans. Miriam Thompson. Cincinnati: Specialty Lithographing, 1979.

Mahoney, Irene, ed. *Marie of the Incarnation: Selected Writings.* New York: Paulist Press, 1985.

### Works about Marie de l'Incarnation

Bremond, Henri. *Histoire littéraire du sentiment religieux en France.* Vol. 6. *Marie de l'Incarnation.* Paris: Bloud et Gay, 1922.

Bruneau, Marie-Florine. *Women Mystics Confront the Modern World: Marie de l'Incarnation (1599–1672) and Madame Guyon (1648–1717).* Albany: State University of New York Press, 1998.

Davis, Natalie Zemon. *Women on the Margins: Three Seventeenth Century Lives.* Cambridge: Harvard University Press, 1995.

Deroy-Pineau, Francois. *Marie de l'Incarnation. Marie Guyart femme d'affaires, mystique, mère de la Nouvelle France.* Paris: Laffonte, 1989.

Mali, Anya. *Mystic in the New World: Marie De l'Incarnation (1599–1672).* Leiden: E. J. Brill, 1996.

Oury, Guy-Marie. *Marie De l'Incarnation (1599–1672).* Solesmes: Abbaye Saint-Pierre, 1973.

Zecher, Carla. "A New World Model of Female Epistolarity: The Correspondence of Marie De l'Incarnation." *Studies in Canadian Literature* 21.2 (1996): 89–102.

ROBERT C. MILLIKEN

# SOR JUANA INÉS DE LA CRUZ
# (1648?–1695)

## BIOGRAPHY

Sor Juana Inés de la Cruz, a seventeenth-century Mexican poet, is celebrated today as the only Spanish American colonial writer to master all the forms of Golden Age Spanish Baroque literature, and as a proto-feminist who eloquently defended the right of women to study and write about all intellectual pursuits. She was born Juana Ramírez de Asbaje on November 12, 1648 or 1651, in Nepatla (near Mexico City), New Spain. Very little is known of her father, a Basque military captain; her mother, a *criolla* (creole), raised Juana, her four sisters, and a half-brother on her own.

As a toddler, Juana manifested a marked precociousness. Growing up on her maternal grandfather's ranch in Panoayan, she spent many hours alone observing the world around her and trying to read books in the family library. According to her autobiography, the *Reply to Sor Filotea*, she learned how to read at age three. Desirous of a complete education, at age seven she dreamed of dressing as a man to be able to attend the University of Mexico. At this time, she also wrote her first literary work—a short play in praise of the Eucharist—which is now lost.

In 1659, Juana moved to the house of an aunt in Mexico City where she continued to nurture her intellectual gifts and taught herself Greek and Latin. With the arrival of a new viceroy, Sebastian de Toledo, the bright little *criolla* soon reached the attention of the court. The viceroy's wife "adopted" Juana as one of her handmaidens. Thereafter, the royal household became Juana's ideal family and the subject of many of her early poems. But as she grew older, this favorite daughter of the Mexican court was confronted by an uncertain future. With no father to provide a dowry or a pedigree for a respectable marriage, the only avenue left for the intellectually ambitious girl was to enter a convent where she could study undistracted by worldly cares. In 1667, Juana entered the community of Discalced Carmelites but departed after three months, claiming the discipline of the order was too strict and oppressive. Consequently, the viceroy arranged for her to enter the more liberal convent of Saint Jerome where she professed her vows in 1669. Now known as Sor Juana Inés de la Cruz, she served as the community's bookkeeper and archivist while also assembling a research library of philosophical and scientific books to assist her in her writing. She remained at Saint Jerome for the rest of her life, and it is here where she composed her greatest poems and plays, both religious and secular; a treatise on music; and various other devotional works.

After returning to Spain in 1673, the ex-viceroy Sebastian de Toledo gathered together all the poems written by the young Juana (many dedicated to his deceased wife) and published them in 1689 under the title *Inundación Castálida* [A Muse's Deluge]. This book established Sor Juana's fame in Europe and earned her the nickname the "Tenth Muse" from Mexico. She herself published a Eucharistic allegory in New Spain in 1689 entitled the *Divino Narciso* [Divine Narcissus], and a year later a second edition of her poetry was published. By 1690 her fame as a poet and religious writer extended throughout the Spanish territories.

In 1689, the bishop of Puebla, a friend of Sor Juana's and a frequent participant in her gatherings of intellectuals at the convent, invited her to comment on a sermon by a Portuguese Jesuit. He published the result, her *Carta atenagórica* [A Letter Worthy of Athena], without Sor Juana's knowledge. Events following this publication are uncertain, but the letter apparently generated controversy in the Church hierarchy. The work was popular in Spain where Jesuits were often the objects of ridicule; however, in Mexico, where the Jesuits maintained a strong presence, Sor Juana's critique of a famous preacher was taken as an insult. Reflecting the negative reaction by some ecclesial authorities, the bishop of Puebla then wrote a mock-chiding letter to Sor Juana under the pseudonym of "Sor Filotea," admonishing her and suggesting that she abandon her intellectual activities as unbefitting a religious woman. Sor Juana's famous *Respuesta a Sor Filotea* [Reply to Sor Filotea] defended her desire to study and write on theology as well as on many secular topics. In this autobiographical statement of her *raison d'être*, she draws on the Bible and the writings of the Church fathers, and she cites great women of intelligence in history and myth in an effort to counter the age-old prejudice that women ought to remain silent. Although the *Reply* indicates that Sor Juana suffered intense criticism as a nun writing non-religious works and daring theological commentary, she continued to write. In the midst of this controversy, for example, another edition of her complete poems was published in Barcelona, and in 1692, music she had written for the Mass was performed at the cathedral in Mexico City. These facts seem to contradict the assertion some have forwarded that she was "silenced" around this time by the allegedly misogynist archbishop. So, it remains a mystery as to why Sor Juana finally decided to renounce her writing in 1693 and sell her library and various scientific instruments. In the same year that the second volume of her works (including her mystical poem *Primer Sueño* [First Dream]) was being published in Spain, she dedicated herself solely to service to her community.

In 1695, a plague spread throughout Mexico City and its environs, and Sor Juana nursed her afflicted sisters at the convent. Contracting the disease, she died on April 17, mourned in the colonies and abroad. As the Mexican historiographer Andrés Cavo noted, recalling the sorrow a century after her death, Mexico "lost . . . a woman of exceptional giftedness, as proven by her writings" (*Historia de México.* Ed. Ernesto J. Burrus, S.J. México, D.F.: Editorial Patria, 1949, p. 368, translation mine).

## MAJOR THEMES

When assessing Sor Juana Inés de la Cruz as a Catholic woman writer, it is important to bear in mind two facts. First, although she is best remembered today for her *Reply to Sor Filotea* and her defense of women's learning, in her lifetime the works that most Spaniards read were her devotions for the Virgin Mary. Second, although many critics try to persuade readers that she was the victim of misogynist Church authorities who tried to silence her, she herself clearly had considerable authority in her community. In fact, to call her "Sor" Juana actually diminishes the level of respect she commanded, for her contemporaries often referred to her as "Madre" Juana. She wore the black veil, which placed her in the highest level of her order's hierarchy. Those with the black veil dedicated themselves to prayer and were exempt from service. Thus, Madre Juana had plenty of time to read, perform her experiments with light and prisms, compose music, host gatherings of Mexico's savants, and write poetry, plays, scientific treatises, and spiritual exercises. Of her extant writings, nearly half are religious in theme. Others mix biblical and mythical metaphors, including references to feminine divinities like Isis and Minerva, in typically complex and intricate Baroque fashion to elevate the mind to ponder the transformative power of line and verse applied to a subject.

To discern the major themes of Sor Juana's spiritual writings, it is necessary to know that her "master" was the Austrian Jesuit and polymath Athanasius Kircher (1601–1680). She cites him as a key influence on her intellectual development in the *Reply*. In addition, Sor Juana even created a verb out of his surname to describe her intellectual approach: "*a veces kirkerizo*" (at times I Kircherize), she states playfully (*Obras completas*, p. 72). Kircher published numerous volumes in his lifetime that attempted to combine or syncretize ancient mythologies, especially those of Egypt, with Christian beliefs in an effort to demonstrate the Catholic faith and the life and person of Christ as the Myth Come True, the fulfillment of pre-Incarnational mythic hopes. This approach to faith and science appealed to Sor Juana, and she frequently employed images from Kircher's writings to illustrate her poems. The mystical poem *First Dream*, for example, is heavily dependent on Kircher for its images of contrasting cones of light and dark, and its landscape of pyramids, all borrowed from his popular *Oedipus Aegyptiacus*. Sor Juana further honored her intellectual mentor by making him the older student who instructs the others in her *Loa del auto al San Hermenegildo* [Praise for St. Hermenegildo], a skit praising the desire to know beyond the limits of knowledge in this world. In this skit, the older student-professor is Kircher, but Sor Juana speaks through him, expressing her own desire to attain wide-ranging knowledge ("*el desear saber*," or "the wanting to know," *Obras completas*, p. 833).

In her Catholic writings, Sor Juana wrote several works dedicated to the Incarnation and various Eucharistic celebrations. Her *villancicos* [songs of praise] celebrate, among other subjects, the birth of Christ (God united to man, including all humanity's purest desires); Mary as the mother of God (giver of his humanity); Saint Joseph as protector of Jesus and Mary (the fullness of the Church, male and female); and Saint Peter as protector of the Church on earth. She also composed numerous song and prayer cycles for the feasts of the Assumption, the Immaculate Conception, and saints' days such as those of Saint Joseph, Saint Peter, Saint Catherine of Alexandria, and Saint Bernard. Many of the texts have glosses indicating they were performed in public settings, including the cathedral in Mexico City. They were also likely sung in religious communities. The emphasis on Eucharistic themes is consistent with the primary mission of the sisters of Saint Jerome to worship and promote devotion to the Eucharist. Other Eucharistic-themed works include the plays *Divine Narcissus* (a clever play on Roman mythology and the sacrifice of Christ), *San Hermenegildo* (a patron saint of her community, a martyr who had refused to deny the teaching of the Real Presence), and a cycle of devotional prayers on the Incarnation.

Sor Juana also celebrates strong women of faith in her writings. In her *Obsequio de María y su concepción* [In Honor of Mary and Her Conception] and her spiritual exercises for the rosary, she reflects on the empowerment of all women through the special grace bestowed on women by God. She observes that it is Mary's flesh and blood that clothe the Son; when we look upon Christ we therefore also look upon his Mother. She emphasizes in one of her sacred poems that Mary herself had come to Mexico in 1531 as the Virgin of Guadalupe to become the Protector of the Americas. In another poem, Sor Juana comments on the bravery of Saint Catherine before her accusers, a woman daring to teach men the True Faith. These women (including the biblical heroes she names in the *Reply*, such as Debra and Mary Magdalene) are for Sor Juana models of women of faith whose voices were heard and respected.

## SURVEY OF CRITICISM

Early Sor Juana studies were largely hagiographic in nature, beginning with Diego Calleja's eighteenth-century "biography," a source of early legends relating to the nun's childhood. Calleja and other early critics played up her uniqueness and her ability to astound her contemporaries with almost other-worldly intellectual powers. In such accounts, Sor Juana attains a near myth-like status.

The late twentieth century has witnessed a renaissance of interest in Sor Juana, much of it fueled by feminist readings of her life (especially the alleged "silencing") and the publication of Octavio Paz's magisterial biographical essay in 1982, *Sor Juana Inés de la Cruz, o Las Trampas de La Fe* (translated as *Sor Juana or, The Traps of Faith* in 1988). Paz's interpretations and conclusions are repeated, often uncritically, in subsequent studies. In fact, one can characterize most of Sor Juana scholarship since Paz's book as scholarship about Octavio Paz's "Sor Juana," a figure who incarnates Paz's familiar critique of Mexican history as a struggle between personal and impersonal forces (see articles by Luciani and Crossen for discussion on how Paz manipulates Sor Juana for his own literary and philosophical purposes). A new, revisionist biography of the actual Sor Juana is long overdue.

Many studies attempt to understand Sor Juana accurately within the context of her times. Still others seek to interpret her as a woman and as a Catholic writer. Arenal's article notes, for example, how the convent became a liberating space for intellectual women in the colonial period. This environment accounts for much of the autonomy and authority that Sor Juana enjoyed. Kirk provides excellent chapters on each of Sor Juana's major themes, especially her vision of Mary and uses of Eucharistic imagery. She also studies Sor Juana's critique of the Jesuit sermon, highlighting the writer's expert use of biblical exegesis to argue Christ's "finesses."

Merrim's 1991 text is still the essential collection of feminist criticism on Sor Juana. It includes helpful commentary on the traditions of convent writers and their milieu. Although published in Spanish, Sabat de Rivers's book is highly recommended for its analysis of Sor Juana's textual uses of Kircher to cast herself as a theological authority in her play *San Hermenegildo*. This book brings together a host of informative essays by Sabat de Rivers discussing various topics, including Sor Juana's struggles with gender and racial identity in Counter Reformation New Spain.

Finally, writing from the perspective of a Roman Catholic theologian, Tavard explores Sor Juana's often confusing but original uses of hermetic traditions, Greco-Roman mythology, patristic sources, Kircher, and other scientific authors of her day. At times, his biographical facts are wrong and one wonders how much of the nun's work he has read; however, his alternate interpretation of Sor Juana's "silence" as a mystic's awe before the Beauty of God is worth serious consideration.

## BIBLIOGRAPHY

### Works by Sor Juana Inés de la Cruz

*Obras completas.* Ed. Francisco Monterde. México, D.F.: Editorial Porrua, 1989.
*A Sor Juana Anthology.* Ed. and trans. Alan Trueblood. Cambridge, Massachusetts: Harvard University Press, 1988.

### Works about Sor Juana Inés de la Cruz

Arenal, Electa. "The Convent as Catalyst for Autonomy: Two Hispanic Nuns of the Seventeenth Century." *Women in Hispanic Literature: Icons and Fallen Idols.* Ed. Beth Miller. Berkeley: University of California Press, 1983. 147–83.

Calleja, Diego. *Vida de Sor Juana.* 1700. México, D.F.: Robredo, 1936.

Crossen, John F. "Sor Juana Inés de la Cruz, ¿ 'Caudilla'?: Octavio Paz en Busca de lo Personal Entre Los Tlatoanis Romanos." *Romance Languages Annual* viii (1996): 424–27.

Kirk, Pamela. *Sor Juana Inés de la Cruz: Religion, Art, and Feminism.* New York: Continuum, 1998.

Luciani, Frederick. "Octavio Paz on Sor Juana Inés de la Cruz: The Metaphor Incarnate." *Latin American Literary Review* 15.30 (July/December 1987): 6–25.

Merrim, Stephanie, ed. *Feminist Perspectives on Sor Juana Inés de la Cruz.* Detroit: Wayne State University Press, 1991.

Paz, Octavio. *Sor Juana or, The Traps of Faith.* Trans. Margaret Sayers Peden. Cambridge, Massachusetts: Harvard University Press, 1988.

Sabat de Rivers, Georgina. *En busca de Sor Juana.* México, D.F.: Facultad de Filosofía y Letras/UNAM, 1998.

Tavard, George H. *Juana Inés de la Cruz and the Theology of Beauty: The First Mexican Theology.* Notre Dame: University of Notre Dame Press, 1991.

JOHN F. CROSSEN

# JULIAN OF NORWICH
## (c. 1342–after 1413)

---

## BIOGRAPHY

Julian (or Juliana) of Norwich was a medieval visionary and recluse in England. Although she is commonly regarded as the first English woman of letters, little is known about her life save the few details contained in her mystical treatise, *Revelations of Divine Love* (1670), sometimes called *Shewings*. We do not know exactly when she was born, when she died, or what her birth name was. She was probably born in Norwich around 1342 and died some time after 1413. She may have been affiliated early in her life with the Benedictine house of Carrow, although it is more likely that she was a highly devout laywoman living at her home. By 1394 she had become an anchoress, enclosed in a cell adjoining the church of St. Julian in Norwich, from which she derived her name. Thereafter, her life consisted of meditation, prayer, and service—a life highly respected by people of the time.

According to her *Revelations*, Julian desired three gifts from God: to have an understanding of Christ's Passion; to experience bodily suffering when she turned thirty (the same age as Christ when he began his public life); and to have the three "wounds" of contrition, compassion, and earnest longing for God. Her desire was fulfilled in May 1373 when she was thirty and a half years old: God sent her a serious illness that debilitated her completely for three days and nights. On the fourth day, Easter morning, the parish priest came and gave her the last sacraments of the Church. The priest visited her again, on May 8, to be with her at her end. When she thought she was passing away and all around her had turned dark, he held up the crucifix before her face, saying, "I have brought you the image of your Maker and Saviour. Look, and be strengthened" (*Revelations*, p. 64). When she fixed her gaze on the face of the crucifix, she saw a light beaming from the cross, and her pain left her immediately. At that moment, the crucifix changed: "And at once I saw the red blood trickling down from under the garland, hot, freshly, and plentiful, just as it did at the time of his passion when the crown of thorns was pressed on to the blessed head of God-and-Man, who suffered for me" (p. 66). The first fifteen visions, which ensued successively during the course of about five hours, granted her an understanding of the mysteries of the Christian faith. The last vision, which occurred the following night, convinced her that the visions were genuinely from God.

Soon after, Julian began, with the help of a scribe, to record her visions in the "short version" of the *Revelations*. In the "longer version," written approximately twenty years later, she added the spiritual meanings of the initial revelations which she had gained through years of study, prayer, and reflection. Consisting of eighty-six chapters, this version deals with not only her personal recollections but also various theological issues such as predestination, the foreknowledge of God, the nature of sin, and prayer. The *Revelations* is now considered one of the most remarkable mystical treatises written by a woman. Although Julian refers to herself as "a simple and uneducated creature" (p. 63), her writing clearly demonstrates that she was a woman of profound intellect and erudition. She acquired a knowledge of biblical and mystical texts from England and Europe. She was also familiar with the Vulgate and the writings of St. Gregory and St. Augustine. Through the great Hebrew scholar of her time, Cardinal Adam Easton from the Norwich Priory, Julian may have had access to Hebrew as well.

As an anchoress, Julian was reputed for her good spiritual counseling. Living in a precarious age beset by the Black Death, the Hundred Years' War, the Great Schism, and the Peasants' Revolt, people sought her out for guidance, consolation, and prayer. Julian's visions of a nurturing and gentle God provided them with an optimistic Christian faith. Notably, Margery Kempe, a controversial English mystic of the time, visited Julian in or about 1413. Kempe, who was ridiculed by some of her contemporaries as a heretic and hypocrite, sought Julian's counsel and approval, for Julian was "expert" in discerning revelations and "could give good advice" to her (Kempe, p. 77). Julian did confirm the authenticity of Kempe's revelations, advising her to remain obedient to Christ's will. "Great was the holy conversation that the anchoress and this creature had through talking of the love of our Lord Jesus Christ for the many days that they were together," recalled Kempe in her autobiography (pp. 78–79).

## MAJOR THEMES

The dominant themes of *Revelations of Divine Love* are theological optimism, God's love, and God as Mother. First of all, theological optimism pervades Julian's book. Living in the late Middle Ages, which was a period of violence, confusion, and unrest, Julian voices a message of hope based on faith and conviction in the sovereignty of God. She declares that God is the supreme ruler and that his design is to bring all humanity, the supreme creation, to the joy of heaven. By his nature, God is gentle, humble, kind, and gracious. He is never wrathful: "God is the goodness that may not be angry" (p. 133). Julian maintains that we tend to envision an angry God precisely because the anger exists within us: "I saw no anger other than human—and that God forgives. This anger is nothing else but perverse opposition to peace and love; it comes from the failure of our own strength, or wisdom, or goodness" (p. 136). Although humans are prone to rage, God tenderly protects them and brings them peace, hence "Everything is going to be all right" (p. 109).

Julian's optimism comes from her transcending earthly things. According to Julian, all sufferings that we go through in this world are momentary and of minor importance, for divine love carries us within itself in love. Thus in Chapter 77 of the *Revelations*, Julian summarizes the message of all her visions by emphasizing God as our keeper: "The remedy is the fact that our Lord is with us, protecting us and leading us into fullness of joy. For it is an unending source of joy to us that our Lord should intend that he, our protector here, is to be our bliss there—our way and our heaven is true love and sure trust!" (p. 200).

Another important subject of the *Revelations* is God's love. With an infinite love, God creates, preserves, and redeems all his creatures. He is a "homely" God who is close by, meeting our everyday needs. There is no aspect of our existence that is untouched by God, and with his foreknowledge and wisdom, he makes everything perfect and good for us. God's love resides within human souls; it unites them to him, and it never fails. God's love finds its ultimate expression in the Cross, where Christ died a redemptive death for all humanity.

One of the interesting aspects of Julian's theology is her reference to God as Mother. Julian envisions a God who is nurturing, tender, and ever-loving—a love like that of a sweet and kind mother. Julian does not characterize the Trinity as a female God but as Father, Mother, and Lord residing in one person. In Chapter 59 of the *Revelations*, Julian elaborates on how the Trinity works by using simple terms: "Our Father decides, our Mother works, our good Lord, the Holy Spirit, strengthens" (p. 168). God's motherhood is revealed in Christ, the Second Person. Indeed, Christ is the origin of all motherhood: "So we see that Jesus is the true Mother of our nature, for he made us. He is our Mother, too, by grace, because he took our created nature upon himself" (p. 168). However, Christ is greater than an earthly mother, for the latter is unable to provide herself as food for her child: "The human mother will suckle her child with her own milk, but our beloved Mother, Jesus, feeds us with himself, and, with the most tender courtesy, does it by means of the Blessed Sacrament, the precious food of all true life" (p. 170). Christ's motherhood, in turn, demands our total dependence on him.

## SURVEY OF CRITICISM

For nearly six hundred years since its composition, the *Revelations* was largely ignored by critics, perhaps due to its abstruseness. In the twentieth century, however, the book has come to receive much attention because of its literary, devotional, and theological values. Edmund Colledge and James Walsh, in their introduction to the 1978 edition of the *Revelations*, compare Julian to Geoffrey Chaucer in her mastery of literary and rhetorical art. Julian also earns the praise of Thomas Merton for her theological insight: "Julian is without a doubt one of the most wonderful of all Christian voices. . . . I think that Julian of Norwich is with Newman the greatest English theologian" (pp. 274–75).

The motherhood of God/Christ metaphor in the *Revelations* has received more critical attention than any other aspect of the book. Benôit du Moustier comments in "Spiritual Childhood and Dame Julian of Norwich" that the *Revelations* is remarkably similar to the writings of the French mystic Marguerite d'Oingt (1286–1310) in its use of motherhood imagery. In "Une Dévotion médiévale peu connue: la dévotion à Jésus, nôtre mère," André Cabussut observes that the idea of God/Christ as a mother not only is biblically sound but also is found in the writings of Christian antiquity, such as that of St. Anselm of Canterbury. Cabassut considers Julian as one of the medieval mystics who speaks of "the maternal aspect of Christ's love and have contemplated it in Christ himself, nay even in the Eternal Word in the bosom of the Trinity. In their meditations . . . they have delighted to address our Lord as 'Mother'" (quoted in Molinari, p. 169). In *Julian of Norwich*, Paul Molinari notes the doctrinal soundness of the motherhood theme in the *Revelations*: "The grounds on which Julian bases her consideration of God as Mother are some amongst the fundamental truths" of the Catholic faith (p. 171). In her article "'Christ My Mother': Feminine Naming and Metaphor in Medieval Spirituality," Eleanor McLaughlin also examines Julian's use of motherhood imagery from the perspective of the medieval Catholic tradition, which includes the works of the Monk of Farne, Marguerite d'Oingt, and Mechthild of Magdeburg. Caroline Walker Bynum's "Julian as Mother and Abbott as Mother: Some Themes in Twelfth-Century Cistercian Writing" is an historical examination of the motherhood theme as found in the *Revelations*. Finally, in "Patristic Background of the Motherhood Similitude in Julian of Norwich," Ritamary Bradley also notes that Julian's motherhood motif is in line with the patristic tradition, which includes Augustine and Philo.

Recent years have witnessed the appearance of a number of critical works focusing on Julian as a Christian feminist. In *The Creation of Feminist Consciousness: From the Middle Ages to Eighteen-Seventy*, Gerda Lerner discusses the feminist theology in Julian's work. According to Lerner, Julian rebels against the patriarchy of the Middle Ages and celebrates women's right to self-expression by using the maternal God/Christ motif. Elizabeth Robertson, in "Medieval Medical Views of Women and Female Spirituality in the *Ancrene Wisse* and Julian of Norwich's *Showings*," contends that "Julian, rather than accepting male views of women, ultimately subverts them, and that rather than being an essentialist herself, she takes an 'essentialist' stance only as a strategy, in an Irigarayan sense: she mocks male views by mimicking and hyperbolizing them, and undoes them by overdoing them" (p. 150). In *Julian of Norwich:* Revelations of Divine Love *and the Motherhood of God,* Frances Beer focuses on such issues as empowerment, women's choices, and attitudes toward women in Julian's writing. "Despite the misogynist climate of her time," she concludes, "[Julian] found the courage to believe in her ability, and to insist on her right, to articulate even the most difficult of the revelations—to act as God's intermediary" (pp. 76–77).

Finally, many critics have written about the theological influences on Julian. In "Some Literary Influences in the *Revelations* of Julian of Norwich," Sister Anna Maria Reynolds holds that the *Revelations* was influenced by the Bible, patristic writings, pseudo-Dionysius thought, and earlier and contemporary English writings, including the *Ancren Riwle.* Hilda Graef, in *The Light and the Rainbow,* discusses Julian's theology in connection with her contemporary, Catherine of Siena. Meanwhile, Sister Mary Paul, in her *All Shall Be Well,* examines the *Revelations* from the perspective of the primitive Judeo-Christian tradition of the "Holy-Spirit, the Mother." Finally, in his dissertation "Julian of Norwich: A Theological Reappraisal," Charles Brant Pelphrey maintains that Julian's theology is in line with Byzantine mysticism and Orthodox theology.

## BIBLIOGRAPHY

### Work by Julian of Norwich

*Revelations of Divine Love.* 1670. Trans. and intro. Clifton Wolters. London: Penguin, 1966.

### Works about Julian of Norwich

Baker, Denise Nowakowski. *Julian of Norwich's* Showings: *From Vision to Book.* Princeton, New Jersey: Princeton University Press, 1994.

Beer, Frances. *Julian of Norwich:* Revelations of Divine Love *and the Motherhood of God.* Suffolk: Boydell Press, 1998.

——. *Women and Mystical Experience in the Middle Ages.* Suffolk: Boydell Press, 1992.

Bradley, Ritamary. "Patristic Background of the Motherhood Similitude in Julian of Norwich." *Christian Scholar's Review* 8 (1978): 101–13.

Bynum, Caroline Walker. *Jesus as Mother: Studies in the Spirituality of the High Middle Ages.* Berkeley: University of California Press, 1982.

——. "Julian as Mother and Abbott as Mother: Some Themes in Twelfth-Century Cistercian Writing." *Harvard Theological Review* 70 (1977): 257–84.

Cabussut, André. "Une Dévotion médiévale peu connue: la dévotion à Jésus, nôtre mère." *Revue d'Ascese et Mystique* 25 (1949): 231–45.

Colledge, Edmund, and James Walsh. Introduction. *A Book of Shewings to the Anchoress Julian of Norwich.* New York: Paulist Press, 1978. 17–122.

du Moustier, Benôit. "Spiritual Childhood and Dame Julian of Norwich." *Pax* 24 (1935): 281–84.

Graef, Hilda. *The Light and the Rainbow*. Westminster, Maryland: Newman Press, 1959.

Krantz, M. Diane F. *The Life and Text of Julian of Norwich: The Poetics of Enclosure*. New York: Peter Lang, 1997.

Lerner, Gerda. *The Creation of Feminist Consciousness: From the Middle Ages to Eighteen-Seventy*. New York: Oxford University Press, 1993.

McLaughlin, Eleanor. "'Christ My Mother': Feminine Naming and Metaphor in Medieval Spirituality." *Nashotah Review* 15 (1975): 229–48.

Merton, Thomas. *Seeds of Destruction*. New York: Farrar, Strauss, 1964.

Molinari, Paolo. *Julian of Norwich: The Teaching of a Fourteenth-Century English Mystic*. New York: Arden Library, 1979.

Paul, Sister Mary. *All Shall Be Well: Julian of Norwich and the Compassion of God*. Oxford: S. L. G. Press, 1976.

Pelphrey, Charles Brant. "Julian of Norwich: A Theological Reappraisal." Diss. University of Edinburgh, 1978.

Reynolds, Sister Anna Maria. "Some Literary Influences in the *Revelations* of Julian of Norwich." *Leeds Studies in English and Kindred Languages* 7–8 (1952): 18–28.

Robertson, Elizabeth. "Medieval Medical Views of Women and Female Spirituality in the *Ancrene Wisse* and Julian of Norwich's *Showings*." *Feminist Approaches to the Body in Medieval Literature*. Ed. Linda Lomperis and Sarah Stanbury. Philadelphia: University of Pennsylvania Press, 1993. 142–67.

Stone, Robert Karl. *Middle English Prose Style: Margery Kempe and Julian of Norwich*. The Hague: Mouton, 1970.

Watkin, Edward Ingram. *On Julian of Norwich and in Defense of Margery Kempe*. Exeter: University of Exeter, 1979.

Windeatt, B. A., trans. Introduction to *The Book of Margery Kempe*. London: Penguin, 1985. 9–28.

## JOHN JAE-NAM HAN

# SHEILA KAYE-SMITH
# (1887–1956)

## BIOGRAPHY

Sheila Kaye-Smith was born on February 4, 1887, in Hastings, Sussex, to an English father and French mother. Her father's side of the family had several dignitaries in the Church of England, and therefore religion was never a foreign topic in the household. Her mother was Presbyterian, although she converted to Low Church Anglicanism after her marriage. Sheila enjoyed a happy childhood; she was an avid reader of the classics as well as contemporary novels, and her powerful imagination and gift for storytelling naturally led her down the path to becoming a writer. She attended Hastings and St. Leonards Ladies' College and then began writing for various magazines. Her first novel, *The Tramping Methodist*, was published in 1908 when she was twenty-one. Nearly every year thereafter, the prolific Kaye-Smith published another piece of writing. Her 1916 *Sussex Gorse*, a local-color work that earned favorable comparisons with Thomas Hardy's close descriptions of Wessex, was her first critical success.

As a child and young woman, Kaye-Smith questioned religion, and she even became an atheist for a short while. In 1918, she converted to Anglo-Catholicism, where she remained for more than a decade. After her return to religion, she penned novels that continued to forge her popularity, including *Tamarisk Town* (1919), *Green Apple Harvest* (1921), *Joanna Godden* (1922), and *The End of the House of Alard* (1923). *Tamarisk Town*—like *Sussex Gorse*, a study of the human toll of all-consuming ambition—sold more than three thousand copies. Kaye-Smith married Reverend Theodore Penrose Fry, a High Church Anglican rector, in 1924. In 1929, however, increasingly ill at ease with Anglo-Catholic beliefs, the couple converted to Roman Catholicism after a trip to Rome. Sheila Kaye-Smith was forty-two years old at the time, and, as she later expressed in her 1937 autobiography, *Three Ways Home*, she had "always been latently and potentially a Catholic—there has been no swing around from a contradictory set of ideas" (p. 14). Fry left the ministry, and over the next few decades the couple worked their small Sussex farm, Little Doucegrove. Kaye-Smith continued to write up to her death at home on January 14, 1956. Her corpus of works consists of more than thirty novels, several volumes of poetry and essays, and three autobiographies.

## MAJOR THEMES

Sheila Kaye-Smith's many works demonstrate a remarkable versatility in subject matter and approach. Her best novels consistently portray the human struggle for survival and fulfillment in difficult situations. Her themes often embrace issues of social-class tensions, gender equality, and religious differences. The latter theme is especially evident in such works as *The End of the House of Alard*, *Superstition Corner* (1934), and *The View from the Parsonage* (1954), novels that mirror Kaye-Smith's own conversion from Low Church Anglicanism through Anglo-Catholicism to Roman Catholicism.

As themes, social class issues and women's roles can be studied from several angles in Kaye-Smith's novels. In *Joanna Godden*, for example, the protagonist is an ambitious woman who refuses to accept her role in society as a typically "female" or purely domestic one. At the opening of the novel, Joanna's father has recently passed away, and she is left with his farm and the care of her younger sister, Ellen. Joanna implements her own management ideas, and the farm grows more prosperous. As a farmer, she assumes that she has earned the right to participate in the local Farmers' Club meetings, but because she is a woman she is not allowed to join the group. As critic Dorothea Walker puts it, "Joanna struggles, not to be a man, but to be a woman with a man's prerogative to act beyond the domestic sphere" (p. 61). But once liberated from the confines of house and domesticity, Joanna finds herself, literally, with nowhere to go.

Meanwhile, Joanna has insisted on providing an excellent education for Ellen so that her sister can become more ladylike; that is, more suitable for marriage to a gentleman from a high social class. Eventually, Ellen does marry such a man, while Joanna herself falls in love with a man who ranks below her in social class. At the end of the novel, impregnated by another man whom she has decided not to marry, Joanna reaches a state of contentment as she finds the courage to withstand society's disapproval of an unwed mother.

*Joanna Godden* was a groundbreaking story for its time of a woman who crosses class and gender barriers. In this and other novels, Kaye-Smith expresses disdain for social class distinctions and for limitations placed on women. Writing of such themes in 1920s England was a bold step for Kaye-Smith who herself broke barriers by achieving both a successful career and marriage. The character of Joanna Godden was one close to Kaye-Smith's heart: strong, ambitious, and willful, she struggles against odds for control of her own life, both financially and emotionally. Although religion does not play as central a role in this early novel as in Kaye-Smith's later works, the author's religious sensibility is evident in Joanna's striving for a fulfillment beyond society's expectations and in her powerful urge to treat others as equals.

A later novel, *The Lardners and the Laurelwoods* (1948) presents another example of Kaye-Smith's frequent theme of the tensions between social classes. The Laurelwood family is of a higher class than the Lardners, their summer servants. Meg Laurelwood is a friend of Bess Lardner, and an incident in their childhood highlights the use of power and control in unequal class situations. Bess's family treats the Laurelwoods as if they were royalty; Bess's mother even ranks them above Bess herself in importance. Her self-esteem fallen, Bess attempts to gain control of the situation by insisting that she and Meg exchange toys. Meg has a very expensive doll, and Bess has a cheap watch; they trade, and Meg has to "serve" Bess and the doll. In another subplot, Dick Lardner falls in love with Diana Laurelwood, but she spurns him for a man of her own class and then leads a life devoid of happiness. Dick becomes an alcoholic, in part because his ego has been stripped to nothing. The domestic situations employed by Kaye-Smith in this novel indicate her continued interest in matters of social equality. By allowing the wealthy and poor girls to switch roles so easily, Kaye-Smith expounds her thesis that humans are not determined by the situation in which they are born. By portraying both Diana and Dick as unhappy adults, Kaye-Smith offers an example of how those who ignore the heart for social trappings or material comfort are bound to lead unsatisfying lives. Again, the social justice that underpins Kaye-Smith's religious sensibility is apparent in this novel: when people have the courage to break free from society's restrictions and treat others as equals, a greater chance exists for joy in life.

Like *Joanna Godden*, *Susan Spray* (1931) presents a strong, independent woman caught up in a male-dominated world. One day Susan, who is from a poor family, comes home early from the fields telling her family that she has heard God speak to her. She subsequently sets out to become a preacher, an unusual occupation for a woman and one at which she proves successful. Her husband supports her decision by assuming all the household chores. After her husband dies, Susan marries again. When she hears that her second husband has drowned, she marries for a third time. However, she later finds out by a letter that her second husband is still alive. But because she enjoys her third husband's wealth, she tosses the letter away and continues her preaching, afraid to reveal her bigamy to her congregation. In *Susan Spray*, then, one sees a twisted religion used to serve one's need for security, power, and money. Susan feels herself one of God's chosen prophets; her valuable time cannot be wasted on household tasks or on raising her children. Her overblown perception of herself makes her a hypocrite, blind to true religious sensibility.

Overt religious themes begin to dominate Kaye-Smith's works with *The End of the House of Alard*, a novel that can be viewed as a treatise on Kaye-Smith's own conversion to Anglo-Catholicism. One of several major themes in this novel is the disintegration of an old, distinguished Sussex family, the Alards, who, when the novel opens, are living in shabby elegance, having little left except the family name. A second major theme is the conflict between the Low and High Churches, manifested overtly in the friendship between George Alard, a Low Church clergyman, and Father Luce, an Anglo-Catholic priest. George is unsatisfied with his work and his parish; he considers himself a failure and cannot understand why his own church feels sterile and is empty during the week while there is always someone praying in Father Luce's church. He begins to find himself longing for the warmth, rich symbols, and liturgical ceremonies that the High Church embraces. He also notes Father Luce's inner peace, something he himself cannot seem to achieve. Stricken with heart failure, George asks Father Luce to administer Extreme Unction to him on his deathbed, a highly symbolic and courageous gesture for the timid and conventional George.

Two other interwoven plots also highlight the superiority of Anglo-Catholicism. George's younger brother Gervase has battled their father over his right to break free of the restrictions placed on him as a member of the gentry. He "lowers" himself considerably in his father's estimation by following his heart, first by becoming an auto mechanic and later an Anglo-Catholic monk. In another plot, the eldest Alard son and heir, Peter, falls in love with a woman he feels forced to reject because she is both a devout Anglo-Catholic and because she has no inheritance; Peter is sure that his father will cut him off if he marries her. He therefore weds a more socially acceptable woman whom he does not love, and he is so miserable at his poor choice that he commits suicide. The need for courage and risk-taking, the novel implies in each of these plots, is necessary in following the promptings of the heart in matters of both human love and religious faith. Learning to take a chance on God, that is, to trust him, is a difficult lesson that each of the younger Alards must struggle with, some succeeding and some failing. Yet, to Kaye-Smith, Catholic values are the only true security in life. As Gervase puts it,

Catholic Christianity stands fast because it belongs to an order of things which doesn't change. It's made of the same stuff as our hearts. It's the supernatural satisfaction of all our natural instincts. It doesn't deal with abstractions, but with everyday life. The sacraments are all common things—food, drink, marriage, birth and death. Its highest act of worship is a meal—its most sacred figures are a dying man, and a mother nursing her child. It's traditional in the sense that nature and life are traditional. (p. 233)

Kaye-Smith returned to the saga of the Alard family in *Superstition Corner,* which relates the dramatic tale of sixteenth-century Reformation persecutions against Roman Catholics in England. After Kaye-Smith and her husband converted to Roman Catholicism, they built a chapel at Little Doucegrove and had Mass said publicly in the area for the first time in centuries. Kaye-Smith found herself intrigued at the time by a local tradition that stated that Mass had been secretly offered in a nearby neighborhood, which had come to be known as "Superstition Corner." Kaye-Smith's novel turns this tale into a romantic account of how a Roman Catholic priest may have remained in the area despite the persecutions. Read in conjunction with *The End of the House of Alard*, *Superstition Corner* relates the saga of how the coming of Protestantism affected the ancient Alard clan, and how the remnants of the family come full-circle back to Catholic beliefs by the beginning of the twentieth century.

In her last novel, *The View from the Parsonage*, Kaye-Smith again compares religious beliefs, this time the Anglican and Roman Catholic traditions. The novel is narrated by a garrulous Low Church Anglican parson, Harry Chamberlin. Harry is a longtime friend of the Cryall family. Blanche Cryall, a woman who professes to atheism and who has suffered the death of two children, leaves her husband and farm several days a week to teach school in London. There, she rekindles an old flame with Anthony Boutflower, a Roman Catholic, and they run off to Paris. After two years, she leaves Anthony, persuaded by Parson Chamberlin that she is pursuing the wrong path. Eventually, Blanche converts to Roman Catholicism and becomes a nun, in part to atone for her sin of seducing Anthony away from his religion. Blanche comes to the place where she begins to understand the meaning of sacrifice and to see that she must have courage in acting not half-heartedly but fully on her new beliefs. W. Gore Allen states that, in this novel, Kaye-Smith "reached the pith of ethical contention between Canterbury and Rome. Canterbury may encourage good people to be better; it does not encourage average people to be good" (p. 526); and Dorothea Walker adds, "In [this novel], the good parson is encouraged to be better, but the average person, Blanche, is encouraged to be good. The risk, the daring, the sacrifice of religion is reserved for Roman Catholicism (or High Church Anglicanism) while the safe, the plodding, the expected is reserved for Low Church Anglicanism" (pp. 121–22).

## SURVEY OF CRITICISM

An immensely popular and prolific writer in the 1920s–1930s, Kaye-Smith's reputation fell off sharply after World War II. Very little criticism has been produced over the last few decades, although her finest works deserve rediscovery. At various times, she has rightly been compared to Jane Austen in her portrayal of strong women characters, to Sir Walter Scott in her evocation of a distant and romantic past, and to Thomas Hardy, the chronicler of Wessex, in her realistic descriptions of Sussex.

In *Sheila Kaye-Smith and the Weald Country*, Robert Hopkins focuses on the settings of Kaye-Smith's works as symbolic backdrops in revealing character. He notes, for example, the parallel drawn in *Sussex Gorse* between the stubborn protagonist, Reuben Backfield, and the harsh plot of land, Boarzell Moor, that Reuben seeks to cultivate. Margaret Mackenzie's and Andrew Malone's articles also emphasize Kaye-Smith's use of local color: Mackenzie examines how the house that Kaye-Smith lived in during the later part of her life influenced her settings, while Malone stresses her resemblance to Hardy in her descriptions of farm life. In "Sheila Kaye-Smith: Convert Novelist," W. Gore Allen studies the correlation between Kaye-Smith's conversion to

Roman Catholicism and the progression of her writings, and suggests that a strong parallel between the two is evident. He concludes that *The View from the Parsonage* best represents the author's conversion experience since in it characters are made to voice the author's own beliefs. Rachel Anderson's introduction to the 1984 Doubleday edition of *Joanna Godden* considers Kaye-Smith's biography in light of the strong female character that she creates in that novel. And Gladys B. Stern's "The Heroines of Sheila Kaye-Smith" intercompares the protagonists of several of Kaye-Smith's early novels in terms of their realism.

To date, Dorothea Walker's 1980 Twayne volume is the only comprehensive and detailed study of Kaye-Smith's writings. Her biography of the author discusses the influences that Kaye-Smith's life and religious experiences had on her writing. Walker examines in depth the two local-color novels, *Sussex Gorse* and *Tamarisk Town*, and the two novels with strong female protagonists, *Joanna Godden* and *Susan Spray*. She also takes a close look at the importance of religion within familial relationships in *The End of the House of Alard* and *The View from the Parsonage*, and she concludes by discussing the issue of social class in *The Lardners and the Laurelwoods*. Overall, Walker presents Kaye-Smith as a novelist whose universal themes make her works still very readable today: "The need for acceptance as an individual, the need for freedom to reach one's potentiality, the need for community with one's fellow human beings. . . . By showing the basis for these human needs and by picturing the constructive or destructive use to which they are put, Sheila Kaye-Smith provides insight into the core of life—human relationships" (p. 152).

## BIBLIOGRAPHY

### Works by Sheila Kaye-Smith

*The Tramping Methodist*. 1908. New York: E. P. Dutton, 1922.
*Sussex Gorse*. New York: Alfred A. Knopf, 1916.
*Tamarisk Town*. London: Cassell, 1919.
*Green Apple Harvest*. New York: E. P. Dutton, 1921.
*Joanna Godden*. New York: E. P. Dutton, 1922.
*The End of the House of Alard*. New York: E. P. Dutton, 1923.
*Saints in Sussex*. Birmingham, England: Elkin Mathews, 1923.
*Susan Spray*. New York: Harper and Brothers, 1931.
*Superstition Corner*. New York: Harper and Brothers, 1934.
*Three Ways Home*. New York: Harper and Brothers, 1937.
*The Lardners and the Laurelwoods*. New York: Harper and Brothers, 1947.
*The View from the Parsonage*. New York: Harper and Brothers, 1954.

### Works about Sheila Kaye-Smith

Allen, W. Gore. "Sheila Kaye-Smith: Convert Novelist." *Irish Ecclesiastical Record* 69 (June 1947): 518–28.

Anderson, Rachel. Introduction. *Joanna Godden*, by Sheila Kaye-Smith. Garden City, New York: Doubleday, 1984. xi-xviii.

Hopkins, Robert T. *Sheila Kaye-Smith and the Weald Country*. London: Cecil Palmer, 1925.

Mackenzie, Margaret. "The House That Sheila Built." *Thought* 6 (June 1931): 108–18.

Malone, Andrew E. "Sheila Kaye-Smith: A Novelist of the Farm." *Living Age* 323 (15 November 1924): 387–90.

Stern, Gladys B. "The Heroines of Sheila Kaye-Smith." *Yale Review* 15 (October 1925): 204–08.

Walker, Dorothea. *Sheila Kaye-Smith*. Twayne's English Author Series, 278. Boston: Twayne, 1980.

ELLEN C. FRYE

# MARGERY KEMPE
## (c. 1373–c. 1440)

---

### BIOGRAPHY

Margery Kempe was a medieval mystic and traveler whose memoir, *The Book of Margery Kempe*, first published in 1501, is the earliest known autobiography written in the English language. The *Book*, written in the third person and dictated some twenty years after her initial vision of Christ, is virtually the only source of information about her. She was born about 1373 in the mercantile town of King's Lynn (then called Bishop's Lynn), Norfolk, England. Her father, John Brunham (or Burnham), was a prosperous merchant and five-time mayor of the town. Nothing is remarkable about her youth except for two things: although she was born into a middle-class family, she was not taught to read and write; and she also committed a hidden sin, probably of a sexual nature, which would later torment her soul immensely.

In about 1393, she married John Kempe, a young merchant and burgess of Lynn, and in due course became pregnant. Her childbirth, the first of fourteen, was a very difficult one. For the next eight months or so, she was gravely ill; during that period she "went out of her mind and was amazingly disturbed and tormented with spirits" (*Book,* p. 1). Fearing death, she sent for her confessor, intending to be absolved of the hidden sin of her youth. The priest's sharp condemnation of her, however, made her lose her mind. She was rescued from insanity, according to her account, by a mystical encounter with Christ in the flesh, which was the first of her many mystical experiences. One day Kempe looked up from her bed, and Jesus was sitting there; he said, "Daughter, why have you forsaken me, and I never forsook you?" and then he ascended into heaven (*Book,* p. 42).

After the miraculous recovery, however, Kempe resumed her worldly life full of covetousness and pride. She wore fancy clothes and, to increase family income, opened several business enterprises in succession, including a brewery, a horse-milling, and a bakery. Her businesses failed miserably one after another, which she regarded as a sign of divine punishment. At this time she was revisited by Christ: one night she "heard a melodious sound so sweet and delectable that she thought she had been in paradise" (p. 46). This, and a later vision of heaven, led her to set her heart on God alone.

As a sign of her conversion, she decided to live chaste for God. Although she suggested to her husband that they sleep apart, he insisted on his conjugal rights. Meanwhile, she faithfully attended the church of St. Margaret in Lynn, for prayer, worship, and contemplation. One night, when she lay in bed with her husband, she heard the melody of paradise. After this incident, she began to display three characteristics of her succeeding life: copious weeping over her sins and trespasses; incessant contemplation of and talking about heaven; and denunciation of all worldly pleasure. She also began practicing extreme bodily penance, fasting, keeping vigils, and wearing a hair-cloth from a kiln inside her gown. Soon her loud sobbing and ascetic lifestyle alienated many clerical and laypeople alike, who called her a "false hypocrite" (p. 48), a heretic, or a Lollard. She refuted all the charges against her, claiming that her actions were dictated by God.

In 1413, at the age of about forty, Kempe finally persuaded her husband to take a vow of chastity, which was confirmed by Philip Repyngdon, Bishop of Lincoln. The couple then visited Archbishop Arundel of Canterbury at Lambeth in the summer or autumn of 1413. Kempe was encouraged by her confessors and spiritual counselors, including the Anchoress Julian of Norwich, whom she visited some time in or about 1413. Then in the autumn, commissioned by Christ, she left Lynn on a pilgrimage for the Holy Land and Italy. In 1414 she visited the chapel of the Portiuncula in Assisi and the chapel of St. Bridget in Rome. In the same year, according to Kempe's account, her marriage to the Godhead took place in the Church of the Holy Apostles in Rome: "The Father [of Heaven] also said to this creature, 'Daughter, I will have you wedded to my Godhead, because I shall show you my secrets and my counsels, for you shall live with me without end'" (p. 122).

Kempe came back to Norwich in 1415, but two years later, she sailed from Bristol for a pilgrimage to Santiago de Compostela. On her return, she resided in Lynn between various journeys throughout England. Her travels were complicated by a series of arrests and trials as a heretic. Between August and September of 1417, she was tried and detained for Lollardy at Leicester, although she was acquitted as thoroughly orthodox in her Catholic faith. In about 1431 Kempe's husband died; in 1433 she made a pilgrimage to Norway and Germany.

On her return to Norwich, the Archbishop of Canterbury encouraged Kempe to write down her mystical experiences. Because she was illiterate, she dictated her story to two different scribes in turn. *The Book of Margery Kempe* survived in a single copy in the family library of Colonel Butler-Bowden, unidentified until 1933, when Hope Emily Allen confirmed it as Kempe's work.

## MAJOR THEMES

The dominant themes of Kempe's *Book* are a mystical union with Christ, temptations and tribulations, and feminine self-empowerment and self-expression. First of all, the *Book* is a spiritual autobiography that describes, in a homely prose style, the author's intensely personal encounters with Christ. As with other medieval spiritual writings, such as the *Ancren Riwle* ("Rule for Anchoresses"), the *Book* demonstrates a passionate attachment to the humanity of Christ. Kempe's first vision of Christ is a good example: he approaches her "in the likeness of man . . . clad in a mantle of purple silk, sitting upon her bedside, [and] looking upon her with so blessed a countenance" (p. 42). While in a trance, Kempe also sees the visions of Christ in bodily form: "And at once, in the sight of her soul, she saw our Lord standing right up over her, so near that she thought she took his toes in her hand and felt them, and to her feeling it was as if they had been really flesh and bones" (p. 249). Throughout the *Book*, Kempe engages in personal conversations ("dalliances") with Christ, who "with great sweetness spoke to [her]" (p. 59), "said to her mind" (p. 137), and "answered her soul" (p. 248).

Moreover, Kempe presents the relationship between Christ and herself by using nuptial imagery, which was common in medieval devotional literature. In the *Book*, Christ appears to Kempe as a bridegroom or husband; she is his bride or spouse. In Chapter 36, for instance, Christ invites her to a spiritual intimacy in terms of the lover-beloved relationship: "You may boldly, when you are in bed, take me to you as your wedded husband. . . . You can boldly take me in the arms of your soul and kiss my mouth, my head and my feet as sweetly as you want" (pp. 126–27).

Second, the *Book* focuses on the temptations and tribulations the author had to overcome on her spiritual journey. She not only had a hidden sin from her earlier life, but also was subjected to temptations to lechery, even after her conversion. In Book I, Chapter 4, she candidly includes a farcical episode in which she was entrapped by lust. In an unexpected answer to her prayer for a miracle, which would silence her critics, God sends her "the snare of lechery" (p. 49). She lusted after a young man at church and proposed to him that they sleep together. Although he had tempted her earlier, he "said he would not for all the wealth in this world; he would rather be chopped up as small as meat for the pot" (p. 50). Utterly ashamed at this rejection, she falls into despair and suffering, which she slowly overcomes with acts of penance.

Kempe was also persecuted by men and women regarding her religious orthodoxy. Because of loud sobbing she was "reproved, scorned or ridiculed" (p. 47) by her contemporaries; and "very many people who loved her before while she was in the world abandoned her and would not know her" (p. 48). She was also deserted by her fellow pilgrims on a pilgrimage to the Holy Land. In a way, the *Book* is the author's attempt at self-vindication for the refusal, false accusations, and slanders she suffered on her quest for salvation. She also remains loyal to the Church, abiding by its rules for Christian faith.

Third, Kempe presents herself as a strong-minded woman who empowers and expresses herself. She made her husband live chaste—partly by persuasion and partly by paying off his debts—and left behind familial obligations in search of spiritual fulfillment. Unlike Julian of Norwich, Kempe declined to be confined as an anchoress and continued to live in the secular world, seeking official recognition from the Church for her spirituality. She challenged the male chauvinism of medieval society, as is shown in Book I, Chapter 53. When Kempe was arrested for heresy near Beverley, she was advised by the townsmen, "Woman, give up this life that you lead, and go and spin, and card wool, as other women do, and do not suffer shame and so much unhappiness." She snubbed determinedly: "I do not suffer as much sorrow as I would do for our Lord's love, for I only suffer cutting words, and our merciful Lord Christ Jesus . . . suffered hard strokes, bitter scourgings, and shameful death at the last" (p. 168). On another occasion, the archbishop of York tried to force Kempe to quit teaching in his diocese. She refused to be silenced, however, declaring that no one could stop her from speaking of God. Another conflict with the clergy took place in Worcester, where the Bishop's men "in clothes very fashionably slashed and cut into points" questioned her, "What the devil's wrong with you?" In reply, she retorted, "No, truly, you are more like the devil's men." Then she "spoke so seriously against sin and their misconduct that they were silent, and held themselves well pleased with her talk—thanks be to God—before she left" (p. 146). Indeed, Kempe was never afraid of reprimanding in public those who displayed moral failings. In Lambeth, for instance, she heard the Archbishop's clerks and "other heedless men" curse and speak "many thoughtless words." She then "boldly rebuked them, and said they would be damned unless they left off their swearing and the other sins they practised" (p. 71).

## SURVEY OF CRITICISM

The keenest debate in Kempe studies has involved the orthodoxy of the author's spirituality. Some critics see Kempe as a religious neurotic and hysteric, regardless of her professed love of God. In her 1940 Prefatory Note to the EETS edition of the *Book*, Hope Emily Allen states that Kempe was "petty, neurotic, vain, illiterate, physically and nervously over-strained; devout, much-travelled, forceful and talented" (p. lxiv). Evelyn Underhill, in a review of the *Book*, is skeptical about Kempe's mysticism: "There is very little in Margery Kempe's book which can properly be described as mystical—unless we dignify her romantic dreams of Christ as the soul's husband, and similar emotional phantasies, by this name" (p. 642). Clare M. Bradford's view of Kempe is similarly unfavorable. In her article "Julian of Norwich and Margery Kempe," she observes that Kempe as a visionary is incoherent, random, and haphazard. Bradford adds, "The picture of Margery which emerges from her writing is that of an eccentric and neurotic woman, to whom the motive of self-glorification is apparently very important" (pp. 154–55).

Nonetheless, Margery Kempe also has admirers, who defend her mystical visions as theologically sound. For instance, Henry C. Mann, in "Margery Kempe," strongly defends Kempe as a genuine and godly mystic, comparing her to Angela of Foligno, John of the Cross, and other visionaries. In "A New Version of a Classic," Leonard Bacon labels the *Book* "an English prose classic," characterizing its author as a "lady with sufficient sincerity, humility, and courage" and "the curious heroine, part saint, part incurably natural woman, full of self-forgetfulness, full of self-pity, and eager to expiate on each" (p. 12). Katharine Cholmeley, in *Margery Kempe: Genius and Mystic* (1947), defends Kempe's sincerity and holiness. Meanwhile, Martin Thornton contends, in *Margery Kempe: An Example in the English Pastoral Tradition*, that Kempe's *Book* is more useful to the ordinary Christian than either Julian of Norwich's *Revelations* or *The Cloud of Unknowing*. In *Mystic and Pilgrim*, Clarissa W. Atkinson argues for Kempe's religious orthodoxy, maintaining that Kempe's affective piety is centered on Christ.

Some critics have discussed Kempe and her work from a feminist perspective. For instance, David Aers argues in *Community, Gender and Individual Identity* that Kempe's suffering originated from her husband who imposed upon her "years of compulsory sexuality, what Sheila Delaney rightly names as 'legal rape,' against which Margery expresses the deepest repugnance and pain" (p. 75). In *Margery Kempe's Dissenting Fictions*, Lynn Staley proposes that the *Book* is a feminist work of fiction in which Kempe "seems deliberately to offer the possibility of an alternative society" (p. 65). Nona Fienburg, in "Thematics of Value in *The Book of Margery Kempe*," argues that Kempe was a strong and independent-minded woman who challenged the male-dominated value system of medieval society.

Still other critics have utilized the insights from psychoanalysis in their study of the *Book*. In "'And Most of All for Inordinate Love,'" for instance, Nancy Partner observes, "Inordinate love, love without bounds, limits, prudence, or restraint, the occasion of transient pleasure and lasting grief, remorse, or guilt, is the self-confessing motif at the center of Margery Kempe's extended confession, her *Book*" (p. 154). According to Partner, Kempe's life consisted of two conflicting sides: one, the desire to live a holy life; the other, "denied desires and repressed knowledge" (p. 255). Partner's essay focuses on the role of the denied desires in Kempe's life, which, the author observes, exemplified the lives of women of late medieval society. Finally, Clarissa W. Atkinson and Mary Hardiman Farley clinically examine Kempe's struggle. In *Mystic and Pilgrim*, Atkinson speculates that Kempe's case prior to her initial vision "resembles 'postpartum psychosis'" (p. 209), which is more severe than depression; in "Religion, Feminist Criticism and the Functional Eccentricity of Margery Kempe," Farley concurs with this conclusion, stating that during most of her adult life, Kempe was clearly the victim of postpartum psychosis.

# BIBLIOGRAPHY

## Work by Margery Kempe

*The Book of Margery Kempe*. 1501. Trans. and intro. B. A. Windeatt. London: Penguin, 1985.

## Works about Margery Kempe

Aers, David. *Community, Gender and Individual Identity: English Writing, 1360–1430*. New York: Routledge, 1988.

Allen, Hope Emily. Prefatory Note. *The Book of Margery Kempe*. Ed. Sanford B. Meech and Hope Emily Allen. EETS, o.s. 212. London: Oxford University Press, 1940. liii–lxviii.

Atkinson, Clarissa W. *Mystic and Pilgrim: The Book and the World of Margery Kempe*. Ithaca, New York: Cornell University Press, 1985.

Bacon, Leonard. "A New Version of a Classic." *Saturday Review of Literature* 4 November 1944: 12.

Bradford, Clare M. "Julian of Norwich and Margery Kempe." *Theology Today* 35 (1978): 153–58.

Cholmeley, Katharine. *Margery Kempe: Genius and Mystic*. New York: Longmans, Green and Co., 1947.

Colledge, Eric, ed. *The Mediaeval Mystics of England*. New York: Charles Scribner and Sons, 1961.

Collis, Louise. *Memoirs of a Medieval Woman: The Life and the Times of Margery Kempe*. New York: Harper and Row, 1983.

Farley, Mary Hardiman. "Religion, Feminist Criticism and the Functional Eccentricity of Margery Kempe." *Exemplaria* 11 (1999): 1–21.

Fienburg, Nona. "Thematics of Value in *The Book of Margery Kempe*." *Modern Philology* 87 (1989): 132–41.

Glasscoe, Marion. *English Medieval Mystics: Games of Faith*. London: Longman, 1993.

Knowles, David. *The English Mystical Tradition*. London: Burns and Oates, 1961.

Mann, Henry C. "Margery Kempe." *Pax* 26 (1937): 257–60; 276–79.

McEntire, Sandra J. *Margery Kempe: A Book of Essays*. New York: Garland, 1992.

Partner, Nancy. "'And Most of All for Inordinate Love': Desire and Denial in *The Book of Margery Kempe*." *Thought* 64 (1989): 254–67.

Staley, Lynn. *Margery Kempe's Dissenting Fictions*. University Park: Pennsylvania State University Press, 1994.

Stone, Robert Karl. *Middle English Prose Style: Margery Kempe and Julian of Norwich*. The Hague: Mouton, 1970.

Sumner, Rebecca Louise. "The Spectacle of Femininity: Allegory and the Denial of Representation in the *Book of Margery Kempe, Jane Eyre*, and *Wonderland*." Diss. University of Rochester, 1991.

Thornton, Martin. *Margery Kempe: An Example in the English Pastoral Tradition*. London: Society for Promoting Christian Knowledge, 1960.

Underhill, Evelyn. "Margery Kempe." *Spectator* 16 Oct. 1936: 642.

Watkin, E. I. *On Julian of Norwich, and In Defense of Margery Kempe*. Exeter: University of Exeter, 1979.

Windeatt, Barry, ed. *English Mystics of the Middle Ages*. Cambridge: Cambridge University Press, 1994.

JOHN JAE-NAM HAN

# ROSE HAWTHORNE LATHROP
# (1851–1926)

## BIOGRAPHY

The youngest of writer Nathaniel Hawthorne's three children, Rose Haw-thorne Lathrop was born on May 20, 1851, in Lenox, Massachusetts. She first encountered Catholicism at age seven when her family lived in Italy. Around age ten, she expressed an interest in writing, but her father forbade her from pursuing this interest partly because he himself had struggled to establish a lit-erary career, and partly because he believed most women writers at the time produced "trash" (quoted in Valenti, p. 24).

Nathaniel Hawthorne died the day before Rose's thirteenth birthday, in 1864. In 1868, his widow Sophia and her children moved to Germany, where Rose fell in love with fellow American George Parsons Lathrop. Rose and George married in England on September 11, 1871. Once they married, they both embarked on literary careers. She wrote poetry and short fiction; he wrote poetry and literary criticism (including a book on his famous father-in-law) and eventually became an associate editor of *Atlantic Monthly*.

The Lathrops' only child, Francis Hawthorne Lathrop, was born on No-vember 10, 1876. Rose suffered from postpartum psychosis and was briefly in-stitutionalized. Francie, as he was called by the Lathrops, died suddenly of diptheria on February 6, 1881. His death evidently marked the beginning of the end of their marriage. As early as 1883, Rose was considering a legal sepa-ration from George, who was reputedly alcoholic and abusive.[1]

On March 19, 1891, the Lathrops shocked the nation by entering the Catholic Church. Their conversion was disconcerting to many Americans be-cause, in the late nineteenth century, most Catholics in the United States were lower-class immigrants. By contrast, the Lathrops were "a conspicuous and an established New England couple" (Valenti, p. 100). Their writings indicate that George was attracted intellectually to Catholic authority, and Rose emo-tionally to Catholic worship (pp. 101, 102).

Rose left George in 1895 and received permission from the Church in 1896 to separate from him permanently, reportedly due to his "increasing intemperance" ("Lathrop," p. 412).[2] Concurrently, she made retreats with several religious orders. She then sought training in nursing and rented rooms on the destitute Lower East Side of Manhattan to found a hospice for poor cancer patients. Rose Hawthorne Lathrop's decision to found such a hospice resulted chiefly from grief over the death of one of her friends, poet Emma Lazarus, from cancer. This decision was particularly heroic because cancer patients were the lepers of Lathrop's lifetime. At the end of the nineteenth century, cancer was considered contagious and it manifested itself wretchedly: people with cancer were usually disfigured, and they emitted nauseating smells. But Lathrop perceived God's image in each suffering person and treated each as she would have treated her Lord. Most people with cancer were driven from their homes and warehoused in hospitals that subjected them to experimentation. Lathrop insisted instead that they die with dignity, at God's pace and in a loving environment.

After the death of her estranged husband in 1898, Lathrop and the other women working at the hospice sought to be recognized as a religious order. In 1901, after surmounting a number of bureaucratic hurdles, Lathrop and her growing number of helpers were finally recognized as a full Dominican sisterhood, the Servants of Relief for Incurable Cancer. The Servants eventually cared for both men and women, of all religions, in New York City and in the countryside.

Once she embarked on a life as an active-contemplative nun, Rose Hawthorne Lathrop, or Mother Mary Alphonsa as she later came to be known, continuously wrote letters and essays to recruit sisters, to solicit donations, and to change attitudes towards cancer patients. From 1901 to 1904, she even published her own magazine, entitled *Christ's Poor*. When she died on July 9, 1926, after a night of letter writing, Lathrop passed into the next life doing what she loved most in this one. As of December 1999, Lathrop's order, now known as the Dominican Sisters of Hawthorne, was considering her cause for canonization.[3]

## MAJOR THEMES

In the years before her conversion, Lathrop's writing was marked by dark images and themes. Most of her poetry was published in 1888 as a collection entitled *Along the Shore*. Almost every poem in this volume dwells on death. Lathrop reflects on her father's death, on her friend's death, and on her son's death. Filled with apparitions, it also depicts a woman lamenting over her dead lover and harps on the dreary theme of *tempus fugit*. "A Song Before Grief" typifies the poems in *Along the Shore*. It begins:

> Sorrow, my friend,
> When shall you come again?

The wind is slow, and the bent willows send
Their silvery motions wearily down the plain
The bird is dead
That sang this morning through the summer rain! (p. 41)

To some degree, such dark poetry may be conventional. Lathrop may have been attempting to write the kind of poetry women typically wrote in the late nineteenth century (Valenti, p. 83). Yet, the poems in *Along the Shore* convey the sense of futility Lathrop evidently felt after her son's death, as she wrangled with her husband and struggled to sustain a literary career. *Along the Shore* was likely written by a woman who did not believe she had much to live for.

The short stories Lathrop wrote at this time seem equally autobiographical. Her children's stories range from a profile of a squirmy girl sitting for a portrait, to an account of a happy family celebrating Christmas Eve. Lathrop based such stories on her own life: she grudgingly sat for a portrait as a child, and members of her family had received the same gifts as the characters in the Christmas story (Valenti, pp. 16, 76). Almost all of her stories for adults may have been inspired by the tumult of her own marriage. These stories feature inconstancy and manipulation on the part of both sexes, although they tend to be more critical of women. Military imagery abounds. For example, "For a Lord," which depicts a coquette stringing along two men, speaks of "the art of love-war" (p. 614). "Saagenfreed" recounts a "battle" between a woman and the fiancé whose inconstancy she exposes. An undercurrent of violence flows through the story: a black wig is likened to a decapitated head (p. 742), and musical instruments are said not to have played a "difficult passage" but to have "sawed away" at it (p. 745). When Lathrop wrote these stories, she was apparently happily married. In fact, when "Saagenfreed" was published, she was pregnant. Yet, she had already suffered for loving George Parsons Lathrop—marrying him estranged her from her brother and sister—and, evidently, she was willing to confront the underside of passion.

After her conversion to Catholicism, Lathrop's writing turned primarily to prose and poetry reflecting on her family and her new faith. In 1897, she published her most acclaimed book, *Memories of Hawthorne*. This book consisted of letters her mother had written about her father. Lathrop provided introductory and concluding reflections as well as links between the letters. At this stage of her career, she also wrote several essays in periodicals on her father's writing habits. The first was so popular that it led her to embark on a brief career as a lecturer.

The religious works Lathrop composed in her conversion period foreshadow her impending vocation. For instance, the poem "The Choice" suggests that to choose Christ is to choose suffering. Undoubtedly, this very Catholic theme accounts, in part, for Lathrop's decision to become a self-renouncing nun. Even more suggestive of her decision is her 1894 *A Story of Courage*, a history of the Visitation convent at Georgetown University. Significantly, Lathrop and her husband were billed as co-authors, but Lathrop essentially wrote the book on her own. Evidently, she became enamored of convent life as she did so. In the preface to the book, Lathrop insists, "Indeed, there are no happier or cheerier persons on earth than the members of religious sisterhoods" (p. iii). She proceeds to present a rhapsodic defense of religious life. She also profiles the many Visitation sisters who, as biographer Patricia Dunlavy Valenti put it, "became nuns in midlife, some leaving their families to do so" (p. 121). The most prominent of these sisters was St. Jane de Chantal, a widowed baroness with a tumultuous love life who cofounded the Visitation order while continuing to care for her family. Given the enthusiasm Lathrop displays towards religious life in *A Story of Courage* and the parallels between her experiences and those of the women she wrote about, it is quite likely that this book project helped Lathrop see what her vocation would ultimately be.

During the last stage of her career, as Mother Mary Alphonsa, Lathrop found fulfillment in putting her writing skills to practical use, waging what she called a "pen war" against apathy about the plight of the poor and sick (quoted in Valenti, p. 163). She wrote continuously to solicit donations and recruit sisters for her order. In 1899, she published "A Cheerful View of a Hard Problem," an essay in the periodical *Catholic World* which explained her mission and predicted it would succeed with "women's work and men's money" (p. 669). To encourage women to commit their lives to this work, Lathrop appealed to a long-running theme of her writings: suffering. She said she was seeking assistants "who have the good sense to realize that the life of an earnest woman, wherever she is, is one of suffering" (p. 667). Lathrop suggests that, in working with victims of cancer, other women would discover what she had learned: that Christ has imbued suffering with meaning, and that suffering can be embraced for the sake of the Kingdom of Heaven.

## SURVEY OF CRITICISM

Rose Hawthorne Lathrop's writings have not fared well with critics. Her own brother, Julian Hawthorne, lamented the "obscurity" of her fiction (quoted in Maynard, p. 198), and at least one early reviewer considered her poetry graceful but simplistic ("Recent Poetry," p. 299). Of all her works, *Memories of Hawthorne* attracted the most interest, although critics faulted Lathrop for invading her parents' privacy and for tediously lionizing her family. In an 1897 review of the book, the *Nation* vented irritation with the "gushing sentiment and sensibility" of Sophia Hawthorne's letters and sneered that her daughter's "literary methods [were] inherited entirely from her mother's side" (p. 404).

Lathrop's biographers have not offered a much more positive assessment of her work. Katherine Burton's *Sorrow Built a Bridge* (1937) seems to show more of an interest in George Parson Lathrop's writings than in those of his wife. Theodore Maynard's *A Fire Was Lighted* (1948) insists that Lathrop's works were published only because she was Hawthorne's daughter and hobnobbed with publishing luminaries (p. 198). Although Maynard finds "bits" of "real feeling" in her poetry, he sees nothing of value in the short stories (pp. 201, 200). In fact, he warns, "If anybody wants to go and look these things up, let him do so at his own risk" (p. 201). Maynard suggests that Lathrop was a literary failure because she was too lazy and impatient to expend "intense labor" on most of her writings (p. 203). Patricia Dunlavy Valenti's *To Myself a Stranger* (1991) devotes an entire chapter to analyzing Lathrop's poetry and fiction. Like Maynard, Valenti prefers the poetry to the fiction, suggesting that the poetry "more satisfyingly unites technique and idea" (p. 81). Valenti even suggests that Lathrop's poetry may have influenced that of T. S. Eliot (p. 87).

While some of Lathrop's critics have put a more positive spin on her work than others, none would consider her a great writer. As Lathrop's brother noted, her greatness lay outside the literary realm: "The gift of expression in art . . . was beyond her own control. Something else was needed to satisfy her soul and release her energies" (Hawthorne, p. 373). Ultimately, Rose Hawthorne Lathrop is memorable less for her writing than for the reason she wrote.

## NOTES

1. Most biographers of Lathrop and her family have depicted George in this light, but Lathrop's most recent biographer, Patricia Dunlavy Valenti, has challenged the depiction, citing a lack of "manuscript evidence" (p. 148).

2. Current canon law for the Latin Rite of the Catholic Church allows spouses to separate if one "causes serious danger of spirit or body to the other spouse or to the children, or otherwise renders common life too hard" (*Code of Canon Law: Latin-English Edition*, p. 417, Can. 1153 §1). The victimized spouse typically makes the separation official by obtaining "a decree of the local ordinary" (*Code*, p. 417, Can. 1153 §1). Because Rose Hawthorne Lathrop received Church permission to separate from her husband, and since it is probable Church law permitted no other reason for separation in 1896 besides the reasons listed above, it is likely the Lathrops separated because George did pose a danger to Rose.

3. Personal telephone interview with Sister Teresa Marie, Dominican Sister of Hawthorne, December 10, 1999.

## BIBLIOGRAPHY

### Works by Rose Hawthorne Lathrop

"Saagenfreed." *Appleton's Journal* 10 June 1876: 741–45.
"Fun-Beams." *St. Nicholas Magazine* 11 (1884): 226–31.
"Lindie's Portrait." *St. Nicholas Magazine* 14 (1887): 512–14.
*Along the Shore.* Boston: Ticknor and Co., 1888.
"For a Lord." *Harper's Bazaar* 30 July 1892: 613–15.
"The Choice." *Catholic World* 56 (October 1892): 17.
*A Story of Courage: Annals of the Georgetown Convent of the Visitation of the Blessed Virgin Mary.* With George Parsons Lathrop. Boston: Houghton, 1894.

*Memories of Hawthorne.* Boston: Houghton, Mifflin, 1897.
"A Cheerful View of a Hard Problem." *Catholic World* 68 (February 1899): 659–69.

### Works about Rose Hawthorne Lathrop

"A Book and Its Story: Hawthorne the Man." *Critic* 5 June 1897: 389.
Burton, Katherine. *Sorrow Built a Bridge: A Daughter of Hawthorne.* London and New York: Longmans, Green and Co., 1937.
Hawthorne, Julian. "A Daughter of Hawthorne." *Atlantic Monthly* 142 (September 1928): 372–77.
"Lathrop, Alphonsa, Mother." *New Catholic Encyclopedia.* Prepared by an Editorial Staff at the Catholic University of America. Vol. 8. New York: McGraw-Hill, 1967. 411–12.
Maynard, Theodore. *A Fire Was Lighted: The Life of Rose Hawthorne Lathrop.* Milwaukee: Bruce Publishing Co., 1948.
"Recent Poetry." *Literary World* 15 September 1888: 299.
Rev. of *Memories of Hawthorne*, by Rose Hawthorne Lathrop. *Nation* 27 May 1897: 403–04.
Valenti, Patricia Dunlavy. *To Myself a Stranger: A Biography of Rose Hawthorne Lathrop.* Baton Rouge: Louisiana State University Press, 1991.

REBECCA L. KROEGER

# MARY LAVIN
## (1912–1996)

## BIOGRAPHY

Mary Lavin is closely associated with Ireland, her primary home and fictional setting, yet she was born in East Walpole, Massachusetts, on June 11, 1912, and lived there until she was nearly ten years old. Her father, Tom Lavin, was a County Roscommon native of great strength and vitality but with little formal education who worked as a groom and caretaker for a wealthy Massachusetts family. Her mother, Nora Mahon, a lovely middle-class Galway woman, was the second oldest in a family of twelve children, and she was sent to visit her cousin in America partly in the hope that she would marry and thus ease the family's financial pressures. Discovering that she disliked America, Nora returned to Ireland, meeting her future husband on the boat. After several years of courtship conducted largely through Tom's ardent correspondence, Nora returned to America and married him, apparently more out of filial duty than love, and in spite of her lack of enthusiasm for her new home and her husband's working-class status.

Nora was determined to return to Ireland, and in 1921 she left Massachusetts for her grandparents' home in Athenry, accompanied by nine-year-old Mary, who attended a local school. The eight months she spent in this Irish village had a great influence on Lavin's life and work; she told Zack Bowen, "For years whenever I wrote a story, no matter what gave me the idea, I had to recast it in terms of the people of that town" (Bowen, p. 18). A year later Tom Lavin joined them in Dublin, but he soon moved to Bective to manage property owned by his Massachusetts employers. In Dublin Mary enrolled in the Loreto convent, where she excelled in English, catechism, and debating. She then attended University College, Dublin, where she took first honors in English and continued on to write a first-class master's degree thesis on Jane Austen. Lavin then returned to the Loreto convent to teach French as she worked toward her Ph.D. in literature.

Lavin selected Virginia Woolf as her dissertation topic, and it was while writing her thesis that she suddenly "made the connection between the work and the hand that wrote it" (Peterson, p. 20). She turned over the typescript of her dissertation and wrote her first story, "Miss Holland," on the back, which was accepted in 1938 for publication in *Dublin Magazine*. More stories and poems followed. Lord Dunsany, one of the first admirers of her work, encouraged her and brought her stories to the attention of editors in the United Kingdom and United States; he even wrote a glowing introduction to her first collection, *Tales from Bective Bridge* (1942), that compared her work to the great Russian realists. This volume went on to win the James Tait Black Memorial Book Prize as the best work of fiction in 1942. Also in 1942 Lavin married former classmate and Dublin lawyer William Walsh, and when in 1945 Tom Lavin died, they bought the Abbey Farm in Bective with her inheritance.

Walsh and Lavin had three daughters: Valentine, born in 1943, Elizabeth, born in 1945, and Caroline, born in 1953. The family divided their residence between Dublin, where Walsh practiced law, and Bective. Lavin, farm wife and mother of three, could write only in those snatches of time left between these full-time duties, and so concentrated primarily on the short-story form, publishing four volumes between 1944 and 1951. Her two novels also came from these years: *The House in Clewe Street* (1945), first published serially in *Atlantic Monthly*, and *Mary O'Grady* (1950). In 1953 Walsh became seriously ill with heart trouble and died in 1954, leaving the grieving Lavin with a farm to manage and three daughters to raise alone with little money. For several years, despondent, she did not write, but in 1958 the *New Yorker* published her short story "The Living," and Lavin continued to be a steady contributor to that magazine through the 1970s. She received a Guggenheim award for 1959–1960, and made what was clearly a mistake in using the money to live with her daughters in Florence, a time later recorded in her few stories set outside Ireland. But she received a renewal of the money and spent the next year at home, writing most of the stories in *The Great Wave and Other Stories* (1961) and *In the Middle of the Fields and Other Stories* (1967).

Lavin published several short-story collections through the 1970s, and garnered numerous literary prizes, including the Katherine Mansfield Prize, the Eire Society Medal, and the Gregory Medal. She gave readings at American universities, and was writer-in-residence at the University of Connecticut at Storrs. Lavin's great friend and advisor during these times was Michael Scott, a Jesuit priest living in Australia whom she had known since her University College days. While Lavin was highly critical of some Catholic dogma, she respected Catholicism's moral teachings and its spiritual reverence, and believed strongly in God and the endurance of religious structures: "Religion is like race or nationality. It's what you are, and you can't throw it off" (Stevens and Stevens, p. 44). Scott shared her views, and in 1969 he received laicization and returned to Ireland to marry Lavin in a Jesuit chapel. They lived at Abbey Farm and in Dublin, where he was Dean of the School of Irish Studies. In 1971

Lavin was named president of the Irish Academy of Letters, and for the last two decades of her life she played a significant role in Irish literary life, encouraging and entertaining young writers. In the early 1980s her health began to fail, and she stopped writing. Scott died in 1990, and in 1992 Lavin moved to a nursing home, where she died at age eighty-three on March 25, 1996.

## MAJOR THEMES

Mary Lavin, unlike James Joyce or Edna O'Brien, does not write in open rebellion against Ireland's social, sexual, and religious strictures, and she rarely examines its infamous political battles. Instead, she writes of the individual consciousness in one small place, probing particular patterns of mind that enable people to maneuver their quotidian lives with some joy and excitement. Yet these same states of mind can prevent her characters from transcending narrow environments and points of view, as in "A Happy Death" (*The Becker Wives and Other Stories*), when a wife's fixed belief that religious revelation must accompany death makes her miss her husband's actual "happy death" of romantic reminiscence. In "Sunday Brings Sunday" (*The Long Ago and Other Stories*), a young girl's optimistic sense of traveling toward a satisfying maturity enables her to live her life of drudgery hopefully, yet this same sense blinds her to present joys and to the dangers that threaten this vision's fulfillment. Such duality marks Lavin's portrayals of human life: those aspects that make it worthwhile, such as family, sexual love, nature, and social rewards, also cause the most misery, and many of her stories are deliberately inconclusive, as if to mirror the reality and complexity of a life that does not fit expected or satisfactory patterns.

Lavin often portrays the destructive consequences of ingrained social and gender divisions. In *The House in Clewe Street*, the characters have difficulty finding a happy medium between convention and autonomy, and a young girl's quest to transcend a working-class life ends in her death. Yet overt feminism rarely appears in Lavin's work. Such stories as "Asigh" (*A Memory and Other Stories*), which blames the ruin of a woman's life on a tyrannical father, are less typical than sympathetic portrayals of beloved, underappreciated fathers and carping mothers, like those in "A Cup of Tea" (*The Long Ago and Other Stories*), and "A Happy Death." Generally Lavin's stories present men and women as equally alive to the world around them, struggling with similar philosophical and social dilemmas. Still, most of Lavin's stories focus on women, and the pathetic lives of some—like Ella in "The Long Ago" (*The Long Ago and Other Stories*), who in her narrow spinster's life is obsessed with the past—constitute Lavin's quiet protest against women's limited opportunities. Lavin's women, like the autobiographical Vera who appears in numerous "widow" stories, often accept male help and strength with conventional feminine gratitude, and many long for the male companionship and protection they have lost or never found. But several find amazing strength without men, and within their traditional roles as mothers and homemakers, like the title character of *Mary O'Grady*, who endures tragedies of mythic proportions but dies with a religious vision of a mother's paradise as she tends her small children.

Lavin's characters, of which Mary O'Grady is a prime example, are ordinary, limited people who cling to convention as truth even as they rail against its limitations, and this is particularly obvious in her depictions of Irish Catholicism. Lavin typically attempts to portray realistically what it is to live within the parameters of Catholic culture and morality, and her characters do not suffer crises of faith or leave the Church. The specifics of Catholic doctrine concern them very little, and they accept its moral structures as the closest approximations to truth that humans can reach; often, as in "Villa Violetta" (*A Memory and Other Stories*), priests are her finest characters since they represent the attempt to discover and live a truly moral and spiritual existence. But the heavy irony of many stories indicates Lavin's sense of conflict between true faith and created doctrine, and the disparity between professed beliefs and actual human lives. Lavin shows certain aspects of Catholic dogma as ideas that block rather than reveal the divine. For instance, "The Nun's Mother" (*The Long Ago and Other Stories*) deplores the Church's repression of women's sexual knowledge; "The Lost Child" (*Happiness and Other Stories*) criticizes the masculine dominance of Catholic doctrine, which denies that the soul of an unbaptized child can enter heaven; and "An Akoulina of the Irish Midlands" (*The Patriot Son and Other Stories*) presents the Protestant/Catholic split as ideological absurdity. Lavin's preoccupation with death, which can be traced through several stories set in or centered on graveyards, seems partly to criticize the Catholic focus on the sin and pain of earthly life versus the desirability of heaven.

Moreover, Lavin's stories often conflate myth and folklore with Catholic rites and symbols, implying that Christianity may be one possible interpretation of divinity among many rather than the only truth. Her characters' greatest epiphanies are Platonic rather than Christian, revelations of a spiritual presence outside the material world that come through ecstatic communions with nature, as in "The Cuckoo Spit" (*In the Middle of the Fields and Other Stories*) and "At Sallygap" (*At Sallygap and Other Stories*). Similarly, her most common symbols are universal rather than Christian. Crosses sometimes appear as evidence of human misunderstandings and burdens, as in "A Memory" (*A Memory and Other Stories*), where both Myra and James crucify themselves for useless obsessions. More common, however, are images of water, soil, and light that imply the human connection to earthly cycles and divine creation, symbols that her characters only dimly comprehend.

Nevertheless, Lavin shows that Catholicism can bring her characters strength and peace, even when specific questions about life's paradoxes and cruelties cannot be fully answered. "The Great Wave" (*The Great Wave and Other Stories*) pits a seminarian and a young boy against an apocalyptic storm from which they emerge the sole survivors of an entire town. It frames their struggle as one of human faith versus the forces of nature, and its conclusion indicates that neither wins or loses, nor that embracing or rejecting religion will ensure human success. Yet "The Great Wave" communicates the power and comfort of Catholic ritual for people who eke out lives in difficult natural surroundings and who continue in spite of such disasters. The life-affirming mother in "Happiness," whose best friend is the admirable Father Hugh, rejects the passive, fatalistic belief that life is a "vale of tears": "It takes effort to push back the stone from the mouth of the tomb and walk out" (*Happiness and Other Stories,* p. 24). As Lavin said of her stories, "If there is affirmation, it only means that I think life is worth living anyway—no matter how hard it is" (Stevens and Stevens, p. 44). Ultimately, Lavin champions human love and resilience in the face of life's tragedies, and advocates a full-blooded life of risk rather than a cautious avoidance of pain, a life that incorporates the Christian virtues of spiritual awareness, empathy, and humility as well as a sensual love of this world.

## SURVEY OF CRITICISM

Many critics have hailed Mary Lavin as one of the masters of the short story in the twentieth century. V. S. Pritchett, introducing her 1971 *Collected Stories,* calls Lavin "a great artist; we are excited by her sympathy, her acute knowledge of the heart, her truthfulness and, above all, by the controlled revelation of untidy, powerful emotions" (p. xii).

Leah Levenson's biography *The Four Seasons of Mary Lavin* presents the only full treatment of Lavin's life. Zack Bowen's short monograph *Mary Lavin* summarizes Lavin's life, major themes, style, structures, and imagery, and effectively introduces readers to her work. Richard F. Peterson's longer study examines Lavin's canon chronologically, tracing particular themes and subjects within each period through detailed readings of her major stories. In the last two decades, feminist critics have newly explored Lavin's subtle portraits of women's lives, most notably in Patricia K. Meszaros's discussion of the creative temperament of Lavin's women, and in Rachael Sealy Lynch's analysis of the destructive "male gaze" in *The House in Clewe Street.*

A. A. Kelly's *Mary Lavin: Quiet Rebel* contains the most thorough discussion of Lavin's Catholic themes and imagery. Kelly examines the irony Lavin aims at religious hypocrisy, particularly her implications that Catholics are more hesitant to break Church rules than God's commandments, and that they are obsessed with outward rather than inward manifestations of mystical experience. Augustine Martin, in his afterword to *Mary O'Grady,* usefully places the novel within its specifically Catholic worldview in an attempt to answer critics' complaints that Mary's piety is unrealistically pure and simple. Marianne Koenig explores Lavin's mingling of fairy tale and folklore traditions with Catholic rituals and symbols, while Catherine A. Murphy discusses the pantheistic epiphanies experienced by Lavin's protagonists. Thomas J. Murray looks at Lavin's criticisms of the Catholic sense of sin and guilt. Jeanette Roberts Shumaker compares "A Nun's Mother" and "Sarah" (*Tales from Bective Bridge*) with two Edna O'Brien stories in an effective demonstration of "the female martyrdom (en)gendered by the Madonna myth" in Lavin's nuns, wives, mothers, and "fallen women," in which "their varieties of sacrifice stem from self-disgust fostered by failing to reach the standards of the Madonna myth" (p. 185).

## BIBLIOGRAPHY

### Works by Mary Lavin

*Tales from Bective Bridge*. Boston: Little, Brown, 1942.
*The Long Ago and Other Stories*. London: Michael Joseph, 1944.
*The House in Clewe Street*. London: Michael Joseph, 1945.
*The Becker Wives and Other Stories*. London: Michael Joseph, 1946.
*At Sallygap and Other Stories*. Boston: Little, Brown, 1947.
*Mary O'Grady*. London: Michael Joseph, 1950.
*The Patriot Son and Other Stories*. London: Michael Joseph, 1956.
*The Great Wave and Other Stories*. London and New York: Macmillan, 1961.
*In the Middle of the Fields and Other Stories*. London: Constable, 1967; New York: Macmillan, 1969.
*Happiness and Other Stories*. Boston: Houghton Mifflin, 1970.
*Collected Stories*. Boston: Houghton Mifflin, 1971.
*A Memory and Other Stories*. London: Constable, 1972; Boston: Houghton Mifflin, 1973.
*The Shrine and Other Stories*. London: Constable, 1977; Boston: Houghton Mifflin, 1977.
*A Family Likeness and Other Stories*. London: Constable, 1985.

### Works about Mary Lavin

Bowen, Zack. *Mary Lavin*. Lewisburg, Pennsylvania: Bucknell University Press, 1975.
Kelly, A. A. *Mary Lavin: Quiet Rebel*. Dublin: Wolfhound Press, 1980.
Koenig, Marianne. "Mary Lavin: The Novels and Stories." *Irish University Review* 9 (1979): 244–61.
Kosok, Heinz. "Mary Lavin: A Bibliography." *Irish University Review* 9 (1979): 279–312.
Levenson, Leah. *The Four Seasons of Mary Lavin*. Dublin: Marino Press, 1998.
Lynch, Rachel Sealy. "'The Fabulous Female Form': The Deadly Erotics of the Male Gaze in Mary Lavin's *The House in Clewe Street*." *Twentieth-Century Literature* 43.3 (1997): 326–38.
Martin, Augustine. Afterword. *Mary O'Grady*, by Mary Lavin. New York: Virago, 1986.

Meszaros, Patricia K. "Woman as Artist: The Fiction of Mary Lavin." *Critique* 24.1 (1982): 39–54.

Murphy, Catherine A. "The Ironic Vision of Mary Lavin." *Mosaic: A Journal for the Comparative Study of Literature* 12.3 (1979): 69–79.

Murray, Thomas J. "Mary Lavin's World: Lovers and Strangers." *Eire-Ireland: A Journal of Irish Studies* 7.2 (1972): 122–31.

Peterson, Richard F. *Mary Lavin.* New York: Twayne, 1978.

Pritchett, V. F. Introduction. *Collected Stories*, by Mary Lavin. Boston: Houghton Mifflin, 1971.

Shumaker, Jeanette Roberts. "Sacrificial Women in Short Stories by Mary Lavin and Edna O'Brien." *Studies in Short Fiction* 32 (1995): 185–87.

Stevens, L. Robert, and Sylvia Stevens. "An Interview with Mary Lavin." *Studies* 86.341 (Spring 1997): 43–50.

ANN V. NORTON

# DENISE LEVERTOV
## (1923–1997)

### BIOGRAPHY

Denise Levertov, one of America's foremost contemporary poets, was born in Ilford, Essex, England, in 1923. Her religious heritage was a rich one, simultaneously Jewish and Christian. Her father Paul Levertoff was a descendant of Schneour Zalman, the founder of Habad Hasidism. He was a Russian Jewish scholar who converted and later became an Anglican priest. He wrote throughout his life about the connections between Judaism and Christianity. He also created liturgies to which he welcomed Jews at St. George's, Bloomsbury, and he helped Jewish refugees in London during World War II.[1]

Levertov's Welsh mother, Beatrice Spooner-Jones Levertoff, was raised a Congregationalist and was, like her husband, involved with political and human rights' issues; she canvassed on behalf of the League of Nations Union and worked on behalf of German and Austrian refugees from 1933 onward. So it was natural that an interest in humanitarian politics came early into Levertov's life.

Levertov believed that inherited tendencies and the cultural ambiance of her own family were very strong factors in her development. She felt that her father's background in Jewish and, after his conversion, in Christian scholarship and mysticism, along with his fervor and eloquence as a preacher, ignited her imagination, even though as a child she refused to recognize that fact. She admitted in a 1986 interview for *Sojourners* ("'Invocations of Humanity': Denise Levertov's Poetry of Emotion and Belief") that although she rejected her parents' world as restrictive and embarrassing, she could not help seeing, despite her teenage doubts, that the church services were beautiful with their candlelight and music, incense and ceremony, and stained glass, and she treasured the incomparable rhythms of the King James Bible and the *Book of Common Prayer* (Hallisey, p. 33). Similarly, Levertov felt that her mother's Welsh intensity and lyric feeling for nature were deeply influential, a fact that she more readily acknowledged.[2]

Levertov recalled in the *Sojourners* interview what she had also expressed in the introduction to her section in the *Bloodaxe Anthology of Women Poets* (1985)—that part of her knew she was an "outsider":

Among Jews a Goy, among Gentiles (secular or Christian) a Jew or at least half Jew, (which was good or bad according to their degree of anti-Semitism), among Anglo-Saxons a Celt, in Wales a Londoner who not only did not speak Welsh, but was not imbued with Welsh attitudes; among school children a strange exception whom they did not know whether to envy or mistrust—all of these anomalies predicted my later experience: I so often feel English, or perhaps European, in the United States, while in England I sometimes feel American . . .

But these feelings of not-belonging were positive for me, not negative. . . . I was given such a sense of confidence by my family, in my family, that though I was often shy (and have remained so in certain respects) I nevertheless experienced the sense of difference as an honor, as part of knowing from an early age—perhaps by 7, certainly before I was 10—that I was an artist-person and had a destiny. (Hallisey, pp. 76–77)

Levertov was privately educated and served as a nurse in London during World War II. She immigrated to the United States in 1948 after she married Mitchell Goodman. She lived in Somerville, Massachusetts, for a number of years while teaching at Brandeis, MIT, and Tufts. In 1989, she moved from Somerville to Seattle and settled close to Lake Washington, in the shadow of Mt. Ranier. She taught part-time at the University of Washington and continued as a full professor at Stanford University for the first quarter of each year, as she had been doing since 1982. Levertov brought her own distinctive spirit and goals to the English Department, especially to her students in the Creative Writing program where she was valued as a superb teacher in the American tradition of poetry.[3] After her retirement from Stanford in 1993, she did several poetry readings and benefits a year in both the United States and Europe. In spite of failing health, she endeavored to keep up her correspondence with other poets and her many friends. Levertov died of complications due to lymphoma on December 20, 1997.

## MAJOR THEMES

Levertov's pilgrimage as an "artist-person" was enriched in the United States by the poetry and poetic theory of William Carlos Williams. Though some critics considered her an "aesthetic compatriot" of some of the poets of the Black Mountain School, she did not consider herself (in 1991, anyway) part of any "school" of poetry.[4] She brought her own distinctive voice to poems concerned with multiple aspects of the human experience: love, motherhood, nature, war, the nuclear arms race, the environment, mysticism, poetry, and the role of the poet. Levertov addressed these themes throughout her career, but all of them appear in her writings from *The Jacob's Ladder* (1958) on-wards and are connected intimately with Levertov's understanding of the awesome responsibility she assumed in her "vocation" as poet.

"Poetry, Prophecy, Survival" reiterates a theme that Levertov addressed on several occasions throughout her career: the poet or artist's call to "summon the divine." She speaks clearly about this "vocation" in a number of works, es-pecially in her 1984 essay "A Poet's View" (reprinted in *New and Selected Es-says,* 1992):

To believe, as an artist, in inspiration or the intuitive, to know that without imagination . . . no amount of acquired scholarship or of brilliant reasoning will suffice, is to live with a door of one's life open to the transcendent, the numinous. Not every artist, clearly, ac-knowledges that fact—yet all in the creative act experience mystery. The concept of in-spiration presupposes a power that enters an individual and is not a personal attribute; and it is linked to a view of the artist's life as one of obedience to a vocation. (p. 241)

Levertov was definitely reflecting not only on her vocation as a poet but also on her own faith journey as she was composing the poem "Mass for the Day of St. Thomas Didymus" in the late 1970s. We learn from Judith Dunbar in "Denise Levertov: 'The Sense of Pilgrimage'" that when she began the poem she considered herself an agnostic, but that she was drawn to the "possibilities of the form of the Mass as an aesthetic structure for poetry. Several months later, writing the final movement, the 'Agnus Dei,' she found herself in a changed relation to the dynamics of doubt and belief. Now her quest would continue with another wager: that of the believer" (p. 24).

For a deeper appreciation of this "wager" that Levertov was continuing with, one must not fail to recognize that she truly valued both her Hasidic and Christian roots. The visionary and prophetic elements of her poetry are en-lightened and enhanced by her interpretation of the Hasidic understanding of the meaning of *hitlahavut* and *avoda.* Buber tells us in *The Legend of the Baal-Shem* that a person's life may be a fusion of *hitlahavut,* "the burning" or the "ardour of ecstasy," and *avoda,* "service" (1955, pp. 17, 23). *Hitlahavut* is embracing God beyond time and space, and *avoda* is the service of God in time and space (p. 23). Levertov celebrated a comparable sense of vocation in Cath-olics like Julian of Norwich, St. Francis of Assisi, Dorothy Day, Thomas Mer-ton, Archbishop Oscar Romero, and Dom Helder Camara. Once their hearts and spirits were ignited, they too were compelled to act.

Levertov recognized the ramifications of this "burning" or "ardour of ec-stasy" overflowing into "service" in the dramatic "conversion" of Archbishop Oscar Romero. His commitment to the poor people of El Salvador was un-equivocal. (One remembers with a sense of irony the words of a member of the Church hierarchy before the Archbishop's installation in the movie *Romero:* "He's a good compromise choice. He'll make no waves. The military will keep a lid on things.")[5] Levertov's appreciation of Romero's prophetic integrity moved her to consider writing the libretto for W. Newell Hendricks's oratorio about El Salvador. When he consulted her about doing the libretto, she suggested El Salvador as a theme and the martyrdom of the four American women as a focus. This was a reasonable recommendation because, as she mentions in "Work That Enfaiths" (reprinted in *New and Selected Essays*), the thought of Romero was constantly before her at that time, and it became instrumental in helping her stop making a "fuss" in her mind about various points of doubt. After all, she asks, "[i]f a Romero or a Dorothy Day, or an Anthony Bloom, a Raymond Hunthausen, a Jean Sulivan, or a Thomas Merton—or a Pascal, for that matter! could believe, who was I to squirm and fret, as if I required more refined mental nourishment than others?" (p. 251).

Though Levertov speaks in "A Poet's View" about her move from a "regretful" skepticism to a position of Christian belief and states that her conversion was not a sudden or dramatic one (p. 241), her poetry of the time gave clear evidence of what she calls in "Work That Enfaiths" the interaction of "artistic and incipient faith" (p. 250). Even though in the late 1970s she considered herself "agnostic,"[6] the "artistic labor" she was working on indicated that she was embarking on a spiritual journey that would culminate in her entering the Roman Catholic Church.

Early in 1997, the year of her death, Levertov brought together in *The Stream and the Sapphire* poems from seven separate volumes that she tells us in her foreword she believed, to some extent, traced her own spiritual journey (p. vii). Several of the poems that testify to this movement are "St. Thomas Didymus," "The Incarnation," "On a Theme by Thomas Merton," and her poems that celebrate Dom Helder Camara's life, "Protesting at the Nuclear Test Site" and "Dom Helder Camara at the Nuclear Test Site." For those interested in tracing Levertov's faith journey through her poetry, *The Stream and the Sapphire* is an excellent resource.

Levertov treasured her copy of the translation of some television interviews by French journalist Roger Bourgeon with Dom Helder Camara, *Through the Gospels with Dom Helder Camara*. It is a collection of thought-provoking and inspirational reflections on Gospel narratives that simply and creatively relates individual texts to the modern world. Dom Helder's reflections—whether on his vocation as priest, the institutional Church, the role of the prophet, miracles, the presence of evil in the world, the poor and others who are disenfranchised— have both an Hasidic and Franciscan tone to them that Levertov felt a kinship with.[7]

Judith Dunbar's article convincingly traces Levertov's journey into Roman Catholicism. Dunbar mentions that in the mid-1980s, Levertov had a strong connection to Emmanuel Episcopal Church in Boston because of both its inspiring liturgies and its commitment to peace and justice issues. The pastor "practically commissioned" her to write her poem "Annunciation" for an Advent service there. She later participated in liturgies and activities at the Paulist Center in Boston. Levertov valued Roman Catholic leadership in social justice issues, and Dunbar is correct to say that along with her appreciation of the

Catholic Church's sense of leadership in social justice movements, she had a perception that "Roman Catholicism was more thoroughly international, as well as culturally and socio-economically more diverse, than the Anglican Church as she had known it when growing up" (p. 25). From personal conversations I had with Levertov, it is easy to support Dunbar's conclusion that it was both the activist in "Denise Levertov and the poet drawn to the sacramental who sought vital currents in the Roman Catholic Church. She remained aware of tension over the issue of authority, yet decided that those she most admired in the Church shared the tension and acted courageously out of conscience" (p. 25).

The story of Denise Levertov's entry into the Catholic Church recalls her friendships with Mary Luke Tobin, S.L.; Thomas Merton; Franciscan priest/poet Murray Bodo; Brother David Steindl-Rast, O.S.B.; Irish priest, poet, and broadcaster, Patrick O'Brien; poet Catherine de Vinck; and Irish poet Eavan Boland, her successor as director of the Stanford Creative Writing program, among others.

Levertov was an active parishioner at St. Joseph's in Seattle, Washington, at the time of her death in 1997. The Jesuits administer St. Joseph's, and she welcomed their genuine commitment to human rights and social issues, as well as their thoughtfully planned liturgical celebrations.

Levertov authored over twenty volumes of poetry and essays, and she received numerous awards for her work, including the Jerome J. Shestack Prize (*American Poetry Review,* 1989), and a 1990 National Endowment for the Humanities Senior Fellowship. In 1995 she was the sixty-first winner of the Academy of American Poets Fellowship.

## SURVEY OF CRITICISM

*Denise Levertov: Selected Criticism* (1993), edited by Albert Gelpi, provides the most extensive and balanced interpretation to date of Levertov's work. Gelpi believes that Levertov was at the center of the American poetic scene from the time she emigrated from England in the 1940s and "remade" herself as a poet in response to the ferment of American poetry in the postwar period. The essays, book reviews, and discussions collected in this study all confirm Levertov's place as one of the most important and influential, most respected and readable, poets of the second half of the twentieth century. After Albert Gelpi's insightful introduction, the first section assembles selected reviews chronologically from Kenneth Rexroth's enthusiastic response to her first American collection, which brought her early recognition, to a wide-ranging review by Ronald Revell of a more recent work, *A Door in the Hive* (1989). Part Two of Gelpi's work offers articles by distinguished critics on several of Levertov's themes: poetics, politics, gender, and religion.

The Fall 1997/Winter 1998 issue of *Renascence* offers a special tribute to Levertov and further enhances our understanding of the variety and riches of

Levertov's poetry that relate to her faith journey. The issue begins with an interview with Levertov by *Renascence* editor Ed Block, Jr., and is replete with reflections on "Spirit in the Poetry of Denise Levertov." Two entries deserve special consideration, however: Paul A. Lacey's "'To Meditate a Saving Strategy': Denise Levertov's Religious Poetry" and Eavan Boland's "A Visionary Element." The issue opens with Lacey's strong essay where he concentrates particularly on two of Levertov's later volumes, *Evening Train* (1992) and *Sands of the Well* (1996), to call attention to some of her poetic strategies for examining what he calls "this new borderland, the one between her intense, descriptive poems about the natural world and poems of her spiritual quest." Lacey convincingly demonstrates that this later poetry not only shows evidence of her earlier work but also continues to be exploratory and "that she continues to build on what William Carlos Williams taught her about form, returning to old themes and subjects while reaching out to new ones, reclaiming older mentors, notably Rainer Maria Rilke, while learning from the wilderness poets of the Pacific Northwest" (p. 19). Lacey believes that in "her quest for salvation—for the world, the tiny egg God gives into Julian's hand and our own—[Levertov] remains pilgrim and wanderer, explorer and creator." He sees Levertov "locating the Gospel story in the dust, grit and heavy clay of our own lives, trying 'to live in the mercy of God' by using 'what is at hand' to construct hopes for wholeness in the human community, in the natural world, and the deepest self" (p. 31).

Eavan Boland in "A Visionary Element" lauds Levertov's "Uncertain Oneiromancy" (*Sands of the Well*) as a "rare" poem. She believes that "[i]t has the exact qualities which Eliot admired Tennyson for: it is a poem of doubt by a poet of faith" (p. 153). Boland's insightful reflections on the poem evoke memories of other earlier Levertov poems that wrestle with the themes of faith and doubt, dream and reality, blindess and seeing. Many of these poems are included in *The Stream and the Sapphire*: "Candlemas," "Agnus Dei," "Flickering Mind," "On a Theme by Thomas Merton," "Standoff," "Suspended," "The Tide," "To Live in the Mercy of God," "Primary Wonder," and "On Belief in the Physical Resurrection of Jesus," among them. All of these poems were steps along Denise Levertov's journey into the Catholic Church and might be fruitfully examined in light of "Uncertain Oneiromancy," a persuasive poem that Eavan Boland believes "will stand at the center of Denise Levertov's achievement" (p. 158).

On his editor's page, Block sensitively muses that, in retrospect, the subtle, understated intensity of Levertov's more recent verse, even in its religious fervor, might be explained by her precarious health. Block believes that, like Keats, against whose reputation she measured her own, Levertov sang more poignantly in her last works because she knew more closely than most of us ever will the nearness of death.[8]

## NOTES

1. See not only Levertov's *The Poet in the World* (1973) but also Judith Dunbar's article "Denise Levertov: 'The Sense of Pilgrimage'" in *America* 30 May 1998: 22–28.

2. Although these thoughts were taken from the interview that Levertov did for *Sojourners* ("'Invocations of Humanity': Denise Levertov's Poetry of Emotions and Belief," February 1986, 32–36), they are reinforced by her own writings in *The Poet in the World* (1973), *Light Up the Cave* (1982), and *New and Selected Essays* (1992).

3. Memorial Resolution, Denise Levertov (1923–1997) by Eavan Boland, Chair; John Felstiner; and Albert Gelpi. At <http://portfolio.stanford.edu/106061>.

4. This topic came up while I was interviewing Levertov in 1991 for the introduction to *Range: A Tribute* (limited edition, 1991). She was commissioned to produce this volume in celebration of the one hundredth anniversary of women at Brown University.

5. See *Romero*, directed by John Duigan, starring Raul Julia. Vidmark Entertainments, 1989.

6. This topic came up in 1977 when I was interviewing Levertov while writing my dissertation at Brown University ("Walt Whitman, Hart Crane, and Denise Levertov: Poet/Prophets in the Tradition of Ralph Waldo Emerson").

7. Levertov gave me a copy of Roger Bourgeon's *Through the Gospels with Dom Helder Camara* (New York: Orbis Books, 1986), and she spoke at length about how much she respected Dom Helder's deep faith and vibrant Catholic spirit.

8. Though Levertov was a very private person, this "awareness" was evident in her conversations with a few of her close personal friends.

## BIBLIOGRAPHY

### Works by Denise Levertov

#### Poetry

*The Jacob's Ladder*. New York: New Directions, 1958.
*With Eyes at the Back of Our Heads*. New York: New Directions, 1959.
*The Sorrow Dance*. New York: New Directions, 1963.
*O Taste and See*. New York: New Directions, 1964.
*Relearning the Alphabet*. New York: New Directions, 1966.
*To Stay Alive*. New York: New Directions, 1971.
*Candles in Babylon*. New York: New Directions, 1982.
*Oblique Prayers*. New York: New Directions, 1984.
*Breathing the Water*. New York: New Directions, 1987.
*A Door in the Hive*. New York: New Directions, 1989.
*Evening Train*. New York: New Directions, 1992.
*Sands of the Well*. New York: New Directions, 1996.
*The Life Around Us*. New York: New Directions, 1997.
*The Stream and the Sapphire*. New York: New Directions, 1997.
*This Great Unknowing: Last Poems*. New York: New Directions, 1999.

## Prose

*The Poet in the World*. New York: New Directions, 1973.
*Light Up the Cave*. New York: New Directions, 1981.
*New and Selected Essays*. New York: New Directions, 1992.

## Works about Denise Levertov

Archer, Emily. "A Conversation with Denise Levertov." *Image* (Winter 1997–1998): 55–72.
Block, Ed, ed. *Renascence: Essays on Value in Literature*. Special Levertov issue. Vol. 50 (Fall 1997–Winter 1998).
Breslin, James E. B., ed. "Denise Levertov." *From Modern to Contemporary American Poetry 1945–1965*. Chicago: University of Chicago Press, 1984. 143–75.
Brooker, Jewel S. *Conversations with Denise Levertov*. Jackson: University Press of Mississippi, 1998.
Dunbar, Judith. "Denise Levertov 'The Sense of Pilgrimage.'" *America* 30 May 1998: 22–28.
Gelpi, Albert, ed. *Denise Levertov: Selected Criticism*. Ann Arbor: University of Michigan Press, 1993.
Hallisey, Joan F. "Denise Levertov's 'Illustrious Ancestors' Revisited." *Studies in American Jewish Literature* 9.2 (Fall 1990): 163–75.
———. "Interview with Denise Levertov." *Sojourners* (February 1986): 32–36.
Janssen, Ronald, ed. *Twentieth Century Literature*. Special Levertov issue. 38.3 (Fall 1992).
Lacey, Paul A. "The Poetry of Political Anguish." *Sagatrieb* 4.1 (Spring 1985): 61–71.
Marten, Harry. "Exploring the Human Community: The Poetry of Denise Levertov and Muriel Rukeyser." *Sagatrieb* 3.3 (Winter 1984): 57–61.
———. *Understanding Denise Levertov*. Columbia: University of South Carolina Press, 1988.
Middlebrook, Diane Wood, and Marilyn Yalom. "Poetry and Political Experience." *Coming to Light: American Women Poets in the Twentieth Century*. Ann Arbor: University of Michigan Press, 1985. 138–44.
Rodgers, Audrey T. *Levertov's Poetry of Engagement*. New Jersey: Fairleigh Dickinson University Press, 1993.
Sakelliou-Schultz, Liana. *Denise Levertov: An Annotated Primary and Secondary Bibliography*. New York: Garland, 1988.
Wagner-Martin, Linda. *Critical Essays on Denise Levertov*. Boston: G. K. Hall, 1991.

JOAN F. HALLISEY

# CLARE BOOTHE LUCE
## (1903–1987)

### BIOGRAPHY

Clare Boothe Luce had an extensive and varied career as a playwright, journalist, editor, politician, and diplomat. Her fame has derived largely from her marriage to publisher Henry Luce and from her celebrity as a socialite, social critic, and political conservative. Yet also important in understanding her influence is her mid-life conversion to Roman Catholicism, a decision that she wrote about and which redefined her literary career.

Born in New York City on March 10, 1903, to William and Ann Boothe, Clare learned early the arts of performance and social climbing. William Boothe was a violinist, Ann Boothe an actress. The struggling family moved frequently; as a consequence, Clare and her older brother, David, had only sporadic schooling. William Boothe left the family in 1911, and the couple divorced in 1913.

Clare represented her mother's hopes for social advancement. Ann Boothe pursued the girl's marital and theatrical prospects, arranging for Clare to become Mary Pickford's understudy in a stage production. She also learned to invest successfully in the stock market and financed a private education for her daughter. Clare attended Cathedral School of St. Mary in Long Island before beginning tenth grade at the Castle School in Tarrytown, New York. Her writing distinguished her at school, and in 1919 she graduated early, first in her class.

Clare's brief attempts at employment and secretarial school left her unfulfilled; reading philosophy and writing poetry suited her better. Ann Boothe having remarried, the family went abroad in 1920, and Europe's cathedrals and theater captivated Clare. While traveling, she met and impressed the wealthy social reformer and feminist Alva Belmont, who in 1921 hired Clare as her assistant in promoting the National Women's Party. Meanwhile, her mother continued efforts to arrange a well-to-do marriage for Clare. On August 10, 1923, at the age of twenty, Clare married George Brokaw, who was twice her age. Their daughter Ann was born the following year. Heir to a fortune, Brokaw belonged to an exclusive social hierarchy that ostracized Clare as an interloping opportunist. He was also an alcoholic prone to violent behavior, and Clare divorced him in 1929.

Although financially established, Clare Boothe wanted to work. Since having a profession was largely unprecedented for women of her era and social status, she had to apply extraordinary drive and originality in launching a career. She asked Conde Nast, a social acquaintance and publisher of *Vanity Fair* and *Vogue*, for a job. Although openly doubting the commitment of women of her status, he referred her to *Vogue*'s editor, Edna Chase. When Chase turned her down, Boothe later revisited the office while both Chase and Nast were away, found an empty desk, requested an assignment, and began writing captions. Boothe's bold demonstration of writing talent and initiative got her hired. She soon moved to *Vanity Fair*, where she mastered various editorial duties and wrote satirical pieces under the pseudonym Julian Jerome; she later rose to managing editor of that magazine. In 1931 she published *Stuffed Shirts*, an essay collection satirizing high society. In 1934, she left the magazine to travel in Europe, where she observed fascist tyranny rising in Italy and Germany. While abroad she wrote weekly political columns for the Hearst newspapers, but her interventionist political views alienated the editor.

Back in New York, Boothe worked on writing a play. She also met Henry Luce, publisher of *Time* and *Fortune* magazines, who, although married, quickly fell in love with her. In 1935 Boothe's play *Abide with Me* opened on Broadway, and shortly after the opening, Boothe and Luce married. While she had intended to continue her journalism career, the editors at both *Time* and *Fortune* balked at hiring the publisher's wife. However, Henry Luce and staff were in the early stages of developing a new magazine that would eventually become *Life*, and Clare Boothe Luce not only helped start this magazine but also later wrote for it. Meanwhile, she also resumed writing plays. *The Women* opened on Broadway in 1936, where it achieved long-running success. She next penned another successful Broadway play, *Kiss the Boys Good-bye*, which opened in 1938. *Margin for Error* followed on Broadway in 1939.

Concern about impending war in Europe drove Clare Luce to travel abroad as a journalist once again in February 1940. Despite escalating conflict, she stayed in Europe to gather material for her book, *Europe in the Spring* (1940), which became a bestseller. In 1941 the Luces traveled together to observe military action in Asia, with Clare Luce writing as *Life*'s war correspondent.

Always interested in politics, Luce ran successfully for Congress in 1942. A Republican, she represented Connecticut for two terms, from 1943 to 1947. In 1944, her daughter's accidental death sent Luce into a profound depression, and she later declined her party's encouragement to seek a third term or a Senate seat.

Luce converted to Roman Catholicism on February 16, 1946, having undertaken instruction from well-known Catholic author and speaker Father

Fulton J. Sheen. While her decision was based on multiple reasons and, largely, her intellectual agreement with Catholic teaching, personal anguish and observation of both the world's suffering and its shallowness also compelled her to seek spiritual renewal and the experience of divine, Christian love. After her conversion, her focus shifted to public expression of her new faith. In 1947 *McCall's* published Luce's extended essay about her conversion, "The 'Real' Reason." She also began lecturing on such topics as "Christianity in the Atomic Age," and she explored religious themes in her writing for stage and screen. In 1947, she encountered insurmountable studio conflicts over her screenplay adaptation of C. S. Lewis's *The Screwtape Letters,* but she later succeeded in seeing another of her religious story lines made into a 1949 film, *Come to the Stable* (nominated for multiple Academy Awards, including Best Story). Luce also wrote a play adapting the life of Saint Maria Goretti to an American setting, entitled *Child of the Morning;* it ran briefly in Boston with Margaret O'Brien playing the lead. In 1952, Luce edited *Saints for Now,* an essay collection relating Catholic hagiography to mid-twentieth-century culture.

From 1953 until 1956 Luce resumed her political career, serving as the United States' ambassador to Italy and distinguishing herself as the first woman to hold a top-level American diplomatic position. In 1959 President Eisenhower nominated her to become ambassador to Brazil, but Senate politics caused her to decline the nomination. Her political counsel, however, was sought by government leaders well into the 1980s. She earned several awards, including the Presidential Medal of Freedom in 1983. She died on October 9, 1987, and is buried at the former Luce estate in Mepkin, South Carolina, which she had donated to a Trappist order for conversion to a monastery.

## MAJOR THEMES

While much of the journalism and drama that Clare Boothe Luce wrote prior to her conversion to Catholicism are works of social satire, this view of the world in its extreme vanity merits reconsideration from the perspectives of religious and gender studies. Luce's satire takes on a culture composed of shallow relationships, materialism, sexism, and petty cruelty—realities of life that her elite social companions took for granted. *The Women* (1937) is a comic challenge to social conventions that destabilize female relationships and autonomy, marriage and family, interpersonal relationships, and moral agency. Among the social problems the play explores are the fashionability of adultery and divorce, the commodification of marriage, the subjugation of women, and ruthless social competition driven by materialism. Luce's depiction in the play of women as vicious gossips and deceitful manipulators may appear anti-feminist, yet this criticism overlooks the author's larger concern here about women in American culture being reduced to exploitable labor, idle consumers, or objects of physical glorification. To Luce, American society pits women against each another in competition for wealthy marriages at the expense of their humanity. In "sharpening [her] claws," the relatively decent Mary Haines in the play learns to counter mistreatment with some mean maneuvering of her own (rev. version, p. 90). Yet Mary's admission that she has no pride left because "that's a luxury a woman in love can't afford" suggests more moral and psychological depth than powder room brawls or seeking vengeance through divorce can account for (p. 89). Mary's jaded admission that she has learned not to trust other women reveals a world-weary voice venting cynicism. The "women" of the play's title are women of the world, which is clearly not a nice place; to suggest that they lack charity is an understatement, but such extreme characterization is indeed the basis for Luce's scathing satire.

Luce's post-conversion writing often validates religious faith, and particularly Catholicism, in a modern, secular, and materialistic age. Her introductory essay in and her editing of *Saints for Now* show her pondering the contemporary and personal relevance of traditional Catholic presentations of holy men and women. The film *Come to the Stable,* which depicts the missionary efforts of nuns who must engage a community's support to build a hospital, emphasizes the enduring potential of faith, hope, charity, and Catholic tradition, even in unlikely secular contexts and against tremendous odds.

Regarding conversion as a public expression of complex personal reckoning as well as a decision based on multiple reasons, Luce recounts her own spiritual progress in essays, most notably "The 'Real' Reason" and "Under the Fig Tree." Her candid reflections on her personal experience blend with ideas about history, politics, contemporary society, philosophy, and Catholic doctrine and tradition. Luce describes conversion as often beginning with "convergence," a powerful confrontation with total experience and its pain and limitations, causing one to seek larger, spiritual understanding ("The 'Real' Reason," pt. 3, p. 76).

"Most converts are Good Friday converts. They have entered His kingdom through the gates of pain," Luce writes in "Under the Fig Tree" (p. 217). Luce's own "convergence"/conversion narrative allows her to demonstrate, in personal writing for a public audience, a Catholic interpretation of pain, loss, and discontent as vehicles for divine grace. "The 'Real' Reason," for example, emphasizes her own early frustrations with society's alluring yet unsatisfying glamour; this disillusionment ultimately leads her to embrace the Catholic faith that she had once dismissed. In this essay, Luce also confronts grief frankly, seeking to understand the untimely deaths of both her daughter and the victims of war she had observed firsthand as a correspondent. In facing death and despair, she ultimately confronts larger questions of the existence of an afterlife and the higher purposes of earthly life: "whatever meaning Death had was given to it by Life . . . But what did Life mean?" (pt. 1, p. 126). She concludes "The 'Real' Reason" by describing intimately her profound convergence of pain and loss, which she experienced one night in 1945 when, overwhelmed with her life's empty pursuits, memories of war, and images of deceased loved ones, she was reduced to tears and desperate prayer in a lonely hotel room.

Luce's writing about her conversion also critiques modern skepticism and the cultural domination of the physical and social sciences over religious faith. In both global and personal terms, she explores the limitations of science and earthly achievement and the primacy of faith. Explaining why Freudian psychology failed her, for example, she asserts, "My psychoanalyst was a soul-quack" ("The 'Real' Reason," pt. 2, p. 16). In addition, humor as a source of humility, faith, and divine grace is also an important aspect of Luce's religious essays and of *Come to the Stable*. Her willingness to embrace Catholicism at the cost of being considered unfashionable or enduring personal mockery suggests an altered comic vision, one offering spiritual renewal and affirmation of powers even higher than her own.


## SURVEY OF CRITICISM

Aside from popular reviews of her books and dramatic works, most criticism of Luce's works centers on *The Women*. While yet finding the play's presentation of women problematic, recent literary scholars have reconsidered the work as a satirical critique, however flawed, of misogynistic, materialistic culture. Susan L. Carlson, for example, finds the play's harsh characterization, intense conflict, and unsettling resolution disturbing. She identifies the play's primary weakness as Luce's failure to distinguish clearly the protagonists' personal flaws from society's larger problems. "The effect," Carlson concludes, "is that [Luce's] lampooning of the women seems cruel because it is practiced upon characters who are already the victims of comic and social convention" (p. 211).

Joan T. Hamilton examines the play's scrutiny of the "fragmentation of female desire, its diffusion and misdirection" (p. 32). This treatment of women, she argues, reveals society's failure. Hamilton examines Luce's characters from the perspective of Michel Foucault's concept of "absent authority," as self-subjugating prisoners in their own social roles (pp. 34–37). While sharing the view that the play is troubling, Hamilton nonetheless advocates reconsideration of the mixed messages the play appears to send, particularly regarding Mary's assumption of a moral high ground through destructive tactics. Such contradiction "underscores the instability of the feminine position in this economy," Hamilton maintains (p. 51). Mary Maddock views *The Women* as a social critique of capitalistic competition as well as of sexism. Maddock sees the play's feminist message as one actually empowering women: "Without being didactic, [Luce] shows women in her audience how to stop being manipulated by their environment and how to control it" (p. 95).

Luce's overtly Catholic writings have not always impressed popular or literary critics. Reviewing *Come to the Stable* for the *New York Times,* Bosley Crowther found her amusingly romantic depiction of Catholic nuns and their funny-yet-faithful missionary endeavors "impulsive," unconvincing, and tire-some: "Mrs. Luce's story, made into a screen play by Sally Benson and Oscar Millard, dishes up generous portions of idyllic make-believe," he contends (p. 1). Wilfrid Sheed also laments the damage done to Luce's dramatic reputation by the insipidly sentimental *Come to the Stable*. Sheed, who knew Luce well, re-calls her admission to him in 1949 that Catholicism seemed to have dimin-ished her powers of literary expression and invention (p. 17). He observes that she seemed unable to reconcile Catholic piety with her acerbic wit and artistic talents, a loss that even then she viewed as an appropriate sacrifice (p. 20). However, Sheed finds "The 'Real' Reason" significant in that it reveals the re-ligious basis of Luce's political convictions regarding the need to combat evil (p. 144).

Mark Fearnow explains the contemporary waning of Luce's reputation by suggesting that generalized perceptions of her conservative political ideology often alienate artistic and scholarly audiences. Fearnow notes that Luce's dra-matic writing declined after her conversion, as she became preoccupied with politics. "What happened to the sharpened, painfully hilarious Luce of the 1930s?" Fearnow asks; "The mind that created *The Women* and *Kiss the Boys Good-bye* had moved on to what Luce had come to see as more important terri-tories" (p. 11).

Nonetheless, Luce's drama, nonfiction, journalism, and screenwriting, of-ten produced in a complex, secular, war-weary, and somewhat anti-Catholic America, merit further consideration. Understanding Luce as a woman who addressed, through her writing and her politics, both feminism and Catholi-cism as fundamental aspects of her worldview may prove illuminating in un-derstanding the twentieth-century American experience.

## BIBLIOGRAPHY

### Works by Clare Boothe Luce

*Stuffed Shirts*. Salem, New Hampshire: Ayer, 1931.

*The Women*. New York: Random House, 1937; rev. ed. New York: Dramatists Play-Service, 1966.

*Kiss the Boys Good-bye*. New York: Random House, 1939.

*Margin for Error*. New York: Random House, 1940.

*Europe in Spring*. New York: Alfred A. Knopf, 1940.

"The 'Real' Reason." *McCall's* 74 (February 1947): 16+; 74 (March 1947): 16+; 74 (April 1947): 26+.

*Come to the Stable*. Screenplay. Story by Clare Boothe Luce. Directed by Henry Koster. Twentieth Century Fox, 1949.

"Under the Fig Tree." *The Road to Damascus: The Spiritual Pilgrimage of Fifteen Converts to Catholicism*. Ed. John A. O'Brien. Garden City, New York: Doubleday and Company, Inc., 1949. 213–30.

*Child of the Morning.* Hardbound copy, 1951. Clare Boothe Luce papers in special collection. Folder 1, Box 326, Library of Congress, Manuscript Division, Washington D.C.

"The Catholic Mind and the Protestant Heart." *Catholic World* 174 (1952): 246–53.

*Saints for Now.* Ed. Clare Boothe Luce. New York: Sheed and Ward, 1952.

*Abide with Me.* Production script. Clare Boothe Luce papers in special collection. Folder 15, Box 325, Library of Congress, Manuscript Division, Washington D.C.

### Works about Clare Boothe Luce

Carlson, Susan L. "Comic Textures and Female Communities 1937 and 1977: Clare Boothe and Wendy Wasserstein." *Modern American Drama: The Female Canon.* Ed. June Schlueter. Cranbury, New Jersey: Associated University Presses, 1990. 207–17.

Crowther, Bosley. Rev. of *Come to the Stable,* by Clare Boothe Luce. *New York Times* 28 July 1949: 19.1.

Fearnow, Mark. *Clare Boothe Luce: A Research and Production Sourcebook.* Westport, Connecticut: Greenwood Press, 1995.

Hamilton, Joan T. "Visible Power and Invisible Men in Clare Booth's [sic] *The Women.*" *American Drama* 3.1 (Fall 1993): 31–53.

Lyons, Joseph. *Clare Boothe Luce.* American Women of Achievement series. New York: Chelsea House Publishers, 1989.

Maddock, Mary. "Social Darwinism in the Powder Room: Clare Boothe's *The Women.*" *Journal of American Drama and Theater* 2.2 (Spring 1990): 81–97.

Martin, Ralph G. *Henry and Clare: An Intimate Portrait of the Luces.* New York: G. P. Putnam's Sons, 1991.

Morris, Sylvia Jukes. *Rage for Fame: The Ascent of Clare Boothe Luce.* New York: Random House, 1997.

Sheed, Wilfrid. *Clare Boothe Luce.* New York: Dutton, 1982.

VICTORIA CARLSON

# MARY MCCARTHY
# (1912–1989)

## BIOGRAPHY

Born in 1912 in Seattle to Tess Preston and Roy McCarthy, Mary McCarthy lived the life of a fairy princess with parents who adored her and her three brothers. Tess converted from Protestantism and became, like many converts, much more Catholic than any McCarthy, impressing upon her children how lucky they were to be Catholic. Roy's heart illness often kept him home with his children, and Mary's brief six years with him affected her greatly. Both her parents died in the 1918 flu epidemic when Mary was six. Mary and her brothers stayed first with their paternal grandparents, strict Catholics living in Minneapolis. Her grandmother McCarthy's materialistic Catholicism contrasted greatly with both the spiritual, communal Catholicism her mother had instilled in her, and the intellectual, romantic Catholicism she later encountered at school as a young teenager. Eventually, the orphans were shuttled off to an elderly aunt, Margaret, and her husband, also living in Minneapolis.

After six years of unhappiness, Mary was claimed by her Grandfather Preston and taken with him back to Seattle; her brothers were left in a Minnesota boarding school. At first, she was nervous about the "Protestants getting her" as she had so often been warned by Grandmother McCarthy. But she was enrolled in a Catholic school, the Ladies of the Sacred Heart, a girls' version of the Jesuit school attended by James Joyce and as powerful an influence on the budding intellectual.

After graduating from Vassar in 1933, McCarthy began writing articles for the *Nation, New Republic,* and *Partisan Review;* she served as drama critic for the latter journal from 1937–1944. Later, she taught at Bard College and Sarah Lawrence College. She married three times, the second time to literary critic and writer Edmund Wilson with whom she had her only child, Reuel. Wilson, whom she married in 1938 and divorced in 1946, is credited with encouraging McCarthy to write fiction.

McCarthy died on October 25, 1989, full of anger at the Church that she thought had failed her: she wrote an unpublished essay assaulting Catholic education just a few years before her death, and she refused to see a priest when she was in the hospital dying. As she promised in her autobiography *Memories of a Catholic Girlhood* (1957), "For myself, I prefer not to play it safe, and I shall never send for a priest or recite an Act of Contrition in my last moments" (p. 27).

## MAJOR THEMES

Mary McCarthy wrote in *Memories of a Catholic Girlhood* that it was difficult to respond to the oft-asked question of whether she retained anything from her Catholic heritage: "This is hard to answer, partly because my Catholic heritage consists of two distinct strains" (p. 21). She refers here to the Catholicism of her parents and of Sacred Heart school, versus the "sour, baleful doctrine" of Grandmother McCarthy (p. 21). This apparent discrepancy in "Catholicisms," as well as the influence of her Protestant grandfather, keenly influenced McCarthy's ambiguous relationship to Catholicism. In her first novel, *The Company She Keeps* (1942), the heroine, Meg Sargent, contrasts her Catholic Aunt Clara's section of the house with her secular father's: "red votive lamps, altars and holy pictures (the Sacred Heart, Veronica's veil with the eyes that followed you about the room . . . ), a rich, emotional decor that made the downstairs with its china shepherdesses, Tiffany glass, bronze smoking sets, and family photographs look matter-of-fact and faded" (pp. 265–66). Aunt Clara is modeled after both the hated Aunt Margaret and Grandma McCarthy. Meg's bedroom, like McCarthy's feelings for the Church, is somewhere in between.

McCarthy wrote little about growing up Catholic, but what she did write was explosive. In *Memories of a Catholic Girlhood*, she details both the positive (love of beauty and learning, Latin) and the negative (vulgarity, lies, hypocrisy) aspects of her Catholic education. Yet, although this is her only book that focuses explicitly on the Church, even a cursory reading of her fiction and essays reveals the influence of Catholicism on her writing and thinking. Ecclesiastical allusions abound, and in her strong sense of morality, punishment, and self-criticism, McCarthy's sensibilities are clearly Catholic. In addition, she portrays Catholic characters, such as Meg in *The Company She Keeps;* in this novel, Meg's psyche is permanently damaged by her upbringing, and she is caught between what critic Thelma Shinn defines as "two sets of values": the modern, intellectual, bohemian woman that she aspires to be, and the anti-modern woman paralyzed by the "traditional values of feminine stereotypes and Catholic dogma in which she was raised" (p. 91). McCarthy's heroines all suffer from this tension, and it is never resolved.

Meg romantically believes that she has the freedom to break away from her past, roughly similar to McCarthy's own orphaned past, and make her own choices. But in the end she fears that her true self has been determined by her past, and that she is doomed, as McCarthy recognized about herself in her first autobiography, to repeat the moral decisions and events of the past. Her internalization of this fatalism stems from both her Catholicism and her psychology; in any event, it undermines her self-esteem. When she does visit an analyst, Dr. James, they desperately avoid discussing her childhood: "The subject frightened them both, for it suggested to them that the universe is mechanical, utterly predictable, frozen, and this in its own way is quite as terrible as the notion that the universe is chaotic. It is essential for our happiness, [Meg] thought, to have both the pattern and the loose ends" (p. 262).

McCarthy's next novel, *A Charmed Life* (1954), is an ironic fable about the dangers of doubt, not just in God, but also in one's self. Seven years after her divorce from the devilish Miles Murphy, Martha Sinnot (whose first name evokes the parable) returns to the charming town of New Leeds with her second husband, John, in hopes of becoming pregnant. Within months she has sex with Miles and becomes pregnant. Like Meg, Martha is reluctantly hopeful—reluctant because she fears that free will is an illusion. She is tired of seeing the truth that always seems to her to get in the way of hope; although she recognizes such insight as a sign of maturity, "she didn't care for it, she would rather be dead" (p. 22). Martha possesses a hopeful, romantic outlook, similar to Meg, but she also has a fatalistic side. Neither proves very helpful or mature, despite her conclusion that "[t]he fatalistic side of her character accepted Miles as a punishment for the sin of having slept with him when she did not love him" (p. 103).

The women of McCarthy's best-selling novel *The Group* (1963) were educated to believe that they have the autonomous capacity as well as the Vassar education and privileged background to do just as they please in life. Ironically, this makes them less free than their mothers, who are portrayed much more positively than the daughters. All the younger women have blithely escaped any religious or parental control, yet they are still controlled and unfulfilled. Kay is the McCarthy figure who has escaped her middle-class parents and reached, however precariously, the upper class through Vassar and her friends. But she is not completely assimilated; she is foiled by the conflicting internal desires of idealism and security. The other members of the group also relinquish their dreams and retreat to the security of authority. Dottie blindly follows a man she has just met to his apartment and gives up her virginity without even a guilt-induced struggle; later, despite herself, she falls in love with him, but refuses to pursue the relationship and instead marries an older man for shelter. Surprisingly, her mother prefers that Dottie test her love for the young lover before she marries the older man; she fears that Dottie is repeating some "dreadful pattern" by retreating into safety. "You'd like God to arrange for you to have something that you know would be wrong for you if you chose it of your own free will," she admonishes her daughter (p. 182). The other mothers are equally liberated. Priss's mother was thrilled at the invention of bottled milk for babies, and she watches with horror as her daughter succumbs to her own husband's strict, even sadistic, breast-feeding schedule. Polly allows fate to decide if Gus will visit her one night, and it does: "Fate sealed the night she got her father's letter. Fate had sent her father as a sign that it would be kind to her so long as she did not think of men or marriage" (p. 299). In fact, all the members of the Vassar group allow fate to lead the way. Even the seemingly strong ones are not immune: as biographer Doris Grumbach wryly points out, Lakey's lesbianism, for example, is probably the result of a Vassar teacher telling her to live without love (p. 50). The irony is that, like all college-educated, upper-class women, they all believe they have complete freedom to make their own decisions.

McCarthy's critical eye was particularly harsh on the bohemian, intellectual woman who toys with sex and politics in order to avoid an essential truth about herself or about the world around her. Interestingly, she never exposes in her fiction the group she is most familiar with—Catholics—despite the fact that she spent most of her early life in Catholic schools. But as critic Wilfred Sheed once wrote, "A Catholic novelist need never mention Catholics. You can recognize the sensibility" (Cryer, p. 21). McCarthy used what she found worthy in Catholicism and discarded the rest; however, she was unable to reject the most important influences since her moral perceptions and everyday actions were guided by her Catholic heritage. And in her strong sense of morality, punishment, and self-criticism, her sensibilities are clearly influenced by Jansenist Irish American Catholicism.

## SURVEY OF CRITICISM

From the start of her career as a critic, composing biting theater reviews for the *Partisan Review* and book reviews for the *Nation,* to the beginning of her career as a novelist in 1942, Mary McCarthy has been called heartless, lying, cold, savage, and brutally honest. Her Vassar English teachers told her to stick to criticism and she did: McCarthy herself admitted in her 1987 autobiography *How I Grew* that when she wrote in anger, "[t]he aesthetic urge was secondary. I had 'something to say'" (p. 101).

*The Company She Keeps* is generally considered her best fictional work, although there are critics who prefer *The Groves of Academe* (1952), a satire of a liberal arts college. The best-selling novel *The Group* was obviously the public's favorite choice. *Memories of a Catholic Girlhood*, an autobiography with many fictional elements, is acclaimed by both critics and the public; many readers consider it and McCarthy's other autobiographies as the author's public confessions, following in the tradition of Catholic confession. Louis Auchincloss writes, "in *Memories* [McCarthy] rises to a pitch of something like passion that makes it the noblest utterance that she has yet produced" (p. 186). However, Timothy Dow Adams complains that McCarthy is deliberately parodying the sacrament of confession in this memoir, boasting of her sins rather than seeking penitence.

Several critics have accused McCarthy of writing fiction that is dry, devoid of emotion, or too objective. McCarthy herself wrote that, compared with others in her family, she was the only one who "ever let his [sic] private feelings be seen" (*How I Grew,* p. 189). Repressing emotions is often the result of a fear of being mocked, as in the Irish American McCarthy household, or a fear of being out of control, which was perhaps the case in the Protestant Preston household. Critics have also not always responded positively to McCarthy's wry sense of humor, which allowed her the distance necessary for satire. For example, in *How I Grew,* she describes with dark comedy a suicide attempt at age fifteen: "I cannot say exactly why I was roaming around his backyard with a bottle of iodine in my hand all dressed up to kill myself" (p. 189). And in *The Company She Keeps,* Meg attempts to see her disturbing sexual encounter with the bourgeois, middle-aged, and chubby Mr. Breen in farcical terms: "She could accept and even, wryly, enjoy it. The world of farce was a sort of moral underworld, a cheerful, well-lit hell where a Fall was only a prat-fall after all" (p. 111).

Although some critics, such as Paul Schleuter, fail to recognize any moral background in McCarthy's fiction (he finds her novels morally "sterile"), others argue that, despite her own convictions and the often "immoral" affairs she depicts, McCarthy's morality is loyal to the Jansenism of her Irish Catholic girlhood. To still other critics, however, this is her downfall as an artist. Bruce Cook, writing for the conservative journal *Catholic World,* states (with almost McCarthyesque malicious glee), "By some cruel trick of the psyche, she has been frozen in the haughty moral posture of her Catholic girlhood" (p. 34). McCarthy's biographer Carol Brightman believes that the author clung to a dualistic view for most of her life. But Mary McCarthy recognized that "goodness" as a moral concept connected to religion is an idea that one unfortunately grows out of, and she indirectly responds to those who would denounce her dualistic worldview:

The idea that religion is supposed to teach you good, an idea that children have, seems to linger on. . . . Very few people appear to believe this anymore, it is utterly out of style among fashionable neo-Protestants, and the average Catholic perceives no connection between religion and morality, unless it is a question of someone else's morality, that is, of the supposed pernicious influences of books, film, ideas, or someone else's conduct. (*Memories,* p. 23)

## BIBLIOGRAPHY

### Works by Mary McCarthy

*The Company She Keeps.* New York: Simon and Schuster, 1942; New York: Harcourt, 1970.

*Cast a Cold Eye.* New York: Harcourt, Brace, 1950; New York: Harvest/Harcourt, 1992.

*A Charmed Life.* New York: Harcourt, Brace, 1955; New York: Harvest/Harcourt, 1992.

*The Groves of Academe.* New York: Harcourt, Brace, 1952; New York: Harvest/Harcourt, 1992.

*Memories of a Catholic Girlhood.* New York: Harcourt, Brace, 1957; New York: Harcourt/Harvest, 1981.

*The Group.* New York: Harcourt, Brace and World, 1963; New York: Avon, 1980.

*Mary McCarthy's Theatre Chronicles 1937–1962.* New York: Farrar, Straus, 1963.

*Cannibals and Missionaries.* New York: Harcourt, 1979.

*How I Grew.* New York: Harcourt Brace Jovanovich, 1980.

### Works about Mary McCarthy

Adams, Timothy Dow. *Telling Lies in Modern American Autobiography.* Chapel Hill: University of North Carolina Press, 1990.

Auchincloss, Louis. "Mary McCarthy." *Pioneers and Caretakers: A Study of Nine American Women Novelists.* Minneapolis: University of Minnesota Press, 1965. 170–86.

Brightman, Carol. *Writing Dangerously: Mary McCarthy and Her World.* New York: Clarkson Potter, 1992; San Diego: Harvest/Harcourt, 1994.

Cook, Rev. Bruce. "Mary McCarthy: One of Ours?" *Catholic World* 199 (1964): 34–42.

Cryer, Dan. "The Examined Life of Mary McCarthy." *Newsweek* 29 (March 1987): 18–21.

Gelderman, Carol. *Mary McCarthy: A Life.* New York: St. Martin's Press, 1988.

———, ed. *Conversations with Mary McCarthy.* Jackson: University Press of Mississippi, 1991.

Grumbach, Doris. *The Company She Kept.* New York: Coward-McCann, 1976.

Schlueter, Paul. "The Dissections of Mary McCarthy." *Contemporary American Novelists.* Ed. Harry T. Moore. Carbondale: Southern Illinois University Press, 1964. 54–64.

Shinn, Thelma. *Radiant Daughters: Fictional American Women.* Westport, Connecticut: Greenwood Press, 1986.

Stwertka, Eve and Margo Viscusi, eds. *Twenty-Four Ways of Looking at Mary McCarthy: The Writer and Her Work.* Westport, Connecticut: Greenwood Press, 1996.

STACEY DONOHUE

# RIGOBERTA MENCHÚ
## (1959– )

---

## BIOGRAPHY

Rigoberta Menchú was born January 9, 1959, in the small village of Chimel in the northern highlands of Guatemala. A Quiché Maya, one of the twenty-two ethnic Indian groups in Guatemala, Menchú grew up during a time of right-wing military dictatorship and guerrilla resistance in her country. Her large peasant family often worked long hours on the *fincas*—coastal coffee, sugar, and cotton plantations—to support themselves while trying to maintain their own small farm. As a young girl, Menchú rebelled against such injustice by entering the struggle against the oppressive landowners and soldiers of Guatemala. Her father, Vincente, a catechist and community leader, became a political figure when he opposed the military government through the Committee for United Campesinos; he was repeatedly imprisoned and beaten, and was eventually killed in 1980 at the burning of the Spanish Embassy of Guatemala while protesting human rights abuses. The military kidnapped, raped, tortured, and eventually murdered Menchú's mother, Juana Tum—a midwife, healer, and revolutionary. At least two of Menchú's brothers also were killed by government security forces during the barbaric violence, destruction of villages and crops, and forced relocation and military service that took place in Guatemala's Indian communities in the 1960s–1980s. During this time, as many as one hundred fifty thousand people are estimated to have been murdered by death squads or the army in Guatemala, and another fifty thousand disappeared.

In 1982, Menchú traveled to Paris to flee persecution and continue her work toward Guatemalan peasant solidarity. It was there that she met and told her story in Spanish to Venezuelan ethnographer Elisabeth Burgos-Debray, who recorded, organized, and edited Menchú's narrative into *I, Rigoberta Menchú, An Indian Woman in Guatemala*. First published in 1983 as *Me llamo Rigoberta Menchú y así me nació la concienca,* the memoir was translated into English the following year. Because of her writing and continued work toward human rights in Guatemala, Menchú was awarded the Nobel Peace Prize in 1992, during the week marking the five hundreth anniversary of Christopher Columbus's arrival in the Americas. With the award, Menchú set up a foundation in her father's name to work toward peace and civil rights in Guatemala. Also largely because of her work, the United Nations declared 1993 the International Year of the World's Indigenous Peoples; for the same year, the Secretary-General of the World Conference on Human Rights named Menchú Goodwill Ambassador.

Although she returned to Guatemala a number of times, Menchú moved back there permanently in 1995 to continue to demand, through legal channels, accountability for the crimes perpetrated by the Guatemalan government. In 1998, she released *Crossing Borders: An Autobiography,* a second autobiographical collection of narratives and essays on subjects about her life, community, and politics. She currently runs the Rigoberta Menchú-Tum Foundation in Guatemala City, continuing her advocacy for human rights, working toward voting rights in Guatemala, and attempting to preserve her cultural heritage.

Menchú's early life history, however, does not lay itself out as neatly as she reports it in her first autobiography, *I, Rigoberta.* In fact, what is most contentious about the figure of Rigoberta Menchú are the facts of her life, which remain difficult to determine. In 1999, David Stoll, an anthropology professor at Middlebury College, released his findings about Menchú's autobiography in his book, *I, Rigoberta Menchu and the Story of All Poor Guatemalans.* Based on his research and interviews, Stoll calls into question many of the particulars of Menchú's memoir. Soon after Stoll's book was released, the *New York Times* investigated and corroborated his claims.

It is in the details of Menchú's narrative that it becomes difficult to identify fact from fiction—or, perhaps more appropriately, individual history from collective history. Indeed, the truths at issue remain complicated precisely because of our differing definitions of truth: while Menchú's autobiography has been accused of taking license with specific events in her family history, such events did occur, albeit perhaps not within the context of the lives she discusses. For example, *I, Rigoberta* reports such events as the kidnapping, torture, and burning alive of her younger brother Petrocinio. Later versions of Petrocinio's murder suggest that he was killed by gunfire, but such horrific actions as she describes were not an uncommon practice of the Guatemalan government in dealing with subversives. Menchú's education is also at issue: her autobiography claims that, as a young adult, she learned how to read and write as part of her struggle to fight the Guatemalan government. Stoll's book, however, points out that the young Rigoberta attended Catholic boarding schools. Menchú has responded that she worked as a housekeeper in the schools, and that the nuns allowed her to attend classes on the side—an explanation that Stoll himself corroborates in interviews, although not in his book.

Many in the press have been less than satisfied with Menchú's answers to Stoll's accusations, particularly with her contention that her autobiography is part of her historical memory of Guatemala. Menchú's defense offers us substantial insight into the ongoing battle between fact and fiction, reality and fabrication, that plagues our postmodern world. Thus her memoir brings to a head questions about the validity of enduring truths in the face of individual perceptions.

## MAJOR THEMES

The dominant themes of Menchú's two autobiographical texts, as well as her various essays, are colonialism, religious syncretism, testimony and advocacy, diversity, community and the individual's role within it, and concern for the rights of indigenous peoples and women. Yet while *I, Rigoberta* is frequently viewed as a political discourse decrying the atrocities of a Third World totalitarian government, one of the main issues taken up by both this text and her later work, *Crossing Borders,* is the role of Catholicism in the life of a young girl. The latter text especially evinces Menchú's esteem for the Church, particularly manifested in her respect for her personal Catholic mentors, such as Monsignor Samuel Ruiz Garcia, Bishop of Chiapas; Julia Esquivel; Mario Colen; and participants in the Christian Coordinating Committee for Guatemala.

Perhaps more critically, *I, Rigoberta* examines the role Catholicism plays within the larger political and ideological struggles of the colonized. In *I, Rigoberta,* Menchú writes of first learning about Catholicism through the work of missionaries, particularly the group Catholic Action, which she joined as a young catechist. Menchú tells how, growing up, she became aware of the oppression of the *indios* in her country, and how some of the Catholic missionary groups supported her people in their resistance against the dominating Spanish landowners, or *ladinos,* even joining the peasant and guerrilla organizations that Menchú advocated. From the Catholic priests and nuns, young Rigoberta learned the power of language, particularly to attain solidarity among her people. She writes, "No-one had taught me how to organise because, having been a catechist, I already knew" (*I, Rigoberta,* p. 122). But the Catholic missionaries offered material as well as spiritual aid, particularly by helping to hide from the military those who, like Menchú's parents, became political targets.

Yet *I, Rigoberta* also investigates the Church's complicity in colonialism, a duality within Catholic teachings that represents a split within the Church itself—between the institutional Church of the wealthy, which supports the class hierarchies of Guatemala, and the liberationist Church of the poor, which joins in Menchú's struggle against poverty and oppression. Ironically, it is the same Church that teaches rebellion that also preaches compliance and submission to one's lot in life: "Their religion told us it was a sin to kill while we were being killed. . . . It kept our people dormant while others took advantage of our passivity" (pp. 121–22).

*I, Rigoberta* works through these conflicting attitudes toward Catholicism through religious syncretism, the hybridization of religions. For example, discussing the mixing of ancestor worship with Catholicism in relation to the religious holidays and ceremonies of her community, Menchú refers to "the Saints' Days, from the Catholic Action. But ours are not the Saints of the pictures. We celebrate special days talking about our ancestors" (p. 65). This acculturation allows Menchú's people to retain their own traditional beliefs while choosing those aspects of Catholicism that are most useful to their struggles, such as certain passages in the Bible, which become tools supporting liberation theology. Such religious syncretism also allows Menchú's people to circumvent some of Catholicism's more repressive teachings, a strategy especially valuable to the women of Guatemala, who bear a large share of the burdens placed on the poor. For example, Menchú discusses the tolerance demonstrated by her people toward women who seek divorce, an allowance that lightens the severity of Catholic teachings that prohibit the dissolution of the marriage vows under any circumstances, even if the woman is suffering.

Menchú is also critical of the *machismo* that is common throughout Guatemalan culture. While she writes of the suffering that mothers face when seeing their children die of starvation or torture, she also addresses the strength of the women who battle against such tyranny. She demonstrates how men and women joined together to fight the soldiers, and how the lack of task differentiation for gender allowed them to work more quickly and effectively. Her commitment to gender equity translated into her early organizational work as well, because she resisted setting up different organizations for men and women. Both she and her mother encouraged women to join the struggle against oppression: "My mother's words told them that any evolution, any change, in which women had not participated, would not be a change, and there would be no victory" (*I, Rigoberta,* p. 196).

Another theme central to Menchú's writing is her sense of community. Concerned about linguistic barriers, she writes of the necessity of learning Spanish—not just in order to master the oppressors' tools, but also as a way to break down barriers among the various groups of Indians, as well as an attempt to create solidarity with the poorer *ladinos,* whom she comes to see as similarly oppressed by those in power. In *I, Rigoberta,* she speaks not just for herself but for all the peoples she represents: she both *is* and *is of* the indigenous peoples of Guatemala. Her experiences of colonialism, exploitation, and rebellion are common to many Indians throughout the Americas; her testimonial, then, is not just for herself but for her people in their political struggle. Menchú becomes an everywoman, the collective voice of the oppressed, regardless of gender, race, class, or ethnicity.

## SURVEY OF CRITICISM

To discuss the critical reception of Menchú's works, one must look to both the literary academy and the popular press. Academic critics of Menchú's *I, Rigoberta* discuss its use of the testimonial genre to connect literature to anthropology, and personal history to social movements; its clumsy plot but articulate, Christian message; and its Third World relationship to its First World audience. Social critics, more interested in the political agenda of the text, accuse Menchú of changing the facts of her story for political reasons; some call her a pawn while others accuse her of purposefully advancing North American liberal ideologies. Dinesh D'Souza, in his 1991 *Illiberal Education,* finds *I, Rigoberta* to be a calculated promotion of Marxist and feminist critiques of the West and their role in Third World politics. David Stoll's book further insinuates that Menchú's writings are more political than personal. Its release coincided with the 1999 publication of the United Nations Commission for Historical Clarification, which found the Guatemalan military, financed by the United States, responsible for political massacres that resulted in the death or disappearance of approximately two hundred thousand Mayans during Guatemala's thirty-six-year civil war. Many worry that Stoll's criticism of Menchú threatens the reaction of the international community to the military reign of terror in Guatemala.

But supporters of Menchú refuse to be disturbed by the media frenzy surrounding the release of Stoll's book, arguing that the truth of her texts resides in the disclosures about the atrocities of the Guatemalan military and in the promise of freedom and change that her writing offers. Despite recent controversy about the veracity of her story, Menchú's *I, Rigoberta* is credited with drawing the attention of the major American and international news media to the Guatemalan army's brutal and extensive repression and destruction of its own peoples. For many readers, teachers, and researchers, *I, Rigoberta* remains a significant contribution to contemporary autobiography and a crucial testament to the role of the contemporary Catholic Church in the struggles of working-class peoples. The text likewise remains a useful tool in the classroom, as evidenced in the many essays included in Allen Carey-Webb and Stephen Benz's *Teaching and Testimony: Rigoberta Menchú and the North American Classroom.* Menchú herself endures as a legendary human rights champion and central figure in the struggle for social justice for women and indigenous peoples.

## BIBLIOGRAPHY

### Works by Rigoberta Menchú

*Me llamo Rigoberta Menchú y asi me nació la concienca.* Barcelona: Editorial Argos Vergara, 1983. Trans. by Ann Wright as *I, Rigoberta Menchú, An Indian*

*Woman in Guatemala*. Ed. and intro. Elisabeth Burgos-Debray. London: Verso, 1984.

*La nieta de los mayas*. With Dante Liano and Gianni Mina. Santillana Publishing Co., 1998. Trans. and ed. by Ann Wright as *Crossing Borders: An Autobiography*. London and New York: Verso, 1999.


## Works about Rigoberta Menchú

Carey-Webb, Allen, and Stephen Benz, eds. *Teaching and Testimony: Rigoberta Menchú and the North American Classroom*. Albany: State University of New York Press, 1996.

DelRosso, Jeana. "Veiled Threats: Contemporary International Catholic Girlhood Narratives." Diss. University of Maryland, 2000.

D'Souza, Dinesh. *Illiberal Education: The Politics of Race and Sex on Campus*. New York: Free Press, 1991.

Graham, Judith, ed. "1993." *Current Biography Yearbook*. New York: H. W. Wilson Co., 1993. 398–402.

Leigh, David J. "Rigoberta Menchú and the Conversion of Consciousness." *Historicizing Christian Encounters with the Other*. Ed. John C. Hawley. Houndsmill, Basingstoke, Hampshire: Macmillan, 1998. 182–93.

Preston, Julia. "Guatemala Laureate Defends 'My Truth.'" *New York Times* 21 January 1999: A8.

Stoll, David. *I, Rigoberta Menchu and the Story of All Poor Guatemalans*. Boulder: Westview Press, 1999.

JEANA DELROSSO

# ALICE MEYNELL
# (1847–1922)

## BIOGRAPHY

Alice Meynell was born in Surrey, the second of two daughters of Thomas
Thompson and his wife, Christiana. The family moved frequently, living a
rather bohemian existence in various places in England, France, and Italy.
Thomas undertook his daughters' education, and he was rigorous about it; the
outcome can be seen in Alice's mature writings, with their rich habit of allusion
and intimate knowledge of English and European literatures, art, and music.

Alice grew into an introspective teenager, reading widely and keeping a diary that shows her awareness that her sex would count against her in her desire
to succeed as a writer and thinker. Her mother quietly converted to Catholicism in the 1860s, and Alice followed her in 1867. Catholicism in the 1860s
presented a heady prospect for the young English intellectual; Newman's *Apo-
logia* was published in 1864, and a wave of conversions spread out from Oxford to all parts of England. Alice's conversion was in part intellectual and in
part emotional: tellingly, she fell in love with the priest who instructed her, Father Augustus Dignam, who had to be re-posted to avoid further trouble. The
experience led to one of her very finest poems, the sonnet "Renouncement,"
which remains her best known work; written in 1870, it was not published until 1882. Another factor in her conversion was her own sense of moral insecurity and her felt need for discipline, for she viewed the Church as providing a
haven of stability.

In 1875, Alice published her first volume of poems, *Preludes* (with illustrations by her sister); it drew praise from Christina Rossetti, Tennyson, Ruskin,
George Eliot, and many others. One reader who was particularly struck by it
was the young Wilfrid Meynell, who became determined to meet her. Meynell,
also a Catholic convert, was working as a journalist in London for various
Catholic periodicals. He was by no means among the first rank of intellectuals,
nor was he financially comfortable, but he was an indefatigable worker, and it is
natural to assume that Alice saw in his loyalty and stability—perhaps one

should say his normalcy—the best sort of husband for her. The marriage took place in London in 1877.

The Meynells entered upon a busy life of journalism, and Alice's poetry slowed to a trickle for many years (her next book of poems and her first book of essays were published in 1893). She gave birth to eight children over the ensuing years. As her reputation as an essayist and poet grew, her ability to combine the role of intellectual with that of wife and mother turned her into something of an icon of the perfect woman to many, including the poet Coventry Patmore. His widely popular poem *The Angel in the House* was a semi-mystical hymn of praise to marriage and the feminine ideal, and soon he saw that ideal embodied in Alice Meynell. The two became very close friends, although Patmore wanted the relationship to be more than that. Others who fell in love with Alice Meynell, or with what she seemed to represent to them, included Francis Thompson and George Meredith, as well as the young American poet Agnes Tobin. In 1901 Tobin convinced Meynell to embark on a speaking tour in America, a tour that included a lengthy stay with the wealthy Tobin family in San Francisco. Later in her life, Meynell told her son that among her greatest regrets had been her inability to return fully the love of Patmore and Tobin.

Meynell was now writing essays for the *Pall-Mall Gazette*, the *Observer*, and other periodicals, reprinting the best of them in a series of books. She also produced several more volumes of poetry and, in collaboration with her husband, continued working on a wide number of journalistic tasks, including translations from French and Italian. She became involved with the women's suffrage movement, on the less militant side, and she and her family took part in many of the mass marches of the era. In addition, she traveled frequently, either with a friend or one or two of her older children, spending much time in her beloved Italy. The family's finances had gradually grown comfortable—in part due to the earnings from Alice's books—and in 1911 Wilfrid bought a country home in Greatham, Sussex. Alice and her family divided their time between their London and Sussex homes, and they continued to attract a stream of literary visitors at both places. The onset of World War I caused Meynell great emotional and physical stress, and she began having difficulties with her health; however, out of this suffering, she produced some of her finest poems. Finally, after a seven-week illness, she died on November 17, 1922.

## MAJOR THEMES

Alice Meynell wrote a great deal of ephemeral journalism, much of it unsigned. She also produced many essays and articles, only some of which were collected and reprinted; there were nine such collections in all. In addition, she wrote criticism, biography, and a book-length essay, *Mary, The Mother of Jesus* (1912). And she published nine separate collections of her poems. Though the essays and poems share some themes, it is best to treat them separately.

Meynell's first volume of poetry, published under the name of A. C. Thompson, was *Preludes;* it consisted of thirty-seven pieces in an impressive variety of forms and meters. In addition to this striking technical mastery, the poems' epigraphs—from Petrarch, Dante, Hugo, Musset—announce a poet of formidable intellect. Many of the poems evince a post-Romantic nostalgia and world weariness that in 1875 had the aura of newness about it; the book is an early example of what we now recognize as the English *fin de siècle* mood. Poems such as "To the Beloved Dead," "A Tryst That Failed," and "To a Poet's Grave" are suffused in a controlled, melancholic lyricism much like that of the early Yeats. Meynell's Catholicism is evident, although not insistent, in this first collection in poems such as "Soeur Monique" and "San Lorenzo Giustiniani's Mother," which contrast spiritual stability with earthly change. Perhaps the book's most striking poem is "A Letter from a Girl to Her Own Old Age," a quietly powerful meditation on anticipated loss and change that also asserts the inner, hidden permanence of the self.

*Preludes* announces most of the themes that would continue to dominate Meynell's later poetry, especially those of time, change, and isolation. The inner life in many of the poems compensates for the losses in the outer one, as in the great "Renouncement." Meynell left this poem out of *Preludes,* fearing it might be read by Father Dignam, the beloved of whom the poem speaks. Agreeing that she must not think of or see him, she still finds that in dreams, the will is removed like clothes, and in that inner world, "I run, I run, I am gathered to thy heart" (*Poems of Alice Meynell,* p. 13). Meynell's husband recognized that the poem's value went beyond any risk of its being seen as indecorous, though, and urged her to contribute it to a sonnet anthology printed in 1882. (It's interesting to note that a 1998 BBC poll ranked "Renouncement" in the top ten of listeners' favorite poems.)

In Meynell's later poems, the sense of isolation and loss is often overcome by religious experience, as in "A General Communion" (*Poems of Alice Meynell,* p. 50), where the Eucharist transcends the boundaries between people, or in "Aenigma Christi" (p. 181), where Jesus' self is contained within Mary's, like a face in a mirror. Meynell had been an admirer of Donne and Herbert long before they became fashionable in the 1920s, and her verse, as in "Aenigma Christi," often turns on a complex metaphor or conceit, much as the seventeenth-century poets' work had. The conceit, for Meynell as for Donne, allowed her to bring together disparate images and states of being, and provided the means for her to move from a poetry of isolation to one of communion. Such communion with others is also explored in a number of poems that deal with the relation of the poet to poets of the past and even of the future, as in "Singers to Come" (pp. 14–15), which addresses future writers and asserts that "Something of you already is ours" (p. 14). The religious quality of Meynell's verse became more explicit with the years, in poems like "The Unknown God," "The Crucifixion," "The Lord's Prayer," and the remarkable "Christ in the Universe" (p. 63), which imagines the future discovery of extraterrestrial life into which God will have also become incarnated. In some instances, she is able to combine Catholic themes with feminist ones, as in "Saint Catherine of Siena" (pp. 42–43), which contrasts the heroic grandeur of Catherine with the empty bravado of the modern man, "stern on the Vote" for women and women's rights (p. 43).

Meynell's poetry during the Great War often concerns the pity of the war, most memorably in "Summer in England, 1914." The war poems also often invoke the suffering Christ, especially "Easter Night" and "Nurse Edith Cavell," and in the last lines of "Summer in England, 1914," which imagine the dying soldiers in the trenches being kissed by Christ. Such imagery has been criticized as glorifying war, but when read in the context of the other poems, it clearly suggests a world gone mad with wasteful, frightening violence, a world that only finds its redemption in the sympathy of a God who also suffered human violence.

Another major theme in Meynell's work after *Preludes* is that of motherhood, which is the subject of dozens of poems. Some of these are addressed to her own children and grandchildren, but not all of the maternity-related poems are warm and celebratory. Rather, there is often a deep ambivalence: for example, in "The Girl on the Land" (*Poems of Alice Meynell*, p. 180) the mother is the earth while the daughter is the reaper, and this disturbing sense that the next generation somehow uses up the present one is perhaps a distant echo of the naturalistic Tennysonian theme of "Nature red in tooth and claw." Other poems, such as "The Modern Mother" (p. 31), suggest that what someone who gives birth most needs is not thanks but forgiveness.

Most of Meynell's best-known essays were written for newspapers and periodicals, including major Catholic ones. But to call the essays journalism would be misleading: they are subtle, demanding, allusive, and stylistically as finely crafted as her poetry. Her favorite prose stylists were, again, seventeenth-century writers such as Richard Hooker, Jeremy Taylor, and Sir Thomas Browne. Their influence is evident in the essays, which move from the personal to the philosophical with ease and grace and often make use of implication and imagery rather than formal argument. Her sentence style, like theirs, is often complex and elaborately balanced.

The essays for the *Pall Mall Gazette* were written between 1893 and 1905, for a column entitled "The Wares of Autolycus," which refers to the mythical trifler. Meynell and a number of other women wrote under this heading, one which suggests that what a woman has to say will be charming, light, and ultimately trivial. Meynell's work, though, is anything but trivial. Her most famous essay from this column is "The Rhythm of Life," with its opening line, "If life is not always poetical, it is at least metrical" (*The Rhythm of Life*, p. 1). This whimsical tone soon deepens into gravity, as Meynell contemplates the rhythms of loss and gain in our lives, and sees in life's "periodicity" our best hope in coping with sorrow (pp. 3–6). The essay is a modern evocation of the Christian stoicism of a Boethius, and its poignancy is even greater when one realizes that it was written shortly after the death of her infant child (she wrote to her daughter, "we have something to forgive God for" [quoted in Badeni, p. 45]).

The essays range over a broad spectrum of topics: there are travel pieces (often set in Italy), philosophical pieces, critical works (including discussions of Patmore, Oliver Wendell Holmes, Shakespeare, and a host of other writers and painters), and a number of essays having to do with women and women's issues. "Penultimate Caricature" (*Rhythm of Life*, pp. 101–6), for example, quietly and effectively demolishes a certain kind of vulgar humor aimed at wives in popular cartoons. Meynell wrote widely on women authors, including Jane Austen and George Eliot, as well as on women in history, such as Samuel Johnson's wife and Hester Thrale. One of the best of these latter essays is "Steele's Prue" (*Alice Meynell: Prose and Poetry*, pp. 189–93), an exploration of the character of Richard Steele's wife, which turns on the fact that while all Steele's letters to his wife have been preserved, none of hers to him exist: what does it mean, the essay asks, to have been so silenced by history?

In her essays, Meynell also wrote on motherhood and children, taking anecdotes from her own children's lives as starting points to consider such issues as the meaning of play to a child, or a child's love of repetition. These essays are often warm, but they are never sentimental; here, as in almost all of her prose, the reader is vividly aware of the writer's powerful intelligence as it probes deeply into even the minutiae of life and finds surprising meaning there. Finally, *Mary, The Mother of Jesus* brings together many of Meynell's themes and characteristic methods. By 1912, Meynell's style was somewhat less baroque and mannered, but it is still recognizably her own, as is the thought that drives this book. She considers Mary as depicted in popular traditions, in the apocryphal Gospels, and in literature and art. Especially provocative is her discussion of the treatment of women in Shakespeare and Milton; in these authors' Puritanism she finds the origins of the modern "artificial inequality" of the sexes (*Mary, Mother of Jesus*, p. 51).

## SURVEY OF CRITICISM

While Meynell's writing was very well known in her day, and almost every modern critical work on women writers of her era mentions her, there have been few extended critical treatments of her since her death. This is partly due to the revolution in taste that occurred in our century: there is nothing Modernist about either her poetry or prose. Indeed, while the Modernists were, in Pound's phrase, "making it new," Meynell's work consciously looks back to tradition for its style and structure. And while feminist criticism in our day prefers the marginalized and socially radical writer, Meynell may seem to represent a comfortably successful middle-class writer, wife, and mother. But to read her work is to see that she cannot be so easily dismissed.

The best place to begin reading about Alice Meynell is in the many memoirs that treat of her, beginning with *Alice Meynell: A Memoir*, written by her daughter Viola, whose gifts as a novelist and short-story writer are evident in her fine book on her mother. Viola's later memoir, *Francis Thompson and Wilfrid Meynell,* concerning the relationship between her father and the poet, also provides much helpful background. What Alice Meynell meant to other women writers can be seen in Edith Wharton's treatment of her visit to London in *A Backward Glance;* from a male perspective, G. K. Chesterton's *Autobiography* describes her in almost saintly terms. And memoirs such as those of Marie Belloc Lowndes and Phyllis Bottome show a side of her that neither the family nor the general public saw. Bottome's depiction in particular is dramatic and evocative; she sees Meynell as an unhappy angel chained down in domesticity and not so much protected by a loving family as smothered by it. June Badeni's biography goes into some detail beyond Viola Meynell's, but is less analytical than one could wish.

The only book-length study of Meynell is that by Anne Kimball Tuell. Its often florid style is typical of the literary criticism of its era (the early 1920s), but it remains worth reading, especially for what it has to say about Meynell's views of women and about her prose. It makes the point correctly, that for Meynell, considerations of audience were far less important than those of style. Tuell's analysis of Meynell's prose rhythm is highly valuable, as is her demonstration that Meynell was trying to do in prose what contemporary impressionists were doing in painting. She sees Meynell as not a strictly Catholic poet, but a "liberally Christian" one, an interesting but highly debatable judgment (p. 246). To date, Tuell is the only critic who has specifically addressed the religious element of Meynell's poetry.

After Tuell, Meynell's work, like that of many late Victorian writers, fell out of fashion, and there is little sustained criticism to be found in the ensuing decades. More recently, Nosheen Khan has examined her war poetry, noting its combination of feminism with anti-war sentiment. And perhaps the most provocative modern criticism of Meynell is Angela Leighton's, which reads the poetry closely and finds in it a disturbing ambivalence regarding the author's role as mother and wife. Leighton probes Meynell's deep consciousness of gender issues, and in so doing opens up new ways of reading both individual poems and her life and work as a whole. She points out that we have been accustomed to reading Meynell's writings through the lenses provided by her male admirers (such as Patmore and Thompson) who saw her primarily as an erotic muse. Leighton's work suggests the depth, complexity, and richness of Meynell's poetry, and in doing so helps recover this important and extraordinarily gifted writer for a new generation of readers.

## BIBLIOGRAPHY

### Works by Alice Meynell

*Preludes.* London: H. S. King, 1875.
*The Rhythm of Life, and Other Essays.* London: Elkin Matthews and John Lane, 1893.

*The Colour of Life, and Other Essays on Things Seen and Heard.* London: John Lane, 1896.

*The Spirit of Place, and Other Essays.* London: John Lane, 1898.

*Ceres' Runaway, and Other Essays.* London: Constable and Co., 1909.

*Mary, The Mother of Jesus: An Essay.* London: Philip Lee Warner, 1912.

*Hearts of Controversy.* London: Burns & Oates, 1917.

*The Second Person Singular, and Other Essays.* London: Humphrey Milford, 1921.

*Alice Meynell: Prose and Poetry: Centenary Volume.* London: Jonathan Cape, 1947.

*The Poems of Alice Meynell.* Westminster, Maryland: Newman Press, 1955.

### Works about Alice Meynell

Badeni, June. *The Slender Tree: A Life of Alice Meynell.* Padstow, Cornwall: Tabb House, 1981.

Bottome, Phyllis. *The Challenge.* London: Faber and Faber, 1953.

Chesterton, G. K. *Autobiography.* New York: Sheed and Ward, 1936.

Khan, Nosheen. *Women's Poetry of the First World War.* Lexington: University of Kentucky Press, 1988.

Leighton, Angela. *Victorian Women Poets: Writing Against the Heart.* Charlottesville: University of Virginia Press, 1992.

Lowndes, Marie Belloc. *The Merry Wives of Westminster.* London: Macmillan, 1946.

Meynell, Viola. *Alice Meynell: A Memoir.* New York: Charles Scribner, 1929.

——. *Francis Thompson and Wilfrid Meynell.* New York: E. P. Dutton, 1952.

Tuell, Anne Kimball. *Mrs. Meynell and Her Literary Generation.* New York: E. P. Dutton, 1925.

Wharton, Edith. *A Backward Glance.* New York: Appleton-Century, 1934.

RAYMOND N. MACKENZIE

# PILAR MILLÁN ASTRAY
# (1879–1949)

## BIOGRAPHY

Pilar Millán Astray was born in 1879 during the *Restauración,* the Spanish equivalent of the Victorian period, in a family that belonged to the bourgeoisie of conservative La Coruña in the province of Galicia. She was the daughter of José Millán Astray and Pilar Terneros; her father was a bureaucrat and writer. The family moved to Madrid when don José was named director of the Madrid Prison. When Pilar was little more than twenty years old, she married Javier Pérez de Linares of the high society of Valencia in the Spanish Levant. They had three children, Javier and Carmen who were born in Valencia, and Pilar who was born in Madrid. When her husband died young, Pilar Millán Astray decided to become a professional writer to earn a living. She won the *Blanco y Negro* literary award in 1919 with her short novel *La hermana Teresa* [Sister Teresa]. *Blanco y Negro* was a very prestigious, monarchic, illustrated magazine. She also published frequently in newspapers and other magazines during the Primo de Rivera dictatorship, among them *ABC, La nación, El espectador,* and *El Sol.* These were first-class publications; *ABC* and *Blanco y Negro* still exist today, and they represent the best of conservative journalism in Spain.

Millán Astray soon moved to theater, the genre that made her famous. She became the most important writer of *sainetes* of her time, at a moment when *sainetes* were very popular. These one-act plays, with a strong comic component and moralizing ending, and often featuring members of the middle class as protagonists, had held the favor of the public since the seventeenth century. Millán Astray extended the *sainete* to a three-act play, creating a hybrid between the *sainete* and bourgeois high comedy. The results are irregular, and sometimes it is obvious that a one-act play was artificially extended to get a longer performance. However, her success was extraordinary. She was the most performed playwright in Madrid during the 1923–1924 season, with more than one hundred performances. In 1926, critics declared her one of the three most popular playwrights, besides Muñoz Seca and Carlos Arniches. Her most popular play, *La tonta del bote* (1936) [The Tin Can Fool Woman] had more than one hundred forty presentations in the Teatro Lara in Madrid. During 1934 seven of her plays were shown in Madrid alone, two of them premieres. Millán Astray belonged during this period of time to the *tertulia*, or literary circle, of the El Gato Negro café, which was presided over by the conservative playwright Muñoz Seca.

Millán Astray was in Madrid when the Civil War started, and she was considered an important prisoner of war because she had been an advocate of conservative Spain and because she was the sister of one of the most important rebel generals. Her brother, General José Millán Astray, had been the co-founder with Francisco Franco of the Foreign Legion in Spain. Francisco Franco was the leader of the military coup d'état that started the Spanish Civil War and was dictator of Spain between 1937–1975. Millán Astray spent the war years imprisoned in Alicante and Murcia where she contracted illnesses that left her infirm the rest of her life. After the war, she published *Cautivas. 32 meses en las prisiones rojas* (1940) [Incarcerated, 32 Months in Red Prisons], a book of conventional Fascist and religious poems that express her feelings while in prison. She stopped writing plays and was forgotten by the histories of literature. It is only a partial paradox that the triumph of Fascism and its misogynist backlash were what silenced Pilar Millán Astray. She died in 1949.

## MAJOR THEMES

Before considering Pilar Millán Astray's major themes, it is best to understand the contexts in which her writing arose. The religious situation of twentieth-century Spain can be defined as intellectually liberal but in the context of a culture that is not yet secularized. At the root of this situation are the political and social developments of the first half of the nineteenth century when the Spanish Catholic Church suffered fierce attacks and was weakened by *desamortizaciones,* or the confiscation, seizure, and closure of thousands of religious institutions. But by the second half of the century, the Church was solidly back as part of the establishment and supporting the conservative-liberal capitalism of the restored Borbón monarchy. However, Spanish society and culture and the Church were moving at different speeds. It was very difficult for organized religion to catch up with the rapid changes of the Spanish nation. Leo XIII (1878–1903) promoted the collaboration of Catholics in the new liberal political systems with *Rerum Novarum* (1891) and other encyclicals, but his successor Pius X (1903–1914) kept a firm grip on the Church, reaffirming his absolute authority and repressing those who wanted to bring secular modernism to the Catholics. One of the most important reactions in Spain was the appearance of a virulent antireligious anticlericalism in the rapidly growing socialist, communist, and anarchist groups. It did not help that the Church was identified with the upper classes and completely dominated secondary education. At the same time, the Church was almost completely removed from the urban lower classes and the landless peasants. Antonio Maura (1853–1925) is the father of modern conservatism in Spain, which is a combination of Catholic orthodoxy, capitalism, and legal and cultural conservatism.

In the 1920s the Spanish Church entered the popular culture wars, attacking the revolutionary changes in dressing and habits. The worst mistake it made was its sanction of the dictatorship of Miguel Primo de Rivera (1923–1930) because after that, the liberal middle class joined the urban proletariat in their understanding of the Church as the main obstacle to the modernization of Spain. The resulting increase in the animosity of the attacks led to the burning of convents in 1931 under a socialist-radical government that refused to protect the Church. The mobs sacked and burned more than one hundred religious buildings in three days. Furthermore, the new secular Constitution of 1932 unilaterally annulled the Concordat and banned the Jesuits from any activity in Spain. It was not merely the separation of church and state; it was an attempt to suppress Catholic culture and education in Spain. Divorce was legalized, the cemeteries were secularized, and most of the religious schools were taken over by the state. The anticlerical sentiments were manifested in the assassination of seven thousand priests and nuns during the Spanish Civil War (1936–1939).

It is in this context that Pilar Millán Astray joined the popular culture wars of the 1920s and 1930s. From her earliest writings on, she was a champion of conservative and Catholic causes and was able to create a public who adored her plays. She entered the cultural wars of the twenties at the time of the first sexual revolution when urban masses moved from the courting system to dating. She was one of the first writers, male or female, liberal or conservative, who detected that this was the beginning of the most important revolution of the twentieth century, that of the birth of the independent woman, especially in urban contexts. As a result, her plays frequently feature a strong, self-reliant, hard-working woman as the main character. Millán Astray vehemently defended this more active role for women, including their right to work, at a moment when the Church and conservative Spain were very confused regarding this important matter and had adopted misogynist positions. She publicly condemned the battering of women by their own relatives (following a tradition started by the lay writers of nineteenth-century Naturalism) and exposed what is known today as sexual harassment. She defended the indissolubility and sacredness of marriage. Although she upheld the moral superiority of the Catholic Church, she attacked corruption within the clergy and the Church hierarchy's lack of concern for the proletariat classes. In similar fashion, although she was a defender of "true" aristocracy, she attacked the idle members of this class, asking them to conduct their business in a manner that could benefit society as a whole.

In her play *Al rugir el león* (1923) [When the Lion Roared], Millán Astray advocates the exploitation of wastelands to avoid emigration. The protagonist is a Christ-like figure, Jesús, who chooses as his wife the good peasant, Maruja, instead of Magda, the marchioness. *Ruth la israelita* (1923) [Ruth, the Jew] follows the religious path of the previous play. It presents evil men, both Catholics and Jews, and good women, both Catholics and Jews. The Catholics try unsuccessfully to convert Ruth, but at the end of the play the spectator gets the impression that the seeds of Catholicism and the love for the Virgin Mary are in Ruth's heart. *El juramento de la Primorosa. Sainete en tres actos, en prosa* (1924) [The Oath of Primorosa] is a play that defends the need for literacy among the poor, the right of women to work, and the honor of working-class women. Primorosa, a hairdresser in a working-class neighborhood of Madrid, is a matriarch responsible for preserving the honor of her daughter and her employees. Rather than accusing the play of a reactionary message, it is more accurate to place it on the puritan side of feminism. According to Millán Astray, the independent but conservative working-class Primorosa is a synecdoche of genuine Spain; she represents the traditional and true values of the country.

*Pancho Robles* (1926) is a defense of Romantic love and a condemnation of the marriage of convenience. *El millonario y la bailarina* (1930) [The Millionaire and the Ballerina] is a failed attempt to rewrite the myth of Carmen; once the myth is dispossessed of her characteristics, that is, sexual freedom, she is reduced from a legend to an ordinary woman. In *Los amores de la Nati* (1931) [Nati's Loves], Millán Astray proposes education as the solution to Spain's problems and warns about the dangers of cinema for the morality of working women. Nati is the archetypal and paradoxical woman Millán Astray wished to represent: fierce and independent while she is fighting to win the love of her life, she is nevertheless humble and servile once she gets her man. *La mercería de la dalia roja. Comedia asainetada en tres actos* (1932) [The Red Dahlia Notions Store] takes place in Madrid during the profound changes brought by the Second Republic (1931–1936). It is a moral drama (not the comedy announced by the title) which tells the story of Alicia, Marchioness of San Clodio. Abandoned by her husband after he squandered the family fortune, Alicia uses her last seventy-five thousand pesetas to buy a notions store in a working-class neighborhood of Madrid. There, she lives a decent life and dedicates herself to helping poor families, teaching young women good manners, and instructing them in how to read and write. She falls in love with Rafael, an Andalusian doctor, but cannot wed him because she is still married. Her friends recommend that she divorce, an idea introduced by the Republic, but she refuses to abandon her Catholic beliefs. By the play's end, her husband is again in Madrid and is prepared to force her to live with him. Nonetheless, Alicia refuses to go with Rafael, and instead denounces Republican immorality and its attempt to introduce non-Christian doctrines in Spain. Alicia perceives divorce as an attack against Spain because the only possible interpretation of Spain is that of a Catholic country as dictated by tradition. The Catholic Kings defined Spain as a Christian country with the expulsion of the Moors and Jews, and Philip II (1527–1598), as a Catholic country with the wars against the Protestants. These overly simplified explanations became a commonplace during Franco's dictatorship. A very fine critic, Díez-Canedo, attacked the play not for ideological reasons but for Millán Astray's failure to put together a thesis comedy in a *sainete* format.

Millán Astray's most famous play is *La tonta del bote*. It tells the story of Susana, a Cinderella or Eliza Doolittle-like character who gains fame and wealth when discovered by Felipe, a man who transforms her into the most famous Spanish dancer of her time. Susana represents virtue; she tries to help everyone, and the worse she is treated the better she responds. This is the nineteenth-century tradition of melodrama linked to popular entertainment; it is close to the French manner in which melodrama was enjoyed by the lower and middle classes. The Manichaeism of such melodrama can be viewed as the attempt of literature after the French Revolution to compensate for the loss of the sacredness of the ancient régime. The subtext of *La tonta del bote* is Catholic popular culture: an arbitrary God who can give favors at will; doubts about the existence of free will; the need of charity; Judas Iscariot as the symbol of treachery; sacraments to mark the stages of life such as baptism, first communion, and marriage; a medieval conception of purgatory; the *virgencita,* or the young Virgin Mary as a symbol of purity; and Judgment Day as the moment of true democracy. This play represents very complex sexual and social relationships and the need of the public to cope with the challenges of modern society: three young single mothers, two young women wandering in the dangers of the streets of the big city, sexual harassment, cohabilitation, abandoned children, battered women, and female unemployment. The artificial solution given to the problems underlines the inability of the Catholic Church and the conservative forces to give a solution to these questions.

There are two successful cinematographic versions of the play. Gonzalo Delgrás directed a stylized, Hollywood-like rendition in 1939, with Josita Hernán and Rafael Durán imitating Fred Astaire and Ginger Rogers. In 1970 Juan de Orduña directed the great starlet Lina Morgan in a version closer to the revue genre, which is more similar to the *sainete* form.

Millán Astray represents the nostalgia for the lost values of traditional society, especially those that were shared by the Church, but she perceived that most of these changes were permanent. Her literature thrived while she was free to compete with other writers in the cultural wars, but once Fascism triumphed she was silenced, because the independent women she envisioned had no room in the anachronistic attempt of the Franco dictatorship to restore the ancient régime and the indissolubility of Church and State.

## SURVEY OF CRITICISM

Although a popular writer in her day, Pilar Millán Astray has been almost totally ignored by contemporary critics. In a brief entry on the author in *Dictionary of the Literature of the Iberian Peninsula,* Janet Pérez expresses the typical attitude of such modern critics when she states, "[Millán Astray's] works are conservative and conventional, with few values beyond simple entertainment" (p. 1090). Such a dismissive approach fails to take into account that to read Millán Astray's work with appreciation, it is extremely important to understand the development of feminist, conservative thought in contemporary Spain. Read in this context, Millán Astray emerges as an important contributor to that dialogue. An illustration of this may be seen in the fact that it is not by chance that the second cinematographic version of *La tonta del bote* was made during the sexual revolution of the 1970s and directed by a Falangist director like Orduña.

Millán Astray is the typical example of divorce between critics and public. Díez Canedo, the most influential critic during her time, considered her plays confusing, because she used *sainete,* comedy, and drama indistinctly. He also criticizes the lack of depth of the characters and how foreseeable they are. Díez-Canedo applauded the musical numbers and the fact that many of the best stars on the stage wanted to represent her plays (Dicenta, Caba, Isbert, Guerrero, and others). The silence about her theater during Francoism is intriguing, even when some of her plays were represented with success. Pilar's brother, General Millán Astray, was famous because he had threatened the Catholic philosopher and writer Miguel de Unamuno during an homage to Unamuno in Salamanca. He yelled, "Death to intelligence!" and threatened to kill the philosopher, who died a few weeks later of natural causes. One has to think the fear of the naked fascism represented by General Millán Astray (he was an impressive character with only one eye and one arm) convinced the critics the best thing to do was just not write about Pilar Millán Astray. Since democracy was restored in Spain, she has been perceived as one of the many unimportant fascist writers, without critics realizing she wrote most of her plays before the beginning of the dictatorship.

## BIBLIOGRAPHY

### Works by Pilar Millán Astray

*Al rugir el león. Comedia.* Madrid: R. Velasco, 1923.
*El juramento de la Primorosa. Sainete en tres actos, en prosa.* Madrid: Sociedad de Autores Españoles, 1924.
*La tonta del bote. Sainete en tres actos, prosa.* Madrid: R. Velasco, 1925.
*Pancho Robles. Comedia en tres actos.* Madrid: Sociedad de Autores Españoles, 1926.
*El millonario y la bailarina.* Madrid: Sociedad de Autores Españoles, 1931.
*Ruth la israelita.* Madrid: R. Velasco, 1931.
*La mercería de la dalia roja. Comedia asainetada en tres actos.* Madrid: Sociedad de Autores Españoles, 1932.
*Cautivas. 32 meses en las prisiones rojas.* Madrid: Saturnino Calleja, 1940.

### Works about Pilar Millán Astray:

Díez-Canedo, Enrique. *Artículos de crítica teatral. El teatro español de 1914 a 1936. IV. La tradición inmediata.* Mexico City: Joaquín Mortiz, 1968.

Ena Bordonada, Angela. "Pilar Millán Astray." *Novelas breves de escritoras españolas (1900–1936)*. Madrid: Castalia, 1989. 351–52.

McGaha, Michael D. *The Theatre in Madrid during the Second Republic*. London: Grant & Cutler, 1979.

Nieva de la Paz, Pilar. "Tradición y vanguardia en las autoras teatrales de preguerra: Pilar Millán Astray y Halma Angélico." *El teatro en España entre la tradición y la vanguardia 1918–1939*. Ed. Dru Dougherty and María Francisca Vilches de Frutos. Madrid: CSIC, 1992. 429–38.

Payne, Stanley G. *Spanish Catholicism. A Historical Overview*. Madison: University of Wisconsin Press, 1984.

Pérez, Janet. "Pilar Millán Astray." *Dictionary of the Literature of the Iberian Peninsula*. Ed. Germán Bleiberg, Maureen Ihrie, and Janet Pérez. Westport, Connecticut: Greenwood Press, 1993. 1090.

SALVADOR A. OROPESA

# KATHLEEN NORRIS
## (1947– )

## BIOGRAPHY

Kathleen Norris, poet and essayist, was born on July 27, 1947, in Washington, D.C. Her family lived in Beach Park, Illinois, until she was eleven, and then moved to Hawaii where Norris graduated from high school. She attended Bennington College and received a B.A. in 1969.

Following graduation, Norris worked in New York City as an arts administrator, then moved to Lemmon, South Dakota, with her husband, David J. Dwyer (a poet, translator, and computer programmer). Norris has worked as a poet-in-residence with the North Dakota Arts Council, and as an assistant librarian, teacher, editor, and essayist while managing a family-ranch corporation.

The decision to move to Lemmon, the birthplace of her mother and grandmother and a town of only sixteen hundred residents, has greatly impacted Norris's life and career as a writer. Although a poet, Norris has gained broad recognition primarily through the unexpected best-seller popularity of her personal essays, *Dakota: A Spiritual Geography* (1993) and *The Cloister Walk* (1996). Both books draw directly from her life in the American Midwest and her religious quest that began in earnest because of living there. Her religious background is a mix of Protestant affiliations now intermingled with a devoted relationship with the Benedictines, as an oblate (lay associate) attached to Assumption Abbey in North Dakota. She also preaches at Hope Church (Keldron, South Dakota) and at Spencer Memorial Presbyterian (Lemmon).

Norris has published more than seven books of poetry, four works of nonfiction, and numerous journal and anthology articles. She has won various awards including the Big Table Poetry Series Younger Poets Award (1971), a Bush Foundation grant (1993), and a Guggenheim Foundation grant (1994).

## MAJOR THEMES

Norris may not say that she is Catholic, but when in 1986 she became a Benedictine oblate, she made vows to the Catholic Church, committing herself to a monastic order, to a specific monastery, and to the promise that she would follow the Rule of St. Benedict to the extent that her life situation allows. This commitment, this covenant relationship with the Catholic Church through a Catholic monastic community, infuses and centers all of her writings. Norris is one of our most adept contemporary women writers on spirituality as well as one of our best monastic guides; her texts go beyond the monastery and introduce an enormous audience to Catholic life, theology, and praxis. With humor, earthiness, compassion, and poetic prose, Norris conveys the power and relevancy of the Christian faith, Catholic monasticism, and personal spiritual renewal.

In *Dakota*'s twenty-six essays and eighteen meditative vignettes, Norris explores, in nonlinear fashion, her personal pilgrimage of faith, the challenges of living with few people in a harsh climate, and the vocation of a poet in "America's outback." Her narrative self-portrait emerges less from revelations about her inner thoughts and momentous life experiences than from a portrayal of her surroundings: the land, the sky, the climate, and the people.

For Norris, the landscape that she sees surrounding herself is a spiritual environment populated by open hearts that accept her as a woman, a poet, and a friend. She writes to demonstrate how lack can act as a catalyst, setting in motion opportunities that might otherwise be unavailable in a context of abundant resources. In monasteries that do not receive as many guests as monasteries in highly traveled regions, Norris can know the monks more personally. In a small town that cannot regularly fill its pulpits, Norris receives an invitation to preach. The silence of the plains allows Norris to break her spiritual silence, to examine that part of her life that she had set aside and not given a voice to while in New York City. Norris returns to the faith of her family, but she reconstitutes it in new ways that resemble what sociologists have described as typical of the post-1960s era, a willingness heretofore unimaginable: Christians crossing denominational and doctrinal boundaries, even crossing what historically has been considered the largest and most entrenched divide, the separation between Protestantism and Catholicism.

Part of the process of traversing formerly closed borders often involves letting go of personal and cultural presumptions. Norris admits her initial difficulties with learning from Catholic monks. In a passage where she discusses how the gifts of monastic disciplines have been valuable in her non-monastery settings, she writes:

I learned that this receiving and giving of gifts moved freely across ecumenical boundaries when I found that *lectio,* a monastic practice which means, among other things, immersion in the contemplation of scripture, made it possible for me to write the sermons that several Presbyterian churches had asked of me. And in turn, writing the sermons deepened my experience of *lectio.* But this flow of gifts was open to me only as I became open to it, through a period of doubt and testing when I wondered why I had wandered so far afield of my Protestant upbringing, why I was drawn to a community of celibate Roman Catholic men. But the gifts kept coming, despite my doubts, and gradually I realized that their hospitality was functioning as true hospitality should, helping me to become who I wanted to be as a writer, as a wife, even as a Presbyterian, and that this was as it should be. (*Dakota: A Spiritual Geography,* pp. 198–99)

While *Dakota* wrestles with demonstrating that what seems empty (Christian faith, the West, the desert) is actually full, *The Cloister Walk* is written out of Norris's experiences during two extended stays at the Institute for Ecumenical and Cultural Research at St. John's Abbey and University, a Benedictine institution in Collegeville, Minnesota. In *The Cloister Walk,* Norris highlights the ordinariness of devoted religious people and what it means to be a sexual being with spiritual passions. The Church appears as a joyful commitment for adherents who maintain their individuality.

By asserting the individuality of monks and nuns, Norris attempts to reveal their humanness, purposely displaying struggles of the flesh to destabilize stereotypical images of religious people as sexless creatures. Norris finds that young men new to the life of celibacy are "edgy," still dealing with a "raging orchestra" of hormones. A sister who recalls an infatuation she had for a priest, even though she let go of it, admits "It was quite an experience . . . to discover that I was a floozie at heart, *after* having entered the convent" (p. 251). Norris comes to learn that many of her Benedictine friends believe that "falling in love is a normal, necessary but painful part of one's formation as a celibate . . . and if we deny or repress it in the name of holiness we end up with a false religion" (p. 253). Sexualizing a group of people who are typically characterized as attempting to de-sexualize themselves fits in with Norris's larger task of making Christian praxis applicable for adults.

Celibacy and virginity are two topics related to sexuality that Norris engages in *The Cloister Walk.* To be a woman who loves God and is also a sexual being, to honor one's body and others, even in difficult or humiliating circumstances: these are themes that Norris explores through stories about the Christian virgin martyrs who preferred being killed to losing their virginity. Norris seeks to honor virgins, of both past and present times, as women who dare to take control of their own bodies and defy cultural demands that deprive them of full physical authority and autonomy.

In part, Norris's fascination with virginity and celibacy results from her disillusionment with the spirit of the age that occurred during the 1960s when she was in college and developing a sense of her own womanhood:

And now I am doing what I've often longed to do, what my education and cultural conditioning have trained me not to do: bring the nun and the whore together, only to find that they agree . . . and the point I am making is that the great lie (or lay) of sexual liberation expected us, conditioned us, to play the whore. . . . I am grieving now for the girl I was back in the 1960s, who struggled with cultural definitions of a woman as someone attached to a man; who had to contend with a newly "liberated" definition of sexual freedom as that which made me more sexually available to men. (p. 201)

Reclaiming the right to abstain from sex becomes something Norris admires about monks and nuns because their refusal espouses the value of community over individual preference. Moreover, it acknowledges physical passion as powerful but worthy of going unfulfilled for a higher passion, a passion for loving God and people.

Norris rejects views that claim celibacy stunts individual growth and that "celibate hatred of sex is hatred of women" (p. 116). She contends that celibacy allows people to love others more freely and fully. The most unexpected capturing of celibate love is in a story that Norris relates about herself, a confessional moment about her own sexuality and her commitment to spiritual integrity above her personal preferences. Norris acknowledges her affection for a monk whom she calls "Tom" that could have transgressed the covenants they both had made: hers to marital fidelity and his to celibacy. She writes,

Tom and I were fast approaching the rocky shoals of infatuation, a man and a woman, both decidedly heterosexual, responding to each other in unmistakably sexual ways. . . . The danger was real, but not insurmountable; I sensed that if our infatuation was to develop into love, that is to ground itself in grace rather than utility, our respect for each other's commitments—his to celibacy, mine to monogamy—would make the boundaries of behavior very clear. We had few regrets, and yet for both of us there was an underlying sadness, the pain of something incomplete. Suddenly, the difference between celibate friendship and celibate passion had become all too clear to me; at times the pain was excruciating. (p. 122)

This exposé of her life requires transparency, a willingness to let readers, all readers—husband, family members, and monastery friends—know such intimate details that most of us would not be willing to admit. Norris disarms us with such difficult information, and she does so again when she describes the depressions that she and her husband have experienced, her rocky marriage, and her sister Becky's traumatic birth. By confessing pain, longings, and desires in her life and the lives of monks and nuns, Norris seeks to identify with an American secular sensibility that demands truth telling about life's realities. Critic Michael Milburn avers that such "honest perspectives win the reader's trust" (p. 19). They also make language about religious sentiments alive with earthly connection, an incarnational language dependent on practical experiences rooted in daily involvements and routines. The incarnational component of Norris's work has captured the interest of many readers and is representative of a vibrant American stream of writing about spirituality that has become more experimental than prior writings in generating new conventions for Christian reflection and memoir.

## SURVEY OF CRITICISM

To date, little extended analysis exists of Norris's work. Book reviews constitute the bulk of discussion about her writings; only a few articles and a dissertation chapter examine her texts in any depth.

Most reviewers praise Norris's writing and then summarize her major pre-occupations: moving and adapting to life in South Dakota; making little-known places accessible to outsiders; embracing emptiness to experience full-ness. Norris is often depicted as a visionary who writes with, in the words of Robert Coles, "meditative intensity" (p. 12). Dale Jacobs proposes that "like all good essayists, Norris offers us the process of a fertile mind at work, medi-tating and reflecting so that we might do the same" (p. 147). Jacobs notices that her writing becomes a form of "lectio divina, or 'holy reading,' in which she can read the world and her place in it while causing us to think about these same issues" (p. 147).

Reviewers often comment that Norris helps readers want to act upon what they read in her books. Mary Louise Buley-Meissner explains this phenome-non as having our own lives opened to the depths. Elizabeth McCloskey writes that Norris helps us appreciate the value of prayer, worship, and liturgical time.

Renée Hausmann Shea situates Norris within a tradition of women's *bil-dungsroman,* a mature woman's "coming of age through deepening connec-tions to place" (p. 37). She argues that Norris "contributes to contemporary America's search for belonging, for personal meaning in a collective past, and for enduring values amid flux" (p. 37).

One of the most insightful readings comes from Jeanne Braham, who de-scribes not only what Norris writes about but also how she writes. Braham gives credit to Norris's poetic training for her ability to "deploy memory and metaphor so distinctively in the service of [her] message, using these to create structure by providing what the poet Charles Simic has called 'the ways in-wardness seeks visibility'" (p. 189). Verlyn Klinkenborg also refers to Norris as having a "poet's particular eye" along with a sense of humor and "genuine so-cial acuity" (p. 8).

Martha Henderson approaches Norris's work from the standpoint of geog-raphy and sees her using "the concept of place as a means of human identity" (p. 469) and as "a medium to understand human spirituality" (p. 472). Finally, my own work on Norris explores the author's use of space and place in render-ing the sacred and a sense of self; I propose that Norris's discourse of space augments our understanding about what her texts value and makes the sacred realm imaginable without using revivalistic religious language.

## BIBLIOGRAPHY

### Works by Kathleen Norris

*Falling Off.* Chicago: Big Table, 1971.
*From South Dakota: Four Poems.* Chicago: Editions du Grenier, 1978.
*The Middle of the World.* Pittsburgh: University of Pittsburgh Press, 1981.
*How I Came to Drink My Grandmother's Piano: Some Benedictine Poems.* Marvin, South Dakota: Blue Cloud Abbey, 1989.
*The Year of Common Things.* Indian Hills, Colorado: Wayland Press, 1990.

*Dakota: A Spiritual Geography.* New York: Ticknor and Fields, 1993.
*The Cloister Walk.* New York: Riverhead Books, 1996.
*The Psalms.* New York: Riverhead Books, 1997.
*Amazing Grace: A Vocabulary of Faith.* New York: Riverhead Books, 1998.
*Little Girls in Church.* Pittsburgh: University of Pittsburgh Press, 1998.
*The Quotidian Mysteries.* Mahwah, New Jersey: Paulist Press, 1998.
*Meditations on Mary.* New York: Viking Studio Books, 1999.

### Works about Kathleen Norris

Braham, Jeanne. "Passionate Inwardness." *Georgia Review* 48 (1994): 188–94.

Buley-Meissner, Mary Louise. Rev. of *Dakota: A Spiritual Geography,* by Kathleen Norris. *Cream City Review* 18 (1994): 255–57.

Coles, Robert. "A School for Love." *New York Times Book Review* 5 May 1996: 12.

Henderson, Martha L. "What Is Spiritual Geography?" *Geographical Review* 83 (1993): 469–72.

Jacobs, Dale. Rev. of *The Cloister Walk,* by Kathleen Norris. *Journal of Popular Culture* 32 (1999): 146–47.

Klinkenborg, Verlyn. "The Prairie as Act of Devotion." *New York Times Book Review* 14 February 1993: 8.

McCloskey, Elizabeth. Rev. of *The Cloister Walk,* by Kathleen Norris. *Commonweal* 125 (1998): 27–28.

Milburn, Michael. "The Lord's Lexicon." *New York Times Book Review* 5 April 1998: 19.

Shea, Renée Hausmann. "Where on Earth We Are." *Belles Lettres* 8 (1993): 37–38.

Tan, Elizabeth Bachrach. "Standing on Holy Ground: The Sacred Landscapes of Annie Dillard, Kathleen Norris, and Frederick Buechner." Diss. University of Massachusetts, 1995.

ELIZABETH BACHRACH TAN

# EDNA O'BRIEN
# (1932– )

## BIOGRAPHY

Born in Tuamgraney, Ireland, on December 15, 1932, Edna O'Brien entered a world that would not only profoundly influence her development but also provide an imaginative resource for her fiction. The fifth child of Michael and Lena O'Brien, Edna was introduced to the life that was predetermined for Irish young girls in the 1930s. Speaking about her mother, O'Brien foreshadows the heroine of many of her stories: "I think my mother was exhausted, spent. She was a woman of considerable ambition, which she hadn't realized" (McQuade, p. 48). O'Brien attended the National School of Scariff from 1936 to 1941 and then the Convent of Mercy in Loughrea. Her memories of the convent life are vividly portrayed in her memoir, *Mother Ireland* (1976), where she documents the conflicts between the rigidity of the religious system and the natural enthusiasm of the young women. Escaping from the parochialism of small-town existence, O'Brien traveled to Dublin in 1946 to work in a chemist's shop and study at the Pharmaceutical College of Ireland at night. Living in Dublin transformed her life. Once she had broken the bonds of place and experienced the freedom of discovery, her natural gifts as a writer began to emerge.

O'Brien is often asked what prompted her transformation from student to writer. She eagerly retells the story: "The first book I ever bought—I've still got it—was called *Introducing James Joyce* by T. S. Eliot. . . . Reading that book made me realize that I wanted literature for the rest of my life" (Guppy, "The Art of Fiction," p. 29). Joyce has been and continues to be a powerful influence on O'Brien. Besides writing a memoir of Joyce entitled *James and Nora: A Portrait of a Marriage* in 1981, her most recent analysis of Joyce, entitled simply *James Joyce,* was published in 1999. Joyce provided O'Brien with the perspective of a Catholic in Ireland. However, while Joyce captured the male reaction to Catholicism, O'Brien revealed the feminine confrontation with the patriarchal Church.

In 1952, Edna O'Brien married the writer Ernest Gebler and they had two sons. The family moved to London in 1959 where O'Brien began working as a manuscript reader, and then published her first novel, *The Country Girls*, the following year. This book documents the adventures of two naive Irish girls from a rural village who seek fulfillment in Dublin, and it captures the lives of young Catholic girls who attempt to negotiate a hostile urban world with few resources from their repressive childhood. In 1962, O'Brien continued the tale of her doomed heroines in *The Lonely Girls*. The trilogy was completed in 1964 with the publication of *Girls in Their Married Bliss*, and O'Brien's reputation as an innovative Irish writer was solidified.

In 1964, O'Brien and Gebler divorced. Living abroad, O'Brien gained the perspective necessary to transform her childhood memories into vivid depictions of the marginalized Catholic, Irish women of County Clare. Her portrayals of Irish women struggling against cultural and religious forces, however, were condemned by the Irish Censorship Board, which banned her novels in the 1960s. O'Brien protested against the censorship without success.

O'Brien's next two novels, *August Is a Wicked Month* (1965) and *Casualties of Peace* (1966), were set outside of Ireland. In each, a troubled Irish woman in exile confronts the burdens of the past that have tragically influenced the present. *A Pagan Place* (1970) experimented with an alternative narrative technique in which the heroine speaks in the second person, referring to herself as "you." O'Brien's innovation in this novel was recognized when she was awarded the Yorkshire Post Book of the Year award. In 1990, she also won the *Los Angeles Times* Book Prize for *Lantern Slides* (1988), a series of short stories partially inspired by Joyce's *Dubliners*.

In addition to novels and stories, O'Brien has written for the stage and film. Her screenplay for *The Girl with Green Eyes* was based on her second novel *The Lonely Girls*, and she rewrote her novel *A Pagan Place* for a 1972 London stage production. Her best known play, *Virginia* (1985), is a lyrical and poignant depiction of the life of Virginia Woolf.

In the 1990s O'Brien scrutinized the Irish female experience as it related to contemporary dilemmas. *House of Splendid Isolation* (1994) presents a confrontation between an isolated, lonely Irish woman and an IRA gunman, and *Down by the River* (1996) dramatizes the clash between past and present as a young, pregnant girl is sacrificed on the altar of Irish cultural ideology. In 1999 O'Brien continued her exploration of Irish themes and authors with the publication of a short biography of James Joyce and the premiere of her newest play, *Our Fathers*. Her latest novel, *Wild December*, will be published in 2000.

## MAJOR THEMES

Born into a traditional Irish Catholic family in rural County Clare, Edna O'Brien responded to the teachings and rituals of the Church with youthful enthusiasm. Religion dominated every aspect of existence and influenced her life and her fiction. When she relocated to Dublin and distanced herself from family, community, and Church, O'Brien began to re-evaluate her Irishness and Catholicism. In particular, she questioned the impact of both on marginalized Catholic women.

O'Brien's primary themes center around the plight of Irish women molded by the limitations of society and religion. Her heroines—mothers, sisters, wives, and children—struggle to define themselves and inevitably fail. Her female characters simply want to get through life, yet their humble yearnings are thwarted because of the lasting influence of the past, specifically their Catholic upbringing, in conflict with the reality of the present. Inevitably, O'Brien's women confront sexuality and the implication of sin and guilt. The representatives of the conservative Irish Catholic Church—priests and nuns—are also paradoxical and powerful figures influencing the fate of O'Brien's characters. Finally, beyond thematic material, the language and images in O'Brien's stories also reflect her continuing involvement with the Church. Her many vivid descriptions rely on the power of religious symbols as she interweaves religious metaphors and Christian rituals, prayers, and iconography into her moving narratives of loss.

O'Brien chronicles the lives of women who are created by their society, particularly by the religious aspects of their lives. Living in an isolated community, their experience is limited and no alternative authority presents another point of view. Even if such a choice existed, who would believe strangers rather than family, friends, and the Church? In dramatizing the influence of Catholicism on her characters, O'Brien expresses the love-hate relationship that so characterizes many people's association with the Church. The institution can be viewed as oppressive and thoroughly patriarchal, employing the power of spirituality, guilt, and fear to subordinate and control the faithful, yet promising eternal salvation as the reward for compliance and passivity.

O'Brien can be savage in her indictment of the inequities and injustices surrounding Catholicism. For example, in *A Pagan Place,* the young protagonist is beaten by her father after a young priest attempts to sexually abuse her. The girl feels tremendously betrayed by both her religion and her parents. In *The Country Girls,* Kate, one of two rural girls who attempt to survive in Dublin, is actually kidnapped by her father and forced back home because of her sexual experiences and other sinful transgressions in that city. Later, in a confrontation with the local priest, it is obvious that the cleric is not at all concerned with Kate as a person, but simply wants to keep her from an evil situation and return her to a stifling existence with an abusive father. O'Brien manages to convey the inconsistency of Church interpretations while confronting the double standard of morality under which many Irish women live. When Kate complains to the priest that her father is a drunkard and an abuser: "It's as big a sin for my father to be [abusive] as for a man to have two wives"; he responds: "I'm surprised at you, to speak of your good father like that. Every man takes a drink. It's the climate" (p. 271). The message is clear: sexuality (female) is a mortal sin; drunkenness and domestic abuse (male) is a mere weakness.

Yet, in spite of the inequities, O'Brien cannot forsake Catholicism and neither can her characters. The same character in *A Pagan Place* who was unfairly punished for the priest's transgressions leaves home to join a convent—not a very promising future but one she chooses, nevertheless. And Kate in *The Country Girls* continually reverts back to her anchor in religion. In spite of "living in sin," she remains rigidly bound to the past and the Church. She asserts, "I won't get married . . . unless I get married in the Catholic Church" (p. 329).

O'Brien's continued reliance on the Catholic Church is seen in the images she creates that enhance her already "Irish" gift for effective and vivid descriptions. And these impressions were embedded early and frequently in O'Brien's childhood: Jesus scourged and tortured for sins; holy cards representing Mary as a perfect, asexual mother; beautiful young women saints ready to sacrifice their lives for chastity; colorful rosary beads and lovely prayer books. O'Brien incorporates these symbols with vivid language and powerful metaphor. In "A Scandalous Woman" (*A Scandalous Woman and Other Stories,* 1974), the narrator states, "We spent the time wandering through the stalls, looking at the tiers of rosary beads that were as dazzling as necklaces, all hanging side by side and quivering in the breeze, all colors, and of different stones" (p. 28). And so young girls empower traditional religious artifacts with a more secular vision—religious artifacts as jewelry and possessions. Herein lies the paradox that makes O'Brien's females so complex. The tenets of Catholicism, while part of young Irish girls' psyches, do not prevent them from seeking worldly fulfillment—sexual love, affirmation—even if the quest proves futile. Yet religion continues to exert an influence on their thought processes and remains a part of their lives. So guilt becomes part of their existence and influences perception and behavior. In "A Scandalous Woman," for example, the protagonist discusses her dilemma with the Church and the secular world: "One day all these sins would have to be reckoned with. I used to shudder at night when I went over the number of commandments we were breaking" (p. 26).

Sometimes the religious fervor and iconography take on sexual overtones. In *Mother Ireland,* O'Brien relates the sexual tension that her mother and she felt when a young priest, who was soon to leave for the foreign missions, unexpectedly visits. Both women experience heightened emotions as the mother prepares tea and cakes: "We knelt on the stone, side by side, closed our eyes and awaited his blessed hands. Once he was gone my mother was overactive . . ." (p. 54).

The influence of Catholicism and its clash with the imaginations and expectations of young characters are vividly depicted in O'Brien's creation of nuns, especially in *Mother Ireland* and in the novel *The Country Girls*. The naive protagonists of these works reinterpret the reality of a religious situation in order to create a romanticized Catholicism: nuns become nuns, they conclude, because of broken love affairs or tragic encounters. Nuns were also mysterious creatures, living in their own, secret world and sheltered from the daily problems of uninvolved husbands, rebellious children, and lack of resources that plagued Irish women. Charged with the task of educating young Irish girls, the nuns reinforced the strict codes of the Church: normal childhood pleasures were suddenly fused with profound choices of good and evil, and the legacy of negativity and guilt remains a part of Irish girls' experience into adulthood. However, O'Brien manages to transcend the stereotypical portrayal of nuns in her poignant story "Sister Imelda" (*Returning*, 1982). Here, the author traces the complicated interaction of two individuals within the convent structure—a student and her mentor, Sister Imelda. As their relationship develops, the narrator begins to understand that Sister Imelda is human and vulnerable. Nuns are still Irish women, and their lives involve sacrifice and loneliness. The story ends on a melancholy note as the student takes leave of the convent, and Sister Imelda also leaves for the secular world.

The influence of Catholicism on Irish women is one of Edna O'Brien's primary themes. When creating her young characters, O'Brien can be poignant and playful. The reader often smiles at some of the misconceptions and misinterpretations of doctrine, ritual, and life that children perceive. However, when O'Brien delves into the lasting effects of Catholic constructs on adult women, the characters she creates are inevitably portrayed as unhappy and unfulfilled. Mothers and daughters fail to bond, burdened by the past and the pressures of conforming to a religious ideal. For example, the characters in "Cords" (*The Love Object*, 1968) present a vivid example of the sadness engendered by a constricted life. Claire, the daughter, cannot forgive her mother. When her mother quarrels with Claire about Claire's unconventional friends, "Claire said hurtful things about her mother being narrowminded and cruel" (p. 125). And the portrait of the mother is equally tragic. She is a humble woman who cannot understand why her daughter is not grateful and loving. The mother laments, "I am a good mother. I did everything I could, and this is all the thanks I get" (p. 125).

O'Brien creates a world where Catholicism plays a pivotal role in the lives and tragedies of her female characters. The memories of the language, images, and dogma of the religion—embracing beauty, power, and fear—are transformed through her fiction and produce a lasting impression of women and Irish Catholicism.

## SURVEY OF CRITICISM

Since 1960 when her first novel was published, reaction to Edna O'Brien's fiction has generally been favorable. Critics suggest that her first novels (*The Country Girl Trilogy*) are her best works. Commenting on *The Country Girls*, V. S. Naipaul writes, "She [O'Brien] offers her characters and they come to us living. Everything that comes out of the novel has a quality of life which no artifice could achieve" (p. 97). Darcy O'Brien comments, "She [O'Brien] has no literary predecessors, this Catholic, female, literary migrant" (p. 183). O'Brien's territory is original, a lonely, desolate world that reveals the restricted lives of rural, Irish Catholic women.

O'Brien's fiction resonates with echoes of Catholicism in her use of language, description of landscape, and depiction of characters. Raymonde Popot states, "Indeed, throughout her writings she records the dread of Hell . . . the fear of everlasting punishment, encouraging mortification and its excesses, fostering the sense of sin and sacrilege and a feeling of guilt that cannot be remedied in later life" (p. 267). This sense of guilt overwhelms her characters, particularly with regard to sexuality. "She is renowned for her anguished female characters, lonely Catholic girls in search of adventure," states Richard Woodward (p. 42). The unhappy consequences of love and sexuality are central motifs in O'Brien's works, but the presentation of these themes is occasionally flawed. As Lorna Sage puts it, "Again and again, she'll [O'Brien] veer dangerously from irony to dewy sentiment" (p. 83).

Critics praise O'Brien's short stories about Ireland. According to Mary Ann Wiggins, "In the short story, O'Brien is a lucid, economical, informing writer. In the short form her timing is, more often than not, impeccable" (p. 60). O'Brien's short fiction highlights her strengths as a writer. Realistic protagonists, vivid settings, and lyrical language all reflect her lifelong link with Catholicism. Woodward notes, "The charged atmosphere of a Catholic girls' education—rituals, prayers, miracles, lives of the saints—was as important to O'Brien as the stories she took in" (p. 50).

The remote Irish countryside, O'Brien's typical setting, infuses her fiction with the literal and figurative constructs of landscape. The brutal and unyielding terrain creates a mythic background for her characters' lives, and descriptions of spaces both vast and intimate contribute to the sense of isolation and alienation. According to Lorna Sage, "Her domestic interiors and inventories, in particular, marvelously evoke the emotional squalor of setting as survival" (p. 88). In fact, the settings seem to exit beyond time, echoing O'Brien's description in *House of Splendid Isolation:* "History is everywhere—it seeps into the soil, the sub-soil. . . . It is like no other place in the world. Wild. Wildness" (p. 3).

Evocative images are reinforced through O'Brien's use of lyrical language. Novelist Mary Gordon states that "Miss O'Brien combines the romantic's passionate feeling for language and the material world with the classicist's unerring sense of form" (p. 39). O'Brien infuses ordinary descriptions, from squalid farm to religious rituals, with vivid details and startling images. From a drop of water in a muddy puddle to the endless colors of rosary beads, she captures both the decay and beauty of rural Irish life. According to Philip Roth, "The result is prose like a piece of fine meshwork, a net of perfectly observed sensuous details that enables you [O'Brien] to contain all the longing and pain and remorse that surge through your fiction" ("Conversation," p. 39).

Edna O'Brien is considered one of the important contemporary Irish women writers of the late twentieth century. Through her Irish Catholic characters and settings, she evokes themes that are timeless. As Thomas Cahill has put it, "Edna O'Brien writes about love and death, the only two things that can ever matter to a great writer. She tells the truth" (p. 11).

## BIBLIOGRAPHY

### Works by Edna O'Brien

*The Country Girls.* New York: Knopf, 1960.
*The Lonely Girls.* New York: Random House, 1962.
*Girls in Their Married Bliss.* New York: Simon and Schuster, 1964.
*The Love Object.* London: Penguin, 1968.
*A Pagan Place.* 1970. London: Penguin Books, 1971.
*A Scandalous Woman and Other Stories.* New York: Harcourt, 1974.
*Mother Ireland.* New York: Harcourt, 1976.
*Returning.* 1982. London: Penguin Books, 1983.
*Virginia.* New York: Harcourt Brace Jovanovich, 1985.
*Lantern Slides: Short Stories.* New York: Farrar, Straus and Giroux, 1988.
*House of Splendid Isolation.* 1994. New York: Plume, 1995.
*Down by the River.* New York: Farrar, Straus and Giroux, 1997.
*James Joyce.* London: Weidenfeld and Nicolson, 1999.

### Works about Edna O'Brien

Cahill, Thomas. "On Edna O'Brien's *Lantern Slides.*" *Los Angeles Times* 4 November 1990: 11.
Eckley, Grace. *Edna O'Brien.* Lewisburg, Pennsylvania: Bucknell University Press, 1974.
Gordon, Mary. "The Failure of True Love." *New York Times Book Review* 18 November 1984: 1, 38.
Guppy, Shusha. "The Art of Fiction IXXVII: Edna O'Brien Interview." *Paris Review* 26 (1984): 23–50.
——. "Edna O'Brien." *Writer at Work Seventh Series.* Ed. George Plimpton. New York: Viking, 1986. 241–65.
Leavitt, David. "Small Tragedies and Ordinary Passions." *New York Times Book Review* 24 June 1990: 9.
McQuade, Molly. "PW Interviews Edna O'Brien." *Publisher's Weekly* 18 May 1992: 48–49.
Naipaul, V. S. "Review." *Modern Irish Literature.* Ed. Denis and Carol McCrory Lane. New York: Ungar, 1988. 431.
O'Brien, Darcy. "Edna O'Brien: A Kind of Irish Childhood." *Twentieth Century Women Novelists.* Ed. Thomas F. Staley. New York: Barnes and Noble, 1982. 179–91.

Popot, Raymonde. "Edna O'Brien's Paradise Lost." *The Irish Novel in Our Time*. Ed. Patrick Rafroidi and Marcus Harmon. France: Universite de Lille III, 1975. 255–87.

Roth, Philip. "A Conversation with Edna O'Brien: 'The Body Contains the Life Story.'" *New York Times Book Review* 18 November 1984: 38–40.

——. Foreword. *A Fanatic Heart*, by Edna O'Brien. New York: New American Library, 1984. vii-viii.

Sage, Lorna. *Women in the House of Fiction—Post-War Women Novelists*. London: Macmillan, 1992.

Wiggins, Mary Ann. "Nell and Void." *Nation* 13 July 1992: 60.

Woodward, Richard. "Reveling in Heartbreak." *New York Times Magazine* 12 March 1989: 42; 50–52.

KATHLEEN JACQUETTE

# FLANNERY O'CONNOR
# (1925–1964)

## BIOGRAPHY

Flannery O'Connor was born March 25, 1925, in Savannah, Georgia. She attended parochial school there as a child. Her father, Ed, was a real estate agent. The O'Connors moved to the small Georgia town of Millidgeville toward the end of the 1930s, when Ed became ill with lupus erythematosus, at that time an incurable disease. He died in 1941. O'Connor stayed in Millidgeville, completing graduate work at the Women's College of Georgia. She finished an M.F.A. in the writing program of the State University of Iowa, where a half dozen short stories, one published contemporaneously, comprised her Master's thesis.

An extra year at Iowa, employed as a teaching assistant, allowed her to begin work on her first novel, *Wise Blood* (1952). This project required five years, a few months of which were spent at the Yaddo writers' colony in Saratoga Springs, New York. There she met Robert Lowell, and became entangled in the acrimonious accusations surrounding the FBI's 1949 investigation into supposed communists at the colony. The investigation prompted O'Connor and the three other artist-residents to leave *en masse* for New York, where she met Robert Fitzgerald, a Catholic poet and English professor, and his family. When the Fitzgeralds moved to a country home shortly thereafter, O'Connor became their boarder, and she continued work on her novel. During a 1950 Christmas visit to Millidgeville, at age twenty-five, O'Connor learned that she, too, had lupus. After a stay in an Atlanta hospital, she moved to a farm, Andalusia, outside Millidgeville, where her mother Regina cared for her over the remaining years of her life. O'Connor completed *Wise Blood* while adjusting to her illness and life with her mother.

With her father's quick demise in mind, O'Connor imagined her writing career would be quite short. Yet she lived with her illness for another fourteen years, combining a careful, craftsman-like writing process, involvement with the farm, and occasional trips for medical purposes or speaking engagements.

In the three years following *Wise Blood,* she produced nine short stories, pub-lished as *A Good Man Is Hard to Find and Other Stories* (1955). Another novel, *The Violent Bear It Away,* was published in 1960. Though she began, briefly, a third novel, her last years were primarily preoccupied with a group of short sto-ries (published posthumously in 1965 as *Everything That Rises Must Converge,* a title borrowed from Teilhard de Chardin). O'Connor died on August 3, 1964, of complications associated with her disease and its treatment. She is bur-ied in a simple plot in Millidgeville, where her alma mater (now renamed Geor-gia College) maintains a Flannery O'Connor Memorial Room in its library.


## MAJOR THEMES

Most often identified as an author of Southern Gothic (more accurately, Southern Grotesque), Flannery O'Connor's violent and darkly humorous sto-ries capture a peculiarly Southern lifestyle with its inherent racial and class conflicts. Simultaneously, her work is intrinsically connected to her Catholic world-view. Her fiction always centers around one major theme: the com-plexities of redemption through faith, or to use O'Connor's key term, grace. For O'Connor, grace is the fundamental core of Catholicism, involving God's efforts to awaken each human individual to an understanding of his or her fun-damental condition: lostness and incompleteness due to sin. To produce such an experience, God places a person in an excruciating experience of pain or hu-mility, often a brush with death, to force the individual into an awakening. This is a profoundly humbling experience for those few O'Connor characters that God successfully reaches; most of his efforts, however, are not successful.

Underpinning her portrayal of the action of grace is O'Connor's sacramen-tal view of life. For O'Connor, all reality is imbued with the spirit of God, a fact which makes all reality worthy of artistic treatment since all circumstances can show a person's proper place under God's hierarchy. Thus O'Connor often re-lies on small details—a town named Toombsboro in a story climaxing in mass murder; a rude girl named Mary Grace intruding into the life of a woman des-perately in need of grace—to foreground her theme. Yet the details are not merely symbols or foreshadowing; rather they are divine eruptions into the lives of her characters. While disavowing a didactic purpose for her fiction, O'Connor wishes her readers to understand the divine intrusions into their own lives, to counter the natural *hubris* that, as her characters show, prevents the acceptance of God's grace.

"A Good Man Is Hard to Find" illustrates O'Connor's Catholic orienta-tion. The scene is mundane: a family (mother, father, two children, a baby, and, most importantly, the children's grandmother) are traveling from Georgia to Florida. A series of apparently accidental mishaps places the family in a trau-matic situation, an automobile accident, after which they quite literally face death and judgment in the form of The Misfit, a murderous escaped convict. One by one, The Misfit executes the family members, culminating with the grandmother. Throughout the story, O'Connor reveals the grandmother as shallow, prideful, and self-righteous: in other words, in need of grace. Only as she faces death does she begin to glimpse her true spiritual condition: in reality, she is no better than The Misfit. As the story's antagonist observes, "She would of been a good woman . . . if it had been somebody there to shoot her every minute of her life" (p. 29). Critics debate whether the grandmother accepts grace before she dies, but the confrontation with spiritual reality within the mundane exemplifies O'Connor's understanding that God fills the world with symbolic meaning.

Reading O'Connor's nonfiction prose contributes to an understanding of her themes. Her letters, collected as *The Habit of Being* (1979), occasionally (and only briefly) touch on the issues of her faith and its impact on her stories. O'Connor's essays, collected in *Mystery and Manners* (1969), state most clearly her goals as a writer. The four essays in section five of this collection emphasize the conjunction of fiction and Catholic belief, as do the somewhat misnamed essays "The Fiction Writer and His Country" and "On Her Own Work." The latter essay includes O'Connor's statement that her "subject in fiction is the action of grace in territory held largely by the devil" (p. 118).

In part because of the centrality of Catholic themes in O'Connor's work, gender issues are more difficult to analyze, often appearing subsumed to the primary theme of grace. While O'Connor identified herself as a woman writer, she separated her work from that of "lady" writers of her time; her emphasis on violence and the grotesque may stem in part from such a strategy. O'Connor often portrays strong, in fact obnoxious, female characters, treating them satirically as possessing traits to be avoided rather than emulated. In addition, while most stories involve parent-child, frequently mother-child, relationships, such relationships are rarely comforting to O'Connor's characters. Feminist recuperations of O'Connor have been hampered largely because of O'Connor's overt espousal of Catholicism, which would seem to position her in support of the patriarchy as endorsed by the Church. O'Connor herself claimed she never thought "of qualities which are specifically feminine or masculine" (*The Habit of Being*, p. 176). Thus one can conclude that while she was very conscious of the theological themes which work their way into the lives of her characters, she was much less aware of the impact of gender on those characters' lives or her own Catholic orthodoxy. As many critics suggest, all other issues are, or at least seem at first glance, subsumed into O'Connor's sacramental vision and her theme of grace.

## SURVEY OF CRITICISM

Though O'Connor published only a handful of books, she has generated a huge quantity of critical reaction and commentary. Almost all O'Connor criticism mentions the relevance of religious, if not overtly Catholic, themes in her work. But since shortly after O'Connor's death, critics have debated the centrality of those themes. Critical appreciation of the stories' theological implications began almost immediately after her death, as seen in the little-circulated O'Connor memorial issue of *Esprit,* containing tributes from critics, theologians, and fellow writers. The collection has been re-published in book form as *Flannery O'Connor: A Memorial,* edited by John J. Quinn.

Frederick J. Hoffman is among the first to have analyzed at length O'Connor's theology in a 1966 essay. Hoffman claims her central theme is a struggle with sin; "a confrontation with Jesus" forms the narratives' primary crisis (p. 35). Carter W. Martin undertakes a more extensive survey of O'Connor's Catholic (and other) themes in *The True Country* (1969). Martin describes grace as a supernatural offer of love, which humans may accept or reject. To Martin, O'Connor's focus, at least in the short stories, is not on the results of grace, but on "junctures . . . when grace is made available and the drama of . . . decision regarding the offer" (p. 84).

Since Martin, similar themes have been explored by Leon V. Driskell and Joan T. Brittain, who argue that O'Connor's view is more Augustinian than Thomistic; Gilbert H. Muller, who suggests that there is an idiosyncratic trope in the stories which he labels "the Catholic grotesque"; Edward Kessler, who analyzes end-of-the-world imagery; and Robert H. Brinkmeyer in *Art and Vision,* who offers a Bakhtinian analysis of O'Connor's resistance against a facile, watered-down Catholicism. James A. Grimshaw's *The Flannery O'Connor Companion* offers a concise appendix summarizing a number of theological influences, Catholic and otherwise, on O'Connor's work.

The extensive critical response to theological themes has prompted Sara Mott in a 1987 essay to suggest, "Any attempt to plow new ground to uncover anything astoundingly different about Flannery O'Connor as a . . . Catholic seems both futile and unnecessary" (p. 217). Yet other writers since the late 1980s have sought to correct what they see as inappropriate interpretations and emphases. John F. Desmond examines O'Connor's biblical view of history, which he suggests has been misunderstood by critics. Ralph C. Wood stresses O'Connor's comic aspects, attributing them directly to her Catholic vision, while Richard Giannone focuses on O'Connor's expression of the joy of atonement from sin through love, rather than the violence and trauma of the initial experience of grace. Joanne Halleran McMullen in *Writing Against God* sums up the various critical approaches toward O'Connor's Catholic themes while arguing (against Desmond) that O'Connor is best understood as presenting hidden mystery.

As critics began analyzing O'Connor's Catholic themes in the 1960s, almost simultaneously others began first, to suggest O'Connor's themes are more akin to Protestant than Catholic theology, and second, to argue that other aspects of O'Connor's fiction deserve more attention than her theology. An essay by Louis D. Rubin, published in the same anthology as Hoffman's groundbreaking essay on O'Connor's Catholic themes, argues that O'Connor seems equally interested in satirizing Southern Protestantism as she is in thematizing grace. Albert Sonnenfeld echoes this theory with greater subtlety in an essay appearing a few years after Rubin's; he posits O'Connor's role is not Catholic but Baptist.

By 1970, shortly after Carter W. Martin's lengthy study, Josephine Hendin perceived an overemphasis on the theological dimension of O'Connor's work, which tended to hide O'Connor's authentic voice and artistry. Andre Bleikasten, writing one of the first overtly postmodern studies of O'Connor in 1978, recognizes the importance of O'Connor's Catholicism, but submits it to a deconstructive gesture; suggesting that language uses a writer as much as the writer uses language, he pits her Catholic religious belief *against* her stories, finding grace an aggression ("God's violence responding to Satan's violence" [p. 152]). Robert Coles de-emphasizes theology through a materialist study of O'Connor's regionalism, and Jon Lance Bacon similarly places O'Connor within 1950s American cold-war culture.

Gender studies of O'Connor's work have been rather late in coming, and often oppose the critical emphasis on theological themes. Among the few early feminist reactions to O'Connor are several works each by Claire Kahane and Louise Westling. Kahane's 1974 "Flannery O'Connor's Rage of Vision" includes a brief psychoanalytic discussion of O'Connor's "contempt" for women. Westling's "Flannery O'Connor's Mothers and Daughters" examines female parent/child relationships, and is also critical of O'Connor. Westling's *Sacred Groves and Ravaged Gardens* associates depictions of place with feminine identity in the work of O'Connor and others. Suzanne Morrow Paulson includes a detailed study of male-female relationships in the short stories, as well as excerpts from earlier feminist analyses by Kahane and Westling. Alice Walker examines the genesis of one O'Connor story from the conjunction of race and gender studies.

Gender studies of O'Connor in the 1990s have incorporated poststructuralist theories and strategies. Katherine Hemple Prawn examines O'Connor the writer, rather than her fictional characters, suggesting her Catholicism stems from a desire for conformity. The anthology *Flannery O'Connor: New Perspectives*, edited by Sura P. Rath and Mary Neff Shaw, contains four noteworthy gender studies: Jeanne Campbell Reesman and Patricia Yaeger examine in separate essays the conjunction of women's bodies and the grotesque ("Women, Language and the Grotesque in Flannery O'Connor" [pp. 38–56] and "Flannery O'Connor and the Aesthetics of Torture" [pp. 183–206]); Marshall Bruce Gentry analyzes the "rigidly patriarchal females" typical of O'Connor's fiction to suggest such characters often "find redemption as they move toward androgyny" ("Gender Dialogue in O'Connor" [pp. 57–72]); and Richard Giannone, in one of the few gender studies to appreciate O'Connor's Catholic themes, argues that she looks beyond gender to enact a feminism of mystical insight ("Displacing Gender: Flannery O'Connor's View from the Woods" [pp. 73–95]).

At the time of this writing, a critical biography of O'Connor is reportedly underway by Sally Fitzgerald. The best biographical sketches at present are those by Fitzgerald and her husband Robert, personal friends of O'Connor, which accompany several of the author's published works. Another useful sketch can be found in Preston M. Browning's *Flannery O'Connor,* with a brief literary biography available in Lorine M. Getz's *Flannery O'Connor.*

## BIBLIOGRAPHY

### Works by Flannery O'Connor

*Wise Blood.* New York: Farrar, Straus and Giroux, 1952.
*A Good Man Is Hard to Find and Other Stories.* San Diego: Harcourt Brace Jovanovich, 1955.
*The Violent Bear It Away.* New York: Farrar, Straus and Giroux, 1960.
*Everything That Rises Must Converge.* New York: Farrar, Straus and Giroux, 1965.
*Mystery and Manners: Occasional Prose.* Ed. Sally and Robert Fitzgerald. New York: Farrar, Straus and Giroux, 1969.
*The Habit of Being: Letters of Flannery O'Connor.* Ed. Sally Fitzgerald. New York: Random House, 1979.
*The Presence of Grace and Other Book Reviews.* Ed. Carter W. Martin. Athens: University of Georgia Press, 1983.

### Works about Flannery O'Connor

Bacon, Jon Lance. *Flannery O'Connor and Cold War Culture.* Cambridge: Cambridge University Press, 1993.
Bleikasten, Andre. "The Heresy of Flannery O'Connor." *Les Americanistes.* Ed. Ira D. and Christiane Johnson. n.d. Friedman and Clark, 138–58.
Brinkmeyer, Robert H. *The Art and Vision of Flannery O'Connor.* Baton Rouge: Louisiana State University Press, 1989.
Browning, Preston M., Jr. *Flannery O'Connor.* Carbondale: Southern Illinois University Press, 1974.
Coles, Robert. *Flannery O'Connor's South.* Baton Rouge: Louisiana State University Press, 1980.
Desmond, John F. *Risen Sons: Flannery O'Connor's Vision of History.* Athens: University of Georgia Press, 1987.
Driskell, Leon V., and Joan T. Brittain. *The Eternal Crossroads: The Art of Flannery O'Connor.* Lexington: University Press of Kentucky, 1971.
Friedman, Melvin J., and Beverly Lyon Clark, eds. *Critical Essays on Flannery O'Connor.* Boston: G. K. Hall, 1985.
Getz, Lorine M. *Flannery O'Connor: Her Life, Library and Book Reviews.* New York: Edwin Mellen Press, 1980.
Giannone, Richard. *Flannery O'Connor and the Mystery of Love.* Urbana: University of Illinois Press, 1989.
Grimshaw, James A. *The Flannery O'Connor Companion.* Westport, Connecticut: Greenwood Press, 1981.

Hendin, Josephine. *The World of Flannery O'Connor*. Bloomington: Indiana University Press, 1970.

Hoffman, Frederick J. "The Search for Redemption: Flannery O'Connor's Fiction." *The Added Dimension: The Art and Mind of Flannery O'Connor*. Ed. Melvin J. Friedman and Lewis A. Lawson. New York: Fordham University Press, 1966. 32–48.

Kahane, Claire. "Flannery O'Connor's Rage of Vision." *American Literature* 46.1 (1974): 54–67. Rpt. in Friedman and Clark, 119–30.

——. "Gothic Mirrors and Feminine Identity." *Centennial Review* 24 (1980): 43–64.

Kessler, Edward. *Flannery O'Connor and the Language of Apocalypse*. Princeton: Princeton University Press, 1986.

Kinney, Arthur F. *Flannery O'Connor's Library: Resources of Being*. Athens: University of Georgia Press, 1985.

Magee, Rosemary M., ed. *Conversations with Flannery O'Connor*. Jackson: University Press of Mississippi, 1987.

Martin, Carter W. *The True Country: Themes in the Fiction of Flannery O'Connor*. Kingsport, Tennessee: Vanderbilt University Press, 1969.

McMullen, Joanne Hallern. *Writing Against God: Language as Message in the Literature of Flannery O'Connor*. Macon, Georgia: Mercer University Press, 1996.

Mott, Sara. "Flannery O'Connor's Unique Contribution to Christian Literary Naturalism." *Realist of Distances: Flannery O'Connor Revisited*. Ed. Karl-Heinz Westarp and Jan Nordby Gretlund. Aarhus, Denmark: Aarhus University Press, 1987. 217–26.

Muller, Gilbert H. *Nightmares and Visions: Flannery O'Connor and the Catholic Grotesque*. Athens: University of Georgia Press, 1972.

Paulson, Suzanne Morrow. *Flannery O'Connor: A Study of the Short Fiction*. Boston: Twayne, 1988.

Prown, Katherine Hemple. "Riding the Dixie Limited: Flannery O'Connor, Southern Literary Culture, and the Problem of Female Authorship." *Having Our Way: Women Rewriting Tradition in Twentieth-Century America*. Ed. Harriet Pollack. Lewisburg: Bucknell University Press, 1995. 57–78.

Quinn, John J. *Flannery O'Connor: A Memorial*. Scranton: University of Scranton Press, 1995.

Rath, Sura P., and Mary Neff Shaw, eds. *Flannery O'Connor: New Perspectives*. Athens: University of Georgia Press, 1996.

Rubin, Louis D. "Flannery O'Connor and the Bible Belt." *The Added Dimension: The Art and Mind of Flannery O'Connor*. Ed. Melvin J. Friedman and Lewis A. Lawson. New York: Fordham University Press, 1966. 49–72.

Sonnenfeld, Albert. "Flannery O'Connor: The Catholic Writer as Baptist." *Contemporary Literature* 13 (1972): 445–57. Rpt. in Friedman and Clark, 108–19.

Walker, Alice. *In Search of Our Mothers' Gardens: Womanist Prose*. San Diego: Harcourt Brace Jovanovich, 1983.

Walters, Dorothy. *Flannery O'Connor*. New York: Twayne, 1973.

Westling, Louise. "Flannery O'Connor's Mothers and Daughters." *Twentieth Century Literature* 24 (1978): 510–22.

——. "Flannery O'Connor's Revelations to 'A.'" *Southern Humanities Review* 20 (1986): 15–22.

——. *Sacred Groves and Ravaged Gardens: The Fiction of Eudora Welty, Carson McCullers, and Flannery O'Connor.* Athens: University of Georgia Press, 1985.

Wood, Ralph C. *The Comedy of Redemption: Christian Faith and Comic Vision in Four American Novelists.* Notre Dame: University of Notre Dame Press, 1988.

SAM MCBRIDE

# EUNICE ODIO
## (1919–1974)

## BIOGRAPHY

"She passed through the world, small, with her great eyes of green hope, fragile but proud, filled with dreams, loves, and misfortunes. . . . A rebel, inevitable, lost within herself . . . she died alone, withdrawn, murdered by water, without a friendly hand to stop her relentless descent." Such is the portrait that Chilean writer Humberto Díaz-Casanueva gives of the troubled life of poet Eunice Odio (p. 9).[1] Born in Costa Rica in 1919, Odio was from her childhood at odds with the provincial character of her small country. Precocious and fiercely independent, she would sneak out of her house at the age of four to wander the streets alone. Her wild spirit was partially tamed at the age of eight when, within the space of two days, she learned to read and quickly immersed herself in the world of books. It was just a matter of time before the reader turned writer: her first volume of poetry, *Los elementos terrestres* [The Earthly Elements] won an important literary prize in Guatemala in 1947 and was published the following year.

Odio next embarked on what would prove to be her defining project, *El tránsito de fuego* [The Passage of Fire]. Completed in 1955 and published in 1957, this immense work (456 pages in its first edition) cemented her reputation as a serious and profoundly challenging poet. Much of the text recalls the surreal images and fluid lyricism of Federico García Lorca, but it is also suffused with elements of biblical and mythological discourse far removed from the predominant literary currents of her time and place.

By 1962 Odio had moved to Mexico and established citizenship there. Although she became friends with many of the preeminent Latin American writers and intellectuals of the day, she was never able to reconcile herself to the politics of the Mexican literary world and consequently lived outside of it, intransigent in her disdain of social and literary fashion. "If I were told that I could be given a single poem in exchange for extreme poverty," she once wrote, "and that it would be a great poem, I would choose the great poem"

(*Antología,* p. 186). Her outspokenness on political issues further alienated her from her peers: having abandoned the radical political left of her youth, she became its fiercest critic. She also had harsh words for the feminism she saw taking hold in the United States. Having lived there from 1959 to 1962, she feared that its net effect would be the homogenization and repression of sexual difference. Odio consequently led a life as economically and socially marginal as it was artistically and spiritually rich, subsisting on the meager income provided by her literary translations and infrequent newspaper and magazine articles.

It was during her residence in Mexico that she became keenly aware of paranormal phenomena, and her fascination with the unseen world came to be reflected not only in her study of Rosicrucianism and the Kabbalah, but in an intense personal devotion to the Archangel Saint Michael, who provided the inspiration for much of her later work. While little information is available regarding Odio's institutional connections to Catholicism, it is clear that it was through the figure of St. Michael that her personal devotion and creative inspiration were most fully united. Indeed, her veneration of St. Michael is one of the primary themes discussed in her letters that have been published in *Antología* [Anthology].

Alcohol abuse and failing health took their toll in her later years, and the increasing isolation in which Odio lived was dramatically underscored by the circumstances of her death: she passed away at home in her bathtub in 1974 and her body lay undiscovered for more than a week afterward. Funeral arrangements were hastily made and she was buried with only four or five people in attendance.

## MAJOR THEMES

Although Eunice Odio published a handful of critical essays and some short fiction, she was first and foremost a poet. Each of her major works of verse is marked by a search for the deep roots common to poetic experience and experience of the divine. The eight poems of her first work, *Los elementos terrestres,* for instance, commingle an unabashed sensuality with a longing for spiritual union with the Other. Texts such as "Posesión en el sueño" [Possession in the Dream] and "Canción del esposo a su amada" [Song of the Bridegroom to His Beloved] are particularly effective in reconciling the imagery of the literary avant-garde with the tradition of Catholic mysticism. The collection speaks powerfully to Odio's ability to engage simultaneously the thoroughly secular (and masculine) love poetry in the tradition of Pablo Neruda's *Veinte poemas de amor y una canción desesperada* [Twenty Love Poems and One Song of Despair] and the more feminine, theologically charged eroticism of the Song of Solomon and St. John of the Cross.

*Zona en territorio del alba* [Zone in the Territory of the Dawn] was published in 1953 and reprinted with modifications in 1974 under the title *Territorio del alba y otros poemas* [Territory of the Dawn and Other Poems].

The collection is thematically and stylistically eclectic, containing some of Odio's earliest poetry, occasional poems, tributes to friends, and other diverse texts. Of particular interest is "Pro Sancto Michaele" [For St. Michael], first published in 1965 and revised in 1971. The poem, considered by some critics to be her finest work, is notable for weaving together an intimate, personal voice of devotion with a fluency of expression—again, informed in part by the innovations of the avant-garde—that avoids falling into didacticism or sentimentality. Alfonso Chase has argued that, in fact, the figure of the angel is of paramount importance in Odio's work: "[she] dedicated much of her life to searching for [angels], first in her relations with other human beings and second in her relations with poetry. This search for the angel is . . . the result of a dualist conception of nature, which she traces in almost all her poetry: that opposition between the divine and the earthly, between man and angel, between woman and man" (p. 5). In many respects, this search comes to its most complete and satisfying conclusion in this poem dedicated to Saint Michael.

"All I want in this world is to realize myself as a human being, to realize myself through poetry, as I understand it," Odio once wrote (*Antología*, p. 88). This is a primary task of her unquestioned masterwork *El tránsito de fuego*. Composed of four organically related long poems, the text is organized in a semi-dramatic, dialogical form, with a gallery of mythological and invented personae taking on speaking roles. Although the character named Ion—an emblem of the poet par excellence in the work—is clearly the central figure, the diversity of voices that gives shape to *Tránsito* belies Odio's interest in exploring what she called the *pluránimo* ("pluranimous") nature of poetry. With respect to this neologism, she explained that the poet must see him or herself in terms of a collectivity in order to broach the Sacred: "If a poet is not the sum of all souls, he is in error. And how can you dedicate yourself to grandiose abstractions that draw you away from Adam's dolorous flesh, and lead you, *and you alone*, to the heights of Divinity?" (*Antología*, p. 90). The poet's obligation is to give voice to the plurality of Being.

*El tránsito de fuego*, then, is Odio's most thorough exploration of the divine nature of the poetic vocation and, conversely, the poetic essence of the divine. From the first verse of the text—"Nada estaba previsto" [Nothing was foreseen]—the focus is on the act of creation that, *ex nihilo*, comes to populate a world through the power of the Word. In her edition of Odio's works, Peggy von Mayer has argued that the sum of the book could therefore be understood as a gloss on the initial verses of the first chapter of the gospel of John (pp. 20–54). Predominant here as throughout all of Odio's work is a sustained interrogation of the notion of "creation" understood in all its literary as well as spiritual valences, for she hardly distinguished between the two.

## SURVEY OF CRITICISM

Although Eunice Odio's poetry was for a long time known only to a handful of friends and fellow poets, there are indications that it has begun to find a larger audience. Those most familiar with her work have been unrestrained in their praise. Carlos Zener, for example, has called her "the great female poet of the Americas" (*Antología*, p. 25). Her appearance in English translation in a recent, widely distributed poetry anthology (Stephen Tapscott's *Twentieth-Century Latin American Poetry*) may do a great deal to bring her work to the attention of a broader public. A handful of critics share the credit for having kept Odio's legacy alive through scholarly articles and new editions and translations of her writing; primary among these is fellow Costa Rican writer and critic Rima de Vallbona, whose critical and bibliographical work has been uniformly excellent. A valuable overview of Odio's persona and poetry is to be found in Venezuelan poet Juan Liscano's "Eunice hacia la mañana," a prologue to the anthology of her work that he edited. Liscano exchanged letters with Odio over a period of ten years; thirty-one of those letters are reprinted (in edited form) in the anthology as well. They offer a fascinating perspective on Odio's complex and passionate personality and uncompromising literary vision.

While there is yet much work to be done regarding the religious dimensions of Odio's work, preliminary inroads have been made by Burdiel de las Heras and Chase in the studies listed below. Burdiel de las Heras's study finds that Hebraic rhetorical devices in the Bible are paralleled in Odio's *Los elementos terrestres,* while Chase catalogues the deployment of angelic motifs throughout the breadth of Odio's work. Peggy von Mayer's introduction to Odio's *Obras completas* [Complete Works] is notable as well for its attention to the biblical underpinnings of Odio's poetic praxis. Nevertheless, as Eunice Odio begins to attract more attention from critics and scholars, one of the most pressing needs continues to be a detailed study of her interweaving of Catholic figures and tropes with her complex and provocative view of the office of the poet.

## NOTE

1. This and all subsequent translations are my own.

## BIBLIOGRAPHY

### Works by Eunice Odio

*Los elementos terrestres.* Guatemala: Editorial El Libro de Guatemala, 1948; San José: Editorial Costa Rica, 1984.
*Zona en territorio del alba.* Mendoza, Argentina: Brigadas Líricas, 1953.
*El tránsito de fuego.* San Salvador: Editorial del Ministerio de Cultura, 1957.
*Territorio del alba y otros poemas.* Ed. Italo Vallecillos. San José: Editorial de Universidades Centroamericanas, 1974.
*Antología: rescate de un gran poeta.* Ed. Juan Liscano. Caracas: Monte Avila Editores, C.A., 1975.

*La obra en prosa de Eunice Odio.* Ed. Rima de Vallbona. San José: Editorial Costa Rica, 1980.

*Eunice Odio en Guatemala.* Ed. Mario A. Esquivel. San José: Instituto del Libro, Ministerio de Cultura, 1983.

*Obras completas.* Ed. Peggy von Mayer. 3 vols. San José: Editorial de la Universidad de Costa Rica, 1996.

## Translations of Eunice Odio's Works

Bellver, Catherine G., trans. "The Trace of the Butterfly" [El rastro de la mariposa]. *Five Women Writers of Costa Rica.* Ed. Victoria Urbano. Beaumont, Texas: Asociación de Literatura Femenina Hispánica, 1978. 33–43.

Collins, Martha, trans. "Creation" [Creación]. *Twentieth-Century Latin American Poetry: A Bilingual Anthology.* Ed. Stephen Tapscott. Austin: University of Texas Press, 1996. 284–85.

——. "Letter to Carlos Pellicer" [Carta a Carlos Pellicer]. *Twentieth-Century Latin American Poetry,* 289–90.

——. "Prologue to a Time That Is Not Itself" [Prólogo del tiempo que no está en sí]. *Twentieth-Century Latin American Poetry,* 287–89.

Espadas, Elizabeth, trans. "Once There Was a Man" [Había una vez un hombre]. *Five Women Writers of Costa Rica,* 22–32.

Levine, Suzanne Jill, trans. "Memory of My Private Childhood" [Recuerdo de mi infancia privada]. *Twentieth-Century Latin American Poetry,* 283–84.

Vance, Birgitta, trans. "The Vestige of the Butterfly" [El rastro de la mariposa]. *When New Flowers Bloomed: Short Stories by Women Writers from Costa Rica and Panama.* Ed. Enrique Jaramillo Levi. Pittsburgh: Latin American Literary Review Press, 1991. 68–80.

## Works about Eunice Odio

Albán, Laureano. "Eunice Odio: una mujer contra las máscaras (*Los elementos terrestres* ante 'Máscaras mexicanas')." *Revista Iberoamericana* 53.138–39 (1987): 325–30.

Baeza Flores, Alberto. "Tras un ángel que bajó a la mañana." *Evolución de la poesía costarricense.* San José: Editorial Costa Rica, 1978. 201–10.

Burdiel de las Heras, Leda María Cruz. "La poesía bíblica y Eunice Odio." *Foro Literario: Revista de Literatura y Lenguaje* 10.10 (1987): 42–50.

Chase, Alfonso. "Imágenes en la poesía de Eunice Odio: los ángeles." *Repertorio Americano* 2 (1975): 3–9.

Díaz-Casanueva, Humberto. "Tránsito de Eunice Odio." *Antología: rescate de un gran poeta.* Ed. Juan Liscano. Caracas: Monte Avila Editores, C. A., 1975. 9–14.

Duverrán, Carlos Rafael. "Eunice Odio: su mundo transfigurado." *Andromeda* 3 (1987): 2–5.

Liscano, Juan. "Eunice hacia la mañana." *Antología: rescate de un gran poeta.* Ed. Juan Liscano. Caracas: Monte Avila Editores, C. A., 1975. 27–70.

Mayer, Peggy von. Prologue. *Obras completas,* by Eunice Odio. Vol. 1. San José: Editorial de la Universidad de Costa Rica, 1996. 9–57.

Tapscott, Stephen, ed. *Twentieth-Century Latin American Poetry*. Austin: University of Texas Press, 1996.

Vallbona, Rima de. "Eunice Odio." *Spanish American Women Writers: A Bio-Bibliographical Sourcebook*. Ed. Diane E. Marting. Westport, Connecticut: Greenwood Press, 1990. 382–93.

——. "Eunice Odio, a Homeless Writer." *Five Women Writers of Costa Rica*. Ed. Victoria Urbano. Beaumont, Texas: Asociación de Literatura Femenina Hispánica, 1978. 44–50.

——. "Eunice Odio: rescate de un poeta." *Revista Interamericana de Bibliografía/ Interamerican Review of Bibliography* 31 (1981): 199–214.

——. "La palabra ilimitada de Eunice Odio: *Los elementos terrestres*." *Los elementos terrestres*. San José: Editorial Costa Rica, 1984. 11–36.

DAVID LARAWAY

# SISTER CAROL ANNE O'MARIE
# (1933– )

## BIOGRAPHY

Carol Anne O'Marie (pronounced "O-MARY") is a Sister of St. Joseph of Carondelet and the author of a popular series of mystery novels featuring an elderly Catholic nun-turned-sleuth, Sister Mary Helen. While religious mysteries and cinematic/television representations of nuns have become well established in twentieth-century literature and popular culture, Sister O'Marie is considered the first American Catholic nun (if not the first nun altogether) to have published a mystery series. While her stories primarily entertain, O'Marie's depictions of Catholicism and women religious challenge stereotypes and invite wider understanding of religion in contemporary life.

Carol Anne O'Marie was born on August 28, 1933, to John and Caroline O'Marie in San Francisco, California. The half-Irish, half-Italian middle-class Catholic family was "very loving," the author remembers. (The communication between her parents inspired the Kate Murphy–Jack Bassetti alliance that figures prominently in O'Marie's novels.) Another daughter, Kathleen, was born seven years after Carol.

Into this secure home crept mystery, in vicarious form: young Carol enjoyed the radio suspense melodramas of the late 1930s and early 1940s, including "The Shadow" and "I Love a Mystery." The O'Marie girls' Irish grandmother also amused them with stories from *True Detective* magazine. Carol developed a lifelong fondness for mystery.

Upon graduating from Star of the Sea High School in San Francisco, Carol countered the family's plans for her to attend college and then marry: she decided to become a nun. In 1951 she entered the Sisters of St. Joseph of Carondelet, the order that had taught her. A vocations recruiter advised at least trying convent life because it was easier to leave than marriage would be. The family did not entirely approve; Caroline O'Marie expected the order to find Carol an unsuitable novice and send her home.

O'Marie continued her education at Mount St. Mary's College in Los Angeles. After making her first vows in 1954, she taught elementary school and, later, seventh and eighth grade. She made her final vows in 1957. She taught for fifteen years at various schools in California and Arizona, eventually serving as principal. She later worked for four years as a journalist for two Catholic newspapers in Sacramento and San Francisco. She then began a ten-year career phase working in development, raising funds for a school run by her order (and working in a position like that held by her protagonist, Sr. Mary Helen).

Seeking a hobby to relax from fund-raising demands, O'Marie turned to creative writing in 1980. An adult education course taught at a community center challenged her to undertake a novel, a project that she worked on for several years but did not expect to publish. O'Marie wrote about what she knew best: convent life, San Francisco, and the mystery genre. She asked her friend and former principal, Sr. Mary Helen Pettid, for permission to use her name and personality in developing a fictional sleuth. The original Sr. Mary Helen cheerfully agreed, quipping that she expected to be dead before the book was done (she actually lived to autograph copies alongside the author). O'Marie intended to create an elderly nun who was secure in her identity and religious vocation, yet also adventurous, intelligent, and witty enough to interest readers.

Encouraged by her class's response, O'Marie sent the manuscript to several literary agents. Charles Scribner III personally asked to see the submission and published *A Novena for Murder* in 1984. A series was begun. O'Marie continued both fund-raising and writing. She researched and consulted with police for information to use in the mysteries. As her books became popular, O'Marie was asked to give public readings and lectures, during which she offered such views as her desire to see the mystery story reconsidered as a contemporary morality play.

Before one such speaking engagement at a San Francisco women's club in the late 1980s, O'Marie observed two homeless women, one urinating in the street. Their desperation and the alarming contrast between posh exclusivity and impoverished street compelled O'Marie to respond. In 1990 she co-founded A Friendly Place, a shelter in Oakland, California, for homeless women. Earnings from O'Marie's books and speeches fund her stipend to work there, while her writerly renown encourages contributions for the shelter's operation.

O'Marie divides her time between working at the shelter and writing. As of July 1999, she was anticipating the spring 2000 publication of another novel, *Requiem at the Refuge,* in which Sr. Mary Helen also begins working in a homeless shelter. O'Marie also had contracted to write a tenth book in the series; however, her recent diagnosis of Parkinson's disease has begun to slow the pace of her activities. Currently, she lives with her religious community in Oakland, California.

## MAJOR THEMES

The Sr. Mary Helen novels are entertaining and comic, yet thematically developed by combining both the religious and the traditional, "cozy" mystery conventions. As "cozy" mysteries, the books feature pleasant domestic or social circumstances that are disrupted by crime, prompting the efforts of an observant amateur sleuth (often an unlikely detective who must rely on her perception, such as an elderly woman in the tradition of Agatha Christie's Miss Marple) to restabilize the situation and to uphold propriety and higher values. O'Marie's informed characterization of the elderly female sleuth as a Catholic religious raises issues of morality, spirituality, social justice, and women's experiences. Major themes in the series include the following: one's personal responsibility to pursue justice actively; female friendship as collaborative strength; the importance of family life in individual and social stability; and the reality and vitality of contemporary Catholic women in professed religious life. These themes also represent Catholicism as a sustaining institution of both tradition and transition, and composed of human beings who are capable of good works and wisdom, foibles and mediocrity, mistakes, and even wrongdoing; the destructive nature of sin (more readily recognized in secular culture as emotional issues such as anger, jealousy, and greed); and God's unfailing mercy and unconditional love extended to all, including sinners.

Sr. Mary Helen and her longtime friend Sr. Eileen work together to solve mysteries that they encounter during their everyday lives. Their shared penchant for becoming involved with news-breaking crime investigations in perilous situations frustrates others: their religious community that welcomes neither publicity nor danger; police inspectors Dennis Gallagher and Kate Murphy, who prefer that the two nuns stay out of homicide investigations; and those whose wrongdoing they seek to expose. As elderly women religious who become sleuths, the duo challenges traditional roles within both the Church and the larger culture, in order to restore moral order but also to effect social and personal change for others in need. The sisters respond to mysterious wrongdoing out of curiosity and the conviction that justice must prevail. As intelligent and perceptive women who are both spirited and spiritual, the nuns are adept at finding and using information, observing human character, and venturing into difficult situations. Although their involvement sometimes vexes the police (particularly Gallagher), his partner Kate Murphy comes to appreciate the sisters for their charm and helpful contributions; a sense of female solidarity is evident in the collaboration and friendship between the sisters and Murphy.

The crimes and failings of O'Marie's culprits and suspects throughout the series could be interpreted as representing all seven deadly sins, although her contemporary psychological treatment of human problems and personalities makes such character flaws seem less obviously didactic or allegorical. O'Marie's first novel took up the subject of the economic exploitation of immigrants, and the series has continued to explore timely issues both social and personal. Several of the novels involve crimes related to love affairs gone wrong, with betrayal, infidelity, jealousy, and anger leading to violence and murder. Anger is a frequent issue for O'Marie's characters; *Death Takes Up a Collection* (1998) particularly explores this human problem as different personalities confront hypocrisy, greed, dishonesty, and insensitivity.

Marriage and family life figure prominently in the books, represented most positively through the ongoing Kate Murphy–Jack Bassetti relationship. Although reflecting contemporary values and challenges, their marriage comes about and grows through references to faith as directing and sustaining family life. *Death of an Angel* (1997) is a study of the power of family for either good or ill. The Murphy-Bassetti union and their extended family undergo extreme adversity yet endure and are strengthened, while the two criminals (one an angry, gluttonous person, the other a shiftless, vengeful ne'er-do-well), who are engaged in separate crimes yet intersecting activities, are both revealed as adult children of abusive families. In *Death Takes Up a Collection*, Catholic marriage and family take on deeper significance than the mere obligation to follow conventional religious practices. This is clear in the problems and progress of the Rodimans, who must grow beyond religious platitudes and parish involvement in order to realize a more mature marriage, a process that requires Tony to listen not only to Church teaching but also to his wife, who must first learn to assert herself.

O'Marie's depictions of convent life challenge stereotypes by presenting nuns as real people. The fictional order in the novels operates a college in San Francisco. The nuns represent different generations and have distinct personalities, creating both tension and harmony, but the small community remains active and faithful. It is a place of prayer and service, and its daily realities include petty annoyances and disagreements, humor and fun, and overall warmth, acceptance, and support.

The novels' Catholic elements are both obvious and integral to the plot, setting, characterization, and theme. The books follow a timeline established by direct reference in each chapter to the liturgical calendar (and this dual relationship between mystery solving and liturgical time is humorously reiterated in Sr. Mary Helen's practice of hiding mystery novels in her prayer book). Various liturgical seasons, holy days, and feast days contribute to the novels' thematic development. O'Marie's Catholic characters include the faithful, the fallen, and the faltering, as well as those who struggle to live ordinary, decent lives. Gradually O'Marie has, in addition, developed characterizations of priests and nuns who have serious problems (e.g., Father Harrington's alcoholism in *Death Goes on Retreat*, 1995); who abuse their authority through acts of pride, greed, or envy (clerical suspects in *Death Goes on Retreat* and Monsignor Higgins in *Death Takes Up a Collection*); and who fall away not only from their religious vocation but also from basic Catholic teachings (Monsignor Higgins and the former Sister Mary Deborah in *Death Takes Up a Collection*). Other characters reveal themselves as lapsed Catholics who have become alienated through negative encounters with clergy members (Beverly in *Death Goes on Retreat;* Tillie Greenwood in *Death of an Angel*). Sr. Mary Helen observes this common problem with a faithful and analytical perspective that allows her (and possibly readers) to recognize divine power as more significant than earthly authority. As she reflects in *Death of an Angel,* "She wondered . . . why people allowed imperfect ministers to drive a wedge between them and the source of such grace and comfort. During her long life she'd never found any priest, or layperson, for that matter, whom she thought was important enough to cause her to leave the church" (p. 265).

Finally, all of the novels conclude with a scene of spiritual meditation during which Sr. Mary Helen, having solved the mystery, reflects on its larger significance and prays. Her dialogues with God reveal an intimate spiritual relationship bolstered by time, humor, and honest expression of faith and humanity. Although O'Marie's characters have been revealed as flawed and even evil and destructive, the ultimate mystery of divine love and mercy establishes a larger context that precludes judgment by encouraging forgiveness and reaffirming faith.

## SURVEY OF CRITICISM

As popular fiction, O'Marie's series has received most of its critical attention through book reviews in mainstream and trade publications. Reviewers note the appeal and insight of Sr. Mary Helen's character, as well as the author's deft plotting that becomes more complex and satisfying as the series continues.

In the scholarly sector, Mary Jean DeMarr regards O'Marie's *Advent of Dying* as "a very Catholic book" (p. 56). DeMarr observes that Sr. Mary Helen's actions and overall characterization demonstrate traditional religious devotion, but that Catholicism also reveals Sr. Mary Helen's human weaknesses and problematizes Kate Murphy's professional choices and family obligations. DeMarr offers the following points regarding the book's essential Catholic nature, its depictions of nuns and laity, and its representation of Advent symbolism to achieve a meaningful tension between criminal investigation and spiritual search: "Through [Sr. Mary Helen], the novel dramatizes the daily life of the religious, while through Kate and Jack it parallels the experiences of lay people trying to practice an ancient faith in the modern world. Through the use of the Advent season, the novel is given shape and an ironic contrast between the Christian promise of new life and the reality of brutal death represented by the murder of the ex-nun" (pp. 60–61).

## NOTE

I gratefully acknowledge the cooperation of Sr. Carol Anne O'Marie in allowing me to interview her for this article on July 28, 1999. I also thank mystery-fiction bibliographer Willetta L. Heising for her assistance in confirming Sr. O'Marie's distinction as the first and, to date, only American Catholic nun to have published a mystery series.

## BIBLIOGRAPHY

### Works by Sister Carol Anne O'Marie

*A Novena for Murder.* New York: Charles Scribner's Sons, 1984.
*Advent of Dying.* New York: Delacorte Press, 1986.
*The Missing Madonna.* New York: Delacorte Press, 1988.
*Murder in Ordinary Time.* New York: Delacorte Press, 1991.
*Murder Makes a Pilgrimage.* New York: Delacorte Press, 1993.
*Death Goes on Retreat.* New York: Delacorte Press, 1995.
*Death of an Angel.* New York: St. Martin's Press, 1997.
*Death Takes Up a Collection.* New York: St. Martin's Press, 1998.

### Works about Sister Carol Anne O'Marie

Bartlett, Kay. "Nun Develops a New Habit: Murder Novels." *Los Angeles Times* 25 January 1987, bulldog edition, Pt. 1: 3.
DeMarr, Mary Jean. "Advent of Mystery: Pre-Christmas Rituals and Customs in Novels by Marian Babson, Carol Anne O'Marie, and Isabelle Holland." *Clues: A Journal of Detection* 14.1 (Spring/Summer 1993): 49–67.
Horowitz, Joy. "Mysteries from a Novelist Nun." *New York Times* 30 August 1987, late city final edition, Sec. 6: 34.
Peters, Ellis, William X. Kienzle, Harry Kemelman, and Sister Carol Anne O'Marie. "Religious Detective Fiction: A Symposium of Practitioners." *Synod of Sleuths: Essays on Judeo-Christian Detective Fiction.* Ed. Jon L. Breen and Martin H. Greenberg. Metuchen, New Jersey: Scarecrow Press, 1990. 127–36.
Rev. of *Death Goes on Retreat. Publishers Weekly.* 25 September 1995: 46.
Rev. of *Death of an Angel. Publishers Weekly.* 4 November 1996: 66.
Rev. of *Murder in Ordinary Time. Publishers Weekly.* 16 August 1991: 50.
Ross, Deborah. "Murder, She Wrote." *Phoenix Gazette* 13 November 1993, final edition: D6.

VICTORIA CARLSON

# EMILIA PARDO BAZÁN
# (1851–1921)

## BIOGRAPHY

Emilia Pardo Bazán was born in La Coruña in the northwestern province of
Galicia on September 16, 1851, to a well-placed family. Although she did not
receive a formal higher education, she had access to private libraries that enabled the precocious young woman opportunities to read widely in Spanish
and other literature and to study the classics. Her determination to learn in
spite of conventions that ruled against higher education for women marked
her early on as a rebel. Her refusal to accept rules for women was a distinctive
mark throughout her life and long literary career.

Pardo Bazán's marriage is one illustration of her quest for independence.
She married José Quiroga Pérez Pinal in 1868 and had two daughters and one
son. Her husband apparently was no match for the strong woman; the couple
separated in 1885. Pardo Bazán took up permanent residence in Madrid
where she enjoyed life at Spain's cultural and artistic center. She even established a salon, which attracted well-known intellectuals and artists of the day.
Neither personal nor intellectual independence, however, persuaded her away
from her Catholic heritage; she remained fervently Catholic throughout her
life.

Pardo Bazán's zest for travel took her away from Madrid periodically as it
had from Galicia. As early as 1871 she had traveled in France, Italy, and England; she learned enough English to read Shakespeare. A year later she was in
Vienna, this time learning German and translating the poetry of Heine. In
1886 she was in Paris where she met Emile Zola, the Goncourt brothers, and
Huysmann. While in France she came into contact with French Naturalism,
*fin de siècle* literature, and contemporary Russian literature, which she read in
French translation. Her interest in Russian letters led to her 1887 book on the
subject of the revolution and novel in Russia. Further trips took her to Rome
(1887), Portugal (1888), and Belgium and Holland (1902).

In 1916 Pardo Bazán was awarded a chair in romance literature at the University of Madrid. A brilliant and famous author and scholar, she nonetheless was shunned by students who could not accept a woman as their professor. Further honors came her way, however. She was the first female president of the literary section of the Athenium in Madrid, and in 1908, in recognition of her literary achievements, King Alfonso XII bestowed on her the title of countess. She died on May 12, 1921, distinguished by a long career of writing: novels, short stories, biographies, literary criticism, and history. Hundreds of her stories and numerous essays on literature and culture appeared in the foremost journals of the day as well as in *El Nuevo Teatro Crítico* [The New Critical Theatre], the monthly journal that she founded and to which she was the sole contributor for the two years of its existence. Pardo Bazán was, quite simply, a prodigious writer.

## MAJOR THEMES

The three major themes in Pardo Bazán's writings, including nonfiction and fiction, are Naturalism, feminism, and Catholicism. Whereas Naturalism is associated with her early period of writing, the themes of feminism and Catholicism inform all her works. Pardo Bazán already had published three novels of Galician setting before the publication of *La cuestión palpitante* [The Palpitating Question] in 1883. This study of French Naturalism made her something of a *cause célèbre* in the literary world; a Catholic woman had dared to champion the French movement of Naturalism with its theoretical basis in scientific determinism and painfully realistic depictions of the sordid side of life. Battle lines quickly formed. Conservatives were especially harsh in their criticism: they attacked Pardo Bazán both for espousing determinism, which was against the Catholic doctrine of free well, and for writing about matters deemed inappropriate for a lady to know.

For decades the question of Pardo Bazán's Naturalism has intrigued scholars: was she truly a Naturalist writer in the mode of Zola? Study of the two novels that were most controversial and yet earned her strong critical praise over the years reveals that Pardo Bazán did not adhere strictly to the tenets of Naturalism. In *Los Pazos de Ulloa* (1886) [The House of Ulloa] and its sequel, *La madre naturaleza* (1887) [Mother Nature], Pardo Bazán describes rural Galicia with the profusion of realistic detail that typifies a Zola novel: descriptions of the physical appearance of characters, interior of buildings, and landscapes are exacting in detail. These realistic descriptions of a rural life fraught with cruelty and ignorance are Pardo Bazán's strongest gesture to French Naturalism. Such descriptions are also characteristic of the nineteenth-century realistic novel that was popular in Spain at the time. In terms of the determinism that carried a Zola character unremittingly to a sordid and unforgiving demise, Pardo Bazán's writings are clearly of another order. True, the brutality of rural Galicia in Pardo Bazán's time affects to their detriment both the people who are native to the area and the outsiders who try, unsuccessfully, to adapt to a hostile environment. But the environment, as harsh as it is, does not necessarily predict corruption or destroy goodness.

Early in her novelistic career, Pardo Bazán featured a heroine who embodied a theme that for the author was a personal statement. In *La Tribuna* [The Tribune], written in 1882, Pardo Bazán depicts a young woman of the working class who emerges as the workers' tribune in their struggle to improve the lot of the working class through social revolution. Although the "tribune" suffers the personal disgrace of bearing the child of a wealthy man who wooed and betrayed her, she feels the hope of a better life as she holds the newborn infant with cries of revolution ringing in her ears. Amparo, the people's spokeswoman, is the precursor of strong female characters who appear throughout Pardo Bazán's novels and short stories.

Three novels with such protagonists are *Insolación* (1889) [Sunstroke], *Memorias de un solterón* (1891) [A Bachelor's Memories], and *El tesoro de Gastón* (1897) [Gastón's Treasure]. This triad represents both the increasing liberation of the female and her growing importance to the psychological growth of the male with whom she relates. In the first of the novels, an attractive widow in Madrid struggles against the urge to return to the safety of her native Galicia as she feels herself dangerously attracted to a man she scarcely knows. To accept his love is to rebel against the strict social conventions of Madrid. That she makes the decision to reject the force of convention can be interpreted as an act of self-liberation. The protagonist, who is just breaking free from the prison of convention, develops into the liberated young woman of the second of the three novels. Seduced by books and learning rather than fancy clothes and suitors, Feita is the fictional face of Pardo Bazán. In her relationship with a man, it is she, the liberated woman, who effects in him psychological awakening, much as the man had done for Asís in the preceding novel. Like Asís, the third protagonist, Antonia, is a widow, but there the likeness ends. Antonia is the mature Feita, liberated and liberating for the man who falls in love with her. Pardo Bazán's feminism was ingrained in her own behavior, translated into fiction, and bolstered by polemic and essays in leading journals of the day.

These three "liberated" protagonists emerge in novels of what has been called the second period of Pardo Bazán's writing, after she wrote the novels associated with Naturalism and before the three novels inspired by *fin de siècle* writing and strongly informed by the theme of Catholicism. Pardo Bazán appears as a Catholic writer from two perspectives. First, she wrote about Catholic subjects and experiences, as in her studies of St. Francis (1882), the Franciscans and Christopher Columbus (1892), Christian epic poets (1894), and traveling through Catholic Europe (1902). Second, her Catholicism is not defined in terms of the Catholic Church as a religious institution but rather in the spiritual or mystical relationship between the soul and God. This relationship is expressed primarily in the literature of such Catholic mystics as St.

Teresa of Avila, St. Catherine of Siena, St. Bernard of Clairvaux, and St. John of the Cross. Certainly, Christians who are not Catholics claim this spiritual heritage, but strictly speaking, the main corpus of mystical writing is in the Catholic tradition.

This spirituality grounds Pardo Bazán's writings. With respect to her novels, spirituality in the Catholic mystical tradition may be traced through characters both female and male from the first period until the end of her novelistic career. So strong is the spiritual in Pardo Bazán's fiction that it qualifies as her aesthetic center; on that basis she deserves to be identified as a Catholic writer. Such characters as the priest, Julián, and Nucha in *Los Pazos de Ulloa*; and Carmen, the protagonist of *Una cristiana* [A Christian Woman] and *La Prueba* [The Test], the latter two novels written in 1890, reveal Pardo Bazán's understanding of Christian mysticism, which she gained from study and probably personal experience as well. These characters prefigure the protagonists of the last three novels, *La quimera* [The Chimera], *La sirena negra* [The Black Siren], and *Dulce Dueño* [Sweet Master], 1905, 1908, and 1911, respectively, in which the mystical theme dominates. In all three novels, the protagonist undergoes a spiritual transformation whereby he or she is turned away from preoccupation with self and the world to enjoy the mystical embrace of God. In the case of *Dulce Dueño*, Pardo Bazán's last novel, the protagonist, Lina, is modeled on St. Catherine of Alexandria; like her namesake, she experiences mystical marriage.

## SURVEY OF CRITICISM

The subject of much critical speculation in her own day, Pardo Bazán as a writer and intellectual continues to elicit abundant discussion. Understandably, her position vis-à-vis French Naturalism has been much questioned. Donald Fowler Brown in *The Catholic Naturalism of Pardo Bazán* and Fernando J. Barroso in *El naturalismo en la Pardo Bazán* [Naturalism in Pardo Bazán] represent the majority position that she advocated Naturalism in technique but not in theory. Her feminism has also come under consistent scrutiny, notably in the 1950s with the work of Ronald Hilton, and in the last twenty years, inspired by the immense popularity of feminist criticism. New Criticism brought to Pardo Bazán studies interest in the inner texture of her fiction, its structure, narrative and descriptive techniques, and imagery and symbols, as seen in *Estructuras novelísticas de Emilia Pardo Bazán* [Novelistic Structures of Emilia Pardo Bazán] by Benito Valera Jácome. Finally, study continues on the spiritual themes as in *Naturalismo y espiritualismo en la novelística de Galdós y Pardo Bazán* [Naturalism and Spirituality in the Novelistic Art of Galdós and Pardo Bazán] by Mariano López-Sanz. From the critics' point of view, Pardo Bazán as a writer does not go out of style.

# BIBLIOGRAPHY

## Works by Emilia Pardo Bazán

### Fiction

*La Tribuna*. Madrid: Alfredo de Carlos Hierro, 1882.

*Los Pazos de Ulloa*. Barcelona: Daniel Cortezo, 1886. Trans. as *The House of Ulloa* by Paul O'Prey and Lucia Graves. New York: Penguin, 1990.

*La madre naturaleza*. Madrid, 1887.

*Isolación*. Barcelona: Imprenta de Sucesores de N. Ramírez y Cía., 1889.

*Una cristiana*. Madrid, 1890.

*La Prueba*. Madrid, 1890.

*Memorias de un solterón*. Madrid, 1891.

*El tesoro de Gastón*. Madrid, 1897.

*La quimera*. Madrid, 1905.

*La sirena negra*. Madrid: M. Pérez Villavicencio, 1908.

*Dulce Dueño*. Madrid: V. Prieto y Cía., 1911.

### Nonfiction

*San Francisco de Asís*. Madrid, 1882.

*La cuestión palpitante*. Madrid, 1883.

*La revolución y la novela en Rusia* [The Revolution and the Novel in Russia]. Madrid, 1887.

*Polémicas y estudios literarios* [Literary Polemics and Studies]. Madrid, 1892.

*Los franciscanos y Colón* [The Franciscans and Columbus]. Madrid, 1892.

*Los poetas épicos cristianos* [Christian Epic Poets]. Madrid, 1894.

*Por la Europa católica* [Through Catholic Europe]. Madrid, 1902.

*La literatura francesa moderna* [Modern French Literature]. Madrid, 1910–1914.

## Works about Emilia Pardo Bazán

Barroso, Fernando J. *El naturalismo en la Pardo Bazán*. Madrid: Editorial Playor, 1973.

Brown, Donald Fowler. *The Catholic Naturalism of Pardo Bazán*. University of North Carolina Studies in Romance Languages and Literatures 28. Chapel Hill: University of North Carolina Press, 1957.

Clémessy, Nelly. *Emilia Pardo Bazán como novelista: De la teoría a la Práctica*. Madrid: Fundación universitaria española, 1981.

Dendle, Brian J. *The Spanish Novel of Religious Thesis 1876–1936*. Madrid: Editorial Castalia, 1968.

Eoff, Sherman H. *The Modern Spanish Novel. Comparative Essays Examining the Philosophical Impact of Science on Fiction*. New York: New York University Press, 1961.

Giles, Mary E. "Feminism and the Feminine in Emilia Pardo Bazán's Novels." *Hispania* 63 (May 1980): 356–67.

González-López, Emilio. *Emilia Pardo Bazán, novelista de Galicia*. New York: Hispanic Institute of the United States, 1944.

Hemingway, Maurice. *Emilia Pardo Bazán. The Making of a Novelist.* New York: Cambridge University Press, 1983.

Hilton, Ronald. "Pardo Bazán and Literary Polemics about Feminism." *Romanic Review* 44 (1953): 40–46.

Jácome, Benito Valera. *Estructuras novelísticas de Emilia Pardo Bazán.* Santiago de Compostela: Anejo XXII, 1973.

López-Sanz, Mariano. *Naturalismo y espiritualismo en la novelística de Galdós y Pardo Bazán.* Madrid: Editorial Pliegos, 1985.

Pattison, Walter T. *Emilia Pardo Bazán.* New York: Twayne, 1971.

MARY E. GILES

# CHRISTINE DE PIZAN
# (1365–c.1430)

## BIOGRAPHY

Christine de Pizan (also spelled Pisan) was born in Venice, Italy, in 1365, but she matured in the French court. Her father, Thomas de Pizzano, an Italian government councilor and a noted astrologer, accepted an invitation by Charles V to visit France. Thomas was so impressed by Charles's humanist approach to government that he relocated his family to Paris and later changed his last name to Pizan. They thus followed the seat of the Catholic Church which had relocated from Rome to Avignon, France, in 1309 under the leadership of Pope Clement V. Christine de Pizan would later ground many of her writings in Roman Catholic doctrine.

As she enjoyed her privileged childhood at court, young Christine offered little sign that she would later become the most accomplished woman writer of medieval Europe. Thomas recognized his daughter's intelligence and procured for her an education in the languages, including French, Italian, and probably Latin. He also obtained a husband for her in 1380. At the age of fifteen, de Pizan made a match with Etienne de Castel, a French courtier, who would later serve as secretary and notary to the king. She rapidly gave birth to two sons and a daughter with Etienne, toward whom she apparently felt great love.

Several crises served to destroy de Pizan's happy existence. Charles V's sudden death in 1380 caused her husband to lose his position, and economic disaster threatened the couple. By 1390 Thomas had died, and Etienne took responsibility for supporting Christine's mother along with his own family. His prospects strengthened in 1390 with an invitation to accompany Charles VI on a journey. Again the medieval Dame Fortune, a figure who later appeared in de Pizan's writings, struck when Etienne died abruptly following a brief illness.

Finding herself a reluctant family head, de Pizan considered her future. Few options existed for fourteenth-century French widows outside of remarriage or convent life, neither of which appealed to her. Not only did she need to support her extended family, but she also discovered that Etienne had left debts to be paid. A search for any written advice for women in her situation proved fruitless, causing de Pizan to later write her own advice book for widows. For the time being, she chose an unusual vocation for a medieval woman. Building on her knowledge of languages, she began a course of self-education with the goal of becoming a professional writer. She equated her transformation to that of a gender change, writing in *The Book of Fortune's Transformation* (1403), "I who was formerly a woman, am now in fact a man" (Blumenfeld-Kosinski, *Selected Writings*, p. 91).

De Pizan achieved her goal, producing at first hundreds of pages of well-received occasional and amorous verse; she soon became popular with the reading public. The topic of widowhood, new to lyric poetry, appeared repeatedly in her works, and she also grew adept at adopting the male voice and in writing devotional texts. Practicing the common habit of dedicating her works to specific aristocrats, de Pizan gained patrons. Later, she wrote a biography of Charles V, *The Book of the Deeds and Good Conduct of the Wise King Charles V* (1404), at the request of his brother, the Duke of Burgundy, and she also engaged in the first written literary dispute on record. In that dispute, she contested the misogynistic presentation of women in Jean de Meun's famous continuation of the *Romance of the Rose* by Guillame de Lorris; she urged the celebration of marriage rather than the sex outside of wedlock encouraged by de Meun's lengthy verse. De Pizan based two allegorical works, *The Book of the City of Ladies* and *The Treasure of the City of Ladies* (both written about 1405), on Roman Catholic precepts; they describe the first all-female utopias. Like her utopias, *The Path of Long Study* (1402–1403) and *Christine's Vision* (1405) frame political and social views with autobiography. As her final work, de Pizan produced the sole contemporary tribute to the young French warrior girl, *Tale of Joan of Arc* (1429).

Deeply interested in politics as well as social issues, Christine de Pizan cautioned in writing against the warring factions in France that would arise in reaction to the unrest brought about by feuding barons. In her *The Lamentation on the Evils That Have Befallen France* (1410), she predicted the horrors that would occur during the destructive court revolution of 1413. In reaction to that power struggle between factions represented by the Duke of Burgundy and the assassinated Duke of Orleans, she wrote an open letter begging for peace. She later warned the young French Dauphin in *The Book of Peace* (1412) against continuing the unpopular practice of appointing commoners to state positions, a practice raising the ire of his barons. Domestic tension boiled amid the violence that had raged all of de Pizan's life due to The Hundred Years War, in which English claims against the French territory caused a constant division of loyalties within France's borders. Her advice, and that of others, was ignored, and de Pizan fled the armed conflict in Paris to take up convent life in 1418, perhaps joining her daughter, a nun at Poissy. No record of any writings by de Pizan exists until her tribute to Joan of Arc appeared. Her exact date of death and place of burial are unknown as all convent records were eventually destroyed by decay when the convent was deserted.

Because de Pizan presented copies of each of her works to the Duke of Berry, a private collector with a magnificent library, her large number of writings were preserved. Some still await translation.

## MAJOR THEMES

Earl Jeffrey Richards, in his edition of *Book of the City of Ladies*, considers Christine de Pizan a "polyscribator" due to her adoption of so many different subjects for her poetry, prose, and epistles (p. xxv). Dominant themes in all her works include love, the value of women, civic peace, virtue, and reason, many of which she informs with an emphasis on spirituality. In *One Hundred Ballads* (1402), de Pizan adopts male and female voices to speak of love's joys as well as the suffering caused by its loss. Frequently, she calls upon God to legitimate her claims, as in poem "18" when she adds to her testimony of melancholy, "may God recognize this"; and in "67" when a male voice pleads, "may God give me the power/to deserve this!" (*Selected Writings*, pp. 7, 9). *The God of Love's Letter* (1399), a lengthy work which sealed the author's fame, uses Ovid's Cupid as its voice, speaking in epistle form to all lovers to counter the misogyny of the *Romance of the Rose*. Taking a stance that anticipates later approaches to legal defense, Cupid addresses the topics of female deception by would-be lovers and male writers who seek to sully women's reputations. De Pizan defends women by offering "a new 'feminist' exegesis" characterizing Eve as sin-free in her original state (*Selected Writings*, p. 16).

De Pizan employs figures such as Lady Reason, Wealth, Nobility, Wisdom, and Chivalry in her allegorical-vision prose piece *The Path of Long Study*. As first-person narrator, de Pizan herself accompanies a Sybil to a utopic court where world rule is discussed. De Pizan accepts the charge to return to her own culture with a positive message regarding the use of reason to achieve civic peace (Richards, *Book of the City of Ladies*, p. xxvii). She emphasizes God's allowance of earthly discord in order to encourage a desire for heaven on the part of mortals where they will experience "peace, joy, concord, love, the loss of which is never to be feared" (*Selected Writings*, p. 66). This work represents the first of several pleas for peace, including *The Book of the Body Politic* (1406–1407), *The Lamentation on the Evils That Have Befallen France*, and *The Book of Peace*. In a portion of this latter book, dedicated to the young dauphin Louis of Guienne, de Pizan reminds her readers of the many biblical stories in which God used children as his mouthpiece, concluding her rendition by addressing God directly: "with all Your past goodness you have now decided to help us again in a similar way, to be with us and comfort us in our great affliction through a child, inspired in speech and deed by Your Holy Spirit." She adds that "the voice of true prayer" combines with God's pity on man, to invoke a peace to halt and heal the wounds resulting from "vicious hatred and horrible bloodshed suffered by Your Catholic kingdom of France where everything perished" (*Selected Writings*, p. 232). *The Treasure of the City of Ladies or The Book of the Three Virtues* and *The Book of the Deeds of Arms and Chivalry* (1410) both act as conduct books, the first for women in all positions in life, from the prostitute to the queen, the second for men engaged in military art.

De Pizan's best known work, *The Book of the City of Ladies*, supports the virtuous character and the often-disregarded intellectual capacities of women. She writes that the female intellect does not differ in nature from that of the male. Rather, girls suffer more barriers to education than do boys, in part due to the attitude of the older generation of women that learning is wasted on girls (*Selected Writings*, p. xii). Appearing as the first-person narrator, de Pizan utilizes the aid of three allegorical female figures, Reason, Rectitude, and Justice, to help construct a utopia. In his introduction to a recent edition of this volume, Richards points out that the title of the work alludes to Augustine's *City of God*, and that de Pizan's "political vision" should "be understood as participating in a Christian tradition of political philosophy" (p. xxxiii). While adopting Boccaccio's approach in *Decameron* and *Concerning Famous Women*, de Pizan shifts her emphasis toward morality, considering "good" women from all social classes. Especially important to her is making readers understand that a learned woman presents no problem to society; rather the studious woman must overcome society's narrow-mindedness in order to reach her intellectual potential. Sacred history guides the author's choice of figures with whom to populate her utopia: she includes various martyred virgins and then establishes Mary, Mother of Christ, as her city's sovereign (p. xli). The Virgin's origin as a "lowly handmaiden of the Lord" proves important to de Pizan's discussion of women in general. Women represent a "historical confinement, humility, and obedience before the eternal divine order" which allows them to serve as perfect representative figures for all humanity. Emphasizing that God is her authority, de Pizan even adopts the exact wording used in the biblical rendition of the Annunciation (pp. lx-lxi). She concludes her book with an address to all ladies, beginning by inviting those "who love glory, virtue, and praise" to enjoy lodgings in the city (p. 254). Her admonition to avoid "misuse" of the "inheritance like the arrogant who turn proud" she supports with a call to "follow the example of your Queen, the sovereign Virgin" who presents a model of humility (pp. 254–55). According to de Pizan, conduct with honesty and integrity will lead her city's inhabitants "to be all the more virtuous and humble" (p. 255).

Possibly the strongest example of de Pizan's grounding of her knowledge and her own authority in the authority of God appears in her *Tale of Joan of Arc*, written at the time of the warrior girl's greatest fame and triumph. De Pizan makes clear in verses 49–52 that Joan's victory is also God's, writing that God has "accomplished all this through His grace" (*Selected Writings*, p. 374). Returning to her favored theme of the utility and virtue of women, she informs her readers in verses 203–8 that "the prowess of all the great men of the past cannot be compared to this woman's whose concern is to cast out our enemies. This is God's doing: it is He who guides her and who has given her a heart greater than that of any man" (*Selected Writings*, p. 376). As Brownlee notes, de Pizan presents in this work "an implicit figural presentation . . . in terms of authoritative Biblical models of active heroism in a politico-religious context" (*Selected Writings*, p. 377).

As Blumenfeld-Kosinski and Brownlee note, despite all of de Pizan's anti-misogynistic literature, she never supported any change in social structure. Rather, her goals remained the encouragement of marriage, personal responsibility, a unified France, and the valuing of women and education (*Selected Writings*, p. xvi).

## SURVEY OF CRITICISM

*Christine de Pizan, Her Life and Works* (1984), by Charity Cannon Willard, remains the most detailed and respected biography of the writer. Willard offers in one chapter a critically astute discussion of de Pizan's involvement in the centuries-long *querelle des femme* through her written reaction to the *Romance of the Rose*. The discussion achieves clarity without giving in to a narrow editorial agenda of any kind. Sarah Lawson's highly regarded translation of *The Treasure of the City of Ladies or The Book of the Three Virtues* (1985) offers an introduction with an easily understood summary of de Pizan's biography. Lawson emphasizes the fluctuation in critical regard of the author's works. She reviews attitudes toward writings evaluated not only as literature but also as historical documents and as treatises emphasizing ideas that prefigured the later cultural and political movement known as feminism.

A detailed discussion of de Pizan's *The City of Ladies*, Maureen Quilligan's *The Allegory of Female Authority: Christine de Pizan's "Cité Des Dames"* (1991) offers a more strident feminist perspective. Quilligan guides readers through an insightful reading of this work, explaining how de Pizan gained her own authority as a writing female by basing her work upon, then varying her approach from, that of male-authored writings such as those produced by Dante, Ovid, and Boccaccio. Quilligan emphasizes the importance of de Pizan's demand for attention, characterized by the opening words of her biography of Joan of Arc, "Je, Christine." The appearance of this phrase throughout *City of Ladies* acts as "a signal mark of Christine's authority, a 'signature,'" that calls unmistakable attention to the author (p. 12). Quilligan explains how de Pizan's framing of all women, regardless of social or religious status, within the Christian community headed by the Virgin Mary represents a departure from techniques of earlier writers. De Pizan embraced women both living and dead as exemplary figures in her allegory, which results in a vision similar to that of Dante. Earl Jeffrey Richards's edition of *City of Ladies* contains an introduction with an annotated bibliography of de Pizan's works as well as a brief survey of critical response.

Out of more than two hundred late-twentieth-century scholarly writings in English on de Pizan, Benjamin M. Semple's "The Critique of Knowledge as Power: The Limits of Philosophy and Theology in Christine de Pizan" most directly deals with religious influence. Focusing on the restrictions of theoretical theology that de Pizan discovered as she attempted to make practical application of religion to medieval women's everyday lives, Semple demonstrates how de Pizan claimed experience as a way of knowing available to women. This approach allowed her to ground her discussion of the value of experience in Catholic theology.

Editions of Christine de Pizan's works continue to appear, with translations of new works expanding her accessible canon. Renate Blumenfeld-Kosinski and Kevin Brownlee offer new translations in their *Selected Writings of Christine de Pizan* (1997), accompanied by a brief critical introduction to each translated piece.

## BIBLIOGRAPHY

### Works by Christine de Pizan

*The Treasure of the City of Ladies or The Book of the Three Virtues.* Trans. Sarah Lawson. New York: Penguin Books, 1985.
*The Selected Writings of Christine de Pizan.* Trans. Renate Blumenfeld-Kosinski and Kevin Brownlee. Ed. Renate Blumenfeld-Kosinski. New York: W. W. Norton, 1997.
*The Book of the City of Ladies: Christine de Pizan.* Trans. Earl Jeffrey Richards. New York: Persea Books, 1998.

### Works about Christine de Pizan

Bell, Susan Groag. "Christine de Pizan (1364–1430): Humanism and the Problem of the Studious Women." *Feminist Studies* 3 (1976): 173–84.
Desmond, Marilyn, ed. *Christine de Pizan and the Categories of Difference.* Minneapolis: University of Minnesota Press, 1998.
Lawson, Sarah. Introduction. *The Treasure of the City of Ladies or The Book of the Three Virtues.* Trans. Sarah Lawson. New York: Penguin Books, 1985.
Quilligan, Maureen. *The Allegory of Female Authority: Christine de Pizan's "Cite Des Dames."* Ithaca, New York: Cornell University Press, 1991.
Semple, Benjamin M. "The Critique of Knowledge as Power: The Limits of Philosophy and Theology in Christine de Pizan." *Christine de Pizan and the Categories of Difference.* Ed. Marilyn Desmond. Minneapolis: University of Minnesota Press, 1998.
Willard, Charity Cannon. *Christine de Pizan, Her Life and Works.* New York: Persea Books, 1984.

——. "A Fifteenth-Century View of Women's Role in Medieval Society: Christine de Pizan's *Livre des Trois Vertus.*" *The Role of Women in the Middle Ages.* Ed. Rosmarie Thee Morewedge. Albany: State University of New York Press, 1975. 90–120.

Zimmerman, Margarete and Dina De Rentiis, eds. *The City of Scholars: New Approaches to Christine de Pizan.* Berlin: Walter de Gruyter, 1994.

VIRGINIA BRACKETT

# KATHERINE ANNE PORTER
## (1890–1980)

**BIOGRAPHY**

Katherine Anne Porter was born in Indian Creek, Texas, on May 15, 1890, the daughter of farmers Harrison Boone Porter and Mary Alice Jones. Christened Callie Russell Porter, she was not quite two when her mother died in childbirth. Porter and her siblings were raised by their paternal grandmother in Kyle, Texas, until the grandmother's death in 1901. The family then moved to San Antonio, where Porter attended private schools.

Porter married John Henry Koontz, the son of a local rancher, in June 1906 in Lufkin, Texas, and converted to Roman Catholicism, her husband's faith. Following her divorce from Koontz in 1915, Porter legally took the name Katherine Anne, after her paternal grandmother. She moved about for several years, hoping to fulfill her childhood dream of becoming an actress. After a brief second marriage, later annulled, to H. O. Taskett in Fort Worth, she was hospitalized for tuberculosis in Dallas and Carlsbad, Texas. Porter had started writing in 1916 as a reporter for a Dallas paper, and when a fellow patient at the hospital, who was also a journalist, moved to Denver, Porter followed and became a society writer and drama critic for the *Rocky Mountain News*. In 1918 she nearly died during the influenza epidemic that struck the United States near the end of World War I. Upon her recovery, she moved to New York's Greenwich Village with literary ambitions.

An interest in revolutionary politics in Mexico led Porter to travel to Mexico City in the fall of 1920, just in time to witness the turmoil created by President Alvaro Obregón's effort to suppress Bolshevik elements. She returned to the United States within six months' time, but reaped the harvest of her experiences in Mexico when her first serious fiction, "María Concepción," was published in *Century* magazine in 1922. Porter returned to Mexico in 1922 and again in 1923, but she continued to make her home in New York City. In 1925, she married British painter Ernest Stock; they divorced in 1928. Two other important early works, "Theft" and "The Jilting of Granny Weatherall," appeared in 1929. Her first major story, "Flowering Judas," was published in the spring of 1930. That same year she published her first collection, also entitled *Flowering Judas*, and she returned again to Mexico, this time on a Guggenheim Fellowship. An encounter with the Soviet film director Sergei Eisenstein provided material for her first short novel, *Hacienda* (1932).

Awarded a second Guggenheim, in 1931 Porter traveled to Europe, where she resided in Paris, Berlin, and Basel. In Berlin, she garnered material for the later short novel *The Leaning Tower* (1941). Material for her only full-length novel, *Ship of Fools* (1962), came as well from this particular journey. In Europe, Porter also began a relationship with Eugene Dove Pressley, whom she married in 1933.

In 1936, Porter completed the short novels *Old Mortality* and *Noon Wine*, which she had begun in 1928, and composed her masterpiece, *Pale Horse, Pale Rider*. Divorced from Pressley, she married her fifth husband, Albert Erskine, in New Orleans in April 1938. They, too, would subsequently divorce. The 1939 publication of *Pale Horse, Pale Rider*, a volume which collected the three short novels, sealed her critical reputation as a chief Modernist writer. Elected to membership in the National Institute of Arts and Letters in 1941, she published *The Leaning Tower and Other Stories* in 1944. A collection of essays, *The Days Before*, appeared in 1952. By the 1960s, Porter was residing in the Washington, D.C., area; *Ship of Fools*, her long-awaited magnum opus, appeared in April 1962 to much celebrity despite a mixed critical reception. The novel was awarded the Emerson-Thoreau Gold Medal of the American Academy of Arts and Sciences, and a successful film version finally brought her economic independence.

*The Collected Stories of Katherine Anne Porter*, published in 1965, was much better received and, to many, is Porter's crowning achievement. She was honored with a National Book Award, the Gold Medal for Fiction of the National Institute of Arts and Letters, election to the American Academy of Letters, and the Pulitzer Prize for fiction in 1966. *The Collected Essays and Occasional Writings of Katherine Anne Porter* appeared in 1970, and *The Never-Ending Wrong*, a nonfiction account of her participation in 1927 in the protest against the Sacco-Vanzetti execution, was published in 1977.

Porter devoted the last years of her life to establishing the Katherine Anne Porter Room of the McKeldin Library at the University of Maryland. She died in Silver Springs, Maryland, on September 18, 1980, and is buried in Indian Creek.

## MAJOR THEMES

While Porter's fiction is best characterized as Modernist, she can also be appreciated for the fact that her works exhibit her unique perspective as an independent woman struggling to be herself in what was then largely a man's world. Her Roman Catholicism, too, appears to inform her best work in ways that are far more pervasive than the Mexican settings of her earliest fiction can account for. Even her Anglo characters, despite their roots in the overwhelmingly Protestant American South, mainly Texas, are generally identified as Roman Catholics.

For a writer as highly conscious of depth and atmosphere as Porter is, it would be unfair to imagine her works' Catholicism as merely an incidental detail. Catholicism's emphasis on guilt, suffering, and the mysteries of iniquity in the midst of a sanctified creation appears to have deeply appealed to Porter's own moral and aesthetic sensibilities. Certainly this is true of her virtual obsession with the themes of betrayal and of motives gone awry. We might, then, expect the Mexican peasant woman and title character of Porter's first important work, "María Concepción," to be a person for whom it was both very important and a mark of honor that she and her somewhat wayward husband, Juan Villegas, were married "in the church, rather than behind it" (p. 4).[1] And Laura, the American protagonist of "Flowering Judas," was not only born Roman Catholic but, in spite of her credentials as a fellow traveler with Mexican revolutionaries, "slips now and again" into a church to say "a Hail Mary on the gold rosary she bought in Tehuantepec." Ultimately, we are told, her faith, which has become her own "private heresy," is "no good" (p. 92). Laura does nevertheless cling to her Catholicism—and Porter feels compelled to use it as a key element in creating the characterization.

Both Laura and María Concepción portray women who are victimized not as much by the men in their lives—in Laura's case, it is the unctuous but politically correct revolutionary leader Braggioni—as by their own overwrought moral consciences, out of which, indeed, their capacity for self-betrayal arises. María can kill María Rosa, her rival for Juan's affections, without batting an eye, but then must rely helplessly on the machinations of the otherwise useless Juan to save her from the law. Laura patiently endures Braggioni's amorous but illicit affections, but she cannot overcome an inchoately nightmarish guilt when she fails to save the political prisoner Eugenio from suicide.

These moral and, in Laura's case, spiritual confusions are based as much on the tenets of the Catholic faith as on the plight of female characters existing in a world peopled by self-centered, self-serving, and exploitative males. Porter's fictions inevitably expose this, in very Catholic terms, as a fallen creation consisting of individuals who, trying to prop themselves up without recourse to the otherness of belief, find themselves, in the end, depending on a selfhood that thereby must signify nothing. The result is ultimately self-betrayal, and such betrayals are all fundamentally Catholic in scope, inasmuch as the true culprit is a self-centeredness that allows any crisis, from the most trivial setback to an event as momentous as death, to leave the protagonist bereft of the capacity for an effective and sustaining response.

So, then "The Leaning Tower" portrays a male protagonist, Charles Upton, whose deferential clumsiness masks a social ineptitude that leads him invariably into pathetic self-betrayals: for example, he finds himself in the bland boredom of post-Weimar, pre-Nazi Berlin simply because a boyhood friend had always spoken highly of the city. In "The Jilting of Granny Weatherall," the title character's crotchety matriarchal tough-mindedness has not quite prepared her for an antagonist as indifferent as death, so that, in her dying delirium, she "could not remember any other sorrow because this grief wiped them all away" (p. 89). In "Theft," the unnamed female protagonist is exploited by an unscrupulous woman janitor, who takes an almost instinctive advantage of the vulnerabilities created by the protagonist's politically fashionable concerns about the less fortunate.

This emphasis on the poverty of self-reliance, a perennial Catholic theme, is capped by Porter in the central metaphor of her final fiction, *Ship of Fools*, in which we are, all of us, portrayed as caught up in the folly of worldliness and selfishness, at a loss as to just how or why things are the way they are—and all too often turn out even worse. Nowhere in Porter's canon is the bottomless pitfall of American Puritanical self-reliance better illustrated, however, than in the story of Miranda Gay, the protagonist of the two short novels that, together, compose what is undoubtedly Porter's most enduring literary achievement, *Old Mortality*, and her masterpiece, *Pale Horse, Pale Rider*.

Generally thought of as Porter's alter ego, the youthful Miranda must battle for self-identity against the romantic legend of her high spirited Aunt Amy, who had lived fast and died young; the sexism rampant in a wartime economy that needs young women to take on traditionally male jobs as long as they do not become too uppity or forget to be feminine; and her love for Adam, a vibrantly healthy young officer's candidate who is all male, and as in love with her as she is with him. As headstrong as headstrong can be (in an Amy-like revolt against the disciplines of her Catholic girlhood, Miranda had quit school in order to elope, or vice versa, much to her father's dismay), she weathers the storms of self-defining self-determination well enough, surviving Cousin Eva's deconstructing the legend of Amy into a rather tawdry affair, the jingoism of war bond salesmen, and her inability to be as hard-boiled a reporter as her male colleagues expect her to be. Clearly, Miranda will not betray either self or her gender.

But self is not enough in Porter's universe, and when a new antagonist, the Flu Epidemic of 1918, enters the picture, Miranda's already limited resources are sorely tested. She survives but learns, upon her recovery, that Adam had succumbed to the virulence. "What do you think I came back for, Adam, to be deceived like this?" she thinks of this unexpected betrayal (p. 317). Despite a stoical acceptance on her part, we must imagine that her sacrifice, bereft of any overarching spiritual significance, will become grist for some future romantic legend, to be deconstructed by some later Cousin Eva. It is in such hollow victories and shallow defeats as these that virtually all Porter's protagonists find their most apt and enduring accommodations with an experience that is bare and unadorned largely because of the lack of a belief in something greater than self. For the Catholic faith, which Porter hints at through her references, is ei-

ther absent from the lives of, or has been consciously abandoned by, her protagonists. Indeed, it is especially in Catholicism's absence as an active element
in her protagonists' lives that their remnant links to the Catholic faith are able
to underscore most effectively those same protagonists' very isolation from any
self-sustaining spiritual overview.

## SURVEY OF CRITICISM

Porter has attracted critical attention virtually from the start of her literary
career. During the heyday of Modernism, her meticulous craftsmanship in fictions that expanded the Impressionist aesthetics of the likes of Henry James
drew the attention of Ivor Winters, Edmund Wilson, Allen Tate, and Cleanth
Brooks. By the early 1940s, Robert Penn Warren had placed her in the company of such other modern masters of the short story as James Joyce, Katherine Mansfield, Sherwood Anderson, and Ernest Hemingway (Warren, p. 93),
and the earliest full-length treatments of her work, such as Harry John Mooney, Jr.'s *The Fiction and Criticism of Katherine Anne Porter* (1957, 1962),
placed her themes and techniques within a Modernist context.

More recently, particularly as Women's and Gender Studies programs have
become broadly established in the academy, Porter has also become a suitable
subject for the increasing critical inquiry into particularly feminine views of human experience. Jane Krause DeMouy, in *Katherine Anne Porter's Women*
(1983), is one of the first to ask us to recognize Porter's fiction as one which
chronicles "particularly how women were affected psychologically by attitudes
in their society and by other women they encountered" (p. 5).

For the most part, criticism has treated Porter's Catholicism as a somewhat
tangential matter. Although a convert, until the 1950s Porter had passed herself off as a Catholic from birth, and so, while some general attention has been
paid to how her faith may or may not be revealed in her fiction, the focus has
been more on Porter's personal views of Catholicism as she expressed them in
her letters and interviews, rather than on how its tenets inform her fiction.

As early as 1969, George Core and Lodwick Hartley, in their introduction
to *Katherine Anne Porter: A Critical Symposium*, observed that while "the effect of her early training in the Catholic Church is rarely obtrusive in her writ-
ing, it is everywhere a felt presence" (p. xv). Likewise, Robert H. Brinkmeyer,
Jr.'s 1993 study, *Katherine Anne Porter's Artistic Development*, concludes that
Porter is "clearly less interested in the institutional role of the [Catholic]
Church than she is in the power and beauty of its great thinkers," particularly
Augustine and Aquinas, and he goes on to observe that even that interest is altered for the worse by her fears of a Fascist-Catholic alliance during World War
II (p. 195). This view is seconded by Janis P. Stout in her 1995 study, *Kather-
ine Anne Porter: A Sense of Time*, wherein she argues that Porter's view of Catholicism "varies" throughout her lifetime (pp. 160–61). James T. F. Tanner,
in *Katherine Anne Porter and Texas Writers* (1990), weighs in with a similarly

dismissive approach when he considers Porter's interest in Catholicism not to be a spiritual or religious one but rather one based on "the aesthetic and cultural connotations of the Roman Catholic faith" (p. 159), in contrast with the "mush" of the fundamentalist Christianity of her childhood (p. 25). Thomas F. Walsh, in *Katherine Anne Porter and Mexico* (1992), goes as far as to comment on the "anti-Christian bias" of her early fiction (p. 34) and even imagines that Porter had very likely "rejected Christian dogma and probably religion itself before coming to Mexico" (p. 18).

Nevertheless, M. M. Liberman, in *Katherine Anne Porter's Fiction* (1971), makes an attempt to understand Porter's Catholicism by focusing on Thomist elements in her fiction. Thus, he can cast Miranda's anti-heroic heroism in wholly Catholic terms: "Miss Porter will hope, without hope, that God will make his appearance to justify the supposition that life has a meaning; meanwhile what choice has one but to proceed" (pp. 50–51). And in her biography of the author, *Katherine Anne Porter: A Life*, Joan Givner argues that despite certain ambivalences, Porter "never regretted her decision to convert to Catholicism and said at the end of her life that no other religion had ever attracted her" (pp. 101–2).

## NOTE

1. All references to the texts of Porter's fiction are from *The Collected Stories of Katherine Anne Porter*. 1965. New York: Harcourt, Brace, 1979.

## BIBLIOGRAPHY

### Works by Katherine Anne Porter

*Flowering Judas and Other Stories*. 1930. New York: Harcourt, Brace, 1935.
*Pale Horse, Pale Rider*. 1939. New York: Harcourt, Brace, 1990.
*The Leaning Tower and Other Stories*. New York: Harcourt, Brace, 1944.
*The Days Before*. New York: Harcourt, Brace, 1952.
*The Old Order*. New York: Harcourt, Brace, & World, 1955.
*Ship of Fools*. Boston: Little, Brown, 1962.
*The Collected Stories of Katherine Anne Porter*. 1965. New York: Harcourt, Brace, 1979.
*The Collected Essays and Occasional Writings of Katherine Anne Porter*. New York: Seymour Lawrence/Delacorte Press, 1970.
*The Never-Ending Wrong*. Boston: Atlantic-Little, Brown, 1977.

### Works about Katherine Anne Porter

Brinkmeyer, Robert H., Jr. *Katherine Anne Porter's Artistic Development: Primitivism, Traditionalism, and Totalitarianism*. Baton Rouge: Louisiana State University Press, 1993.

Core, George, and Lodwick Hartley. *Katherine Anne Porter: A Critical Symposium.* Athens: University of Georgia Press, 1969.

Givner, Joan. *Katherine Anne Porter: A Life.* New York: Simon and Schuster, 1982.

DeMouy, Jane Krause. *Katherine Anne Porter's Women: The Eye of Her Fiction.* Austin: University of Texas Press, 1983.

Liberman, M. M. *Katherine Anne Porter's Fiction.* Detroit: Wayne State University Press, 1971.

Mooney, Harry John, Jr. *The Fiction and Criticism of Katherine Anne Porter.* Pittsburgh: University of Pittsburgh Press, 1957. Rev. ed. 1962.

Stout, Janis P. *Katherine Anne Porter: A Sense of Time.* Charlottesville: University Press of Virginia, 1995.

Tanner, James T. F. *Katherine Anne Porter and Texas Writers.* Texas Writers Series, No. 3. Denton: University of North Texas Press, 1990.

Walsh, Thomas F. *Katherine Anne Porter and Mexico: The Illusion of Eden.* Austin: University of Texas Press, 1992.

Warren, Robert Penn. "Irony with a Center." *Katherine Anne Porter: A Collection of Critical Essays.* Ed. Robert Penn Warren. Englewood Cliffs, New Jersey: Prentice-Hall, 1979. 93–108.

RUSSELL ELLIOTT MURPHY

# ADELAIDE ANNE PROCTER
# (1825–1864)

## BIOGRAPHY

Born in London on October 30, 1825, Adelaide Anne Procter was the eldest child of Bryan Waller Procter ("Barry Cornwall") and Anne Skepper Procter. A precocious child, she had the advantage of living in a home frequented by William Wordsworth, Charles Dickens, William Thackeray, Frances Kemble, and Mary Howitt. Dickens wrote that before she could read she carried about like a doll a little book of favorite poems her mother copied for her ("Adelaide," p. 740).

Educated entirely at home, Adelaide learned French, German, and Italian, as well as mathematics and the required "lady like" pursuits of piano playing and painting. Her great love, however, was writing poetry. In 1843, at the age of eighteen, she contributed her first poem to *The Book of Beauty*. Ten years later, when Dickens was editing the magazine *Household Words*, she began submitting poetry under the pseudonym of Miss Mary Berwick, reasoning she wanted no unfair advantage over other contributors simply because she was a friend. Dickens was delighted with her work and tried repeatedly to discover her true identity. Only after he had praised her while dining one evening with the Procters did he learn the truth. It has been calculated that a full sixth of the entire output in Dickens's magazine was Procter's work. She also contributed to other periodicals. Many of her poems, notably "The Lost Chord," were set to music and used as Catholic and Protestant hymns.

Procter and two of her sisters converted to Catholicism in 1851. Their aunt, Emily de Viry, who was a Catholic, may have influenced their decision. Converting was an act of bravery for the three women since it occurred at a time of heightened anti-Catholic feeling in England. All published accounts agree, however, that their decision had no ill effect on the household.

Although she never married and lived at home her whole life, Procter demonstrated an independence of spirit through her intellectual and philanthropic endeavors. She belonged to the Langham Place circle, a group of women who met periodically to listen to and encourage each other's work. She also was a member of the Portfolio Club. In 1853, she traveled to Italy for an extended visit with her aunt, Emily de Viry, during which she studied the area closely.

Procter's concern about the socioeconomic condition of women and children was evident when she became secretary of the Society for Promoting the Employment of Women in 1859. After Emily Faithfull founded the experimental Victoria Press which employed women in all phases of production, Procter was asked to edit a special collection, *The Victoria Regia* (1861), a showcase of contemporary writers. She also wrote *A Chaplet of Verses* (1862) to support the Providence Row Night Refuge, the first Roman Catholic shelter established in England solely for homeless women and children.

Procter's busy life exacerbated the tuberculosis from which she suffered. A trip to Malvern to regain her health was unsuccessful. After returning home she spent fifteen months in bed. She died on February 2, 1864, at the age of thirty-nine.


## MAJOR THEMES

The power of prayer is a recurrent theme in Procter's poetry. "A Legend" (*A Chaplet of Verses*, p. 108), for example, contrasts the difference between the pompous monk's vain preaching and the humble monk's sincere prayers. The narrator of "Per Pacem ad Lucem" [Through Peace to the Light], one of the poems set to music, does not wish for a "pleasant road" but rather for Christ to lead her through all life's troubles to a final peace (pp. 106–7). The soldier in "The Warrior to His Dead Bride" admits his strength has come from his lady's prayers. Her continued intercession for him in heaven has removed his grief and filled him with a hitherto unknown peace (*Complete Works*, pp. 303–4).

The Virgin Mary also figures heavily in Procter's religious poetry. Sister Angela, the "fallen woman" in "A Legend of Provence," is seduced by the wounded knight she has been assigned to nurse. He takes her away from the convent, then abandons her. As the half-dead Angela returns to the convent, she is met by the Virgin who reveals she has taken the young nun's place for the entire time she has been absent (*Complete Works*, pp. 204–16). Mary is also the central figure in a number of poems in *A Chaplet of Verses*. The speaker of "Ora Pro Me" [Pray for Me] calls upon her as a helper and guide in times of trial (pp. 49–50). "The Annunciation" retells the biblical story of how Mary was informed she would be the mother of God (pp. 26–28). In "Threefold," Mary is presented with three gifts, the Past, the Present, and the Future (pp. 45–46). And "The Names of Our Lady" attempts to define all the euphemisms attributed to Mary (pp. 14–17).

Procter did not hesitate to include politics in her religious poetry. "The Church in 1849" describes the anti-Catholic sentiment common in England at the time (*Chaplet of Verses*, p. 51). "The Jubilee of 1850" is a prayer that Catholicism will be restored to England (pp. 33–35). "An Appeal" asks that England not strip Ireland of her Catholicism. The speaker chastises the English for systematically denying the Irish food and shelter and begs that their only remaining possession, their religion, not be wrenched away as well (pp. 29–32). Perhaps Procter's finest politico-religious poem is "Homeless." Here she points out that England's animals, criminals, and material wealth are all cared for, while the poor, whom she compares to Lazarus lying outside the rich man's door, go without adequate food and shelter (pp. 125–26).

## SURVEY OF CRITICISM

Charles Dickens was the first to recognize Adelaide Anne Procter's poetic talent. He published over fifty of her poems in his *Household Words*. After her death, he wrote an encomium about her life and works that would later be used as the preface of a volume of collected verse. He praised her fiercely independent nature, sense of humor, and lack of paranoiac poetic introspection ("Adelaide," pp. 742–43). *The English Woman's Journal* also made her one of its chief poetic contributors (Armstrong, p. 472). The *Journal's* obituary paid tribute to Procter's theory that poets were no less responsible for the obligations of daily life than others: "She would argue that if poetic genius really did unfit its owners for the practical business of life, then its possession was a misfortune, and poets ought to be classed with cripples and other helpless or deficient beings" (quoted in Armstrong, p. 472).

Procter's popularity extended to Queen Victoria herself. For many years, in fact, Procter's only rival was Tennyson (Crawford, p. 334). Up until World War I, her books were constantly reprinted. Literary historians point out that Procter's themes appealed to middle-class sympathies. For example, the Victorians venerated motherhood, and Procter's "Links with Heaven" (*Victoria Regia*, pp. 335–36) was guaranteed to tug at the heartstrings of any woman who had lost a child.

Critics are divided over the quality of her work. Her contemporaries were likely to see the sweet sentiment expected of a female poet of the time, completely overlooking her feminist leanings. Writing in 1883, Eric Robertson noted that her conversion to Catholicism "perhaps prejudiced many who had early admired her writings" (p. 226), but he added that a "nun-like" charm was evident in her poetry (p. 226). Of her post-conversion texts, critic H. J. Gibbs noted, "though her special views of religion are not obtruded in her works, a generally devout tone, deep admiration for Christian heroism, devotion, and self-abnegation are conspicuously manifest in her subsequent writings" (p. 360). One reviewer, although faulting several texts in *Legends and Lyrics* (1858), nevertheless concluded, "The number of Miss Procter's poems, however, which attain to a positive degree of merit, is quite large enough to give her book a pleasant tone, and to render it an agreeable addition to the stock of modern poetry" (*North American Review*, p. 255). Still others deem Procter's narrative poetry as some of her finest work. In fact, Ward and Waller in *The Cambridge History of English Literature* favorably compare her skill in verse narrative to that of William Morris (p. 198).

Procter's most overtly Catholic volume, *A Chaplet of Verses*, has produced a less favorable response. An 1862 *Athenaeum* reviewer chastised her for making this collection "so exclusively Papistical" (p. 781). Contemporary critic Susan Drain concurs that the book is "the repository of her worst verse, showing all the sentimental excesses of the Roman Catholic convert" (p. 234).

Despite such mixed reception, Procter has lately attracted the notice of feminist theoreticians. Angela Leighton, for example, uses "The Legend of Provence" to discuss the Victorian female imagination (p. 351). Generally, however, her work awaits a definitive examination.

## BIBLIOGRAPHY

### Works by Adelaide Anne Procter

*Legends and Lyrics.* First Series. London: Bell and Daldy, 1858.
*Legends and Lyrics.* Second Series. London: Bell and Daldy, 1861.
*The Victoria Regia.* Ed. and contributor. London: Victoria Press, 1861.
*A Chaplet of Verses.* London: Longman, Green, 1862.
*The Poems of Adelaide A. Procter.* Boston: Ticknor and Fields, 1863.
*The Complete Works of Adelaide A. Procter.* London: Bell, 1905.

### Works about Adelaide Anne Procter

Armstrong, Isobel, et al., eds. *Nineteenth-Century Women Poets: An Oxford Anthology.* Oxford: Clarendon Press, 1996. 471–90.
Crawford, Anne, et al., eds. *The Europa Biographical Dictionary of British Women.* Detroit: Gale, 1983. 333–34.
Dickens, Charles. "Adelaide Anne Procter." *Atlantic Monthly* 10 (July–December 1865): 739–43.
Drain, Susan. "Adelaide Anne Procter." *Dictionary of Literary Biography: Victorian Poets Before 1850.* Ed. William Fredeman and Ira Nadel. Vol. 32. Detroit: Gale, 1984. 232–35.
Gibbs, H. J. "Adelaide Anne Procter." *The Poets and the Poetry of the Nineteenth Century: Joanna Baillie to Jean Ingelow.* Ed. Alfred H. Miles. London: Routledge, 1891. 359–76.
Herbermann, Charles, et al., eds. *The Catholic Encyclopedia.* New York: Encyclopedia Press, 1911. 450–51.
Hickok, Kathleen, and Natalie Joy Woodall. "Adelaide Anne Procter." *An Encyclopedia of British Women Writers.* 1988. Ed. Paul and June Schlueter. Rev. ed. New Brunswick, New Jersey: Rutgers University Press, 1998. 519–20.
Leighton, Angela. "'Because Men Made the Laws': The Fallen Woman and the Woman Poet." *New Feminist Discourses.* Ed. Isobel Armstrong. London: Routledge, 1992. 342–60.
Rev. of *A Chaplet of Verses.* *Athenaeum* 1807 (14 June 1862): 781–82.
Rev. of *Legends and Lyrics.* *North American Review* 88 (1859): 255.

Robertson, Eric. *English Poetesses. A Series of Critical Biographies and Illustrative Extracts.* London: Cassell, 1883.

Rogal, Samuel J. *Sisters of Sacred Song: A Selected Listing of Women Hymnodists in Great Britain and America.* New York: Garland, 1981. 62.

Ward, Adolphus W. and Alfred R. Waller, eds. *The Cambridge History of English Literature.* Vol. 13. New York: Macmillan, 1932. 198.

NATALIE JOY WOODALL

# ANTONIA PULCI
## (1452–1501)

## BIOGRAPHY

The playwright Antonia Pulci was born in 1452, most likely in Florence, to Jacopa de Roma and Francesco d'Antonio Tanini. Antonia was one of nine children. She received a classical and religious education and was familiar with the works of Petrarch and Dante. At eighteen she married Bernardo Pulci, whose brother Luigi wrote *Il Morgante*, a heroic poem based on thirteenth-century chivalrous sources. Both Antonia and Bernardo wrote sacred dramas for popular performances. The marriage produced no children, and Antonia helped care for her relatives. She dedicated her life to literature, religion, and the composition of sacred dramas. She eventually became an Augustinian tertiary. After her husband's death in 1488, she established an Augustinian convent, Santa Maria della Misericordia, in Florence. Pulci was evidently ill for several months before she died at the end of September 1501.

## MAJOR THEMES

At least four works (*sacre rappresentazioni,* or sacred plays) are directly attributable to Antonia Pulci: *The Prodigal Son* (date unknown), *The Play of St. Guglielma* (c.1500), *The Play of St. Domitilla* (1483), and *The Play of St. Francis* (date unknown). In their 1996 edition of English translations of Pulci's plays, *Florentine Drama for Convent and Festival*, James Wyatt Cook and Barbara Collier Cook include several other plays that may be Pulci's: *The Play of Saint Anthony Abbot, The Play of Saint Theodora,* and *The Play and Festival of Rosana and the Second Part of the Festival of Ulimentus and Rosana.* As is customary for the genre, Pulci drew her plots from the Old Testament and hagiography. While in medieval religious drama, narrative interests prevailed over character depiction and dramatic conflict, Pulci's plays focus on characters at crucial stages in their lives. Her saints are portrayed very realistically and humanly. Their petty foibles are not dismissed, and Pulci shows how their individual choices affect others in their families or communities. Pulci also added topical and contemporary flavor through lively dialog and references to contemporary events, which added life to the performances. The use of elaborate scenery and singing and dancing also rounded out the productions.

Pulci's plays are based on the lives of saints and biblical characters, and her concerns with women's life choices are especially reflected in her plays based on the lives of female saints. At a time when women were expected to be passive and submissive, Pulci portrays female saints and secular women as strong protagonists. Her holy heroines are energetic, articulate, persuasive, and able to debate both sides of a question. The main themes of Pulci's sacred plays are the triumph of faith over adversity and persecution, and the virtues of obedience and chastity. Although her *sacre rappresentazioni* are didactic in their aim, they focus on issues relevant to her contemporary culture. Her plays concerning the lives of female saints promote and celebrate celibacy and virginity as preferable states for women over marriage.

Pulci's plays reflect her personal experiences and her own concerns. *The Play of St. Domitilla* examines women's choice in fifteenth-century Italy: marriage to her "lord" or to "The Lord." Women could live socially acceptable lives in marriage or in a convent, but not outside either. Because women were excluded from other institutions that would lend them power and legitimacy, the convent was a viable alternative. Allowing women to choose the convent provided them with agency in a world in which males were in control. The choice between marriage or life as a consecrated virgin in the convent faced virtually every woman in Renaissance Italy. Both ways of life required submission to authority, but the convent offered a freedom of sorts, and for learned women provided them with an acceptable context in which to continue their studies. This choice had been an issue in Pulci's own life, although her marriage seems to have been a companionable one.

Pulci's dramatic vehicles educated her audience about the lives of several early Christian saints, but Pulci did not always choose the obvious stories recorded in hagiographies. *The Play of St. Francis*, for example, focuses on Francis of Assisi's relationship to his parents and his community rather than on the more dramatic aspects of his life, such as his receiving the stigmata. *The Play of St. Guglielma* explores the issue of parental obedience, since the saint's parents force her to marry the King of Hungary against Guglielma's wish to remain chaste. In fact, although she herself was childless, Pulci often includes domestic and child-raising issues in the plots of her sacred plays. She explores with empathy the challenge of raising children and the grief parents suffer when their children do not turn out as they expected.

While humanists of the sixteenth and seventeenth centuries throughout Europe defined women's participation in culture and her limited roles in public life, through her plays Pulci engaged in the discourse on women's roles through representations of the social institutions in which women lived and positioned themselves in their society. Her plays also allowed her to enter the contemporary debate between humanists and clerics over the use of pagan culture as a support for Christian morality, as, for example, the dialogue in *St. Domitilla* bears out.

*The Play of St. Guglielma* deals with lust, violence, rape, and the gender and power issues that connect them, while celebrating the saint's virtue and the redeeming quality of Christian faith. Ordered by her parents to marry the King of Hungary, St. Guglielma remains behind for the good of the kingdom when the King joins the Crusades. She proves to be a wise politician and a just ruler. But she becomes an immediate temptation to her brother-in-law, who loses no time in seducing her. Guglielma refuses his advances and keeps silent to avoid a political scandal. When the King returns, the brother-in-law shifts the blame to Guglielma. Without hearing her side of the story, the King condemns his new wife to death. Guglielma's executioner, however, is moved by her piety and her prayers to God and the Virgin Mary, and he sets her free. In the desert, Mary appears to Guglielma; two angels in disguise then lead her to a port where they leave her under the care of a pious captain. Guglielma heals the captain's sick men, and eventually joins a monastery where she continues to heal others, including her perfidious brother-in-law who has been cursed with leprosy. Finally, she also forgives her husband, who renounces his kingdom to live a holy life with his saintly wife.

Perhaps Pulci's first play, *The Play of St. Domitilla* lays bare what marriage meant for a young woman and forcefully argues against it, recommending the life of a professed nun instead. The play extols the superiority of chastity over marriage, and provides solid arguments against the disconcerting changes marriage brings to a woman: "To every pleasure of his, transform your life," it cautions (1, pp. 141–44). The play's plot derives from Jacobus de Voragine's collection of saints' lives, *The Golden Legend*. Basing her work on de Voragine's writing about the male saints Nereus and Achilleus, Pulci shifts the focus to their female convert, Domitilla, the niece of the Emperor Domitian who was notorious for his persecution of Christians during his reign (A.D. 81–96). In the play, the emperor has given his niece in marriage to Aurelian, one of his barons. But Domitilla defends her virginity and represents it as a precious commodity, the one thing a woman inherits at birth and can choose to keep. The dialogue lists arguments against marriage: the possibility of a husband's infidelity, physical abuse, and angry outbursts; the pain of childbirth; the sorrow of giving birth to handicapped children; and the risk of death in childbirth. But unlike the grim picture of earthly husbands presented in this list, the heavenly Lord is extolled as a compassionate and just spouse. Pulci emphasizes Domitilla's strength of character in seeing her decision to remain a virgin through. Not only does she remain unmoved in the face of reasoned arguments to the contrary, but she has the power to convert others to Christianity and convince them that this passing world is false and that Christ is the eternal, loving spouse.

The success and popularity of Pulci's writings can be attributed to her powerful and simple style combined with dramatic structure. Fifteenth-century Italian women humanists wrote in classical languages, but women poets wrote in the vernacular. Religious drama consisted of poetry in *ottava rima* (hendecasyllable meter in octave stanzas) written in the vernacular. In addition, popular literature of the day was written in the vernacular following a program promoted by the humanist Leon Batista Alberti and patron of the arts Lorenzo de'Medici. Its aims were to dignify Italian nonclassical literature, to promote the Italian language, and to upgrade popular genres such as medieval religious drama whose productions were presided over by lay guilds. The literary level of these much-attended productions rose thanks to writers like Antonia Pulci, her husband Bernardo, and Lorenzo de'Medici. Pulci's simple yet eloquent style, her good sense of dramatic structure, and her adaptation of hagiographic and biblical sources to include contemporary issues contributed to her success.

In the context of political order and institutionalized authority, *sacre rappresentazioni* persuade, inform, engage, and entertain. Works based on the lives of women saints show these women as powerful, eloquent, persuasive, and influential. In these plays' original audiences were certainly women about to make the decision between marriage and convent life, as well as women who already belonged to religious communities and needed reaffirmation that their choice had been the correct one. Pulci's distinguishing trait was her ability to humanize divine intervention and to emphasize the fact that morality's rewards are not exclusively found in heaven but also in this life. Among other contributions, Pulci helped imbue this popular genre with wit and humor, adroit word play, and keen psychological insights.

## SURVEY OF CRITICISM

Criticism concerning Pulci's work is limited. This is true in Italian letters and especially so in English. Alessandro D'Ancona was the first modern critic to recognize Pulci's importance, and he included her *St. Guglielma* in his 1872 edition of mystery plays. In 1885, Francesco Torraca mentions Pulci's name along with the Pulci brothers, Luigi and Luca; Lorenzo de'Medici; and Renaissance poet Angelo Ambrogini (Poliziano) for their contributions to vernacular poetry. Antonia Pulci is also noted in Francesco Flamini's article about her husband written in 1888, "La vita e le opere di Bernardo Pulci"; in this article, he states that her work is deemed worthy of being included with other principal authors of mystery plays.

Despite the scant critical reception and lack of commentary on her work, the longevity and popularity of Pulci's plays speak for themselves. Many copies of the plays, which were repeatedly staged in the fifteenth and sixteenth centuries, were found in several Tuscan libraries. While the popularity of their performances peaked in the mid–fifteenth century, the plays themselves continued to be read for the next three hundred years. There were at least twelve editions of *St. Domitilla* between 1500 and 1648, and twenty-five editions of *St. Guglielma* in the sixteenth and seventeenth centuries.

In modern criticism, James Wyatt Cook and Barbara Collier Cook's anthology contains the only English translations so far of Pulci's plays. The Cooks remain faithful to Pulci's Italian, foregoing rhyme to focus on the overall themes. Their introduction, "Antonia Pulci and Her Plays: The Other Voice, the Nobler Deed, the Womanly Concern," helps situate the playwright within the larger literary picture of fifteenth-century Florence. They also provide a list of secondary works on Pulci and suggestions for further reading. Not all scholars agree that Antonia Pulci was the author of all the plays the Cooks attribute to her in their anthology.

Rinaldina Russell's brief entry on Pulci in *An Encyclopedia of Continental Women Writers* provides a basic biography of the author. In Russell's later volume, *Italian Women Writers*, Bernard Toscani's entry on Pulci reiterates her scant biography but also includes several thorough analyses of her plays, a summary of her themes, a survey of criticism, and other useful materials. Unsure of Pulci's death year, Toscani claims Pulci was the daughter of Francesco Gianotti. However, in her 1999 review of the Cooks' collection of Pulci's plays, Elissa Weaver corrects Toscani's biographical errors. According to Weaver, who studied the Florentine tax records of the period, Pulci's father was actually Francesco d'Antonio Tanini, her dates are 1452–1501, and, evidently ill, she drew up two wills, one in July of 1501 and one in September of 1501. Weaver's work continues to help fill in the many gaps and correct the misinformation about Pulci's life.

Not directly related to Pulci's life or writing but providing interesting contextual studies are the Winstead and Schulenburg books listed in the bibliography. Winstead's work on virgin martyrs discusses how the monastic legends of female saints were transformed in late medieval England. She offers an interesting section about what she terms "The Generic Virgin Martyr." In addition, her explanation of Jacobus de Voragine and the popularity of his collection *Legenda aurea* [The Golden Legend] is good background reading for how this work influenced other writers, including most likely Pulci herself. Finally, Schulenburg's book provides an important source on the history of the cult of early women saints, pointing out how virginity, or *integritas,* was considered an essential prerequisite for a Christian life.

## BIBLIOGRAPHY

### Work by Antonia Pulci

Cook, James Wyatt, and Barbara Collier Cook, eds. *Florentine Drama for Convent and Festival.* Chicago: University of Chicago Press, 1996.

**Works about Antonia Pulci**

D'Ancona, Alessandro. *Le origine del teatro italiano.* Second edition. 2 vols. Turin: Loescher, 1891.

——. ed. *Sacre rappresentazioni dei secoli XIV, XV e XVI.* Florence: Le Monnier, 1872.

Flamini, Francesco. "La vita e le opere di Bernardo Pulci." *Il Propugnatore* n.s. 1 (1888): 224–48.

Jordan, Constance. "Listening to the 'Other Voice' in Early Modern Europe." *Renaissance Quarterly* 1 (Spring 1998): 184–92.

Matter, Ann E., and John Coakley. *Creative Women in Medieval and Early Modern Italy: A Religious and Artistic Renaissance.* Philadelphia: University of Pennsylvania Press, 1994.

Newbigin, Nerida. *Nuovo 'corpus' de sacre rappresentazioni fiorentine del Quattrocento.* Bologna: Commisione per i testi di lingua, 1983.

Russell, Rinaldina. "Antonia Pulci." *An Encyclopedia of Continental Women Writers.* Ed. Katharina Wilson. New York: Garland, 1991. 1018–19.

Shulenburg, Jane Tibbets. *Forgetful of Their Sex: Female Sanctity and Society, ca. 500–1100.* Chicago: University of Chicago Press, 1998.

Torraca, Francesco. *Il teatro italiano dei secoli XIII, XIV, XV.* Florence: Sansoni, 1885.

Toscani, Bernard. "Antonia Pulci." *Italian Women Writers: A Bio-Bibliographical Sourcebook.* Ed. Rinaldina Russell. Westport, Connecticut: Greenwood Press, 1994. 344–52.

de Voragine, Jacobus. *The Golden Legend: Readings on the Saints.* 2 vols. Trans. William Granger Ryan. Princeton, New Jersey: Princeton University Press, 1993.

Weaver, Elissa B. "Antonia Pulci: Florentine Drama for Convent and Festival: Seven Sacred Plays, trans. James Wyatt Cook." *Speculum* 74 (January 1999): 474–76.

Winstead, Karen A. *Virgin Martyrs: Legends of Sainthood in Late Medieval England.* Ithaca: Cornell University Press, 1997.

ROSEANNA M. MUELLER

# CHRISTINA ROSSETTI
## (1830–1894)

## BIOGRAPHY

Born in London to an Italian expatriate father, Gabriele Rossetti, and Frances Mary Lavinia Polidori, a devout Anglican of Italian ancestry, Christina Rossetti is one of the great Victorian poets. She came from a literary family: her brother Dante Gabriel Rossetti was a famous painter and poet; her other brother William was a respected critic; her sister Maria, an Anglican nun, wrote a highly regarded essay on Dante; her father and maternal grandfather were both translators and scholars; and her uncle, Dr. John Polidori, was Lord Byron's physician and the author of *The Vampyre*. She was especially close to her mother and wrote her first poem in 1842, when she was eleven, for her mother's birthday. Rossetti's maternal grandfather, Gaetano Polidori, encouraged her poetry writing from the time she was a child and privately printed her first small volume of poems, *Verses: Dedicated to Her Mother* (1847).

As a child, Rossetti was exuberant and outgoing, and she had a bad temper. During her teen years she transformed herself into a reserved and self-effacing adult. At twelve years old, she became a member of the Tractarian parish of Christ Church, Albany Street, and was strongly influenced by Tractarian teachings. Tractarians were adherents to the principles of the Oxford Movement, which began in the 1830s. A reaction against secular encroachments on the authority and power of the Anglican Church, the Oxford Movement called for a return to the faith of the early Christians, emphasized the sacredness of the apostolic succession, and sought to reform Anglican worship along more Catholic lines. In 1845, one of the most respected leaders of the Oxford Movement, John Henry Newman, converted to Roman Catholicism, inspiring many High Church members to follow him. These events resulted in a huge national scandal, and throughout the 1840s, the danger of conversion to Catholicism was a topic that was debated with increasing antagonism.

These events affected the life of the young Christina Rossetti in a number of ways. In 1848 she became engaged to James Collinson, but she broke off the engagement when he converted to Roman Catholicism. He gave up his new faith and they resumed their plans to marry, but in 1850—the year the Roman Catholic Church was re-established in England—Collinson re-converted to Roman Catholicism, and this time their engagement was canceled for good. Although her Italian father, Gabriele Rossetti, was anti-Catholic and hated the papacy for political reasons, her maternal grandparents had a successful inter-faith marriage: her grandfather Gaetano Polidori (also Italian-born) was a non-practicing Catholic, and his wife, formerly Anna Maria Pierce, was an Anglican Englishwoman. They raised their daughters—including Rossetti's mother, Frances—as Anglicans, and their sons as Catholics. As for Rossetti herself, her brother William said that she saw Roman Catholics as "authentic members of the Church of Christ, although in error upon some points" (quoted in Marsh, p. 91). One wonders whether she would have objected to marrying Collinson had it not been for the turbulence surrounding Catholicism and issues of conversion at that moment in Victorian culture. Jan Marsh speculates in her biography that during this crisis, Rossetti may have suffered from the question of whether she should follow her fiancé into the Roman Catholic Church (pp. 113–14). But Rossetti remained a devout Anglican her entire life, and she never married. Her later relationship with Charles Bagot Cayley was also affected by religious differences. Although she did not marry Cayley because of his atheism, they remained good friends until his death in 1883.

Rossetti suffered from poor health throughout most of her life. In 1871 she was diagnosed with Graves disease, a thyroid disorder. She died of cancer in London on December 29, 1894. After her death, Rossetti was lauded by one contemporary admirer as a "sweet lady, and poet, and saint"—a view that many of her readers would have shared (Lootens, p. 158).

Although Rossetti wrote several popular volumes of devotional prose from the late 1870s until her death, her primary passion throughout her life was the writing of poetry. *Goblin Market and Other Poems* (1862) was her first major publication. The title poem tells the story of Laura and Lizzie, two young sisters who are tempted by a sinister bevy of goblin men who offer them myriad luscious fruits. When Laura yields and eats their fruit, she begins to die; Lizzie performs an act of self-sacrifice and obtains an antidote that saves and completely restores her fallen sister. Many of Rossetti's poems employ such fairy-tale settings along with irregular or nursery rhyme meter to convey an essentially religious message. *Goblin Market* was followed by *The Prince's Progress and Other Poems* (1866) and *Sing-Song: A Nursery Rhyme Book* (1872). A collected edition of her works, *Goblin Market, the Prince's Progress and Other Poems*, was published in 1875.

Rossetti's fourteen sonnet sequence, "Monna Innominata," appeared in *A Pageant and Other Poems* in 1881. Inspired partially by Elizabeth Barrett Browning's *Sonnets from the Portuguese*, Rossetti characterized this series of love poems as ones that Barrett Browning might have written had she been unhappy instead of happy. The sonnets are narrated by a *donna innominata* (nameless lady) to her beloved. This figure may be a real man (Rossetti's brother William believed the sonnets were addressed to Charles Cayley, who proposed to Rossetti but was turned down); or, following Rossetti's consistent use of religious analogy, these sonnets, which explore the many-sidedness of love, may be addressed to God.

Editions of Rossetti's poems were reprinted many times during her lifetime. Her devotional texts are mainly meditative works on the scriptures and aids to reflection and prayer. These include *Annus Domini: A Prayer for Each Day of the Year, Founded on a Text of Holy Scripture* (1874), *Seek and Find: A Double Series of Short Studies of the Benedicte* (1879), *Called to Be Saints: The Minor Festivals Devotionally Studied* (1881), *Letter and Spirit: Notes on the Commandments* (1883), *Time Flies: A Reading Diary* (1885), and *The Face of the Deep: A Devotional Commentary on the Apocalypse* (1892). These works were read by a large and devoted audience.

## MAJOR THEMES

Rossetti's poetry and prose are replete with themes of transience, the deceptive allure of the material world, loss, resignation, betrayal, the afterlife, and temptation. She believed profoundly in the need for, and the efficacy of, Christian charity in the postlapsarian world. Indeed, charity—especially sisterly charity, such as that exemplified by Lizzie toward Laura in "Goblin Market"—is one of the most prevalent themes in her canon. Rossetti has often been characterized as a religious recluse; but even though she lived a contemplative, almost clerical life, she was actively engaged in the details of the world around her. In fact, her writings reveal a sharp, observant, resilient character and an incisive wit. A lover of nature and animals, she was always drawn to the small and seemingly insignificant elements and creatures of God's creation. Her poems were carefully crafted and revised, and yet they retain their mystical force. Intensely attracted to the material world and its sensual pleasures, she was nevertheless suspicious of its enticements; her poetry and devotional works continually look ahead to the rest and consolations of the next world.

Rossetti's Catholic influences derive primarily from her Tractarianism. The doctrines and cultural practices of the Oxford Movement shaped her religion and her art, particularly, as Mary Arseneau and others have pointed out, in her belief in and extensive uses of sacramentalism and incarnationalism. Arseneau explains,

The Tractarians saw the incarnation as the vital core of the Church, its sacraments, and God's plan for humanity's redemption. In addition to this intense incarnationalism, the Tractarians were known for their sacramentalism, a term which refers both to their reverence for the sacraments of the Church and to the broader concept of their awareness of the transcendent as sacramentally and analogically present in the material world and in human life. ("Incarnation and Interpretation," p. 80)

Rossetti believed that Christ's Incarnation—God becoming man, the Word being made flesh—gave objects in the material world spiritual meaning. But an earthly object—a particular flower, stone, or bird—can convey a spiritual message only if a person is looking for evidence of God's creation rather than for mere sensual satisfaction. Elements in nature are symbols of God's presence and divine plan; for the understanding Christian, therefore, all objects in the world have a sacramental value. We find this principle operating in almost all of Rossetti's poems: her Tractarian aesthetics are especially strong in "Charity," "Consider," "Amor Mundi," "A Rose Plant in Jericho," "Endure Hardness," "There is a budding morrow in midnight," and "Symbols." In the 1849 "Symbols," for example, the speaker is waiting for a perfect rose to bloom and for a nest of bird's eggs to hatch, but both fail to happen. In her anger, she crushes the branch and the eggs. These destroyed elements of nature then speak, reproaching her for her violence and teaching her that, in God's eyes, she likewise fails to achieve her potential: "And what if God, / Who waiteth for thy fruits in vain, / Should also take the rod?" (lines 22–24; *Poems and Prose*, pp. 18–19). Finally, Tractarian sacramentalism is at the core of the meaning of "Goblin Market." Lizzie is wise enough to recognize the sacramental and saving power of the very fruits that lead to her sister's fall. After the goblins attack Lizzie, the juices from their fruits, now smeared all over her battered body, represent her own loving sacrifice, and she can use these juices to save her sister.

In many ways, Rossetti exemplifies the fascinating contradictions and tensions inherent in Victorian Anglo-Catholic identity. She was not a Ritualist, one who supported the use of incense, candles, vestments, and other Catholic-inspired ceremonial trappings and rituals in the Anglican service. But her Anglo-Catholicism was distinctive, and even radical, especially in her emphasis on both the joys and the temptations of the material world. On the one hand, she celebrated the lushness of God's creation; on the other hand, she lived an ascetic lifestyle, which her brother William characterized as "puritan[ical]" (quoted in Battiscombe, p. 32). Rossetti was also extreme, and particularly Catholic-leaning, in the importance she placed on the veneration of saints and martyrs, especially in her prose works *Called to Be Saints* (1881) and *Time Flies* (1885). Many Victorians viewed glorifying and praying to the saints as "Romish" and idolatrous, but in *Called to Be Saints*, Rossetti defends this devotional practice: "[L]est any one in reading what I write should condemn me as dwelling too prominently on the servant in lieu of the Master . . . [o]r if one say, 'Was Paul crucified for you?' I answer that I desire to follow St. Paul not otherwise than as he bade us thus follow Christ" (Kent and Stanwood, p. 248).

Finally, Rossetti's interest in Anglican sisterhoods also accords with her Catholic sympathies. Although she did not become an Anglican nun like her sister Maria, whom she revered, Rossetti did work with prostitutes and other female outcasts at the St. Mary Magdalene Home for Fallen Women at Highgate Hill. Her work as a poet and writer of devotional texts was for her a kind of religious vocation. Although it is unlikely that Rossetti ever seriously considered conversion to Roman Catholicism, like many Tractarians she desired the unity of the universal Church and regretted the rift between the Church of England and the Church of Rome. She describes her idea of Catholicism:

It seems that to grasp, hold fast, adore the Catholic Mystery leads up to man's obligation to grasp, hold fast, adore the Christian Mystery; rather than this to the other. What is Catholic underlies what is Christian: on the Catholic basis alone can the Christian structure be raised; even while to raise the superstructure on that foundation is the bounden duty of every soul within reach of the full Divine Revelation. (*Letter and Spirit*, pp. 8–9)

As P. G. Stanwood explains in "Christina Rossetti's Devotional Prose," Rossetti believed in " 'the Catholic religion' . . . which teaches the unity and trinity of the Godhead" (p. 240). Rossetti considered herself to be a Catholic, just not a *Roman* Catholic.

## SURVEY OF CRITICISM

Rossetti has been associated primarily with two Victorian aesthetics: Pre-Raphaelitism and Tractarianism. Members of an artistic movement founded by Rossetti's brother Dante Gabriel in 1848, the Pre-Raphaelites filled their canvases and poems with highly wrought detail and often employed medieval and religious themes and symbols. For many years Rossetti was regarded merely as a minor Pre-Raphaelite poet, and her brother's reputation preceded hers. But in the last two decades, Christina Rossetti has moved to the center of the nineteenth-century poetic canon, mainly due to reassessments by feminist literary critics and by critics who recognize the influence of Tractarian aesthetics on her work.

The text by Rossetti that has attracted the most critical attention is the title poem of *Goblin Market and Other Poems* (1862). Angela Leighton observes that in "Goblin Market" Rossetti "treads a breathtakingly thin line between nursery rhyme, sexual fantasy, religious allegory and social criticism" (p. 135). Critics have held widely differing views about this poem, reading it variously "as an allegory of the origin of evil, a psychological study of a split personality, an exploration of conflict in the soul of an artist, and a lesbian tract" (Spivack, p. 53). "Goblin Market" is especially notable in terms of Rossetti's Anglo-Catholicism because the culmination of the poem is Lizzie's Christlike eucharistic ritual, in which she offers her body as a vehicle for her sister's redemption. The poem dramatizes the saving power of Holy Communion. As Arseneau points out in "Incarnation and Interpretation," even when Rossetti's poems do not appear to be explicitly devotional, they contain religious meaning (p. 80). Moreover, Anthony H. Harrison has argued that Rossetti's Anglo-Catholic religious sensibility was not incompatible with, and in fact fostered, the "feminist subversiveness of her writing" ("Christina Rossetti and the Sage Discourse," p. 95).

Little has been written about Rossetti in relation to Roman Catholicism, but Harrison and Arseneau have done considerable work on the specifically Anglo-Catholic themes in her writings. P. G. Stanwood's essay, "Christina Rossetti's Devotional Prose," is an excellent introduction to its subject; for more on the key Christian and Anglo-Catholic tenets in Rossetti's devotional prose, see Kent and Stanwood's *Selected Prose of Christina Rossetti.* Diane D'Amico focuses on issues of religious faith and gender in Rossetti. Her article "Eve, Mary, and Mary Magdalene: Christina Rossetti's Feminine Triptych" is a good starting point for readers interested in the ways in which Rossetti both draws on and challenges the typology of Eve and traditional representations of women in Christianity.

## BIBLIOGRAPHY

### Works by Christina Rossetti

*Letter and Spirit: Notes on the Commandments.* London: Society for Promoting Christian Knowledge, 1883.

*The Complete Poems of Christina Rossetti: A Variorum Edition.* Ed. R. W. Crump. 3 vols. Baton Rouge: Louisiana State University Press, 1979–1990.

*Christina Rossetti: Poems and Prose.* Ed. Jan Marsh. London: Everyman, 1994.

*Selected Prose of Christina Rossetti.* Ed. David A. Kent and P. G. Stanwood. New York: St. Martin's Press, 1998.

### Works about Christina Rossetti

Arseneau, Mary. "Incarnation and Interpretation: Christina Rossetti, the Oxford Movement, and *Goblin Market.*" *Victorian Poetry* 31.1 (Spring 1993): 79–93.

Arseneau, Mary, Antony H. Harrison, and Lorraine Janzen Kooistra, eds. *The Culture of Christina Rossetti: Female Poetics and Victorian Contexts.* Athens: Ohio University Press, 1999.

Battiscombe, Georgina. *Christina Rossetti: A Divided Life.* London: Constable, 1981.

Carpenter, Mary Wilson. "'Eat me, drink me, love me': The Consumable Female Body in Christina Rossetti's *Goblin Market.*" *Victorian Poetry* 29.4 (Winter 1991): 415–34.

D'Amico, Diane. "Eve, Mary, and Mary Magdalene: Christina Rossetti's Feminine Triptych." *The Achievement of Christina Rossetti.* Ed. David A. Kent. Ithaca: Cornell University Press, 1987. 175–91.

Harrison, Antony H. "Christina Rossetti and the Sage Discourse of Feminist High Anglicanism." *Victorian Sages and Cultural Discourse: Renegotiating Gender and Power.* Ed. Thaïs E. Morgan. New Brunswick, New Jersey: Rutgers University Press, 1990. 87–104.

——. *Christina Rossetti in Context*. Chapel Hill: University of North Carolina Press, 1988.

Kent, David A., ed. *The Achievement of Christina Rossetti*. Ithaca, New York: Cornell University Press, 1987.

Leighton, Angela. *Victorian Women Poets: Writing Against the Heart*. Hemel Hempstead: Harvester Wheatsheaf, 1992. 118–63.

Lootens, Tricia A. "Competing Sainthoods, Competing Saints: The Canonization of Christina Rossetti." *Lost Saints: Silence, Gender, and Victorian Literary Canonization*. Charlottesville: University Press of Virginia, 1996. 158–82.

Marsh, Jan. *Christina Rossetti: A Literary Biography*. London: J. Cape, 1994; New York: Penguin, 1995.

Spivack, Charlotte. "'The Hidden World Below': Victorian Women Fantasy Poets." *The Poetic Fantastic: Studies in an Evolving Genre*. Ed. Patrick D. Murphy and Hyles Vernon Ross. Westport, Connecticut: Greenwood Press, 1989. 53–64.

Stanwood, P. G. "Christina Rossetti's Devotional Prose." *The Achievement of Christina Rossetti*. Ed. David A. Kent. Ithaca, New York: Cornell University Press, 1987. 231–47.

KATHLEEN VEJVODA

# MARY ANNE SADLIER
# (1820–1903)

## BIOGRAPHY

Because her mother died early, Mary Anne Madden was raised mostly by her father, Frances Madden, a well-to-do merchant in the Irish midlands. At eighteen, with her father's encouragement, she began to publish poetry. After her father's death in 1844, twenty-four year old Mary Anne moved to Montreal where she worked at various odd jobs before marrying James Sadlier in 1846. Sadlier was the manager and owner of the Canadian branch of the Catholic publishing company founded by himself and his brother Denis, D. & J. Sadlier Company. The company eventually became the largest Catholic publishing house in America after buying the backlist of fellow Irish American publisher John Doyle. During the fourteen years that the Sadliers spent in Montreal, Mary Anne raised six children and began her career as a novelist and essayist. By the time the family moved to New York City in 1860, Sadlier was the best known Irish Catholic writer in America.

After her husband's death in 1869, Sadlier returned to Montreal to live with her married children. Toward the end of her life, she was undermined by her nephew, William, who took control of the publishing company and the copyrights to her works. Yet friends came to the rescue with monetary support and recommendations. Sadlier also spent time founding and endowing several charities in the 1870s: the Home for the Aged, the Foundling Asylum, and the Home for Friendless Girls. In 1895, Notre Dame University awarded her the Laetare Medal for literature, and in 1902, she received a "special blessing" from Pope Leo XIII in recognition of her "illustrious service to the Catholic Church" (Lacombe, p. 105). She died in 1903 at the age of eighty-three and is buried beside her husband, James, in Calvary Cemetery, Woodside, Long Island.

## MAJOR THEMES

Sadlier was a prolific writer of sentimental and didactic romances, many of which promote Irish Catholicism in Protestant North America. Several novels detail the struggles of Irish immigrants, while others are Irish historical romances. Her ten historical novels were popular with her nostalgic Irish immigrant readers, particularly the one that concerns the Great Famine, *New Lights; or, Life in Galway* (1853). Although the novel takes place during the starving decade of the 1840s, it does not describe the effects of the famine in any great detail. Yet it does angrily depict the traveling Protestants who offered soup to starving Catholics in exchange for conversion. The story focuses on the Catholic Bernard O'Daly family, and in the historical romance tradition, there are two pivotal scenes: one in which Bernard's wife, Honor, dies, and the other in which the family is evicted. The eviction could have been prevented if O'Daly had converted, but he refuses. Two of O'Daly's sons immigrate to Philadelphia in search of work and money to help prevent the eviction, but they are too late. The money they do earn, however, helps care for O'Daly in his forced retirement.

*New Lights* illuminates several of Sadlier's key themes in her other Irish American novels: the pull of Catholicism against the strength of invidious Protestantism, and the idealized portrait of the suffering mother. The novel also illustrates a key moral issue for Sadlier: the need for women to have a proper work ethic. In the novel, Mrs. O'Daly's house is clean and well-kept despite the poverty of the family, whereas the Gallagher daughters play the piano and speak French but refuse to do housework. Thus, Victorian virtues of work and cleanliness find their way into Sadlier's Catholic moral sensibilities.

Two of her immigrant novels, *The Blakes and the Flanagans: A Tale Illustrative of Irish Life in the United States* (1850) and *Bessy Conway; or, The Irish Girl in America* (1861), best illustrate another of Sadlier's recurring themes: the dangers of immigration for Irish Catholics. Indeed, in nearly all of her works, the worst sin a character can commit is to relinquish one's religion or culture. Along with her publisher husband, Sadlier shrewdly marketed her books to Catholic working-class immigrants, the audience she desired to reach.

Like her contemporary Harriet Beecher Stowe, Sadlier "claimed to be working not for fame but for God and country—in this case the Catholic faith and the Irish nation in America," but she was rewarded with fame nonetheless (Lacombe, p. 101). Her literary fame in America began when her first immigrant novel, *Willy Burke; or, The Irish Orphan in America*, was printed in the popular Catholic magazine *The Pilot* in 1850, and subsequently published as a book. In her preface, she clearly identifies the didactic goal of her immigrant fiction: "[This book is] written for the express purpose of being useful to the young sons of my native land, in their arduous struggle with the tempter" (p. 3).

*The Blakes and the Flanagans*, Sadlier's most popular novel, depicts one of the central issues in Irish American politics in 1850, the so-called "schools question." Irish Catholics objected to the Protestant-controlled public school system and set out to create a separate Catholic system. In the novel, the idealized, "good" Catholic Flanagan family finds success in America as a result of their piety: their children attend Catholic schools. The Blakes, on the other hand, send their children to the public schools, and, as a result, the children reject both their parents and their religion in their attempt to assimilate: thus the Blakes are justly punished for their betrayal of Catholicism. In Sadlier's works, religion is more important than other values, such as assimilation or economic and social success. And in her novels, Sadlier's women characters are charged with the Victorian role of religious and moral guardians. Thus it is not surprising that it is Sadlier's women characters, such as the pitiful Mrs. Blake, and not the men, who first recognize the evil influence of the public schools.

Sadlier was quite blunt in her desire to reinforce the Catholic values of her mostly immigrant readership. In her preface to *The Blakes and the Flanagans,* she writes,

Reader, there is a moral contained in this story, and you will not read far till you find it out. It relates to a subject of all others the most important, and, if read with that attention which men usually give to momentous affairs, it cannot fail to make a salutary impression. The world is, and I believe has ever been, divided into two great classes, believers and unbelievers: the children of the one true Church, and the children of the world. It is needless to say that all my writings are dedicated to the one great object; the illustration of our holy faith, by means of tales or stories. The drama of these in general, and of this one in particular, is taken from every day life. The world around us is full of Blakes and Flanagans. (p. 1)

The novel also explicitly notes that the virtue of working does not mean, for good Catholics, that money is the sole object. Mr. Blake is criticized for spending more time earning money than watching over his family. Sadlier particularly feared that social mobility in America threatened what she saw as the impermeable safety nets for Irish immigrants: religion, family, and ethnicity. According to scholar Colleen McDannell, the author feared that to give up one meant to lose them all (p. 71). The Blake children learn to reject both Catholicism and all things Irish while in public school; this, in turn, destroys family ties between generations. By maintaining ethnic and religious ties, however, the Flanagan family stays intact, and they earn a comfortable living at a family-run business.

Sadlier had the same fear of the women's movement, which in her day was generating momentum, especially among Protestant women. She portrays these "feminists" as cold, unwomanly, and immoral in all of her novels: in her opinion, to promote women's rights meant to destroy the family structure where the father is the patriarch and the mother is the moral guardian. In Sadlier's world, only non-married Catholic women (like the protagonist in *Elinor Preston,* 1861) and widowed women have both social and moral power. Ironically, this was a very unrealistic expectation in the nineteenth century since a large percentage of Irish women immigrants remained unmarried and were virtually powerless.

Although Sadlier merely hints at the real-life domestic and social problems of Irish immigrants in her earlier novels (perhaps to avoid racist stereotypes), by the time she wrote *Bessy Conway*, she highlights them. Alcoholism, poverty, and spousal abuse exist within the Irish community, and in this novel they are not just viewed as punishments for Protestants and lapsed Catholics. Here, Sadlier takes the more typical American stance of blaming the individual rather than the circumstances. The novel depicts the tale of hard-working Bessy who refuses to convert to Protestantism in order to save her job, and who is rewarded at the end with a return to Ireland and with a pocket full of money. "Keep your girls at home!" she warns her Irish neighbors (p. 296). However, the rest of the novel's characters do not fare so well. One cousin becomes an alcoholic and wife beater; his sister-in-law marries a fool who leaves her to care for a crippled daughter; and another character is eventually killed by her abusive husband, and their son is adopted by Protestants who turn him against Catholicism. Meanwhile, pious Bessy has returned to Ireland in time to save her family from eviction and so impresses the landlord's son that he converts to marry her. The self-sacrificing religious woman, who manages to avoid the negative effects of immigration, is rewarded at the end, in this world and, implicitly, in the next.

## SURVEY OF CRITICISM

Charles Fanning is one of the few literary critics today who has rediscovered the works of Sadlier in his ongoing attempt to define an Irish American literary tradition. In *Exiles in Erin*, he classifies nineteenth-century Irish American fiction into three "literary generations": pre-Famine, Famine immigrants, and the children of Famine immigrants (p. 3). Sadlier is of the Famine generation, those authors who wrote didactic, melodramatic novels that shared ways with their fellow immigrants of surviving in the new world. Fanning calls Sadlier "the most prolific and influential of the Famine generation's writers" (p. 100). And this feeling was shared by some of her contemporaries. In 1850, Catholic convert Orestes Brownson, editor of the *Quarterly Review*, suggested that someone should write a moral tale about the trials of life of an Irish or Catholic orphan. Patrick Donahue, the editor of the Catholic journal *The Pilot*, immediately offered a fifty dollar prize plus publication of the piece to whomever met this challenge. The winner, as judged by Brownson, was Mary Anne Sadlier for her book *Willy Burke; or, The Irish Orphan in America*. However, upon the publication of *The Blakes and the Flanagans*, Brownson's opinion of Sadlier weakened: he thought the novel "too" Irish and not Catholic enough, and he worried that its anti-assimilationist message was too strong (Fanning, *Irish Voice*, p. 26).

Fanning criticizes Sadlier as a cold, judgmental propagandist, a sort of Dr. Laura for the Irish immigrants, who praises those who sacrifice themselves for others and condemns those whose life choices do not meet her strict moral standards (*Irish Voice*, p. 140). Most twentieth-century critics also dismiss Sadlier as overly sentimental and didactic, only useful for sociological and historical insights. However, critic Liz Szabo disagrees in part: she sees Sadlier's works as quite complex and not at all sentimental. To her, the novels negatively depict the process of assimilation for most Irish Catholic immigrants.

## BIBLIOGRAPHY

### Works by Mary Anne Sadlier

*Willy Burke; or, The Irish Orphan in America*. Boston: Donahoe, 1850.
*New Lights; or, Life in Galway, A Tale*. New York: Sadlier, 1853.
*The Blakes and the Flanagans: A Tale Illustrative of Irish Life in the United States*. Dublin: Duffy, 1855; New York: P. J. Kennedy, 1855.
*Elinor Preston; or, Scenes at Home and Abroad*. New York: Sadlier, 1861.
*Bessy Conway; or, The Irish Girl in America*. New York: Sadlier, 1862.
*Confessions of an Apostate; or, Leaves from a Troubled Life*. New York: Sadlier, 1864.
*Con O'Regan; or, Emigrant Life in the New World*. New York: Sadlier, 1864.

### Works about Mary Anne Sadlier

Diner, Hasia R. *Erin's Daughters in America: Irish Immigrant Women in the Nineteenth Century*. Baltimore: Johns Hopkins University Press, 1983.
Fanning, Charles, ed. *The Exiles of Erin: Nineteenth-Century Irish-American Fiction*. Notre Dame, Indiana: University of Notre Dame Press, 1987. Second ed. Chester Springs, Pennsylvania: Dufour Editions, Inc., 1997.
——. *The Irish Voice in America: Irish-American Fiction from the 1760s to the 1980s*. Lexington: University Press of Kentucky, 1990.
Lacombe, Michèle. "Frying Pans and Deadlier Weapons: The Immigrant Novels of Mary Anne Sadlier." *Essays on Canadian Writing* 29 (Summer 1984): 96–116.
McDannell, Colleen. *The Christian Home in Victorian America, 1840–1900*. Bloomington: Indiana University Press, 1986.
——. "'The Devil Was the First Protestant': Gender and Intolerance in Catholic Fiction." *U. S. Catholic Historian* 8 (1989): 51–65.
Szabo, Liz. "'My Heart Bleeds to Tell It': Women, Domesticity and the American Ideal in Mary Anne Sadlier's 'Romance of Irish Immigration.'" *Religions of the United States in Practice*. Ed. Colleen McDannell. Princeton, New Jersey: Princeton University Press, forthcoming.

STACEY DONOHUE

# Dorothy L. Sayers
## (1893–1957)

### BIOGRAPHY

Dorothy Leigh Sayers was born in 1893 in Oxford to the Anglican Reverend Henry Sayers and his wife, Helen Mary, both of whom were educated, highly literate, and, by Dorothy's account, caring and solicitous parents. The majority of Sayers's childhood was spent with her parents in East Anglia, where she received a private education at the hands of her father and a governess. By her early teens, she was writing and performing plays and experimenting with writing poetry in a variety of verse forms. She was sent to boarding school in 1908, where she cultivated a love of languages, music, literature, and drama. Entering Sommerville College at Oxford in 1912 and concluding her studies in 1915, she enjoyed a lively social and academic experience, participating in dramatic and choral productions, and evincing a strong enthusiasm for German and French.

After unsuccessfully attempting to train as a nurse, Sayers accepted a post as schoolmistress in Hull, at the same time writing poetry that was published by *Oxford Magazine*. During her summer vacations, she worked on translating the *Chanson de Roland* into rhymed couplets (eventually published in 1957). In 1917, Sayers's father arranged a position for her as an apprentice to the publisher Basil Blackwell, and the following year she published her collection of poems, *Catholic Tales and Christian Songs*. At this time, Sayers fell in love with Captain Eric Whelpton, and in 1919, she accepted his invitation to work as his assistant at a boarding school in Normandy. When Whelpton gave up his position, Sayers returned to England and was in the first group of women to be formally invested with a B.A. and an M.A. at Oxford in 1920. Taking a copywriting position at an advertising firm, Benson's, in 1922, Sayers also began to work on her novels, producing such famous Peter Wimsey detective stories as *Whose Body* (1922), *Clouds of Witness* (1926), *The Five Red Herrings* (1931), *Murder Must Advertise* (1932), *Gaudy Night* (1935), and *Busman's Honeymoon* (1937). In 1930, Sayers introduced the character of Harriet Vane into her Wimsey novels, an independent, original, and witty heroine often seen as a reflection of Sayers's own character. After a failed relationship with the highbrow novelist John Cournos, Sayers became pregnant with the child of Bill White, a motorcyclist and car salesman. Abandoned by White and frightened of the effect the news would have on her family and friends, Sayers kept the birth of John Anthony in 1924 a secret from all, with the exception of her cousin Ivy Shrimpton, who agreed to raise the boy. Eventually, Sayers told her journalist husband, Atherton Fleming ("Mac"), whom she married in 1926, but he refused to adopt Dorothy's son until later in their marriage, and John Anthony grew up apart from his mother, knowing her only as the visiting "Cousin Dorothy" and later as his adoptive mother.

At the same time as she pursued her successful career in detective fiction, Sayers devoted herself to more scholarly interests; she published a complete translation of *Tristan* in 1929, was appointed president of the Modern Language Association in 1938, and gave lectures on such diverse topics as metrical form and detective fiction. At the invitation of author Charles Williams, Sayers wrote the Christian drama *The Zeal of Thy House* (1937). After the successful performance, Sayers became known as a "religious" as well as literary figure, and she took an increasing interest in Christian dogma. In 1939, she wrote a letter to the *Times* urging that churches be kept open during the war. Upon invitation from the publisher Victor Gollancz, she wrote a Christmas message for the nation, and she consistently urged and embodied active social responsibility. In 1940 and 1941, she produced her two most important Christian works, *The Mind of the Maker* and the drama *The Man Born to Be King*. The Church Assembly asked her advice about religious drama, the Archbishop offered her the Lambeth Degree of Doctor of Divinity (which she declined), and she helped to establish the Guild of Catholic Writers. In addition, she was the only woman to speak at a conference in 1941 to discuss the role of the Church in social reconstruction after the war.

Increasingly disillusioned with various political pressures in the Anglican Church and uncomfortable with the public perception of herself as a theological authority, Sayers wished to distance herself from such organized constitutions and resolved in 1943 to back away from writing on explicitly religious subjects. She concentrated on translating Dante's *Divine Comedy*, seeing in it the potential for a successful channeling of her theological, creative, and scholarly interests. But she also went on to produce two more religious plays, *The Just Vengeance* (1946) and *The Emperor Constantine* (1951), both of which focus on the formulation of the Nicene Creed. She died suddenly in 1957. The remaining third of Sayers's translation of Dante's *Paradiso* was completed by Barbara Reynolds in 1962.

Although she never converted to Roman Catholicism, Sayers strongly sympathized with many of its tenets. Despite being an admirer of the "bravery" of converts, Sayers preferred to remain in the Anglican faith into which she was baptized by her father, but corresponded and sympathized in great measure

with Anglo-Catholic and Roman Catholic members of the clergy, most particularly the Reverend Patrick McLaughlin, with whom she ran St. Anne's House
as a Centre of Christian Discourse on and off after the war.


## MAJOR THEMES

The themes of Sayers's early detective fiction concern independence and
creativity of thought; the latter theme came to greater prominence in her later
overtly religious works. Although she greatly admired the prose and fiction of
G. K. Chesterton, Sayers did not impart a distinctly religious ethic to her detective stories, preferring instead to offer subtle explorations of the nature of
good and evil within a primarily entertaining fictional context. In her play *The
Devil to Pay* (1939), Sayers most fully explored this question of good and evil.
Toward the end of her novelistic career, Sayers increasingly emphasized the
importance of work to the individual and to society, and the importance of
equality and mutual appreciation in human relationships. This was effectively
emphasized in her detective fiction's depiction of the relationship between
Wimsey, who matures socially and intellectually, and her independent, clever
heroine Harriet Vane. But Sayers eventually abandoned the detective fiction
form after the psychologically involved *Gaudy Night* and *Busman's Honeymoon,* arguing that moral problems could not be solved simplistically, and
should not be represented as such in fiction.

This close connection between creativity, morality, and eventually theology
became Sayers's primary concern in her later works, and it was in her religious
dramas, translations, short essays, and *The Mind of the Maker* that she most explicitly defined her various concerns. With her series of radio plays, Sayers embodied in art what she continually asserted in her personal writings, that is, the
dramatic nature of Christian dogma. These assertions had already been published in the *Sunday Times* in 1938 as "The Greatest Drama Ever Staged Is the
Official Creed of Christendom" and "The Dogma Is the Drama" (both collected in *The Whimsical Christian*). Influenced by the writings and plays of T.
S. Eliot in particular, Sayers recognized the potential for creative and religious
expression in drama, emphasizing the importance of accessibility and lucidity.
Asserting that the dogma of the Incarnation was the most important and dramatic element of Christianity, Sayers diligently (and controversially) sought to
make the drama of Christ's life and Incarnation as realistic and therefore accessible as possible. Her work emphasized realistic dramatic presentation and language, while at the same time decidedly avoiding the reduction of biblical
events to staged historical fact.

Often commended by theologians for her "accurate" and thorough representation of dogmatic truth, Sayers claimed such goals to be less her aim than
imparting a social relevance to the moral truths inherent in Christianity. In *The
Man Born to Be King*, for example, Sayers shows the kingdom of God conflicting with earthly ideas of government, and thereby implies the need for social

reform as well as for religious awareness. Throughout her writings, Sayers denounces menial, mechanical labor, objecting that it is only through creativity that men and women can truly discover themselves and God, and thereby contribute positively to society. Sayers did not attempt to provide a platform of social reform, however, and chose instead to emphasize the importance of reflecting an awareness of the beauty and singularity of humanity in all forms of government and social interaction.

Sayers greatly appreciated G. K. Chesterton, C. S. Lewis, and Charles Williams not only for their opinions on religion, but also for the ways in which they rendered moral concerns accessible and enjoyable through fiction, poetry, and prose. This perceived ideal is most clearly realized in *The Mind of the Maker*, in which Sayers offers a clear explanation (rather than "proof") of the doctrine of the Trinity. In discussing the three parts of the Trinity, Sayers asserts that all are aspects of one creative act. In stating this, Sayers addresses the presence of the Trinity in creative writers, isolating the way in which some, despite a wonderful original plan, have no skill with which to execute that plan, while others have the technique without any plan worth realizing. Sayers uses the process of creating art as a metaphor for the Trinity, and in so doing clearly delineates her own artistic and religious ideals and demonstrates a way in which religious truths can be tested by artistic practice and experience. To Sayers, since the human creative process mirrors the Trinity, humans are most fulfilled and godlike when they are actively creating. Again, this theme is closely related to the emphasis in her detective novels on the importance of individual freedom and responsibility.

Throughout her life, Sayers, despite her interest in dogma and theological concerns, felt herself distanced from the organized structure of the Church. Arguing that she was unable to come to God naturally through intuition, emotion, or service, Sayers asserted that the only way in which she could do so was through the intellect. In her writings, she not only expressed but manifested the importance of creativity and intellectual energy in the realization of moral and religious truths.

## SURVEY OF CRITICISM

The first major (and authorized) biography of Sayers is that of James Brabazon; through the use of letters, unpublished manuscripts, and comments from acquaintances, it provides a portrait of Sayers without much literary discussion. This is also characteristic of Barbara Reynolds's more recent (1993) work, which nonetheless provides more insight into the context in which some of Sayers's works were produced. Perhaps the most successful literary survey of Sayers's writing is provided by Ralph Hone. Catherine Kenney provides a thorough assessment of Sayers's primary contributions to literature and culture and is one of the few authors to give considerable attention to Sayers's concern with the position of the modern woman. This concern is also emphasized by Alzina Stone Dale.

Contemporary reviews of Sayers's religious dramas and essays on religious issues provide insight into the intellectual and social context in which Sayers was working. The Hannay collection offers papers on such topics as Sayers and Wilkie Collins, Christian aesthetics in Sayers's dramas, good and evil as themes in the detective novels, and the importance of Harriet Vane as an influence in Sayers's novelistic development. Most recently, John Thurmer's collection of essays on Sayers's Christian thought has provided a much-needed contemporary examination of Sayers's theology, while the collection of essays edited by Christopher Dean and presented to Sayers specialist Barbara Reynolds contains contributions from leading Sayers scholars on such various themes as the author's personal qualities, her work as a translator, her drama, and her spirituality. Finally, Janice Brown's recent study provides a more precise theological study of Sayers's work, focusing on how the seven deadly sins appear in the detective novels.

## BIBLIOGRAPHY

### Works by Dorothy L. Sayers

*Catholic Tales and Christian Songs.* Oxford: Blackwell, 1918.
*Gaudy Night.* London: Gollancz, 1935.
*Busman's Honeymoon.* London: Gollancz, 1937.
*The Zeal of Thy House.* London: Gollancz, 1937.
*The Devil to Pay.* London: Gollancz, 1939.
*The Mind of the Maker.* London: Methuen, 1941.
*The Man Born to Be King: A Play-Cycle on the Life of Our Lord and Saviour Jesus Christ.* London: Gollancz, 1943.
"Are Women Human?" *Unpopular Opinions,* by Dorothy Sayers. London: Gollancz, 1946. 106–16.
"Making Sense of the Universe: An Address Given at the Kingsway Hallon Ash Wednesday March 6th 1946." Pamphlet. London: Claridge, Lewis and Jordan, 1946.
*The Just Vengeance.* London: Gollancz, 1946.
*The Comedy of Dante Aligheri: The Florentine: Cantica I: Hell.* Middlesex: Penguin, 1949.
*The Emperor Constantine: A Chronicle.* London: Gollancz, 1951.
*The Comedy of Dante Aligheri The Florentine: Cantica II: Purgatory.* Middlesex: Penguin, 1955.
"Christian Belief about Heaven and Hell." *London Sunday Times* 16 January 1958: 8.
*The Comedy of Dante Aligheri The Florentine: Cantica III: Paradise.* With Barbara Reynolds. Middlesex: Penguin, 1962.
*The Whimsical Christian: Eighteen Essays by Dorothy L. Sayers.* New York: Macmillan, 1978.

### Works about Dorothy L. Sayers

Basney, Lionel. "God and Peter Wimsey." *Christianity Today* 17 (1973): 27–28.

Brabazon, James. *Dorothy L. Sayers: A Biography.* New York: Scribners, 1981.

Brown, Janice. *The Seven Deadly Sins in the Work of Dorothy L. Sayers.* Kent, Ohio: Kent State University Press, 1998.

Dale, Alzina Stone. *Maker and Craftsman: The Story of Dorothy L. Sayers.* Wheaton: Harold Shaw Publishers, 1978. Rev. ed. 1992.

Dean, Christopher, ed. *Studies in Sayers: Essays Presented to Dr. Barbara Reynolds on Her 80th Birthday.* West Sussex: smallprint, 1994.

Gilbert, Colleen B. *A Bibliography of the Works of Dorothy L. Sayers.* Hamden: Archon, 1978.

Hannay, Margaret P., ed. *As Her Whimsey Took Her.* Kent, Ohio: Kent State University Press, 1979.

Hone, Ralph E. *Dorothy L. Sayers: A Literary Biography.* Kent, Ohio: Kent State University Press, 1979.

Kenney, Catherine. *The Remarkable Case of Dorothy L. Sayers.* Kent, Ohio: Kent State University Press, 1990.

Lewis, C. S. Rev. of *The Mind of the Maker*, by Dorothy L. Sayers. *Theology* 43 (October 1941): 248–49.

Reynolds, Barbara. *Dorothy L. Sayers: Her Life and Soul.* London: Hodder and Stoughton, 1993.

——. *The Passionate Intellect: Dorothy L. Sayers's Encounter with Dante.* Kent, Ohio: Kent State University Press, 1989.

Thurmer, John A. *Reluctant Evangelist: Papers on the Christian Thought of Dorothy L. Sayers.* West Sussex: smallprint, 1996.

IRENE MORRA

# VALERIE SAYERS
## (1952– )

---

## BIOGRAPHY

Valerie Sayers—the middle child of seven siblings, five sisters and a brother—had ample opportunity in her native town of Beaufort, South Carolina, to grow up learning about the complexities of navigating human relationships, choices, triumphs, and compromises. Influenced powerfully as a Southern Catholic woman writer by the inexorable vision and style of Flannery O'Connor—who once quipped that "the truth shall make you odd"—Sayers figured out quickly while learning her art that the challenge of Southern fiction is in rendering the grotesque, that startling convergence of willful, radical character; dark comedic drama; and the burden of history and religious tradition in the "Christ-haunted" landscape of the South, as O'Connor puts it. Predictably, then, Sayers has declared that she is "interested in pursuing people in trouble; I'm not just interested in looking at perky, well-adjusted people" (Farrell, p. 24).

Born on August 8, 1952, and raised a feisty Irish Catholic girl in the fundamentalist, Protestant South, Sayers also acquired an acute sense of what it means to be a stranger because of her anomalous religion and because of her rebellious proclivity to question the prescribed roles for women in Southern culture. As one critic notes, "[Sayers] is a Catholic, which is to say an outsider in the overwhelmingly Protestant rural South, and the characters who most clearly interest her are those whose relationship to the majority is uneasy and ambiguous" (Yardley, p. 3). In *Who Do You Love* (1991), for example, Dolores Rooney—a transplanted Catholic New Yorker in Due East, South Carolina, Sayers's fictional setting modeled after the author's low-country hometown—feels as if visitors from up north could identify her "as surely as if they wore radar and she beamed signals that said: 'Outsider. Stranger Just Like You'" (p. 6). In both published and unpublished essays, interviews, and letters, Sayers has made much of her Catholicism and regional stakes; for instance, in the typescript of a conference keynote address in Spring 1993 at Columbia College, South Carolina, Sayers writes,

I grew up in Beaufort . . . a coastal town that, like many other Southern coastal towns, has plenty of Catholics. But we were still a distinct minority, and as a child I thought this was pretty wonderful. For one thing, Catholics danced and drank and smoked cigarettes incessantly, which gave scandal and made us, or so I thought, exotic in the eyes of Protestant Beaufort. It troubled me that we did not learn chapter and verse the way Protestants did, but Catholics had a breezy, intuitive air when it came to the Bible, a reverence that focused on the general spiritual drift rather than the literal words. Catechisms, not Bibles, were meant for memorization. ("Creating Saints," p. 1)

The influence of religion and place on Sayers's life and work is distinctive. Her father, now deceased, was a psychologist at the Parris Island Marine base during Sayers's youth in Beaufort. In a May 9, 1998, interview with Charline R. McCord, Sayers has described the important formative impressions she collected there as she watched the "Yankee liberalism" (p. 137) that pervaded her family placed into sharp relief against the background of arch Southern language, customs, and topography. Her parents moved to Beaufort from New York, and they were "befuddled by the South and the manners of the South and kind of resistant to it" (p. 137). Valerie, alert and imaginative, the first of the children born in the South, quickly intuited that she "came from a family of misfits" (p. 137) and her mother "pegged" her "as the writer at a very early age" (p. 135).

Sayers left Beaufort for college in 1969, a time fraught with the tensions of civil rights activism, the so-called sexual revolution, the drug culture of the decade, and the growing power of the feminist movement, all key influences in her development as a contemporary novelist. She writes lyrically about the trip north in a paper delivered at the 1995 Modern Language Association:

1969 Beaufort County, in the South Carolina lowcountry. The West Coast Champion, on its nightly way north, pulled into the Yemassee railroad depot just after dark. . . . We lurched off into the night, leaving behind the dank rich smells that spread out over the fields and marshes of the lowcountry, leaving behind family on the platform, leaving in the locked train station that tightly strapped valise of sin, sex and segregation that was set off in the corner of the South's imagination but just waiting to be unlocked by the rest of the world. As we sped through the southern seaboard by night, we could only imagine looming outlines of cypress swamp, soft roll of tobacco fields. By daybreak we knew that the light that drenches the South would fill the trees, as they are filled in "A Good Man is Hard to Find," with "silver-white sunlight," and we knew that "the meanest of them [would] sparkl[e]." Not so easy to leave a place where the meanest trees sparkle. ("Pilgrimage," pp. 1–2)

Sayers enrolled at Fordham University at Lincoln Center with aspirations of becoming an actress. She left acting, but finished her degree and returned to the South, where she remained for a year until relocating again in New York with her husband, Christian Jara, a film producer and director.

While in New York, Sayers served as a 1992 Literature Fellow of the National Endowment for the Arts, taught at New York University, and participated in various writing circles and workshops. She disclosed humorously in a classroom conversation in Spring 1993 in Columbia, South Carolina, that "the writer's life is very difficult. . . . [In New York] everyone is severely neurotic in a city that has the largest per capita count of neurotics than anywhere. Everyone has to get in touch with his or her unconscious, and so everyone sleeps a lot. But you have to be awake, don't you? Writing has to be disciplined: every day or nothing."[1] Her own persistent craft has resulted in numerous essays, reviews, and five published novels. *My Sister Has Left Me*, her first novel, unpublished, is a brooding reflection on "women's imaginative lives" and the biblical theme of "rivalrous sisters" ("Genesis (Rebecca)," p. 47). Her current novel in progress is entitled *Cab Ride to Dixie*.

In Fall 1993, Sayers, her husband, and their two teenage sons moved from Brooklyn to South Bend, Indiana, where Sayers currently serves on the faculty of the creative writing program at the University of Notre Dame, an enclave of midwestern Catholicism hospitable to her imagination. Sayers, however, continues to write from the vantage point of the South, of quaint but complicated fictional Due East, her inescapable true home.


## MAJOR THEMES

Despite her admission of the profound legacy of Flannery O'Connor and other Southern comic writers, Sayers does not people her fiction with aberrant, grotesque characters in a background setting of rural violence, dispassionate humor, or physical and spiritual deformity. Rather, Sayers's fictional world is masked by a gilded façade of Southern respectability and seeming contentment in a more urban setting. The truth is that Sayers's characters are as displaced as O'Connor's or Walker Percy's, wandering lonely and often shocked in a confused, fallen world, seeking their own paths to redemption against a backdrop of seemingly sedate, civilized, middle-class ways. Jonathan Yardley notes that Sayers is acutely aware of the legacy of her Southern predecessors but more interested in "today's battles than yesterday's" (p. 3) since she is a writer whose cultural context has been the post-Kennedys, post-Martin Luther King, post-Vietnam, post-Watergate era, a world where the once-acute modernity of the great Southern writers of the first two-thirds of the century has lost its keen edge to complacency and cynical detachment.

Not that Sayers shies from the rigorous social analysis and psychological penetration of her forebearers or that she delivers a simple, painless narrative, for her fiction has been praised as "hard-eyed if not . . . hardhearted . . . [giving] nothing up to sentimentality" (Butler, p. 9). No complacency or cynicism here, only the gaze of a storyteller who admits modestly that while good fiction begins not "with an idea, but rather with an image or a strong sense of character or with [a dramatic] incident," she regretfully does not have "from my own work an example as vivid as Faulkner's vision of Caddy with her muddy drawers" ("Creating Saints," p. 7). What she does have, though, is a clear view of the force of Catholic sensibility that lends her an ironic sense of humor concerning nothing less than the earnest, ultimate matter of grace. She half-jokes in a letter that what she finds in Catholic comic novelists such as O'Connor, Percy, Muriel Spark, and J. F. Powers is a "reassurance" that "modern religious thought has not been entirely ceded to reactionaries" and "there are still plenty of reactionaries to battle."[2] She can do so because she is convinced that the mystery of faith is necessarily wedded to original sin, the human condition which is the half-understood discovery of the little girl in O'Connor's "A Temple of the Holy Ghost" or young Mary Faith Rapple and Kate Rooney in Sayers's novels. But such knowledge is, of course, not reserved for the young, for in *Brain Fever* (1996) a grown up Mary Faith and Tim Rooney struggle to earn the peace of emotional and spiritual accord while continually dealing with the gloom of doubt and madness, a darkness represented at the end of the novel by the blackened, grimy Holland Tunnel from Manhattan to Jersey: "We were heading home. And the weight of Tim Rooney's head was a comfort on my lap, a comfort for the moment. Even if he was a mess" (p. 308). "A comfort *for the moment. Even if* he was a mess": those are powerful and loaded conditions typical of Sayers's unsentimental fiction.

Again, the unsentimental renderings stem from Sayers's Catholic wit, astringent method, and sharp eye for realistic details of character, event, and place. Religion, for instance, is not something her characters merely "get," as a Southerner might say; it is as systemic and palpable as Dolores's prayerful memory of her dead father and the "close damp air of . . . summer press[ing] down on her" (*Who Do You Love*, p. 324), or as physical as "the smell of pine and marsh" and "home fires" when Franny has an epiphanic moment in such "gray-green" light that "You'd think the Holy Ghost was descending" (*The Distance Between Us*, p. 496). Sayers's is the tough religion of an Aquinas, Marcel, Kierkegaard, Teresa of Avila, Tolstoy, and Dostoevsky, all of whom her characters read with passion. Sayers says in a piece on the special charge of the Catholic novelist, "What is most striking about . . . American chroniclers of Catholic life . . . is their insistence on the 'hard things,' on the presence of evil and the possibility of redemption." She adds that Catholic fiction is "stark" and "fierce," definitely not like much contemporary writing, "with its detached narrative voices and its desultory ironic stances. It is, I submit, impossible to find a desultory narrative about the Church" ("When the Catholic Novelist," p. 26). Such an appraisal illuminates why Sayers's characters live up to O'Connor's comment about the "Christ-haunted" South as they struggle for spiritual rest and atonement against a world decidedly turned away from miracles and faith. But even out of the South, her troubled people wrestle with agonizing choices, like the screenwriter Michael Burke and promiscuous Franny Starkey in *The Distance Between Us* (1994), careening through a marathon of sex and drugs, a volatile marriage, and dangerous gunrunning in Ireland, and trying all the while simply to return to the comforts of home and the grace of love. In *Due East* (1987), Mary Faith Rapple, in fact, jokes that her illegitimate, unborn baby was immaculately conceived, not entirely untrue, since by the end of the novel the infant child is the pure miracle that helps bring about the potential reconciliation of Jesse Rapple (the forlorn father, crippled by the loss of his wife to cancer) and Mary (the spunky yet vulnerable fifteen year old separated from all community, longing for a moment of genuine love amidst the chaos of her young but woeful life). Grace is never easily encountered in Sayers's settings of Due East, New York, or Killorglin.

Evidently, miracle and faith are not oppressive or fundamentalist in Sayers, for they are stained, necessarily, with a deep sense of imperfection, the kind of burdensome Catholic sense of guilt that shatters a simple, dichotomous view of the world where flesh and spirit, sin and salvation, who and whom, lie flatly separated as antonyms. The latter pair comes from the grammatically flawed line *Who Do You Love*, drawn from the Bo Diddley lyrics, that give the novel its title. In the novel, Bill Rooney, Dolores's sulking, volatile, but faithful husband, squirms whenever Dolores corrects his usage. "Everything," as Bill reflects earlier, "was black and white for Dolores. . . . Dolores wanted everyone to see the world as a spiritual dichotomy" (p. 65). One of Dolores's journeys in the story, particularly because of her adultery for the second time while pregnant, is to get beyond mere irony and ambiguity in spiritual matters to actual, corporeal experience of religious dilemmas and the lingering torment of guilt—the daily physical reality, that is, of the fall. Faith and deed, then, are truly inseparable in the authentic spiritual life: flesh and spirit converge; Christ is the incarnate Word; the blood of Jesus does stain the cross; the communion wafer is not a symbol: "[N]o one with a religious inclination would ever dream of calling Christ a symbol. . . . Communion wafers—which we rightly call hosts, you see—are the body of our Lord Jesus Christ" (*Who Do You Love*, p. 259).

The seemingly ordinary lives of Sayers's characters do not mask for long the truly dysfunctional nature of the author's imaginary community. In Due East, the provincial setting of her first three published novels, and in New York, the dominant setting of her fourth and fifth novels, people wander through a maze of sin, guilt, and agony, which is disturbing and ultimately transfiguring. Sayers focuses on a cast of characters who appear normal and content in satisfied lives but who quickly discover that they crave the gift of grace. A tired, transformed Mary Faith in the last paragraph of *Brain Fever* states, "It felt good to have someone else drive the car" (p. 308).

The disparity between the safe, snug Southern landscape, especially as it touches and limits the lives of women, and the personal, domestic, and universally felt human crises that play out in her fiction forms the core of Sayers's work, a fiction of her own brand of odd, displaced persons in "territory held largely by the devil," as O'Connor once stated. Being a Catholic, a woman, a stranger, and odd are central to Sayers's fiction. Sayers knows that despair and grace, too, grow in frenetic Brooklyn and in the heart of cozy Due East, the new South of considerably amorphous boundaries and increasing heterogeneity. Sayers's characters progress from exile to redemption, but reconciliations and new lives are earned tentatively through suffering and guilt, a condition defined by the "ferocity" of her Catholic strain, which, as she notes generally about the Catholic imagination, presses her work to "an absolutely vivid insistence on matters of faith and salvation" ("When the Catholic Novelist," p. 29).

## SURVEY OF CRITICISM

Most of the criticism available on Sayers's work is in the form of book reviews. Critics agree that Sayers has a gift for unsentimentally uncovering the immense, sudden, fleeting power of grace in a disordered, fallen world. Jack Butler's comment on *Due East*, for example, represents much of the criticism on Sayers. He focuses on the novel's "texture, the density of its observation," as the characters participate in a "domestic comedy of errors" which takes them "into total confusion" until a miracle transforms their lives with "warmth, peace and affection in the midst of unrelenting woe" (p. 9). In a review of *Who Do You Love*, Howard Mosher admires Sayers's "humor and irony" in developing "family history, an unusual and fascinating setting, affecting characters . . . along with a racy, light-handed prose style" (p. 29). Jonathan Yardley adds that Sayers's predecessors are clearly William Faulkner, Eudora Welty, and especially Flannery O'Connor, pointing out that Sayers's Catholicism makes her "connection to her regional literary heritage . . . an eccentric one." Sayers's fiction, he continues, sometimes walking "a fine line between comedy and melodrama," moves us "toward a point of no return, a shock to the system that leaves almost nothing untouched or unaltered"; she offers us "imperfect people and makes us like and care about them, an essential task for any novelist" (p. 3). One might add "Catholic novelist" to his judgment. Michael Farrell's review of *The Distance Between Us* highlights Sayers's "authenticity of voice. The words are not so much imaginative fabrications as recognizable echoes of real life, untidy and uncertain" (p. 25). Moreover, his article's title itself goes to the heart of Sayers's fiction: "Sayers' Folks Stagger Toward Redemption."

In addition to such reviews, Charline R. McCord's interview with Sayers appears in a recent edition of *Southern Quarterly*, and Anita Gandolfo includes Sayers in her overview of post-Vatican II Catholic American literature.

## NOTES

1. Notes of classroom conversation taken by John Zubizarreta. Columbia College, March 23, 1993.

2. Letter from Valerie Sayers to John Zubizarreta, April 17, 1993.

## BIBLIOGRAPHY

### Works by Valerie Sayers

*Due East.* New York: Doubleday, 1987.

*How I Got Him Back; or, Under the Cold Moon's Shine.* New York: Doubleday, 1989.

"When the Catholic Novelist Portrays the Church." *Catholic Commission on Intellectual and Cultural Affairs Annual* 9 (1990): 21–32.

*Who Do You Love.* New York: Doubleday, 1991.

"Guilt and Gone with the Wind." *The Movie That Changed My Life.* Ed. David Rosenberg. New York: Viking, 1991. 89–106.

"Creating Saints." Unpublished address delivered at South Eastern Conference on Christianity and Literature, Columbia, South Carolina. 26 March 1993.

*The Distance Between Us.* New York: Doubleday, 1994.

"The Pilgrimage North." Unpublished paper delivered at the Modern Language Association Conference, Chicago. 29 December 1995.

*Brain Fever.* New York: Doubleday, 1996.

"Genesis (Rebecca) and Luke." *Communion: Contemporary Writers Reveal the Bible in Their Lives.* Ed. David Rosenberg. New York: Anchor, 1996. 39–48.

Interview with Mark Allison. "A View from Due East: An Interview with Valerie Sayers." 18 February 1998. Online posting, 22 December 1999, at http://arts.endow.gov/artforms/Lit/Sayers.html.

Interview with Charline R. McCord. 9 May 1998. *Southern Quarterly* 38.2 (Winter 2000). 135–52.

### Works about Valerie Sayers

Butler, Jack. "Mary Faith Pleads Virginity." *New York Times Book Review* 8 March 1987: 9.

Farrell, Michael J. "Sayers' Folks Stagger Toward Redemption." *National Catholic Reporter* 27 May 1994: 17+.

Gandolfo, Anita. *Testing the Faith: The New Catholic Fiction in America.* Westport, Connecticut: Greenwood Press, 1992.

Mosher, Howard Frank. "24 Hours in Due East, S.C." *New York Times Book Review* 7 April 1991: 3+.

Yardley, Jonathan. "Southern Discomforts." *Washington Post Book World* 24 February 1991: 3.

JOHN ZUBIZARRETA

# SOPHIE ROSTOPCHINE, COUNTESS DE SÉGUR (1799–1874)

## BIOGRAPHY

In 1799 Sophie Rostopchine was born into an aristocratic Russian family. Her father, Count Feodor Rostopchine, was Czar Paul I's advisor, and as governor of Moscow during the Napoleonic wars, may have given the order to burn the city in order to save it from French conquest in 1812. From this Russian Orthodox and still feudal background, Sophie was to develop into a fervent Roman Catholic, loyal to her new country, France, and concerned with the challenges of a society undergoing transformation through urbanization and class conflict.

Sophie's father was a strong figure, tender yet volatile and eccentric. Rostopchine influenced Sophie's relations to men and to authority in general, as her later writing shows respect for worthy authority figures alongside a rebellious mockery of petty defenders of order. Her mother, a strict disciplinarian who believed in Spartan habits and who withheld demonstrations of affection, was responsible for the inculcation of strong moral expectations and for Sophie's sense of the mother figure as central to the development of children.

Raised in the Russian Orthodox faith, Sophie was influenced by her mother Catherine's conversion to Roman Catholicism, an act that provoked the anger of the Czar himself and created a schism within the family. Although her father and siblings remained in the Russian Orthodox Church, Sophie converted to Catholicism at the age of seventeen.

In 1816 inquiries into Rostopchine's role in Moscow impelled him to move the family to Paris, in what the count perceived as an exile. Intelligent and lively, well educated and able to speak several languages, Sophie entered into a brilliant social circle in which religious life ranged from conventional observance of Roman Catholic practices to skepticism or agnosticism. In 1819, she married the aristocrat Eugène de Ségur, a former page of Napoleon and later an administrator for the national railways. Although the couple had eight children, the marriage was marred by the handsome Eugène's infidelities and absences and by Sophie's jealousy. In later years their relationship mellowed as Eugène became a supporter of his wife's literary career.

Politically, Sophie was acquainted with a range of conservatives and liberals. Although her works were published by the liberal Hachette press, she was nevertheless a strong admirer of Louis Veuillot, a conservative Catholic. While she left no political writings, her letters and the biographies written by her children indicate that she favored strong leadership in order to prevent the violence that had rocked France in 1789, 1830, and 1848. Initially supportive of Napoleon III, she was proud that her eldest son, Gaston, served for some time as his representative to the papal court. Her enthusiasm waned as Napoleon III's commitment to the Pope weakened and as he supported nationalist movements. An ultramontaine, Sophie believed that the authority of the Pope was greater than that of the French Church or of any secular power.

Gaston de Ségur was a significant influence on his mother's development as a Christian and as a writer. A gifted painter, he chose to devote his life to the priesthood. Initially this decision grieved Sophie, but as her own spiritual life deepened, she took guidance from her son. Gaston's career in Church diplomacy ended when he lost his eyesight. He turned to work as a prison chaplain, and his commitment to the urban poor inspired Sophie to greater identification with the marginalized. She joined a women's group associated with the Society of Saint Vincent-de-Paul, which collected money in support of Catholic workers' programs, and in 1866 she became a Third Order Franciscan and took the name Sister Marie-Françoise.

Ségur had a passion for children's education. When their father's work took her granddaughters to England, Sophie put her bedtime tales in written form and became an author at the age of fifty-five with *New Fairy Tales* (1857). Her works were quickly adopted for the series La Bibliothèque Rose Illustrée [The Illustrated Pink Library], published by Hachette. Ségur was the most successful writer of the series and the only one to remain in print to this day. At her death at the age of seventy-four, she had become known as a beloved grandmother figure to a broad readership.

## MAJOR THEMES

Ségur is best known for her twenty children's books published in the Pink Library Series. The novels combine a unique blend of realism, sentimentalism, humor, and clearly articulated religious and moral values. One trilogy (*Les Petites Filles Modèles* (1857) [The Model Little Girls]; *Les Malheurs de Sophie* (1858) [The Misfortunes of Sophie]; *Les Vacances* (1859) [The Vacation]), often referred to as the "Sophie cycle," shows an aristocratic child struggling from early youth to obey the demands of her mother, facing abuse from a stepmother, and reintegrating into a new family that reforms her troubled nature. These works have been read as psychologically compelling depictions of mother-child relations and of the socialization of a young aristocratic girl. The "General Dourakine" novels (*L'Auberge de l'Ange Gardien* (1861) [The Inn of the Guardian Angel]; *Le Général Dourakine* (1864) [General Dourakine]) broadens the perspective to depict a wider range of social classes and situations. Issues of order and authority shape these novels with the volatile General representing a sometimes arbitrary and even unjust patriarchal authority that Ségur both supports and judges. The demand that authority be based on justice and on the well-being and consent of the governed becomes a theme in later novels for an older audience; two examples are the character Jeannot, who blames his criminal activities on a corrupt and neglectful employer in *Jean qui grogne et Jean qui rit* (1865) [Jean Who Groans and Jean Who Laughs], and Charles who leads a revolt against a brutal schoolmaster in *Un Bon petit diable* (1865) [A Good Little Devil].

In Ségur's works, the true basis for justice and social unity comes from the Christian faith. Catholicism openly shapes the lives of the protagonists, particularly in the later novels. Ségur's final work, never completed, was to have been a lives of the saints for children. Yet, as Laura Kreyder has argued, it is possible to read Ségur's fictions as examples of saintly children living amidst the demands of familial and secular society. Influenced by the hagiographic tradition popular in the mid–nineteenth century, Ségur depicts child protagonists in a range of situations from working class through the aristocracy who illustrate the virtues of charity, faith, sacrifice, solidarity with the marginalized, hope, and obedience. Prayer is extolled as a source of consolation and guidance and as an expression of gratitude. Emphasis is placed on the joys of Christian life, not on concepts of sin or restriction, although the consequences of disorderly and disobedient lives are demonstrated through unrepentant characters. Biblical principles are frequently quoted, with this educative role confided to protagonists, principally children, and not to moralizing adults or the narrator. In keeping with the Catholic Church's endeavors to revitalize belief after the 1789 revolution, much emphasis is placed on catechism and first communion, with the latter often portrayed as an exceptional event, a turning point in a protagonist's life. Novels such as *François le Bossu* (1863) [The Little Hunchback] and *Pauvre Blaise* (1860) [Poor Blaise] feature dramatic moments of conversion. At a time in which religion was considered mainly the domain of women, Ségur includes strong figures of both genders and of all ages as role models in her fiction.

Ségur was highly influenced by the movement of social Catholicism typified by the Society of Saint Vincent-de-Paul, and she used her novels to argue for respect for the poor and for blacks, and for the equality of all before God. Protagonists include the son of a gatekeeper, whose integrity, kindness, and piety convert his master and his master's son (*Poor Blaise*), a physically handicapped child (*The Little Hunchback*), and a mentally impaired boy (*La Soeur de Gribouille* (1861) [Gribouille's Sister]).

Although current studies of Ségur mainly focus on her fictional works, of greater importance to Ségur herself were her works designed to help children physically and in their faith. *La Santé des Enfants* (1856) [The Health of Children] is a collection of medical advice, frequently relying on homeopathic remedies. Three catechismal works, *L'Evangile d'une Grand'Mère* (1865) [A Grandmother's Gospel], *Actes des Apôtres* (1867) [Acts of the Apostles], and *La Bible d'une Grand'Mère* (1869) [A Grandmother's Bible], aim to make Bible stories and teachings comprehensible to children and to help well-intentioned parents who "do not know the path to follow to form Christians in the bosom of the home" (Donnet, p. v). Although Ségur reworked the Scriptures (e.g., she reformulated the four Gospels to make one continuous narrative and paraphrased the texts), she was careful not to depart from their meaning, submitting the work to careful scrutiny by her son Gaston and a series of Church leaders. In keeping with her taste for dialogue and with contemporary styles of pedagogy, her *Grandmother's Gospel* is not a "reading" of the Scriptures but a telling of the Gospel by a grandmother who addresses thirteen children from the ages of four to seventeen. The children interrupt to ask for clarification of terms or of events, and the resulting discussions show Ségur's faithful rendering of contemporary theology as well as a sense of the struggles and questions of new believers. The children question teachings that contradict their understanding; when told that they must not be angry against their brothers, Little Louis asks, "But a poor man, for example, or even a worker, isn't my brother?" allowing the grandmother to introduce the concept of equality and brotherhood before God (p. 84). Budding anti-Semitism and naive patriotism are quelled as she touches on the role of the Jews in Christ's death: "Valentine: 'The French would never be so evil.' Grandmother: 'There are millions of them who are just as evil and who act just like the Jews. They do not persecute Jesus as a man, because they cannot, they do not see him, but they insult God as man by their words, by their actions; they crucify him by their desire'" (pp. 76–77). Conservative in its depiction of the family as the source of Christian values, the *Grandmother's Gospel* can also be read as daring, allowing a polyphony in which female and children's voices question and discuss an authoritative text generally received as univocal.

## SURVEY OF CRITICISM

Much critical attention to the Countess de Ségur has been biographical. Based perhaps on affectionate accounts by her son Gaston and daughter Olga, early studies often emphasized her sentimental appeal. Others examine the sufferings and tensions of her life in order to understand her impulse to write or to see the influence of her family history on the fictional families that she created. Such works generally limit their comments on her writing to the children's novels, particularly the cycles of novels centered around Sophie, read as a self-portrait, and those concerning General Dourakine, seen as a father figure. Biographers Yves-Michel Ergal and Marie-José Strich briefly consider Ségur's religious works, declaring that they "were to form generations of children" (p. 457).

Because of the realistic approach of the novels, historians and sociologists have mined them as sources of information about daily life in Second Empire France. The varieties of Ségur's settings and characterizations led Robert de Montesquiou to call her "the Balzac of childhood" (p. 22). Controversy has centered on Ségur's sometimes painful depictions of physical discipline and death scenes, with critics such as Laurent and Chalon debating the effects of such passages on child readers.

Blending biography, history, and literary criticism, Laura Kreyder presents a unique "biography" of Ségur as a writer, discussing her novels and their production as a kind of second life for the Countess. Perhaps the most comprehensive and even-handed treatment of Ségur to date, Kreyder's study examines some of the received notions about her, testing them against an extensive reading of not only her novels but also her religious works. Particularly attentive to the value systems of the texts, Kreyder relates them to the changing society of mid-nineteenth-century France and considers the enduring popularity of the novels.

Literary criticism has often drawn on psychological constructs to interpret the novels, as in Marc Soriano's Freudian speculations on the effects of Ségur's painful childhood. Ideological readings include Marie-Christine Vinson's study offering a feminist and Marxist interpretation of the Sophie cycle as a socializing text that maintains aristocratic dominance; Sylvie Mathé's reading of Ségur's psychological and ideological struggle with issues of order and disorder; and Marie-France Doray's article which argues that Ségur advocated greater Christian acceptance of the poor by upper-class people who were offended by the outward signs of poverty.

## BIBLIOGRAPHY

### Works by Sophie Rostopchine, Countess de Ségur

*La Santé des Enfants*. Paris: Hachette, 1856.
*Les Petites Filles Modèles*. Paris: Hachette, 1857.
*Les Malheurs de Sophie*. Paris: Hachette, 1858. Trans. as *The Misfortunes of Sophy*, by Honor and Edgar Skinner. New York: Putnam's Sons, 1936.
*Les Vacances*. Paris: Hachette, 1859.
*Pauvre Blaise*. Paris: Hachette, 1860.
*L'Auberge de l'Ange Gardien*. Paris: Hachette, 1861. Trans. as *The Angel Inn*, by Joan Aiken. Owings Mills, Maryland: Stemmer House, 1978.
*La Soeur de Gribouille*. Paris: Hachette, 1861.
*François le Bossu*. Paris: Hachette, 1863. Trans. as *The Little Hunchback*, by C. Mulhooland. Dublin: Gill and Son, 1884.
*Le Général Dourakine*. Paris: Hachette, 1864.
*Un Bon petit diable*. Paris: Hachette, 1865.

*Jean qui grogne et Jean qui rit.* Paris: Hachette, 1865.
*L'Evangile d'une Grand'Mère.* Paris: Hachette, 1865. Adapted by Mary Virginia
    Merrick as *A Life of Christ for Children as Told by a Grandmother.* St. Louis:
    B. Herder, 1909.
*Actes des Apôtres.* Paris: Hachette, 1867.
*La Bible d'une Grand'Mère.* Paris: Hachette, 1869.

### Works about Sophie Rostopchine, Countess de Ségur

Bleton, Pierre. *La Vie Sociale sous le Second Empire: Un étonnant témoignage de la
    comtesse de Ségur.* Paris: Les Editions Ouvrières, 1963.
Chalon, Jean. "Pour adultes seulement, la comtesse de Ségur." *Figaro Littéraire* 9
    February 1974: 10.
Donnet, Cardinal. "Approbation de Son Eminence le Cardinal Donnet, Archevêque
    de Bordeau." Prefatory materials to *L'Evangile d'une Grand'Mère* (listed
    above), v-vi.
Doray, Marie-France. "Cleanliness and Class in the Countess de Ségur's Novels."
    *Children's Literature* 17. Ed. Francelia Butler, Margaret Higonnet, and
    Barbara Rosen. New Haven: Yale University Press, 1989. 64–80.
Ergal, Yves-Michel, and Marie-José Strich. *La Comtesse de Ségur.* Paris: Perrin, 1990.
Kreyder, Laura. *L'Enfance des saints et des autres. Essai sur la comtesse de Ségur.*
    Fasano, Italy: Schéna, 1987.
Laurent, Jacques. "Etrennes noires." *Au Contraire.* Paris: La Table Ronde, 1967.
    157–67.
Mathé, Sylvie. "La Poupée perdue: Ordre et Désordre dans Les Petites Filles Modèles
    de la Comtesse de Ségur." *Theory and Practice of Feminist Literary Criti-
    cism.* Ed. Gabriela Mora and Karen S. Van Hooft. Ypsilanti, Michigan: Bi-
    lingual Press, 1982. 117–30.
Montesquiou, Robert de. "Le Balzac de l'Enfance." *Le Figaro* 7 September 1907: 22.
Soriano, Marc. *Guide de littérature pour la jeunesse.* Paris: Flammarion, 1975.
Vinson, Marie-Christine. *L'Education des Petites filles.* Lyon: Presses Universitaires de
    Lyon, 1987.

RUTH CARVER CAPASSO

# MURIEL SPARK
## (1918– )

## BIOGRAPHY

Muriel Spark was born Muriel Sarah Camberg in Edinburgh in 1918 to a Jewish father and a Gentile mother. Despite her father's Jewishness, Spark has claimed that the influence of Judaism on her faith and fiction has been more cultural than religious, and she received an essentially Presbyterian upbringing. Spark attended James Gillespie's School for Girls in Edinburgh, where she was encouraged to nurture her literary interests. Soon after leaving school, she married S. O. Spark and moved to Rhodesia; her son Robin was born in 1938. Although she was not writing at this time, Spark made many observations of Africa that provided material for subsequent short stories. With the end of her marriage in 1944, Spark returned to England, and worked in political intelligence at the Foreign Office. Following the war, Spark was employed as a journalist, and in 1947 she became the General Secretary of the Poetry Society, a duty which included editing *Poetry Review*. Leaving the Society in 1949, Spark started a magazine, *Forum*, which issued two numbers. At this time, she produced her first book-length publications, all of which were non-fiction studies of such literary figures as Mary Shelley and Emily Brontë, and she edited a collection of essays on Wordsworth. Some of these texts were written in collaboration with Derek Stanford. Spark's interest in historical female literary figures at this time indicated her general concern for the position of women in society; this thematic interest is also reflected in her volume of poems, *The Fanfarlo and Other Verse* (1952).

In 1951, Spark produced her first short story, "The Seraph and the Zambesi," winning a contest sponsored by the *Observer* newspaper. It was at this time that Spark became interested in the works of John Henry Newman. Asserting that until 1951 she had been almost completely indifferent to religious concerns, she now experienced a kind of spiritual crisis, the effects of which were to heavily influence her subsequent writings. Baptized into the Church of England in 1953, Spark rejected Anglo-Catholicism for Roman Catholicism nine months later, and was baptized in 1954 after having received instruction from a Benedictine monk. At the same time, she was undergoing periods of psychological distress, a near-breakdown to which Spark has attributed the mental and emotional stress of her religious upheaval and her simultaneous attempts to write. After her baptism, she temporarily retreated to Aylesford Priory, a Carmelite house in Kent, to recover from her emotional stress and occasional hallucinations.

In 1955, Spark was invited by Macmillan publishers to write a novel, and it was this work, *The Comforters* (1957), which not only established her as a unique satirical novelist, but also allowed her to recover from her nervous turmoil. Returning to London, she produced a number of novels in quick succession; seven novels were published in seven years. With *The Prime of Miss Jean Brodie* (1961), Spark became a popular and critical success. She was encouraged in various projects, and produced one play, *Doctors of Philosophy* (1962), as well as stories and radio plays for the BBC, and a children's book, *The Very Fine Clock* (1968). Finding the pressure of such projects difficult, Spark moved to New York in 1962, producing one novel during her time in the United States, *The Hothouse by the East River* (1973). After three years, she moved to Italy, where she currently resides. Although her outlay is not as prolific as it had been in the 1960s, Spark has published twelve novels since 1965 and continues to be an extremely popular writer.

## MAJOR THEMES

In her essay "Edinburgh-Born," Spark asserts that it is upon the "nevertheless principle" that much of her literary composition is based, and that it was on the "nevertheless principle" that she became Catholic (p. 180). In Spark's writing, this "nevertheless principle" seems to be defined as an acceptance of the potential for multiple interpretations and understandings of a character, an event, or a work of fiction. Thus, in the novel *Memento Mori* (1959), the narrator evinces strong sympathy for all of the very different characters. Spark uses this "nevertheless principle" not only as a moral emphasis in her work, but also as a means by which to structure her fiction. Much of her fiction presents what might seem to be paradoxical treatments of time, place, or reality, to suggest a greater absolute truth to life. Spark treats real life, replete with its political and social realities, with satirical realism, while at the same time treating supernatural events and apparitions in the same realistic tone. In so doing, she emphasizes the presence of the spiritual in life, and attests to its fundamental reality.

Despite her attestation of a connection between her conversion and the discovery of her creative abilities, Spark insists that she does not think of herself as a Catholic when she is writing. She asserts that her approach to Catholicism has been intuitive rather than intellectual. Thus her fiction is rarely concerned with matters of doctrine; instead, it provides what she terms a Christian norm from which to evoke and evaluate freely actions, characters, and reality. Indeed, Spark does not hesitate to question certain practices within the Church. She implicitly treats premarital sex sympathetically in her novels, and by her own admission, she questions the psychological implications of birth control on women in *The Bachelors* (1960). Spark is nonetheless moralistic in her novels; her most prominent emphases are on spiritual health and the recognition of the self. In a sense, this recognition of the self is linked to Spark's appreciation for Catholicism, which she asserts has enormous scope, thus allowing human creative and intellectual freedom within a solid religious framework. Many of Spark's works emphasize individual complexity of emotion and thought. The consequent emphasis on the importance of self-realization is particularly evident in her treatment of women characters, who figure largely in her fiction. Emphasizing the humility of the creator, Spark in no way likens her moralistic narration to dogmatic truth; instead, it is a vehicle to present the potential for multiple readings of events, thereby emphasizing compassion and openness as well as the co-existence of material and spiritual reality.

Despite the fundamental compassion suggested by the narrative structure of her works, Spark is often accused of flippancy in her treatment of characters and events. The author defends her satirical, potentially distanced approach as a means to more actively discourage a complacent and sentimental acceptance of poverty and social evil. In her novels, she promotes active awareness rather than mere acceptance of social evils by awakening in readers a sense of the absence of compassion existing in many humans. In so doing, she attempts to encourage readers toward action rather than literary sympathy towards social and political difficulties. Despite her commitment to the Catholic Church, Spark is bothered by what she perceives as the complacent hypocrisy of many Catholics, and often uses her novels to expose and denounce that hypocrisy. Both *The Comforters* and *Robinson* (1958) explore the problems of adjusting to Roman Catholicism in a secular world as the protagonists, both Catholic converts, confront questions of chastity, charity, and self-sacrifice. In *Memento Mori*, Spark is less introspective and more religiously self-assured in evoking the presence of the spiritual and supernatural in life. Instead of having a single character cope with conversion, she explores through various characters the need to accept death and recognize the presence of the divine in life. Despite this argument, the novel is essentially pessimistic in that none of the characters take advantage of this realization.

Since the mid-1960s, in fact, Spark's novels have become increasingly pessimistic. *The Mandelbaum Gate* (1965) is perhaps the last novel in which Roman Catholicism is a central concern. Critics have speculated that this is largely due to Spark's increasing disillusionment with the Church as an institution, particularly with the changes that have resulted from Vatican II. Spark has changed her thematic interest in her more recent works from God's "design," a theme prominent in her early work and often used as an allegory for the novelistic process itself, to the relationships between people. This is not to say that Spark's religious concerns in her fiction have diminished. Her more recent novels, however, have tended to be more profoundly cynical in their emphasis on the lack of genuine faith in present society. The fact that they point to this despair indicates Spark's continuing concern with faith, its place in society, and its importance as a literary concern.

## SURVEY OF CRITICISM

No biography exists of Muriel Spark as yet, and the most reliable and thorough accounts of her life and spiritual concerns largely remain those that have been provided by the author herself in various interviews, articles, and her 1992 autobiography, *Curriculum Vitae: Autobiography.* Derek Stanford's book, though limited in context, is interesting primarily for its detailed account of Spark's early career and spiritual conversion. The most thoroughly researched text probably remains that of Ruth Whittaker. Exemplary critical treatments include the Hynes collection, which offers excerpts from interviews with Spark, as well as a variety of critical responses to her fiction tempered by a thoughtful and thorough introduction. A similarly useful collection is Alan Bold's *Muriel Spark: An Odd Capacity for Vision.* Norman Page's recent study offers a much-needed survey of all of Spark's fiction, and provides welcome attention to her social and theological concerns. This attention is also provided by Whittaker's text and that of Edgecombe. Judy Sproxton's text is one of the most notable works to address the importance of the numerous female characters in Spark's fiction and their literary, religious, and social implications.

## BIBLIOGRAPHY

### Works by Muriel Spark

*The Fanfarlo and Other Verse.* Aldington: Hand and Flower Press, 1952.
*The Comforters.* London: Macmillan, 1957.
*Letters of John Henry Newman.* Edited with Derek Stanford. London: Peter Owen, 1957.
*Robinson.* London: Macmillan, 1958.
*Memento Mori.* London: Macmillan, 1959.
*The Bachelors.* London: Macmillan, 1960.
*The Ballad of Peckham Rye.* London: Macmillan, 1960.
"How I Became a Novelist." *John O'London's Weekly* 1 December 1960: 683.
*The Prime of Miss Jean Brodie.* London: Macmillan, 1961.
"My Conversion." *Twentieth Century* 170 (Autumn 1961): 58–63.
"Edinburgh-Born." *New Statesman* 10 August 1962: 180.
*Doctors of Philosophy.* London: Macmillan, 1963.
*The Mandelbaum Gate.* London: Macmillan, 1965.
*Collected Poems I.* London: Macmillan, 1967.
*The Very Fine Clock.* London: Macmillan, 1969.
*The Hothouse by the East River.* London: Macmillan, 1973.

*The Abbess of Crewe.* London: Macmillan, 1974.
*Loitering with Intent.* London: The Bodley Head, 1981.
*A Far Cry from Kensington.* London: Constable, 1988.
*Curriculum Vitae: Autobiography.* London: Constable, 1992.
*Open to the Public: New and Collected Stories.* New York: New Directions, 1997.

### Works about Muriel Spark

Bold, Alan. *Muriel Spark.* Contemporary Writers Series. London and New York: Methuen, 1986.

——, ed. *Muriel Spark: An Odd Capacity for Vision.* London: Vision Press, 1984.

Edgecombe, Rodney Stenning. *Vocation and Identity in the Fiction of Muriel Spark.* Columbia: University of Missouri Press, 1990.

Hynes, Joseph, ed. *Critical Essays on Muriel Spark.* New York: Macmillan, 1992.

Kemp, Peter. *Muriel Spark.* Novelists and Their World Series. London: Paul Elek, 1974.

Malkoff, Karl. *Muriel Spark.* Columbia Essays on Modern Writers Series. New York: Columbia University Press, 1968.

Massie, Allan. *Muriel Spark.* Edinburgh: Ramsay Head Press, 1979.

Page, Norman. *Muriel Spark.* Macmillan Modern Novelists Series. London: Macmillan, 1990.

Sproxton, Judy. *The Women of Muriel Spark.* London: Constable, 1992.

Stanford, Derek. *Muriel Spark: A Bibliographical and Critical Study.* Fontwell: Centaur Press, 1963.

Stubbs, Patricia. *Muriel Spark.* Writers and Their Work Series. Harlow: Longman for the British Council, 1973.

Tominaga, Thomas T. and Wilma Schneidermeyer. *Iris Murdoch and Muriel Spark: A Bibliography.* Scarecrow Author Bibliographies, 27. Metuchen, New Jersey: Scarecrow Press, 1976.

Whittaker, Ruth. *The Faith and Fiction of Muriel Spark.* New York: St. Martin's Press, 1982.

IRENE MORRA

# EDITH STEIN
## (1891–1942)

### BIOGRAPHY

Edith Stein was born in Breslau, Germany (now Wroclaw, Poland) on Yom Kippur, October 12, 1891. The last of eleven children of Siegfried and Auguste Stein, her devout Jewish parents celebrated the coincidence of her birth with this holiest of Jewish days with great joy. But her parents were unable to pass their faith on to their daughter who, by the age of fifteen, as she reveals in *Life in a Jewish Family* (1933–1935), had become a "Jewish atheist." Later, during her formative years as a philosophy student, Stein found herself among other Jews who had converted to Christianity, some for career advancement, others, as in the case of Stein, for spiritual reasons.

Stein came to Catholicism by way of philosophy. Among the first women admitted to university studies in Germany, academic excellence led Stein to a career in philosophy, first at the University of Breslau, then to Göttingen University, where she studied under Edmund Husserl, who was then in the process of establishing a major twentieth-century philosophical movement—phenomenology. Stein received her doctorate with highest honors and became Husserl's first assistant. During this period, she took the responsibility of editing Husserl's manuscripts for *Ideas Pertaining to a Pure Phenomenology and to Phenomenological Philosophy* (*Ideas II*) (1993), a work that was to have central importance after World War II when read by Maurice Merleau-Ponty and others at the Husserl Archives in Leuven, Belgium, before its publication. It is in sections on the body in this work that contemporary existentialism finds early inspiration, and it is in this work that Husserl developed a philosophy of intersubjectivity and empathy that has much in common with Stein's own work done under his guidance, *On the Problem of Empathy* (1916).

Stein's youthful atheism weakened under the influence of others in the phenomenological movement of the time who had already converted to Christianity, including Husserl, Adolf Reinach, and Max Scheler. Despite success in the academic world, a dual track becomes noticeable in Stein's thinking at this point in her life. The contemplative life of the philosopher became balanced by a deep and genuine humanity that demanded of her an active life. In the midst of her phenomenological research during World War I, the active life of service beckoned, and Stein joined the Red Cross as a nurse's aide, requesting to work with soldiers suffering from cholera, dysentery, typhus, and other infectious diseases.

On New Year's Day 1922, a day as full of symbolic religious significance as her day of birth, but on this occasion one of choice, Stein converted to Catholicism. Soon thereafter, she began a successful series of lectures throughout Germany on women's concerns and feminist issues from a Catholic perspective. At the same time, she continued her scholarly work, translating John Henry Cardinal Newman's letters into German and attempting in the late 1920s a synthesis of the philosophies of Thomas Aquinas and Husserl. Her application in 1931 for a teaching position at the University of Freiburg was rejected, however, because of Germany's growing anti-Semitic hysteria. At the time of the rejection, Martin Heidegger, a former colleague in Husserl's circle and, after Stein, Husserl's next assistant, held the chair in phenomenology at Freiburg. At the time, Stein could not understand Heidegger's antipathy toward her, but his entry into the Nazi Party in 1933 spoke for itself.

In the same year that Heidegger announced his embrace of National Socialism, Stein became a Discalced Carmelite. This step fulfilled her long-cherished wish to be a cloistered nun. She took the name Sister Teresa Benedicta of the Cross. To protect her from the Nazis, the Carmelites transferred her to Echt, Holland; yet despite these efforts, she was arrested and sent to Auschwitz. She died in the gas chambers of that abattoir along with her sister, Rosa, on August 9, 1942. She was fifty-one years old.

Since Stein's martyrdom, two miracles have been attributed to her and verified by the Church. She was beatified by Pope John Paul II in 1987. These events led to her being proclaimed a saint on October 11, 1998, but controversy accompanied Stein's canonization at every step of the way. In his "Papal Homily at the Canonization of St. Edith Stein," Pope John Paul II reminded Catholics that because she was Jewish, Stein, her sister Rosa, and other Catholic Jews from the Netherlands were sent to Auschwitz and murdered there. But from the Jewish perspective, Stein's canonization as a Catholic saint created a storm of controversy.

When the Nazis arrested Stein and her sister at the Dutch convent, it is reported that the last words her religious sisters heard her speak to Rosa were, "Come, let us go for our people" (Oben, p. 36). It is in this context that Saint Edith Stein takes a deserving place next to other martyrs of the holocaust such as Anne Frank, and other intellectual Jewish women of the time such as Simone Weil, also a convert to Catholicism.

## MAJOR THEMES

In 1921, while Stein was on holiday with friends, she discovered a copy of the autobiography of St. Teresa of Avila, the founder of the Carmelite Order.

After an enthralled reading that has hallmarks of a mystical experience, she is reported to have exclaimed, "This is the truth!" (Oben, p. 17). She then rapidly moved toward converting to Catholicism. The day after reading St. Teresa of Avila, Stein bought a Catholic catechism and began a life of study and devotion that would continue to the day of her martyrdom. When Stein sought entrance into the convent some years after her baptism, the Carmelites believed that her cloistering would come as a serious shock to her mother. But they also understood that the Church needed a woman of Stein's renown and abilities. As is the case in all of her writings, Stein explains her conversion and entry into the Carmelites candidly in "How I Came to the Cologne Carmel" (Batzdorff, pp. 13–30).

During the 1920s, Stein became a significant voice for feminism in Germany and one of the key spokeswomen for the Catholic Women's Movement. Her work in the movement was especially important in formulating a Catholic feminist perspective grounded in principles rooted in her own philosophical background and thought. With this intellectual strength, she became a speaker of power and eloquence, addressing conferences in Heidelberg, Zurich, Salzburg, and other locations throughout the nation in the troubled times of the Weimar Republic. When Hitler came to power in 1933, Stein was already a recognized figure in the struggle for women's rights as well as a prominent figure in the German academic world. In fact, the rising prominence of Hitler and attendant Nazi vituperative attacks on Jews led Stein to ask for a private audience with Pope Pius XI in the Spring of 1933, at which time she intended to urge him to release an encyclical to counterbalance Hitler's maniacal anti-Semitism. For reasons unknown, the meeting never took place.

In the decade leading up to her martyrdom, Stein maintained her philosophical career, writing, translating, and developing what became a well-known position on women's questions. In her lectures, she frequently dealt with social and cultural as well as ethical and spiritual issues of importance for women in modern society. Her written work, reflecting the themes and topics of her talks, is a forceful reminder of the avant-garde nature of her feminist thought. Between 1928 and 1933, Stein published a series of articles that today remain unsurpassed among those concerned with women's rights and place in society: "The Ethos of Women's Professions," "The Separate Vocations of Man and Woman According to God and Nature," "The Spirituality of Christian Women," "Fundamental Principles of Women's Education," "Problems of Women's Education," "The Church, Woman and Youth," and "The Significance of Woman's Intrinsic Value in National Life." In these articles, in addition to her own autobiographical and philosophical works, Stein situated herself as a progressive feminist for her time. This stance demanded ethical awareness of women's contributions and the just treatment of women, and, beyond these immediate concerns, proposed a resolution to the "crisis" of European culture and civilization that her mentor, Husserl, had belatedly outlined in his last work. Stein suggested that women are the source of healing for this world in crisis; in fact, she identified the healing of western civilization as the essential role of the Christian woman.

Stein believed that the essence of womanhood was motherhood and companionship. But this essentialism is not to be taken as solely a biological function, for while the existential situation of a woman varies from wife, professed nun, or single woman, the nurturing essence of all women remains unchanged. A woman's personhood, Stein maintains, develops by a woman exercising this nurturing quality in her particular state of life.

Politically, Stein was aware of the oppression of women under Nazism, and she warned that the loving and caring essence of woman should not be sacrificed to any leader other than God, in whom the capacity for human love is fulfilled. Woman's "divine privilege," in fact, is her special relationship with children, all children. Stein warns against the fallacy of the "hyper-feminine" that detaches women from their motherly essence. Her comments on the single woman are particularly revealing. She believes that in becoming "the spouse of Christ," a woman fulfills her essence and becomes a beacon of love as she lives a mystical union. Moreover, she believes that a woman's essence is emotion-centered. This essence is the primary force for "total humanity" because, unlike men who achieve objectivity at the cost of complete humanity, women are adaptive. As a consequence, women can do any job a man can do, but the opposite is not necessarily true of men. In arguing for women's full development as human beings, Stein insists that modern women could no longer be confined solely to children, kitchen, and church. Stein's thinking about women's roles and destiny was well ahead of its time. Theologically, she even argued for the position of the Blessed Virgin Mary as the Co-Redemptrix of humanity, an idea suggested in similar language in Pope John Paul II's *Redemptor Hominus* (1979). Stein's articles on women's issues have been collected in *Essays on Woman* (1996).

Besides her essays on women, after her entry into the Carmelites Stein also wrote a series of occasional poems and prayers celebrating the religious and spiritual life. These writings are marked by an earnest and moving simplicity that stands in sharp contrast to the analytic edge of her philosophical and feminist work. They are collected in Susanne Batzdorff's *Edith Stein: Selected Writings*.

Stein's philosophical perspective eventually outgrew phenomenological methodology. Echoing Husserl's concerns in *The Crisis of European Sciences and Transcendental Phenomenology* but moving beyond what had become the philosophical impasse of solipsism that many saw as her mentor's greatest weakness, Stein suggested that "People have lost their moorings and are in search of something to hold on to. They want a philosophy of life. This is what they find in Thomas" ("Husserls Phänomenologie," p. 329). Stein was acute enough to recognize that an underlying, though indirect, connection between Husserl and Thomas Aquinas already existed. Husserl's teacher, Franz Brentano, had borrowed the concept of intentionality from Aquinas, and an expanded theory of intentionality became the bedrock of Husserl's phenomenology.

In her last work, *Finite and Eternal Being* (1935–1936), Stein proposed a daring philosophical syncretism that has been hailed as a significant contribution to neo-Thomism, which resumed after World War II. The work, attempting to bring Husserlian phenomenology and Thomistic metaphysics into harmony, had been rejected by publishers before the war, although admirers suggested that Stein allow the work to be printed under the name of a Nazi sympathizer. She refused.

## SURVEY OF CRITICISM

Since World War II, an ongoing reappraisal of Stein's importance within both the phenomenological tradition and neo-Thomism has received fresh impetus from her canonization and, although a large body of secondary work on Stein has not yet appeared, numerous projects are underway and a consensus appears to be emerging that places Stein's philosophical work on a high plateau. This high regard for her philosophical work may be attributed to two important aspects of her thought: her work on the lived-body, and the ontological considerations of her later Thomism. Stein's mature thought does not reside solely within the phenomenological tradition, although the important work she did for her mentor established the young scholar as one of Husserl's most important early students. Her doctoral dissertation, later published as *On the Problem of Empathy*, and her edition of Husserl's *Ideas II* are indispensable to an understanding of Stein's importance within the phenomenological tradition. What is important in her study of empathy, which also figures as an important consideration in Husserl's *Ideas II*, is an understanding of empathy as a firm ground for intersubjectivity. But even in this instance, Stein draws from many others besides the Göttingen Circle of phenomenologists. In *The Phenomenological Movement*, Herbert Spiegelberg explains that Stein "tried to incorporate some of Husserl's non-idealistic phenomenology and a good deal of Reinach's, Pfander's, Scheler's, Conrad-Martius's and Heidegger's thought" (p. 238).

Waltraut Stein, the grandniece of the philosopher and a leading Stein scholar, explains that Stein's understanding of the focal importance of the body is that "bodily space (of which the zero point is the "I") and outer space (of which the zero point is the living body) are very different" (p. xix). It is impossible to underestimate the influence of this distinction on later existential phenomenologists such as Merleau-Ponty and dialectic-materialist Husserlians such as Tran Duc Thao.

Among the extensive critical work written on Stein, Waltraud Herbstrith's *Edith Stein: A Biography* is exceptionally sensitive to details that relate the philosopher's thought and life, and Freda Mary Oben's *Edith Stein: Scholar, Feminist, Saint*, though short, is a moving introduction to Stein as a feminist, giving close attention to her ideas on the essence of womanhood. Susanne Batzdorff's *Edith Stein: Selected Writings*, a short anthology of essays and poems written after she was cloistered, reveals Stein at the zenith of her religious experience. And Hilda C. Graef's *The Scholar and the Cross: The Life and Works of Edith Stein* is an early, comprehensive treatment of Stein's twofold path as intellectual and as saint.

## BIBLIOGRAPHY

### Works by Edith Stein

*Essays on Woman*. 1928–1933. Ed. L. Gelber and Romaeus Leuven. Trans. Freda Mary Oben. Second edition, revised. Washington, D.C.: ICS Publications, 1996.

*The Hidden Life*. 1935–1941. Ed. L. Gelber and Michael Linssen. Trans. Waltraut Stein. Washington D.C.: ICS Publications, 1992.

"How I Came to the Cologne Carmel." *Edith Stein: Selected Writings*. Ed. Susanne M. Batzdorff. Springfield, Illinois: Templegate Publishers, 1998.

"Husserls Phänomenologie und die Philosophie des hl. Thomas von Aquino, Versuch einer Gegenuberstellung." 1929. *Jahrbuch für Philosophie und phänomenologische Forschung. Erganzungsband*. Trans. Mary Catharine Baseheart. Dordrecht: Kluwer, 1997. 315–88.

*Life in a Jewish Family*. 1933–1935. Ed. L. Gelber and Romaeus Leuven. Trans. Josephine Koeppel. Washington, D.C.: ICS Publications, 1986.

*On the Problem of Empathy*. 1916. Trans. Waltraut Stein. Washington, D.C.: ICS Publications, 1989.

*Science of the Cross*. 1942. Ed. L. Gelber and Romaeus Leuven. Trans. Josephine Koeppel. Washington, D.C.: ICS Publications, 1998.

*Endliches und ewiges Sein: Versuch eines Aufstieges zum Sinn des Seins* [Finite and Eternal Being]. Published posthumously in *Edith Steins Werke II*. Freiberg: Herder, 1950; 3rd ed., 1986.

### Works about Edith Stein

Baseheart, Mary Catharine. *Persons in the World: Introduction to the Philosophy of Edith Stein*. Dordrecht: Kluwer, 1997. 129–44; 179–80.

Batzdorff, Susanne. *Aunt Edith: The Jewish Heritage of a Catholic Saint*. Springfield, Illinois: Templegate Publishers, 1998.

———, ed. *Edith Stein: Selected Writings, with Comments, Reminiscences, and Translations of Her Prayers and Poems by Her Niece, Susanne Batzdorff*. Springfield, Illinois: Templegate Publishers, 1990.

Collins, James. "Edith Stein and the Advance of Phenomenology." *Thought* 17 (1942): 685–708.

Graef, Hilda C. *The Scholar and the Cross: The Life and Works of Edith Stein*. New York: Longmans, Green, 1955; Westminster, Maryland: Newman Press, 1955.

Herbstrith, Waltraud. *Edith Stein: A Biography*. Trans. Bernard Bonowitz. San Francisco, California: Ignatius Press, 1992.

Oben, Freda Mary. *Edith Stein: Scholar, Feminist, Saint*. New York: Alba Press, 1988.

Spiegelberg, Herbert. *The Phenomenological Movement*. 1960. Third revised and enlarged Edition. The Hague, Netherlands: Martinus Nijhoff, 1984.

Stein, Waltraut. Introduction. *On the Problem of Empathy*, by Edith Stein. Trans. Waltraut Stein. Washington, D.C.: ICS Publications, 1989.

PAUL MAJKUT

# Mary Stuart, Queen of Scots
# (1542–1587)

## BIOGRAPHY

Mary Stuart, Queen of Scots, the daughter of Mary of Guise and James V, was born at Linlithgow Palace on December 8, 1542, and ascended the throne six days later. Her early childhood was jeopardized by "The Rough Wooing" of Henry VIII in 1544–1545 (that is, by English invasions of Scotland after the marriage agreement between Henry's son, Edward, and Mary was dissolved when the pro-French, Catholic faction strengthened in Scotland). In 1548 Mary was sent to France where, for thirteen years, she received the protection of the Guise-Lorraine family and a religious, intellectual, and artistic education. Her marriage to the young Dauphin, François II, ended after his sudden death in 1560, and Mary entered a period of mourning as "*la reine blanche*" (the white queen). In 1561, at the age of nineteen, she returned to a Reformed Scotland. Mary's own exertion of religious authority proved moderate and conciliatory; she herself attended Mass and received communion in private. The early years of her reign were relatively stable, although the issue of her marriage remained contentious in its implications for the English succession and religious power.

In 1565, Mary married Henry Stewart, Lord Darnley, in a Catholic ceremony. Controversy surrounded their marriage: Mary's moral and sexual conduct was increasingly scrutinized, and apparent tensions between Darnley and Mary made the former a useful pawn for the queen's enemies. In March 1566, David Rizzio, an Italian musician promoted to the position of Mary's secretary, was murdered by Protestant rebels in consort with the embittered Darnley who sought to gain the crown matrimonial; speculation had grown about the nature of the Mary-Rizzio relationship and his Catholic allegiance. Mary witnessed the attack, pregnant with the future King James. Mary's seven-year Scottish reign entered its most acute crisis on February 10, 1567, when Darnley was assassinated. Accusations spread that Mary herself was implicated in the murder, intensified by rumors of an adulterous liaison with

James Hepburn, Lord Bothwell, himself under suspicion with other of Mary's nobles. On May 15, she married Bothwell, by Protestant rites (which she took pains to justify to French royalty), but it was an alliance which did not bear the politically ameliorative repercussions Mary had anticipated. The famous discovery of a silver casket on June 20, 1567, containing written material attesting to her alleged adultery and complicity in the assassination, deepened public and private hostilities against Mary.

Mary surrendered on June 15, 1567, at Carberry Hill to the confederate lords; imprisoned at Lochleven Castle in fragile health, on July 24 she abdicated in favor of her son. Finally defeated at the battle of Langside in 1568, Mary sought protection from Elizabeth in England. For the remainder of her life, hopes of monarchical restoration were prevented by her constant imprisonment by the English queen who was threatened by the possibility of Mary's accession and Catholic insurrection. The Babington plot of 1587 resulted in Mary's trial at Westminster where she was found guilty of attempting to overthrow Elizabeth; Mary denied responsibility. She was executed on February 8, 1587 at Fotheringhay Castle, and buried at Peterborough Cathedral until her body was finally interred at Westminster in 1612. Mary's execution caused controversy in Catholic Europe where pro-Marian support was manifested in a wealth of texts and pamphlets that proclaimed the innocence of the martyred Scottish queen. Mary's devout preparations for death were emphasized in the posthumous Marian hagiography: that in her final hours she had requested the freedom to exercise her religion as did other Catholic sovereigns. Throughout her life, Mary publicly declared that she desired to live and die in the Catholic faith, "*avec constante resolution de souffrir la mort pour le maintien & obeissance de l'Eglise Catholique, Apostolique & Romaine*" (with steadfast resolve to suffer death in order to uphold and obey the holy Roman, Catholic and Apostolic Church).[1]

## MAJOR THEMES

Religious, political, and literary discourses, both for and against Mary, made Mary incarnate the twin identities of her name, the Virgin and the Magdalene. This enduring symbolism underlies the poetry in which Mary is enshrined in her own words. Her extant writing principally consists of an elegy on the death of her first husband, François II; poetry to Elizabeth; the series of twelve poems (the so-called "casket sonnets") controversially attributed to her in George Buchanan's incriminatory *Detection* (1571); and a number of devotional texts which stem from her years of incarceration. Creativity served as consolation to Mary, especially in the later poems, found in fragile manuscript hand, which put the poetic in service of the spiritual. In taut dialectical sonnet form, Mary sustains a colloquy with God. Rhetorically and emotionally composed at the point of abandonment, Mary's sacred poetry is full of agony, exploring the afflictions of spiritual imperfection and longing. While contrasting with the resolution of faith in her letters, they display Mary's characteristic linguistic sensitivity: parallelism, oxymoron, and repetition. "*Ayant au coeur ta passion écrite*" (having your passion inscribed upon my heart) ("Méditation"), for example, is a characteristic Marian pun suggesting the enactment of Christ's Passion within Mary herself.

Mary's longest religious poem is the one-hundred line meditation in couplets, the "Méditation sur l'inconstance et vanité du monde" [Meditation on the Inconstancy and Vanity of the World], composed in response to the Latin prose work sent to her by John Leslie, Bishop of Ross, who acted as her chief representative in England, became involved in Catholic agitation against Elizabeth for which he was imprisoned, and to whom Mary referred as "*mon conseiller*" (my advisor). With the sonnet "L'ire de Dieu par le sang n'apaise" [The Anger of God Is Not Appeased by Blood], it was published in Leslie's *Piae Afflicti Animi Consolationes Divinaque Remedia* (1574) [Holy Consolations and Divine Remedies for the Afflicted Spirit]. A combination of Stoic philosophy and personal devotion, "Méditation" is a formal spiritual or meditative exercise composed while "*en prison.*" Rhetorically, the text is divided between an impersonally sententious moral voice, and the intimate, supplicatory tone of the penitent. The former does not obscure the poem's self-reflexive ironies (the "fall of princes" topos reflects Mary's own state as an exiled, powerless queen), nor her private spiritual state as she implores that God "*préserve*" (protect) her. This dynamic between personal identification and "protective" moral generalization is most precarious in the allusion to the Magdalene, "*la femme pécheresse*" (the woman sinner). While anticipating the concept of atonement in the latter comparison with Peter, the analogy evokes the penitential typology of the Magdalene as sexual sinner as well as the melancholic concept of the beautiful penitent. A number of scriptural texts influenced the "Méditation": the Psalms, Proverbs, Corinthians 2 and, in the prevailing *vanitas* theme, Ecclesiastes.

The poem's structural center is desired union with, or return to, "*L'unique Sauveur*" (the one and only Savior). Theologically, both it and the sonnet "L'ire de Dieu" [The Anger of God] contest whether salvation is "*Jà ordonné*" (preordained) or earned by the individual penitent. The sonnet explores the Reformation debate about the efficacy of good works and the nature of "merit." Insisting on the spiritual purity of each individual, Mary's poem ascribes a doctrinal simplicity and beauty to the Catholic faith as an implicit counterpart to the Lutheran or Calvinist position of the doctrine of justification. Immaculate spiritual purity achieved in isolation, "*un esprit en oraison constant*" (a mind in constant prayer) to which she aspires, is contrasted with elaborate ritual portrayed as a pagan offering or sacrifice in allusion to Hebrews 10:4.

The "Méditation" exemplifies the Queen's poetic relationship with her "*pere Souverain*" (Sovereign father) by assuming a loving God in the adoration of His "*douce clemence*" (gentle mercy) and yet communicating fear and doubt

that forgiveness is imminent. Mary's supplicant is abject yet imperious. In re-
vering God as possessing "*grande majeste*," Mary implicitly contrasts divine
sovereignty with fallible earthly sovereignty. The petition for deliverance is often allied with the desire that her fragility, in both spiritual and physical senses,
be forcefully subdued: "*Tu veux, Seigneur, être maître du coeur*" (You desire,
Lord, to be master of my heart). Devotion has a repetitive grammatical structure: "*Donne, Seigneur, donne-moi patience*" (Give, Lord, give me patience).
Mary's colloquy with God (interestingly, she never directly addresses the Virgin, nor draws upon Marian devotion) is characterized throughout by this paradox of abnegation and assertion: in the sonnet "O Seigneur Dieu," she
desires that God expel her fragility and purge and renew her, while also ardently proclaiming that "*Je te défendrai*" (I will defend you), perhaps also a co-
vert allusion to the faith.

The in the "Méditation," Mary's desire to be sanctified becomes a plea that the
faith of "*ma Mère, l'Eglise*" (my Mother Church) be preserved. Here, she prays
for her own faith to be forever strengthened, but "*la foi*" (faith) may also signify the Catholic Church itself, and Mary's desire that it be divinely saved from
the threat of Reforming Protestantism. Mary portrays her devotion as a metaphorical retreat, an inner sanctum, or the cloistered, enclosed space to which
"L'ire de Dieu" speaks. Her religious poetry sustains an underlying dialogue
between the freedom of the soul and the body spiritually and, in Mary's case,
literally, imprisoned and "*Pleine de maux*" (full of sorrow).

The sonnet most likely composed just before Mary's death resembles a final
testament. "*Que suis-je hélas? Et de quoi sert de ma vie?*" [Alas, What Am I?
What Use Is My Life?]: this plangent questioning of identity, depicting the
martyred heart (the dichotomy of "body" and "heart," rather than body and
soul, is always asserted), might be conceived as her spiritual dethroning, a voluntary abnegation. If Mary's religious poetry can be read as the spiritually creative effort to counter adversity, then her last work barely attests this. Here,
Mary exonerates herself from the "burden" of hope by transferring the power
of prayer to those "*amis*" (companions) who remain. The only consolation is
held in the final imagined translation of earthly finiteness into the anticipation
of "*la joie infinie*" (eternal joy).

Interestingly, Mary rarely identifies herself as a specifically female penitent:
does her devotion to God ultimately enable the possession of the spiritual freedom to which she constantly aspires? In devotion, she presents herself unen-
cumbered by the excess of femininity that defined her natural and sovereign
bodies so that she may embody the "*grâces*" of purity, loyalty and humility. Before God, she lays her "*coeur dévot*" (devout heart) on trial.

Fragments of poetry inscribed by Mary in her *Book of Hours*, which she possessed from 1554 until her death, resemble miniature spiritual exercises or acts
of devotion. Three layers of text are presented: the Biblical, the decorative, and
the closely worked quatrains that echo the moral and devotional poetry. The
solid Gothic scripture contrasts with the implied emotional fragility of Mary's

tenuous script; on one leaf she poignantly inscribed at the edge of a prayer to the Virgin "*tres doulce dame*" (most sweet lady). In these quatrains, which recall "emblem poetry," Mary writes tenderly of "*mon ange tutélaire*" (my guardian angel), and the visionary beauty of "*un bel ange*" (beautiful angel) who also serves as an intermediary spirit between herself and God in the "Méditation." (The emblematic qualities of Mary's poetry are tangibly realized in her embroidery which often uses religious motifs: a seventeenth-century account of a bedhanging, now lost, describes "the word her Majesties name turned in an Anagram, *Maria Stuart, sa vertu m'attire* [Mary Stuart, His/Its virtue draws me near] . . . This hath reference to a Crucifix, before which with all her Royall ornaments she is humbled on her knees").[2]

Eloquent intercessions to God that render the written word as almost sacramental—in that sense, they are offertory—Mary's poems of confession, contrition, and devotion place emphasis on the purity and integrity of her true faith, which ironically contrasts both with the accusations of idolatry and duplicity leveled at her throughout her life, and with the accounts of her serene martyrdom in the hagiographical histories. The intense symbolic value of Mary, Queen of Scots, in Catholic history is both enriched and complicated by these poetic records of her faith and spirituality.

## SURVEY OF CRITICISM

The extensive historiographical literature on Mary, Queen of Scots, contrasts with the comparatively slight body of criticism on her poetry. Critical reception has been frustrated by the controversial "authenticity" of the "casket sonnets," while negotiating the dangers of psychological or emotional essentialism and the necessity of granting Mary creative autonomy. The accepted probability of their status as forgeries has obscured their interesting literary position as secular love sonnets written in Mary's name (Mary's voice "ventriloquised") in a period of intense controversy over the Queen. As I have argued in my article "Rewriting the Renaissance Language of Love and Desire: The 'bodily burden' in the Poetry of Mary, Queen of Scots," acceptance of authorship has seemed to entail acceptance of Mary's culpability in Darnley's murder when the texts themselves are not incriminatory. The texts remain as transgressive expressions of female sexual desire which also anticipate the themes of renunciation, devotion, and martyrdom of the later religious poetry. The "canonicity" of Mary's poetry has proven elusive, not easily assimilable into French or Scottish literary contexts, although Travitsky's anthologized selections and Hackett's essay place Mary's writing within a British literary context. Phillips offers an excellent account of Catholic literary and political responses to the Queen's death; in my article "The Creation and Self-Creation of Mary Queen of Scots," I examine the religious poems in the Scottish context of debates over Mary. Bell's is the most recent, accessible anthology and translation of Mary's poems, while Arbuthnot's remains a sensitively edited collection.

## NOTES

1. Adam Blackwood. *Martyre de la Royne d'Éscosse*. Edinburgh: Jean Nafeild, 1587. 401–2.

2. William Drummond of Hawthornden. Cited in Alison Saunders, *The Sixteenth Century French Emblem Book*. Geneva: Droz, 1988. 267. Note that the translation of Mary's anagram is ambivalent. "*Sa vertu m'attire*" can be glossed as either "Its virtue draws me near" or "His virtue draws me near"; in the context cited, it most probably refers to the crucifix but it may also allude to God.


## BIBLIOGRAPHY

### Works by Mary Stuart, Queen of Scots

Arbuthnot, P. Stewart-Mackenzie, ed. and trans. *Queen Mary's Book*. London: Bell, 1907.

Bell, Robin, ed. and trans. *Bittersweet within My Heart: The Collected Poems of Mary Queen of Scots*. London: Pavilion, 1992.

Labanoff, Alexandre, ed. *Lettres, Instructions et Memoires de Marie Stewart reine d'Ecosse*. 7 vols. London: Dolman, 1844.

Sharman, Julian, ed. *Poems of Mary Queen of Scots*. London: Basil Montagu Pickering, 1873.

Travitsky, Betty, ed. *The Paradise of Women: Writings by English Women of the Renaissance*. Westport, Connecticut: Greenwood Press, 1981.


### Works about Mary Stuart, Queen of Scots

Bingham, Caroline. "The Poems of Mary Queen of Scots." *Royal Stuart Papers X*. London: The Royal Stuart Society, 1976.

Dunnigan, Sarah M. "The Creation and Self-Creation of Mary Queen of Scots: Rhetoric, Sovereignty, and Femininity in Sixteenth Century Scottish Poetry." *Scotlands* 5.2 (1998): 65–88.

——. "Rewriting the Renaissance Language of Love and Desire: The 'bodily burdein' in the Poetry of Mary, Queen of Scots." *Gramma* 4 (1996): 181–96.

——. "Scottish Women Writers c.1560–c.1650." *A History of Scottish Women's Writing*. Ed. Douglas Gifford and Dorothy Macmillan. Edinburgh: Edinburgh University Press, 1997. 15–43.

Fraser, Antonia. *Mary, Queen of Scots*. London: Weidenfield & Nicolson, 1969.

Hackett, Helen. "Courtly Writing by Women." *Women and Literature in Britain 1500–1700*. Ed. Helen Wilcox. Cambridge: Cambridge University Press, 1996. 169–89.

Lewis, Jayne Elizabeth. *Mary Queen of Scots: Romance and Nation*. London: Routledge, 1998.

Phillips. J. E. *Images of a Queen: Mary Stuart in Sixteenth Century Literature*. Berkeley: University of California Press, 1964.

SARAH M. DUNNIGAN

# TERESA OF AVILA
# (1515–1582)

## BIOGRAPHY

Teresa Sánchez de Cepeda y Ahumada was born in the walled city of Avila, Spain, on March 28, 1515. The third of eight children, she was a lively, charming child, her father's darling. After the death of her mother in 1528, Teresa prayed before the statue of the Blessed Mother in the cathedral asking Mary to be her mother. By the time Teresa was a teenager, her frivolous behavior and questionable company so worried her father that he arranged for her to live as a boarder with the nuns at the Augustinian convent. Initially, Teresa had no intention of entering the religious life, but under the influence of an especially devout nun she began to consider becoming a nun. The decision did not come easily, but during a serious illness, fear for her immortal soul seized the day. She decided to enter the Carmelite convent of the Incarnation, outside the walls. Knowing that her father would be devastated by the decision, she entered without his permission and made her profession on November 3, 1537. Nearly twenty years of inner struggle were to follow.

Teresa was in turmoil for several reasons. First, she was aware that her commitment to the religious life was thin: fear, rather than love for God, had motivated her to become a nun. Second, her health deteriorated and she suffered a life-threatening illness that left her paralyzed for almost three years. Third, she was emotionally fragile: the death of her father in 1543 and an attraction to a priest she met while recuperating were profoundly unsettling. Fourth, she suffered under the weight of hypocrisy: having learned from a devout uncle the practice of mental prayer known as recollection, she in turn taught the nuns in the convent how to think about the words they said rather than merely recite them in rote fashion. While the nuns praised her sanctity for leading them inward in prayer, Teresa knew she was a sham: unbeknownst to them she would abandon prayer for long periods of time and turn lukewarm in her devotions.

Teresa likened her suffering to being swept about by an ocean storm; on the one hand she desired God, on the other, the things of the world. The divided will she describes is reminiscent of St. Augustine, whose autobiography she knew. Like him, she was plunged into the despair of indecision, then raised up by God's grace. Just as Augustine set eyes on a passage by Paul as he heeded the child's voice telling him to take up and read and was washed clean of pride and indecision with tears of repentance, so was Teresa graced with weeping at the sight of a statue of the crucified Christ. The Teresa who fell to her knees in tears arose profoundly changed: the oscillating woman gave way to a resolute Teresa, bound for a rich spiritual life that was defined outwardly by her work to reform the Carmelite order, advise men and women of all stations in society, and write treatises that rank among the most significant in the corpus of Christian mystical literature.

The conversion occurred in 1555. The next years saw stunning growth in prayer. By 1558, she was discussing with a few close friends in the convent the possibility of living a reformed life, consonant with the Primitive Rule. This reform she undertook with caution, if not secrecy, in an Avila that relished little the prospect of more religious communities to support. In 1562 Teresa founded in Avila the first Discalced house, St. Joseph's Monastery, by authority of a papal bull. From 1567 to 1582, the once frail Teresa traveled throughout Spain to found and administer seventeen convents, direct the spiritual lives of her nuns, extend the reform to the Carmelite friars, and counsel the many lay people, including the king, who sought her wisdom.

Acting on orders from her confessor, Teresa began to write about the spiritual life for the benefit primarily of her nuns. *La Vida* [The Life] was completed by the end of 1565, and *Camino de perfección* [The Way of Perfection] shortly thereafter. These were followed by the account of the founding of the convents, *Libro de las fundaciones* [The Book of the Foundations], completed in 1588. In 1577 *Las Moradas* [The Interior Castle] appeared, her magisterial cartography of the soul's journey within herself to know God.

Even though Teresa's health was in serious decline by 1582, she remained active in the reform. Negotiations for a new foundation took her to Burgos where she fell gravely ill. Unable to complete the trip home to her beloved St. Joseph's, she stopped at the convent in Alba de Tormes where she died on October 4, 1582. She was canonized in 1622; declared the national saint of Spain (sharing honors with St. James, or Santiago) in 1814 when French troops were being driven out of Spain; and proclaimed a Doctor of the Church by Pope Paul VI in 1970.

## MAJOR THEMES

The theme that informs all of Teresa's writing is the soul's journey to God—the mystical way. In works like *The Life* and *The Book of the Foundations*, the journey is expressed in single mystical experiences that she identifies as her own; they are not necessarily patterned so as to form a sequence of events leading to transformation and union. *The Life* is a spiritual autobiography filled with events and people, from childhood until the time of writing the book. Teresa describes her supernatural experience of hearing and seeing the Lord, her years of struggle before her conversion, her difficulties with confessors and learned men, and the early years of the reform of the Carmelite order. In chapters eleven through twenty-three, she shifts focus away from herself to present a mini-mystical treatise developed through the image of prayer as the watering of the soul. The four ways in which the soul is watered are four kinds of prayer. The first way is by the difficult labor of drawing water from a well. The second is by the less demanding work of drawing water with a windlass. The third way of watering is from a stream or spring, which requires little effort. All work ceases for the soul in the fourth way as the Lord waters her with refreshing rains. The movement in prayer is thus from active to passive, outer to inner.

*The Way of Perfection* further demonstrates Teresa's ability to present delicate understandings in familiar language. In this case, she grounds her mystical theology in the seven petitions of the Our Father. *The Book of the Foundations* is the spiritual journey ingeniously expressed on two levels. On the first level, the book is the story of how each convent came into being; the stories are behind-the-scenes glimpses into Church politics, petty intrigues, and Teresa's genius in negotiations and human relations. On the second level, the *Foundations* expresses outwardly in the work of the reform the interior wonders being wrought within Teresa's soul.

Teresa's masterpiece of mystical writing is *The Interior Castle*, a beautifully elaborated image of the soul as an interior castle where God takes his delight. Teresa recounts in the first chapter how one day, when she had been pondering how to begin this treatise that her confessor had directed her to write, the image of the soul as a castle with many mansions occurred to her. Just as desire for God mysteriously sets one on the path of loving God, so the image of the castle was the gift that generated the writing of the mystical treatise. The seven mansions of the interior castle are different experiences or forms of prayer by which the soul moves and is moved by God ever more deeply within herself until, marvelously, she is brought into the fullness of the divine embrace, known in mystical theology as the Spiritual Marriage.

The mansions are seven in number, divided between the first three where the soul is aware of herself as directing the journey, and the subsequent four where she is made increasingly passive in the relationship. The mansions are distinguished by different forms of prayer. Mental prayer identifies the first three mansions where the soul as a beginner actively works to cultivate virtues and root out imperfections through devotional reading, good conversation, charitable works, and, importantly, mental prayer. One cannot even get into the castle, warns Teresa, without practicing mental prayer, which, contrary to vocal prayer (the rote recitation of formulaic words), requires active consideration of the words being said aloud or to oneself. In strongly advocating mental prayer for her nuns, Teresa went against the religious conventions of her day that forbade women to think and, of course, to teach. The transition from the active, purgative way of the first three mansions to the illuminative way of the fourth and fifth mansions is marked by the experience of passive recollection—the first kind of supernatural prayer in the interior castle. Whereas in mansions one through three the soul was aware of her efforts to love and be pleasing to God, here, in the fourth and fifth, she is more and more aware of being loved and rendered pleasing to God. Recollection is supernatural prayer because the soul does not initiate and direct the prayer; she is aware of her eyes closing without effort on her part and a temple of solitude being built up around her.

As the soul is moved by God more deeply within herself, the senses and faculties gradually cease to function. The fourth mansions are identified by the Prayer of Quiet and the fifth mansions by the Sleep of the Faculties, where the senses and faculties of understanding, memory, and will are not merely quieted but their activities suspended. The chapters on these mansions illustrate Teresa's prudence and wisdom in the spiritual life. Aware of the temptation to court unusual experiences in prayer, Teresa cautions repeatedly that charity and humility are the essential features of the true lover.

The sixth mansions, or the Spiritual Betrothal, are the transition from the illuminative way to the unitive way. These mansions are especially dangerous to the soul because extraordinary phenomena such as wounds of love, raptures, flights of the spirit—all of which Teresa herself had experienced—can divert the soul from the true path. The danger is in thinking that such experiences are necessary for perfection when, in fact, they may be serious disadvantages to the true indicators of spiritual growth, namely, humility and charity. For Teresa, the sixth mansions are not only perilous but agonizing as the soul feels herself suspended between worlds, now delighting in rapturous embrace with the Lord, now gripped by fear of abandonment. This suffering ceases in the seventh mansions when the soul is embraced by God in the Spiritual Marriage. A vision of the Trinity that transcends understanding wrought through the senses and mind marks Teresa's entry into the seventh mansions. The active and contemplative are harmonized as the soul is transformed; her will, which is the highest faculty of the soul, is brought into conformity with the will of God. Prayer, too, is transformed from a single event into a sustained, wordless conversation with God.

Teresa's accomplishment in the *Interior Castle* is to have rendered in accessible language the mystery of divine love. She makes of the mystical journey an experience open to all people, even women and others in the ranks of the spiritually disenfranchised. Feminism was not a rallying cry in Teresa's time, but in her writings she expresses attitudes that exposed and partly disarmed the biased conventions of sixteenth-century Spain. She may appear to accept such biases in calling herself a miserable worm and a worthless uneducated woman, but those words need to be read contextually. Teresa was well aware of what had happened to women in the first thirty-five years or so of the century when in the apparent openness of Erasmian-inspired reform, women fashioned for themselves spiritual careers, teaching prayer, interpreting scripture, healing, and prophesying. Several women became famous as visionaries and ecstatics, some infamous for their independent lifestyles and public association with lay and religious men. Eventually, the Inquisition took these women to task; several were arrested, tried, and imprisoned. Some women, called *alumbradas* (enlightened ones) because they felt themselves enlightened by the Holy Spirit, were tortured and executed as heretics. When Teresa was questioned informally by the Inquisition, she was armed with discretion. Not only had she claimed her ignorance as a woman, but she had written only at the behest of male religious superiors, submitted her writings to Church officials for examination, and consulted theologian after theologian about the orthodoxy of her positions. These strategies served her subversive agenda, which was to affirm the validity of women's spiritual experience.

As a woman of Jewish lineage on her father's side, Teresa was doubly marginalized. Fears that *conversos* (converted Jews, or their descendants) would secretly return to Jewish practices was one reason for the establishment of the Spanish Inquisition. In Teresa's lifetime, *conversos* suspected of relapsing were hunted down, tried, tortured, and punished, even burned at the stake. Her own grandfather had been tried in Toledo, his *sanbenito* (penitential garment) hung in the parish church as a permanent reminder of his guilt. Teresa needed rhetorical and other strategies to gain support for reform of the Carmelite order and acknowledgement that women's spiritual experiences were valid and valuable. In these efforts, Teresa of Avila courted danger. Enflamed by love, she could do no less; she could do no differently.

## SURVEY OF CRITICISM

Until recently the most substantial criticism has interpreted Teresa's writings from within the tradition of Christian mystical theology and literature. E. W. Trueman Dicken's *The Crucible of Love: A Study of the Mysticism of St. Teresa of Jesus and St. John of the Cross* illustrates this focus. Comparison with other mystical traditions is another major approach, as seen in Catherine Swietlicki's *Spanish Christian Cabala: The Works of Luis de León, Santa Teresa de Jesús and San Juan de la Cruz*. New Criticism encouraged study of intrinsic elements like metaphor and narrative structure, as in Joseph Chorpenning's "The Monastery, Paradise, and the Castle: Literary Images and Spiritual Development in St. Teresa of Avila."

The last twenty years have seen increased attention to Teresa as a feminist and a model for women's spirituality. Deirdre Green's *Gold in the Crucible: Teresa of Avila and the Western Mystical Tradition* exemplifies the feminist approach. Most recently, contextual and rhetorical work has carried Teresian studies to new levels of appreciation for her unique stance within the tradition of Christian women's spirituality and on the margins of conventional Catholic religiosity. In this line, Alison Weber's *Teresa of Avila and the Rhetoric of Femi-*

*ninity*, Gillian T. W. Ahlgren's *Teresa of Avila and the Politics of Sanctity*, and Carole Slade's *St. Teresa of Avila: Author of a Heroic Life* are groundbreaking studies.

## BIBLIOGRAPHY

### Works by Teresa of Avila

*The Complete Works of St. Teresa of Jesus*. Trans. E. Allison Peers. 3 vols. London: Sheed and Ward, 1944–1946.
*The Collected Works of St. Teresa of Avila*. Trans. Kieran Kavanaugh and Otilio Rodríguez. 3 vols. Washington, D.C.: ICA Publications, 1976–1985.
*The Letters of Saint Teresa of Jesus*. Trans. E. Allison Peers. 2 vols. London: Sheed and Ward, 1951.

### Works about Teresa of Avila

Ahlgren, Gillian T. W. *Teresa of Avila and the Politics of Sanctity*. Ithaca, New York: Cornell University Press, 1996.
Bilinkoff, Jodi. *The Avila of St. Teresa: Religious Reform in a Sixteenth-Century City*. Ithaca, New York: Cornell University Press, 1989.
Chorpenning, Joseph. "The Monastery, Paradise, and the Castle: Literary Images and Spiritual Development in St. Teresa of Avila." *Journal of Hispanic Philology* 3 (1979): 121–33.
Clissold, Stephen. *St. Teresa of Avila*. London: Sheldon Press, 1979.
Green, Deirdre. *Gold in the Crucible: Teresa of Avila and the Western Mystical Tradition*. Longmead, England: Element Books Limited, 1989.
Luti, J. Mary. *Teresa of Avila's Way*. Collegeville, Minnesota: Liturgical Press, 1991.
Peers, E. Allison. *Mother of Carmel: A Portrait of St. Teresa of Jesus*. Wilton, Connecticut: Morehouse-Barlow, 1944.
Slade, Carole. *St. Teresa of Avila: Author of a Heroic Life*. Berkeley: University of California Press, 1995.
Swietlicki, Catherine. *Spanish Christian Cabala: The Works of Luis de León, Santa Teresa de Jesús, and San Juan de la Cruz*. Columbia: University of Missouri Press, 1986.
Trueman Dickens, E. W. *The Crucible of Love: A Study of the Mysticism of St. Teresa of Jesus and St. John of the Cross*. New York: Sheed and Ward, 1963.
Weber, Alison. *Teresa of Avila and the Rhetoric of Femininity*. Princeton, New Jersey: Princeton University Press, 1990.

MARY E. GILES

# THÉRÈSE OF LISIEUX
# (1873–1897)

## BIOGRAPHY

The modern saint Thérèse Martin of Lisieux, France, who in the centennial year of her death became the youngest of the thirty-three Doctors of the Catholic Church and only the third woman to be so named, is one of the greatest writers in the Christian narrative tradition. Called the "Little Flower" because of the appearance of roses to those who pray to her and seek her intercession, and as a way to distinguish her from "Big" Teresa of Avila, Thérèse of Lisieux embraced the simple, quotidian experiences—the human and earthy— wherein she found God. At the request of her prioress, two and a half years before dying at age twenty-four, Thérèse wrote *Historie d'une Ame*, or *Story of a Soul* (1898), a work that is invaluable for the lessons it presents not only on the author's physical maturation from childhood to young adulthood, but also on her spiritual metamorphosis to Christian perfection. A consideration of Thérèse's narrative underscores her contributions not only to the genre of spiritual autobiography but also to the significance of the writing process itself—bibliotherapy—as a means of affecting a change and a healing in both the writer and reader. This account of Thérèse's life at Carmel clarifies the metamorphosis that occurred in her and, consequently, accommodates the experience of each individual reader. Thus, the deceptively simple recordings of a young cloistered woman from northern France stir in the reader awakenings and reminders of religious sensibility and the gradual unfolding of the soul. Indeed, Thérèse's *Story of a Soul* is a seminal work and one of the most widely read Christian narratives in the literary tradition of spiritual autobiography.

Marie Françoise Thérèse Martin was born on January 2, 1873, to a middle-class family in Alençon, a town fifty-five miles from Lisieux in Normandy. Her mother, Zélie Guerin (1831–1877), had a lace-making business which she supervised in her home. Her father, Louis Martin (1823–1894), helped in choosing the lace designs and dealt with the markets in Paris. He also owned a watch repair and jewelry shop, as well as some property. Four years later, when

Thérèse's mother died of breast cancer, Louis Martin and his five daughters (of whom Thérèse was the youngest) moved to a house with a large garden in Lisieux. Later, in *Story of a Soul,* Thérèse refers to herself as the "little flower" in her father's garden. On April 9, 1888, Thérèse entered the cloistered Carmelite convent nearby, at the age of fifteen, after begging Pope Leo XIII to grant permission, a courageous act particularly in one so young. After some probationary months as a postulant and novice, she took her vows on September 18, 1890, taking the name of Sister Thérèse of the Child Jesus and the Holy Face.

Initially given tasks of washing, ironing, and cleaning, Thérèse eventually became the director or "mistress" of novices. While she approached both her routine and professional duties with a simplicity and dignity, she suffered from what would be diagnosed in contemporary clinical psychology as depression and neurosis, which she tried to hide. Her humanity is further revealed, for example, as she discusses her love for the Blessed Virgin Mary but her dislike of praying the rosary, a Marian devotion. She was a great mystic, but was not at all fond of retreats. She often fell asleep during community prayer, believing that, since parents love their children when they are awake or asleep, so too does God love us even if we doze off while praying. It is not difficult to ascertain the appeal of this saint to contemporary readers who are serious about their spiritual development yet who experience ambiguity and paradox in their lives.

Three of Thérèse's blood sisters—Marie; Pauline, who later edited and published *Story of a Soul*; and Céline— also entered Carmel. While it was rare that the reformed Carmelite order, founded by St. Teresa of Avila, would accept four sisters from the same family, Theresian authorities now believe that the presence of her sisters was providential. The sisters' observations of the youngest sibling convinced them of her holiness and precipitated Thérèse's recording of her spiritual progress. Pauline, known in Carmel as Agnes of Jesus, was elected prioress in 1893, whereupon she made it a priority that Thérèse would set down her spiritual memoirs. Marie also encouraged Thérèse to write the "little doctrine" which reveals how Thérèse had dreamed since childhood of serving God in a variety of ways, including as a priest, yet another bold and courageous statement for a nineteenth-century woman to proclaim. Thérèse gradually came to realize that serving God consists not in great achievements but in great love—the *caritas,* or charity, extolled by St. Paul. One of the greatest contributions Thérèse made to the genre of spiritual autobiography is her disclosure that each moment, accepted and lived in this spirit of love, is an occasion for heroism and a step along the journey to sanctity.

Only seven years after her entrance into the Carmel monastery, Thérèse Martin died of tuberculosis in the convent's infirmary on September 30, 1897. The posthumous publication of her "little way" exerted a strong influence on such people as the French soldiers of World War I, Mother Teresa of Calcutta, Dorothy Day, and Edith Stein. Thérèse's journal of a soul and her powerful writing style cause her to be considered the "sister" soulmate of all who seek a life of spiritual integrity.

In September 1898, the Carmelite monastery distributed 2,000 copies of *Historie d'une Ame* in a version considerably edited by Pauline. While these initial copies went mostly to other Carmelite convents, the book quickly became known to the general public. It is now translated into all major languages and has sold millions of copies. Shortly after *Story of a Soul* became widely disseminated, the Carmelite community and the Vatican received letters reporting favors granted through the intercession of Thérèse. In 1910, a beatification process was opened and on May 17, 1925, Pope Pius XI canonized Thérèse a saint. The next year, she was declared, along with St. Francis Xavier, the patron of missionaries and, later, the secondary patron of France, along with St. Joan of Arc. With Pope John Paul II's action of proclaiming Thérèse a Doctor of the Church on October 17, 1997, St. Thérèse of Lisieux continues to serve as a spiritual healer and teacher of the whole Christian community, as she promised: "I will scatter flowers . . . and these flowers are every little sacrifice, every glance and word, and the doing of the least of actions for love" (p. 156). The feast day of St. Thérèse of Lisieux is October 1.

## MAJOR THEMES

While spiritual autobiography originated with St. Augustine's fourth century *Confessions*, St. Paul's conversion recounted in the Acts of the Apostles is the basis for the genre. St. Augustine, in effect, appropriated the biblical account of St. Paul's experience of personal change and adjusted it to his quest for self-understanding. Whether written by St. Augustine, St. John of the Cross, St. Ignatius of Loyola, Thomas Merton, or St. Thérèse, the language of change and conversion intrinsic to the Christian self-narrative not only records but also effectuates the breakthrough and the journey from oneself to the "Other." Thérèse's language, though reflective of nineteenth-century prosaic idioms, utilizes the discourse of illumination, purgation, and union with God crucial to spiritual autobiography. By its extraordinary sensitivity to the sounds and syllables of spiritual autobiography, *Story of a Soul* charts the dynamic processes associated with self-discovery. Imbued with spirituality and mysticism, spiritual autobiography is a genre of introspection and meditation, though its confessional aspects also make it a public mode of address.

The expression of the experiences of the "dark night of the soul" (p. 70) from a female perspective accounts for Thérèse's far-reaching influence and appeal. Her ability to utilize the written word is quite effective as she paints memorable portraits in human terms of Major Superiors, Mother Pauline (whom she directly addresses throughout the text as "Mother"), sisters in community, the Pope, and friends and family members. In *Story of a Soul*, Thérèse reflects on and interprets past and present experiences and thereby clarifies and charts the development of her soul. Her persistence in finding answers to her restlessness and her curious religious spirit impelled her to read the epistles of

St. Paul to try to find "some cure for my sufferings" (p. 154). In these texts, she was reminded, as she writes, that "we cannot all be apostles, prophets, doctors, that the Church is made up of different members, and that the eye cannot also be the hand. This answer was clear enough, but it did not satisfy me and brought me no peace" (p. 154). So she read St. John of the Cross and returned to St. Paul, now enlightened by the passage that describes "the better gifts . . . a yet more excellent way"; that is, the way of charity as "the most excellent way of going safely to God. I had found peace at last" (p. 154). Her new-found proclamation that "Charity gave me the key to *my vocation*" (p. 155), evolved into a peace that brought her calmness and tranquillity; she discovered a place in the Mystical Body of Christ that allowed her to be both giver and recipient of Christ's love. *Story of a Soul* culminates with "LOVE" in uppercase letters, followed by three exclamation points; it is a passionate injunction to Christ "to choose in this world a multitude of little victims worthy of Your LOVE!!!" (p. 159).

Little did Thérèse know that these recordings of the inner workings of her soul in both its ambivalent and transcendent states would become a classic touchstone with universal appeal. Her belief that she had "expressed myself very badly. . . . But, after all, I am not writing a literary work, and if I have bored you by this homily on charity, you will at least see that your child has given proof of her goodwill" (p. 126) belies a profound spirituality and writing style that serve as a record of the Christian disciple's journey from the illuminating power of God, through the purgative state or "little way," and culminating in the encounter and union with God. Devotional works such as Thérèse's spiritual autobiography establish a sense of the sacred which, ironically, is more apparent in recordings of the three stages of spiritual development and the "dark night of the soul" than in works that explicitly attempt to reinforce and redefine religious tradition and doctrine.

*Story of a Soul* underscores the organic and flexible nature of the spiritual life and authenticates its analysis as spiritual autobiography. Not only does it provide a unique depiction of daily life in a Carmelite monastery as it was experienced by a young woman, but also and most importantly it reflects values and meanings, not merely facts or events, and assigns the final meaning of her vocation and the completion of her soul to the *Logos*, the Lord who reads hearts. St. Thérèse continues to enlighten souls like the prophet and Doctor of the Church she could not imagine becoming. Her spirit and spirituality permeate the world, as she predicted, "preaching Your Name and raising your glorious Cross in pagan lands" (p. 153). The title "Doctor of the Church," with its accompanying characteristic of "healer," is duly awarded this modern woman of the Catholic tradition. The quotidian and human details of Thérèse's short life encourage us to set out on the path of perfection which consists in "the complete abandonment of a baby sleeping without a fear in its father's arms" (p. 150).

## SURVEY OF CRITICISM

The popularity and influence of St. Thérèse are furthered by both verbal and photographic artists. *Saint Thérèse of Lisieux: Her Life, Times, and Teaching* by Conrad DeMeester, O.C.D., provides more than two hundred photographs and includes fourteen chapters on Thérèse by leading Theresian authorities. It serves as a fine tribute to her declaration of sainthood on the centenary of her death and paints a portrait, both literally and figuratively, of a "fellow" Carmelite. The book was published first in Italian and then in eleven other languages. Steven Payne, O.C.D., edited the English edition. Vivid in its verbal and photographic account of Thérèse's life is Tom Morgan's *Saints: A Visual Almanac of the Virtuous, Pure, Praiseworthy, and Good*. This book includes inspirational narratives of saints for the ordinary reader. Also far-reaching in its scope and manner of defining the "saints" of our day is Robert Ellsberg's *All Saints: Daily Reflections on Saints, Prophets, and Witnesses for Our Time*. His 365 figures break open the criteria for canonization by including such literary artists as Flannery O'Connor and Gerard Manley Hopkins.

H. D. Kreilkamp's article, "St. Thérèse of Lisieux," discusses the element of suffering as it furthered the appeal of St. Thérèse for such contemporary spiritual writers as Thomas Merton and Graham Greene, and for the priest-missionaries with whom Thérèse corresponded. Her injunction to "accept ourselves as we are, trying to change what we can" (Kreilkamp, p. 3), furthers her appeal for the current reader and underscores her title of Doctor, or "physician of the soul." Kreilkamp's paralleling of our age of angst with Thérèse's affinity for those "plagued by fear of suffering or death" renders the saint palpable for our time (p. 3).

Jean Guitton's *The Spiritual Genius of St. Thérèse of Lisieux* broadens the perspective of childlike simplicity by which many people have come to regard Thérèse to include an assessment of her as a spiritual giant and an underrated spiritual voice of the late nineteenth century. Guitton, a member of L'Académie Française and the only lay member of Vatican II, identifies themes in her writing, addresses her use of language, and compares her to Edith Stein and Elizabeth of the Trinity. A shorter version of this text was originally published in French in 1954.

Susan Helen Wallace's *Call Me Little Theresa: St. Theresa of Lisieux* serves as a recent autobiography of the young French woman in language reflective of modern parlance and spirituality. And John W. Donohue's "Thérèse of Lisieux: Doctor of the Church" is an informed article on the key elements in Thérèse's life, augmented by remarks from other Theresian authorities and from Thérèse herself. This article provides an historical and personal view as well as a review to date of current studies on Thérèse.

## BIBLIOGRAPHY

### Work by Thérèse of Lisieux

Beevers, John, trans. *The Autobiography of Saint Thérèse of Lisieux: The Story of a Soul.* New York: Doubleday, 1989.

### Works about Thérèse of Lisieux

DeMeester, Conrad, O.C.D. *Saint Thérèse of Lisieux: Her Life, Times, and Teaching.* Ed. and trans. Steven Payne, O.C.D. Washington, D.C.: Carmelite Studies Publications, 1997.

Donohue, John W. "Thérèse of Lisieux, Doctor of the Church." *America* 177.19 (1997): 12–16.

Ellsberg, Robert. *All Saints: Daily Reflections on Saints, Prophets, and Witnesses for Our Time.* New York: Crossroad Publishing, 1998.

Francis Mary, Brother, and Franciscan Friars of the Immaculate. *St. Thérèse: Doctor of the Little Way.* New Bedford, Massachusetts: Franciscan Press, 1997.

Guitton, Jean. *The Spiritual Genius of Saint Thérèse of Lisieux.* Trans. Felicity Lang. Montana: Triumph Books, 1997.

Koenig-Bricker, Woodeene. *365 Saints: Your Daily Guide to the Wisdom and Wonder of Their Lives.* New York: HarperCollins Publishers, 1995.

Kreilkamp, H. D. "St. Thérèse of Lisieux." *America* 34.1 (1997): 2–3.

Morgan, Tom. *Saints: A Visual Almanac of the Virtuous, Pure, Praiseworthy, and Good.* San Francisco: Chronicle Books, 1994.

Wallace, Susan Helen. *Call Me Little Theresa: St. Theresa of Lisieux.* Boston: Pauline Books and Media, 1995.

MARY THERESA HALL

# SIGRID UNDSET
# (1882–1949)

## BIOGRAPHY

Sigrid Undset was born on May 20, 1882, in Kalundborg, Denmark, the eldest of three daughters. Her father, Ingvald Undset, was a well-known archaeologist whose specialty was the Iron Age in Europe. Undset was raised in Kristiania (the name was changed to Oslo in 1925), where her parents moved on account of the failing health of her father. She grew up in a tolerant, free-thinking household, and attended a progressive school. Influenced by her father's work, she devoured Old Norse and Icelandic sagas and gleaned much of her fascination with and knowledge of medieval Scandinavia that would later serve as backdrops to her most famous novels, *Kristin Lavransdatter* and *The Master of Hestviken*. Although she was born into the Lutheran faith, the predominant religion in Norway at that time, Undset's parents were not practicing Christians and allowed their children to form their own opinions concerning religion. Early in her childhood, Undset had already begun to formulate the opinions that would eventually lead to her conversion to Catholicism.

Undset's father died at the age of forty, when she was eleven, and her mother was left to raise three children on a very meager income. At sixteen Undset, instead of pursuing a university career, went to work as a typist for a German firm in Oslo, where she was to stay ten years. Her time as a secretary, although humdrum and unfulfilled, gave Undset great insight into the lives of ordinary working men and women trying to eke out a meaningful existence apart from the mundane routines of their lives. These individuals became the inspirations for her first novels, *Fru Marta Oulie* (1907) [Mrs. Marta Oulie], a story about marital infidelity; *The Happy Age* (1910), a collection of short stories about the "respectable drudges" (quoted in Brunsdale 1991, p. 87) whom Undset observed during her time as a secretary; and *Jenny* (1911), which established her writing career. This latter novel, though well received, caused a great outcry in feminist circles where it was felt that Undset compromised the integrity of women. The heroine is a struggling artist who, unsatisfied in her work, searches for emotional fulfillment in the arms of various lovers. Unhappy with these momentary love affairs, Jenny eventually despairs and commits suicide. Undset was unaffected by this criticism for in these early novels she was already developing the themes that would become prominent in all her later work: those of personal growth, integrity, and responsibility.

At twenty-seven, Undset won a scholarship that enabled her to travel to Rome, which at that time was a popular destination for Scandinavian artists and writers. There she met the naturalistic painter Anders Svarstad, whom she married in 1912; they had three children together before separating in 1919. It is during this time that Undset began her epic novel *Kristin Lavransdatter*. She had earlier published a novel set in tenth-century Iceland, entitled *Gunnar's Daughter* (1909), but it too closely imitated the Icelandic sagas such as *Njall's Saga,* especially in the dashing hero Skarpedhin, whose likeness we see in Erlend Nikulaussøn, Kristin's wayward husband in *Kristin Lavransdatter,* and in Olav Audunssøn in *The Master of Hestviken. Kristin Lavransdatter,* a trilogy of books, was published between 1920 and 1922, followed by the four books of *The Master of Hestviken* between 1925 and 1927. These epic works established Undset as a significant literary figure, not only in Norway but also around the world.

In 1924 Sigrid Undset converted to Catholicism. Her conversion was a process that developed over a period of years rather than any sort of specific religious crisis. Undset had always felt unsatisfied with the Protestant faith, which she believed encouraged self-centered behavior rather than the well-being of the world at large. She embraced neo-Thomist philosophy, which viewed spiritual knowledge as being acquired by hard facts received through the senses (Brunsdale 1991, p. 92). Undset and other neo-Thomists such as Jacques Maritain, who grew up in a similar environment as Undset, applied their religious theories to political and sociological issues. They maintained that only by a return to the principles of the Catholic Church as practiced in the Middle Ages could humankind hope to survive (Brunsdale 1991, p. 92).

In 1928, Undset was awarded the Nobel Prize for literature for her forceful and accurate descriptions of the Middle Ages in Scandinavia. She continued to write and publish actively throughout the next decade. Her novels during this period, *The Wild Orchid* (1929), *The Burning Bush* (1930), and *Ida Elisabeth* (1932), reflect the profound influence of the Catholic faith on her life. These novels, set in contemporary Norway, take the themes she explored in her medieval novels—personal growth, the quest for truth, and the struggle of the spirit over the flesh—even further. Today many critics, among them Undset biographer Mitzi Brunsdale, find the later novels unpalatable due to Undset's dogmatic insistence on Catholic theory as a solution to all of life's problems.

It was during this period that the threat of Fascism was making itself felt around the world as Hitler's power increased. From early on, Undset was a strong opponent of Hitler and his regime, and she made her sentiments known in many speeches and essays. When Norway was occupied in 1940, she fled to the United States, where she remained in exile for the duration of the war. During this time, she wrote essays about her country's history and recent misfortune at the hands of the Nazis, and she released a book recounting her flight from Norway by way of Sweden, Russia, and Japan entitled *Return to the Future* (1942). *Happy Days in Norway* (1943), an account of her life in Norway, was specially commissioned by Eleanor Roosevelt, who wanted authors from allied occupied countries to write books about their homeland for Americans.

Upon her return to Norway, Undset was awarded by King Håkon VII the Grand Cross of the Order of Saint Olav, Norway's highest honor, for her literary contributions and service to her country. But by this time her health and spirit were rapidly declining. Her latest book, a biography of Catherine of Siena, the fourteenth-century reformer of the Church, had been rejected by her publishers. She died three years later in 1949. A multivolume novel set in the eighteenth century entitled *Madame Dorthea,* the first volume of which had been published in 1939, was left unfinished. *Catherine of Siena* was published posthumously.

## MAJOR THEMES

Though the majority of Undset's novels are set in contemporary Norway, she is best remembered for her two medieval works, *Kristin Lavransdatter* and *The Master of Hestviken,* which take place in the fourteenth and thirteenth centuries, respectively. In these stories, Undset combines her love of Scandinavian history and mythology with her growing attachment to Catholicism. For Undset, the Middle Ages represented the epitome of all that Catholicism came to mean for her; she once described it as "the bearer of those ideals which cannot die" (quoted in Brunsdale 1991, p. 89).

In *Kristin Lavransdatter,* Undset develops the themes of the quest for truth, the growth to maturity, and the most difficult lesson for the novel's heroine to learn, the ability to forgive others as God forgives us our sins. Kristin, the beautiful and willful daughter of a wealthy landowner, the pious Lavrans Björgulfsön, falls in love with the beguiling Erlend Nikulaussön. Their relationship is problematic from the start, for Kristin is already betrothed to a man whom her father has chosen for her, Simon Andressön, and Erlend is under a ban from the Church for adultery. The two meet secretly in a house of ill-repute not far from the convent where Kristin is staying. The convent and the brothel represent the struggle of the spirit with the flesh, a theme that frequents much of Undset's work. While Undset recognizes the importance of sex in a relationship, succumbing to passion over reason and deceit over truth can only lead to grief. Kristin's father, after several years and much persuasion, finally submits to the union of Erlend and Kristin. However, their marriage is blighted from the beginning. Even as Kristin wears the traditional virgin's bridal wreath at her wedding, she conceals the child that she has conceived with Erlend. Though the couple later make amends to her parents and the Church for their sin, Kristin is plagued by guilt and is unable to forgive herself or Erlend, whom she blames for their sorrows. Though Kristin believes herself a good and pious Christian, criticizing Erlend for what she feels are his lax ways, she suffers from pride coupled with an inability to be opposed in any way. She keeps the wrongs that Erlend has committed locked up inside her until they strafe like a festering sore. Their marriage falls apart when Erlend, no longer able to withstand his wife's behavior, lays open her faults to her, though she is yet incapable of facing them:

I wot well you are more godly in such-like things than I can ever be—yet, Kristin, 'tis hard for me to see how it should be a right reading of God's word to go on, as your way is, ever storing up wrath and never forgetting . . . but often when you speak so soft and sweet, as your mouth were filled with honey, I fear me you are thinking most upon old wrongs, and God may judge whether your heart is full as pious as your mouth—(p. 150)

The marriage between Erlend and Kristin represents another major theme in the novel, and one that often set Undset at odds with feminist critics. Around the time of the publication of her second novel, *Jenny*, many feminist groups in Norway were attempting to have St. Paul's injunction, "Wives, be submissive to your husbands," excluded from the Norwegian marriage service. Undset, however, believed that the line should remain, stating, "these selfsame words carry nature's own legal prescription for marriage: that woman shall marry the man whom she can call her lord—and no one else" (quoted in Brunsdale 1991, p. 88).

After the death of her husband, Kristin joins a convent in Oslo, leaving the care of the manor to her son Gaute and his wife. As Kristin leaves her worldly life behind her, she gives herself unselfishly to the task of helping and administering to others. During her last days, as she lies dying from the plague that ravishes the countryside, she is at last at peace with herself and with the memory of her husband, whom she now realizes she has wronged: "Disobedience was the chief of my sins . . . All the days of my life have I longed both to go the right way and to follow my own wildered paths as well—"(p. 360).

In *The Master of Hestviken*, the protagonist Olav Audunssøn must wrestle with the guilt that he carries throughout his life, that is, his going against God's will by following his own uncertain course. The influence of the era's pagan myths and beliefs are even more strongly felt in this novel than in *Kristin*. It is, therefore, more difficult for the characters to adhere to the Christian faith, for Christianity's statutes are very different from the Viking codes of old in which a man was obliged to take the law into his own hands when he or a member of his kin was wronged. Olav begins his difficult journey by sleeping with Ingunn, his foster-father's oldest daughter, before they are married. He does this in part to secure the promise that Ingunn will be his bride, which is put into question as the foster-father, Steinfinn, lays dying. Though Olav and Ingunn had been officially betrothed when they were children, Steinfinn has decided to seek another marriage partner for his daughter. The two children, who were raised as brother and sister, had come to rely on their future together as husband and wife as certain; indeed, as the only secure thing in their lives, which are burdened by the many troubles that the Torressøn clan endure.

Olav's troubles multiply when he murders a young Icelandic man who had seduced Ingunn while he was away under service to a Duke. This secret crime becomes a heavy burden for him to bear, and it eventually poisons not only his life but also the lives of those around him. Unlike Kristin, who suffers from pride and hypocrisy (for she uses her piety as a crutch and a weapon), Olav feels alienated from everyone around him and most especially from God, whom he feels is unduly hard on him. Years after the murder, he believes himself beyond redemption. Because he has turned away from God for so long, he no longer thinks it possible to seek his forgiveness. As with Kristin, it is only at the end of his life that Olav comprehends the magnitude of God's love and forgiveness. On his deathbed, he experiences the peace of one who at last has come to terms with his life, leaving his past and his sins behind him. He finally makes the journey he had been too afraid to make before: "For an instant he stared with open eyes straight into the eye of the sun, tried even, wild with love and longing, to gaze yet deeper into God. He sank back in red fire, all about him was a living blaze, and he knew that now the prison tower that he had built around him was burning" (Vol. 4, *The Son Avenger,* p. 985).

The themes of growth to maturity, and the triumph of the spirit over the flesh, are ever present in Undset's works, medieval and contemporary. She was convinced that humans needed a strict religious doctrine to lead them on the right path toward salvation, and for her only Catholicism offered this. The characters who populate her novels, as with all humankind, are flawed, but they possess the potential to develop and to arrive at a mature understanding of their lives. Undset believed that materialism and sensuality restricted growth and therefore impeded the development of society; once again, she maintained that the solution to this problem lay in the teachings of the Catholic Church. We see this, for example, in *Jenny*. The protagonist's quest for fulfillment in the arms of various lovers impedes her moral and spiritual growth and in the end results in her suicide. It is how humans lead their lives, both in regard to themselves and to those around them, that is important. Abusing relationships (as is the case with Kristin, Jenny, and Ida Elisabeth) only leads to one's downfall. After his conversion to Catholicism, Paul Selmer in *The Burning Bush,* for example, sees more clearly his relationship with those around him and the place they have in his life. No longer encumbered by skepticism and free from the tie of material greed, he discovers a peace and contentment he has never felt before.

## SURVEY OF CRITICISM

A. H. Winsnes's *Sigrid Undset—A Study in Christian Realism* is one of the earliest biographies of Undset and contains a detailed account of her childhood and early life as well as her conversion to Catholicism. Mitzi Brunsdale has written numerous articles on Undset's writing, such as "Stages on Her Road: Sigrid Undset's Spiritual Journey," as well as a biography, *Sigrid Undset, Chronicler of Norway*, which combines biographical information on the author, Scandinavian history as it relates to the novels, and critical interpretations of the works. Although the majority of Undset criticism deals with her two medieval epics *Kristin Lavransdatter* and *The Master of Hestviken*, a few works such as Elisabeth Solbakken's *Redefining Integrity: The Portrayal of Women in the Contemporary Novels of Sigrid Undset* focus primarily on Undset's novels set in modern times. Feminist critics like Solbakken often encounter difficulty in finding a place for Undset's later novels in the canon of contemporary women writers' works due to her "old fashioned" views concerning a woman's place as a wife and mother above all things. J. C. Whitehouse's articles, "Religion as Fulfillment in the Novels of Sigrid Undset" and "Concepts and Pictures: Ways of Seeing the Human Person in the Catholic Thought and Literature of Mid–Twentieth Century Europe," help clarify many of Undset's major themes as well as the Catholic philosophy on which they are based. Finally, Margaret Mary Dunn's book, *Paradigms and Paradoxes in the Life and Letters of Sigrid Undset*, and her articles, "*The Master of Hestviken*—A New Reading, I & II," provide clear and concise analyses of the novels and their themes.

## BIBLIOGRAPHY

### Works by Sigrid Undset

*Gunnar's Daughters* [*Fortellingen om Viga-Ljot og Vigids*]. 1909. Trans. Arthur G. Chater. Intro. and notes by Sherrill Harbison. New York: Penguin, 1998.

*Jenny*. 1911. Trans. W. Emme. New York: H. Fretig, 1975.

*Kristin Lavransdatter I: The Bridal Wreath* [*Kransen*]. 1920. Trans. Charles Archer and J. S. Scott. New York: Vintage, 1987.

*Kristin Lavransdatter II: The Mistress of Husaby* [*Husfrue*]. 1921. Trans. Charles Archer. New York: Vintage, 1987.

*Kristin Lavransdatter III: The Cross* [*Korset*]. 1922. Trans. Charles Archer. New York: Vintage, 1987.

*The Master of Hestviken I: The Axe* [*Olav Audunssøn i Hestviken*]. 1925. Trans. Arthur G. Chater. New York: Vintage, 1994.

*The Master of Hestviken II: The Snake Pit* [*Olav Audunssøn i Hestviken*]. 1925. Trans. Arthur G. Chater. New York, Vintage, 1994.

*The Master of Hestviken III: In the Wilderness* [*Olav Audunssøn og hans børn*]. 1927. Trans. Arthur G. Chater. New York: Vintage, 1995.

*The Master of Hestviken IV: The Son Avenger* [*Olav Audunssøn og hans børn*]. 1927. Trans. Arthur G. Chater. New York: Vintage, 1995.

*The Wild Orchid* [*Gymnadenia*]. 1929. Trans. Arthur G. Chater. New York: A. A. Knopf, 1931.

*The Burning Bush* [*Den brændende busk*]. 1930. Trans. Arthur G. Chater. New York: A. A. Knopf, 1930.

*Ida Elisabeth.* Trans. Arthur G. Chater. New York: A. A. Knopf, 1933.
*Madame Dorthea.* 1939. Trans. Arthur G. Chater. New York: A. A. Knopf, 1940.
*Return to the Future.* Trans. Henriette Naeseth. New York: A. A. Knopf, 1942.
*Happy Times in Norway.* Trans. Joran Birkeland. New York: A. A. Knopf, 1942.
*Catherine of Siena* [*Caterina av Siena*]. 1951. Trans. Arthur G. Chater. New York: Sheed and Ward, 1954.

## Works about Sigrid Undset

Bayerschmidt, Carl. *Sigrid Undset.* New York: Twayne, 1970.
Brunsdale, Mitzi. *Sigrid Undset, Chronicler of Norway.* Berg Woman's Series. New York: Berg Publishers Limited, 1988.
——. "Stages on Her Road: Sigrid Undset's Spiritual Journey." *Religion and Literature* 23.3 (Autumn 1991): 83–96.
Dunn, Margaret. "*The Master of Hestviken*—A New Reading I." *Scandinavian Studies* 38 (1966): 281–94.
——. "*The Master of Hestviken*—A New Reading II." *Scandinavian Studies* 40 (1968): 210–24.
——. *Paradigms and Paradoxes in the Life and Letters of Sigrid Undset.* New York and London: Lanham Publishers, 1994.
Hudson, Deal, ed. *Sigrid Undset on Saints and Sinners: New Translations and Studies.* Papers presented at a conference sponsored by the Wethersfield Institute of New York, 24 April 1993. San Francisco: Ignatius Press, 1993.
Lytle, Andrew. *Kristin: A Reading.* Columbia: University of Missouri Press, 1992.
Solbakken, Elisabeth. *Redefining Integrity: The Portrayal of Women in the Contemporary Novels of Sigrid Undset.* Frankfurt and New York: Peter Lang, 1992.
Whitehouse, J. C. "Concepts and Pictures: Ways of Seeing the Human Person in Catholic Thought and Literature of Mid-Twentieth Century Europe." *Journal of European Studies* 16 (1986): 1–27.
——. "Religion as Fulfillment in the Novels of Sigrid Undset." *Renascence: Essays on Value in Literature* 38.1 (May 1985): 2–12.
Winsnes, A. H. *Sigrid Undset—A Study in Christian Realism.* 1949. Trans. P. G. Foote. New York: Sheed and Ward, 1953.

OLIVIA SCHAFF

# SIMONE WEIL
# (1909–1943)

## BIOGRAPHY

Simone Weil was born in Paris, France, in 1909. Her father and mother were well educated and her brother André, a brilliant mathematician, would develop foundational and influential ideas in algebraic geometry and number theory. Weil often felt herself laboring in her brother's shadow, but she soon differentiated herself from him by the intensity of her religious and moral imagination. For her, neither purely abstract worlds and models, nor the engineered forms and homages to power of modern technology, answered to her questioning spirit. A brilliant student, she was among the first women to graduate from the École Normale Supérieure. Whether writing on Descartes or Marx or performing routine factory work, Weil remained preoccupied with ultimate questions. Rejecting Marx's thoroughgoing materialism, Weil searched for her spiritual identity in pacifism, in anti-Fascist political action during the Spanish Civil War, and in reading and writing on philosophy, ethics, and social justice.

The Weils were Jewish—Simone Weil's attitudes toward her Jewish heritage and Judaism as a traditional faith are highly complex—and as the political ideologies of Communism and Fascism with their overt anti-Semitism and violence dominated the war-ravaged European landscape, in 1942 the family immigrated to America. Simone, however, stayed in New York only briefly. Appalled by Hitler's invasion of Czechoslovakia, in touch with the Free French forces, and seeking to oppose the Nazi war machine by sending nurses to the front lines as moral witnesses to the power of love and compassion, she returned to London. Suffering from tuberculosis, consistently eating only the equivalent of the meager rations of the poor in occupied France, still preoccupied in mind and heart with God, justice, and salvation, Weil died at the age of thirty-four at Ashford, Kent, in August 1943. On her deathbed, she was baptized by a non-ordained friend into the Catholic faith.

Although Weil had refused baptism until the very end of her life, she had long been preoccupied with the person of Christ, the mystery and institution of the Church, and the nature of the sacraments. Indeed, one of the last works she wrote before her death—"Theory of the Sacraments" (1943)—expresses her thinking about the sacraments. Further, her "spiritual autobiography" in *Waiting for God* (1951) consists of a series of letters to a blind Dominican priest, Father J. M. Perrin, who had become her close friend. That her baptism was a culmination of her preoccupation with God and faith is made clear by the depth and intensity of her moral and religious thought as well as by several religious experiences she recounts. As Eric O. Springsted delineates them, the first occurred in a poor fishing village in Portugal, the second at Assisi, and the third during Holy Week in 1938 at Solesmes, France, in a Benedictine monastery (p. 18). In this last experience, she described the radiance on the face of a young English Catholic after he had received the Eucharist; she recited George Herbert's poem "Love" in an almost incantatory state and felt Christ's presence as a beloved friend; and she was assured of the reality of God and Christ not abstractly but in the dynamism of its relationship to the earthly and finite soul. So real would this dynamism become that Weil argues that our "longing to love the beauty of the world in a human being is essentially the longing for the Incarnation. . . . The Incarnation alone can satisfy it" (*Waiting for God*, p. 171). Weil's preoccupation with the mystery of the Incarnation—and, indeed, with the Passion and the sacraments—reflects her vision of God as dynamic toward and engaged with the world and the individual soul. Her baptism embodies this vision of a concrete human world touched by an equally real and concrete grace.

## MAJOR THEMES

In her major writings, including *Waiting for God, Gravity and Grace, The Need for Roots*, and her *Notebooks*, Weil addresses a striking range of subjects: Platonic philosophy, metaphysics, science, friendship, justice, ethics, the love of God and the depths of suffering, the need for attentiveness, and what she calls in *Gravity and Grace* "the mysticism of work." Throughout them runs a twofold preoccupation: a contemplative, even mystical concern with the soul, God, salvation, and the mystery of Christ; and a passionate concern for social justice and community in a time rife with war, ideology, technological power, collectivism, and other forms of oppression, all of which threatened to annihilate the individual soul and the life of faith. The intensity and power of Weil's concerns and vision influenced such writers as Camus and T. S. Eliot and continue to resonate strongly.

For Weil, it is the tradition of meditation—at times but not always mystical—that helps to bring the soul to God. To be sure, God comes to us and not the reverse: "We cannot take a step toward the heavens. God crosses the universe and comes to us" (*Waiting for God*, p. 133). Weil's idea of attentiveness, informed at once by rabbinic and Christian views of learning and reading, pervades her vision of God and of grace as experiential. It also informs her view of *malheur*, or affliction, the intense experience of loss and uprooting the Crucifixion embodies and all human beings go through—the dark night of the soul whose distinct and ultimate mark, paradoxically, is not despair but joy. Finally, this attentiveness should issue in compassion and justice, for our most authentic experience of love is not solitary but communal. Although she remained in "exile" from the Church for most of her life and viewed warily all organized social structures—an understandable reserve, given Nazi and Communist collectivism and totalitarianism—Weil believed in and speaks for the common bonds and love that define all authentic communal sharing and faith.

In an essay in *Waiting for God* entitled "Reflections on the Right Use of School Studies with a View to the Love of God," written for students at a Catholic girls' school, Weil argues that real attentiveness in study can be sacramental. By "attentiveness" Weil means not muscular contraction and concentration, but an openness to the object of study—a poem, a verb conjugation, an equation—in faith and expectation. Undertaken in this light, attentiveness retains the very substance of prayer. Here patience is not simply a cardinal virtue but the heart of all real meditation, just as faith is not merely a useful prospect but "the indispensable condition" (*Simone Weil: Selected Writings*, p. 93). Seen and experienced in faith, all acts of reading, writing, and listening are not simply academic exercises but enactments of an attentiveness marked by the presence of the sacred—precious, says Weil, beyond measure.

Yet just as Weil insists that something in our soul is repelled by attentiveness as the body is repelled by fatigue, so she links distractedness and indifference to evil. In this moral drama in turn, evil is part of the affliction that subverts our faith and uproots our longings for stability, for home. Affliction makes us powerless, mocks our hopes, and plunges us into the void—a palpable nothingness in which we count for nothing while separated from everything. G. K. Chesterton described the Crucifixion as "God abandoned by God." Just so, Weil sees the Crucifixion as uprooting, dislocation, abandonment. Yet in this abandonment, she emphasizes, Christ remains obedient even unto death. In the same way, the created order and all matter are obedient to God. By our own obedience, our consenting to God's reality and presence, we become receptive to God's love—a love at once pure and terrifying: "He whose soul remains ever turned toward God though the nail pierces it finds himself . . . [at] the true center" of the universe, in God (*Waiting for God*, p. 135).

In our love of neighbor and in the love we express in our prosaic lives and ways, says Weil, we are "implicitly" loving God. That Weil's gravitation toward solitude and exile—a necessary state, she believed, for the authenticity of her interior life and conscience—could seem self-righteous and prideful is evident. Yet she loved the biblical story of the Good Samaritan because while it may be relatively understandable that members of the same group would try to love each other, a love that is "anonymous"—the Samaritan did not know the wounded Jew, and Jews as a group despised Samaritans—is deeper and more encompassing still. Suspicious of all organizations—political, social, ecclesiastical, cultural, economic—Weil nonetheless values community as she does empathy. The same attentiveness that at its best marks study, she insists, should mark our way of looking at and listening to others. So, "paradoxical as it may seem," she says, studying an academic problem or text "may be of great service one day" in our helping a soul in affliction (*Simone Weil: Selected Writings*, p. 97). Just as it is the key to real study, so attentiveness lies at the heart of all real justice, compassion, and community. Indeed, speaking for all those she influenced—including T. S. Eliot, Hannah Arendt, Camus, and many others—the writer Czeslaw Milosz stated of Weil in his Nobel Prize speech, "Her intelligence, the precision of her style were nothing but a very high degree of attention given to the sufferings of mankind."

## SURVEY OF CRITICISM

Eric O. Springsted's introduction to Weil in his edition of her works, *Simone Weil: Selected Writings*, is a fine consideration of Weil at once analytical and sympathetic. Simone Petrement's *Simone Weil: A Life* is a rich and illuminating biography. Diogenes Allen and Eric O. Springsted's *Spirit, Nature and Community* provides a range of views on dimensions of Weil's thought and writings, as does John M. Dunaway and Springsted's *The Beauty That Saves.*

## BIBLIOGRAPHY

### Works by Simone Weil

*Waiting for God.* Trans. Emma Craufurd. 1951. New York: Harper and Row, 1973.
*Notebooks.* 2 vols. Trans. A. Wills. London: Routledge and Kegan Paul, 1952.
*Gravity and Grace.* Trans. A. Wills. New York: G. P. Putnam's Sons, 1953.
*The Need for Roots.* Trans. A. Wills. London: Routledge and Kegan Paul, 1956.
*Simone Weil: Selected Writings.* Ed. Eric O. Springsted. Maryknoll, New York: Orbis Books, 1998.

### Works about Simone Weil

Allen, Diogenes, and Eric O. Springsted, eds. *Spirit, Nature and Community: Issues in the Thought of Simone Weil.* Albany: State University of New York Press, 1994.
Dunaway, John M., and Eric O. Springsted, eds. *The Beauty That Saves: Essays on Aesthetics and Language in Simone Weil.* Macon: Mercer University Press, 1996.
Petrement, Simone. *Simone Weil: A Life.* Trans. Raymond Rosenthal. New York: Pantheon Books, 1976.
Springsted, Eric O., ed. Introduction. *Simone Weil: Selected Writings.* Maryknoll, New York: Orbis Books, 1998. 11–29.

THOMAS WERGE

# Antonia White
# (1899–1980)

## BIOGRAPHY

Antonia White's life might best be viewed as a collage of troubled relationships: with the Catholic Church, with loved ones, and, most importantly, with herself. White's life looms large behind her fiction, and separating the two is no easy task, but recent feminist literary critical work has done much to broaden the scope of White studies and enrich understanding of the writer's life experiences. Antonia White was born in London in 1899, and was christened Eirene Adeline Botting by her parents Cecil and Christine. Because she was an only child, White spent much time alone. She lived the first years of her life as a miniature adult, remarkably astute and sophisticated in her thinking, evidently not "childlike" at all. She invented games for her stuffed animals to play and imagined that she was somewhere—anywhere—else, performing heroic deeds, living an adventurous life. Her father converted to Catholicism when she was eight and wished to give his daughter the thoroughly Catholic upbringing he never enjoyed. His decision to send her to the exclusive Convent of the Sacred Heart in Roehampton that same year set into motion White's love-hate relationship with the Catholic Church. While in school, she grew increasingly dependent on the approval of others; she longed to develop close friendships with the more wealthy and cosmopolitan girls and suffered from a consuming need to make her father proud of her intellectual achievements. Indeed, her father's desire for her to earn a university degree and become a teacher motivated the young White to earn academic honors and pursue study of the classics.

But White's relationship with her father was far from harmonious. As nearly all studies of White have pointed out, her life seemed to revolve around earning her father's approval. Figuring out how to please him consumed much of her energy and attention. Her diaries and letters indicate that she had a most difficult time defining herself in any but a relational way—as anything except her father's daughter. As she grew into young adulthood, White came to reflect on the shadow her father cast over her life when he converted to Catholicism and introduced her to a new way of life at the convent school. Life and art, from that point on, became for her struggles to rise above the injustices she felt she suffered at the hands of her father.

This particular drama manifested itself in other relationships and in other areas of her life. White's difficulty in maintaining close relationships is described in her own diaries and letters as well as in the memoirs of her two daughters, Susan Chitty and Lyndall Passerini Hopkinson. All three of White's marriages ended in divorce, and the intensive Freudian analysis she underwent later in life suggested to her that conflicted feelings about her father brought about an inability to sustain a healthy relationship with a member of the opposite sex. Although she had a few close friendships with women, these too fell victim to varying degrees to White's apparent unwillingness to let down her defenses and reveal her personal flaws to those close to her.

A bright spot in White's personal and professional life came in her associations with the "Hayford Hall" circle, a group of women (and a few men) who gathered at the estate of Peggy Guggenheim to discuss art, literature, and life. There, White seems to have found the supportive and energetic environment that enabled her to write, critique the work of others, and work through some of her personal issues. Critic Mary Lynn Broe contrasts the positive family dynamics of White's interactions with Djuna Barnes and Emily Holmes Coleman at Hayford with the dysfunctional family relationships portrayed in White's novel, *Frost in May* (1933). White's relationship with Coleman, in particular, was a source of support throughout her life.

Unfortunately, however, the bulk of White's writing years were spent in virtual torment. She was unconvinced of her own intelligence and creativity and was painfully shy about sharing her writing with others. *Frost in May*, for instance, was completed only because her husband insisted that she read to him regularly from the manuscript; after the novel was published, it took seventeen years for her next novel, *The Lost Traveller* (1950), to appear in print. While White had no difficulty working on the writing of others (she translated more than twenty-five French novels, her translations of Colette receiving high praise and awards), she clearly struggled with incorporating her own experiences and ideas into fiction. And while she had trouble writing for a large audience, she was a faithful letter writer and diary keeper. Her voluminous diaries were edited into two volumes by her elder daughter, Susan Chitty, and reveal the depth of her fears as well as a sense of humor and levity rarely seen in her fiction.

That White was a guarded person is obvious, and she kept her most personal struggles private. In addition to debilitating writer's block, she suffered recurrent bouts of insanity that required both hospitalization and lifelong therapy. Like her earlier experiences in school, these struggles are reflected in her fiction. The two novels that followed *Frost in May*—*The Lost Traveller* and *The Sugar House* (1952)—describe the difficult maturation of Clara Batchellor, while White's final novel, *Beyond the Glass* (1954), treats Clara's surrender to madness, clearly one of the most painful topics for White to address. Though she attempted to continue the success of her autobiographical novels with *Julian Tye* and *Clara IV*, both novels were abandoned when White was unable to reconnect with the spirit of her heroines, Nanda Grey and Clara. Having made an uneasy truce with her daughters, White died in 1980, in the company of her beloved cats. Neither her fiction nor her diaries reflect that she made lasting peace with the memory of her father.

## MAJOR THEMES

The major theme of Antonia White's fiction is the struggle for self-definition. Her four novels together tell the story of a precocious girl's awakening to a nascent artistic vocation, rebelling against family and Church, making decisions about family and career, and, finally, confronting the self after battling madness. In *Frost in May*, White's autobiographical heroine is named Nanda Grey; in *The Lost Traveller, The Sugar House,* and *Beyond the Glass,* she is called Clara Batchellor. Though the names are different, the story is clearly a continuing one. Each novel presents a convincing and sensitive portrayal of a Catholic girl's growing up.

White's experiences at the Convent of the Sacred Heart are imaginatively reworked into the plot of *Frost in May.* The author's ambivalent feelings about the Catholic Church are evidenced in her presentation of the fictional Lippington Convent School as a bastion of patriarchal indoctrination and enforced conformity. The entire novel, in fact, is suffused with a sense of Nanda's concurrent fascination with and abhorrence for Catholicism. Like White herself, Nanda is searching for her father's approval yet is a victim of his anger, inflexibility, and coldness. Though she aspires to the ideal of selfless womanhood for which the nuns are grooming her, she is unable to deny her artistic impulses and love of beauty and breaks away, inch by inch, from the stultifying world she is strangely, almost sentimentally, attached to. Nanda decides to become a writer and, while recovering from measles in the infirmary, begins work on a wild tale of lavish lifestyles, sin, and ultimate redemption. But she is unable to pen the "conversions" of her cast of characters before the nuns confiscate the work, summon her parents, and promptly dismiss her from the school. At the novel's end, White leaves the reader with very little sense of where Nanda might be headed next, although it is clear that Nanda is horrified at the realization that she has failed her father.

Curiously, *Frost in May* does not reveal much about Nanda's relationship to her mother. Though it is possible to infer that they enjoyed a close relationship (judging by Nanda's reluctance to leave her mother when Mr. Grey first takes her to Lippington), Mrs. Grey appears infrequently in the text. While there are brief flashes of mother-daughter love and understanding in the novel, their relationship seems almost not to have a history. The story of Nanda and her father is dominant. *Frost in May* appears, at first glance, to have but a single, linear plot trajectory, though in fact it encompasses many non-linear, circuitous stories of women defining themselves against the fabric of Catholicism. The nuns, for example, offer Nanda only negative examples of what it means to be both female and Catholic. While Nanda initially rejects their lessons, she nonetheless finds herself growing close to a few of her teachers and becoming increasingly interested in the almost romantic tales told of the foundress of the order. Her initial fear of the religious life is tempered by respectful curiosity. She experiences other changes as well. The friendships she cultivates with three older girls grow into a network of female support that runs counter to the ideology of convent discipline, which disapproves of female bonding. At Lippington, she is taught to devalue the love of beauty, nature, and imagination that her mother represents. But in her circle of friends, she comes into contact with her intuitive and creative side and experiences the kind of sisterhood that enables her to embark on the writer's life with confidence.

Nanda's journey toward self-definition is fraught with difficulty because of her unwillingness or perhaps even inability to acknowledge her likeness to her mother. By the novel's end, it is clear that, although we see little of Mrs. Grey, the seeds of her love of life are planted in Nanda and are continually growing in opposition to the Catholicism that has already taken root. Both mother and daughter are unmoved by ritual and ceremony and instead seek out sensual satisfaction and deeper meaning in the world around them. These similarities between mother and daughter are even more pronounced in White's other three novels, where it is Mrs. Batchellor who continually comes to Clara's rescue, helping her deal with the accidental death of a child in her charge, the disintegration of her marriage, and her ultimate loss of dignity and hope in the mental hospital. In *Frost in May*, the mother-daughter relationship is harder to define. The world of creativity and beauty symbolized by Nanda's mother is not a simple antidote to the stark sterility of the convent. Nanda's ambivalent feelings toward both her parents are more than the outward signs of simple adolescent rebellion, for Nanda is not the typical adolescent. Like White herself was, she is hypersensitive to her environment. She loathes being thought of as an ignorant child yet is often unprepared to accept the consequences of her actions. Most important, she longs to make sense of the world. Inextricably joined to her mother and receptive to her value system, fascinated yet repelled by the mysteries of her father's beloved Catholicism, Nanda seeks to integrate and reconcile the choices these two different worlds are offering. Although she is no older than fourteen by the novel's end, the acuity of her emotions and depths of her beliefs belie her age.

## SURVEY OF CRITICISM

White is becoming an increasingly important figure in a broadened conception of literary Modernism. Unfortunately, many of the most illuminating studies of White are found in dissertations that are difficult to obtain. While nearly all of the critical studies focus on *Frost in May*, the revival of interest in

White will surely lead to treatments of her other novels as well as her diaries and short fiction.

Because the autobiographical angle is so consistently emphasized in studies of White, virtually every article presents the pertinent biographical facts and considers their reflection in the fiction. Jeanne A. Flood, for instance, contends that writing was a means of therapy for White and that the damaging relationship with her father prevented her from moving beyond strictly autobiographical subjects for her novels. Jane Dunn offers a perceptive and thoroughly researched look at White's life in her biography. Currently the only full-length biographical study, it makes similarly informed connections between White's life and art.

Philip F. O'Mara moves beyond autobiography and considers White's literary sources and influences. Tracing the major themes in White's novels, he notes their origin in her lifelong writer's block. Julietta Benson highlights the contradictions inherent in the Catholic religion and lifestyle; in a close reading of *Frost in May*, she shows how White's conflicted relationship with the Church is borne out in her fiction. Ellen Cronan Rose elaborates on the correspondences between *Frost in May* and Joyce's *Portrait of the Artist as a Young Man*, helping to place White in a gendered, Modernist, and Catholic context.

## BIBLIOGRAPHY

### Works by Antonia White

*Frost in May*. 1933. London: Virago, 1978.
*The Lost Traveller*. 1950. London: Virago, 1979.
*The Sugar House*. 1952. London: Virago, 1979.
*Beyond the Glass*. 1954. London: Virago, 1979.
*As Once in May*. Ed. Susan Chitty. London: Virago, 1991.

### Works about Antonia White

Benson, Julietta. "Varieties of 'Dis-Belief': Antonia White and the Discourses of Faith and Skepticism." *Journal of Literature and Theology: An International Journal of Theory, Criticism, and Culture* 7 (1993): 284–301.
Broe, Mary Lynn. "My Art Belongs to Daddy: Incest as Exile: The Textual Economics of Hayford Hall." *Women Writers in Exile*. Ed. Mary Lynn Broe and Angela Ingram. Chapel Hill: University of North Carolina Press, 1989. 42–85.
Dunn, Jane. *Antonia White: A Life*. London: Jonathan Cape, 1998.
Flood, Jeanne A. "The Autobiographical Novels of Antonia White." *Critique: Studies in Modern Fiction* 24 (1983): 131–49.
O'Mara, Philip F. "Trust Amid Sore Affliction: Antonia White's Novels." *Cithara: Essays in the Judeo-Christian Tradition* 28.1 (1988): 33–43.
Rose, Ellen Cronan. "Antonia White: Portrait of the Artist as a Dutiful Daughter." *LIT* 2 (1991): 239–48.

SARAH MYERS

# Selected General Bibliography

Allitt, Patrick. *Catholic Converts: British and American Intellectuals Turn to Rome.* Ithaca: Cornell University Press, 1997.

Aquino, Maria Pilar. *Our Cry for Life: Feminist Theology from Latin America.* Trans. Dinah Livingstone. Maryknoll, New York: Orbis Books, 1993.

Aveling, J.C.H. *The Handle and the Axe: The Catholic Recusants in England from Reformation to Emancipation.* London: Blond and Briggs, 1976.

Baker, Joseph Ellis. *The Novel and the Oxford Movement.* New York: Russell and Russell, 1965.

Bausch, William J. *Storytelling: Imagination and Faith.* Mystic, Connecticut: Twenty-Third Publications, 1984.

Beer, Frances. *Women and Mystical Experience in the Middle Ages.* Rochester, New York: Boydell Press, 1992.

Bergonzi, Bernard. "A Conspicuous Absentee: The Decline and Fall of the Catholic Novel." *Encounter* 55 (August–September 1980): 44–56.

Bornstein, Daniel, and Robert O. Rusconi, eds. *Women and Religion in Medieval and Renaissance Italy.* Trans. Margery J. Schneider. Chicago: University of Chicago Press, 1996.

Bossy, John. *The English Catholic Community, 1570–1850.* London: Darton, Longman and Todd, 1975.

Bouyer, Louis. *Women in the Church.* Trans. Marilyn Teichert. San Francisco: Ignatius Press, 1979.

Breslin, John B. "The Open-Ended Mystery of Matter: Readings of the Catholic Imagination." *Examining the Catholic Intellectual Tradition.* Ed. Anthony J. Cernera and Oliver J. Morgan. Fairfield, Connecticut: Sacred Heart University Press, 2000. 147–78.

Brinkmeyer, Robert H., Jr. *Three Catholic Writers of the Modern South.* Jackson: University Press of Mississippi, 1985.

Brown, Stephen J. M., S.J., and Thomas McDermott. *A Survey of Catholic Literature.* Milwaukee: Bruce Publishing Company, 1945.

Bruneau, Marie-Florine. *Women Mystics Confront the Modern World: Marie de l'Incarnation (1599–1672) and Madame Guyon (1648–1717).* Albany: State University of New York Press, 1998.

Bynum, Caroline Walker. *Fragmentation and Redemption: Essays on Gender and the Human Body in Medieval Religion*. New York: Zone Books, 1991.

———. *Jesus as Mother: Studies in the Spirituality of the High Middle Ages*. Berkeley: University of California Press, 1982.

Cadegan, Una Mary. *All Good Books Are Catholic Books: Literature, Censorship, and the Americanization of Catholics, 1920–1960*. Ann Arbor, Michigan: UMI, 1988.

Calvert, Alexander, S.J. *The Catholic Literary Revival*. Milwaukee: Bruce Publishing Company, 1935.

Carver, George, ed. *The Catholic Tradition in English Literature*. Garden City, New York: Doubleday, Page, 1926.

Desmond, John F. "Catholicism in Contemporary American Fiction." *America* 170 (4 May 1994): 7–11.

Dolan, Jay P. *The American Catholic Experience: A History from Colonial Times to the Present*. Garden City, New York: Doubleday, 1985.

Dronke, Peter. *Women Writers of the Middle Ages: A Critical Study of Texts from Perpetua (d. 203) to Marguerite Porete (d. 1310)*. Cambridge: Cambridge University Press, 1984.

Dulles, Avery R. *The Catholicity of the Church*. Oxford: Clarendon Press, 1985.

Evasdaughter, Elizabeth N. *Catholic Girlhood Narratives: The Church and Self-Denial*. Boston: Northeastern University Press, 1996.

Fanning, Charles. *The Irish Voice in America: Irish-American Fiction from the 1760s to the 1980s*. Lexington: University Press of Kentucky, 1990.

Fraser, Theodore P. *The Modern Catholic Novel in Europe*. New York: Twayne, 1994.

Gable, Mariella, O.S.B. *The Literature of Spiritual Values and Catholic Fiction*. Ed. and intro. Nancy Hynes, O.S.B. Lanham, Maryland: University Press of America, 1996.

Gandolfo, Anita. "The Demise of Father O'Malley: Reflections on Recent American Catholic Fiction." *U.S. Catholic Historian* 6 (Spring/Summer 1987): 231–40.

———. *Testing the Faith: The New Catholic Fiction in America*. New York: Greenwood Press, 1992.

Gardner, Helen L. *Religion and Literature*. London: Faber and Faber, 1971.

Gelpi, Albert. "The Catholic Presence in American Culture." *American Literary History* 11.1 (Spring 1999): 196–212.

Gerhart, Mary. "Whatever Happened to the Catholic Novel?" *Morphologies of Faith: Essays in Religion and Culture in Honor of Nathan A. Scott, Jr*. Ed. Mary Gerhart and Anthony C. Yu. Atlanta, Georgia: Scholars Press, 1990. 181–201.

Giles, Mary E., ed. *Women in the Inquisition: Spain and the New World*. Baltimore: Johns Hopkins University Press, 1999.

Giles, Paul. *American Catholic Arts and Fictions: Culture, Ideology, Aesthetics*. Cambridge: Cambridge University Press, 1992.

Greeley, Andrew M. *Religion as Poetry*. New Brunswick, New Jersey: Transaction Publishers, 1995.

Griffiths, Richard. *The Reactionary Revolution: The Catholic Revival in French Literature, 1870–1914*. New York: F. Ungar, 1965.

Halsey, William M. *The Survival of American Innocence: Catholicism in an Era of Disillusionment, 1920–1940*. Notre Dame, Indiana: University of Notre Dame Press, 1980.

Hannay, Margaret P., ed. *Silent But for the Word: Tudor Women as Patrons, Translators, and Writers of Religious Works*. Kent, Ohio: Kent State University Press, 1985.

Hardon, John A., S.J. *The Catholic Lifetime Reading Plan*. Royal Oaks, Michigan: Grotto Press, 1998.

Hoehn, Matthew, ed. *Catholic Authors: Contemporary Biographical Sketches, 1930–1952*. Newark, New Jersey: St. Mary's Abbey, 1948–1952.

John Paul II, Pope. *Pope John Paul II on the Genius of Women*. Washington, D.C.: United States Catholic Conference, 1997.

Karaban, Roslyn A., and Deni Mack, eds. *Extraordinary Preaching: Twenty Homilies by Roman Catholic Women*. San Jose, California: Resource Publications, 1996.

Kellogg, Gene. *The Vital Tradition: The Catholic Novel in a Period of Convergence*. Chicago: Loyola University Press, 1970.

Kenneally, James J. *The History of American Catholic Women*. New York: Crossroad, 1990.

Kennelly, Karen, ed. *American Catholic Women: An Historical Exploration*. New York: Macmillan, 1989.

Kessler-Harris, Alice, and William McBrien, eds. *Faith of a (Woman) Writer*. New York: Greenwood Press, 1988.

Killen, Patricia O'Connell. *Finding Our Voices: Women, Wisdom, and Faith*. New York: Crossroad, 1997.

Kolbenschlag, Madonna, ed. *Women in the Church I*. Washington, D.C.: Pastoral Press, 1987.

Labrie, Ross. *The Catholic Imagination in American Literature*. Columbia, Missouri: University of Missouri Press, 1997.

Luker, Ralph. "To Be Southern, to Be Catholic: An Interpretation of the Thought of Five American Writers." *Southern Studies* 23 (1984): 3–7.

Maison, Margaret M. *The Victorian Vision: Studies in the Religious Novel*. New York: Sheed and Ward, 1961.

Marshall, Sherrin, ed. *Women in Reformation and Counter-Reformation Europe: Public and Private Worlds*. Bloomington: Indiana University Press, 1989.

Matter, Ann E., and John Coakley, eds. *Creative Women in Medieval and Early Modern Italy*. Philadelphia: University of Pennsylvania Press, 1994.

McDannell, Colleen. *The Christian Home in Victorian America, 1840–1900*. Bloomington: Indiana University Press, 1986.

Menendez, Albert J. *The Catholic Novel: An Annotated Bibliography*. New York: Garland, 1988.

Messbarger, Paul R. *Fiction with a Parochial Purpose: Social Use of American Catholic Literature, 1884–1900*. Brookline, Massachusetts: Boston University Press, 1971.

Morris, Charles R. *American Catholic: The Saints and Sinners Who Built America's Most Powerful Church*. New York: Times Books, 1997.

Murphy, James H. *Catholic Fiction and Social Reality in Ireland, 1873–1922*. Westport, Connecticut: Greenwood Press, 1997.

National Conference of Catholic Bishops; Bishops' Committee on Women in Society and in the Church. *The Wisdom of Women: Models for Faith and Action.* Katherine Bird, writer and general ed. Washington, D.C.: United States Catholic Conference, 1991.

Neuhaus, Richard John. *The Catholic Moment: The Paradox of the Church in the Postmodern World.* San Francisco: Harper and Row, 1987.

Oden, Amy, ed. *In Her Words: Women's Writings in the History of Christian Thought.* Nashville: Abingdon Press, 1994.

O'Rourke, William. "Catholics Coming of Age: The Literary Consequences." *New Catholic World* 228 (July–August, 1985): 148–52.

Petroff, Elizabeth A. *Body and Soul: Essays on Medieval Women and Mysticism.* New York: Oxford University Press, 1994.

Phayer, Michael. *Protestant and Catholic Women in Nazi Germany.* Detroit: Wayne State University Press, 1990.

——, and Eva Fleischner. *Cries in the Night: Women Who Challenged the Holocaust.* Kansas City, Missouri: Sheed and Ward, 1997.

Quillin, Michael, S.J. "Since Blue Died: Catholic Novels Since 1961." *Critic* 34 (Fall 1975): 25–35.

Ranft, Patricia. *Women and the Religious Life in Premodern Europe.* New York: St. Martin's Press, 1996.

Rapley, Elizabeth. *The Devotes: Women and Church in Seventeenth-Century France.* Kingston, Ontario: McGill-Queen's University Press, 1990.

Reynolds, David S. *Faith in Fiction: The Emergence of Religious Literature in America.* Cambridge, Massachusetts: Harvard University Press, 1981.

Rodriguez, Jeanette. *Stories We Live: Hispanic Women's Spirituality.* New York: Paulist Press, 1996.

Scaraffia, Lucetta, and Gabriella Zarri, eds. *Women and Faith: Catholic Religious Life in Italy from Late Antiquity to the Present.* Cambridge, Massachusetts: Harvard University Press, 1999.

Schulenburg, Jane Tibbets. *Forgetful of Their Sex: Female Sanctity and Society, ca. 500–1100.* Chicago: University of Chicago Press, 1998.

Schuster, George N. *The Catholic Church and Current Literature.* New York: Macmillan, 1930.

——. *The Catholic Spirit in Moden English Literature.* New York: Macmillan, 1922.

Smiley, Pamela. "In the Name of the Father: The Effects of Orthodoxy on Roman Catholic Women Authors." Diss. University of Wisconsin—Madison, 1992.

Smith, Larry. "Catholic, Catholics Everywhere: A Flood of Catholic Novels." *Critic* 37 (December 1978): 1–8.

Sonnenfeld, Albert. *Crossroads: Essays on the Catholic Novelists.* York, South Carolina: French Literature Publications, 1982.

Sparr, Arnold J. "From Self-Congratulation to Self-Criticism: Main Currents in American Catholic Fiction, 1900–1960." *U.S. Catholic Historian* 6 (Spring/Summer 1987): 213–30.

——. *To Promote, Defend, and Redeem: The Catholic Literary Revival and the Cultural Transformation of American Catholicism, 1920–1960.* New York: Greenwood Press, 1990.

Steichen, Donna, ed. *Prodigal Daughters: Catholic Women Come Home to the Church.* San Francisco: Ignatius, 1999.

Surtz, Ronald E. *Writing Women in Late Medieval and Early Modern Spain: The Mothers of Saint Teresa of Avila*. Philadelphia: University of Pennsylvania Press, 1995.

Taves, Ann. *The Household of Faith: Roman Catholic Devotions in Mid-Nineteenth-Century America*. Notre Dame, Indiana: University of Notre Dame Press, 1986.

Thorp, Willard. *Catholic Novelists in Defense of Their Faith, 1829–1865*. New York: Arno, 1978.

Turpin, Joanne. *Women in Church History: Twenty Stories for Twenty Centuries*. Cincinnati, Ohio: St. Anthony Messenger Press, 1990.

Tynan, Daniel J., ed. *Biographical Dictionary of Contemporary Catholic American Writing*. New York: Greenwood Press, 1989.

Warner, Marina. *Alone of All Her Sex: The Myth and Cult of the Virgin Mary*. New York: Knopf, 1976.

Webster, John C.B., and Ellen Low Webster, eds. *The Church and Women in the Third World*. Philadelphia: Westminster Press, 1985.

White, James A. *The Era of Good Intentions: A Survey of American Catholic Writing, 1880–1915*. 1958. New York: Arno, 1978.

Whitehouse, J. C., ed. *Catholics on Literature*. Dublin: Four Courts Press, 1997.

Wiesner-Hanks, Merry, ed. *Convents Confront the Reformation: Catholic and Protestant Nuns in Germany*. Trans. Joan Skocir and Merry Wiesner-Hanks. Milwaukee: Marquette University Press, 1996.

Wilson, Katharina M., ed. *Medieval Women Writers*. Athens, Georgia: University of Georgia Press, 1984.

——, ed. *Women Writers of the Renaissance and Reformation*. Athens, Georgia: University of Georgia Press, 1987.

Wolff, Robert Lee. *Gains and Losses: Novels of Faith and Doubt in Victorian England*. New York: Garland, 1977.

Wood, Ralph C. *The Comedy of Redemption: Christian Faith and Comic Vision in Four American Novelists*. Notre Dame, Indiana: University of Notre Dame Press, 1988.

Woodman, Thomas M. *Faithful Fictions: The Catholic Novel in British Literature*. Philadelphia: Open University Press, 1991.

Zinsser, William, ed. *Spiritual Quests: The Art and Craft of Religious Writing*. Boston: Houghton Mifflin, 1988.

# Index

Boldface page numbers indicate the location of main entries.

# About the Editor and Contributors

VIRGINIA BRACKETT teaches at Triton College in River Grove, Illinois. The New York Public Library included her first book, *Elizabeth Cary: Writer of Conscience* (1996), in its 1997 catalog of recommended reading for teens. Her additional books include *Encyclopedia of Classic Love and Romance Literature* (1999) and *Early Women Writers: Voices from the Margins* (2000).

RUTH CARVER CAPASSO is Associate Professor of French at Kent State University. Her research interests include women writers and children's literature of the nineteenth century, particularly the series La Bibliothèque Rose Illustrée. She has written on the Countess de Ségur's depictions of crime and child development and her messages of philanthropy for children.

VICTORIA CARLSON is a writer and writing teacher in St. Louis. She graduated from the creative nonfiction writing program at the University of Iowa. Her work has appeared in *U.S. Catholic, The Critic: A Journal of Catholic Culture*, and *The Christian Science Monitor*, among other publications. She is currently at work on a memoir.

KRISTINA CHEW is Assistant Professor of Classics and Director of the Program in Classical Civilization at the University of St. Thomas in St. Paul, Minnesota. Her essay on multiculturalism and classics has appeared in the *Classical Journal*; an essay entitled "The Losses of Theresa Hak Kyung Cha's *Dictee*" is forthcoming in a collection on Asian American women writers. She is currently writing an autobiography about being an Asian American classicist.

JOHN F. CROSSEN is Assistant Professor of Spanish at Mansfield University of Pennsylvania. He specializes in the literature of the Long Eighteenth Century in Spanish America (1650–1850). His dissertation is on landscape imagery in the writings of two exiled eighteenth-century Mexican Jesuits, Francisco Clavijero and Andrés Cavo, and he has published essays on Sor Juana Inéz de la

Cruz and Clavijero. In addition to doctoral studies at Indiana University, he holds an M. Div. from Saint Thomas Theological Seminary in Denver.

JEANA DELROSSO earned her Ph.D. in English from the University of Maryland, where she teaches English and Women's Studies. She is currently writing her first book, *Veiled Threats: Contemporary International Catholic Girlhood Narratives.* Publications from her recent research appear in the *NWSA Journal* and *MELUS.*

TERESA DERRICKSON is currently working on her Ph.D. at Indiana University of Pennsylvania. Her research interests include contemporary international novels in English and narrative theory.

STACEY DONOHUE is Associate Professor of English at Central Oregon Community College. She has published essays on Mary McCarthy, Mary Gordon, Mary Lavin, and Robin Morgan.

SARAH M. DUNNIGAN is a graduate of the universities of Glasgow and Edinburgh, and is currently British Academy Postdoctoral Fellow at Edinburgh University. Her interests lie in medieval and Renaissance literature, especially Scottish, and particularly in representations of desire, femininity, and devotion. She has a forthcoming book entitled *Eros and Poetry at the Courts of Mary Queen of Scots and James VI.*

ANNE M. ENENBACH is a Ph.D. candidate at the University of Notre Dame. She teaches first year writing, and is currently engaged in research for her doctoral project on the intersection of labor and gender issues in modern and contemporary Irish drama.

DEANNA DELMAR EVANS is Professor of English at Bemidji State University in Minnesota. She has published articles in the area of Middle Scots Literature and on teaching the Middles Ages in such journals as *Studies in Scottish Literature, Neophilologus, Medieval Feminist Newsletter,* and *Germanic Notes.* Her piece on "The Nine Worthies" is forthcoming in *Medieval Folklore: An Encyclopedia of Myths, Legends, Tales, Beliefs, and Customs,* and her article "Hrotsvit the Dramatist as Teacher" is also forthcoming in a volume edited by Phyllis Brown and Katharina Wilson. She has also published entries on Hildegard of Bingen, Clare of Assisi, Francis of Assisi, and Walter Mape.

ELLEN C. FRYE received her undergraduate degree in Spanish from the University of North Carolina at Chapel Hill, her master's degree in Spanish from the University of Virginia, and her Ph.D. in Spanish from the University of Pennsylvania. At present, she is a Visiting Assistant Professor of Spanish and Director of the Foreign Languages Program at Monmouth University. Her research interests include the seventeenth-century *comedia* of Spain and actor-spectator relationships; rhetorical devices and casuistry in Spanish mysticism; and subjectivity, exemplarity, and religion in the early modern short story.

MARY E.GILES is Professor Emeritus of Humanities and Religious Studies at California State University at Sacramento. The author of seven books and many articles, she is the founding editor of *Studia Mystica* and writes on Christian mysticism, women's spirituality, and Hispanic women writers.

MARY THERESA HALL is Associate Professor of English at Thiel College in Greenville, Pennsylvania, teaching courses in linguistics, introduction to literature, British literature from Beowulf to the present, and composition. She received her Ph.D. in English from Duquesne University; her published dissertation is entitled *Country Parsons, Country Poets: George Herbert and Gerard Manley Hopkins as Spiritual Autobiographers.* She has published and presented papers on such subjects as Chaucer, Hopkins, Bob Dylan's poetry, and educational leadership. She has also taught the Bible as literature and is interested in the parallels between literature and spirituality.

JOAN F. HALLISEY is Associate Professor in the Communication Department of Regis College in Weston, Massachusetts. She is the Denise Levertov editor for *The Heath Anthology of American Literature* and for *American Women Writers: From Colonial Times to the Present* (A Critical Reference Guide), volume 5, Supplement. Part of Hallisey's 1978 doctoral dissertation at Brown University was on Levertov. She has published several articles on Levertov's work and is currently working on a Levertov web page for Oxford University Press's new American Literature series.

JOHN JAE-NAM HAN earned his Ph.D. in English at the University of Nebraska—Lincoln. He is presently Assistant Professor of English at Missouri Baptist College in St. Louis where he teaches British and American literature, world literature, and history of the English language, among other courses. His publications include articles on Flannery O'Connor and Asian American authors.

SHERRILL HARBISON is a lecturer at Trinity College, Hartford, and an Associate of the Five Colleges in Amherst, Massachusetts. She received her Ph.D. in English from the University of Massachusetts at Amherst. She has published on Faulkner, Cather, and Undset; is editor of the Penguin editions of Cather's *The Song of the Lark* and Undset's *Gunnar's Daughter,* and wrote introductions for volumes 2 and 3 of Penguin's new translation of Undset's *Kristin Lavransdatter.*

KATHLEEN JACQUETTE is Assistant Professor at the State University of New York, Farmingdale. Her Ph.D. dissertation was entitled "Irish, Female, and Catholic—the Vision of Patriarchy in the Fiction of Edna O'Brien." She has presented papers about Edna O'Brien at numerous national and international conferences on Irish Studies.

NANCYLEE NOVELL JONZA is the author of *The Underground Stream: The Life and Art of Caroline Gordon* (1995). A full-length narrative and critical biography, *The Underground Stream* won the 1995 Violet Crown Book Award for nonfiction.

REBECCA L. KROEGER is a doctoral candidate in English at the University of Virginia. She earned a B.A. in English and French from the University of Notre Dame, and an M.A. in English from the University of Virginia.

MARIA LAMONACA earned her Ph.D. from Indiana in 1999. She is currently a Lilly Postdoctoral Fellow and Lecturer in English at Valparaiso University. Her teaching and research interests include Victorian literature and culture, nineteenth-century women writers, faith and secularism in the Victorian novel, and religion in popular literature and culture (nineteenth century to the present).

DAVID LARAWAY received his Ph.D. from Cornell University in 1998 in Romance Studies. He is currently Assistant Professor in the Department of Spanish and Portuguese at Brigham Young University where he teaches courses in Latin American literature. He has published articles on figures as diverse as Jorge Luis Borges, Benito Pérez Galdós, and Mariano Azuela, and is currently writing a book on religious discourse in modern Latin American poetry.

RAYMOND N. MACKENZIE is Professor of English at the University of St. Thomas, St. Paul, Minnesota. He has recently completed a biography of Alice Meynell's daughter, Viola Meynell, and he is currently working on a study of the novelist François Mauriac.

PAUL MAJKUT is currently Assistant Professor at National University in La Jolla, California. His career has followed a triple track: community organizing, writing, and teaching. He has won numerous Press Club awards for his writing, most recently covering various aspects of the situation in Chiapas, Mexico. He has taught extensively abroad, including university appointments in Canada, Arabia, and the People's Republic of China. Among his recent publications are "Chiapas: Rain Forests and Revolutions," "'Earth Some Special Good Doth Give': A Phenomenological Reading of Friar Laurence's Earth Monologue," and "The Concept of the Dog Doesn't Bark: Notes Towards a Materialistic Phenomenology of Film Noir."

SAM MCBRIDE teaches writing and humanities at DeVry University, Pomona. He specializes in twentieth-century literature and culture, with emphases on interdisciplinary performance and the conjunction of religion and literature. He is currently collaborating on "Women Among the Inklings: Feminism, C. S. Lewis, and J.R.R. Tolkien."

ROBERT C. MILLIKEN is Lecturer in English at the University of Nebraska—Lincoln. His teaching and research interests include connections between Renaissance art and literature, especially, of late, Hans Holbein's reflections of European courtly and humanist circles.

IRENE MORRA is completing her doctorate in English at the University of Toronto. Her dissertation considers the adaptation of literary works into opera libretti by modern British writers, particularly Auden and Forster. She has contributed entries to the forthcoming *Encyclopedia of Biography*.

MOLLY MORRISON is Assistant Professor of Italian at Ohio University in Athens, Ohio, where she teaches Italian language and literature. She has published articles on Dante and medieval Italian holy women.

ROSEANNA M. MUELLER holds a Ph.D. in Comparative Literature and is the Foreign Language Supervisor at Columbia College Chicago. Her areas of specialization include sixteenth-century literature of Spain and Italy, the pastoral tradition, Italian women's literature of the fifteenth and sixteenth centuries, and contemporary women's Latin American literature. She has contributed articles and reviews to such journals as *Voices in Italian Americana, Hispania, Italica, Renaissance Quarterly, Canadian Review of Comparative Literature*, and such collections as *Latin America and Its Literature, Feminist Encyclopedia of Spanish Literature*, and *Feminist Encyclopedia of Latin American Literature*.

RUSSELL ELLIOTT MURPHY is Professor of English at the University of Arkansas, Little Rock. He is the editor of the *Yeats Eliot Review* and the founding director of the annual St. Charles Borromeo Conference on Catholicism and Literature. He has published widely on Modernist literature, particularly on T. S. Eliot, William Butler Yeats, and Gerard Manley Hopkins.

SARAH MYERS is an independent scholar from Detroit, Michigan. She received an M.A. in English and American literature from Indiana State University. Her current research interests include feminist theory and the American local colorists, particularly Sarah Orne Jewett and Margaret Deland.

ANN V. NORTON is Assistant Professor of English at Saint Anselm College, where she teaches nineteenth- and twentieth-century British literature. She received her Ph.D. from Columbia University, and has written on Edna O'Brien, Virginia Woolf, Antonia White, and A.S. Byatt. Her book, *Paradoxical Feminism: The Novels of Rebecca West*, was published in 2000.

SALVADOR A. OROPESA is Associate Professor of Spanish at Kansas State University. He has recently published his second book, *La novelística de Antonio Muñoz Molina* (1999).

EILEEN QUINLAN, S.N.D., Ph.D., teaches at Notre Dame College of Ohio, where she chairs the Department of English, Communication, and Theater. A member of the Sisters of Notre Dame of Cleveland, she earned her advanced degrees from Loyola University Chicago and Bowling Green State University.

MARY R. REICHARDT is Professor of English and Catholic Studies and the director of the Master's Program in Catholic Studies at the University of St. Thomas in St. Paul, Minnesota. She received her Ph.D. in English from the University of Wisconsin—Madison. She teaches courses and has research interests in early American literature, women's literature, Catholic literature, the short story, and autobiography. She is the author of numerous articles and five books on women writers, and is a contributor to the forthcoming *Encyclopedia of American Catholic Women*. She also works as a freelance editor and writing consultant.

NANCY L. ROBERTS is a professor in the School of Journalism and Mass Communication at the University of Minnesota—Twin Cities. She is also an adjunct faculty member for the Program in American Studies. Her books include *Dorothy Day and the "Catholic Worker"* (with Anne Klejment); *American Catholic Pacifism: The Influence of Dorothy Day and the Catholic Worker Movement; American Peace Writers, Editors, and Periodicals: A Dictionary*; and *The Press and America: An Interpretive History of the Mass Media*, 9th edition (with the late Edwin and Michael Emery).

LISA TREVIÑO ROY-DAVIS is currently completing her dissertation entitled "Mi'ja, Mamíta, Mamá: Constructing the Fictional Self in U.S. Latina Prose" at Indiana University of Pennsylvania. She is also working on an anthology project of Latina life stories and autobiographical writings with Cecilia Rodrígues Milánes of the University of Central Florida. Her work with Latino/a racial issues in literature has been recognized by the Conference on College Composition and Communication. She was honored with the Scholars for the Dream Travel Award for her presentation at the Spring 2000 convention in Minneapolis.

OLIVIA SCHAFF is a postgraduate student at the University of Wales–Cardiff. She is completing a doctoral thesis on historic and religious significance in the medieval novels of Sigrid Undset and Zoé Oldenbourg. She holds a master's degree in medieval British history from the University of Wales—Cardiff, and a master's degree in Victorian Studies from Université Lumière—Lyon 2, Lyon, France.

DEBRA L. STOUDT is Associate Professor of German at the University of Toledo. She earned her Ph.D. in German from the University of North Carolina at Chapel Hill. Her teaching interests include German civilization and German folklore; her research focuses on medieval German mysticism and medieval magic and medicine. She is the co-editor of *Medieval Sermons and Society: Cloister, City, University* (1998), and author of "Medieval German

Women and the Power of Healing" in *Women Healers and Physicians: Climbing a Long Hill*, edited by Lilian Furst (1997).

ELIZABETH BACHRACH TAN is an independent scholar and chaplain at the University of Massachusetts at Amherst. She is a co-editor of *The Academy and the Possibility of Belief: Essays on Intellectual and Spiritual Life* (2000), and writes about American spiritual autobiographies in her dissertation, "Standing on Holy Ground: The Sacred Landscapes of Annie Dillard, Kathleen Norris, and Frederick Buechner." She lives with her husband and two children at The Dock, their home and a ministry center for international and American students.

KATHLEEN VEJVODA is Assistant Professor of English at Metropolitan State University in St. Paul, Minnesota. She received her Ph.D. in English from the University of Texas at Austin in 2000. Her research interests include Victorian literature and culture, Irish Studies, and Women's Studies. She is currently working on a book about Roman Catholicism and idolatry in the Victorian novel.

THOMAS WERGE is Professor of English at the University of Notre Dame. He received his B.A. in English and philosophy from Hope College, and his M.A. and Ph.D. in English from Cornell University. He is co-editor of the scholarly journal *Religion and Literature*. He has written on the religious dimensions of early and nineteenth-century American literature as well as on such figures as Dante, Dostoevsky, and Simone Weil.

NATALIE JOY WOODALL is the senior correspondent for the *Palladium-Times* newspaper, Oswego, New York. She holds doctorates in both classical languages and in English literature. She is the author of numerous articles and reviews.

WENDY M. WRIGHT is Professor of Theology at Creighton University in Omaha, Nebraska. Her area of expertise is History of Christian Spirituality, with a specialty in Salesian spirituality. She has authored or edited a number of books and articles on this tradition including *Francis de Sales and Jane de Chantal: Letters of Spiritual Direction, Francis de Sales: Introduction to the Devout Life and Treatise on the Love of God*, and *Bond of Perfection: Jeanne de Chantal and Francois de Sales*.

JEFFREY T. ZALAR is a Ph.D. candidate in modern German cultural and religious history at Georgetown University, where he is training under Roger Chickering. His research deals with issues of Catholic spirituality and intellectual culture; he has published articles in *Catholic Historical Review* and *Neue Zeitschrift für Missionswissenschaft*.

JOHN ZUBIZARRETA is Professor of English, Director of Honors and Faculty Development, and Dean of Undergraduate Studies at Columbia College.

He has published widely on modern American and comparative literatures, pedagogy, and teaching improvement and evaluation. A Carnegie Foundation/C.A.S.E. Professor for South Carolina, he has also earned recognition for teaching and scholarly excellence from the American Association for Higher Education, the South Atlantic Association of Departments of English, and other educational organizations.

CPSIA information can be obtained
at www.ICGtesting.com
Printed in the USA
BVHW031453231119
564640BV00003B/10/P